ME AND THE GENERAL

ME AND THE GENERAL

ROSEMARY VALENTI GUARNERA

Library of Congress Control Number: 2013923628
ISBN: Hardcover 978-1-4931-5833-1
Softcover 978-1-4931-5832-4
eBook 978-1-4931-5834-8

This book was printed in the United States of America.

Rev. date: 06/20/2014

To order additional copies of this book, contact:
Xlibris LLC
1-888-795-4274
www.Xlibris.com
Orders@Xlibris.com
551105

April 18, 2015

To Clay —

Hope you enjoy

Lee & the General —

[illegible]

ABOUT THE BOOK

ME AND THE GENERAL is a story finally being told after many years. It is the biography of a man named Ralph Liguori, whose life was intertwined with the "infamous" Charles "Lucky" Luciano and a would-be president, Thomas E. Dewey. It relates the twists and turns that change the course of his existence. As a young boy, he suffers his first heartfelt tragedy of the loss of his beloved father—which changes his life forever.

Segue the Roaring Twenties, an era in which he slowly begins to find himself. In the following years of the Great Depression, there are the struggles to find work—only to succumb, at times, to an easier path in the so-called rackets.

His good looks, winning personality, and talents brought him to the attention of the "big boys," who befriended him, and Ralph learned of their nefarious ways.

But more importantly is his lifelong friendship with "Lucky" Luciano—the GENERAL and GODFATHER—linked to the betrayal of Thomas E. Dewey in the famous 1936 New York prostitution trial—a trial that reveals the machinations which caused the incarceration and subsequent exile to Italy for both Ralph and Luciano.

In prison, as well as in exile, we find incredulous episodes—fantastic tales—while many loose ends come to fruition.

It is a compelling, yet sad, story that illustrates the fine line between good and evil.

(The narrative is based on personal interviews on tape and friendship.)

DEDICATION

In Ralph's memory and for his complete faith in me

and

to Eugenio, for his patience and moral support.

ACKNOWLEDGMENT

Special thanks to the memory of Audrey R. Langer, whose most valuable guidance, assistance, and enthusiasm made this project possible.

FOREWORD

This is the story of Ralph Liguori, a man whose entire life was based on loyalty and a sense of duty (even in circumstances that altered his life). He believed that friendship was sacred, and among his closest friends was none other than Charles "Lucky" Luciano. It was Liguori's profound belief in the importance of friendship that cost him ten years in prison, in one of the biggest criminal trials in American history. And it was his friendship with Luciano that betrayed him and saw him exiled to Rome—where he lived for thirty-six years, until his death in 1981.

This book also provides a startling behind-the-scenes revelation of a man named Thomas E. Dewey (the Special Prosecutor), who pulled all the stops to convict Luciano (the Boss) and Liguori (the Accomplice), as they appear in the following three sketches entitled "Introduction."

The story encompasses the transition from the Roaring Twenties to the anger and despair of the Great Depression—an era darkened by gangsters and political corruption. It depicts ambition and the fine line dividing good from evil in society's doctrines—a grim era occasionally brightened by the famous and the infamous, the sinister hoodlums, and the magical celebrities who peopled its days.

Most importantly, *Me and the General* presents the life of Ralph Liguori—a life intertwined with that of Luciano. One cannot be told without the other.

In the face of all that has been written and portrayed of these men's lives, and of the events that have unfolded about them, it is hoped that this book—Ralph's testament—will end some of the falsehoods and exaggerations generally founded on rumors and idle gossip.

It is a candid glimpse of one small segment of American history.

AUTHOR'S NOTE

A man's name is his heritage, and it is his inalienable right to defend it against those who malign, vilify, or defame it. Only the victims really know the insurmountable pain they suffer as a result of such calumny. Ralph Liguori, like others, had a right to vindicate his reputation (controversial to some).

I met Ralph in Rome, Italy, the latter part of 1969 while he was handling sightseeing and airport transfers by private car with driver. His eyesight, troubled by glaucoma, had deteriorated badly by then, and I had easily felt compassion for the man. It was obvious to me that Ralph was a survivor who wouldn't succumb to depression. Soon thereafter, he began to work almost exclusively for me at the travel agency with which I was associated at that time. Without a doubt, he was an interesting personality.

Ralph was a Runyonesque character (his accent, his ways), but a sense of curiosity told me there was much more behind the façade he presented. He was nostalgic for the States, and perhaps it made him happy to find an Italo-American girl (especially of Sicilian origin) with whom he could reminisce. Our initial casual conversations mushroomed into longer and more complicated discussions, revealing in small doses, at first, some of his personal background—including his close friendship with Charles "Lucky" Luciano (the infamous gangster).

I realized, almost from the start, his burning desire to tell his story—of his relationship with Luciano and of the frame-up that caused them both to be exiled.

By now, we were very dear friends; and he began asking me to assist him in writing various letters. The author, Martin Gosch, had contacted him regarding the possibility of writing Charles Luciano's story jointly with him. I then met with Ralph's lawyer, Fausto Cavalaro who asked me to take down Ralph's preliminary notes for discussion with Gosch and an American lawyer.

A previous attempt for a story had been made between Luciano and Gosch but never materialized—because of Luciano's sudden death of a heart attack in 1962.

A similar fate occurred at this time. As various conversations proceeded, Gosch, unexpectedly, died in 1973. And that is how it all began. Ralph was on his own!

Subsequently, Ralph refused many professional writers and, as he put it, "chased" others away; but at one point, obsessed with telling his story, he said, "Rosemary, *you* write it!" Perhaps it was his faith in me that brought about that decision—his faith in the way he knew I would tell it. Other writers came along after that decision, but Ralph wouldn't budge. He had given his word!

It was a big order for me. I was not a professional writer (although a lifelong dream). I began in the only way I thought best, which was, first, to put it all on tape, organizing our interviews chronologically. In each session, we talked about a particular period. This continued for a couple of years. Finally, the tapes were finished. There were however some tales he did *not* want on the tapes. We had many other discussions, elaborating on the material already on tape—adding other stories he had forgotten at the time. Otherwise, his memory was incredible.

In the years that followed, I divided my time between the New York and Rome libraries, painstakingly researching the story and dates; some were incorrect by months. Twice there was a difference of a year, which was understandable because of the time that had elapsed.

In this regard, I would like to give special recognition to the New York papers: the *Journal News,* the *Daily News,* the *Daily Mirror,* the *Herald Tribune,* the *New York Times,* and the *Brooklyn Eagle,* whose coverage of the famous 1936 prostitution trial was invaluable in my research. I would also like to give credit to all the Italian newspapers in Rome, as well as to the *Rome Daily American.*

Unfortunately, Ralph did not live to see his dream come true. He died in 1981 with only his immediate family and relatives around him. During his last agonizing days, his final words to me were, "Rosemary, *the book*!" And I promised.

INTRODUCTION

Dewey

THE SPECIAL PROSECUTOR

The grainy black-and-white photos on the tabloid's front page made those on trial look far worse than they did in person. They emphasized heavy jowls, puffs and patches beneath bleary eyes (often rather askew from the flash of lightbulbs), thinning and greasy hair, five o'clock shadows, and wilted shirt collars.

"Good Lord, what a motley crew!"

The young special prosecutor gasped the words with a pronounced smirk for the benefit of one of his assistants. Among the photos of the accused, he spotted the bloated features of a twenty-six-year-old call girl—one of the key witnesses in the sensational "organized sin" hearings. From his research, he knew that Nancy Presser (Dotty) had once been an exquisitely beautiful teenager whose yearning for the bright lights had brought her to New York to dance in the best chorus lines (George White's Scandals). When lean times came along, the naïve youngster began bestowing her favors on those willing and able to pay. But as far as the prosecution was concerned, Dotty's only value depended on how well her testimony helped to bring about a conviction—a conviction that would bring the Boss of all Bosses to his knees.

The pavement square in front of the stately Woolworth Building glittered like a diamond-strewn carpet in the brilliant spring sunshine. The sharp odor of fresh newsprint assailed the nostrils of Thomas E. Dewey as he extracted one copy of the *New York Times* from beneath its hemp twine fastening.

"They had me down for a milquetoast pushover," he sneered to one of his aides, drawing himself up to his top height and purposefully striding to the corner to make the Broadway traffic light. "Today they'll find out just what kind of Boy Scout in khaki shorts I am!"

A pushcart peddler greeted him with a wave of the arm and a hopeful smile. Dewey paused to place a quarter in the outstretched palm—his contribution to another victim of the Great Depression. As the peddler handed Dewey an apple, he tipped the peak of his cap and mumbled a grateful thank-you. As he stared at the coin, he wondered how far he could stretch the quarter that day.

Traffic was already growing heavier, and the air hummed with the purr of car engines and the echo of horns. It was good to walk, the young special prosecutor told himself, to walk and smell the morning dew in the City Hall Park. The tall slender trees displayed their pale green leaves, swaying ever so slightly. Passersby, recognizing Dewey from news photos, nodded and waved to him. He responded with an ingratiating smile, exposing even white teeth and a carefully trimmed mustache beneath a tip-tilted nose. Dewey touched the brim of his gray homburg to men and doffed it to women. Nobody could ever fault the young prosecutor for a lack of social graces. It was all part of the Dewey persona—the conservative single-breasted suits; the crisp, starched shirt collar and cuffs; the properly understated necktie; and the meticulous parting of his dark brown hair. He exuded perfection and ethics, discipline and class—the gentleman nonpareil. But to his adversaries (and even to some of his friends and acquaintances), he was looked upon as an insufferable stuffed shirt.

Born on March 24,1902, in Owosso, Michigan, Thomas E. Dewey came from a long line of illustrious Republicans; and in his early youth, he was a devotee of Theodore Roosevelt's brand of modern conservative nationalism. An opera buff, Dewey was endowed with a fine tenor voice, which served him well in choral work and student musicales; but sadly, as he grew older, his voice changed, and this talent was relegated to the privacy of his shower. While pursuing a law degree at Columbia University, where he became acquainted with future Supreme Court Justices William O. Douglas and Harlan F. Stone, Dewey arrived in a New York City dominated by Jimmy Walker and Tammany Hall and quickly involved himself in Republican Club activities. It was a disturbing era of Prohibition and speakeasies, of a precarious stock market and organizational crime.

Selected (with other Columbia Law graduates) as assistant to U.S. attorney George Z. Medaglie, Dewey soon became familiar on a daily personal level with rampant crime and gang warfare, in which the L' Unione Siciliana began to figure prominently.

Whatever his failings as a popular president, Herbert Hoover had pulled out all stops in prosecuting underworld kingpins, encouraging the use of broader powers to place the infamous Al Capone behind bars. Also, in the black era of the Lindbergh baby kidnapping and murder, he drew confidence from public outrage to instigate an all-out counterattack on crime.

In the succeeding Democratic administration of Franklin Delano Roosevelt, the campaign against organized crime was to have its star players, and the role of prosecutor was to be handled by the brash, bold, hard-hitting, menacingly ambitious young Thomas E. Dewey. Upon his appointment in 1931 to the office of chief assistant U.S. attorney, at the age of only twenty-nine, one of his Columbia Law classmates congratulated Dewey with the prophetic flattery: "I know you will acquit yourself with great credit . . . And who knows, someday you may be governor . . . or mayhap PRESIDENT!"

Dewey's insistence upon punctuality, his demanding perfectionism, his supercilious attitude toward those who did not immediately comprehend the verbal expressions of his mile-a-minute mind were, for that reason, thereafter shunned. His rigid personality, at times, created more enemies than friends. Dewey, however, ignored most of his critics. "I'm not out to win any popularity contests," he advised those closest to him, who had warned him not to step on too many toes. But that was not exactly true. Dewey was indeed out to win all the popularity contests that came his way—especially among men who had the authority to recognize his skills and pave the way for his advancement. He had convinced himself as a child that he had what it took to be president of the United States. His grandfather had been one of the founders of the Republican Party. His own father and uncle were GOP leaders, and as a natural consequence, Dewey looked upon Tammany Hall as some kind of evil emporium in which people were bought and sold.

Thus, with all that background and with all those merits behind him, Tom Dewey was out to make a name for himself. And he didn't really care how he went about accomplishing this, or how many people he had to hurt in his unbridled race for the fame and power. During his baptism of fire, Dewey, in surprisingly short order, disposed of several gangland luminaries of the late twenties and early thirties. Criminals like Jack "Legs" Diamond (Jack Moran), Waxey Gordon (Irving Wexler)—and their cohorts vanished from the lawless jungle once Dewey took the helm. At one point, however, he had to make a break from the scene, due to political pressures, when President Roosevelt appointed Martin J. Conboy as the new U.S. attorney of New York. Not deterred, Dewey knew how to wait and knew what he could achieve.

When New York governor Lehman appointed him assistant district attorney in the early summer of 1935 (a position some of the finest lawyers in the state had turned down), Dewey was more than ready. Judge Philip J. McCook, at Dewey's swearing in, came up with a more impressive title for the young deputy assistant: SPECIAL PROSECUTOR.

Dewey wasted no time! For his base of operations, he chose Frank Woolworth's skyscraper, the beautiful Cathedral of Commerce, rising sixty-five stories over Broadway, Park Row, and Barclay Street in Lower

Manhattan—within close walking distance of the city hall and the State Supreme Court in Foley Square. Dewey saw to everything—dividing ten and a half thousand square feet on the fourteenth floor into thirty-five cubicles, all arranged around a long hallway, which bisected the entire suite. The building's numerous entrances, including one direct link to a subway line, ensured the safety of witnesses slipping away in the vast commuter congregation—coming and going in the underground of the city. A twenty-four-hour guard service was hired. When everything was precisely as Dewey wanted, he made his famous radio speech. It was an eye-opener of a speech—Dewey's grand appeal to the public—for help in stamping out organized crime!

"Your cooperation is essential . . . ," he told radio listeners. "Your help will be kept secret, and your persons will be protected. If you have evidence of organized crime of whatever kind, however large or small, bring it to us. The rest is our job. We will do our best."

When Dewey set out to assemble his staff, he shrewdly surrounded himself with twenty excellent men, seven of whom were Republicans and six Democrats (to dispel the notion that he would act purely from a political standpoint). Fourteen of the chosen were law graduates from Harvard and Columbia Law; fourteen held Phi Beta Kappa keys; and ten of the twenty were Jewish—a wise move on Dewey's part to counterbalance his prosecution of a bull pen filled with Jewish defendants.

Some of his chief assistants were Murray Gurfein, Frank S. Hogan, and Sol Gelb—seasoned prosecutors who knew the ropes. Nevertheless, Dewey also gave his younger men, like Barent Ten Eyck and Jacob J. Rosenblum, an opportunity to exercise their new profession. But the man who would fill Ralph Liguori with repugnance was Dewey's deputy assistant, Harry S. Cole. Ralph would shudder with cold sweat whenever he thought about Cole and his insidious behavior toward him.

As soon as Dewey had delegated the various tasks to be performed, months and months of investigations followed. He and his assistants zealously prepared to squash the biggest vice racket of that moment—compulsory prostitution. The entire case was masterminded by the crime buster himself—a case meant to make him famous. His whole campaign had been set up to convict the Boss. He was not interested in obtaining convictions of front men only. That sort of thing had been going on for years. Like the surgeon seeking the head of the tapeworm in order to destroy the parasite, Dewey aimed straight for the top.

And the *top*—as he proposed to prove in court—was Charles "Lucky" Luciano.

Luciano

THE BOSS

A hideous gray dust settled over everything and everyone in the tiny Sicilian village of Lercara Friddi, east of Palermo in the sulphur hills—where the very air stank of all that was disgorged from the mines. But an even more disagreeable stench permeated every vestige of life among the residents—the stench of antiquity and rust, decay and putrefaction, human waste and sweat; the sweat of centuries-old battles against hopeless despair; the stench of poverty. It was in this humble setting that Charles "Lucky" Luciano—the middle child of Antonio and Rosalia Lucania—was pulled and slapped into the world on a dreary late November day in 1897.

Impoverishment is not a natural state of being; the planet is bountiful, with abundance for all. It is the regulatory edict of society in which poverty is established—the system that allows one man to prosper while his neighbor starves, in the name of circumstance. Thus, poverty often forges character, builds strength, and creates lifelong challenges. Without his ever being aware of the power budding within him, Luciano (christened Salvatore Lucania) began early in life to recognize the challenges to improve his lot and, more importantly, learned how to fulfill his ambitions.

For the first ten years of his life, Luciano observed the struggle of his family to survive, to overcome the hunger and the cold. He watched his hardworking father scrimp and save, putting away a few tiny coins in a large glass bottle beneath his bed. They were savings representing his dream to immigrate—to travel with his family to the Promised Land across the ocean. But when the miracle at last became reality, when the Lucania family huddled together with the rest of the masses on the deck of the ship that brought them to the safe sunlit harbor of the New World, the ten-year-old immigrant boy could not restrain his skepticism. Somehow he already knew there were no miracles. He instinctively understood that if a man became determined to change his life for the better, it was up to the acuity of his brain, the skill of his hands, and the strength of his muscles to achieve his goal.

Shaking the sulphur dust of the Sicilian hills from his feet, Luciano found himself stepping through the dust of New York City's incredible congestion, where only the hardy survived and where only the faithful and the foolish celebrated the dawn of each new day with a smile. The Lucania family, seven in all, settled into a squalid frame tenement on the lower east side, where a new miasma of odors replaced the stench of Sicilian sulphur. The tottering structure boasted a wall-sweating basement with three stories of four small apartments on each landing. The superintendent and his family lived in the basement, which included the boiler room, coal bins, and supply closets. The apartments consisted of four tiny rooms, in which upward of five family members could be accommodated. A black potbellied stove stood against one wall in the kitchen, alongside the bathtub with its rust and scarring. Toilets were located on the landings—one commode for every four apartments, one pull chain toilet bowl for a minimum of twenty tenants. Overuse would periodically destroy the plumbing, and backed-up pipes would protest their weariness by spilling waste throughout the building's landings, causing new ceiling leaks and untold days of misery for the building's occupants.

In Sicily, there had been outhouses, separated a good distance from the family home. In Lercara Friddi, the people had been poor, hungry, and dirty—tired of their existence. In the Promised Land, they often found themselves wallowing in their own offal, with no escape and no more dreams of a better life.

The impressionable young Luciano bedded down at night on the floor, beside his elder brother Giuseppe and his younger brother Bartolo, smelling the sweat of their bodies, while listening to the grunts and sighs of their dreams. Across the tiny room, stretched out on an old mattress, lay his sisters Francesca and Concetta; and in the chamber on the other side of the wall were the muffled voices of his parents discussing their frustrations—and despair—followed by the hiss and whispers of their couplings. There were other nocturnal noises that kept Charles Luciano awake: mice foraging in the kitchen; the tiny clink of the metal drip pan beneath the icebox; a colony of rats scampering across the roof, attacking the bags of garbage on the fire escape, claws ticking at the windowpanes; horses clip-clopping along cobblestone streets, drawing their wooden-wheeled wagons and carts; and the occasional sputtering and clamor of an automobile engine passing in the humid night air. Someday he too would drive an automobile, he told himself with a grim smile. The luxury of such an extravagant possession was so unattainable that few immigrants dared fantasize about driving a car. But Luciano did, making solemn vows to himself to lull his nerves to sleep. Somewhere in the night, a baby cried, fretting against the heat and the sting of a soaked diaper against acid-reddened flesh. The mournful cry echoed inside young Luciano, aching to escape his lips. He swallowed it back and buried his face in his crossed arms. He felt such despair.

The humiliation of ignorance—as others perceived it—was, for Salvatore Lucania, the harshest torment of all in the New World. At Public School (PS) 10 in south Manhattan, when the teacher learned he did not know a single word of English, Salvatore was cuffed smartly across his forehead and scornfully ordered, with furiously pointed fingers, to seat himself in the last row of the classroom, until he could respond to her questions in English. Stung and bewildered, ashamed before the staring gaze of those pupils who were New York born and fluent in English, Luciano wondered what kind of hell his father had mapped out for the family. The teachers, almost all of whom had names like McKenna and Barrett and Callahan, often spoke a singsong kind of English, which he later learned was a somewhat tarnished Irish brogue. It made him livid to realize that these middle-aged women were immigrants themselves but endowed with the good fortune of emigrating from English-speaking countries, regardless of the accent. Occasionally, a teacher, here or there, would ask if he went to church; and upon learning that he and his family attended the neighborhood Roman Catholic Church, she would soften her attitude and commence to treat her coreligionist with greater compassion and helpfulness.

Lucania was impressed by the natural intelligence of the Jewish kids at PS 10 and, subsequently, at PS 40. They could generally be relied upon to raise their hands with quick answers to questions from the teachers, to do their homework, to keep their notebooks neat and clean, and to be the highest scorers on weekly tests. Salvatore Lucania observed them from the back of the class and envied the ease with which they absorbed their lessons. He listened intently to their interest in the subject material, the way they competed among themselves, and the pride they felt in achieving high marks. He longed to emulate them, to become as brainy as they were, but it seemed a hopeless goal. Nevertheless, he liked what he saw among the Jews; and when he was sufficiently fluent in English, he found himself, once or twice, expressing his congratulations to one boy or another who had scored high on an exam or assignment. His respect for them grew with the years. While the Jewish kids in the neighborhood were mostly poor, there was always an uncle or aunt in their background who lived uptown or who drove a fancy automobile. He came to believe that they knew how to work themselves up in the system. Unlike his other Sicilian and Italian classmates, Luciano befriended the Jewish students and frequently joined them in street games. Somewhere in his developing plans for a better future, he realized that they had brains, were smart and fierce. They could prove outstanding allies someday.

When he was fourteen, Salvatore was punished for truancy, drawing a four-month sentence to the Brooklyn Truant School; and by the time he was released, Salvatore Lucania had developed leadership qualities; his Sicilian contemporaries were awed by the fact that he had already done time. Less impressed was Antonio Lucania, who had tried desperately to encourage his son to finish school. Realizing it was a hopeless cause, he pressed his restless boy to get a job, but a routine of hard work was not for Sal. He resented his family's poverty (had always been ashamed of it), and he intended to become rich (fast). He began as a gambler, successfully rolling dice in the street, and soon formed his own gang of other immigrant teenagers.

Together they embarked upon a life of petty crime, pooling their take to keep from flaunting their newly earned riches at home. They knew all too well how stern fathers could mete out memorable beatings in their efforts to hold on to whatever was left of their self-respect in the eyes of their neighbors and their god. Antonio Lucania was one of those fathers. While he still had no proof, he felt that his relationship with his son, Sal, was beginning to deteriorate.

It did not take long before the periodic "take" from the neighborhood, where Luciano's young gang did their marauding, became rather slim pickings for the daring it entailed—subsequently raising their sights to that Manhattan realm of wealth situated north of Fourteenth Street and south of Harlem. It was in this new wonderland of bulging wallets, fine jewelry, objects d'art, furs, imported leathers, and stores with brimming cash registers that Salvatore Lucania came to realize that intelligence and education were not the exclusive preserves of the Jews. He struck up a lasting friendship with a Calabrian, Francesco Castiglia (later known as Frank Costello), the man who was later to remain his lifelong ally.

Standing on the very first rung of the ladder was no position a determined young man would hold indefinitely. Salvatore Lucania was on his way. He was tough, sometimes vicious—a kid from the streets with little social conscience and a growing penchant for power that would lead him to smash anyone and anything in his way. It was this side of the boy that made Antonio Lucania turn from his son in disgust. But the one side his father did not and would not see was Salvatore's open warmth—his almost naïve ambition, his incongruous eagerness to please and to emulate, his thirst for knowledge, his reliability, and his loyalty.

At eighteen, in his desire to advance himself, the young Lucania dared to hook up with the neighborhood narcotics pusher, George

Scanlon. In the summer of 1916, he was arrested for unlawful possession of narcotics (a phial containing a half dram of heroin) and served six months in Hampton Farms Penitentiary. There he divested himself of the effeminate diminutive *Sal* and emerged a hardened ex-con with the name that stuck: Charlie Luciano.

Twenty years later, almost to the month, the trial of the state of New York versus Charles Luciano et al. opened on a bright, sunny Wednesday morning, May 13, 1936, in the New York State Supreme Court in downtown Manhattan. The charges were "compulsory prostitution" in violation of the New York Penal Law. The presiding judge was the socially prominent Philip J. McCook, seen as the defender of the city's moral outrage. Luciano faced a blue-ribbon jury of twelve middle-class New Yorkers (two alternates)—all upright citizens who were uncomfortable with much of the lurid testimony and dismayed to observe a parade of weary ladies of the night telling their tales of sin and woe. Charlie sat upright, expressionless, aware that all eyes would be upon him. It was a quirk of fate, he thought, that of all the crimes he had committed, the crime of which he was accused was the one of which he was innocent. He shot a glance at the jury, but their gaze was fixed on a short meticulously groomed, impeccably attired man—a man with a pert nose and trimmed black mustache, exuding confidence.

That man, surrounded by a veritable army of assistants whom he had carefully selected, was the special prosecutor Thomas E. Dewey.

Liguari

THE ACCOMPLICE

There was something about the expression on those jurors' faces. The probing looks in their eyes, the disconcerting way in which they fixed their combined gaze upon each of the accused—unemotional, dispassionate, and analytically cold. It unnerved the sturdy young man with the light brown hair crowning a youthful face, with eyes as piercingly blue as any of the Anglo-Saxons in that jury box. Returning glance for glance, Ralph Liguori's expression betrayed nothing at all. He felt an unbidden yawn creeping up the back of his throat and concealed it behind one raised hand. Ralph had lain awake most of the night, trying hard to quell the fear that gnawed at his innards—the fear of what lay ahead. Seated on the hard bench in the cathedral-ceiling courtroom, only two places removed from the Boss himself (Dave Betillo and Jimmy Frederico occupied those two places), Ralph Liguori avoided eye contact with Lucky Luciano and fought to retain his composure.

Arriving in Foley Square earlier, Ralph had felt his flesh prickling with a sense of morbid excitement in the spring air, a kind of "death in the arena" anticipation among the throngs gathered to squeeze in—to witness the biggest criminal trial in history. Hordes of policemen and plainclothesmen had been assigned to the scene but were helpless against the mass invasion of spectators pushing and worming their way through the massive doors of New York's Supreme Court. In the square just beyond those doors, traffic could not budge; cars and taxis and occasional limousines pressed bumper to bumper, horns blaring. Doors slammed as frustrated passengers, late for work, swearing under their breath, left the comfort of the taxis and sedans, attempting in vain to transport them, and tried to hoof it the rest of the way to their offices. No clerk in a law or insurance office could afford to arrive late with the lame excuse of having been caught in a traffic jam.

The Great Depression was just about reaching its peak. Under Franklin Delano Roosevelt's New Deal, some relief was already in sight, a gradual improvement in economic conditions, but it would take another three to four years for real results. Prohibition had been repealed, which had been a farce for many; the population continued to struggle, waiting for the end of the tunnel. For some, fortunately, there was more money, but jobs were still hard to find.

In the courtroom, Ralph gazed at the magnificent paneled walls of dark walnut, the polished wood of the benches and stands. No question, the courtroom with its vaulted ceilings was impressive. Few spectators, Ralph admitted to himself in torment, even among jurors and defendants alike, could ignore the pervasive sensation that they were participants in a historical morality play—an almost holy confrontation between good and evil.

The presiding judge, Philip J. McCook, a staunch Republican from a moneyed family with political connections, had been specially designated by New York's Governor Lehman, at the express wishes of the special prosecutor. McCook's features were a study in piety; he had seated himself with grandiose gestures that reminded Ralph of a Caesar on his throne. Yet for those who knew the man intimately, the piety and grandiosity were merely theatrical. The honorable Judge McCook's narrow-minded prejudice was well-known to many.

Ralph had been written in, so to speak, as defendant number 13, and the superstition hanging over that number added to his sense of uneasiness. Three of the original defendants—Al Weiner, Peter Balitzer, and David Marcus—had defected, having accepted various promises of immunity in exchange for their testimony. Ralph stared at them in contempt; he hated squealers. Apart from Betillo, Frederico, and Pennochio, Ralph realized that the rest of the codefendants—Wahrman, Spiller, Jacobs, Berkman, and Ellenstein—were all Jews. Ralph thought this fact had probably been a hard nut for the special prosecutor. It was clear to him that Dewey, in the public eye, was working his way up, obviously working for the governorship and, from that lofty office, Ralph surmised, directly to the White House. It must have gnawed at his gut to seek the conviction of so many Jews, because Dewey knew damn well it would take the enormous power of the Jewish American influence to put him into the presidency. The special prosecutor, however, cleverly circumvented that problem by openly publicizing that the primary purpose of his crime-busting campaign was to convict the kingpin of the prostitution racket—the Sicilian, Charlie "Lucky," the man whom Dewey entitled the greatest gangster in America.

Ralph glanced over at the attorneys for the defense—some of the finest lawyers in the State, most of them Jews themselves, men who were aware of the driving ambition, the ruthlessness of the Special Prosecutor. Even they—Moses Polakoff, George M. Levy, David Paley, and Samuel and David P. Siegel, to name a few—had professionally no use for Dewey and his tactics. They could sense the political climate, the weight of public opinion, and they brooded solemnly because they knew the odds were against them. Ralph's own attorney, an Italian and, oddly enough, a Republican, was Lorenzo Carlino—an extremely capable man of conviction, alert and sensitive. He was a man of great integrity who had persevered in life to become a well-respected attorney among his peers. He cut a dramatic figure in that courtroom with his dark hair and eyes and strong features. Ralph knew Carlino had guts and would perform with the dedication of his soul, to trouble Judge McCook and to give Dewey a run for his money.

Alongside the group of attorneys sat the special prosecutor himself. Ralph squinted through long lashes to take a scathing look at the man who seemed determined to ruin his life. He seemed to pose like a god in the courtroom, so sure of himself in his dapper pin-striped suit and vest with that rigid collar and cuffs so white they blinded one's eyes. He wore a single-breasted suit, of course, to make him look taller; how he loved the limelight, smiling under the natty, glossy mustache that cartoonists had trademarked. *That Napoleonic sonofabitch!* Ralph steamed inwardly. Dewey had a way of belittling a man with his supercilious, condescending grin. Even among those who supported him, he had his critics and adversaries, but that didn't bother him. "His love of criminal prosecution"—wrote a journalist of Dewey before the trial got under way—"amounts almost to a mania." He had promised reporters much cooperation; Ralph learned from conversations with some of the guys who followed the Luciano people. If a news photographer, however, dared to compromise the dignity of Dewey's office by snapping pictures in an awkward position (with his mouth open or taking a bite out of a sandwich), that hapless photographer would no longer be welcome on his company's staff. It was no secret that Dewey could pull enough strings with the newspaper publishers to have the man fired.

Ralph, reminiscing as he sat waiting on the courtroom bench, remembered Dewey's first speech from his Woolworth offices asking for public help. When the results of that speech had proved inconsequential, Dewey had revealed his hypocrisy with an about-face—subpoenaed witnesses when they would not talk and cited them for contempt, all in the name of virtue, in the name of morality.

Top men in the various gangs had, until then, considered Dewey only a pain in the ass, a flash in the pan, who would rave and rant and then disappear from view. Few thought of rubbing him out because he was so visible, which was his strongest shield of defense. Such an act would not only martyr the man, but would bring down the full force of government law and order upon all their heads. Most men, especially Luciano, wanted no part of that. Ralph had heard various conversations between

Charlie and his underlings. "Getting" Dewey was considered out of the question. It would have led to widespread consequences. When gangland leader Dutch Schultz (born Arthur Flegenheimer) had decided to take matters into his own hands, planning to eliminate the special prosecutor, Schultz lost his own life one desolate day in October 1935. Afterwards, Ralph knew that Charlie, with some bitterness, regretted his decision and, as the trial progressed, cursed himself a thousand and one times for his ambivalence about Dewey's importance.

To make matters worse, one of Dewey's most powerful tools was his Joinder Indictment, a new statute that he sent to Albany for adoption by the State Senate and supported by Governor Herbert H. Lehman and Herb Brownell in the legislature. It was quickly endorsed by the City Bar Association, the State House Assembly, and by Mayor Fiorello La Guardia, and the Joinder Law became known as the Dewey Law. Under this law, an innocent person could be incriminated simply by association with a criminal—a measure that combined more than one law in a conviction. A few civil libertarians had objected to the measure, but their outcries were drowned out by public applause. And for Ralph Liguori, it was the decisive tool that worked effectively to bring him to the defendants' bench alongside Lucky Luciano.

For all but two of his thirty years, Ralph Liguori believed he had been born in New York City, and that he was as much a *Yankee Doodle Dandy* as Tom Dewey himself. Why his parents withheld the truth about his birth from him was one of those ridiculous mysteries that defy explanation. He learned, too late, that he too had emigrated from Trastevere (Rome) to New York in February 1907 with his family when he was only eleven months old. It was something that would haunt him throughout his later life.

Unlike other immigrants, the Liguori family was comfortably settled by Ralph's uncles in a home behind a barbershop equipped with eight barber chairs, which meant that his father, Joseph Liguori, would employ seven barbers—an unheard beginning in those days. Ralph's mother, Agnes, belonged to a family known to be *benestante* (well-to-do) with two brothers in the jewelry business, carrying on the family tradition. For generations, the Ruggeri family had lived in Trastevere, the most popular section of old Rome—across the Tiber River via the Ponte Garibaldi and far enough away from the Vatican. Two of Agnes's sisters had also married well, and since there had never been the slightest hint of hardship among his ancestors, Ralph always wondered why his parents had decided to leave Rome for the New World. But his father's five brothers and three sisters had long before established themselves in

America, and Joseph, the only sibling remaining in Rome, longed to be reunited with his family.

The Brooklyn home, at 291 Fifth Avenue, was by no means luxurious but was equipped with many modern comforts in three rooms with kitchen and bath. It was there that Agnes and Joseph celebrated the birth of their much desired daughter, their fourth child, Anna. Slowly, they acclimated themselves to their new surroundings, not yet fully accepting what they found in their new society, but took comfort from the closeness of numerous relatives who helped make the transition easier. Not easily discouraged, they struggled to master the harsh sounds of the English language, which was not soft and round or musical like their beloved Italian. Gradually, as did most Italians, they created a pasticcio—a hodgepodge of English and Italian. When uncomfortable with a word, they would simply Latinize it, as did everyone else in their social sphere. Thus, they had no trouble communicating among themselves. It was their way of bringing their own language closer to them.

Some years later, Joseph Liguori, tired of barbering, opened a supermarket at 2024 Gravesend Avenue near Kings Highway in Brooklyn, into which he incorporated a meat department. This move included a five-room house above the market. The new home boasted a marvelous kitchen paneled with fine wood and equipped with the most up-to-date appliances. The bathroom, to everyone's delight, contained a large Victorian bathtub. With all new furniture and even a piano in the parlor for little Anna, the family had taken a step upward, and Ralph's mother began feeling more secure in her new country. Agnes trusted her husband completely, as did all who dealt with him in business. Joseph Liguori was a great guy with a warm and winning personality, proud of his ability to pave the way for his three sons. He dreamed of a great American future for them.

Never ever could Joseph Liguori envision his youngest son to be accused of serious crimes—to be seated with a group of gangsters in a courtroom at the mercy of a gangbuster determined to make a sacrificial lamb of him.

BOOK I

CHAPTER ONE

"Your Honor, this is the beginning of a fight for justice!" Those few clipped words rang through the electrified air of the courtroom and were punctuated by the sharp snap of Carlino's briefcase as he darted a grim look, eloquent in its wordlessness, at Ralph Liguori. A look that stated, "Courage. We're not through yet!" Then, with an abrupt turn, the fiery young defense attorney made a hurried exit from the courtroom.

For decades afterwards, the replay of that courtroom scene would appear repeatedly before Ralph's stinging eyes in minute detail. He would study Judge McCook's florid face, the way he nudged the lower rim of his spectacles upward, away from the glistening ridges of his puffy cheeks, and the way his hand clasped the gavel, poised with it in a frozen moment of suspense. Stifling humid heat had been entering through the courtroom's open windows; bright, shimmering waves of sunlight caused spots of color here and there, heightened somehow by the irritating drone of a horsefly fluttering round the room. Ralph leaned forward and saw the mottled faces of the legal adversaries as he strained to hear the judge's grave pronouncement.

McCook mouthed something about having considered Carlino's motion for a separate trial regarding Ralph Liguori on the grounds that the latter's constitutional rights were being violated. Etched forever in Ralph's memory was the cold look exchanged between his dedicated attorney, Carlino, and the presiding judge. Poetically handsome with brooding eyes and a shock of dark hair, his slender hands trembling with fury and agitation, Lorenzo Carlino's open scowl bespoke his contempt for this officer of the court who had been swayed by pomp and politics. The implacable State Supreme Court justice McCook had prejudged the matter and decided it would not be in the best interest of the prosecution—of the gangbuster, Thomas E. Dewey—to agree to a separate trial for Carlino's client, Ralph Liguori.

And so the gavel came down. It was May 5, 1936.

Ralph heard the words, "Motion denied." Finis, fait accompli. Ralph Liguori, innocent of the charges, having had nothing whatsoever to do with organized prostitution, was to be tarred with the same brush Dewey wielded against the one man he wanted out of the way—Luciano.

He already had made a name for himself prosecuting “Legs” Diamond, followed by equally sensational legal assaults against Waxey Gordon and other Jewish gangland figures.

Now he wanted the Sicilian boss!

Just what kind of people were these Sicilians, the public wanted to know. What indeed were these secret societies of criminals, dangerous men banding together in clubs and clans and in “families,” calling themselves by exotic, cultlike names? And what of the dark imprint of a black human hand at the bottom of dire warning notes—letters of veiled threats, already striking terror into the hearts of many a man and woman in New York and other principal cities where masses of immigrants had chosen to settle? The notoriety of the dreaded *Black Hand* had spread insidiously, accompanied by the growth of an even more powerful, sinister organization. Its members regarded it as their “house,” their “family,” permitting a growing army of nondescript, barely literate immigrant men to achieve a measure of importance and respect (*rispetto*) simply by letting it be known that they had ties to the Cosa Nostra—to the Mafia.

To those victimized, the old country codes of *vendetta* and *omerta*—which encompassed ancient tribal rivalries and grudges, unresolved antagonisms, and hostilities with vows to avenge, vows to kill—were unacceptable, intolerable, not to be absorbed into any aspect of American life. Yet nobody could deny the existence of those codes, nor that they had been spilling over daily into the congested streets and alleys of the teeming city. Many a vessel, accompanied by unpredictable winds, made its way across the Atlantic to Ellis Island, carrying in new masses of huddling humanity, the wretched refuse of southern European shores. Gradually, crime itself became synonymous with one ancient Mediterranean designation: Sicily. The ethnic description of the *Sicilian* conjured up in the minds of nervous, frightened, and revolted Americans the sense of criminal power—the sense of evil.

The Italian mainland, struggling through its history to maintain its own existence, had (almost from the beginning) forsaken the beautiful island of Sicily. Historians have traced its oldest inhabitants to the Stone Age, to a people thought to be called the Sicani of Iberian origin who settled in the island’s northwest, together with another ancient people believed to have come from the fertile crescent in Asia Minor: the Elimi or Elymians. The eastern shores of the island were settled by southern Italic immigrants called Siculi who, following the Phoenicians, had been greatly influenced by Greek domination. It is thought that the original intermeshing of inhabitants began with these earliest settlers, and the island became known as Sicily.

Democratization began with the Greeks, under whose rule the arts were encouraged to flourish. Under Roman domination at the end of the third century BC, Sicily became important as the granary of Rome. There followed a series of invasions and conquests: the Byzantines and the Arabs (whose domination lasted two centuries and whose architectural influence is still visible). The Norman-Swabian rule, raising Sicily to new heights under Emperor Frederick II (dubbed King of Sicily), King Frederick joined the island's rule with that of the southern part of Italy, principally Naples, from which emerged references as the Two Sicilies. In his court, the Sicilian dialect became the chief literary language of Italy. Later, the Tuscans took that credit, thanks to Dante Alighieri and his beautiful, flowing pen.

The rule of a Frenchman, Angevin, was greatly unpopular and short-lived, ending in 1282 with the Sicilian Vespers, because of the bloody massacre by the French for their incessant and indiscriminate ravishment of Sicilian women. To their dubious credit, it was the first uprising in which the Sicilians successfully banded together in a common cause, a common battle. A long Spanish (Argonese) rule followed, but despite periodic popular rebellions, the Sicilian peasants could not undo the double stranglehold of the rich barons and monarchy. Following the bitter Spanish and Austrian wars, Sicily found itself assigned to the House of Savoy, only to be swapped for Sardinia and passed to the House of Bourbon. The embattled island miraculously survived one bloodbath after another, often approaching total obliteration, until it was finally unified with Italy in 1860 by Giuseppe Garibaldi. The unification with the mainland, however, did not bring an end to the woes of the island. The Italians looked upon Sicily as a poor, wretched relative who was not really wanted in respectable circles, and the Sicilians remained an embarrassment to their kinsmen up and down the "boot" of mainland Italy.

Is it any wonder that the region's unfortunate history and the blending of bloodlines of some of the fiercest and most passionate people of the world should lend credence to the common belief of natural lawlessness among Sicilians? After centuries of exploitations, and in spite of their temperaments, the Sicilians had learned to be submissive; and in their pursuit for happiness, some had taken adverse and sometimes dangerous byways. But this ancient, sensitive people were also envied for their many inherent artistic talents, acute minds (arborous and loyal attributes), all peppered with a high dose of family love and pride. The island has produced some of Italy's finest writers, poets, musicians, scientists, and, yes, politicians.

Ralph Liguori was not Sicilian. His roots were cultivated in a more noble land. He was Roman. But in the streets of New York, poor Sicilians, Italians, Jews, and Irish were one and the same. Regardless of ethnicity in that early Prohibition era in the melting pots of the New World, they were by and large tempted at one time or another to cross over the straight and narrow. Money was always a primary motive. To test one's own daring and courage, to forge new alliances and find acceptance among one's peers was primary. And for thrills along with a whole variety of reasons. Those reasons were by no means the exclusive property of the Sicilians. But in spite of their good qualities with their large families, their manner of speech and dress, the Sicilians became more visible in the community and more likely to be suspected of crime. Consequently, they outdistanced other ethnic groups on the police blotters. The Irish Catholics and Protestants alike were just as rough and boasted just as many hoodlums. Many had escaped public condemnation and law enforcement harassment, because they had practically taken over the ranks of the New York Police Department and filled the offices of the city's politicians.

Nor were the Jews to be left far behind in statistical surveys of ethnic crime. All too often, however, Jewish lawbreakers had wealthy, respectable relatives (and at least one lawyer in the family) who would pay heavily to keep their irresponsible young kinsman from disgracing them in their new homeland. It was no secret that animosity existed between some of the gangs, regardless of nationalities.

Ralph knew of Charlie Luciano's close brush with death at the hands of a group of New York cops in 1929. It occurred during the pursuit of the independent bandit "Legs" Diamond. Several Irishmen, as ruthless and powerful as any group of Sicilians, decided to get rid of Luciano, the "Wop," the "Goombah," who had been giving them a headache. (Ralph was always convinced that the Winberry Brothers did the job on Luciano because later, he too would be victim of the same Irish cops.) The Winberry team hauled Charlie into a car, took him to some isolated spot in Staten Island, and, after brutally beating the hell out of Charlie, they left him for dead—but not before, as a last sign of horrific punishment, they slashed one side of his face. Miraculously, Charlie survived their merciless beating; and as he touched his slashed face, he thirsted for vengeance. With grim determination, he crawled along a desolate road until pals—frantically searching for him—ultimately found him. The nickname Lucky (which had been given to him in the early days when he was rolling dice on the streets and always winning) began to stick in earnest from then on. Small-time punks, however, were the ones who primarily used that name (of course, history has also adopted the name in reference to him).

Those in Luciano's inner circle began referring to him as the Boss of All Bosses, but his actual code name—used only by his closest allies—became the General.

For those mysterious reasons that sometimes bond people in lifelong friendships, Ralph found himself one of Luciano's close favorites in an association that lasted until the latter's death. Luciano, nine years older than Ralph, took the younger man under his wing in a protective, fraternal manner; and Ralph grew to admire, respect, and, ultimately, love the soft-spoken, polite man with the black hair and dark, fiery eyes. Careful about his appearance, Luciano preferred conservative business suits elegantly tailored and a variety of snappy hats, which he wore slightly tipped to one side. He seldom smoked and rarely raised his voice—unless someone had tickled his funny bone, sending him into a hearty, distinctive, and unmistakable laugh. He had a tremendous sense of humor, was known to be generous with tips and with women, sharing Ralph's abiding interest in pretty girls. Once, after a day at the races in Saratoga, Charlie and Ralph were relaxing over a drink in the bar when a beautiful curvaceous call girl strolled by. Charlie leaned over confidentially and whispered, "She cost me $100 the other night!"

"What? You're crazy. I only paid $50," Ralph smirked triumphantly.

Charlie stared incredulously, then broke into his famous laughter as he gently patted Ralph's shoulder and raised his glass in approval.

This camaraderie pertained only to call girls. In the arena of more serious relationships, each man lived strictly by the code of the fraternal society in which they existed. Neither man ever made a single advance toward any woman who had first attracted the interest of the other. This was an unwritten law among all of their allies.

The heavy atmosphere of the courtroom brought Ralph out of his reverie to pick up sensitively on the shuffling of feet, the coughing of the jurors and spectators, and the whispering in the press box, where columnists Dorothy Kilgallen and Walter Winchell sat, staring fixedly at Dewey. Ralph recognized some of the other newsmen from the *New York Times*, the *Herald Tribune*, the *Journal-American*, the *Daily News*, the *Daily Mirror*, and the *Brooklyn Eagle*—all taking notes while the court reporter tapped away at his stenotype machine, recording Dewey's words as they were spoken. Completely stressed, Ralph thought, *Damn, that bastard has been speaking for four and a half hours!*

Dewey had seated himself informally at the edge of a table, addressing the jurors as if he were conversing with them at a cocktail party. He looked subdued, having gained the confidence of the blue-ribbon jury, but Ralph knew that was all a sham. The special prosecutor was a shrewd, calculating man, with a format minutely planned in advance.

"Convict the boss," he stated dramatically as he rose to face the entire courtroom, "or turn all others out. We've had convictions of front men for years!" Referring to the defense lawyers failing to produce persons who would crack on the stand, he practically shouted, "Everyone in whom Luciano had any faith was called. The whole underworld had spewed up its rotten guts in behalf of Luciano."

From where Ralph was seated, he could see Charlie Luciano staring straight ahead, showing no emotion, but he could tell by the way Charlie's jaw was set hard that he was seething inside and grinding his teeth. The long scar that ran from the outer part of the right cheek to his chin where it was more noticeable (a souvenir of his Staten Island beating by the Irish cops) made him look rather sinister when he was tense. Although it was common street knowledge that the Winberry boys had disfigured Charlie, newspeople had always tried to tie his scar to a gang war between the gang lords Maranzano and Masseria. That was all claptrap. The truth was that the line between cops and robbers was very thin. Corruption in the police force made the existence of crime possible. The one could not exist without the other. Lawmen were never above using the roughest tactics imaginable to force a confession or simply for their own sick, sadistic pleasure. They were known (on the streets) to have eliminated a lawbreaker, disposing of the body and placing the blame on rival gangs. The criminal element had to swallow those revelations in silence. How could they ever press charges?

Dewey was still speaking, not even close to winding down. Still referring to Luciano, the primary target of his entire campaign, he exclaimed that Charles "Lucky" Luciano was no common gambler who stood before the bar of justice. No, indeed. Luciano, he stated, was the greatest gangster and assassin in America and had used fall guys all his life. "We've had enough of sacrificing front men," Dewey said. "Isn't it about time we convict the boss?" One look at the jury and Ralph knew for certain that Dewey had won—that without another single word being uttered, he had won it all.

"There's little purpose in sending any but the big shots to prison," Dewey concluded. "This time, we're out to destroy the entire structure of the industry."

And of course, Ralph steamed within himself; Tom Dewey didn't give a good goddamn if that meant destroying innocent men along the line. Not when *his* career, *his* fame, was at stake. Not when *his* success in the landmark trial would be his stepping stone to bigger and better things.

Ralph kept jarring himself awake periodically as Dewey's voice droned on and on. In the hot, stuffy courtroom, it was impossible to concentrate. Attorneys, jurors, defendants et al. tried hard not to be lulled to sleep by the ongoing voice of the—special prosecutor—but when Dewey mentioned Dotty's name, it jolted Ralph, and he became wide awake and alert. Poor little Dotty. Dewey hadn't the slightest compunction about impugning her character, besmirching her before the eyes of the world as a prostitute and a drug abuser. Ralph knew better than that. He looked at her with compassion and shuddered at what he saw.

Dotty's face appeared swollen, her eyes puffy. The tension of the trial and her long addiction to dope had taken its toll. Dewey was quick to pounce upon THAT vulnerability in Dotty (Dewey insisted on using the name Nancy Presser whenever referring to the beautiful young victim) to extract various confessions and admissions from the girl. He went so far as to imply that she had been on intimate terms with Charlie Luciano!

Ralph wanted to jump from his seat. How could the smug bastard lie like that in a court of law! He had won an enviable reputation with his fists on the streets of New York, and at that moment, with Dewey's scurrilous lie ringing in his ears, it was all Ralph could do to keep from leaping forward and cracking Dewey's jaw. He wanted to stem the tide of that loathsome outpouring of venom. There had never been anything whatsoever between Luciano and Dotty!

Dotty had been Ralph's girl, and the unwritten code of the society prohibited a man from toying with the affections of another man's woman. It was a rule that went back to the dawn of civilization and for the Sicilians and those to whom their family ties extended; it was a rule that survived through the ages of time.

Instantly, Dewey turned to squint at Ralph with a contemptuous smirk, the kind of gloating expression that declares, "Vengeance is sweet." A look that warned Ralph he would nail him for sure. He HAD to nail Ralph, HAD to make sure that Ralph Liguori's voice was silenced. Because Ralph, whom Dewey accused of being the stickup man for Luciano's vice syndicate, was the only man who could speak the truth.

CHAPTER TWO

The headlines of the *New York Daily News* screamed in bold black print: DEWEY RIDDLES LUCKY ON STAND.

The special prosecutor had made Luciano squirm, forcing him to admit knowing a group of criminals like Lepke Buchalter, Jake Gurrah, and Bugsy Siegel—all sterling, upright citizens known throughout the east by many as law-abiding philanthropists. Luciano adamantly denied any personal acquaintanceship with Ciro Terranova or Al Capone, but his testimony was blasted by the introduction into evidence of hotel records and telephone cross-reference slips, clearly linking Luciano's Waldorf Astoria Hotel suite with the unlisted numbers of both gangland bosses.

Lorenzo Carlino, in his no-holds-barred verbal assault on the special prosecutor, referred to Dewey as, "The greatest actor I've ever seen . . . the boy prosecutor . . . a Boy Scout dressed in khaki shorts!" Not only, Carlino stormed, did Dewey condone perjury and offer protection to pimps, prostitutes, and drug addicts whom he used as witnesses, "but," the defense attorney scathingly protested, "he presents his mock evidence . . . with the charm of a beautiful cobra . . . while consuming thousands of glasses of water!"

There was no question that the firepower of the brilliant defense attorneys had begun making inroads into the strength of Dewey's barrages. He had been hurling charges at the accused, fermenting substantial doubts in the minds of the enthralled jurors, and appeared to have been personally wounded by the onslaught of the defense attorneys. Consequently, he worked on his summation well into the wee hours of dawn. Dewey was pale and subdued upon arriving at the courthouse on that morning, but when he began to speak, his indignation at the personal attacks made against him and his staff began rising, and his sarcastic barbs took on a metallic edge as he pierced again and again into the tough hide of the defense strategy.

"I've heard myself described as the greatest actor in America," he stated petulantly, with a glare at Carlino, "and the stupidest dolt. I have heard myself described as an irresponsible child of thirty-two, and as Machiavelli's lineal descendant."

The jurors, picking up on the special prosecutor's personal appeal for understanding and compassion, sat mesmerized, listening to Dewey's recitation of the ordeal he had endured for four and a half months—trying to work with prostitutes, pimps, gangsters, bookers of women; hearing their stories; persuading fifty-five of those lowlives to testify; holding their hands; offering them immunity.

"You cannot convict bookers of women on the testimony of anybody but the people they booked. You cannot convict the men at the very top of a criminal enterprise except upon the testimony of the people who were their associates, their subordinates, or their intimates." Dewey paused, eyes glistening with annoyance, fixed his gaze toward the spellbound jurors, and exclaimed caustically, "Of course, we can't prove that Luciano placed girls in houses. He had graduated from that." Then he admittedly called attention to the telephone calls from the Waldorf Astoria, which had revealed the names of some of Luciano's associates.

But Dewey's stumbling block was Ralph Liguori. Ralph had never betrayed a friendship. From the outset, Dewey had received no cooperation from Ralph, and that failure drove Dewey wild with frustration. For that reason, Dotty (Nancy Presser) had become absolutely essential to the special crime buster as a witness who could refute whatever Ralph testified.

"For two hours, I sat with her, trying to persuade her to testify," Dewey continued in his marathon summation, stating he had personally assured the trembling girl that she would not be *murdered*!

"If you want to know what responsibility is, try to persuade a witness, trembling with terror, to go to the stand," he went on fervently as though Dotty's welfare truly concerned him. "The defense did everything to blast her. They resorted to every device known to corruption to break down her story. Why did they try to destroy her by all their evil means except that they don't dare face the truth?"

Ralph knew that Dewey had coerced the girl, had backed her up against a wall, knowing she was badly in need of a fix—using every trick in the book to use her testimony as a means of driving a wedge between Ralph and Luciano. Ralph felt his eyes smart as he remembered the first time he discovered that Dotty took dope, the first night he sat with her as she torturously went through her first withdrawal. But this kind of sentimentality had no place in Dewey's makeup. Now Dewey had more to say about Ralph and delivered his statements with gusto. "Liguori, the only defendant, except Luciano, to take the stand in his own defense, did so as a human sacrifice for his boss . . ." He seemed to take pleasure in vilifying Ralph and spouted on how Ralph was the stickup man for the syndicate and was heard only to discredit the testimony of his sweetheart, Dotty. "Who had boasted having been on intimate terms with Luciano and having learned his secrets.

"Why was a sacrifice made out of Liguori?" Dewey glowered in Ralph's direction. "Everybody at the defense table knew Luciano would be slaughtered under cross-examination. They knew he wouldn't last fifteen minutes before it became apparent that he was a procurer, and one of the worst perjurers in the courtroom. They were trying to sacrifice the little guy to save the big guy, under orders from the boss. Imagine the power of that man!"

Dewey's words kept reverberating in Ralph's head. "Why was a sacrifice made out of Liguori?" *What a goddamn liar! Carlino was right.* Ralph boiled inside. Dewey was not only a great actor; he could have been one of the greatest con men in history! *What a bastard,* Ralph seethed. He knew practically nothing about Ralph the man but had decided that Ralph would be part of his plan for a victorious conviction. Sure, he had a dossier on Ralph, containing all the vital statistics. He knew that Ralph's sturdy build made him appear larger and more powerful than he actually was; that he was an arresting-looking man with youthful, sensitive features; that he was an elegant dresser who enjoyed driving big expensive cars and who smoked El Producto cigars.

But there were smaller details that Dewey didn't know or, if he did, felt were inconsequential. For instance, it was probably unimportant for Dewey's purposes to know that Ralph was a fastidious man, impeccable in his attire, changing clothes several times a day, insisting on silk shirts and neatly ironed underwear. Or that Ralph was a family man, generous to relatives and friends, a sucker for a sob story. What Dewey SHOULD have known from the very outset was that when Ralph's pride was injured, his temper was formidable; that he was extremely selective in his choice of friends and that, once having made a friend, was loyal to a fault. Finally, Dewey had erred badly in believing that Ralph, like every other man, had his price or could be persuaded to compromise his principles to perjure himself.

Judge McCook took over and began his lengthy discourse, which lasted more than two and a half hours. Everything he said in his instructions to the jury sounded fair and contained in each word the bright ring of justice.

"I have tried to give you a fair picture of the situation. You must consider the form of the testimony. The question of credibility is most important. The majority of the witnesses do not rank very high on the social scale." On the credibility of prostitutes, he lectured, "A prostitute is at once a victim of an enticer, and her life is full of lies, but I say she is not unworthy of belief merely because she is a prostitute. You must give to her story the same weight as a reputable person. If you believe, then the story stands."

Realizing the probable confusion regarding the conspiracy law in the minds of the distraught jurors, the fact that the prosecution had only to establish a common design and unity of purpose among the codefendants, McCook explained, "The act of one was the act of all even though one or more might not have taken part in the crime, or known of it until long after it was committed. If you find one guilty, then all are guilty." He emphasized, "The crimes of which these men are accused are vicious and low, and those who would aid and abet such crimes are not to be met in polite society."

As soon as he concluded his summation, the defense attorneys flung a barrage of objections, shouting for additional charges, and McCook listened. Under pressure from them and to counterbalance his obvious partiality toward the prosecution, he admonished Dewey for his melodramatic statements, which claimed that, "Luciano maintained a reign of terror throughout the course of this case. Failure to prove parts of my opening was due to those terroristic tactics." And he ruled that they be stricken off the record.

He further warned the blue-ribbon jury to disregard damaging statements regarding Luciano's gangster reputation, "There being no evidence before this court." Nevertheless, any analytical mind could determine that McCook and Dewey had played an enchanting duet.

The courtroom was still filled with chaos, a welter of voices resounding, a kinetic scene, a free-for-all, and Judge McCook shouted over and over again for order. Finally, he dramatically spoke his stern last words to the jurors, "You alone are the judges of the facts!"

The gavel came down thunderously.

Court was dismissed!

Once the jury was sequestered to deliberate and the accused were dispatched to waiting for the verdict, Ralph did try his best to relax. Dinner, including Luciano's favorite dish, was delivered to their room by Giovanni of the Grotta Azzurra Restaurant, a friend of the group; and in the presence of four or five policemen on guard inside the room, the men managed to enjoy their meal. Trying valiantly to keep their morale high, the men discussed the brilliant work of their attorneys, whom they considered the finest in the field. For several hours, Ralph and Luciano exchanged gags and maintained an outward expression of stoicism. They excused themselves from playing cards with the others to pass the time and speculated that with the jury taking so long to arrive at a verdict, there was a chance they would be acquitted. When word filtered through that Wall Street was offering two-to-one odds for acquittal, their spirits rose slightly, but no man among them wanted to kid himself. A few prayed silently. The men had made a pact that anyone falling asleep before the verdict came in would get a hotfoot.

Ralph was the first to succumb. Drained of his emotions, he could no longer keep his eyes open and dozed off. Jimmy Frederico quietly produced a pack of book matches and carefully inserted one corner of the cardboard into the binding of Ralph's shoe. As he ignited the matchbook, all eyes were fixed on the tiny fire, which flared up and licked at the sole and toe of the shoe. In silence they waited, not daring to make a sound, restraining their hilarity at the anticipated reaction of the sleeping victim.

Luciano laughed the hardest when Ralph's foot wiggled a few times, then kicked forward. Ralph sat bolt upright, his pale blue eyes bulging, emitting a hoarse outcry as he leaped to his feet and went into a spirited dance. Hearing the laughter, Ralph couldn't help but join the merriment and glanced at his old friend's face, finding it strangely youthful, filled with good-natured mirth. It was an open face, nothing evil about it. *I love this man,* he reminded himself. *I did not betray our friendship. I never could.* They had been too close—had shared too much, possessed too many of the same qualities.

Ralph accepted the affectionate slaps on his back for having been the "designated clown" to lighten their hearts, to break up the monotony, and to temporarily suppress their fears. Then Ralph sat back, clasped his hands, and, head bent down, wondered how the path of his young life had led him to that moment.

CHAPTER THREE

"Ralphy!"

"Yes, ma'am?"

Ralph stood up as Ms. Prime came toward him with a book in her hand, glasses perched on her nose.

"Did you write this?" She had the book opened, and he caught sight of the four penciled letters in his second-grade scrawl. He had seen that word on a hundred walls, but now he knew it was a bad word by the look on her face. "Come with me, Ralphy," she commanded in an outraged voice.

Red-faced, knowing that the rest of the kids were watching, Ralph followed her out of the classroom.

He was told to wait outside the principal's office until, after what seemed an eternity, she motioned him in. Mrs. Daley, the principal, always had a smile for the kids; and now flashing that smile, she said sweetly, "Ralphy, will you go to the janitor and get me some Lifebuoy soap?"

"Yes, ma'am," the boy replied politely, his blue eyes snapping suspiciously, but he scurried off on his mission.

On his way back, he found Ms. Prime and another teacher waiting for him in the hallway. As he stretched out his arm to hand over the soap, he realized he was trapped. Ms. Prime grabbed his hands while the other shoved the soap in his mouth. Ralph felt the burning, distasteful taste in his mouth and struggled desperately against their clutching hands. Finally, he wriggled free and ran all the way home. The minor infraction escalated into a major catastrophe, and Ralph's mother was called to school. Only her wisdom and old country charm saved Ralph from being expelled. He was in the second grade at PS 77 in Brooklyn, and the incident had a far-reaching effect on Ralph. As he grew, and especially in his adult years, in and out of trouble, Ralph never used vulgarity in his speech or habits. There was no doubt, however, about Ralph's toughness. He was highly respected for his adeptness in tight situations, but at times, some of his pals mocked him for his gentlemanly manners, especially when he became a soft touch for someone. It was just good-natured fun because everyone admired Ralph. He was a "champion of the underdog."

For the remainder of his school days at PS 77, Ralph managed to become the principal's pet and began to learn respect and trust from her. He, of course, knew how to use his baby blue eyes to charm even an elderly woman. Ralph was a lively, intelligent boy who brought home a good report card—mostly to impress his father, with whom he had a special bond. Joseph Liguori couldn't resist favoring his blue-eyed, towheaded youngest boy, and Ralph's love for his father mounted to new heights with each passing year. There wasn't anything Ralph wouldn't do for the man. His desire to please, however, would sometimes backfire. In third grade, Ralph imagined himself a sort of Santa Claus, gleefully passing out gifts to his classmates. He had worked out a plan. Knowing that his mother kept loose change in a cloth bag pinned under her pinafore, he waited one morning until his father had left for work, then crept stealthily into the bedroom where his mother was sleeping. He had tiptoed midway into the room. When she tossed and turned, Ralph froze, expecting the worst, but luck was with him. His mother sighed and turned in her sleep.

Noiselessly, Ralph skillfully unfastened the pouch, then sneaked back to bed, grinning as he visualized his friends' grateful smiles. At breakfast, Ralph downed his milk and cereal with unusual speed and enthusiasm, surprising his mother. She watched curiously as her son rushed out for school, not knowing that he was heading straight for the candy store.

As he opened the money bag, Ralph felt a pang somewhere near his heart. He had already picked out the goodies and was about to pay when he realized he was spending his mother's savings. It was however too late. Out of the seventy dollars he discovered carefully folded inside the pouch, he very slowly counted out twenty dollars. His vision of distributing the candy overcame, momentarily, any guilt feelings that had begun to rise.

In the school yard, his generosity was compensated by the children's surprised, happy faces, squealing gratefully. No sooner had he and his classmates seated themselves than his mother appeared, standing very tall and erect in the doorway.

"Ralphy?"

Sheepishly and without a word, glance glued to the floor, Ralph went toward her with the money bag. She did not embarrass him further but leaned over and whispered, "We'll talk about this at home!"

Agnes Liguori never did tell her husband, but Ralph's behind stung for a long time. He was however grateful to her, not only for saving him from a stiffer punishment, but for not having to face the disappointment in his beloved father's eyes. Thus, Ralph learned to curb his enthusiasm over childlike fantasies. It was a fact that although Joseph abounded in love and generosity, he was also a great disciplinarian. His children returned his love but feared his wrath. While Agnes didn't spare the rod, Joseph primarily used his eyes as a tool. He would utter only a few words of reprimand, then fix his errant child with an icy stare, causing instant silence. Once he shifted his gaze, the matter was closed, and the child dared to breathe again.

Shortly after Joseph opened his supermarket, he surprised his family by bringing home a beautiful thoroughbred horse—a racehorse from the Far West. It had cost a cool thousand, a lot of money then, but he considered it an investment as well as a personal joy. The Liguori boys named him Dick, although everyone loved him, especially Ralph, who was enthralled. The horse adored Joseph. They enjoyed a special kind of communication, and when Dick pranced about on the sidewalk (cart and all), it was interpreted that he wanted an apple. Always well-groomed, Dick was kept in a barn a few blocks away; and after dinner, Ralph would rush over to feed him. While Dick munched his food, Ralph talked to him about mundane things. Sometimes Dick would stop eating, gaze at the small wide-eyed boy, as if he fully understood, and continue munching away. Ralph was one happy lad in Brooklyn.

It was three o'clock one morning when Joseph quietly awakened his young son. The night before, he had announced it was time Ralph learned about the family business, and that they would go together to the central market to buy fresh goods and meat for the store. When Ralph heard his father's voice, he sprang to the window to look at the sky. A prophetic thought came to him, *I hope it doesn't rain.* Dick strutted along, creating a pleasant rhythmic clip-clopping on the cobblestones, when suddenly, the skies turned an awesome gray. Ralph could see the jagged lines of lightning in the distance and felt vaguely uneasy. Peals of thunder grew more ominous, and suddenly, a cold rain rushed down. Dick whinnied calamitously as they approached the big hill on Washington Avenue, which ran down to the Wallerby Market. The hill had become very slick with the rain, and Ralph clutched his father's arm, terrified. It felt as though Dick's hooves were slipping, and despite his father's reassurance that the horse knew his stuff, Ralph hung on tightly. He made up his mind to play sick the next time it looked like rain before embarking on another trip to the market.

Ralph eventually outgrew his fears, mostly because Joseph took special care in developing his son's character (his self-reliance) to have confidence in himself. Joseph covertly saw his youngest son, with his alert mind and buoyant personality, as his heir in managing the family business. Al, Ralph's elder brother, was a carefree lad, fonder of his good times than of becoming a store manager. He was instead responsible for selling outside the supermarket. Every morning, except Saturday, he would hitch up Dick, stock the cart with fresh fruits and vegetables, prepared foodstuff, and venture out into the countryside.

"Are you going fishing again this morning?" Joseph asked his eldest son, entering the boys' bedroom. It was Saturday, a day on which Al usually went fishing, or so his father thought. "Why don't you take Ralphy today?" he continued. Al nodded assent while Ralph squirmed in bed with delight. When his father had gone, Al frowned, not too happy about taking his seven-year-old brother.

"Okay, Ralphy," he called. "Get with it! We're going to Coney Island."

When at last they stood in front of the huge billboards of the movie house, Al pulled Ralph close to him. "Listen, Ralphy. I'm going to tell you something, and don't say anything to Poppa OR anybody! I don't go fishing on Saturday. Nobody knows it, but me." He paused, waiting for Ralph's reaction.

Surprised and disillusioned, Ralph avoided his brother's eyes. "Yeah, okay," he replied dejectedly.

"Now, here, take the money for the show. I'll pick you up later," Al urged.

Ralph nodded silently. It was a shoot-'em-up Western, but Ralph didn't enjoy the prospect of watching it by himself. After the movie, Ralph leaned against the wall outside the theater for what seemed like hours, waiting for Al. At last he spotted him approaching with a package under his arm.

"Fresh fish for Poppa," Al grinned, pointing to the parcel. Puzzled by the deception, Ralph remained silent all the way home. It saddened him to learn of Al's hoax, especially because it betrayed their father's love for them.

Joseph walked around the counter to receive Al's package of fish, all smiles while patting his eldest son on the back. "These I'll sell to my best customers." He beamed with pride. Ralph smiled but betrayed nothing. He loved his father and didn't want to lie to him, so he always avoided the subject, happy that Joe Liguori was happy.

Sunday was always a special day, with a festive air brightening the house. Agnes moved about cheerfully in the kitchen preparing breakfast, a pert apron over one of her Sunday dresses. She smelled of sweet fragrances with her hair piled up in the fashion of the season, similar to the Gibson Girl mode. Joseph, clean-shaven and smelling of tangy scents, usually hummed arias by Puccini or Verdi. He too was dressed to the hilt with a stylish vest and a snappy Papillon under his starched white collar. It had become almost a ritual the way the Liguori brothers, in their best suits, would tease their younger sister, Anna—all dolled up in frills and bows, her hair bobbing with curls.

After breakfast, Dick was hitched up to a fine buggy, and the whole family climbed in for their first stop: Sunday mass. Afterwards, Joseph guided Dick, who held his head majestically high, thrusting his magnificent legs forward into Manhattan. From there, it was to the Hoboken Ferry to cross the Hudson into New Jersey. Their destination was Palisades Park, where the children were allowed to play to their hearts' content while Agnes and Joseph sat on a park bench, conversing like newlyweds. For lunch, Joseph took the family to a fashionable restaurant. On Sunday, he always wanted the best. Not only was he a connoisseur of good food, a *buongustaio*; he also enjoyed fine wines. Ralph tried to emulate his father at the table—the ceremonious way in which he consumed his food. Any onlooker could easily see that Ralph had inherited his father's tastes. The merry mood was sustained all through lunch despite Agnes's constant attempts to teach her boys table manners or stop their playful efforts to break down baby sister Anna's prim and proper behavior. After Joseph enjoyed one of his fine cigars, the family would be off again, with Dick strutting around the countryside.

As evening approached, they stopped at a familiar parlor for their favorite *gelato* (ice cream). Agnes watched her children cheerfully eating and chattering away and smiled at her husband. She considered herself very lucky and thanked God for his blessings. They finally returned home about eleven o'clock in the evening while everyone scrambled into the house. Joseph unharnessed his handsome horse, stroked his long mane, and, in a gesture familiar to Dick, solemnly raised his hand. The horse responded with a short snort, raised his noble head, and headed into the stable. Pleasantly exhausted, they all fell asleep—happy and at peace with the world.

The following four years were carefree ones for Ralph. He enjoyed the right doses of motherly love and constant paternal guidance and protection. Among his siblings, he remained the most gregarious, with definite signs of leadership, as his father had always known. But the light in Ralph's piercing blue eyes were to lose their usual luster. The most tragic winter of his life was upon him. Coughing and sneezing, with his eyes watering, Ralph felt his body on fire and, touching his forehead, knew that he was burning with fever. His happy home had turned into an infirmary with his brothers—Armand (fourteen) and Al (sixteen) in the next room—both victims of the Spanish influenza. Al was the worst off; he was practically in a coma, his respiration weak. The epidemic was taking its toll on thousands of people, and Ralph's beloved father was in a hospital bed, fighting for his life.

Ralph's love for his dad was so deep that when he thought of him suffering, his heart ached, and he aged far beyond his eleven years. Agnes was holding her own, although she was beside herself with grief. Her fine upbringing as a child had taught her self-control. True to her Roman heritage, she remained courageous and strong, never faltering in front of her children. Nights found her awake, listening to the coughing and wheezing of her sons. It was four o'clock in the morning, and she had just returned from checking on Al for signs of improvement, but thoughts of her beloved husband prevented her from sleeping. He was so much a part of her that the idea of losing him was more than she could bear.

Ralph sat bolt upright in bed. The shrill sound of the telephone had startled him. He heard his mother move to answer it and instinctively followed her down to the store, keeping a certain distance. Ralph's love for his mother was different from his love for his father, but it was just as strong. He watched her lovingly as she lifted the receiver with trembling hands. In the semidarkness, she looked small and pathetic in her challis robe with her disheveled hair hanging loosely below her shoulders. She did not speak. Rain gurgled in the metal gutters, and the *swoosh* of the wind splashed it against the windows. Ralph noted light streaks of early dawn peeking through. The store had always smelled of enticing aromas to Ralph, but now a certain mustiness seemed to permeate throughout.

He shuddered as he heard his mother mumble, "Yes, Doctor, I heard you. I'll be down as soon as I can."

Agnes slowly hung up, and Ralph saw her shoulders contract. He rushed to her as she turned and saw the tears gushing down. She hugged him desperately, crying softly. "Poppa is dead. Poppa is dead, Ralphy!"

Ralph hung tightly to his mother, not wanting to let go, and together they wept against each other, rocking to and fro. He was in shock. It was impossible for him to believe that his father would not be around for him anymore, and Agnes knowingly stroked his face, brushing away the tears. Her own agony was overcome by the love she had for her children, whom she knew needed her now more than ever. Trying to regain her composure, she sensed that her husband's favorite little boy was about to grow up. She led Ralph back to his bedroom to dress. Then she informed the others. Armand stayed home to watch over Al and Anna while Ralph accompanied her to the hospital.

Hunched over in the hospital chair, Agnes held her husband's cold hand and tenderly placed a kiss on his lips with her fingertips. Ralph took out his clean kerchief and blew his nose, trying to hold back the tears. He looked at his father lying so still, color drained from that handsome face, and he felt something break inside. Standing erect alongside his bereaving mother, he listened to her speaking softly, sweetly, to her husband.

Joseph's brothers rushed to Joe's deathbed and, controlling their own grief, firmly took over the funeral arrangements, thereby sparing Agnes and her children the grueling details. As was the custom then, Joseph's body was laid out in the home's front parlor. Al was still in a coma in the bedroom, Armand was coughing in great paroxysms of breathlessness, and Ralph ignored his own failing condition. He had refused to stay in bed, stubbornly insisting he had to be with his mother. For three days and nights, people came to pay their respects, and all mourned Joseph's early death. He was only forty-five, and Agnes, a few years younger, had become the beautiful widow with four children to raise.

During those trying days, Ralph felt the presence of his five uncles—somber in black suits and ties, obviously shaken by their brother's death, a brother whom they loved and deeply respected. Each took a turn walking to the casket, touching their departed brother's hand, deep in sorrow. Ralph caught his uncle Alfred weeping privately. The aunts were in the kitchen, cooking the meals and preparing refreshments for relatives who had remained with the family. A first cousin of Joseph's through marriage, Tommy Dyke, a tall handsome man, tried to console everyone. He and Joseph had been very close, and he paid particular attention to Ralph, who had always admired him, calling him "uncle" out of respect.

Ralph's bright blue eyes had turned pale, his puffy cheeks drained of their usual color, but he stood like a little soldier, protectively guarding his mother. When night arrived and everyone had left, with a heavy sadness, Ralph locked the door and turned off the lights. He had begun to realize, at his tender age, that an important part of his life had been shut off forever.

CHAPTER FOUR

Death, particularly of a loved one, creates an agonizing transformation for the survivors. The void bequeathed by the decedent to those left behind in mourning is a deception; for it is not a void at all, but a tangible, throbbing, torturous, and living pain afflicting all who come near—wounding, scarring, searing, and changing them forever.

Following his father's death, Ralph was never the same. It was as though his father had left him a legacy of responsibility toward his family—an invisible but totally binding document regulating his future even though he was the youngest of the boys. Agnes, for all her great faith, had difficulty accepting her husband's passing. She saw her beloved everywhere (in the house, the store), and at times, she found herself speaking to him as though he were there in the bedroom with her. But despite her stirring memories and the four children, Agnes pulled herself together and decided to confer with Joseph's brothers about their future. Her brothers-in-law convinced Agnes that the children were still too young, and that she alone could not carry on the family business. Thus, with some reluctance, she was persuaded to sell the store, and the family moved to Van Sicklen Street and Avenue U. It was a nice, respectable, middle-class neighborhood, which was important for Agnes. The older boys were fortunate to land jobs at the Brooklyn Rapid Transit Company.

Still ravaging Europe was the World War, and in the spring of 1917, America joined her allies by declaring war on Germany. Liberty bonds were being sold throughout the land while billboards displayed a stern Uncle Sam in a Lincolnesque stovepipe hat and red-and-white-and-blue outfit, dramatically declaring, "We want you." Everyone sang rousing patriotic songs, such as "Over There . . . Johnny, get your gun." Agnes, having adopted a strong nationalistic spirit, spent much time knitting woolen socks and scarves for the soldiers. She even taught Ralph, who was curious about everything, how to knit; and although his brothers stared amusingly at him, Ralph too had joined the war effort.

Anna and Ralph were still in school—Ralph studying hard and being rewarded with good grades, much to his mother's satisfaction. But life was changing for Ralph, and suddenly, his classmates seemed too immature for him. Until the aftermath of his father's death, Ralph had found school an interesting, demanding challenge; but afterwards, he began to experience intolerable boredom and, when he was in the sixth grade, could not wait to be transferred to PS 95. The transfer meant new teachers, which intrigued Ralph as new adventures always did. According to most of her pupils, Ms. Haley was a tough Irish educator of fifty. Intent on inculcating each child with the day's lessons, she usually kept the class after school doing homework—a practice that Ralph thought was downright mean. He felt sure she did so to cover up her inability to hold the class's attention during regular school hours. Her lack of consideration for her students weighed heavily on him, and he was determined to rid himself of Ms. Haley and her infernal boredom.

Wearily shuffling along the school hall with his best friend of the moment, Mario, Ralph spotted the janitor leaning on his broom, wiping his receding forehead and leering, obviously tired—a weather-beaten man on the nether side of fifty but not too old to enjoy ogling the lovely young girls leaving class. Ralph's wit, always dependable and quick, prepared to illustrate to the janitor a way to put an end to his woes. Naturally, the plan was to enhance Ralph's pockets.

"Hey, Mr. Patterson, I have a proposition to make," he called out as he approached with Mario at his heels.

"Yeah, Ralphy?" the man grinned. "Let's hear it."

"How about if I give you a hand sweeping up the place at night?"

"Hey, not a bad idea, Ralphy," he croaked, his bland eyes brightening. "I sure could use some help. How about ten cents for every classroom you sweep?"

"WOW, that's great. And my friend Mario?" Ralph never neglected his friends. Even as a youngster in his most impressionable years, he always remembered the value of sharing.

"Yeah, sure, why not. You can start tomorrow."

Absolutely elated by this unexpected triumph and slapping Mario joyously about the shoulders, Ralph ran all the way home to tell his mother. At least he wouldn't have to endure the ignominy of bothering her for small change. Of equal importance, he wouldn't have to remain after school in Ms. Haley's wearying presence, listening to her high-pitched brogue. He could now be excused to work. On the first night on the job, Ralph and Mario slipped away, much to the envy of their classmates, and headed down to the boiler room to pick up their brooms. Ralph led the way, and as he pulled open the heavy door, what he saw made him stop abruptly. Mario coming up fast practically toppled over him.

"Oh, my god!" the boys whispered.

There, tangled together, were Ms. Haley and Mr. Patterson. She stood pinned against the wall, her arms embracing him, uttering strange feline sounds. He was clasping her buttocks with both hands as he grunted and groaned, pelvis thrusting rhythmically back and forth. One hand finally released the rounded bulge of her behind to grope roughly over her full breasts, until she uttered such a whoop of climactic abandon that Ralph instinctively understood what he was witnessing—and stared in wide-eyed fascination as he tried to block Mario's view. Ralph had never seen an act of intimacy. His parents had always been discreet, coupling quietly behind closed bedroom doors. But the sensual animalistic scene before him was something new. It aroused not only strange sensations in his young virginal being, but a certain revulsion as well. So this is where the prim Ms. Haley slipped away after school hours! The mean, hypocritical old goat! She kept the kids in class after school because she needed an excuse to fool around with the janitor at night!

Ralph felt weak with nausea. *I'll make her pay for this,* he vowed, breathing hard. Mario, jockeying to catch a glimpse of what was happening, tripped over the brooms so that they clattered against the pails. Then all hell broke loose!

Ms. Haley gasped with unbearable embarrassment as she tried to adjust her rumpled skirt and blouse while the janitor, unable to speak, stood helpless and ridiculous in his underwear. Ralph grimaced, viewing the pair with disgust, as Ms. Haley began a litany of moaning, singsong pleas.

"Oh, please don't say anything, don't say anything, Ralphy," she cried, her crimson face concealed between her hands. By now, the janitor had pulled up his trousers, buttoned his fly, and flung his suspenders over his shoulders. "Now, listen, Ralphy," he began, and fear made his gritty voice quiver.

But Ms. Haley interrupted him. "I'll be ruined," she wailed, fussing with her hair, working her reddish blond ringlets around her fingers. "I'll lose my job," she sobbed and began to offer the boys sums of money as bribes to keep them from betraying her secret.

Before Ralph or Mario, eyes popping and mouth gaping, could respond, the desperate pair offered them ten dollars a week for their silence—quite a hike from ten cents a classroom. Ralph managed to conceal a sinister smile, hugging Mario's shoulders in triumph as the trembling janitor and his schoolmarm paramour slinked hurriedly from the boiler room.

Within weeks, Ralph began to feel the intoxicating joy of handling money. He and Mario boldly hailed taxis to take them to the most popular Broadway shows, frequently stopping for coffee and cake in the finest cafes in Manhattan—even the famous Café Ferrara. Ralph felt very grown-up. Having money meant the difference between having luxuries and doing without. There was no going back to being a dependent child.

The following summer, Ralph worked at the Williams and Morfit Garage on West End Avenue between Sixty-eighth and Sixty-ninth streets, where his uncle, Ralph Conti, who had brought great mechanical expertise with him from Italy, was the body shop manager. Conti had built a special chassis for Ralph De Palma, the world-famous auto car racer who had become a regular customer. Whenever De Palma drove into the garage, Ralph, who idolized the auto racer, hustled to dust his car, yearning for a generous tip. To work with fine cars and mechanics was the ultimate pleasure for Ralph. No doubt he had inherited some of his passion for cars from his uncle. The other mechanics took him under their wing. Not only did Ralph learn everything about driving, but by watching and assisting them, he also quickly absorbed basic technological skills.

Ralph could not spend quickly enough the ten dollars a week he was paid as a mechanics helper, which had made up for the loss of the school money. With school out for the summer and his needs and wants expanding, he felt driven to double his finances. Before long, he and Mario were shooting craps with boys from the neighborhood, soon discovering their natural talent for the game. Their winnings grew to such an extent that after six months, they had advanced to cutting the games. By the time he was thirteen, Ralph had gained valuable experience as a young gambler and enjoyed every minute of it—especially the look and feel of money. How could he continue studying history and geography? Latin and math? He felt confident he was using all the arithmetic he would ever need on the sidewalks of New York. Without a loving father, no longer present to guide him, to protect, Ralph was now alone to follow a path that his father certainly did not intend for him.

Prohibition had been running its course, and whiskey runners were very much in demand—a demand that provided Ralph's next summer adventure. He and Mario were hired by a classmate's father who owned a saloon on Kings Highway and Gravesend Avenue, close to home. People still craved alcohol, Prohibition or not, and saloon keepers had to make a living. (Cognizant of the risks, ways were devised to keep people from being caught breaking the law.) With a bottle of whiskey in his hip pocket, Ralph waited in the saloon's back room. Soon, he knew, he would be called by the barman. When a customer wanted a drink, the barman signaled Ralph by tapping the counter with a glass. The routine took only a minute. Ralph would rush out, hand the whiskey to the barman, who poured the drink, retrieve the bottle, and run into the back room to hide until the next call. One day, however, things did not run so smoothly. A gentleman came in, claiming to be a friend of a friend, and asked for a drink. Ralph emerged as usual, but as he turned to run, the "customer" gave him a sharp kick in the rear end, and Ralph fell flat on his face. Half-smiling, half-sneering, the customer helped him up and showed his police badge.

"Go home, kid, and stay there!" he growled. Embarrassed, Ralph rushed out and ran as fast as his legs could carry him. It had been a lucrative but frightening experience, and Ralph had known the risks. After a cooling-off period, which included a daily examination of the tens and twenties folded in his secret cache, he felt he needed more money. So heeding a voice in his head, he returned to the saloon, rubbing the fading black-and-blue mark on his behind.

In the eighth grade, Ralph definitely made up his mind that he no longer wanted to attend school, determined to help support his mother and sister. Anna's piano lessons were costly, and she was showing promise. Agnes and Joseph had long planned that Anna would be a piano teacher. Therefore, she wasn't allowed to do housework because Agnes repeatedly pointed out that it would ruin her hands. Anna was never to feel the lessening of the good life Joseph had provided, and Agnes did all she could to maintain it. In fact, the entire family agreed on Anna's future. With the two older boys working, and with the money saved from the sale of Joseph's business, it was not necessary for Agnes to go to work; but Ralph felt obliged to do more for his family. Persistent (as was his nature), he explained to his mother why he had to quit school. If Agnes had serious misgivings about Ralph's lack of education, she kept them to herself. Oh, how she missed Joseph. Armand was learning the electrician's trade working as an apprentice at Luna Park and, the following summer, negotiated a job for Ralph—selling soda pop, malted milk, and root beer for a man who owned fifteen stands.

On Sunday, a stand man was out sick, and Ralph was told to fill in for him. As soon as the manager of the stand welcomed Ralph, he said, "Listen, kid, don't put your hand in this tub, 'cause the water's dirty!"

Ralph nodded, but when he saw the manager putting glasses into the same tub, he began to wonder about the remark he had made. If the water was dirty, why would he put the glasses in there? When the manager's back was turned, Ralph, curious as always, reached all the way down into the tub and found a pool of money—nickels, dimes, quarters, pennies. The works!

"Hey," he exclaimed, "look what's in here!"

The manager turned around with a sardonic look on his face. "Okay, so you're a smart kid. Keep your mouth shut, and I'll give you ten dollars a week."

Ralph, in stunned silence, simply nodded his head. As a result, besides his regular salary of ten dollars, Ralph received another ten and began to understand the advantages of keeping his mouth shut.

But it was just another summer job. The family moved again—to Sheepshead Bay, Fifteenth Neck Road, near the Brighton Line Subway, always in Brooklyn; and with school out of the way, Ralph, anxious to succeed, impatiently waited for new opportunities.

CHAPTER FIVE

Ralph's new landlord, Mr. Barone, a butcher from Palermo, belonged to a large family, which included some famous cousins—the Castellanos and the Gambinos. (Ralph thought they were the nicest people he had ever known.)

Like his cousins, Barone was successful in business and became the proud owner of a large three-story building. On the first floor, fully equipped with every time-saving modern device, was an ample butcher shop. Ralph's family lived on the floor above. As soon as the Liguoris moved in, Mr. Barone noticed Ralph and liked what he saw. Consequently, the next time Agnes entered the shop to buy meat, the butcher inquired if she thought her son would work for him, taking orders and making deliveries. Ralph, upon hearing the proposition, thought it was a lucky break and couldn't wait to begin. Like his father, he had a natural affinity for the butcher trade and, as his father had trained him, stole with his eyes by simply watching the fine points of butchering. Ralph was paid fifteen dollars a week and, with his tips, wound up earning about twenty-three.

Barone's butcher shop was open on Sundays until noon, sometimes one o'clock, depending on the crowd returning from church. Mr. Barone, however, didn't work on Sunday; that day was sacred for his family. Ralph, therefore, worked with Tony, the manager. On the first Sunday of Ralph's employment, a good customer entered and made a substantial purchase, handing Tony a large bill in payment. Tony made a point of examining the hundred dollar bill, then turned to Ralph and told him to go out for some change. Ralph inquisitively eyed the cash register, knowing there was plenty of change in it, and he noticed that Tony hadn't even run up the sale. His baby blue eyes narrowed slightly, and Tony realized the boy was hep to him.

After Ralph returned with the "needed" change and the customer left, Tony said softly, "Okay, Ralphy, you're a good kid, but too damn smart. I know you're wise to me already. So, okay, we could all use some extra money. Keep this to yourself, and I'll take care of you too."

Keeping his mouth shut was nothing new to Ralph. His education on making easy money was beginning to expand. One Thursday, after returning from his route taking orders, Ralph reported to Tony that he had taken an order for two rabbits from a Mrs. King, a heavyset Negro woman who ran a boarding house.

Tony's eyes twinkled, and he smiled slyly, "Why, yes, indeed, we have some special rabbits for her!"

Ralph noticed an odd ring to the remark but dismissed it. On Friday morning, when the meat truck arrived, Ralph failed to see any rabbits and questioned Tony about it.

With a mischievous glint in his eyes, Tony replied, "Ralphy, I told you . . . don't worry. We have special rabbits for Mrs. King."

Early that afternoon, Mr. Barone asked Ralph to follow him to the backyard, where, among other things, he raised chickens. He pointed to a cat and told Ralph to catch it.

"Gotta get rid of that little mouser. It's been eating my chicks," he told Ralph.

With his limbs shaking, Ralph carried the trusting feline to Mr. Barone, who swiftly put a knife through its gut; and before Ralph could recover, he was ordered to catch another. Scrambling about the yard, Ralph finally managed to catch a strong young tom, and Barone dispatched it just as neatly. Then they went down into the cellar where a large pail of water was boiling on the stove, and as Barone went through the process of boiling and skinning the cats, Ralph wanted to vomit. Finally, Barone finished and handed the corpses to Ralph with pride of workmanship, smiling maliciously.

"Ralphy, these are Mrs. King's two rabbits! But don't you dare say anything to anybody about what you saw here today."

Ralph nodded dutifully, his eyes bulging. Who the hell would squeal about a thing like that! "Tony, listen," Ralph protested, his young voice crackling, "I ain't going to deliver these cats as rabbits. My conscience bothers me!"

Tony looked at the flustered lad and replied soothingly, "Ralph, just ride your bike over, ring the bell, drop the package, and run like hell!"

Ralph shook his head in disgust but did as he was told. The following Monday, Ralph was routinely washing the outside store windows when out of the corner of his eye, he saw a big black woman in a flowered dress with a matching bandana around her head approaching. Ralph dropped his long-handled brush and tripped over the pail of water as he rushed in, yelling to Tony.

"I'm going! Aunt Jemina's coming!"

Tony grabbed him by the collar. "Relax, kid, just hide behind the iceboxes and listen."

As soon as Ralph crept down, he heard Tony's voice sing out, "Why, good morning, Mrs. King. How were them rabbits?"

"Mmmm, mmmm, Tony, they was the best rabbits I ever had," she replied, smacking her lips. "I'll be back for more in a couple of weeks."

After she left, Ralph wobbled to his feet and blurted, "Gees, how could she say a thing like that?" And holding his revolted stomach, he dejectedly went home.

Agnes was furious when Ralph confided in her what had happened. She assured him that his father would never have done anything like that. "If you ever bring me a skinned rabbit, I'll throw it down the stairs, and you along with it!" she warned him emphatically.

At fifteen, Ralph was an apprentice to Tony and doing quite well at the trade—but not without certain setbacks. Alone in the shop one day, stocking the freezer with choice cuts of beef and pork, he heard the doorbell jingle and, with nervous delight, turned to watch Betty Thompson walk in. She had become his newest secret love; and whenever he saw her, his face flushed, his ears rang, and his whole body throbbed with undefined cravings. He was practically mesmerized as he surveyed her—firm young breasts bobbing, beautiful long reddish blonde hair falling about her slim shoulders, great blue eyes glistening—and oh, the way her tiny waist accentuated her gently rounded hips. Still innocent of his sexual desires, Ralph ached all over. But despite her mature body, Betty, at fourteen, was still childlike and shy—especially when she came with one of her parents. She'd limit herself to an amorous glance, then, blushing, would lower her eyelids if Ralph caught her.

But today, they were alone! "Ralphy," she said nervously, "I need six pork chops in a hurry, because my daddy has to go to work."

Tongue-tied, he gave her one of his sweetest smiles and took the loin of pork out of the showcase. He began preparing the slices, cutting the meat neatly up to the bone, then reached for the cleaver to chop. He looked up to find Betty smiling approvingly and again felt his face on fire. In that moment of distraction, his right hand came down with the cleaver, striking the web between his thumb and forefinger! A sharp pain flashed through his arm, and blood spurted immediately. Trying not to show pain, Ralph quickly tossed a clean cloth over his cut and carefully went on with chopping. Then, smiling through clenched teeth, he somehow managed to wrap the meat. Afraid Betty would say something, he hurriedly handed her the package and, with a strained smile, told her, "I'll put it on your father's bill."

Betty thanked him and rushed out, almost colliding with Tony coming through the door. Tony took one look at Ralph's drained white face and knew something was wrong. "My god, Ralph," he cried, rushing behind the counter, noticing blood accumulating in a small pool beneath Ralph's hand. Swiftly, he produced a bottle of peroxide and a box of gauze, then cleaned and bandaged the wound with the compassion and tenderness of a father. Ralph felt his knees buckling under but refused to faint. True, he had lost an opportunity to woo his heartthrob, but, at least, Betty never knew what a clumsy fool he could be vis-à-vis a woman who captured his fancy.

Barone's backyard was the hub of many activities. It extended to his private home where he maintained a sizable bootlegging operation. Soon, Barone had Ralph delivering some of his whiskey. Thus, while learning the practical butcher trade, the youth gained an inside glimpse into the more dangerous realm of the "big boys."

He had begun helping in the loading operations. One morning, while assisting in transferring five-gallon tin cans of alcohol from a private car to a small truck, Ralph was lifting the last container when he heard a police car approaching. Before he knew what was happening, both the private car and the truck made a screeching getaway, leaving him dumbfounded, covered with soot, and carrying a five-gallon tin can in his arms. The patrol car came to a screaming, rocking stop, and two officers rushed toward him.

"Hey, kid, where d'ya get that?"

Thinking quickly, Ralph replied, "Some guy offered me a dollar to help put this in his car, but before I could, the car and truck took off."

"Is that so?" the cop scowled. "You're a liar, kid. Maybe you'll change your tune at the station house!"

A very anxious Agnes was called to the police station where she witnessed her son's interrogation. They tried to scare him, but Ralph was too well schooled. He knew if he were to talk, it would make things much worse, so he kept repeating his story, insisting that he couldn't give them the names of the men because he didn't know them. Agnes pleaded for her son, emphasizing he was a good boy working to help his widowed mother. Since it was Ralph's first encounter with the police, he was released with a warning to his mother that if he were ever involved in a similar incident, he'd be sent to reform school. Ralph had feared a severe tongue-lashing from his mother, but they went home in silence. Agnes had always considered the whole business of prohibition a foolishness—strange and unnatural. But she made no comment, distressed as she was for Ralph's future.

All day Ralph avoided Barone's house for fear of being watched, but later that night, as he stood on the corner, a young man came up to him saying Barone wanted to see him in the coffee shop. At the door of the café, Ralph spotted his landlord waiting at a corner table, motioning to him.

As soon as he sat down, Barone whispered, "What did they ask you? Did you say anything about me, Ralphy?"

Ralph very calmly told him the whole story. He did not lie.

Barone chuckled. "Okay, okay, you're a smart kid, Ralphy. Here, put this in your pocket." Then waved Ralph off.

Back in his bedroom, Ralph unfolded the wad on his bed that Mr. Barone gave him and counted three hundred dollars. He couldn't believe his eyes! It was a lot of money, and it had come so easy. Immediately, he knew what to do. This time, Ralph did tell a lie. In order to obtain his driver's license, he swore he was eighteen instead of fifteen. Somehow he got away with it. Triumphantly, he bought a nifty model T Ford. Still another plus! To his great surprise, his salary was raised to twenty-five dollars a week.

Ralph Liguori was doing all right for himself.

CHAPTER SIX

Charlie gently placed his hand on Ralph's shoulder to avoid startling him.

"Ralph, you've been daydreaming." He smiled fraternally.

Through the slits of his tired eyes, Ralph looked up at his friend, noticing Charlie's drawn face and puffed lids, obviously from lack of sleep.

"Yeah, guess so," Ralph creaked wearily, rubbing his eyes and face to perk up. "What time is it?"

"Quarter past five—in the morning," Charlie told him.

Suddenly, the door swung open, and a guard shouted, "All right, you guys, it's time. The bailiff is rushing to the judge's chambers right now. They've finally reached a verdict!"

Silence reigned for a moment. It was stifling hot in the room; not even the morning's cool breezes, flowing through the open windows, offered relief. Outside, the skies were streaked with the subtle colors of dawn breaking, as the sun timidly showed its face. A normal day for the advent of summer. The defendants finally scrambled to their feet, brushing their wrinkled trousers and plucking at their sticky shirts to air them. Ralph ran a comb through his hair; those without combs passed their fingers over their hair, trying their best to tidy up their appearances. Some showed signs of five o'clock shadow on their faces. No one spoke; it seemed as though they were all mute. Then, one by one, with guards at their sides, the defendants walked silently to their destinies.

Judge McCook, in the meantime, had hastily put on his robes, splashed water on his face, and rushed down the corridor with the bailiff following at his heels.

Hundreds of people waited for the verdicts outside the courthouse, mingling together in the nearby Mulberry and Foley Parks. To help control the crowds, extra police and detectives had been put on duty, some with tommy guns, inspecting everyone, wary of everything in the vicinity, afraid that someone might try to spring Charlie. But that was the farthest thing from Charlie's mind. It was a far-fetched idea that one of the defendants would attempt to escape. Nevertheless, the lawmen were halting cars, trucks, and anxious-looking people who wandered close to the courthouse entrance. The wives and relatives of the defendants lingered inside, some leaning against the walls of the dreary corridors. When they heard that the jury was returning, they began to mill around the courtroom doors, but the guards had orders to keep them out. Ralph, as well as the others, preferred it that way. Otherwise, it could have been worse than the screaming and lamenting at an Italian wake.

The jurors finally filed in around five thirty. Ralph examined their stern faces and instinctively knew that things were not going well. And yet, Ralph felt confident that things couldn't be that bad for him. Certainly, they couldn't hang him for something he didn't do! The mental strain unnerved him, and he tried with all his might not to lose his composure. Foreman Edward Aderer remained standing as the other jurors took their seats. With their lawyers at their sides, the defendants stood facing the bar.

The austere Judge McCook, somewhat ruffled, dispassionately called out, "Have you reached your verdict, gentlemen?"

"We have, Your Honor."

"The bailiff will take the verdict," McCook ordered. He paused for a moment; then with specific emphasis on Charlie's name, he exclaimed, "How do you find the defendant, Charles Lucania, on the first count of the indictment?"

Another pause. The suspense sizzled to the danger point. The silence was finally broken by the foreman, nervously rustling the papers in his hands. At last, recomposed, he swallowed hard and boldly pronounced, "GUILTY!"

Charlie's head fell forward as though he had been shot. Slowly, he raised his chin and stared expressionless at the judge. He was shattered but too proud to give in to the raging emotions wrenching through him. His lawyers, Moses Polakoff and George Morton Levy, also stood stunned. They felt they had delivered a convincing defense, even with the odds stacked against them, but perhaps, naively, they had been hoping for a small miracle. Levy gently touched Charlie's arm in solidarity as the counts of the indictments against him continued.

"On count 2 of the indictment?" the bailiff's voice went on matter-of-factly.

"GUILTY!" the foreman's voice boomed.

The bailiff continued the routine questioning: "Count 3 . . . 4 . . . 5 . . . 6 . . . 7 . . . 8 . . . 9 . . . 10 . . ."

And the answer always came back as a drumming, "Guilty . . . Guilty . . . Guilty . . ."

The repetition placed the jurors in a state of somnolence. They had debated for five and a half hours, had come up with two ballots before their final verdict of 11-1. As they sat there with the burden of their decision, their tired faces lined with the responsibility of it all, one juror, Martin Moses, broke down. As the single exception, the overstressed juror wept unabashedly at the court's constant chant of "guilty."

When Ralph finally heard Judge McCook utter his name, he stiffened, and the knot in his throat hardened. Something told him it was all over.

"How do you find the defendant, Ralph Liguori, in the first count of the indictment?" bellowed McCook.

"GUILTY!" the foreman replied.

Ralph felt an electrical shock jolt through his body. His face turned ashen, and the ringing in his ears and the pressure against his temples grew so great that he thought his head would explode. At that moment, he swore he heard his mother and Anna cry out desperately. But they weren't alone in their grief. As the word *guilty* sounded through the closed doors, all the women began to howl with pain, like wounded animals, and the wailing continued throughout the reading of the verdicts.

The courtroom was full of newspapermen busy with their steno pads, with photographers focusing their cameras to shoot their pictures. The flashes intermittently lighted the courtroom as the defendants blinked in silent anger.

The voices of the foreman and bailiff had become cold—detached—as their words echoed the same wearisome repetition. "Guilty . . . Guilty." It took about forty minutes for all the verdicts to be read and registered; afterwards, Judge McCook turned to the jury and congratulated them on their decisions, as though a noble act had been performed.

"I congratulate you on the service that you have rendered the people," he told them, "and upon the righteousness of your verdict."

Oh, crap, hissed Ralph through compressed lips, glaring with hatred at Dewey who stood to one side, obviously pleased with his success.

The defendants were then asked to face the court to state their personal data—age, place of birth, address, even religion. When Frederico was questioned about the last, he was so irate he snarled, "Heathen!"

Dewey, still alert on the job and without the slightest vestige of compassion, addressed the court, urging McCook for immediate sentencing. There was an instantaneous outcry from the defense attorneys, especially from a livid Samuel Siegel, who had jumped to his feet to object. Judge McCook, taking note of the vehemence before him, contradicted Dewey, matter-of-factly observing. "There's no need for all the hurry." While consulting his calendar, he casually mumbled beneath his breath, "Let's see now. . . A week from Wednesday." Then looked up sternly to announce, "June 18 at 10:00 a.m.!"

With that, he banged his gavel and made a hurried exit.

Dewey accepted the rebuttal without comment. Trying to avoid everyone, he quietly slipped out of the courtroom. A young woman, someone's wife or relative, ran after him, thrust her highly polished long nails within striking distance of his face, yelling, "Framer upper! You'll get yours!" Dewey paled but neatly evaded her as a policeman dragged the screaming woman away.

Ralph, Charlie, and the others were given twenty minutes to say good-bye to their loved ones and to exchange a few words with their lawyers. In a funeral scene cloaked with grief, men and women clung to one another, weeping their farewells. The defendants were then shackled together and led into a waiting van. At 6:30 a.m., automobiles filled with detectives escorted the van to The Tombs Prison. Charlie, however, was taken to the Raymond Street Jail.

The prosecution staff, lingering in the corridors to continue commenting on the trial, appeared ecstatic over its triumphant finale. Smiles were in abundance as backslapping and victorious handshakes were exchanged. But not quite as jubilant over Dewey's victory was Magistrate Anna M. Kross of women's court, who firmly stated that the convictions did not solve the prostitution problem.

That evening in his Fifth Avenue apartment in Manhattan, Dewey—the victor, the champion gangbuster—issued his statements to the press, pompously opening his well-rehearsed discourse.

"This, of course, was not a vice trial. It was a racket prosecution. The control of all organized prostitution in New York by the convicted defendants was one of their lowest rackets. The four bookers who pleaded guilty were underlings. The prostitution racket was merely the vehicle by which these men were convicted.

"My understanding is that certain of the top-ranking defendants in this case, together with other criminals, under Luciano, have gradually absorbed control of the narcotics, loan shark, policy, and Italian lottery syndicates, the receipt of stolen goods and certain industrial rackets."

To ingratiate himself to all, Dewey also delivered a short speech, giving credit to his assistants—those dedicated attorneys "with the determination to win."

The Tombs, a decaying dump, certainly didn't help Ralph's spirits. His cell had no sink (just two cots) with enough room for an occupant to take two steps (back and forth). It was damp, like a dungeon. There was nothing to do there but read and think. Ralph had memorized all of the comments Dewey had made to the press, and it infuriated him to know that the special prosecutor, in effect, had insinuated that prostitution was not Charlie's racket. Possessed of his own set of rules regarding justice, Ralph couldn't reconcile himself to the fact that men were being framed and sent to prison for crimes they didn't commit—to circumvent the fact that the prosecution had no proof of the defendants' other alleged illegal activities. No one, steamed Ralph, had a license to frame another person! He saw it as a gross miscarriage of human justice.

Whenever Ralph directed his thoughts to his own predicament, he struggled to contain his emotions. Dewey and his boys had vengefully framed him also. He didn't have a chance because no one listened to him; it had been his word against the young prosecutor who had the law on his side. At times, desperation had raged helplessly within him when Ralph thought about his mother and her anguish. But it was when he thought of his father that the tears came to his eyes. Heartfelt memories of his youth and his loving alliance with his father blanketed him with grief. How disappointed Joe Liguori would have been with him! Sometimes Ralph overcame his misery by rationalizing that Judge McCook couldn't be so obtuse—so blind to the truth—and would probably relent in the end with the pronouncement of a light sentence. With that encouraging thought, Ralph lulled himself to sleep.

While waiting for sentencing, the defendants were subjected to psychiatric tests performed by Dr. Perry M. Lichtenstein of the Bellevue Division in the Criminal Courts Building. His reports were to be submitted to Judge McCook before the date scheduled for sentencing to assist the magistrate in his character analysis—especially to enlighten him on the sociopsychological makeup of the various defendants. Charlie received a great deal of publicity. The media said he was shallow! But those close to Charlie (and those who knew him best) protested he was anything but shallow.

Dewey, during the period that followed, continued smearing the defense with additional wild statements, claiming he was moving for disbarment of two of the defense attorneys (no individuals named), alluding to attempts he said had been made to bribe two of his aides. He also demanded that Police Commissioner Lewis J. Valentine investigate Patrolman Heidt's conduct. (Heidt, a defense witness, had testified that the women witnesses whom Dewey had kept in custody had gone to nightclubs and had been given generous amounts of alcoholic beverages.) Valentine communicated back that although Heidt's file was somehow strangely missing, he would proceed with vigor to carry out Dewey's wishes.

The defense lawyers, however, were not sleeping on the job. They already had filed their appeals. It was reported that Charlie had spent a quarter of a million dollars. Ralph wasn't sure, but he did know Charlie had paid Attorney Levy fifty grand, plus weekly expenses, and that he probably paid more for Polakoff. In addition, there were other bureaucratic expenses, such as fifteen grand to have the seven-thousand-page trial record printed for appeal. Charlie's elderly advocate, the wealthy and prestigious Samuel Kops, was perhaps Dewey's strongest legal adversary. He stood adamantly against the Joinder Law, contesting its constitutionality. Kops claimed that the law was unjust because it was passed after the crimes were committed—a clear breach of the ex post facto law, which denied each man the right to have his own day in court. Generally, Kops thought it was also unfair to lawyers in private practice, and he was prepared to take the law all the way to the U.S. Supreme Court to test its constitutionality.

Basically, the appeal for Charlie and Ralph was to be based on that premise, along with new evidence in their favor.

CHAPTER SEVEN

Eleven days of agonizing detention had finally ended. Ralph and the other defendants, handcuffed in pairs to detectives and followed by armed guards, were taken back to the courthouse for sentencing. Ralph couldn't believe his eyes. The courthouse was packed, overflowing with crowds, and it appeared that police surveillance had tripled. *Perhaps they think it's our last chance to escape,* Ralph thought bitterly. About fifty uniformed policemen, some with automatic rifles, kept the crowds from gathering too close to the courthouse. More than a dozen horseback and motorcycle cops circulated around to disperse suspicious characters. Inside, an equal number of uniformed policemen and plainclothesmen, plus regular courthouse guards, stood mingling around, scanning the halls—with half a dozen armed security men stationed at each entrance. Dewey himself was protected by two detectives. Obviously, the prosecution was not taking any chances.

To make matters worse, it was a dark and dismal morning; the brooding clouds forewarned an ill-omened day. Lightning flashed and crackled, followed by the din of clapping thunder. The gloom of the courtroom atmosphere matched everyone's mood, as those present waited for Justice McCook to appear. After forty-five minutes, he finally rushed in, grumbling to himself, and the defense attorneys wasted no time in making their motions.

Ralph's lawyer, Carlino, fought vigorously (until the bitter end), moving to adjourn sentencing, claiming he had obtained new information. The fiery Carlino charged that during the trial, two jurors had received police protection around their homes and offices. "Prejudicial to the defendants," he argued, his dark eyes flashing. He also revealed that family members had visited jurors Smith and Gagnon when, by law, outside influences were prohibited. Carlino strenuously pressed McCook for time to further investigate his findings.

"Without legal merit," Dewey retorted starchily, standing as tall as he could.

McCook, in the eyes of Liguori and Luciano, not to mention the defense, was working in obvious agreement with Dewey. Anxious to get on with the sentencing, he denied all requests as well as a dozen others promoted by the defense.

Shivers ran up and down Ralph's spine when he realized he was at the mercy of that man. He wondered if McCook had ever taken a psychological test to determine if he were capable of judging his fellow man—and of possessing the power to decide their fates. Was McCook a sadist at heart, with preconceived ideas about crime and punishment? Ralph wondered silently, convinced that McCook was not free of political pressures.

Charlie was well dressed in a dark suit and somber tie as he stood stoically before the bench. Ralph knew Charlie was worried, that he had his own misgivings about McCook. With shoulders drooped and head bent, he waited.

"Have you anything to say before sentence is pronounced upon you?" the court clerk routinely called out.

Silence. Levy tugged gently at Charlie's sleeve. He gazed up with a faraway look and, in a soft, earnest voice, stated, "Your Honor, I have nothing to say, except that I am innocent!"

Unperturbed by the statement, Judge McCook nodded absently and turned to Levy for further remarks. There were none. Having read Charlie's psychiatric tests and a special report prepared by probation officer Irving W. Halpern, McCook felt omnipotent. His tone was extremely stern as he censured Charlie.

"The crimes of which you stand convicted are those of placing females in houses of prostitution, receiving money for such placing, and knowingly accepting money from their earnings without consideration . . .

". . . an intelligent, courageous, and discriminating jury has found you guilty of heading a conspiracy or combination to commit these crimes, which operated widely into New York, and extended into neighboring counties. This makes you responsible in law and morals for every foul and cruel deed, with the accompanying elements of extortion by the hand of codefendants. I am not here to reproach you, but since there appears to be no excuse for your conduct, nor hope of your rehabilitation, I will now proceed to administer adequate punishment."

As if in synchronization with Judge McCook's salient remarks, thunder roared, and lightning streaked across the skies, creating an eerie horror story ambiance. No one was relaxed; tensions were high while everyone in the courtroom waited with bated breath for the pronouncement.

"I hereby sentence you to thirty to fifty years imprisonment!" he bellowed.

The entire roomful of spectators gasped. But McCook impassively proceeded to render a breakdown of the years: ten to twenty for placing females in houses of prostitution, ten to fifteen years for taking money for so placing them, and ten to fifteen for accepting money from prostitution.

Charlie stared at McCook incredulously. Stunned, he wanted to shout that the man was crazy, throwing the book at him for something he didn't do! *They're sending me away for life,* he screamed inside himself. Helpless, he looked frantically at Levy. *They* had wanted Charlie out of circulation—incapacitated.

And *they* had succeeded.

To add insult to injury, before Charlie was led out of the courtroom, Judge McCook warned him how any reprisals against the witnesses would be treated and, in a booming voice for all to hear, declared, "Let the record show that should any witness for the people be injured or harassed in the future, this court will ask that the maximum sentence imposed be served by each of the defendants!"

One by one, the defendants took their turn, and McCook had censuring remarks for each. He told Betillo, twenty-eight years old, that he was considered Luciano's most ruthless and dangerous aide and, as such, was to serve a twenty-five- to forty-year sentence. Frederico, thirty-five, who had received two previous felony convictions, was informed he possessed a low, vicious, and brutal character (was an incorrigible criminal); and that he and Pennochio, forty-four (said to be a hardened criminal with nineteen arrests on his record), would receive special provisions. They both received a flat twenty-five years.

The charcoal gray sky suddenly turned black, as though the sun were in eclipse, and the anticipated rain poured down violently, the winds driving it savagely against the courtroom windows. The fierce storm distracted the spectators, creating general apprehension among them. Justice McCook, with his spectacles pushed down on his nose, vigorously banged his gavel to regain their attention, while tossing an intimidating glance in Ralph's direction. Ralph caught the look, and when the clerk called out his name, he quivered with presentiment.

Impatient with Ralph, McCook paid no attention to his claim of innocence and, without hesitating, tore into him.

"Your crime," he began gravely, "which was to supply the routine violence necessary to the combination, under the direction of better minds than yours, while acting as procurer for your personal profit, cannot be condoned. You have a good family and enjoyed an opportunity to live a law-abiding life, but you chose rather, especially of late, a way which better suited your vain and lazy nature. You are a silly imitator of the racketeers you admire . . .

"However," he continued with a supreme air of authority, "you are still young and have no prior convictions against you. Therefore, I am offering you, through a comparatively short sentence, the opportunity for rehabilitation."

Then without further ado, he announced, "I hereby sentence you to seven and a half to fifteen years in prison!"

Ralph almost choked. He was only thirty years old. That was a big chunk out of his young life (*the best years*), and he felt cheated! How could he accept being legally framed, especially when they had also falsely portrayed him (as a *pimp*, among other things)? Ralph was livid. No, he could never forgive Dewey. He turned helplessly to Carlino and saw his face contorted with rage. Carlino tried to console Ralph by reminding him of the appeals, but Ralph had a premonition that it was all over. Over for him and over for Charlie. Charlie, "the General," the commander in chief, had been humiliated and condemned along with his subordinates. The degradation aimed at them that day had left its indelible scarring on both men.

Attorney David P. Siegel had also pleaded for his client, Abe Wahrman, asking the court for clemency in consideration of his youth and the fact that he had no previous record. Judge McCook paused and turned to Dewey for his opinion, who replied acidly that the record showed Wahrman to be a "depraved character" with an utter lack of social responsibility. Without missing a beat, McCook condemned the defendant to fifteen to thirty years. At that moment, Wahrman, a blond boyish-looking lad of twenty-two, suddenly turned old, his face twisted in pain. He and Attorney Siegel walked out in a daze, as the rain drummed angrily against the windowpane.

Everyone had received stiff sentences except the squealers. David Marcus was given three to six years; Jack Ellenstein, four to eight years; while Peter Balitzer and Al Weiner each received two to four years. These men, involved up to their heads in the prostitution racket, were each given only a comparable slap on the wrist.

Sentences for Benny Spiller, Jesse Jacobs, and his office boy Meyer Berkman were postponed until July 1. Dewey wanted a further opportunity to work them over, although he didn't give his reason at the time. (Eventually, Spiller and Jacobs did talk and, for their cooperation, received sentences of about two years. Dewey was even more lenient on Meyer Berkman.)

Before Judge McCook adjourned, defense attorney Levy tried one last time to be heard. He asked that execution of Charlie's sentence be postponed in order for him to settle his affairs.

"In light of a thirty-year sentence," he appealed dramatically, "we are entitled to a thirty-day stay!"

Dewey, who was still there on the sidelines, interjected tenaciously that it was not possible—that a great deal of money had been spent to arrange the police convoys. They couldn't repeat the performance "as much as we would like to consent." He smiled maliciously.

Justice McCook again supported Dewey's argument and denied the motion.

Levy was outraged and cried out sarcastically, "The ruling is so disgraceful that I won't even take exception to it!"

The show was over at almost 12:30 p.m. The women, as usual, were in the corridors, crying their hearts out, clinging to one another. It was one thing to accept the guilty verdicts, but the sentences were unbearable. They rushed upon the defense lawyers emerging from the courtroom, besieging them with questions. It wasn't difficult for Charlie's lawyers to spot his sweetheart, Gay Orlova, among the women. Her blonde beauty was outstanding. They tried to mitigate her sorrow with words of encouragement, advising her they were preparing Charlie's appeal before the appellate division, scheduled sometime in the fall.

On the other side of the courthouse, Ralph, Charlie, and the others were shackled together like ferocious animals and led out to the sheriff's van, ready to be escorted by the usual entourage of policemen and detectives. The rain had symbolically stopped pouring; what remained was a light drizzle. With opened umbrellas, tear-stained women, other relatives, and their lawyers stood on the courthouse steps, solemnly watching as their loved ones pulled away.

Once back at The Tombs Prison, the prisoners were fingerprinted and photographed for the rogues' gallery; and while they were given a modest lunch, the red tape was processed for their transfer to Sing Sing in Ossining, New York. When they returned to the van, with the same escort, they were hustled to Grand Central Station for the 4:15 p.m. Sing Sing train. In addition to relatives and friends, the station was jammed with hundreds of people waiting to say farewell. The trial proceedings had been amply covered in the daily newspapers, and to some of the onlookers, the defendants had become almost heroes in a grotesque way. Everyone wanted a close-up look at the prostitution racketeers.

The trip to Ossining was tedious and exhausting. Ralph called it the milk train because it *chug-chugged* along, stopping at every station. No one was in a mood to talk. Finally, inside Sing Sing, they were unshackled and ushered into the receiving hall where each man went through the demeaning procedure of emptying his pockets of personal belongings and money. Ralph had very little change, only about five one-dollar bills. Betillo "Little Davie" had two, and Charlie had a wad of two hundred. The attendants took everything. Once processed through the usual fingerprint routine, the prisoners were individually placed in solitary confinement, which shocked everyone. It was a precautionary step by prison authorities who were afraid of reprisals against the bookies to whom Dewey had promised protection. It was a temporary stay, however, and they were soon released. The powers that be had made their decisions; the prisoners were to be separated. Only Ralph, Charlie, and Betillo, however, were being transferred to Clinton Prison in Dannemora (sometimes called Siberia).

Ralph was tired of being herded around like an animal, but at least he had learned his new home would be Dannemora. Well, one place was the same as another. Prison was prison. Ralph, however, was anxious to be settled in order to begin work on his appeal. As he boarded the train for Siberia, he thought of Dotty. Dewey had kept his promise; she had her reward. She had been whisked off to Europe with Cokey Flo and another girl. Ralph, however, knew Dotty—knew she wasn't happy in her heart. He envisioned her leaning against the ship's wooden railing—a ship taking her away from him and her troubles. He visualized her staring toward the horizon, her face sad, her eyes tearful.

What a strange twist of destiny! Had Ralph lied, had Dewey gotten what he wanted out of him, he could have been with Dotty. Instead, there he was facing a seven-and-a-half- to fifteen-year prison term. An early release for good behavior would depend solely on the politically influenced parole board (and on the whims of Thomas E. Dewey). Ralph promised himself that once in Dannemora, he would study law. He wanted out!

In the meantime, he would try to get some sleep on the train.

CHAPTER EIGHT

"You're too young! What are you doing here!"

The colorful lights offered a dim, warm glow; the band played a romantic ballad, but the pert redhead refused to budge even though Ralph had conjured up his most charming self in asking her to dance.

"Too young?" he flushed. And throwing out his chest, he exclaimed, "I'm eighteen!"

"Tell me another," she replied saucily, her green eyes twinkling in mirth.

Ralph refused to be put down, especially since his pals, Mario and Frank Russo, were observing his savoir faire, so he reached in his pocket and pulled out his driver's license.

"You don't believe me? Take a look at this!" He smugly boasted, handing her his license.

"Ooooh . . . ," the lovely squealed incredulously. "You are eighteen . . . But what a baby face . . . Ralph," she added sweetly.

Ralph glanced at his friends and winked, and taking the girl in his arms, he whirled her away triumphantly.

It was the inception of one of his nicknames, Baby Face Ralph—a name that would be used disparagingly by some in the future.

At fifteen, Ralph's interest in girls had become paramount, along with his love for dancing and cabarets; and with plenty of money in his pocket, the way was paved for him. Sometimes Ralph was lucky, and he would date one of the older girls he had met at the dance halls; but as soon as they learned the truth about his age, they dropped him. Although he was a very hip teenager, he was still rather innocent with women. Ralph had yet to meet the girl who would free him from his inhibitions to let his passions fly.

Mr. Barone was still acting as Ralph's tutor, and perhaps because Ralph had lost his father, he easily became attached to Barone. He was the first person Ralph knew who could sell something almost every minute. His lucrative bootlegging operation was always growing and, at times, helped can whiskey. It flowed out pint by pint, gallon by gallon. Ralph's greatest enjoyment came however when Mr. Barone acquired his first new automobile.

It was one of those quiet Sundays in spring. The Liguoris had enjoyed one of their classic Sunday lunches—fettuccine with cream sauce, veal scaloppini in white wine, tossed green salad with oil and vinegar dressing, and, Agnes's favorite dessert, *zuppa inglese.* Agnes loved to cook and, especially after Joseph's death, made a special effort to continue the tradition of good food and family cheer on Sunday. After lunch, the older boys took off to indulge their own escapades, Anna played her piano, while Agnes did the dishes. Ralph went to his room to relax. He was a night person and needed to conserve his energy for later. As he reclined, meditating on his bed, enjoying the cool, light breezes flowing through the window, he heard Mr. Barone calling up to him.

"Ralphy, come on down. I've something to show you!"

Ralph went to the window, brushed aside the beige lace curtains, and saw Barone waving up to him. He liked what he saw.

"Okay, be right down," returned Ralph and hustled downstairs.

"How do you like my new car, Ralphy?" Mr. Barone asked beaming as he stood beside a long black Cadillac parked in the driveway.

"Wow," whistled Ralph, totally impressed. He had always dreamed of buying his own Cadillac one day.

"There's only one hitch, Ralphy . . . I can't drive . . ."

"What?" screamed Ralph in disbelief.

Barone nodded, half-embarrassed by the fact that at his age, he had never learned to drive. "Thought you'd like to teach me." He smiled.

"With this car, anytime," laughed Ralph.

Their roles were now reversed. Ralph was the teacher, and every Sunday, he took the older man out for driving lessons. When Barone finally was able to handle the wheel by himself, he wanted to surprise his cousins with his new skills. He took Ralph visiting first to the Castellanos (Paul) then to the Carlo Gambino family. A bottle of homemade red wine was immediately produced, and everyone drank to toast Barone's new accomplishment. Those Sunday jaunts and family visits were pleasant, but toward evening, Ralph always excused himself. He couldn't give up dancing, so he would drive Barone home, put the car in the garage, shower, and take off with his young buddies.

Agnes, however, unwilling to relinquish her young son to the uncertainties of an independent life, was privately orchestrating her own ambitions for Ralph. About two years later, when she was sure that her sons, especially Ralph, had reached a certain maturity (Ralph was eighteen), she held a family conference. It was painful for Agnes to speak about Joseph, but with Anna sitting on the sidelines, the stoic widow revealed to her sons her desire to continue in business where their father had left off. The older boys looked perplexed, and as Agnes tried to encourage them, Ralph watched them vacillate in their decision. His heart went out to his mother, and partially to please her, but mostly because he so strongly resembled his enterprising father, Ralph convinced everyone that his mother had a great idea. Thus, it was agreed to open a supermarket. They would call it the Ideal Meat Market—Liguori Brothers, and they found an excellent location at the intersection of Bath and Bay Avenues on Thirty-first Street. The day the huge signboard was hung on the building, Mr. Barone was on hand to congratulate them. Beaming from ear to ear, he embraced Ralph paternally, genuinely happy to see his young friend spreading his wings.

Ralph soon trained his elder brother, Al, to be a butcher—as his father had taught him. "Al," he would say patiently, "just watch me!" Almost immediately, they were doing good business. Agnes had won her case.

But Ralph was not all work and no play. Dancing was in his blood, and he couldn't give that up.

His circle of friends around the dance halls was growing. One night, with Mario and Frank, he was introduced to a handsome young Italian immigrant, Rodolpho d'Antonguolla, destined to be known to the world as Rudolph Valentino. Rudolph was born in Castellaneta in Southern Italy—a poor, deprived town with a single outlet only a few kilometers from the Gulf of Taranto. He had worked as a gardener in Long Island for a rich family (had even washed windows for a living), but his dream was to become a professional dancer. Rudolph's limited English was still heavily accented, but he was the best tango dancer around the dance halls. When Valentino danced, everyone left the dance floor to watch him. He moved so smoothly, with a particular style and grace, his body embracing the music as he became its master. What class! Squads of girls and women stood around, hoping to catch his favor to enjoy a chance on the parquet with him. Some were lucky. He was always a gentleman, a prince—kind and gentle to everyone without exception. Even though Rudy was older than Ralph, they became very good friends, sharing their mutual love of dancing. Three and four times a week they would meet to make the rounds of the dance halls. Ralph stood in awe of Rudy and watched him dance with deep admiration. There was no one like Rudy!

Once at the Arcadia, while Ralph was dancing, having a great time with the girls, Rudy called him into the men's room.

"Ralphy, come here. I want to show you something," he chattered excitedly. "Tonight we're going cabareting!"

"Yeah? How come?" Ralph laughed. "What's new?"

Rudy opened his hand to reveal a wad of greenbacks.

Ralph's tone immediately became serious. "Where'd you get that?"

Rudy chuckled and began to babble in Italian, which he always did when excited, "*Fantastico, incredibile, quella li.* that old lady gave me $500 just to dance with her! Can you believe it!" He did a little jig. "Come on," Rudy urged. "You pick the place. Let's go!"

The boys took off and made a night of it. There was one problem however. When Rudy was around, no other boy could score with the girls. Rudy's one true love, however, was dancing. They would stay out until two o'clock in the morning, and then Ralph would drive Rudy home to Long Island. Rudy, however, had another dream, and he soon took off for Hollywood. Studying Rudy's Latin good looks and dancing talents, the movie makers quickly claimed him and proceeded to make him one of the industry's most famous movie idols. One of the immortals.

When Ralph was seventeen, he had made another new friend, Tony Piscopel—a man destined to be loyal to Ralph as long as he lived. Tony was a good-looking Sicilian, about 5'8" tall with a great slender build. His dark, expressive eyes, coal black beneath long dark lashes, matched his soft black wavy hair. With his sensuous lips, winsome smile, and well-modulated voice, he could sweep any girl off her feet. Tony Piscopel was a ladies' man (and was no angel).

Tony came from a large closely knit family—five brothers and two sisters. He had a difficult childhood; Mr. Piscopel had many mouths to feed, and honest work with decent pay was hard to find for many illiterate immigrants. Mrs. Piscopel was a saint and couldn't be blamed if some of her sons took a wrong path; it was something that happened often in those troublesome times. One brother was called Cut 'Em Up Morris, an expert with a knife. Ralph met Morris after his release from Sing Sing following a five-year stretch. The felon wasn't out too long before he knifed another man, Charley Mararello (a man well connected), and again, Morris was in deep trouble. There was only one man who could save him—Frankie Yale, head of L'Unione Siciliana. A desperate Mr. Piscopel went running to him, hoping to ward off his son's inevitable death. Sure enough, Yale called Morris and Charley together and told them to shake hands. In those days, when *they* said "shake hands," one shook hands. The affair blew over, but Mr. Piscopel remained in Yale's debt.

Tony, like his hot-tempered brother, was also fast with a knife; and even though he was a more lovable guy, his short fuse involved him into many scrapes. Sometimes Ralph came to his rescue with a pair of steel fists. When Tony was nineteen, two important events took place in his life. He became a bouncer at the Cameo Ballroom and fell madly in love with a beautiful blonde girl. Everyone called her Clara Bow because she was the spitting image of the famous silent screen actress. He was crazy about her, jealous and possessive, and he warned everyone that she was off-limits. But Tony was not lucky. Despite his dire warnings, word reached him that another man had slept with Clara, a man whom Tony knew very well; and for a Sicilian, that was an act of high treason.

A few days later, around closing time at the Cameo, Tony took Ralph to one side and whispered confidentially, "Ralph, get your car. I've something to do."

Ralph immediately recognized Tony's dark mood and knew enough not to question him. He casually replied, "Okay, meet me outside in a couple of minutes."

As Ralph drove his car to the side of the ballroom, he found other cars arriving and lining up behind him. He began to suspect something ominous but shrugged it off. Then he saw Tony, his handsome face drawn tight, dragging a resisting Clara, her lovely blonde hair falling over a face lined with fear. Tony shoved her into the backseat and followed her in.

"Okay, Ralph, hit it," he snarled.

Ralph nodded, and as he pulled away from the curb, he saw the cars following him, as in a procession. Tony told him to drive to an old farmhouse, which they had used on other occasions for business, and not another word was spoken.

It was an eerie night. The roads were deserted as the caravan of cars sped along, out of the city and into the countryside. Almost an hour later, Ralph pulled into the dirt drive leading up to the farmhouse, which was almost hidden by tall forbidding trees. The full moon cast a kaleidoscope of shadows around the yard.

Tony stepped out, forcefully dragging Clara who protested frantically, "Tony, Tony, you're hurting me, please." But he was in a daze, oblivious to her pleas as he pushed her into the farmhouse and threw her on the bed.

Ralph sat transfixed. He had begun to realize what was about to happen, and he stiffened with indignation. He liked Clara Bow. Tony emerged from the farmhouse and stood cold and impassive, signaling the men out of their cars, one by one. And one by one, the men entered the house to brutalize the hapless girl. Ralph could hear her desperate cries, begging her rapists to stop, but he could do nothing. He was powerless against Tony's folly, hated to have been present. When at last Clara's hysterically piteous screams became so unbearable, Tony snapped out of his trance. He stared fiercely at the one young man who was responsible for the entire affair. He was part of the group, but not until that precise moment did the young lad understand what was happening. He broke into a run for his life. Tony, prepared for the flight, caught him and beat him mercilessly, leaving him battered and bleeding in a clump on the ground. Then he ordered the other men back into their cars.

Clara came stumbling out, barefoot, her face distorted with pain, her beautiful features streaked and smeared by what was left of her makeup. Her lovely pink chiffon dress, torn and tattered, hung in strands from her body. Too weak to stand, Clara clung to the porch pillar for support, screaming in a hoarse, groaning delirium, "Sons of bitches . . . You sons of bitches . . . Sons of bitches . . ." Until, beaten and exhausted, she slid to the dirty wooden floor, vomiting bile, as the cars pulled away.

Behind the wheel, a shocked and outraged Ralph drove in silence. He was greatly disturbed. It was the first time he had witnessed such a thing. The beaten young man, on the other hand, was lucky. Ralph had heard stories involving certain "families" where—if a similar betrayal occurred—the traitor would be brutalized and delivered to his relatives in a coma near death, on a cold slab, with his genitalia amputated and stuffed in his mouth. But an outrage of that enormity was alien to Ralph's character, and he found himself questioning his affection for Tony, knowing he would give his chum a very wide berth for a while. When he turned to look at Tony, who sat silent beside him in a daze, he was surprised to find tears streaming down his handsome, tormented face.

Ralph immersed himself in his work and enjoyed observing the family's success. He was also doing very well with a little gambling on the side and was finally able to purchase his dream car—a Cadillac. It was the first of a series of beautiful cars: Stutz, Marmon, Pierce-Arrow, Isotta Fraschini, and a beautiful Cord—each ten years ahead of its time, and each of which he kept no longer than six months. His preference for Cadillacs, however, earned him another nickname: Cadillac Ralph. His mania for beautiful, expensive cars, however, made him a suspect to envious people and especially to the police, who considered him a potential gangster. Ralph was constantly pulled over by some roving patrol car to prove his identity. When he was able to prove his legitimate family business, he would be begrudgingly sent off, but not without a grumble or sarcastic remark.

Agnes was deeply troubled over her son's lifestyle, unhappy about Ralph's late hours, although he never missed work in the morning. Sometimes, when she would see his eyes close from fatigue at the store, she wanted to cry out to him but didn't. One day, however, Ralph unexpectedly caught her weeping in a corner. It was unlike her, and he immediately rushed to her side, demanding to know what was wrong.

"Ralph, I can't see you going on this way . . . You can't work all day and stay out all night . . ." She began wiping her eyes. "Besides, I worry about you and what all these late hours mean. Please . . . stay home tonight . . . Go to bed early. You're killing yourself. Please!" Agnes tenderly touched his soft baby face. Ralph put his arms around her and promised to stay home that night, to go to bed early—anything, just to comfort her, to stop her from weeping. But he couldn't resist the siren call of adventure. He waited until she was asleep, then slipped out to meet his friends.

It was something bigger than life to Ralph. Nightlife and its habitués fascinated him. He was in his element. One evening about a year later, with his friends at the Park Palace Cabaret on Ocean Park West, Park Circle, he met Frankie Yale (Francisco Uale). Of course, Ralph knew about him. There were very few who didn't. He had founded the L'Unione Siciliana, later known as the Italo-American Union, and had organized a big drive across the nation for membership (but the Sicilians always ran the show). L'Unione Siciliana operated throughout the land as a social and cultural club. Its purpose was to aid Sicilian immigrants with their various new problems arising in a country where the laws and mores were foreign to them. Unfortunately, many ignorant immigrants were also exploited. As the organization spread to other major cities, Frankie Yale became national president, thus becoming more and more powerful. Naturally, the club was a potent tool in his hands. What with fund-raising festivities (and the allegiance of its members), it became a political machine for votes coveted by all politicians.

Frankie walked in with his bodyguard, a man known only as Sham, followed by his usual entourage and sat at his favorite table. He was not a good-looking man but was an excellent dresser, nor was he tall, only about 5'6" with a stocky build. His round swarthy face and olive complexion was highlighted by almond-shaped dark brown eyes and a mass of black straight hair. He always wore a hat, mostly wide-brimmed, and a big cigar protruded constantly from his mouth. Frankie Yale looked the picture of the tough guy he was.

As usual, Ralph was enjoying himself. With his winning personality, he knew almost everybody. Because of his apparent popularity, he had also met many of the "big boys" around town, who took to him instantly. It was easy to like Ralph. His motto was, "Mind your own business. Don't step on people's toes because as soon as you do, you will find yourself in trouble!"

That night, Ralph and Tony were entertaining two good-looking, sexy showgirls at their table, drinking and laughing, the girls flirting outrageously with their eyes and gestures, when a waiter carrying a tray of glasses and a bottle of champagne made his way toward them. Ralph was pleasantly surprised. While the waiter uncorked the champagne, intuitively he glanced toward Frankie's table, in time to see the swarthy leader smile and lift his glass in a salute. Ralph raised his in a similar gesture, smiling back appreciatively.

It marked the beginning of a new and lasting friendship.

CHAPTER NINE

For the poor, poverty is not an ennobling experience. Perhaps for saints it is, such as for Saint Francis, who divested himself of his worldly riches to live a life of deprivation in order to redeem himself in the eyes of his god. But for mere mortals, it is very difficult to overcome the pain and humiliation—the anger and trauma—that poverty breeds. For relatively few, poverty can act as a catalyst that tickles the brain, arouses the imagination, and stimulates creativity to inspire those few to emerge as liberators. For Charlie Luciano to be surrounded by an affluent society and be unable to partake of its tempting fruit was hell on earth.

He had his fill of poverty at an early age. After detention at the Hampton Farms Penitentiary, he had tried legitimate work, sometimes with his father, but he couldn't tolerate his father's lifestyle—hard labor for a pittance. With his lack of education and training, Charlie realized his future in the legitimate world was not a rosy one. But in the asphalt jungle (the grimy streets of Manhattan and Harlem), his burning ambition had already found other paths—shortcuts to instant wealth. He became the leader of an impressive group, comprised of equally ambitious men: Frank Costello, Joe Adonis (Giuseppe Antonio Doto), Vito Genovese, and his Jewish pals Meyer Lansky (Maier Suchowljansky) and Bugsy Siegel (Benjamin Siegel).

With Charlie, it began with gambling, at which he was a natural. He and Costello (who was six years older) had learned the ropes from the man known as The Brain—Arnold Rothstein (supposedly the racketeer behind the famous World Series scandal of 1919 involving the Chicago White Sox). They both navigated well in and around the Jewish community. Costello even married a nice Jewish girl, Loretta Geigerman, whose parents lived on prestigious Park Avenue. Charlie's business acquaintances gradually grew (Waxey Gordon and Dutch Schultz were two more); and his family of friends widened, as his reputation spread throughout the city, to include Johnny Torrio, Carl Gambino, Willie Moretti, and, of course, Frankie Yale.

It is hard to understand why in 1923, Charlie permitted himself to be again involved in a drug crime. Basically a contemplative and reticent man, he allowed Vito Genovese, in a moment of weakness, to convince him to handle a big money drug deal—with Big Nose Charley (Charles Lagaipa). It was something Charlie had promised himself he would never do. But Vito, who had no scruples about drugs, insisted it was a one-time-only shot and the take too big to pass up, so Charlie was precipitated into a vulnerable situation where he personally was to deliver some samples to their destination. It was a naïve move on his part, which only proved what a greenhorn he was in the racket. Charlie had set out for his rendezvous with a few packets of heroin in his pockets when a Federal Narcotics agent caught up with him on West Fourteenth Street. He was arrested on the spot, and the sky fell for Charlie. It was an injunction from heaven; he would say later, never to touch drugs again. Not even his best political connections could help him. The narcotics agents could not be bought. With his back against the wall, Charlie became what he hated most—a stool pigeon—and collaborated his freedom against a trunkful of narcotics. He won his plea and sent the agents scurrying to a basement at 164 Mulberry Street where he had arranged for the trunk to be found. Charlie was released, but it was a traumatic time for him, an experience he would never forget. For the rest of his life, he had a hard time convincing people that, indeed, he personally never dealt with the white powder again.

Three years later, after that eventful affair, Ralph met Charlie. He was first introduced to him by Frankie Yale at the bar on Fourteenth and Fifteenth Avenue—Yale's favorite hangout. Charlie and Costello were sitting at the bar, having a drink with Frankie, when Ralph walked in with Tony. It was a casual introduction, everyone shaking hands with one another, but Ralph had time to study Charlie and was impressed with him, as well as with Costello. He thought they looked like two successful businessmen—the way they were dressed. Costello was suave, with nice features, and a great talker. Charlie, his dark eyes glistening, smiled continuously, leaving the limelight to his companion. From then on, they would always nod to each other as their paths crossed in the dance halls and cabarets they frequented. Ralph was then barely twenty and a newlywed while Charlie, almost thirty, was involved in his climb to power. Their close friendship was destined to start a few years later.

Ralph too had had his moment of weakness, and sometimes his naiveté' involved affairs of the heart. At sixteen, he had lost his innocence with an older girl but had not allowed himself to be the target of any one woman. He loved them and left them—at times without pomp and circumstance. One evening, however, at Souchers Dance Hall in Coney Island, he met Evelyn.

They spotted each other across the dance floor. Ralph noticed a shapely blonde girl turning to gaze at him from the other side of the room. He was intrigued, but for Evelyn, it was love at first sight. She waited for the handsome youth to come to her. Fascinated, Ralph walked toward her, silently took her into his arms, and drew her out onto the dance floor, their bodies intertwining as one. As they parted slightly for air, Ralph watched her toss her shoulder-length blonde hair to one side, her limpid green eyes intently scanning his face. He felt his blood surging through his body. He instantly knew that he would definitely be seeing Evelyn again.

Night after night they met. Ralph learned that Evelyn Nelson was of Irish descent; that her parents owned a candy store on Eighth Avenue near Prospect Avenue, but that her family life was not happy. When they were together, Evelyn clung to Ralph, completely overwhelmed by him—his looks, his money, his Cadillac, his loving ways. She had made up her mind that Ralph would be hers, and it didn't matter to her at all that she was slightly taller.

About a week later, behind the butcher counter, engrossed in sectioning and cutting up a side of beef, Ralph felt someone watching him. He looked up to see those familiar green eyes fixed upon him.

"Evelyn, what are you doing here?" he asked, surprised.

"Ralphy, I must talk to you!" she replied, with a certain urgency.

Ralph looked around the store to see if his mother had seen her, but she appeared busy at the cash register with some customers. He quickly came from behind the counter, sensing something serious was amiss, and took Evelyn away from other eyes and ears. Agnes, however, had witnessed the whole scene but betrayed nothing. In the back room, Evelyn began weeping (something Ralph could never handle in a woman), explaining between sobs that she had had a family argument and had run away from home to be with him. She told him she loved him, wanted only him, and didn't care about anything else in her life. There was just one thing for Ralph to do. He embraced her tenderly, whispering words of comfort.

"It'll be okay, Evelyn. I'll take care of you. Don't worry."

Furtively, he slipped out of the store with her, but Agnes looked up from her books to watch their stealthy departure.

Ralph found a furnished room for Evelyn about fifteen blocks away from the store where their trysts continued every night after work. Ralph, however, did not give up his nightlife, which caused their first lovers' quarrel. At eighteen, he was not ready to settle down, no matter how he was smitten with Evelyn, so he took her back to her parents. Mrs. Nelson, who had been drinking excessively, assaulted him with the worst tongue-lashing he had ever heard, demanding that he marry her daughter! Ralph quietly left without a word, but Evelyn would not be deterred from remaining with the love of her life. Parting was sweet sorrow, and the lovers' spat didn't last. This time, Ralph took her to a rooming house near Coney Island, and the romance was on again.

Agnes was frowning more and more those days, not because of Ralph (he told her very little of Evelyn) nor of the business (they were doing very well), but because her elder son, Al, had also fallen in love with a woman who lived near the store. The problem was that Al not only was neglecting the store, visiting her two and three hours a day, but also draining the family bank account for her. Ralph was also discouraged, and although he would defend his brother when customers complained, he told both Al and Agnes that it just wasn't good business. Al, however, was completely bitten by the love bug and wouldn't listen. In order not to create a family feud, Ralph tenderly told his mother he was leaving, and he joined Evelyn in the rooming house.

Of course, Agnes, depressed about the way her family was splitting up, could not just stand by and accept what was happening. A resourceful woman, she finally tracked Ralph down at his rooming house, and they held an emotional tête-à-tête.

"If your father were alive today," she began tearfully, "his strong guiding hand would have prevented all of this, and many, many other things."

Ralph felt a knot in his throat at the mention of his father. He listened calmly to his mother's soul-stirring sermon. When necessary, Agnes could thrust forth her own inner strength, a strength not easy to combat. Ralph was convinced to return home to open up a second store. It was near the saloon where he had worked as a whiskey runner, at 475 Kings Highway. Again, it was a successful enterprise, but it lasted only two years. Al began to bet heavily on the horses and lost constantly, causing him to siphon off the family accounts.

"Damn, someone left the light on!" Ralph mumbled as he glanced toward the store. He slowly brought his Cadillac to a stop and parked a few doors down the street. A precautionary measure.

As he stepped out of the car, he looked at his watch and frowned. If he didn't hurry, he would be late for his appointment with Tony.

"Why can't they be more careful!" he fumed silently while he fumbled for his key. It seemed that whenever Ralph didn't lock up, something always happened.

The overhead bell rang as he pushed the door open, and instantly, Ralph heard the slam of the cash register drawer.

"Who's there?" he called. "That you, Al?"

There was a hesitant silence. "Uh . . . yeah, yeah . . . it's me," Al finally managed.

Ralph walked toward the cashier's cage, an overhead light was burning, and found his brother fidgeting beside the cash register. He looked sickly pale, and although the night was cool, there were beads of perspiration on his forehead and upper lip.

Al, not much taller than Ralph, always nattily dressed, was just lighting a cigarette, and Ralph caught the slight tremor in his fingers as he placed the white shaft between his lips.

"Hi, Ralphy," Al murmured nervously. Noticing his youngest brother all spruced up, he added innocently, "You going out?"

"Yeah, but I saw the light on, as I was driving by. Christ, it could have been a burglar! What gives? You working late?" Ralph asked, not hiding his irritation and edging close to the counter.

He had already sized up the situation. Ralph knew what his brother was up to. It was not the first time!

"How'd we do today?" he asked Al, forcing a grin.

"Oh . . . n-nothing special," Al stammered. "Just the usual . . ."

Ralph nudged his brother aside and pushed open the cash register. He noticed the metal baskets holding the singles and fives were there, intact. The holders for the tens, twenty, and fifty dollar bills were bare. The metal glinting up at Ralph in the light confirmed his suspicions.

"We . . . uh . . . we had a pretty lousy day," Al told him unevenly.

"Cut it out, Al," Ralph warned. "What'd you do with the rest of the bills? You were at the cash register when I came in."

"Rest of the . . . hey, Ralphy, what're you talking about?" Al began to protest, color rising in his cheeks. "You accusing me—"

"Oh, stop the crap, Al," Ralph interrupted, choking back his fury. "You're losing again on the ponies, and you're taking Ma's money to cover your losses! Right, Al?" he pressed.

"Hey, Ralphy! You got no right!"

"I've got *every* right! Don't lie to me! This is *my* business *too,* you know!"

"So I took a few bucks!" Al cried defensively. "I'll put it back tomorrow! You got no right to make me feel like a thief!"

With a stare of cold contempt, Ralph slammed shut the register drawer and forcefully shoved his brother aside. He couldn't take it.

"Hey!" Al called after him in a strangled voice. "Don't tell Ma! Don't say anything to Ma, Ralphy!"

Ralph had reached the door. He turned around and stared frostily back at a wilting Al Liguori.

"I don't have to tell her, Al. She's not a fool. She knows. But . . . *I* can't take it! *I* can't stand watching you steal us blind any more. You can keep the store, Al. I want out!"

The overhead bell jingled as Ralph left, and his whole body seemed to quiver. He could not handle an open breach with his elder brother. It was too great a drain on his energy. Hell, he didn't need the income from the store, not if it meant having to always look the other way while Al stole from them. It was time to move away, to cut the umbilical cord and set out more independently. He felt sorry for his mother. Nevertheless, he decided to call it quits. Within weeks, Ralph relinquished the business to the family and left home for good—a move that led him to marriage.

It was one of those $2.00 weddings in Brooklyn's city hall. Evelyn was eighteen; Ralph, almost twenty; and their two witnesses, not much older. But Ralph's marital problems were just beginning. Evelyn's home life had never been a loving one, and she expected to find her salvation in Ralph and in her marriage. Unfortunately, she had picked the wrong man. Although Ralph was capable of great love, he was not the stay-at-home type; and her possessive nature, combined with her bad temper, made for a turbulent relationship. Their $2.00 wedding didn't stand a chance. It was over practically before it began.

Ralph was ambitious and dynamic, too young to be curbed. He was working his way up to independence, and that took time. With Tony, he was organizing crap games around Brooklyn, which put an extra fifty dollars weekly in his pocket—since he was the cutter of the games. They were very well organized, with lookouts at strategic points to warn them if the police cars came—in time to break the game and scatter.

In addition to the crap games, they were asked by two Greeks, owners of cafes on Ninth Avenue between Forty-sixth and Forty-seventh streets, to protect them against hoods who were pestering them. Ralph had now entered the protection racket, earning large additional sums of money. On weekends, he joined Tony as a bouncer at the Cameo Ballroom, strengthening his reputation as a tough personality. Although a young man, small of stature, Ralph was built like a bull with steel fists. Mr. Goldstein, his boss, paid him fifteen dollars for his services.

On the legitimate side, after Ralph left the family business, he made the rounds of the butcher shops. He was first hired by Carl Graham Bean on Risen Avenue and worked for him six to seven months. He then transferred to the prosperous Lionel Brothers on Bath Beach. Afterwards, his friends in the business all clamored for him, beginning with the Castellano Brothers (who conducted a butcher business as a front for their bootlegging operations). Ralph worked for them about six months before moving to Castellano's son-in-law, Frank Gambino, on Grayson Avenue and Avenue U; and finally, with Castellano's "okay," he joined the Gambino family's butcher shop. Ralph was constantly hustling to make extra money.

Especially since he was soon to become a father!

Evelyn was pregnant and making the most of it. Despite the fact that he was working around the clock, Ralph tried to be patient with her—considering her condition—and, time permitting, showered her with attention. As her pregnancy advanced, however, she became more and more capricious—demanding. Dead tired one morning, Ralph arrived home around four o'clock and found Evelyn wide awake, waiting.

"Ralph," she moaned, "I can't stand it. I'm so hungry. Please, please get me a watermelon!"

"A watermelon! Where the hell could I find a watermelon at this hour? Go to sleep, Evelyn. You must have had a bad dream."

"No, Ralph . . . please. My stomach hurts. If you don't, it'll burst. Really, it will," she continued pleading.

Rather than argue a hopeless cause, Ralph turned around and went out to find a watermelon. At that hour, it was impossible to find a store open; but as he drove by the Waldorf Astoria Hotel, it hit him. He turned the car around, rolled onto the curb, parked, and ran in to buy Evelyn her watermelon.

Evelyn nearly jumped with joy at the sight of it.

"Oh, Ralphy . . . my hero . . ."

Can anyone really understand women? mused Ralph.

Joey Liguori was born on August 20, 1926, in Brooklyn. He was a beautiful boy with his father's baby blue eyes. Ralph felt he was in seventh heaven!

Unfortunately, not even Joey's birth helped to improve their marriage. Evelyn's behavior became insufferable with her obsessive jealousy, and a few months later, they separated. It was a tragic moment for Evelyn. At nineteen, and perhaps because of her family situation, she lacked the maternal instincts to raise her son. Without obtaining Ralph's approval, she placed Joey in the care of friends and refused to disclose his whereabouts. It was of course a vindictive move and not the kind of thing one could do to Ralph with impunity. He did not intend to permit his son to be raised by strangers, and Evelyn was playing with fire.

It took a few months, but Ralph discovered that Joey, then six months old, was being sheltered in an apartment on West End Avenue and Sixty-fifth Street. That morning, a resolute Ralph stood before the mirror, combing his hair; he would tolerate no nonsense. After he retrieved a clean white handkerchief from the dresser drawer, he patted the revolver in his trouser pocket and took off. Upon approaching the house, he noticed that the shades were being quickly drawn, which only triggered his anger. When no one would respond to his rapping at the door, he became furious. With a dangerous roar of exasperation, Ralph lunged twice against the door, drawing his gun as it fell open, and lined three or four people up against the wall. Shouting menacing words to them to stay put, he rushed into the bedroom, lifted Joey out of the crib, and, still pointing his gun, rushed out, leaving the people all petrified.

He took Joey directly to his mother and Anna where he knew the baby would receive the warmth and loving care from his own flesh and blood. What Evelyn lacked as a mother, Ralph made up as a loving father. While Agnes and Anna raised Joey, he vowed to be with them every Sunday and faithfully followed that pattern through the years.

Evelyn, however, was not easily discouraged and, instead, nurtured love-hate emotions. She continued to spy on Ralph, trying to catch him with another woman, and when that failed, she devised one last vengeful act. Ralph had traded in his old Cadillac for a new one. Late one Saturday night, he parked in front of the garage near his mother's house. In the morning, Ralph found all the beautiful upholstery slashed, the inside completely destroyed. Naively, he never thought of Evelyn; instead, he had come to the conclusion it was, perhaps, the union man objecting to his car parked in front of the garage and dropped the issue. The following Sunday morning, Evelyn phoned to speak to her son.

"Joey, ask your daddy how he likes his new car . . ."

When little Joey innocently repeated his mother's smug question, Ralph shrugged his shoulders and held his silence. He never spoke badly about his wife to his son. He had other things on his mind.

Evelyn became a closed chapter in his life.

CHAPTER TEN

The Roaring Twenties represented an era memorable for sweeping change—marked by a strong, stimulating wind of carefree lifestyle. It gradually ushered in the Jazz Age—a period that introduced George Gershwin, Irving Berlin, and Cole Porter; colorful sports figures Babe Ruth, Gene Tunney, and Jack Dempsey; and "blazing youth" epitomized in the novels of a passionate young writer, F. Scott Fitzgerald. Calvin Coolidge had inherited the nation's woes in 1923 from President Warren G. Harding, who died while in office. After Cooledge's election in 1924 to a full four-year presidency, he did his best to clean up the corruption in the previous administration—the most shocking of which was called the Teapot Dome scandal. Harding's secretary of the interior had accepted bribes for leasing government-owned oil reserves to private companies. President Coolidge was a man of few words and few deeds, and toward the end of his office in 1927, he announced, "I do not choose to run."

The nation's presumed prosperity was riding on thin air, and the winds of the Great Depression were arriving. More and more workers were losing their jobs.

Ralph was no exception.

Even the Gambinos were tightening their belt as various cuts of meat became authentic luxuries. Ralph eventually left their store, deciding to abandon butchering for the moment. He applied for a cab driver's license (known as a hack license on the streets) through the police department. Fortunately, once he obtained it, Ralph almost immediately began working for a respectable German, Carl Van Grice, who had married a nice Italo-American girl. Grice had a fleet of ten cabs, and Ralph drove a Hupmobile two shifts a day. Sometimes, in between shifts, he would stop at Frankie Yale's favorite hangout—the bar on Fourth and Fifth Avenue.

"Ralph, come over and meet my kid brother," Frankie called, waving him to his reserved table.

Frankie and Angelo Yale immigrated to the States with their parents when they were respectively fifteen and ten years old. They were poor immigrants, but Frankie had become the boss, *un pezzo di novanta*, and Angelo leaned heavily on his prestige and power. As big brother, Frankie had persuaded Angelo to become an undertaker, conveniently making the funeral parlor one of their legitimate fronts. Of course, Frankie had many other enterprises, including a cigar factory and the Harbor Inn nightclub in Coney Island. His good friend Johnny Torrio shared partnership for a while.

Everyone cordially shook hands. As Ralph studied Angelo, he came to the conclusion that all Angelo had in common with his brother was the shade of his dark eyes. They were clearly not in the same league. Angelo was taller (about 5'8"), and despite being five years younger than Frankie, he had salt-and-pepper hair, which helped his average looks. *Kind of arrogant,* thought Ralph as they talked about the dance halls they both frequented—Ben Modern's Riviera Ballroom where Glenn Miller often played and the Meadowbrook, a great dance hall in New Jersey (also a meeting place for many of the boys). Angelo spoke and grinned pompously, particularly when he mentioned the beautiful girls he met at the dance halls. "He thinks he's irresistible," laughed Ralph inwardly and decided to add "vain" to his opinion of Angelo.

"Ralphy," the sound of Frankie's baritone voice revealed his cast iron character. "I'd like you to take care of Angelo for me. He's got a knack for getting into trouble!"

"Sure, Frankie, why not," Ralph replied lightly, trying not to look surprised. Angelo was fifteen years older than Ralph. *It's absurd,* thought Ralph, but he surmised that it was Frankie's way of paying him respect for his age. To return this trust, Ralph began to socialize with Angelo, regularly taking him to the dance halls and cabarets. He learned soon enough that Angelo was a troublesome guy whom no one liked. Tony couldn't stand him and complained when Ralph brought him along, but Ralph explained he was doing it for Frankie's sake.

Basking in the aura of his brother's protection, Angelo felt he had carte blanche to do as he pleased. He was an unscrupulous character who continuously enjoyed shaking people down. Frankie, however, was not lenient with him. When Angelo created problems, not only did Frankie fly off the handle, but was also extremely tough and cold in punishing his kid brother. Once when Frankie learned that Angelo was pestering someone he knew, he told his brother to lay off. But stubborn Angelo wouldn't listen; he dared to challenge his elder brother's dictates. Frankie, livid, ordered his gorillas to find him and to tie him to the back of his Lincoln. When Angelo realized what was about to happen, he struggled to escape, kicking and punching, but the gorillas were too tough. They dragged him to the car and fastened him tightly to the rear bumper, arms outstretched. As Frankie slipped behind the wheel, Angelo kept shouting, "Frankie, don't do this, Frankie! Listen, don't . . ." But

Frankie belligerently put his foot on the gas pedal and drove off. He dragged him around the block until Angelo's screams became so pathetic that Frankie's fraternal instincts made him stop. He pulled into the funeral parlor's drive and, without a word, motioned to his men to untie a bloody and badly bruised Angelo . . . then disappeared into the house. Frankie's explosive temper was well-known. Angelo should have known better, but he was a complete screwball.

At times, Frankie asked Ralph to help him out on a job. One day, while Ralph was resting between shifts, Frankie called.

"Ralph, I need you to do something for me."

"Sure, Frankie, what's up?" Ralph replied, knowing he couldn't refuse.

"There's a strike going on at the Borden Milk Company . . . and they've got scabs working . . . Now here's what I want you to do . . ."

As instructed, Ralph went out to case the place and did find that some drivers with their horses and wagons were scabbing. Ralph was basically a kind and caring person; times were difficult, and he realized that the drivers were just trying to make a living. Before he went into action, he approached one of them.

"Look," he said sympathetically, "the boys don't want you here, and orders are orders. Now, I don't want to hurt you, so do as I tell you. At a certain point, as I come behind with my car, you jump off your wagon and make out like you ran away because I'm going to hit real hard."

The poor man thanked him profusely, then, trembling, mounted his wagon, which was tied to his horse on the trolley tracks. He swiftly and furtively loosened the horse's reins and, as Ralph advised, jumped off just in time. Apparently, the sound of the car racing up behind had also frightened the horse, and he too vanished. Ralph never did see him! The reverberating crash alerted the other scabbers who, upon viewing the scene, scrammed out of sight. The place was suddenly deserted. The job was accomplished. Ralph received fifty dollars for his services.

Driving a cab was more an enjoyment than work for Ralph. He had an opportunity to meet many people (good, bad, and indifferent), but his career as a hackie was short-lived.

One cold night in March 1927, in downtown New York, he picked up three men with four suitcases. Two of the men looked familiar, but he couldn't place them. They asked to be taken to an address in Coney Island, adding that one of them was moving. Ralph wasn't too happy about having to make the return trip, but he drove them out anyway, hoping to pick up a fare in that area. Fortunately, the men asked him to wait, and Ralph agreed, happy to have the return fare. He didn't even mind the half-hour wait, and in the end, they gave him a very generous tip. Ralph went home satisfied that night.

About three or four days later, Ralph was called to the Bath Beach station house for questioning. A detective named Fitzsimmons began badgering him.

"Did you take anyone around in your cab on the night of March 7?" he sneered.

"Sure, I picked up a few people. That's my job," Ralph replied firmly.

"Wise guy, heh? Well, you don't happen to remember picking up some guys and driving them out to Coney Island?" he continued with scorn.

"Yeah, I do remember three guys with suitcases. They were supposed to be moving, or at least that's what they told me. Anyway, that's none of my business. My job is to take them where they want to go!" Ralph answered.

"Ah, so. Well, you don't happen to know them, do you?" the detective persisted, completely irritated.

"No! A couple of them looked vaguely familiar, but I didn't know them," Ralph retorted, growing visibly angry.

"Yeah?" the lawman snarled. "Well, you're under arrest!"

"Arrest," Ralph exclaimed. "For what?"

"Burglary, that's what!"

With no further ado, guards were ordered to take Ralph away.

Ralph tried to make the detective listen to reason but to no avail. He was taken to jail. It was there he learned that the men he took to Long Island had burglarized a factory of women's high-fashion clothes. They were caught on the street peddling the merchandise. One of them, Johnny Williams, squealed to the cops, then ran off to join the navy. After ten days, Ralph was released on bail fixed for $25,000.

A few days later, a very good friend of Ralph's, Frankie Marlowe, alias Big Marlowe (because of his height and size), contacted Ralph.

"Ralph, you know who wants to see you?"

"No. Who?" Ralph replied matter-of-factly.

"Don Pepe Periano, the Clutch'n Hand!"

"What the hell does he want of me!" Ralph practically screamed. Don Pepe Periano was a man who didn't think twice before he killed someone.

"Ralphy." Marlowe leaned in close. "Did you know about the robbery . . . did you know it was his nephew's plant?"

"No! Christ, had I known, I wouldn't have gone," Ralph retorted.

"Okay. Ralphy, okay . . . but you'd better go see what he wants." Marlowe smiled reassuringly.

Ralph was worried, but he was nobody's fool. Before he went, he told Tony and another friend about his predicament, and they agreed to accompany him in case there was *real* trouble. Ralph drove toward Don Pepe's house and dropped the boys off a block away. They synchronized their watches.

"Okay, now if I'm not out in fifteen minutes, you guys come marchin' in!" a plucky Ralph instructed.

Ralph parked in front of the house. Dismissing the twinges in the pit of his stomach, he climbed up the staircase and rang the doorbell. The Clutch'n Hand personally opened the door, and Ralph felt a throb in his chest. Don Pepe Periano was a horrific-looking man. He was huge, with fat discolored lips, which supported a half-smoked cigar. His left arm, paralyzed at birth, hung limp and lifeless while his right arm was oversized with the hand of a gorilla, hence his nickname.

Don Pepe pulled the cigar out of his wide mouth with his thick dark fingers and snickered. "Well, well, Little Ralphy, Baby Face Ralph. You know, everybody says you got a lot of nerve. I can't believe it . . . you come to Don Pepe's house all alone!" His laugh was made up of short funny grunts, and his presence was repulsive, but Ralph calmly stood his ground. "Yeah, you got a lot of goddamn nerve," Don Pepe added, still chuckling as he motioned Ralph in.

Ralph followed him silently into the parlor. Don Pepe motioned him to be seated in a high-back armchair, making himself comfortable opposite him. Many a tête-à-tête had taken place there in those two armchairs, Ralph theorized, probably changing the lives of certain people. Ceremoniously, Don Pepe offered him a drink; Ralph nodded and finally spoke up softly.

"Don Pepe, I understand you wanted to see me."

"Yeah, Ralphy," the Don began, taking a puff on his cigar. "I sent word, because I wanted to meet this up and comin' young man called . . . Baby Face Ralph." With that, he smiled suspiciously.

"Well, now you've met me," Ralph returned.

"Yeah, and a young punk who dares step into my territory!" he snapped, his color and tone changing dramatically.

"What territory?" Ralph asked, holding his own.

"What territory . . . what territory," the older man growled. "Ralphy," his voice went down an octave as he stared with piercing eyes. "Did you know that was my nephew's place?"

Don Pepe had tried to throw him off guard with the sudden query, but Ralph was no easy prey. He knew that some of the old-timers were a bit theatrical, but inwardly, he was not so cocksure of himself.

"Listen, Don Pepe," he said as respectfully as he could, showing no emotion, "I didn't know about your nephew's plant . . ."

Ralph continued to maintain his innocence very convincingly and calmly explained what actually happened.

Don Pepe stared at him, silently making a mental decision; then his face lightened up. "Okay, Ralphy, forget about it! Your word's enough." He rose from his chair, signaling Ralph that the inquisition was over, and extended his hand.

As they approached the door, the doorbell rang; Don Pepe turned curiously to Ralph before opening. "Ooooh . . ." He chuckled when he saw Ralph's two friends. "I didn't think you'd be such a fool to come here alone. You're a smart young fella, Ralphy . . . Take care of yourself."

He paternally patted Ralph on the back and waved them all off. Ralph couldn't wait to get away. Once behind the wheel of his car, he heaved a deep sigh of relief.

Ralph was one gutsy guy at twenty-one.

Still waiting for the trial on the charge of burglary, Ralph received word that Frankie Yale wanted to see him. They met at the bar where Frankie immediately assured him of his support.

"Ralphy, don't worry . . . I'll help you out. Go ahead with the trial . . . and stick to your story about not knowing the guys!"

Frankie proceeded to tell him what to do and what not to do. Fortunately, Ralph was acquitted on no evidence. Johnny Williams, the stool pigeon, was not present at the trial; but three years later, when he returned from having served with the navy, he was mysteriously murdered.

Although he was acquitted, Ralph lost both his driver's licenses. He agonized over this new dilemma—in a state of prostration—but not for long. He called his uncle, Tom Dyke, in Albany.

Ralph had always had a special rapport with Tom. In the ten or so years following Joseph Liguori's death, Dyke had climbed high in politics. He was involved in Tammany Hall and very close to the powerful Irish politicians "Upstate"—the O'Connell Brothers. Tom Dyke also owned a large prosperous cigar factory; Dyke cigars were sold throughout New York. Contrary to Frankie Yale's similar enterprise years earlier, Dyke manufactured a good product and had become a very rich, influential man. Property investments were high on his list. Ralph was to meet his uncle at his restaurant on Eighth Avenue and Thirty-fourth Street, near the garment center, which Dyke used as a meeting place.

When they spoke on the phone, Tommy Dyke kindly soothed Ralph's anxieties. Thus, it was with some confidence that Ralph climbed the flight of stairs to the restaurant. He quickly scanned the room and saw his uncle speaking softly to a man with a friendly face, dressed in a state trooper's uniform. Dyke looked up and gave Ralph a broad smile of welcome.

"Ralphy, come here . . . and meet Commissioner Harnett."

Ralph nodded his head respectfully and shook hands with the uniformed man.

"Commissioner, this is my nephew, Ralph Liguori, the unfortunate boy I told you about . . . Not only did they take away his livelihood by withdrawing his hack license, but they also took his regular license away. I'd hate to see him get into further troubles . . ."

As he elaborated on Ralph's family background, Tommy Dyke spoke in a soft, authoritative manner, using great tact—and coming across as the self-assured man he was. The commissioner couldn't help but embrace Ralph's cause.

"Don't worry, kid. We'll have your license back in no time." Harnett assured him, smiling. "Stop by the station house the day after tomorrow, and it'll be ready."

Ralph couldn't believe his ears. He was overwhelmed and totally impressed with his uncle Tom, who was beaming at him. Politely, he thanked them both, leaving them to discuss more serious matters.

In those days, one had to have connections!

CHAPTER ELEVEN

Angelo was showing off again!

It was with his two-seater Marmon car, an expensive beauty with a fantastic horn made up of four tubes. Oh, how Angelo loved to blast that horn to let people know he was passing by—apart from the fact that he was a crazy driver!

He and Ralph were returning one night from the Meadowbrook, after dancing to Glenn Miller's swinging music; they were driving through the Hudson Tunnel when Angelo began blasting that horn like a nuthead throughout the length of the tunnel. Ralph asked him to stop blowing the damned horn, but Angelo loved to hear the sounds ricocheting and laughed his silly head off—until the end of the tunnel. There they found the police waiting.

As usual, it took Ralph's quick wit to sidetrack them with double-talk about how great the tunnel was (it had recently been completed). He was however extremely nervous since they had two guns in the car. Fortunately, the cops were friendly; after admiring the car, they lightly scolded Angelo about his horn and discharged them. Undoubtedly, Angelo was a hardhead and continued to make a spectacle of himself, at times portraying a first-class buffoon.

Tony rarely joined Ralph when he was with Angelo. Angelo and Tony just did not hit it off; their personalities clashed. Ralph suffered through many evenings without Tony, but with so many other friends around, he usually managed to enjoy himself—in spite of Angelo. A couple of weeks after the horn-blowing tunnel affair, Ralph went nightclubbing with Angelo at Parkway Palace at Ocean Parkway and Park Circle in Brooklyn and met a couple of lovely showgirls. In the morning, after Sunday brunch with the girls, they decided to end the party and drove to Long Island to visit Charley Gelado at the College Inn. Gelado's real name was Gerardo Scarpato, but he had long been famous for his love affair with ice cream (*gelato*). He was always craving ice cream; consequently, the boys had nicknamed him Charley Gelado, exchanging the *t* for the soft *d* as in the Sicilian dialect.

Charley Gelado was the big man in charge of Long Island and well respected. His winning personality combined with his good looks—milk white complexion, chestnut-colored hair, and crystal clear hazel eyes—made up for his short, medium frame. He was known to be a gentle person but could change to unexpected brutality. To be boss, one had to have guts! Gelado was also bright and became successful in the restaurant business. Ralph had met him years before when Gelado married the sister of Ralph's boyhood friend Mario; thus, the gang would get together at the College Inn for a beer or to discuss business. Sometimes, they would shift meeting places and have lunch at Charley's Villa Nuova Restaurant in Coney Island.

Ralph and Angelo arrived at the inn around one o'clock, and as soon as they walked through the entrance, Ralph could feel a certain tension permeating the atmosphere. Intuitive by nature, he could always smell trouble in the air. A few of the boys seated around the room greeted them solemnly, and Charley immediately beckoned Ralph into the back room.

"Hey, Ralphy, got a minute?" he called, pretending a smile.

Ralph nodded and followed him.

"Listen, Ralphy, I've got some bad news. If Angelo asks you to go with you . . . don't go!" Charley was tense, his face dark.

Ralph automatically stiffened. "Why?" he demanded.

"Frankie Yale just got killed!"

"God . . . No . . . Where?" Ralph felt his knees weakening.

"In Borough Park. They found his body slumped in the front seat of his car full of lead from a submachine gun."

"A machine gun?" exclaimed Ralph. "Poor Frankie," he winced, feeling his stomach giving way to the nausea creeping up. What he needed was a good, stiff drink. *I have to be calm*, thought Ralph. *My own life could be in danger*. He had been such a close friend and "babysitter" for his brother, Angelo.

Charley interrupted his musing. "Remember, Ralphy, I'm telling you for your own good! The boys don't want any further problems with this!" he concluded sternly.

"Okay, Charley, don't worry," replied Ralph in a daze. "I'll do my best to keep him here."

He then tried to walk out nonchalantly, as though nothing had happened, but Angelo, anxiously awaiting his return, was not a complete fool.

"What'd he want, Ralphy? Any trouble?"

"No, Ang . . . Why should there be trouble? He wanted to tell me something about Mario, that's all."

Angelo didn't bite. "Yeah? We'll see!"

He sprang up and went straight to the back room where Charley had remained. Ralph sat drinking his beer, not knowing what to expect. Finally, Angelo came out white as a ghost, completely shaken.

"Come on. Load up," he hissed. "Let's go, Ralphy." His jaw was set tight.

"Go? Where?" Ralph responded, trying to be composed. He was nervous as hell.

"Ralphy . . . load up!" Angelo insisted, his face contorted in pain.

Ralph felt compassion for him, for himself, and for everyone else at that moment, but he tried to reason with Angelo.

"Load up . . . Like hell!" he retorted, keeping his tone muffled. "You're crazy! You heard what Charley said. We can't move, and, man, when he says we can't move, *we can't move*! Sit down . . . Ang . . . Behave yourself . . . Try to be calm," Ralph half-pleaded.

Looking around the room, Ralph saw several determined faces, which clearly indicated that they weren't going anywhere. Three hours later, they were finally allowed to leave the inn.

Ralph used the long wait trying to calm Angelo who was still shaking with tears, terribly upset. His brother had been shot down in cold blood, and *his* brother was Frankie Yale! It wasn't easy to comfort Angelo, but Ralph kept trying, begging him to accept the fact that it was done, and that he had to let it be. Angelo, however, was tormented and kept theorizing about "who done it," coming out negative every time.

The underworld knew what happened! Scarface Al had shown his hand! Frankie had been leaning too hard on one of Capone's friends even though Al had warned him to lay off. Frankie Yale, however, was his own man. As national president of the L'Unione Siciliana, he continued to use his strength and influence regarding the coveted vacant presidency of the Chicago chapter. The conflict had triggered Capone's violent side. At that stage of the game, Capone had already stopped obeying anyone and had issued his own orders to kill his old friend Frankie Yale, his onetime mentor and protector. It was no surprise to Ralph that the Sicilians never really accepted Al Capone!

The hours, days, and weeks that followed were very tense for Ralph. He didn't want to drive in the same car with Angelo, afraid he would be shot with him, perhaps killed! For a couple of weeks, he changed cars daily.

One morning after Frankie Yale's assassination, Ralph tried to pacify Angelo and drove him to the Borough Park police station in Brooklyn to retrieve Frankie's beautiful maroon-colored Lincoln coupe. The police refused to release the car, and none of Ralph's or Angelo's arguments could convince them to do otherwise. The police had their instructions. Then Angelo noticed Frankie's hat, which was still in the car, and asked *at least* for the release of the hat. The cops gave Angelo a weird look, shrugged their shoulders, and handed him the hat. Ralph followed as

Angelo solemnly walked out, his head bent, staring at the hat in his hands, eyes transfixed, as if in prayer. Eventually, Angelo received the car as well as the diamonds, which were found on Frankie's body.

Frankie Yale had one of the biggest funerals ever held in New York, if not as lavish as some of those held in Chicago. Many men would miss his leadership, and Ralph felt he had lost a very good friend. Frankie had always had a special liking for him, and although Ralph was not considered one of *his* boys, Frankie had helped form Ralph's reputation with the older men. For a young lad, Ralph enjoyed an unusual position of respect because of this affection. In Frankie's memory, Ralph promised himself to keep an eye out for Angelo.

The underworld was fermenting, undergoing a state of transformation. New men were appearing on the scene; old ones were disappearing or fading away in diverse ways. The power structure was changing as well as the caliber of leaders.

Back in 1920, "Big Jim" Colosimo of Chicago had met his demise at the hands of one of Frankie Yale's boys, as requested by his friend Johnny Torrio. Frankie did not carry out the job personally (not that he wasn't capable). He had amassed enough gorillas to do his bidding. In those days, it was very rare for a top man to take care of the actual hit himself; top men were involved at a higher level. It was true, however, that Johnny Torrio (the Fox) had asked his friend Frankie to help him become the new bootleg king of the windy city.

At that time, Alphonse "Al" Capone (a Neapolitan who never really received the Sicilian blessing) was one of Frankie's boys and hung around the Harvard Inn, sometimes acting as a bouncer. He was also a dance hall bully—a boisterous young punk with no class. With Frankie, he was always on his best behavior, afraid of Frankie's wrath, but things changed later. It was Frankie who introduced Ralph to Al at Souchers Dance Hall in Coney Island. Al was quite a bit older than Ralph, and the two never did become real friends; Ralph didn't like Capone's style. Instead, he became close friends with Al's brother, Ralph, named Bottles, who was altogether a different type of person, even in their looks. Ralph Capone had a nice, open, friendly face as opposed to Al's harsh features. Ralph would meet Bottles and his cousin Willy Fischetti at the clubs, and they'd pass the hours enjoying good camaraderie. Bottles and Fischetti were both good-looking guys, well built, a little on the hefty side but classy dressers—wearing their fedoras perched neatly to one side. Later, they followed Al to Chicago when he took over that city.

Al Capone was a husky guy who used his weight to push people around—an agitator, always ready for a fight. At times he could be pleasant, but his crude personality and violent nature betrayed him.

It happened one night in a dance hall on Fulton Street. Al made some smutty remarks about Frank Gallucci's sister. No man could ever insult a Sicilian's sister! Little Galuch (as Frank Gallucci was known) became so furious that he slipped up behind Al and slashed the left side of his face with a stiletto. It was a night of nerves and frenzy! Gallucci went into hiding, fearing Capone's violent revenge. Again, it was Frankie who induced them to make peace. But Al was disfigured for life and became Scarface Al. With his face spoiled by the slash, he became even more violent. It did not take long before a couple of murders were attributed to him. Finally, to clear the air, Frankie sent him to Chicago, to his friend Johnny Torrio (at times referred to as Johnny the Fox).

After his uncle Jim Colosimo was conveniently eliminated, Torrio found he had his hands full with the Irish gangs for control of the booze. He had democratically divided Chicago into a pie, assigning to the various gangs their slice (their territory) in which they called the shots for the area. But after a short period of seemingly peaceful activity, the South Side O'Donnell Brothers, troublemakers by nature, abruptly refused to acknowledge Torrio's dominance; and the gunfire erupted. Capone, however, was a real enforcer, and it wasn't long before the O'Donnell gang faded into oblivion. Capone received his reward and became the number 1 man in Torrio's organization—a full partner, sharing the profits straight down the middle.

Then it was Dean O'Banion's turn, and he was also a tough cookie. O'Banion supposedly controlled the north-northeast side of Chicago for his bootlegging operations, but the Gennas (the Terrible Sicilians) who ran Little Italy on the South Side were trying to muscle in by underselling their whiskey. A Genna truck was hijacked, and the war was on! At that particular time, Torrio tried to be neutral; but when O'Banion made the wrong move by double-crossing him in a deal, which would have ensured a jail sentence for Johnny Torrio, the war soared to a peak!

With Frankie Yale's support, O'Banion was killed in his flower shop located across the street from the Holy Name Cathedral (well-known to movie fans of that era). It happened just hours before the less spectacular funeral of Michele Merlo—Chicago's president of L'Unione Siciliana—a nonviolent leader who had died of cancer. After O'Banion's death, however, peace still did not reign. Shortly thereafter, Hymie Weiss, a Jewish crony of the Irish who had taken over O'Banion's gang and territory, began to demonstrate his strength; and the battles continued. Weiss had tried to dispose of Torrio in 1925, after the latter returned from a visit to Italy. Johnny Torrio managed to escape death but, weary of all the violence and bloodshed, decided to call it quits. After being released from the hospital and sitting out a short spell in jail, Torrio turned over his empire—once and for all—to Alphonso "Scarface Al" Capone.

It did not end there! A year later, Hymie Weiss was gunned down by Capone's men. Al, however, still had problems; not only did the O'Banion mob continue under the leadership of another aspirant, George "Bugs" Moran, but he also had to contend with the Sicilian clan of the now powerful Aiello brothers. The streets of Chicago continued to be arenas of bloodshed. But Scarface Al triumphed over all. After the notorious St. Valentine's Day massacre in 1929, he obtained so much publicity that he secured the undisputed position as boss of Chicago.

Gangs were also mushrooming throughout the eastern states and gave rise to the formation of many independents. In Detroit, the Purple Gang, a group of tough Jewish boys who preyed on their own kind, gained notoriety when bootlegger "Big Maxey" Greenberg left the city for greener pastures. Greenberg had entered into an alliance with Arnold Rothstein (supposedly, Waxey Gordon was also involved) in a big liquor deal—importing alcohol directly from England to the wharfs of New York City, which remained the number one port for smuggling.

Man's greed continued to consume all who became contaminated. In November of 1928, at the Park Central Hotel in New York, Arnold Rothstein was found dead, a bullet in his stomach. (A few years later, in 1933, "Big Maxey" Greenberg, who had become a top man of Waxey Gordon, was shot down by one of Dutch Shultz's men in a dispute between the two groups.) Meanwhile, the Purple Gang continued to romp around, finally branching out into rum-running. They met with a high-level man, Moe Dalitz, who collaborated with them on certain liquor enterprises, but the gang was too wild for Dalitz; and he decided to move to Akron, Ohio, where he joined forces with men like Morris Kleinman, Lou Rothkopf, and Sam Tucker. Continuing gang wars, involving numerous deaths and a few prison terms for group members, forced the Purple Gang to temporarily disperse. Soon it reconstituted itself under the leadership of a new man, Pete Licavoli—then under the auspices of the Cleveland Syndicate.

Cleveland had long before produced gifted sons of the rackets on different fronts. It began in the early 1900s with the Irish—men like Mickey McBride, who began as circulator of the *Cleveland News*—and moved on to control the Cleveland Cab System. He became the power behind the national wire service and, finally, amused himself as owner of the Cleveland Browns football team. He was rivaled only by another Irishman, Thomas McGinty, the Cleveland Plain Dealer circulator who stretched his talents to control racetracks and gambling casinos, reaching all the way west to Las Vegas and internationally to Havana, Cuba.

On a different level, the Lonardo Brothers, led by "Big Joe" Lonardo, began controlling the Cleveland Woodland District, dominated by Sicilian-Italian immigrants. By the time Prohibition rolled around, they were the uncontested bosses. They ingeniously subordinated immigrants living in the area to work cheap stills for them. Since times were difficult, and the idea of Prohibition foreign to them, many of these poor immigrants were only too happy to make some money. Besides, if they were approached, it was very difficult to refuse. Big Joe reigned for quite some time, but, as always, a rival gang yearned for power, and he was challenged by the Porrello Brothers. On his way to a trumped-up meeting to discuss business with one of the Porrellos, "Big Joe" Lonardo was shot down, and the Porrello Brothers became the all-powerful leaders. To confirm matters, a meeting of the Mafia was held at the end of 1928 in Cleveland's Hotel Statler (the first known reunion of its kind) to proclaim Joe Porrello as *capo* (the boss). The Porrello dynasty was later toppled by the Mayfield Road Mob (the Milano and Polizzi boys), which was later allied with the Cleveland Syndicate—running from Detroit to Buffalo. Other cities—Pittsburgh, Philadelphia, Boston, and Atlantic City—also had their own combinations, but the main criminal gang action was still in New York City.

The nation believed that 1928 would bring a change to the White House. In New York, Tammany Hall was officially supporting Al Smith, one of the favorite sons. Working his way up from early youth, Smith had become an important Democratic leader. As a boy (after quitting school), he had labored many years in the Fulton Fish Market, which was controlled by the Mafia. He had grown up among other disadvantaged urchins, learning the street language and becoming acquainted with many of the "boys." In his early twenties, he actively entered politics.

In 1919, the Happy Warrior, as Franklin Delano Roosevelt called him, Smith became governor of New York; and in 1928, Roosevelt helped him with the Democratic presidential nomination. Later, the two men became opponents for the Democratic presidential nomination in 1932. Roosevelt won the presidency against Herbert Hoover, who ran for reelection.

Roman Catholic Smith, already handicapped by his religion, was however defeating himself (perhaps unconsciously) by preaching against Prohibition and the power and wealth of bootleggers. His stand to repeal the Prohibition law (Volstead Act) would certainly cut out the mainstream of revenue for the gangs. But Tammany Hall had many friends among the bootleggers (some covertly allied to other important party members).

Obviously, they would not be pushing for Smith's election. Hundreds of thousands of votes controlled by these men were lost.

It was no surprise that Charlie Luciano was not too keen on him. Al Smith had to wait another four years to gain Luciano's attention and support. Charlie was very busy finalizing his own plans to reorganize the underworld, and those plans included big politics. Alfred E. Smith, Democratic presidential candidate, lost the election in 1928 to Herbert Hoover, the somber pudgy-faced Republican. America was to remain under Republican leadership, and consequently, Prohibition continued, and bootlegging flourished.

Although the ensuing years were destined to be dark and difficult for most Americans, ironically the underworld enjoyed a period of unprecedented growth.

CHAPTER TWELVE

In Brooklyn, Ralph was still struggling for a legitimate livelihood. The police had reissued only his regular driver's license. Therefore, without his hack license, he was unable to drive a cab. Work as a butcher was also difficult to obtain. In the summer of 1928, he turned to his uncle Alfred, who had become the father figure of the Liguori family after Joseph's death.

Alfred Liguori first began his profession in America as a printer, but in those tumultuous years of the 1920s, the printing trade was not very lucrative; whereas bootlegging was paying big dividends. He decided that a change of occupation was in order and set up shop as an independent bootlegger with offices on Lafayette Street. Before long, he had become one of the biggest bootleggers in the business.

Alfred had an imposing frame, standing six feet tall with a strong, husky build; his light skin contrasted with his black hair; and when he smiled, his large, wide hazel eyes seemed to glisten like polished gems. But he wasn't just a handsome man; he had those qualities that automatically produce a leader. He possessed an easygoing disposition, but, like most in command, Alfred Liguori could be very tough when necessary; and in his operations, there were some very rough moments. When dealing in business, he spoke in low tones; but in his lighter mood, especially when he was told a good joke, his exuberant laughter was contagious and could be heard far and wide. Alfred was a family man, happily married, with two children, and filled with an old country sense of responsibility toward his brother's family. He had remained close to Agnes and her youngsters. He put Ralph on his payroll in order to help him, but Alfred also knew that Ralph was resourceful, and a trustworthy family member was just what he needed.

Ralph's uncle Alfred's favorite hangout was Ferrara's Café on Grand Street near Mulberry and Mott. All the biggest bootleggers in the United States transacted business there, and Ralph, along with the others, did plenty of money counting in the back room. One evening, after a long negotiating session with some men in his uncle's behalf, Ralph lingered over an espresso. Savoring the toasty aroma of his coffee, he turned at the sound of someone entering and found "Wild Bill" Ercolini strutting toward him.

Ralph liked Bill. The man wasn't heavy on looks but was a good-natured guy, respected by everyone. Bill was brother-in-law to Alfred Liguori and Tommy Dyke, for both men had married Bill's sisters. Ercolini had also become a successful bootlegger and had made a lot of money investing in real estate. Wild Bill's first love was playing the ponies; next came driving big cars—either Packards or Lincolns.

"Hey, Ralphy, how you doing? You're just the guy I wanted to see!" Bill grinned and sat down with Ralph.

"Yeah, how come?" asked Ralph, laughing lightly.

Without preamble, Bill blurted, "Ralph, could I use your car tonight?"

"My car?" exclaimed Ralph, a little annoyed. "Everyone knows I never lend my car to anyone, unless I go with it. Why? What's happening?" Ralph asked, pressing for an answer.

"Oh, hell! Old man Ferrara asked me to get him a car for tonight . . . He's got an appointment with someone," Bill replied, not at all happy with his assignment.

Ralph stopped him from going any further.

"Bill, I'm sorry. It's my rule. Besides, I'm busy tonight," he added, trying to alleviate Bill's discomfort.

"Yeah, okay, Ralphy, forget it. I understand," Bill mumbled and ordered a drink for himself while Ralph nodded for the same.

It ended there, but not for Bill. He ultimately lent his own beautiful new Lincoln to Ferrara—never to see his car again. Ferrara, it turned out, had been dealing heroin; but that night, a federal agent had set him up. It was the appointment that ended his career. Ferrara was arrested on the spot—Lincoln and all. He was sent to Leavenworth Prison, where he died at the age of seventy-five. Fortunately, Bill did not become involved. Ralph regretted the loss of the car but thought Bill should have known better. The aftermath of the event served to firm up his resolve never to lend a car to anyone—not even to a friend.

Bootlegging was not an easy trade. Someone was always trying to swindle someone else, muscle in on another's territory, and bootleggers were always vulnerable to hijacking. Ralph had had a first glimpse of the business with Barone, his boyhood mentor, but after a few months of learning the trade with his uncle, he saw its more sinister side.

Alfred Liguori had received a huge order of alcohol. Naturally, he was very happy. Being a highly respected man, word had reached him that payment would be in counterfeit money. He informed Ralph of the intrigue, as well as of his own plot, and kept their secret. When the time arrived to consign the alcohol, Alfred had two of his most trusted men fill the alcohol cans with water; after which, they calmly waited for their "customers." At the hour of negotiation, Ralph sat silently in a corner to observe his uncle in action, prepared to glower menacingly at the appropriate moments. Alfred quietly but sternly informed the would-be swindlers that he was aware of their counterfeit money scheme and "persuaded" them to reconsider—to return with genuine greenbacks. With no choice but to capitulate, the customers agreed. Alfred's men escorted them away. The plan was carried out under tight surveillance, and they returned with the money. It wasn't until later that the foiled swindlers learned they were double-crossed—that they had purchased water instead of alcohol. They did not retaliate. They knew better. But those were the rules. If one sets out to cheat another, the plan would usually boomerang. The cheater was himself deceived in the end. It was a lesson many learned the hard way.

Hijacking was a more dangerous game. In order to deliver the liquor safely to its destination, trucks loaded with alcohol were always heavily guarded along the way. Some bootleggers had one or more men stationed in the back of their trucks, armed with tommy guns, and it was not unusual to hear gunfire reverberating through the night.

Ralph and his uncle had their own methods. Armed with more conventional guns, Ralph and Alfred's hired men escorted the truck in three cars. Ralph led the procession in the first car behind the truck. After traveling a few blocks, Ralph shot ahead of the truck. Another block or two and the second car overtook the truck and Ralph. Then as the third picked up speed to pass, Ralph and the second car swerved around the block, scanning the area for possible trouble. As soon as they were sure the surrounding streets were clear, they fell back into line, repeating the routine as frequently as possible. Once they reached their destination, Ralph and the men remained on guard to oversee the unloading process. Mission accomplished.

A couple of years later, Ralph was accompanying one of his uncle's trucks to Long Island, in the usual fashion. Suddenly, the truck driver, unable to stop because of his speed, went through a yellow light. Ralph's acute ears picked up the sound of a motorcycle cop roaring down on them. As the policeman motioned the truck to pull over to the side, Ralph drove up also, hoping to intercede in time. He casually stepped out of his car, then tipped his hat, smiling at the policeman.

"Sir," Ralph began kindly, "I have a card for you."

The cop scrutinized Ralph from under his helmet, took what looked like a business card, glanced at it, took it, and then, without a word, waved his hand to signal permission for Ralph and the truck to leave.

Ralph, needless to say, was relieved but at the same time agitated. It was two o'clock in the afternoon, and he knew he had to return quickly to town in order to reach Central Park West before the motorcycle cops changed shifts at four o'clock. (They used the park to change shifts and assignments every eight hours.) Ralph needed his card back!

The card was one of the few in existence. During the bootlegging era, violence was an everyday occurrence. It appeared that the bootleggers were truly *the untouchables*. The government was besieged with outcries of indignation by law-abiding citizens and organizations to smash the racket and arrest the criminals, many pressing their representatives in Congress.

One man to embrace the alarming situation was Fiorello Henry La Guardia, first as state representative for New York (1923-1933) then as mayor of New York City in 1933, an office he held until 1945. While he was mayor, he became one of Frank Costello's worst enemies, in his efforts to rid the city of the slot machine racket. Pressured into decisive action, law enforcers had the roads constantly surveilled; and in response, bootleggers had sought ways to circumvent their risks. Those with political contacts were the winners, and a system of identification cards was devised—a sort of passport to travel freely, untouched by arrest. Ralph had one, and he felt privileged to own it.

Once he accompanied the truck to its destination, and was assured that the delivery was in good hands, Ralph sprang into his classy Auburn Cord and, hugging the road, sped straight for Central Park. He arrived a few minutes before four and rushed toward his good friend Gus who was conversing with a couple of motorcycle cops. Gus was a tough guy with a big heart AND was head of the New York department's Motorcycle Squadron—commanding the five boroughs.

"Ralph, what brings you here?" he asked cheerfully.

"Gus, I had to give my card away today!" Ralph exclaimed, a little breathless.

"Okay, Ralphy, relax. Tell me about it. Where did it happen?" Gus replied calmly to ease Ralph's agitation.

At that moment, they heard a motorcycle roar into the park and turned to see the same cop who had stopped Ralph on the highway. He strolled over, and as he took off his helmet, he handed Gus the card.

Gus wasted no time in introducing Ralph. "John, this is my good friend, Ralph Liguori. Understand you met him today."

"Yeah, that's the card he gave me." John smiled knowingly. "I assume all is in order?"

"All in order." Gus nodded and returned the card to Ralph, making light of Ralph's thank-you. The matter concluded, he said, "Listen,

Ralph." Confidentially grasping Ralph's arm. "We're having a party at the Special House on Long Island tonight. Come on over and bring a couple of cases of scotch with you . . . It's going to be a blast!" Gus smiled, his eyes twinkling with mirth. "I'll have two of my men meet you to escort you there—for safety's sake. Okay?"

Ralph couldn't help laughing. "Okay, Gus. See you tonight . . . and thanks again."

With his card back in his wallet, Ralph felt a strong sense of security. The squadron leader, on secret orders, had issued them to selected people to assist them in any awkward situation they encountered on the road. The motorcycle cops knew about the cards and understood their instructions. A very contented Ralph leisurely drove home.

At that time, Ralph lived in the Central Park West Hotel near Sixty-fourth Street. It had once been called the Park West Hotel, then Monticello, and then the Montel. The owners were obliged to change the hotel name often in order to survive its bad publicity; many of the racket men who lived there were inevitably shot down—in, on, and around the premises. Ralph's appointment with Gus was for eight o'clock at the Big Foot Restaurant, which was located near the hotel. First, however, he drove over to the Thompson Street warehouse—Vito Genovese's general headquarters, run by his lieutenant, Tony Bender (Anthony Strollo)—and loaded his car with two cases of scotch for Gus. A few minutes before eight, as Ralph approached the restaurant, he could see the motorcycle cops waiting. He pulled up alongside, exchanged greetings with the young policemen, then turned his Auburn Cord around to follow them out to Long Island. Ralph felt very important as he sped along with his escort, but soon, he became somewhat embarrassed. Those damned cops were in such a festive mood; they began sounding their sirens, chasing everyone off the road!

Their lively spirits, however, were contagious, and Ralph began laughing out loud. "Aaah, if only 'Little Fiorello' La Guardia could see me now!"

CHAPTER THIRTEEN

What was Charlie Luciano doing?

He was busy becoming a "high priest" of New York, although he was not completely in charge—yet. Like so many, except on a larger scale, Charlie was knee-deep in bootlegging, involved in all facets of gambling, and had embraced the protection racket. But he and his associates, whose names would eventually become synonymous with organized crime (Costello, Genovese, Adonis, Anastasia, Lansky, Siegel), were *also* paying for protection (political protection)—a sort of politico-criminal alliance. And it paid off! Charlie's group was becoming the most powerful and profitable around town.

New York, however, was still more or less divided between two major forces. Two racket czars who both wanted to become the Boss of all Bosses: Giuseppe "Joe" Masseria, an illiterate Sicilian who ruled with a bloody hand, and Salvatore Maranzano, a highly educated Sicilian from Castellammare del Golfo (hence, later, the name of the Castellammarese War). They were two distinctly diverse personalities determined to have it their way.

Both parties were courting Charlie, having heard of his organizational talents. He was definitely a man to have on their side, especially since he already had a very impressive crew working with him. But both Masseria and Maranzano should have thought beyond their immediate ambitions because Charlie possessed all the leadership qualities to be a *real* boss, superseding each of them. As a street urchin, Charlie had learned all the angles, had developed the necessary guts to kill (although that was a decision he made in extremis), and he had matured into an intelligent albeit complicated personality. Perhaps the secret to his success in the underworld could be found in his democratic theories. Charlie was not obsessed with greed; therefore, he was able to give everyone a piece of the action, and he knew how to share the wealth with his political contacts. His word was sacred, and his handshake alone sealed a decision.

Charlie was also a good listener. All his associates and lieutenants were able to voice their opinions, without fear, and to offer advice. He respected each man for his particular know-how. For instance, Meyer

Lansky was consulted for financial matters; Frank Costello, for political intrigue; and Johnny Torrio as advisor honorarium. Charlie always weighed all the pros and cons and was known to acquiesce in a decision if a point was well made.

Torrio, who had returned to New York after abandoning his Chicago kingdom to Capone, had become an advisor to Charlie. He was still a man of great respect, and although he was basically retired, he possessed enough experience to be an asset to any group. Johnny and Charlie thought along the same lines. Both thinkers, they painstakingly planned ahead, organizing each step of the action, and, when necessary, attacked the enemy by surprise. Their friendship lasted many years.

During the courtship by both Masseria and Maranzano, Charlie could not help having some misgivings about his choice, which he had been nurturing for some time. Initially, it was Torrio who advised Charlie which road to take. After revealing his decision to his associates, Charlie finally agreed to join Masseria. For this alliance, Charlie stipulated two conditions: firstly, he was to be the number 2 man in the outfit; and secondly, he was to maintain his independent operations. Masseria agreed, elated to have him, but, in return, as his requirement, insisted that Luciano be his constant companion—a sort of bodyguard and chauffeur. Assured of this extra strength, Joe Masseria let it be known that he had appointed himself boss. Charlie, with the brains of a corporate man, began to revamp Masseria's organization while keeping his own operations clicking like clockwork.

Maranzano was not very happy about this new alliance and never stopped harassing Masseria, always hoping to entice Charlie away from Joe the Boss, but Charlie was not interested, for the moment.

While the assassination of Frankie Yale had disturbed the underworld (especially since it was an act of utter defiance on Capone's part), it offered the opportunity for Charlie and his gang to expand. Joe Adonis, at that time, advanced to Boss of Brooklyn after Augie Pisano, the heir apparent, left for New Jersey. Charlie loathed Capone's violent methods, which were, according to him, as bad as those of the old-timers (or Mustache Petes, as some people called them). And when Capone committed his St. Valentine's Day bloodbath, Charlie and his associates had had enough.

Charlie thought of Chicago as a nuthouse, with "guys shooting all the time!"

A few months after Hoover began exercising his presidential powers, Charlie organized a summit meeting in Atlantic City, with the collaboration of Enoch "Nucky" Johnson, king of the city. It was May 1929, five months after the first reunion in Cleveland. The progressive young mob was beginning to show its new face—the spirit of cooperation for success of all. "There is enough for everyone" became their new creed. Joe Masseria and Salvatore Maranzano were not invited. It was clear by this move that Charlie had not included them in his long-range plans.

One of the items of the agenda was how to keep Scarface Al from the spotlight. He had aroused too much concern on Capitol Hill and was causing tidal waves of public alarm and official outrage, destined to handicap certain underworld operations. The members attending the Atlantic City meeting approved a new dictum to avoid publicity at all costs. Capone was ostracized at the meeting for the violence in Chicago, and he was energetically asked to call off the bloodletting. Having to submit to other pressures in his own city, Capone consented to collaborate (at least temporarily). He agreed to cool off in jail on a concocted charge, and he did so at the Holmesburg County Prison in Chicago.

After his release in 1930, Al's yearning for prestige and status continued. He was too much of an egocentric to stay behind the scenes and was ready to resume his number one position. The next year, *he* hosted a national convention at the Congress Plaza Hotel in Chicago for the boys. He paid all the bills, provided all the fun. As he was re-proclaimed Boss of Chicago, he joyously chewed on his cigar, smiling widely at the crowd like a king.

This madness for the limelight, however, was eventually his downfall. His passion for baseball provided that one moment of excess exposure. Being an avid baseball fan, he had secured a special reserved box at the stadium, and he seldom missed a game. In those days, the Chicago White Sox was a fantastic team, offering great excitement for the fans. On that particular day, Scarface Al was ecstatic; the president of the United States, Herbert Hoover, was in the next box. He believed it to be a sign that he had truly arrived. With a smiling face, Al leaned out from his box and attempted to strike up a conversation with the president, who stared solemnly at him, his jowls hanging in bulldog fashion. Imagine! Hoover ignored him completely and turned to his aide to ask who was the "laughing boy with the big cigar." Much to the chief executive's chagrin, he learned the man was none other than public enemy number one of the times. Hoover, highly insulted after that incident, personally promoted and solicited the income tax investigation already in the works against Capone, determined to rid society of him for a long time. That was the real beginning of Al's downfall. The Federal men finally compiled all the evidence they needed, and eventually, he was arrested.

The records show that Capone was convicted in October 1931 for income tax evasion and sentenced to eleven years. He was sent to the

Atlanta Penitentiary after a short detention in the county jail. But even the Atlanta prison was thought too good for Capone, and two years later, he was transferred to the infamous Alcatraz Prison in the San Francisco Bay (sometimes called The Rock). There, his life was made very difficult; but despite harsh disciplinary actions against him, Capone managed to become a model prisoner. Many of the other hardened criminals disliked him, especially after Capone had refused to join them in a mutiny spree. Some were jealous of his fame, and it was not surprising that several attempts were made on his life. The first time, someone tried to poison him; then a prisoner tried to choke him. The third attempt almost proved fatal. A jailbird struck him from behind with a pair of scissors, causing a four-inch gash, but Al Capone had again escaped death at the hands of his enemies. His wife, however, was panic-stricken and pleaded with the authorities to allow him to be transferred to another prison. His brother, Ralph "Bottles," went to Washington to solicit the transfer but failed. Al was doomed to Alcatraz. The one thing from which Capone didn't recover was his bout with syphilis. The slow deterioration of his brain had begun, and it wasn't long before the disease had taken hold of his senses. It was rumored that he was ready for the insane asylum. After eight years, however, he was released on good behavior. Capone retired from all activities in Key Biscayne, Florida, where he died a natural death in 1947.

After Atlantic City, Charlie became the center of attention. All eyes focused on him—from the very depths of the underworld up to the reigning lords. The police department kept tabs on him, and the political machinery in New York became interested. The more Charlie tried to keep behind the scenes, the more men sought him out to make decisions, but being in the limelight had its drawbacks. This was when Charlie had become the target of the two unorthodox policemen (Winberry) who, with a squad of cops, had taken him for the famous ride—practically killing him, slashing his face. They wanted to destroy the *dagos* (those *guinea* bastards), beginning with Charlie Luciano—perhaps too simple a personal reason for their savagery. Most likely they were urged and supported by their higher-ups. It is difficult for many people to accept the fact that police brutality existed then, but unfortunately, it did.

1929 was a crazy year full of berserk happenings in which the political and economic crisis had come to a head. It appeared to be the culmination, the breaking point of years of the nation's foolhardiness. Americans behaved erratically, somehow sensing an encroaching danger. And suddenly, the explosion. All hell broke loose as Wall Street crumbled in October. The stock market crash was like a sinking ship at sea, everyone overboard trying to save himself. The Great Depression had begun with many heartbreaking situations. Heads of families were desperate for work, not having money for their daily bread. There appeared to be lines for food—everything. The poor became poorer and more destitute. Immigrants, with their hopes and dreams shattered, entered into a state of hopelessness. It was not uncommon for many of the poor (especially the young men) to bypass the law. Middle-class Americans also suffered, finding it difficult to make ends meet. Everyone was hustling to make some kind of living—survival of the fittest. In many ways, it was tougher on the upper middle-class, accustomed to the presumed prosperity of the earlier twenties, to suddenly become poor, losing all they owned in the crash. But the really rich just got a little less rich. Hunger, unrest, and unhappiness swept the nation. Suicides were prevalent.

During those troubled times, the underworld pot kept brewing, and the Masseria and Maranzano blocs were still violently fighting, recruiting young men to enlarge their ranks. The Castellammarese skirmishes had broken out into a full-fledged war. Mistrust was everywhere (spies infiltrated into the enemy camps), and almost no one was above suspicion. Masseria was the more aggressive of the two, not because he had more guts, but because he was less civilized. Maranzano's wrath was at its peak when Masseria ordered one of Maranzano's best friends—Gaspare Milazzo, a native of Castellammare and capo of Detroit—killed. Masseria believed that the killing would intimidate Maranzano's men, especially since he then issued a personal death warrant for Maranzano. Instead, the Castellammarese boys (including Stefano Magaddino from Buffalo and, initially, the Aiellos of Chicago) tightened their alliance; and plans for Masseria's demise became the constant topic of discussion. But while Maranzano's men talked, Joe the Boss struck again.

An important and influential man, Gaetano "Thomas" Reina, was the next target and the first prominent boss of New York to be murdered in the war. He was essentially a Masseria supporter in charge of the Bronx, but he was also friendly with Maranzano. Reina had met with the Castellammare boss socially several times, and Maranzano never lost an opportunity to convince Reina that Masseria was a greedy, bloodthirsty individual. He expressed the need for more intelligent leaders, and that the present mob system had to be reorganized. Maranzano's arguments against Masseria seemed much more logical and more in line with what Reina himself had always thought. But spies were all over, and "Joe the Boss" Masseria received word that Reina was going over to the enemy (Maranzano). That was treason. The penalty was death. Masseria understood the implications and ordered Reina's death—a sign to discourage others who thought of deserting him. Reina was murdered on February 28, 1930.

Retaliation was soon in the works. Gaetano Reina was a well-respected man, and plots to avenge his life were soon put into operation. Masseria, slippery as an eel, was known to dodge more bullets than anyone. He escaped all his would-be assassins and continued to provoke Maranzano. With cold-blooded determination, he ordered all Castellammares around the country murdered—a message that meant Maranzano's days were numbered. There was constant bloodshed in the streets day and night, and the unscrupulous war between the two Mafia lords began having repercussions in different circles. Civic leaders and politicians began to demand a stop to the bloodbaths; newspapers began to preach for a cleanup (headlines screamed), and the hotline to the police commissioner never stopped ringing. The time had come for Luciano to step in. He would now make the move he had planned for a long time, and his allies had become legion.

Tom Gagliano, the new boss of the Reina Family (after Masseria's appointed leader, Joe Pinzolo, was mysteriously murdered also in 1930), and Tommy Lucchese, (Three-Finger Brown) were good friends of Charlie's, especially Lucchese. Both men began to approach Maranzano to pave the way for Charlie, and soon, a secret alliance emerged with Maranzano. It was decided that Luciano would take over Masseria's operations, simultaneously continuing his business affairs with his private group. But Charlie insisted on still another condition: no more reprisals—the bloodshed had to stop. Everyone agreed, and the demise of Masseria was left to Charlie.

Charlie picked Villa Nuova, Charley Gelado's restaurant in Coney Island, as the place of assassination. Plans called for Masseria to be taken there for lunch. It was prearranged (so as not to arouse Masseria's suspicions) to have a few people dining there, in order for them to be halfway through their meals when Charlie arrived with Joe the Boss. There were to be no witnesses! It was no secret Masseria loved to eat, so a sumptuous lunch, befitting a king, was prepared with plenty of excellent wine. Charlie planned everything with the precision that had built his reputation. He created a scenario to give his actors enough time to take their cues by inviting Masseria, mellowed by the wine, to play cards. At a given time, Charlie excused himself to go to the men's room; and not a minute later, the triggermen walked in, fired away, and rushed out. Charlie calmly washed his hands as he heard the gunshots and, after two to three minutes, walked out to call the police. Masseria was dead, half-slumped in his chair, still holding a card in his hand. It was a balmy spring afternoon—April 15, 1931.

Of course, Charlie was arrested on the spot but later released due to insufficient evidence. The job had been assigned to someone

Charlie trusted, someone from his group. Most likely, that choice was Vito Genovese, his second in command, who, together with Anastasia, decided on the gunmen. The policeman who made the arrest was Abati, whom Ralph had met as a rooky cop in Coney Island. After that celebrated arrest, Abati went straight up the ladder to become Inspector Abati. (More than thirty years later, in 1967, Ralph met Abati in Rome, and they reminisced for some time about *those* days.)

A few months after Masseria's death, Charley Gelado and his brother-in-law, Mario, took a trip to Italy. Mario was a terrific singer (he idolized the Italian tenor Enrico Caruso) and wanted to go to Italy to hear the music—the operas—he loved so much. Charley just wanted to get away from all the bad publicity. They stayed about four or five months, and when they returned, they went to see Ralph to report about their trip. Mario was especially animated.

"Ralph, you should have seen the LaScala Opera House in Milan—beautiful!" exclaimed Mario, kissing his fingers in remembrance.

"Yeah, but those people are poor," Charley interrupted Mario's enthusiastic remarks. "The gasoline costs a fortune over there," he complained.

Mario continued as though he hadn't heard Charley. "And, Ralphy, Rome . . . unbelievable. The Colosseo . . . the fountains . . . St. Peter's . . . the Vatican . . . a masterpiece . . . Ralphy, you gotta go there someday!" Mario cried passionately.

Ralph, who at that time still didn't know that he had been born in Rome, smiled kindly at his boyhood pal with whom he had shared many adventures. *He's still a kid at heart,* thought Ralph and, not wanting to dampen Mario's obvious infatuation with Rome, tried to look interested.

"Okay, okay, Mario . . . Someday . . . Someday I'll get there!" He laughed.

Ralph couldn't have imagined then that one day, Rome would become his home!

A few days after the visit, Ralph heard that Charley Gelado was dead—murdered. He was shocked to hear the news but asked no questions. Later, Charlie "Lucky" would tell him that after Masseria's death, Gelado kept asking for special considerations; and although he personally liked Gelado, his group thought he was getting too big for his boots. Reluctantly, Charlie acquiesced to their "recommendation" but confessed to remorse about the decision. Ralph's feelings were that Gelado should have known better. After all, he was doing very well in business and should have been content with his already respected position. *But this is what greed does,* Ralph realized. *When you begin to step on people's toes, you automatically become a pest to be wiped out.* Still, Ralph felt badly. Gelado had always been good to him.

To celebrate the victory of Masseria's demise, and to pass out the rewards, Maranzano held a huge meeting in Upstate New York where the princes, dukes, and barons of the Mafia met, along with all their underlings. Maranzano had indeed become a sort of Julius Caesar. As befitting an emperor, he dictated to everyone present how the new organization would operate—who would have what territories, who would belong to what families, and how the wealth would be divided. And peace reigned for a short while!

Meanwhile, Charlie had some private meetings of his own to consolidate his allies and to put his house in order. He was already considered the real number one leader by many. On the other hand, Maranzano was not as gullible as Masseria. He did not completely trust Luciano and looked with suspicion at his close companions, whose loyalty to Charlie was practically unheard of then. He began to premeditate Charlie's assassination, and Vincent "Mad Dog" Coll, a hired killer, was called to do his bidding. Maranzano, however, did not know the breadth and scope of Charlie's organization. Charlie was informed of his death warrant—time and place—and swiftly retaliated by designing a scheme of his own to rid the underworld of Maranzano.

It was preordained that Maranzano would receive a tip from official sources that the IRS was interested in him and, therefore, to expect visitors from that office. In September 1931, some of Luciano's boys, dressed as Federal men, paid a friendly visit to Maranzano in his real estate offices in the Grand Central Building on Forty-sixth Street and Park Avenue. Maranzano, despite all his wary intellect, actually believed them to be the Feds and cordially received them. Suddenly, they attacked him, but the job was not well done. It was an agonizing scene. First, the killers tried stabbing him to death, but Maranzano, resisting with all his might, managed to stay alive. Undeterred, one of the hired men pulled out a gun and blew out Maranzano's brains. Ironically, it was the same day that "Mad Dog" Coll was to keep his appointment with Maranzano to decide the demise of Charlie Luciano. Coll was slowly climbing the stairs as the killers rushed down, screaming at him to leave the building, that Maranzano was dead. Everyone vanished from sight.

Thus, the man who had worshipped Caesar was betrayed like Caesar, by those closest to him.

Ralph did not know Vincent Coll personally, but some of his friends did. Coll was known to be one of the most bloodthirsty bastards around—proud of his cold, ruthless reputation as a highly paid hired killer. This notoriety, however, was short-lived. Like others in his profession, he was never satisfied with the money he received for the contract and would put the squeeze on the side for a little blackmail money. He tried that tactic for the last time with Owney Madden. In his youth, Madden had been the leader of the terrible Gophers in New York and, for valid reasons, was nicknamed Killer. No one stood in his way! Later, he became one of the biggest non-Italian bootleggers operating on the West Side and, as boss of the Irish, highly respected. Coll was cocky enough to believe that everyone was afraid of his gun—that he could muscle in as he pleased. When he tried to exert pressure on Owney, he was playing a losing game. Owney was too polished an operator for him. By chance, Ralph saw Coll in the last moments of his life. He was in the drugstore on the corner of Eighth Avenue and Twenty-third Street (it was around the first months of 1932) when Coll was shot to death in the phone booth.

Shortly thereafter, Owney, tired of all the killings, quit everything and moved to Hot Springs, Arkansas. He married the postmaster's daughter and went legitimate. But he never forgot his friends! Costello was having problems operating his slot machines in New Orleans after Huey "Kingfish" Long's death. (Senator Long, who had been Louisiana's Democratic governor, was assassinated in 1935 by a political foe, amidst the marble columns of the capitol building in Baton Rouge.) Owney intervened for Costello and talked to the new mayor of the city. The problems were resolved. Sometime later, when Charlie needed help because Dewey was trying to extradite him from Arkansas, Owney was there to help. Ultimately, Madden retired to Florida.

With Maranzano eliminated, the old ways were definitely gone. Charlie, heir to the throne, would not accept any title, such as Boss of All Bosses. He felt it was time to push forward with a completely new type of organization. It would be a national syndicate (a commission), and everyone would have his say with periodic meetings to iron out their differences. No more pricking of fingers to become blood brothers under Charlie. It was the autumn of 1931, and symbolically, as nature's colors changed and the trees shed their leaves, the Mafia shed its taboos—changed its style. The members would look like businessmen with conservative suits as their new attire; they would reach out like the tentacles of an octopus to encompass many diversified activities. They were planning for a very prosperous future, and the rewards were to be greater than their expectations.

But at that particular moment, for most Americans, the specter of the Great Depression loomed like a hideous, hollow-cheeked skull.

CHAPTER FOURTEEN

Strengthening its stranglehold on the nation, the truculent Depression, an unwelcomed treacherous intruder, continued to spare no one on its indiscriminate, demoniacal path to economic and social-psychological destruction.

In the beginning, President Hoover was reluctant to interfere. ("A temporary halt in the prosperity of a great people," he had said guilelessly.) But soon realizing the deadly breadth and scope of the situation, he tried his best to resolve some of the problems, which had engulfed "a land rich in resources." After Hoover's inauguration, his administration began by establishing the Federal Farm Board to assist the farmers. But Hoover signed another congressional bill, which raised tariffs on nonfarm products, seriously damaging America's foreign trade and contributing to the sad state of the nation. When the stock market crashed in October 1929, the Great Depression had indeed paralyzed America. Angry farmers armed themselves with pitchforks to fend off mortgage foreclosures on their farms; many other Americans, unable to keep up mortgage payments, were forced to leave their homes to live in shacks—dubbed "Hoovervilles." Unemployed workers staged hunger marches and demonstrations. Hoover kept telling the nation they had nothing to fear; prosperity was "just around the corner." Despite his continuous reunions with businessmen, industrialists, and labor leaders in which Hoover called for everyone's cooperation, his other attempts in Federal aid programs, economic conditions did not improve; and the Depression grew steadily worse. In utter desperation, many took strange and mysterious paths to cope with the moral and physical hunger generated by the Great Depression.

Ralph had already embarked on the road to illegitimate enterprise. After his father's death, all the older men he knew were, in one way or another, involved in bootlegging or some other racket. He had slowly learned how they operated, and now, as a young man, there was no turning back. Still, in the back of his mind, he was obsessed with working legitimately—on the surface at least. He had many reasons for seeking legitimate work, other than receiving a regular salary. Ralph knew he needed an alibi for the lifestyle his unlawful activities afforded him, and was tired of having to justify his luxury cars to scornful police. Their accusatory words kept ringing in his ears, "Hey, bud, wha d'ya do for a living?" But subconsciously, Ralph could not completely break away from the straight life he knew his mother desired for him; and he was still haunted, deep in his heart, by his father's memory.

Ralph was a people person, but as gregarious a man as he was, as he aged, he also became more and more contemplative. He enjoyed his moments of solitude; he needed time to think—to govern himself and his life. Lying on his bed, arms tucked under his head, gazing at the ceiling of his room, fantasizing a bit, he came to the conclusion that at twenty-five, he still had not achieved the success to which he aspired. He needed his luck to change! Times were tough, but, oh, if he could only find a butcher's job, then he could concentrate on expanding to other things.

The phone jingled.

"What . . . what . . . you're kidding!" Ralph screeched.

He had jumped at the sound of the phone and was astonished to hear his brother, Al, on the other end, advising him that a reputable butcher—having heard of Ralph's reputation in the trade—was offering him a job. Carl Schwartz, he was told, was opening up a new store on the corner of Fifth Avenue and Sixtieth Street in Brooklyn.

Ralph was beside himself with joy. He practically danced into the bathroom, splashed water on his face, and gave himself a big smile in the mirror. *You handsome son of a gun!* He changed into a fresh shirt, grabbed his hat, and closed the door behind him, whistling a happy tune.

Carl Schwartz, a German Jew, was a champion of the butcher business. He and his two brothers had been very successful in their other stores on West Seventh and Fifth streets near Kings Highway and West Fiftieth Street. At thirty-five, Carl had become a shrewd businessman, coordinating purchases for all three of their stores, thereby obtaining good quality at convenient prices. Carl was honest (legitimate and in no way connected with the rackets), always fair and serious in his dealings with everyone. Even tempered, sociable, Carl always enjoyed a good joke. And the customers loved him.

Ralph found Carl waiting for him at the entrance of the store—a tall strapping man, blond hair combed neatly to the side, with a slight forelock hanging down to the right of his forehead. As Ralph examined Carl's milk white complexion and friendly sky blue eyes, he thought, *Now here's a good-looking Jew!*

"Ralph, I'm happy you came." Carl smiled, displaying large even white teeth, and he heartily extended a strong hand. Ralph responded just as warmly and sensed they would become good friends.

Carl didn't waste time in reconfirming his interest in him. "Everyone tells me you're one of the best butchers around, Ralph. I'd like you to come to work for me. What do you say?" he asked, his eyes narrowing.

"Yeah, I'd like that, Carl. Thanks for the offer," replied Ralph with dignified restrain.

"When can you start?" asked Carl.

"Tomorrow," responded Ralph.

Ralph worked behind Carl on the second bench, beyond which worked several other butchers—one of whom was George, an Irishman in his midfifties, with a pleasant face, white hair, and pale brown eyes. He carried his heavy frame well even though he shuffled, somewhat like a clown, when he walked. George was a good butcher, polite and very accommodating to the customers. But Ralph soon learned he was a two-faced character.

After observing Ralph for about two months, Carl called him aside.

"Ralph, I've been watching you," he began, and Ralph stiffened. He would hate to lose his job. "And I like what I see. They were right. You know your trade. I'd like to leave you in charge!"

Carl was smiling broadly.

"Well, this is a surprise. Thanks, Carl." Ralph grinned, more than pleased with the trust and promotion. Carl Schwartz was an intelligent man. He understood Ralph was an excellent butcher, as well as a capable businessman.

Ralph undertook his new function very seriously and, although he was younger than most of the men in the shop, was capable of managing with a firm but sensitive hand. He knew the butcher trade was very tricky and perspicaciously allowed the men to take home meat, knowing all too well that if the butchers wanted to deceive him, they could easily do so behind his back. In his exaggerated generosity (part of his lifelong personality), every morning Ralph offered the men coffee and donuts from the nearby coffee shop. Then it was all work! Ralph succeeded in running a good shop without dictator tactics. Everyone *appeared* happy.

Thursday mornings, Carl made the rounds of his stores, delivering the new stock of meat—always smiling and exchanging pleasantries with the men. Shortly after Ralph's promotion, he arrived one morning looking solemn, without his usual outward display. Ralph was busy running through the day's orders, but one glance (as usual) told him something was amiss. When Carl called him into the icebox, his gut feelings told him he was right.

"You know . . . Ralph . . ." Carl began with great difficulty. "You know . . . I heard something in the market . . . but I don't believe it," he added quickly.

"Yeah, what was it?" Ralph asked bluntly, expecting the worst.

"Well," Carl fumbled, then paused. "Well . . . somebody told me that you steal." His face reddened with embarrassment.

"I *steal!*" exclaimed Ralph. "Well, Carl, if you think I steal . . . I quit right now!" concluded Ralph, taking off his white smock.

"No, Ralph . . . wait!" pleaded Carl. "Please don't misunderstand me. I just wanted you to know what I heard. You have a right to know, and I'll tell you another thing. If you steal, you sure must know how, because as far as profits are concerned, this store makes more than the other two put together! So you must know what you're doing."

Ralph said nothing. He was deeply hurt by the accusation.

"I want to tell you where it came from," continued Carl, relieved of the burden of the news. Ralph stiffened as he heard the words. "It comes from George."

"George?" grunted Ralph.

"Yeah, good ole George," Schwartz replied sickly. "Listen, Ralph, you're the boss here . . . If you want to fire him . . . do as you please!"

"Yeah, okay," Ralph mumbled, his anger rising.

Mrs. Schwartz, Carl's mother, was Ralph's able assistant on Saturdays. It was their busiest day, and Mrs. Schwartz handled the cash register for him. She was a nice Jewish mother, with some of the same qualities as Agnes, and perhaps that was why she and Ralph were compatible. They made an average of two thousand dollars on that day, which was good money in those trying times. After Ralph paid the men, Mrs. Schwartz took the balance home to Carl.

This time, George was the last to be paid.

"Come and get your money, George," Ralph called apathetically.

George took off his butcher's coat and shuffled over to him.

Ralph slowly counted George's salary, and as he extended his hand with the money, he glared sternly at an unsuspecting George. "You have a long tongue, George. You're fired!" he stated with finality.

George's mouth opened wide in surprise; his eyes rolled, and without a word, he fell senseless to the ground. Ralph, fearing a heart attack, rushed for the whiskey and forced some down George's throat. Slowly, George came to his senses and wobbled to his feet. Still in shock, his face ghastly white, he picked up his money and silently went home.

On Monday morning, Ralph heard a soft, meek voice addressing him.

"Are you Mr. Ralph?"

He looked up from slicing an order of steaks and nodded, surveying the timid young woman before him. George's wife, he immediately surmised—younger than George by ten years. *Bet they have a bunch of kids,* mused Ralph, picturing her over a washtub, scrubbing clothes. There was a respectable aura about her. Ralph noticed that the nervous woman was plainly dressed, and that her shoes were worn-out. Two large clasps held her golden brown hair in a neat bun. *Hmm, nice color,* thought Ralph. Her delicate features were constricted, as if in pain, and while she clasped an old handbag with her fingertips, she spoke demurely.

"Ralph," she said softly, her voice interrupting Ralph's silent observations. "Did you really fire my husband?"

"Yes, I did. Your husband has a long tongue," Ralph replied emphatically. Damn, he hated these situations.

"Please." Her cheeks were flushed. "Let me explain. I think that . . . maybe . . . it's my fault . . . and I'm sorry. You see, every night when George comes home . . . I badger him, calling him stupid for being bossed around by a twenty-five-year-old kid. I taunted him all the time . . . because *he* wasn't the boss. Now I realize . . . I pushed too hard. Oh, Ralph, times are so bad. I get so frustrated . . ." The disconsolate woman lowered her face in shame, trying to control her emotions.

"Listen, I can't help it if I happen to know the butcher business better than your husband. I was practically born in it. My father was a butcher, and age or no age, I learned my trade well," Ralph told her harshly.

"But, Ralph, my husband really likes you a lot . . . ," she began pleading, her hands trembling.

"Oh yeah? He liked me so much that he tried to get my job, bad-mouthing me behind my back. George thought that with me out of the way, he could be boss!" Ralph shouted, further releasing his anger. He turned his head because he saw what he had expected. Tears. The dejected woman tried to fight them back, brushing them aside one by one as they fell on her crimson cheeks.

"Listen, if George wants my job so badly," Ralph snapped, frustrated. He could never handle a woman's tears. "I'll give it to him!"

Shocked at his words, the young housewife stood still, alarmed.

Ralph, sensing he had gone too far, calmed down. Baby Face Ralph could always be turned on by a pleading wife, mother, or sister (sometimes by hard men whom he saved). Also, with the Depression, he did not have it in his heart to deprive anyone of a livelihood.

"Okay . . . Okay," he said softly. "Tell your husband he can come back to work. Tell him to come back tomorrow."

Overwhelmed with relief, she repeatedly stammered her profuse gratitude. Taking her leave, she kept looking back at Ralph, half-giggling with happiness.

And George returned to work.

The older butchers relished teasing Ralph about the young girls who entered the shop, and he played along, to be a good sport. But Ralph definitely was not interested in settling down; he liked playing the field. One marital experience was enough. One slow afternoon, the men, including Ralph, were ogling a voluptuous girl of eighteen wearing a tightly fitted dress. As she swung and swayed her way out with her package of veal cutlets, Ralph shifted his gaze to a gentleman at his counter, who was laughing as he too watched the departing damsel.

He was an average-looking guy of medium height, around fifty, with a touch of gray at the temples; and at that particular moment, his dark eyes twinkled with mirth. The man was John Foley, a perfect gentleman from Brooklyn and personal secretary to the Democratic senator Heffernan. Both Ralph and John were naturals at making friends; thus, it followed that John had become a steady customer and a very good friend. Like many Irishmen, he loved good camaraderie, was loquacious, and liked to drink. Ralph genuinely enjoyed his company. Many nights on his way home from the office, Foley opened the door to the shop, stuck his head in, and called out, "Ralph, let's have a drink."

Other evenings, Ralph was still enhancing the contents of his wallet by organizing poker games, except that now he had become the protector. It was another form of the protection racket. The players had to be protected, not only from the police, but also from underworld characters who would crash in on the winnings. Therefore, a protector would offer his services for a price, guaranteeing that the game would go undisturbed by both factions. Most of the time, the gangs knew who was protecting who, and their code demanded respect for each other's territory. Sometimes, however, some became greedy, and trouble would break out. In the event of a police raid, regular cards would be substituted, and the money would disappear ahead of time. But usually, Ralph was tipped off. Survival was not possible without the collusion of friendly police.

With his new butcher job down pat, Ralph was restless to expand his outside interests—always on an independent basis. For some time, he had been secretly nursing a plan and, once he thought he was ready, had promised himself to talk to John Foley about it.

John, however, was psychic. As he sipped his drink, he noticed Ralph wasn't laughing at his jokes with the usual spontaneity. "Okay, Ralphy, what is it? What's on your mind?" he finally asked quietly.

"I'm sorry, John. You're right. I did want to talk to you about something very personal. I've been wanting to do this for some time . . . but . . . You know, all the swells around here like to drink . . . and . . ." Ralph was hesitating, not too sure of John's reaction. "Well, hell," he continued, "I'll lay it on the line. I'd like to open up a speakeasy around here somewhere." He stopped and scanned John's face for a negative sign. Instead, he heard what sounded like a father patronizing his son.

"That sounds like a good idea, Ralph. Go ahead."

"Well, you know, it takes contacts," Ralph murmured. "Would you give me a hand?"

"Of course, I would. Go to it and don't worry . . . I'll take care of the problems. Now, let's have another drink." He dismissed the subject and called the waiter.

Speakeasy was a descriptive word, easy to define—speak in low tones, go quietly, for you're drinking illegally. Ralph also went quietly in setting up his first speakeasy. He chose a bottom flat in an attractive building on Forty-seventh Street between Fourth and Fifth Avenues. It had five rooms, which could accommodate private parties. In the main room at the far end was a cozy bar with a piano, while small tables were placed to one side. Ralph hired a singer-piano player and only one waiter. There was also the mandatory peephole through which clients were identified. The speakeasy, although decently decorated, was not lavish. One couldn't be too fancy in the business because one might have to change locations unexpectedly. Those were the risks. One day you're there, the next day you're gone! But with good political connections, many remained in the business for a long time.

Ralph's spirits were definitely up. He was beginning to see more and more money coming in. He stopped in his speakeasy every evening and waited until closing time—sometimes three to four o'clock in the morning, depending on what was happening.

Several months after the speakeasy was in operation, he parked his blue Cadillac, as usual, a block and a half away (Ralph *never* parked in front of the speakeasy). As he stepped out, he noticed a policeman strolling toward him. In a nonchalant manner, Ralph began strutting the other way.

"Hey, you're goin' the wrong way, ain't ya? Hey, bud, I'm talking to you!" the cop yelled.

Ralph casually turned around and innocently replied, "Officer, I think you have the wrong man."

"Who you kidding? It ain't the first time I seen this car here," the lawman snarled.

"Well, maybe you've seen my car, because I have a lady friend around here," Ralph responded smoothly. "I'm sorry to disappoint you, Max, but I'm going this way."

As Ralph continued walking, the policeman shouted after him. "Listen, buddy, who ya think you're foolin'? I'm coming back with the squad, and we're gonna break up the joint!"

That night, a worried Ralph called his friend John to relate what happened. John calmly listened. "Okay, Ralph, I have to make a contact. I'll call you back."

Within a short time, he was telling Ralph, "Tomorrow look for the cop. He should be on the beat until 12:00 midnight. Go over and tell him to call the captain . . . And relax, Ralph, it's taken care of. You can sleep now."

The next night, as he climbed out of his Cadillac, he spotted the policeman, who appeared to be waiting for him at the corner. Both men strode toward each other—the cop with a more pleasant look on his face.

"Why'n hell didn't you tell me you knew the captain?" the cop blurted.

"Buddy, I never tell anyone who I know or don't know," Ralph replied whimsically. "Anyway, let's forget it," he added more kindly. "Come on in and have a drink." And as he spoke, he slipped twenty dollars into the policeman's hand. The lawman looked at the money and smiled. Ralph was never disturbed again.

Feeling more confident, Ralph decided to open up another speakeasy just a block away on Forty-eighth Street. *Easier to control both,* he thought. It was more or less set up as the first, except that it was smaller—more cozy. One day, the police squad *did* arrive. Fortunately, it was early, and the patrons consisted of only two men, accompanied by a girlfriend. She was a short young redhead, pretty and round all over. When the cops barged in, she became so frightened that she ran and hid under the piano. She looked like a stuffed doll, trying to conceal herself. Crouching on all fours, she had her buttocks propped up in such a peculiar fashion that the cops could not stop laughing.

"Come on out, honey. Poppa Bear's not gonna hurt ya," teased one.

As she timidly crawled out, the squad leader's mood changed to one of merriment and shouted, "Okay, let's have a drink on the house!" Everyone had a few laughs while Ralph personally served the drinks.

With his speakeasies' successfully launched, and his butcher job intact, Ralph extended himself further into the protection racket. Several Greek coffeehouses on Eighth, Ninth, and Tenth Avenues requested his services, which put another twenty-five to thirty dollars a week in his pocket. He was a very busy man. His fortune had changed.

Lady Luck, for the moment, was treating him well!

CHAPTER FIFTEEN

A sleek and highly polished gray Rolls-Royce pulled up to Schwartz and Bros. Butcher Shop on Sixtieth Street. A neatly dressed chauffeur, his tailored suit matching the car, rushed to open the door for Ms. Christy. She graciously stepped out like a European countess, accustomed to having people do her bidding. A maid scurried out; a black cape hung loosely on her shoulders over the classic uniform—black dress and white pinafore; her maid's white corona perched high on her ash brown hair. She followed behind as the chauffeur pushed open the doors to Schwartz and Company.

All motion ceased in the shop—as if a film projector had put the action on hold—while Ms. Christy and her entourage regally walked in.

"Now I've seen everything," Ralph mumbled under his breath.

The attractive lady, past fifty, concealed her age very well with a trim figure and a rather smooth face. Her elegant, expensive clothes told the rest. Ms. Christy made a pretext of glancing about the shop, but she *knew* where she was going.

"They tell me you are one of the best butchers in town," she simpered, her pale green eyes fixed on Ralph's face.

"Well, no, ma'am," Ralph replied politely, "I just do my job . . . seriously." He had to focus in on her; the scene was so unreal. But she was too stiff and "proper" to appeal to him.

"Well, word has it that you're a master at your trade . . . and I settle for nothing but the best. My maid will be coming here in the future to purchase our meat." Her voice was cool, in a low-key, and her English perfect. "May I ask what your first name is?" she inquired demurely, still holding everyone's attention.

"Ralph, ma'am."

"*Raffaele*," she murmured in Italian, "very poetic and such a baby face!"

Ralph blushed and said nothing. Although he had developed a certain savoir faire with women, paradoxically, there still remained a flavor of youthful shyness in him.

"Well, good day, *Raffaele*," Ms. Christy purred and strutted proudly out the door, held open by the chauffeur, and disappeared into the backseat of the car. The maid remained for a few minutes while Ralph cut up her order of meat. Then she too vanished.

"Man, was that for real?" whistled George.

Everything had happened so swiftly; Ralph was still speechless.

Henceforth, Ms. Christy became one of Ralph's steady customers, but she never entered the store again. On occasion, she waited in the car like a lovesick adolescent to sneak looks at Ralph while her maid did the shopping.

One day, George, who loved to gab, blurted, "Ralph, you know . . . Ms. Christy's after you. She likes *butchers*!" And he laughed heartily.

Ralph stared fiercely at him, but George grinned from ear to ear.

"Oh, yeah?" Ralph snapped. "She's not my type! Hell . . . she must be around fifty-five . . . I'm twenty-six. For Chrissake . . . do you think I'd go with an old bag like that?" he wildly objected.

But George did not give up. No, not good ole George. "You know, Ralph . . . she's got a lot of money," he continued, still teasing. "You know that big building . . . two blocks down? Well . . . she owns it!" Although they had become friends, George had a way of irritating Ralph.

"I don't need her money!" exploded Ralph.

"Okay . . . okay, Ralph . . . Don't get sore." George decided to lay off.

The subject was momentarily closed.

The next day, the maid appeared; but this time, she leaned over the counter; and in a rather secretive tone, she whispered, "You know, Ralph, Ms. Christy likes you a lot. I mean *a lot*. Why don't you come up to the apartment sometime for tea?"

Ralph was polite but evasive. "Well, don't get me wrong, but I just don't have the time. Someday . . . maybe . . . I'll come up and say hello." He dismissed her gently.

The routine, however, was repeated, repeated, and repeated until it was all Ralph could do to maintain his composure.

About a month or so later, Ralph had just traded in his old Cadillac for a new one and was testing it, making the rounds of his speakeasies. Impulsively, the thought hit him. Hell, why not? He would stop and visit Ms. Christy! She lived in the neighborhood. As he rode up in the elevator, he told himself he was crazy, but somehow he was in the spirit of the thing. He rang the doorbell, smiling at the sound of musical chimes. There was Ms. Black and White opening the door.

"Oooh, Mr. Ralph . . . what a pleasant surprise," the maid squealed. "Ms. Christy will be *so* pleased to see you."

Ralph smiled, glancing around the spacious entrance hall and up at the crystal chandelier. He knew he was in a very classy place. As the maid led him into the parlor, he caught a glimpse of himself in the huge gold leaf, framed mirror above an antique neoclassical pier table. Ralph sank into a large armchair with huge goose-down cushions and felt like an idiot with all the fluff and puff around him. Uncomfortably seated, with his hat still in his hands, he watched Ms. Christy make her regal entrance. Her figure never looked so good! She wore an elegant evening dress, of satin sheen, clinging to her slender curves; a two-strand necklace of cultured pearls adorned her graceful neck. Her blonde hair was neatly swept up to one side. She wasn't bad to look at, not at all, mused Ralph. Very aristocratic. Well, why not? She was rich, well-bred—an English Ms. Christy. She came forward with a charming smile and held out her hand. Ralph had some difficulty getting out of that damned puffed chair, but somewhat awkwardly, he finally succeeded. They exchanged greetings, and Ralph timidly and cautiously moved over to a Chippendale chair (*without* cushions).

Ms. Christy offered him tea. Ralph declined. She offered whisky. He heartily accepted. Ralph needed it. *Whatever possessed me to come,* he admonished himself. The maid was finally dismissed for the evening, and the two strangers were alone. Ms. Christy wanted to know all about Ralph's life (she seemed to be fascinated by it) and listened starry-eyed, as if Ralph was a famous personality. Then, quite suddenly, she slowly rose and said sweetly, "Ralph, would you like to see the apartment?"

Ralph nodded and, without a word, followed her around. It was a beautiful penthouse, fabulously furnished with expensive paintings in handsome frames, and artistic tapestries adorned the walls. Ralph didn't know very much about painters, but he was smart enough to recognize the paintings were the works of well-known artists. The shimmering margins of the parquet floors framed several beautiful Oriental rugs; the furniture was antique, and plush brocaded drapes fell in thick loose folds at the windows. No gaudy opulence in Ms. Christy's home, only genuine elegance. She gently took Ralph's arm and paused as they reached the doorway of her bedroom.

"Very nice," was all Ralph could shyly say. The room was what one could call Hollywoodish—a study of beige shades with splashes of white and delicate blue. The wall-to-wall carpeting was plush pale blue. Oriental lamps created subdued lighting.

Ralph followed her gaze to the bed, on which he saw a beautiful pair of fine blue silk pajamas. She nudged him closer and said coyly, "Ralph, these are yours. These are for you."

Without daring to look at her, Ralph, in stupid innocence, replied, "What am I to do with them?"

"Put them on," she whispered.

"What?" Ralph gasped, his face reddened.

"Put them on," she repeated softly.

Flushed, his jaw set, a nerve throbbing in his cheek, Ralph gently led Ms. Christy back into the parlor. This was not for him. He wasn't ready for this interlude. Soon, a successful combination of Ms. Christy's charm and the warm sensation of a few more potent drinks, Ralph was persuaded to try on the blue silk pajamas.

In the bathroom, Ralph stared at himself in the mirror, his head whirling and his heart clamoring. Then he shrugged his shoulders and mumbled, "Hell . . . why not!" When he entered the bedroom, he found Ms. Christy standing near the window, in a loose-fitting, provocative black peignoir, twisting her hands in anxiety. She slowly turned to him admiringly, surveying him with admiration and approval. He saw the hungry look of lust in her eyes, which signaled the course of events.

Ralph was a smooth lover, gentle and considerate with his women, but somehow, he sensed Ms. Christy wanted to play games. As he moved toward her, he heard a tippy squeal of anticipated rapture, and her eyes were gleaming. Ralph found her warm and eager as he pulled her to him, and his mouth savagely found her lips. She wound her arms around his neck, her fingers digging into his shoulders. Her young butcher boy was finally in her arms. He swept her up and carried her to the bed where he firmly deposited her. Ms. Christy clung passionately to him, but Ralph pinned her neatly beneath him, deftly raising her gown and returning her wild kisses, as his own passion soared. Ecstatically, she guided his hand along her trembling thighs, and his fingers explored—pressing and squeezing—until guidance was no longer needed as he lost himself in her warm flesh. She climaxed quickly, reaching a state of ecstatic transport. But her need was insatiable, and throughout the night, she seduced her young lover again and again; her convulsive cries of wanton abandon filled the room.

The next morning, at breakfast, Ms. Christy was as elegant as ever in a flowing pink chiffon gown, with a slight trace of makeup on her glowing face. She tried very lovingly to convince Ralph to live with her.

"Ralph, stay with me . . . I'm absolutely crazy about you," she pleaded. "I'll pay for everything. You can leave your job . . . I'll buy you an Isotta Fraschini car! Oh, I know it will be . . . oh, so grand." Ms. Christy clutched her hands dramatically to her breast as she spoke.

Ralph, embarrassed by the situation, mustered his best act to dissuade her of her infatuation with him. He honestly felt sorry for her. Basically, she was a nice lady and *very* lonely. Tenderly, he took her hands in his and gently murmured, "Look, Ms. Christy, I like you a lot. You're something real, different for me, but money doesn't interest me. I have enough of my own . . . and then I would never stay with you for that reason. I have too much respect for you."

When she was about to protest, Ralph added firmly but kindly, "It's no use . . . I'm too independent. I have to lead my own life."

Ralph stood up and took Ms. Christy in his arms. Kissed her affectionately on the cheek, then slowly let himself out. At the door he turned for one last smile, leaving Ms. Christy stunned, in a dramatic pose. Once outside the door, Ralph rushed out of the building, wishing he had wings.

Ms. Christy, however, did not give up. She had to have him! Determined, she personally went into the shop a few times, but Ralph always politely excused himself, saying he had administrative work to do. Very diplomatically, he instructed George to serve the beautiful lady while he hid in the back room, counting money—anything, in order to avoid a scene with her.

One day, however, she cornered him when he was alone in the shop.

"Ralph, I miss you so . . . Please come and stay with me," she supplicated, her eyes searching his. "You said you liked me, loved my apartment. I am prepared to live with you . . . knowing just that. If you must work," her eyes became misty as she begged him to listen, "I'll set you up in your own butcher shop. My lawyers will arrange for your divorce . . . so you'll have nothing to worry about. Oh . . . Ralph," she cried.

"Ms. Christy," Ralph said gently, trying to interrupt, but she was on a roll.

"Remember, I promised you an Isotta Fraschini?" she continued. "Well, it'll be one of the most beautiful you've ever seen!"

The Isotta Fraschini was supposed to be the icing on the cake because at that time in the USA, it cost between $25,000 and $30,000, depending on the extras; some very plush ones ran almost double that amount.

Ralph was literally backed up against the wall as Ms. Christy pressured him. In defense, he stammered, "M-Ms. Christy, let me think about it. I need time."

He had uttered the magic words. She squeezed Ralph's hand, kissed her two forefingers, placed them against his lips, and left.

Ralph was relieved but embarrassed. When she came, they had become the main attraction in the shop; and the men, enjoying the romantic interlude, were neglecting their clients. Ralph found himself shouting, "Haven't you guys anything better to do? Get the hell to work!"

Of course, Ralph had made up his mind. He could not be bought, especially where his heart was concerned. He was a free spirit and couldn't be possessed by anyone. *Ralph loves 'em and leaves 'em*, were words especially true during that period of Ralph's life. Also, his son, Joey, growing up in his mother's care, needed a father, which was very important to Ralph.

He finally told her it was useless. She would have to look elsewhere for a lover. Ms. Christy's face was gray, expressionless. She walked haughtily out of the shop, her shoulders stiff with pride, while the men sadly shook their heads.

The *coup de grace* was delivered about a month later when a beautiful Isotta Fraschini pulled up and parked *purposely* in front of Schwartz and Bros. George wasted no time in commenting.

"Ralph, looks like she's fallen in love with another *butcher*! Aaah . . . hell hath no fury like a woman scorned," George recited poetically. "I told you . . . you was a damned fool. Now ain't that a beauty of a car?" he teased.

"Yeah . . . well, she can have him! Nobody *buys* Ralph! I make my own money. Now for Chrissake . . . let's get to work!" Ralph yelled.

And to hell with Ms. Christy.

The country was still in a terrible economical crisis because of the Depression. Work at Carl Schwartz's was not bustling the way it ordinarily did. Ralph's sixty dollars a week and his 2 percent commission were a strain on Carl. Eventually, he had to discharge Ralph, taking over the manager's position himself. Fortunately, while Ralph was employed by Carl, he was being courted by two other successful butchers, Louis Goldner and Benny Becker (brothers-in-law), who operated a large store on Sixtieth Street and Fifth Avenue. They were also suppliers to restaurants and hotels, and miraculously, were still doing well. They hired Ralph on the spot, matching only the sixty dollars a week. Ralph was very happy; at least he had his "legitimate job."

But Ralph's job was taking too much of his time during the day, making it difficult for him to control his other enterprises. Without the commission Carl Schwartz had been paying him, the sixty dollars a week he was earning was not worth all the hours he worked. He made more money on the side. His lifestyle required that he increase his finances and resolved to make the break—once and for all. He would quit his butcher job and take the risks involved. Ralph had come to terms with himself; he had accepted his destiny!

In his moments of quiet meditation, Ralph had toyed with the idea of entering the numbers racket—but only independently. He had always refused to be a part of any particular group, refusing a tight alliance with anyone, including Charlie. It kept his friendships intact, gave him more room to move about, and was, all in all, a healthier situation. The numbers racket, or policy trade (as some people called it), had become very profitable, and Ralph was anxious to try his luck. But being one's own boss didn't mean one went around and did things on the sneak. One let his friends know. Respect was the name of the game.

Before he acted on this new venture, Ralph decided to have a talk with Charlie.

CHAPTER SIXTEEN

Ralph was seventeen when he first met Joe Adonis (Giuseppe Antonio Doto) at Soucher's Ballroom in Coney Island. Adonis, at that time, hung around with Good-looking Georgie and Frankie Marlowe, the two best pickpockets in town. Joe was a smart kid and was calm by nature. He didn't possess the aura of an underworld man, but rather, that of a typically serious businessman. Always debonair in his pin-striped suits, he was easily referred to as The Businessman. Slowly, Joe's financial situation improved, and he opened a restaurant on Fourth Avenue and First in South Brooklyn—with the unpretentious name Joe's Restaurant. Not satisfied with owning just a restaurant, enterprising Adonis branched out into slot machines. He soon became one of the leaders in the racket—and raking in big profits.

About that time, he received an urgent call from Detroit. Could he break up a strike?

"Sure," Joe answered confidently. "Tell me about it and I'll tell you how much it'll cost."

He was told it was not just a small ordinary strike. It was one of the biggest Ford Motor strikes of all time.

To Adonis, it was business as usual. He could garner enough underlings to muster up a task force whenever he wanted—for whatever reason he deemed necessary. To comply with this particular request, he mobilized a large group of men and personally took command. Undoubtedly, it set the union movement back somewhat, but Joe became a hero to the Ford Motor Company, which helped extend his contacts into the Anglo-Saxon world. Shortly thereafter, Adonis opened a Ford Dealership near his restaurant with two men, Kirwin and White, whom he jocularly named his Two WASP Partners. The dealership was known by the two latter names—a very respectable front. Joe had received his reward. With that added activity, Joe Adonis had truly become a very respected Mr. Big as boss of Brooklyn. (Later, Joe Adonis expanded into the trucking business, hauling interstate goods.) Ralph and his brother, Al, were one of the first to purchase a Ford truck from him for their supermarket business.

It wasn't long before the boys understood what a gold mine there was in promoting the unions. Some played both sides of the fence. Greed.

After Frankie Yale's death, Ralph maintained his promise to look after Angelo. He felt sorry for Angelo because without his famous brother, Angelo was a nobody. Yet there wasn't anything important Ralph could do, so one day, he talked to Adonis.

"Can't you give him a piece of some action?" Ralph asked, half-pleading. "He's a headache, I know, but we should, in Frankie's memory, give him a chance."

"Okay, Ralphy . . . you're always playing the big brother routine," Joe replied sympathetically. "I'll talk to Vito (Genovese). He'll have some ideas. But do me a favor . . . stay away from that guy! It ain't healthy for your reputation. Tell him to come and see me first . . . so I can have a 'heart-to-heart' talk with him. AND tell him to come alone!" Joe concluded, as though he had just closed a business deal.

Ralph was grateful to him for being understanding, realizing that whatever Joe would do was because he, Ralph, had asked him. Actually, Adonis couldn't have cared less for Angelo.

About two days later, Ralph received a call from Vito to meet him that evening at Ferrara's Café. When Ralph arrived, Vito was sitting at a corner table, deeply engaged in conversation with two men. Vito was a natty dresser, but there was always something sinister about him. The darkness of his deeply set eyes (oft times covered by sunglasses) framed by shadowy circles, and thick unruly black eyebrows, seemed to cast a spell of foreboding evil. His long thin lips curved slightly upward at the corners, giving him a sort of permanent ironic smile. Vito was short with small feet, but when he wore one of his expensive hats, or simply with his crop of black hair piled high on his head (in his younger days), he managed to look a bit taller. Vito Genovese was a Mr. Big with whom you had to watch yourself—and Ralph was glad that Vito liked him.

As Ralph approached the table, the two men rose slowly, nodded slightly, and left without a word. Vito sprang up energetically and stretched out his hand.

"Ralphy, good to see you, kid." Vito laughed, his face lighting up. "Playing good samaritan again, heh?"

Ralph smiled, and after exchanging pleasantries, Vito continued more seriously. "I talked to Joe . . . and you're right . . . we should do something in Frank's memory. Angelo's a troublemaker, but we'd like to help him straighten out. So . . . it's okay. But we're not taking any chances. It's no deal, unless *you're* with him." Vito paused to study Ralph's reaction, then leaned over and, in low tones, revealed his plan. "Ralphy, we want you to organize the ice racket in Rockaway. You'll have everything you need. We'll take care of you . . . don't worry about money, or nothing. We've already got the okay for you to go there."

Measuring his words, not wanting to offend, Ralph began to object politely, "Vito, you know I got lots of things of my own going . . ." But as he spoke deliberately, Ralph gazed into Vito's eyes and found them to be intense, resolute, and he understood the message. "Yeah . . . well . . . okay, I'll do it for you, Vito—and to give Angelo a break!" He finally consented.

"Okay, pal!" Very pleased, Vito flung one arm around Ralph's shoulder and added, "But, Ralphy . . . just don't get into any trouble. No slipups! Keep your eyes on Angelo, *and* keep me informed."

Ralph left quite satisfied, not only for Angelo, but also for himself. Vito had confirmed that he held a very respected position.

The day they finally arranged to drive out to Rockaway, Angelo was all spruced up like a real dude on his first job. Ralph winced when he saw his outfit: a green-and-white plaid jacket with a thin yellowish thread outlining the squares, a dark green shirt, and the tie? Shocking white! *What taste,* thought Ralph as he shook his head in disgust. Apparently, Angelo felt very important with the assignment because he had acquired a cocky stance and thrust out his chest more boldly than usual. Ralph, instead, was all business, in a dark gray serge suite, and well prepared with a definite plan to organize the icemen.

Ralph and Angelo began by canvassing the area, letting their presence and purpose be known, and found that the icemen were indiscriminately scattered. Ralph hired a couple of stoolies to mingle among them, to inform him about what the icemen were thinking, and learned that they gathered every day at a nearby lunch wagon. When Ralph felt enough of their curiosity had been aroused, he drove up in his shiny black Cadillac, with Angelo at his side, and parked near the wagon. He felt very much the politician as he went around shaking hands, introducing himself and Angelo. He gave the icemen their packaged pep talk. Actually, Ralph was not acting. He believed in the project, thought it to be beneficial for the men—and when he spoke, he was sincerely enthusiastic. Most of the icemen appeared to be in favor in the idea of a union and listened with interest to what Ralph had to say. Initially, Ralph used a low-key approach, not wanting to alienate the icemen by aggressive tactics. He gave them time to savor the new concept in their minds, waiting a day or two before he made another appearance to resume talks. Ralph changed cars often during those days to demonstrate that there was real money behind him.

Meanwhile, Ralph learned that there was only one plant in the area producing ice, Murray's Ice Plant, and Mr. Murray enjoyed his monopoly.

He raised prices arbitrarily without notice and played this game especially around Christmas. Some icemen became so discouraged that they traveled to New York to obtain their ice.

There was also a great deal of animosity and bickering among the icemen. Those who had ice shacks were undercutting the prices of the horse and buggy icemen (a few had small trucks), who naturally required more maintenance and overhead expenses. And the times being what they were, many people went directly to the shacks, with their pans and pails, to purchase the ice more cheaply. On top of it all, the icemen had to contend with the unethical pricing methods of Mr. Murray. Obviously, the horse and buggy men were more than happy to have a sympathetic ear and easily became allies to the plan. Ralph and Angelo, therefore, concentrated their efforts toward the shack men, which was not easy. Some would not yield. For the most part, however, the idea of a union had been successfully assimilated, so much so that Ralph received word that Mr. Murray wanted to see him. Ralph kindly declined—for the moment.

Ralph's next step was to organize a meeting for all the icemen, a big rally, at which the functions of the union would be explained. He rented a large hall, set the date, printed posters to announce the event, displaying them in strategic places, and generally spread the word around. Two New York lawyers (chosen by Vito) were sent down to explain some of the legal aspects of forming a union. The hall was jammed to capacity with a noisy crowd, creating a real hubbub, and was more or less divided between the two groups. Ralph, Angelo, and the two lawyers sat behind a long wooden table on a small stage rigged up for the occasion. The meeting was meant to initiate a big membership drive; Ralph had prepared an excellent opening speech, emphasizing brotherhood and a fair break for all. He stood erect, sure of himself, as he spoke telling them what they would be receiving for their money. When he announced that medical care and hospitalization would be free, he was interrupted by a pleasant stir of consenting individuals. At this point, Ralph believed he had them in the palm of his hands and decided to toss out his important clincher.

"AND, we're going to build another ice plant!" he shouted, "bigger and better than Murray's. It'll create competition and regulate prices!"

Loud cheers and applause filled the hall. The icemen were completely and favorably animated. Angelo acted like some kind of cheerleader, raising his arms in triumph. Ralph gave him a good hard look, and he settled back a little. The lawyers smiled complacently.

Ralph, however, also had some disturbing things to say, which he knew would be received by hissing, but now was the time to throw the bomb. Ralph raised his hands to quiet the audience.

"My friends," he began solemnly, "we must also make some drastic changes!"

Silence reigned.

"All the ice shacks MUST close," Ralph declared, and as he expected, there was an uproar. He tried to calm them down, shouting over their disapproval. "I understand your feelings," he cried out, "but let me explain . . ."

To Ralph's surprise, Angelo produced a whistle from his pocket and blew loud and clear to subdue the shouting. It wasn't something Ralph would do, but it worked, and Angelo smiled proudly.

In a soothing but loud voice, Ralph explained, "We are offering those men who close their shacks, horses and buggies or trucks, as they wish, for which they can pay back the union a little at a time—without interest!"

The men continued to murmur amongst themselves.

"AND," Ralph continued, "all the routes will be divided among all the icemen equally. FURTHER, if a man gets sick, we'll have another iceman take his route, so he won't lose out. IN ADDITION, if one fella loses a customer, he'll have to exchange one with the iceman who got his!" Ralph was using all his savvy, and with his clean, innocent face and blue eyes, he was finally capturing the crowd. He shrewdly paused to make sure he had everyone's attention.

"FINALLY," he shouted, "everyone will be insured. For example, if one iceman's truck breaks down, we'll provide another truck to replace it, so he won't lose any business!"

Many in the audience began applauding. Ralph emphasized that they had security with the union—everything to gain and very little to lose. Most of the icemen were overwhelmed; many were ready to sign on the dotted line. The lawyers then took over for the question-and-answer segment. The rally was a big success! But some of the shack men held out. Ralph and Angelo still had to convince the stubborn ones.

Ralph had cased the neighborhood for weeks and knew all the ice shack locations by heart. He drove toward one of their biggest opponents. His informers had told him that an Italian immigrant from Bari, known as Joe, was creating the most static. Angelo was fidgeting in his seat, and Ralph could tell he couldn't wait to use a little muscle on the iceman. That was Angelo's main problem—always restless, always eager for a fight. The shack was located at the end of a long row of streets, dissected by alleys, in an empty, unkempt field. Like most, it was a simple wooden shack, built well, with a long wooden platform in front extending around to the drive. As Ralph pulled up, he spoke to Angelo in stern terms.

"Listen, Ang, there's not going to be any action here. Just talk! We've done a good job up to now, and we're not going to spoil it with any rough stuff. I'll do all the talking," Ralph warned emphatically.

"Yeah, okay, but if he tries any funny stuff—"

"No, Ang," Ralph interrupted, "I said no muscle . . . nothing . . . just talk!"

Angelo nodded sullenly. He couldn't compete with Ralph's iron fists.

They pulled themselves out of the car in slow motion, each inhaling the cool breeze, which gently touched their faces. It was not yet dusk, and the sun still glowed, casting fantastic colors across the sky, as though an artist had wielded an impressionist's brush with strokes of pink hues against gray-toned clouds—providing the right shadings for the forlorn wooden ice shack.

A little dark man appeared in the shack's doorway. His black hair was parted along the middle and plastered down with gel, and his pencil-thin black mustache was just as sleek. He wore a sweaty undershirt, half in and half out of his baggy brown pants, held up by a pair of bright red suspenders. Leaning against the door, holding a shiny round ice pick in his right hand, the swarthy-complexioned middle-aged iceman glared intently at the two strangers approaching.

"I'ma not gonna close!" he blurted, his English poor and heavily accented.

Expecting the hostility, Ralph smiled pleasantly at his adversary. "Relax, Joe, we just want to talk to you," Ralph called out as he and Angelo walked up the creaky planks.

Joe tightened his grip on the ice pick, anticipating the worst.

Ralph's blue eyes gazed kindly at the little man as he spoke gently, "Look, we're not looking for trouble, Joe. We just thought if we talked to you, you'd change your mind—because we're offering you a chance to make more money, more than you realize . . ."

"Yeah, Joe, think about it!" Angelo added, taking a stance of importance.

Ralph's icy stare at Angelo demanded instant silence. Turning to Joe, he continued in conciliatory tones. "I understand how you feel . . . You hate to give up what you have here, but, believe me, you won't be losing anything. You'll be better off in the long run . . ."

Still fixed in the same pose, Joe was undaunted. "Naw, I'ma not gonna join you . . . I'ma not gonna pay you guys no money." And shifting his body menacingly, he ordered them to leave. "Now, get out. I know Palmiotti, the boss . . . I no have to do nothin'!"

There was indeed a boss from Bari, named Joe Palmiotti, in New York, but what the poor little immigrant didn't know was that he was a good friend of Ralph's. Palmiotti was in the shylock racket and practically owned a piece of every Barese in town.

"Okay, Joe, you go and see him," Ralph said, ready to conclude, "but be sure to tell him you spoke to Ralph."

Angelo was flustered. As they walked toward the car, he quipped, "Chrissake, Ralph . . . you should have let me rough him up a bit!"

"Ang, you'll never learn. There are *other* ways," Ralph replied calmly.

That night, Ralph advised Vito of the obstacle; and in about two days, he received a call to meet Joe Palmiotti at Ferrara's. This time, Ralph took Angelo with him in order to demonstrate how some things worked. Joe, the iceman, was already there, silent and respectful in a clean suit and tie, holding a straw hat in his hands, waiting. As Ralph sauntered in, a jolly, swarthy-looking Joe Palmiotti, in a spotless white linen jacket, greeted him affectionately, looked at Angelo, and gave him his hand. Tall for a Barese, Palmiotti was a dapper dresser; his tailor-made clothes had just the right cut. He constantly smoothed his pomaded mustache with his left forefinger and thumb, so that the diamond ring on his little finger would be more conspicuous. Everyone waited for him to speak.

Palmiotti turned to the now humble immigrant and authoritatively asked, "These boys came to see you?"

"Yea, they wanna me to join a union . . . give up my ice shack," he replied, trembling in Palmiotti's presence.

"Did they make you a proposition?" Palmiotti continued evenly.

"Yeah, they say lotsa things. They tell me I gotta pay two hundred dollars to join the union," Joe exclaimed, exasperated.

"Joe," Palmiotti interrupted in fatherly tones, "these are good boys. They were sent to Rockaway to do a job . . . for all the icemen's good. Maybe, you didn't understand them, Joe?"

"Well . . . I tella them I wanna see you first, to maka sure," Joe respectfully answered.

"Okay, now you see him, and now you do as they tell you. How much did you say you had to pay?" Palmiotti asked.

"Two hundred dollars, Joe," he said meekly, looking at his straw hat.

"Well, it just went up to three hundred dollars for all the trouble you cause," Palmiotti scolded. "This is a lesson . . . The next time good people come to you . . . you listen to them. *Va bene*, okay, it's finished. You can go!"

Just as though Joe were his child, Palmiotti dismissed the iceman, who retreated like a fugitive. Ralph felt rather sorry for him.

Palmiotti shook his head and waved his hands in harmony. "Ralphy, sorry about this. Let's have a drink."

The first part of the next week, while Ralph and Angelo were making their rounds in Rockaway, Mr. Murray solicited a meeting with them. Ralph agreed it was time for them to talk and sent word he would be at the plant in an hour. It was an extremely hot day, one of those muggy, no-air days, in which the blazing sun seemed determined to burn the sidewalks of the city. Ralph and Angelo had loosened their ties, but Ralph insisted they keep their jackets on to maintain a proper business decorum.

Murray's ice plant was located on the outskirts of Rockaway in what was classified as a commercial section. It was a plain rectangular dark red brick building with black window trims. The front lawn, emerald green and immaculately kept, had been neatly divided into two squares, enclosed by a low black iron fence made of thin pipes. A long cement sidewalk ran through the squares up to the front entrance, which sported huge oak double doors. To the left of the doors was a large black sign with gold letters reading, MURRAY'S ICE PLANT. The driveway, to the right of the building, continued around the back to the loading and unloading platforms. Ralph opened the front door and noticed a middle-aged woman, around forty-five, with frizzy reddish blonde hair, sitting behind a rather modern desk. She was busy, acting as receptionist, clerk, and secretary all rolled into one—a regular girl Friday type. The men were obviously expected because she quickly and nervously ushered them into Murray's office. They saw him standing near the window in his shirtsleeves, his tie hanging down unknotted. As Murray turned to face his visitors, Ralph's eyes stared directly at the special belt he wore, with his pistol propped neatly in the holster.

"Watch out, that pistol might go off!" Angelo half-snorted.

"Yeah," Ralph added casually, not wanting Murray to think they were worried about his gun. "You sure you know how to handle it?"

It was obvious that Murray wanted to portray himself as a tough guy. Ignoring the remarks, he very evenly said, "How much do you boys want to leave town?"

With an impatient gesture, Ralph calmly replied, "We're not here to be bribed, but to talk business. We're here to ask *you*, if you want to sell your ice plant?" Ralph eyed him steadily.

"NEVER!" Murray shouted angrily.

Ralph sized him up to be around forty, a tough bastard, wirily built, with firm, sinewy arms. His face was thin, with a narrow, straight nose; and at that moment, his light brown eyes were filled with resentment. The room was stifling, not the best day to negotiate. Murray began to perspire; tiny beads of sweat formed along the lines of his receding forehead. As he reached into his pocket for a handkerchief, Angelo tightened for a moment, thinking Murray was going for his gun.

"Sorry to hear that," continued Ralph placidly. "It's only fair to tell you that we're here to build another ice plant, bigger and better . . . and I'm afraid you're going to have some tough competition!"

"Listen, you guys," Murray's voice was angry. "I've been here a long time, and I've built up this business from nothing . . . built up this area. I've provided work for a lot of men . . ."

"Yeah, we see how—taking advantage of them . . . raising prices . . . monopolizing everything," replied Ralph sarcastically. "It ain't enough to just provide work, Mr. Murray. You're behind the times!"

"Okay, you're smart bastards. How much is it worth to you?" Murray snapped.

Angelo stared at Murray with a sarcastic grin, then turned to Ralph. "Ralph, tell this man who he's dealing with, will you?"

Murray interrupted, "Is fifty grand enough to make you forget this whole damn business?" The smug look on his face betrayed his satisfaction, thinking he had outwitted them.

His eyes locked with Murray's, Ralph quietly but provocatively responded, "My friend's right, Mr. Murray. You've got us all wrong. We don't take bribes . . . You can't buy us! We're here to start a legit business . . . form a union to really help the icemen you've been screwing for a long time!"

Angelo began throwing his chest out, and Ralph knew it was time to leave before trouble occurred.

"Okay, Ang, let's give Mr. Murray time to think about our proposition," Ralph said, concluding the interview.

"Get out, you bastards," Murray stormed, the sweat now gleaming on his cheeks.

Ralph tossed him a salute, and as he and Angelo took their leave, he could see, from the corner of his eye, Murray slumping down into his chair, frantically wiping his brow.

Toward the end of the week, Ralph had another chat with Vito to report his progress and to advise him that the project would be finalized in approximately two weeks. Vito's normal smile broadened as he complimented Ralph.

"I knew you had it in you, Ralphy . . . You've done an excellent job—and with no ripples from the police!" He leaned closer to Ralph as he always did when he wanted to share a confidence. "You know the right people in the police department had given us the go-ahead for the Rockaway affair—on condition there wasn't any rough stuff. AND, Ralph, I gave my *word*!"

Ralph understood Vito's last message very well and was relieved that he had pulled it off without causing any waves.

That weekend, however, unbeknownst to Ralph, Angelo drove to Rockaway ALONE. He wanted to be the big shot on his own, was tired of being the number 2 man. He cruised up and down the streets looking for some action when suddenly, his eyes lit up. He had an idea, and with a sardonic look on his face, he swerved the car around and headed for the ice shack belonging to the little man from Bari.

Joe was bent over, gathering the leftover pieces of ice for his family, when suddenly, someone pushed open the door. Frightened at the crashing sound, he turned abruptly to find Angelo grinning diabolically at him.

"What you want here?" he snapped, alarmed at the unexpected visit.

"Aah, still playing the tough guy," quipped Angelo. "You don't learn your lessons very well . . . do you, Joe?"

The poor iceman didn't like Angelo and cared less for his sinister look. His eyes searched frantically for his ice pick and caught sight of it lying upright in a corner. Slowly, he moved toward it, shouting to keep Angelo off guard, "I ask you . . . whatta you want?" But Angelo was quick, and just as Joe was ready to snatch up the ice pick, he grabbed the iceman by his undershirt and threw him against the wall.

"So . . . you want to hurt me . . . you no-good bastard! A guy comes to talk to you . . . and you want to hurt him . . ." Angelo went wild, lifted him up, and swung a nasty blow to the side of the iceman's head. In a daze, Joe squired loose and ran outside, but Angelo caught up to him. The poor would-be rebel was no match for Angelo, who continued to whip him to a pulp—until he could no longer stand on his feet. Then Angelo administered the finishing blow. He walloped Joe so hard that the poor little man fell, striking his head against the wheel rim of an abandoned wagon near the shack. As he lay there, half-dead, Angelo snapped out of his craze and panicked as he stared at his blood-streaked hands. It was then that the hothead ran to Ralph in a sweat and blabbed everything to him.

"What . . . what . . . did you do!" Ralph yelled. "Ang, you son of a bitch! After all I preached to you about no trouble . . . you go ahead and do something so damn stupid?"

"Ralphy, I don't know what got into me . . ." Angelo ran his hands through his hair in a desperate gesture. Ralph, enraged, felt only repugnance and interrupted his whining.

"For your sake, I hope that guy lives . . . because if he dies . . . after what the big boys said, and what they tried to do for you . . . you're dead too!" Ralph turned away from Angelo in disgust. "Ang, I've had enough . . . I'm through with you . . . Just don't bother me anymore, Ang."

No matter how pathetically Angelo begged to be forgiven, Ralph would not listen. The episode nauseated him; he was completely exhausted with Angelo's hoodlum tactics. It was over between them.

As Ralph expected, Vito called; he and Adonis wanted to see him at Ferrara's. He had no choice but to go; he knew he would be read the riot act. In a deeply depressed mood, Ralph pushed through Ferrara's doors. They were both waiting for him with grim faces—Vito's face darker than ever.

"Sit down, Ralph," Vito said gloomily. "You see, Ralphy, do a guy a good turn and you see what happens?" He shook his head sideways in antipathy.

"Angelo's always the same guy . . . He'll never change. We're not blaming you, kid . . . You did your best, but the operation is now closed! Luckily, by some miracle, that guy will live." Vito paused and looked at Adonis, who was listening attentively. "Ralphy," he concluded sternly, "we have to let everything cool off for a while."

Adonis tried to soothe Ralph's feelings, knowing how disheartened he was.

"Joe," Ralph wailed, "I worked damn hard on the project . . ."

"Yeah, I know, Ralphy. Forget about him. I told you he was a bad egg. Just don't go vouching for him anymore. He ain't worth it!"

With a wave of the hand, Adonis ordered a round of drinks. Ralph said nothing more. The two older men looked at him sympathetically. After all, Ralph had performed an excellent job. They spent the next half hour trying to elevate "Baby Face" Ralph's spirit.

The Rockaway affair had ended—and with it, Ralph's friendship with Angelo.

CHAPTER SEVENTEEN

Charlie studied the blue-eyed young man seated in front of him. He had been told by Vito of the Rockaway fiasco and knew it had nothing to do with Ralph's efforts. On the contrary, he had done an excellent job, and Ralph was the kind of person Charlie wanted in his "family." Ralph was indeed a young man who commanded respect. He was bright, capable, and endowed with a wonderful personality.

Charlie spoke quietly, "Ralph, I'd like you to join me—you know . . . my group." Of course, Ralph was flattered, knew it was a sign of deep respect, and, with equal feelings, declined his offer to join him. Charlie smiled admiringly at the enterprising lad but was disappointed. For a young man, Ralph was doing all right for himself, and Charlie understood his desire to be independent.

"So, now you want to go into numbers?" Charlie said casually.

Ralph nodded assertively. "I've already found offices in the Browning Building . . . on Sixtieth and Broadway," he replied enthusiastically.

"Oh yeah . . . great . . . that's where Frank (Costello) directs his slot machine operation," Charlie said approvingly. "As a matter of fact, if you ever want to go into that racket, Frank can teach you the ropes. Yeah . . . Yeah . . . on your own," he added laughing.

Ralph lifted his eyebrows and chuckled. "Charlie, I can't help it. That's the way I am. I've got to do my own thing. I think I took after my father . . . well . . . in being independent, I mean." Ralph became pensive, knowing that Joe Liguori would never have taken such a path in life.

Noticing Ralph's facial expression change at the mention of his father, Charlie gazed intently at Ralph. He understood. Fathers always had a way of remaining in your gut all your life, dead or alive, Charlie mused.

"I've got to tell you, Ralph . . . Once Frankie (Yale) told me that you're a young guy to be respected. He was right. Now, if you need any names for controllers and runners for the numbers, let me know," Charlie offered affectionately.

Ralph left Charlie in a happy state. It wasn't that he had to ask permission; he didn't have to answer to Charlie. It was a matter of paying respect—an opportunity to check out the neighborhoods where he intended to operate. A fast rule was that you never sponged in on someone else's territory. Charlie was the big man of the racket. He knew everything and everybody. Vito also did well for himself, but he was outclassed by Frank Erickson, an ex-disciple of Arnold Rothstein. Erickson had perfected his operation in a secret alliance with Costello, who always enjoyed playing a behind-the-scene game.

In a week's time, Ralph had special telephone lines installed and, with a secondhand desk and a couple of chairs, went into business. Numbers was something like the speakeasy operation; one invested very little in furniture and spared the interior decoration because one could be here today, gone tomorrow. In order not to be confined to the office, Ralph hired one girl to assist in answering the phones. The numbers racket was still in its embryonic stage, compared to what it became, and Ralph was determined to grow with it.

At first, Ralph hired three, then four collaborators, called controllers, who reported directly to him. The number of controllers was not necessarily important, but rather, the areas in which one operated—plus the contacts the boss and his controllers had. Each of Ralph's controllers had about four or five runners working (running) for him, who communicated only to him; after which, the controller checked in with Ralph. Runners rarely knew their boss; they were not supposed to. It reduced the risks involved. Because the runner was more exposed to the elements, he followed determined rules. He was never to stand still, could not be conspicuous. He was to be sharp enough not to be caught with the betting slip on him. If the runner was arrested, he was to immediately destroy the slip—the evidence. "Try not to get caught with the slip," Ralph drummed into his controllers' heads, who, in turn, preached the same gospel to the runners.

When a runner was arrested, Ralph needed to know *exactly* where the arrest occurred. Time was of the essence in order to make the right connections to *fix* things. Who were Ralph's connections? In this operation, not city hall, *but the cop on the beat.* (Some were on Ralph's payroll; others were not easily corrupted.) Ralph would contact the sergeant or captain, to discover who the arresting officer was, and then would promptly reach him for a fix. Once the fix was on, the arresting cop modified his testimony at the hearing. When questioned about the betting slip, he said that he found it NEAR the runner; he was never to say he found the slip ON the runner. The case was then naturally dismissed. When a fix was impossible, the runner could receive up to ten days and, occasionally, from two to six months in jail. Those were the risks. In these cases, Ralph assisted the runner's family—providing money for food and bills—until he was released.

People from all walks of life played the game of chance. One could find a runner anywhere—in a bar, restaurant, tea parlor, social club, anywhere people congregated. After choosing one's favorite numbers, any amount of money could be placed with him; even a nickel was good in those days. The runner wrote up betting slips for "win," place," or "show," keeping one copy for the house. If someone bet a large sum of money (and odds were great), Ralph turned the bet over to a different outfit with a bigger bank, in case the number would hit. He lessened his own gains, but if the number did come through, he had protected himself against a bustout (bankruptcy).

Ralph obtained the winning numbers mostly from the race wire (the trotters) at Belmont, Saratoga, Jamaica, and the Aqueduct in Long Island. For the Italian immigrants, he used the Italian lotteries and Italian numbers—based on the Italian stock market. The calls to Italy, however, became expensive and were soon easily traced by the police. Ralph dropped that source and stuck to the race wires. As usual, he learned fast, and his operation became very successful. Operating speakeasies, numbers, and the rest, Ralph thought it wise to hire a bodyguard.

Johnny Orzo was a big guy, over six feet, with a powerful build. He was a good dresser and walked in a light, nonchalant manner. When he wasn't wearing a hat, he constantly ran his hand through his abundant mop of brown hair, which matched the color of his doleful eyes. Because of his height and build, one could call him attractive. HE thought he was! The only thing about him that irritated Ralph was when he tried to imitate Charlie's laugh. Somehow, it rubbed Ralph the wrong way.

One afternoon, as Ralph was leaving his office building, he spotted two plainclothesmen talking to Johnny. Apparently, they were looking for Ralph because he could see Johnny trying to signal him away. He succeeded in shaking the detectives, just as Ralph casually sauntered up to him.

"What happened, Johnny?" Ralph teased.

"For Chrissake, Ralph . . . beat it. They might be back any minute," he muttered.

Ralph laughed. Johnny was around thirty-two but acted ten years younger—like an overgrown kid. He wasn't very bright, often a pathetic dolt. All he loved to do was eat, smoke cigars, and go with girls—pretty much in that order. Johnny could be a real hardhead (at times a troublemaker with no heart); otherwise, he was pleasant, a sort of schizo. Ralph, at any rate, knew how to handle him.

"Relax, Johnny," Ralph chuckled. "Don't be so naïve, man . . . They just wanted to get staked . . . that's all. Come on . . . Let's get some lunch!"

Johnny gave him an absent look, rolled his eyes toward heaven, and followed Ralph.

Later that evening, the plainclothesmen returned, and Ralph paid his dues. That's the way it went. Graft was everywhere. Everyone in those days was in on the take.

It was early spring; the fresh breezes, slightly crisp and fragrant after the last snow had disappeared, permeated the air as a blithe, exhilarating spirit. Ralph and Tony stood in front of the Brent Hotel, deeply inhaling the breezy, invigorating bouquet, when they saw a mutual friend strolling up the street.

"Betty," Ralph called cheerfully. "What brings you downtown?" As if Ralph didn't know.

"Hi . . . Ralph . . . Tony. I went to a matinee to see George's latest film. Wanted to see it again . . . but can't today," she replied wistfully.

"Ah yeah, George . . . He's great, isn't he?" Ralph responded, feeling sorry for her. The George she was referring to was George Raft, her ex-boyfriend. Betty and George had been lovers and had lived together downtown, before he went to Hollywood. She was still pining for him and found solace in watching his films over and over again—sometimes two and three times a sitting. Ralph thought it was such a waste. Betty was a very beautiful girl, with shiny black hair, expressive dark eyes, and a terrific figure. George Raft was no fool; he was a connoisseur where women were concerned. With the latter attribute, plus the fact that George was a great dancer, an easy friendship had sparked between him and Ralph. They frequented the same dance halls and sometimes made a night of dancing around Manhattan, enjoying wine, women, and song. George was born on New York's West Side and knew most of the boys from the dance halls. It was rumored that the racketeer, Owney Madden, helped George break into the movies. In those days, an abundance of talented people were just waiting to be discovered.

Ralph tried to convince Betty that with her good looks, she could easily begin a new life, but she replied sincerely that she needed time. While Ralph and Tony stood reminiscing with her about George, two well-dressed men approached them.

"Excuse me," said the taller huskier man politely, "are you Ralph?"

"I am," Ralph replied, curious. Neither man looked familiar, but he waited to hear more.

"A couple of friends from Detroit are here . . . and they'd like to see you," the same man added convincingly.

Ralph did have friends in Detroit, so he thought it was perfectly logical that they wanted to see him; perhaps they needed assistance in some matter. It was Ralph's way—sometimes ingenuous.

"Oh, yeah? Where are they staying?" Ralph asked casually.

"At the Graystone Hotel on Ninety-third and Broadway." It was always the taller man speaking. The other man, on the short side, resembled a real moron.

"Okay," agreed Ralph. "Tony, let's go."

They said their good-byes to Betty, then followed the two men to their car, not suspecting anything underhanded, especially since Ralph had no quarrel with anyone. Once at the Graystone, they rode up in the elevator without speaking. As Ralph casually watched the floor numbers, he began to wonder about the men from Detroit. They stopped at the fifth floor, and without breaking silence, Ralph and Tony followed their guides. They approached a room down the corridor. The shorter man knocked lightly. A nondescript man of medium height opened the door. Ralph noticed another fellow inside but didn't recognize either one of them. Just as an alarm bell went off in his head, Ralph felt a gun being shoved hard into his ribs; he and Tony were fiercely pushed into the room.

"Well, this is a surprise!" Ralph remarked sarcastically.

"Yeah, ain't it!" the exclamation was uttered by a man waiting inside, a man whom Ralph assumed to be the leader. He was a homely man, wearing a suit that had seen better days, and had a certain air of arrogance about him. Without further conversation, he quickly ordered his henchmen to blindfold both captives. Ralph and Tony were dragged across the room and roughly shoved into two separate chairs. Their legs and arms were tied to them and their mouths taped. It was a first experience for Ralph; he was angry with himself for falling into such a stupid trap. It was even too late to create a rumpus in the hotel. Ralph was convinced it was a phony setup because if someone were to be killed, he wouldn't be taken to a hotel room to be murdered. That would be risky since names, even if false, had to be registered at the front desk. Ralph racked his brain, trying to figure it out.

"I suppose you're wondering why we brought you guys here?" the leader said toughly. "I'll get to the point . . . fast. It's Wild Bill we want. We know he's a good friend of yours, Ralph. He's worth a lot of money . . . and we want you to finger him for us!"

These unknown characters had plenty of nerve, thought Ralph. Bill Ercolini was more than a good friend; he was tied to Ralph through relatives. Although they did not frequently pal around with each other, there were times when Bill, Tony, and Ralph attended the races together at Saratoga. But the kidnappers were right about one thing—Bill was a millionaire. He was also the finance man for one of the boys' combinations downtown. Snow, however, would have to cover the equator before Ralph would finger a near relative. *These rats don't know what's in store for them, as soon as I get loose,* Ralph fumed inwardly.

"We'll leave tomorrow morning . . . You'll have all night to think about it," the leader's raspy voice announced.

Ralph and Tony were kept as hostages all night—without a thing to eat or drink in that awkward, tiring position, completely ignored, as if they didn't exist. The captors, two at a time, took turns guarding them. During the night, in the darkness behind his blindfold, Ralph kept his ears perked up to try to determine what was happening around them. About three o'clock in the morning, two of the men returned, complaining to the others that they had been in an automobile accident. Ralph surmised they probably had two cars on the street and wondered which one was damaged.

"We let the guy go . . . because we didn't want to stop and, maybe, bump into the cops . . ." It was the tall husky man talking. "We had to tie the Oakland bumper with a rope . . . so it wouldn't hit the ground and make a racket . . ."

"Yeah . . . you did right. We don't want to attract attention," the leader replied.

Ralph now knew that once he freed himself, he would look for an Oakland car with a tied bumper. He forced himself not to doze in order to hear every word spoken between the small-time hoods. Ralph began contemplating his revenge. He was convinced he was involved with amateurs, but they would definitely have to pay for this offense. They'd been reading too many Dick Tracy comic strips, mused Ralph sardonically.

At long last, the hoods untied Ralph's hands and feet, removed the blindfold, and brusquely ripped off the mouth tape. Ralph's lips smarted, but he didn't move a muscle. There were guns pointed at his and Tony's head. Ralph glanced at his hapless companion and wasn't surprised to find him trussed up and blindfolded as before. Then he understood; Tony was to remain as hostage. Ralph's watch showed ten o'clock in the morning.

"Okay . . . let's get a move on," said the boss man. "No funny stuff, Ralph . . . Otherwise, we bump off your friend Tony here. You can kiss him good-bye!"

"Don't worry," snarled Ralph. "That'll never happen." Then, addressing Tony, he added, "Don't worry, Tony. I'll be back for you!"

The slovenly boss took the wheel of the Oakland while his tall husky crony pushed Ralph into the backseat, climbing in beside him. Wild Bill's garage was on Fifty-third Street near Broadway, but Ralph told them to park the car a block away on Fifty-fourth Street. Unbeknownst to his kidnappers, Ralph wanted to walk there, specifically on the left side of the street. There was a reason; he had to gain time for his next move. As the two men flanked Ralph on each side, they slowly began approaching the garage. From a distance, Ralph spotted Wild Bill talking to a group of friends. With him was another Bill—William "Big Bill" Dwyer, a tough Irishman who had received his training on the waterfront. He was one of the pioneer bootleggers in New York and a very good friend of Owney Madden and Frank Costello. Not a man with whom to tangle. Ralph also saw Frank Erickson, a stout, friendly Scandinavian and one of the most important bookmakers in New York. Ralph remembered him first as a waiter in Coney Island—before Erickson met Rothstein who taught him the ropes. Sometime later, Erickson helped organize the race wire and subsequently formed his silent partnership with Costello.

The three men were chatting with Polly Adler, the one and only madam of the times. She had the biggest plushest bordello in New York with the most beautiful girls. Nothing less than one hundred dollars a crack at her place. She ran a prosperous business. Her celebrated house on Central Park West was host to the most famous politicians, high police officials, millionaires, and, of course, to the kingpins of the underworld. But to look at her, one realized Polly had never been a beauty queen. She was short, rather hefty, and at sixty-five, her features had hardened, giving her a somewhat masculine look. Polly was however a shrewd businesswoman, known for her great sense of humor, and she enjoyed a marvelous rapport with the boys.

The group glanced down the street and noticed Ralph, with his face tightly drawn, coming toward them with two strange men, one on each side of him.

"Ralph's in trouble," observed Wild Bill, and the others agreed.

Suddenly, Ralph swung at the tall man on his left, his steel fists slamming him up against the store window. Before the tall man's crony could react to Ralph's lightning attack, he felt his jawbone splinter beneath Ralph's powerful blow. Grunting in pain, he staggered and tripped, falling against a parked car, then fell to the curb. Ralph's friends came running, breathless, but Ralph barred them from coming any closer and shouted, "Let 'em alone, let 'em go! They've got Tony at the Graystone."

Behind Ralph, the two hoodlums were scrambling to safety, but Ralph raced toward the garage with Wild Bill at his heels; the others followed. Ralph and Bill jumped into one of the cars and, with screeching tires, sped out of the garage. Upon reaching the Graystone, they rushed up to the fifth floor, but the room was empty.

"They must have been tipped off," exclaimed Ralph.

"Okay, Ralph," Bill said coldly, "let's go back to the garage and mobilize!"

"I-if they touch Tony . . . if they do anything to him—" Ralph stammered, and his complexion was ash pale.

"Come on, kid . . . don't worry," Bill interrupted. "We'll find them."

Ralph rushed to leap into Bill's car, and they soared back into the garage. Bill shouted to his attendants, "Get two cars ready—fast!" Meanwhile, Big Bill and Frank (Erickson) had called in some troops who were waiting in the garage.

"Load up, you guys," Bill ordered. "We've got some serious business to take care of!"

Nine men were equally divided into three cars. Ralph informed them of the Oakland car with the tied bumper, and he drove the lead car. They cruised up, down, and around downtown Manhattan all afternoon. By five o'clock, Ralph was desperate.

Wild Bill sat next to him, cursing, "So those sons of bitches wanted to kidnap me! They're as good as dead!"

But Ralph's mind was on Tony—his bosom buddy. He couldn't let those amateur bastards finish him off! He swerved around a corner and suddenly spotted the Oakland on Chatham Square, approaching Broadway. Throngs of people were crossing the street. Ralph stomped on the gas pedal, pulled alongside the Oakland, then cut directly in front of it, forcing it to mount the curb. A second car raced to its side while a third blocked its rear end. The Oakland was trapped. The kidnappers panicked; one flung open his door and tried to escape, but the boys grabbed him.

Again, Ralph shouted to let him go. "I want the boss man behind the wheel!" he yelled.

Hearing Ralph's directive, one of the boys jumped into the Oakland's front seat, shoving his pistol into the driver's ribs, while another pushed in from the opposite door, crushing the driver between them. Still another climbed into the backseat, just to be on the safe side. Then they all drove away like speed demons, racing to get away before the cops arrived on the scene.

"Ralph, drive to the Mulberry Street Garage," Bill hissed.

Ralph nodded. It was another one of Bill's garages, which he used for such happenings. Ralph was a whiz behind the wheel, but the others, screeching and reeling at high speed, kept close behind him. As soon as they wheeled into the garage, the doors were slammed shut, and everyone stepped out of the various cars. Death in his eyes, Ralph propelled his ashen-faced captive into the office. The terrified man stood motionless as Ralph frisked him up and down.

"Well . . . well . . . look what we have here!" he remarked caustically, bouncing in the palm of his hand the gun extracted from the man's inside pocket. "A real fine piece! Why, it must be brand new—so nice and shiny!" Ralph sneered contemptuously. "Let's see if you've used it yet." Inwardly, Ralph was trembling, wondering whether Tony was still alive, but his hands did not betray him. He gently released the clip. All bullets were there.

Just then, one of Ralph's boys dashed in, panting. "Ralph . . . we got word that Tony's okay! They turned him loose . . . Guess they got scared. He's on his way down!" The knot in Ralph's chest disappeared, but he didn't soften; the bum in front of him had something coming.

"O-K-A-Y . . . ," Ralph drawled with ominous deliberation. "I'm sure Tony will enjoy watching your funeral with us." He dragged out a chair and forced the panic-stricken man into it. "Tie his hands behind the chair," Ralph ordered, placing the gun on the desk beside him. "And wash this guy's car . . . 'cause we're gonna leave this bastard in the rumble seat in front of his house in Detroit!"

The kidnapper sat shocked, never uttering a sound.

"Now, I'll show you how to be a real gangster," Ralph remarked sarcastically. "First, you're gonna eat a good meal, since it's your last . . . That's one of the rules . . ."

The captive's eyes bulged.

"Okay, Mr. Big Shot," Ralph persisted, "why'd you want to kidnap Bill? Didn't you know who he was?"

"Well . . . I heard he was a *good fella*," the man reluctantly murmured.

Bill stood impassively, letting Ralph handle the whole show. When Ralph heard the words *good fella*, he went wild. All the tension he had managed to control suddenly became unleashed. Like a madman, he snatched up the pistol and whacked it across the man's mouth, sensing the crunching of teeth. Instantly, blood streaked down the man's chin and spattered his shirt. He was squinting with pain. Ralph took a deep breath and eased off, calling for a basin of water for the man to wash out his mouth.

Ralph's sudden brutality stemmed from the unwritten rules of the underworld. In this case, it was *respect.* If the man had said he was only trying to make money, Ralph would have been more sympathetic. Everyone is entitled to make a buck. But the aspiring hoodlum wanted to hurt Bill, heard he was a good fella—that was the wrong thing to say. One never touched the *good fellas.* In the rackets, before a guy did anything, he first found out who his victim was, to what outfit he belonged, and who his connected friends were. That way, he would never find himself in deep trouble.

All eyes were fixed on Ralph, waiting for his next move. Ralph realized the man in the chair was a pathetic sight, but he wasn't through with his lesson. After the boys cleaned the hapless man up a bit, Ralph launched into a stern interrogation.

"Where do you come from?" Ralph demanded.

"Brooklyn," the man groaned.

"Brooklyn?" exclaimed Ralph. "Buddy, I thought you said you were from Detroit?"

"No . . . I'm from Brooklyn," came the hoarse admission.

"Who do you know in Brooklyn?" Ralph badgered.

"Happy Maiori," the man responded weakly.

Ralph's eyebrows lifted. "Who else do you know there?"

"Bugsy Goldstein."

"You know Bugsy?" Ralph retorted, and the weakened man nodded without a word. "Well . . . well . . ."

Ralph's keen ears heard the door open. He turned to see Tony leaning against it with a smile of triumph. Tony had quietly slipped in, not wanting to interrupt Ralph's act. They exchanged a salute of camaraderie, and Ralph smiled, realizing how fond he was of the handsome son of a gun.

"Tony, do me a favor," Ralph called affectionately. "Charlie's at Ferrara's Café . . . Go tell him our gangster friend here knows Happy Maiori and Bugsy Goldstein. Tell him to get hold of one of them . . . to come down here."

Tony grinned. "Right, Ralph . . . leave it to me."

Charlie, however, had already been informed. The first thing he said to Tony was, "Tell Ralph to be calm . . . not to do anything rash!" He would send word to Joe Adonis to contact Happy. Adonis made the call, and Happy immediately showed up at the restaurant.

Meanwhile, Tony, who was famished after his ordeal, returned to the garage with sandwiches, pizzas, and wine for everyone. Ralph's rumbling stomach reminded him how the bastards had starved them, but he had promised the man a meal. He allowed the suffering fool to be untied to enjoy some food.

About an hour and a half later, in walked Happy Maiori. Charlie had had someone drive him to the garage. "Hi, Ralph . . . boys." He shook hands with Tony and Bill; then, extending his hand to Ralph, he exclaimed, "Ralph . . . what the hell is goin' on?"

"Hi, Happy, do you know this punk here?" Ralph asked, pointing to the hoodlum with disgust.

"Yeah, he's a crumb from the city sanitation department."

The man with the gaping front teeth began to plead desperately, "Happy . . . please save me . . . Please, please save me for my two children. I beg you . . . please!"

"I'm sorry. I can't do anything," Happy answered apathetically. "You're in Ralph's hands now. You've done it too raw." Happy's decision was final.

"Happy . . . please . . . think of my family!" the man supplicated.

"You should have thought of that first," Happy replied flatly. "You shouldn't have done anything like this. You always ask before you do anything, so you don't get yourself in no trouble." Happy was not about to give absolution. He turned to Ralph and said, "Do whatever you want, Ralph." Then he stood aside.

The man began to sob, and Ralph grimaced. He just couldn't stand tears. Another message arrived from Charlie, telling Ralph to hold off (not to do anything) and to bring the man down to Ferrara's. Ralph stared at the distraught man in the chair, waiting to get clobbered at any moment, and he softened. After all, Ralph was no killer.

"Look here," Ralph stated toughly. "I'll say this in front of Happy and the others. Then, after . . . somebody else . . . will tell you. Just because Happy's here . . . I'm going to leave you . . . like on parole. Don't let me ever catch you trying to make a crooked dollar . . . because I'll come and get you in your own house!"

Happy clapped Ralph's shoulder, indicating his approval, and left.

Wild Bill begrudgingly agreed.

Everyone went to Ferrara's where Charlie was patiently waiting in the back room. Charlie turned to Ralph sympathetically and said, "Ralph . . . shake hands with him . . ."

"Charlie," Ralph replied, asserting himself, "I will . . . only on one condition . . . That he goes back to working honestly . . . that he doesn't try to be a racketeer anymore, because he's not made for it!"

Acting very much the judge, Charlie turned to the would-be gangster with the missing front teeth and quietly stated, "Give Ralph your word of honor . . . and shake hands on it!" Then to Happy, he added, "See that this guy stays in line . . ." Happy nodded in agreement.

Everyone shook hands. The kidnapping affair had ended. Years later, Ralph heard that the man whom he'd brutalized had gone so straight that even if he saw a wallet or pocketbook lying on the ground, he wouldn't pick it up for fear he would be accused.

Ralph laughed to himself. He had put something like the fear of God into the man. Hah! In his way, he had saved another soul.

CHAPTER EIGHTEEN

"Ralphy . . . if you need any slot machines, just go up to my place and take whatever you want!" Frank generously offered his young friend.

If there was anyone else, besides Charlie, whom Ralph admired, it was Frank Costello. Leaving his office in the Browning Building, Ralph met him by chance, and the seasoned, debonair Frank invited Ralph to a coffee break. Ralph considered Frank, fifteen years older than him—a fascinating, intelligent, enterprising, and successful businessman, very much in charge.

Born on January 26, 1891, in Lauropoli (a small Calabrian town facing the Ionian Sea in Southern Italy), Frank, at the age of five, left with his mother and brother to join his father, Luigi Castiglia, already in America, who had opened a small grocery store. The family had settled in East Harlem—where the slums had already begun to blight the original beauty of the area and where other immigrants, in a similar plight, fought for their existence. Frank experienced the same difficulties growing up, as all other youngsters in the neighborhood, but he was a natural to succeed. He simply used his brains and innate qualities as a low-key convincing orator—a born politician and diplomat. It is no small wonder that he became known for his political intrigues in the underworld and dubbed a "prime minister." In his late twenties, Frank formed a company that created the first punchboards sold in drugstores, candy stores, and even in stores selling school supplies. The prize at that time was a pretty little doll. It wasn't long before he was making big money—money which he invested in real estate. This was before the controversial Volstead Act was passed; after which, Frank rose rapidly to new heights with his bootlegging empire.

"Frank, I appreciate your offer. Maybe I'll give it a try someday," replied Ralph gratefully. "But it's more complicated . . . takes more time."

"Listen, Ralph . . . if you need any help, just let me know," answered a congenial Frank.

"Okay . . . I'll let you know . . . thanks." Smiled Ralph. He really liked Frank. Apart from everything else, he had a great personality—an advisor to many.

Ralph later did go into slot machines on his own, but the racket did not appeal to him. Too many problems involved, as far as he was concerned. Furthermore, Ralph's worst enemy was the twenty-four-hour clock; his major efforts and energies were necessary to succeed in the numbers racket. Ralph eventually dropped the machines.

After leaving Frank, Ralph entered into his Cadillac and headed toward Brooklyn. Suddenly, there it was again—a police siren. The cops had spotted his car and sped up alongside. "Pull over!" one cop shouted to Ralph.

"What is it this time?" Ralph asked with resignation.

"House robbery," the officer replied while examining Ralph's license.

"House robbery? Hey, Officer, I never robbed a house in my life," squealed Ralph.

"Yeah, tell it to the judge," was the sarcastic response.

In his cell, Ralph had time to think things over. He had overcome his virtuous ideals about an honest job, but without an occupation, he was left wide open for police harassment. It was his third arrest. The first was the cab incident, which cost him his hack license. Then in 1930, it was his two-seater Caddy sports car that attracted the attention of the patrolling police. Ralph was stopped, interrogated, and arrested on the spot for grand larceny. It was a routine roundup, but with his classy car, Ralph looked like one of the local hoods. Ralph remembered he was taken to the Bath House precinct in Brooklyn and booked. Grand larceny was a grave offense. He was not immediately discharged, and it took Ralph's lawyer, Sammy Rosenblat, to arrange the $25,000 bail. He was released about a week later.

But it didn't matter. If one's case was dismissed, or discharged, that person's name went on the blotter; and from then on, Ralph had a police record. Ralph had become a hood—a gangster to the police. As a result, he found himself again in a cell on another bum rap.

He recalled how his mother fretted about these arrests, how he tried to explain in simple terms for her the arrest procedures. Ralph clarified the words for her—*dismissed* and *discharged*. When someone is arrested for a crime, the police have to have evidence against him; someone has to point him out, identify him. (For that, the lineup is sometimes used.) The prosecutor compiles and presents his evidence to the judge for examination. It is the judge's prerogative to dismiss the case before it even comes to a hearing or trial stage—at which point the accused could be automatically discharged. If the judge orders a hearing or trial, the accused could also be discharged at that time, if found innocent. The case is *dismissed*. The person is *discharged*. Agnes tried very hard to understand.

Ralph also touched on what was meant by *habeas corpus*. If one was found guilty and is in prison awaiting appeal, he has a recourse, through his lawyer, to a writ of habeas corpus. It is a final personal appeal (an order obtained from the court) that allows one to appear in person before the judge to plead his case. The judge, based on the evidence presented, can either set him free or send him back to prison—as he deems appropriate. If the judge has been prejudiced or "bought," the accused can forget about his release. If, on the other hand, one were to be set free, the court's prosecutor could always, depending on new evidence, take out a warrant for his rearrest.

Charlie had tried a writ of habeas corpus a few times—twice in 1936 during the commotion Dewey had caused in Hot Springs and Little Rock, Arkansas, trying to extradite Charlie to New York for the prostitution rap. It had been touch and go for a while, but Charlie's lawyers were outwitted by Dewey, and a writ of habeas corpus had failed. In a final attempt, Charlie had tried to use the writ of habeas corpus soon after he arrived in Dannemora Prison, but that also failed.

Of course, it was important to have a good lawyer, as well as close friendships—contacts with the bail bondsmen. Most of them at that time in New York City were Jewish—although many of the "boys" had their own finance men who handled such matters. If a man had connections (belonged to a combination), that service was free. The bondsmen received anywhere from 10 to 15 percent of the full amount—depending. Ralph was an independent, but he had many friends who helped resolve these types of problems. He never paid the full amount.

When Charlie was jailed in Little Rock, Dewey, after much finagling, was able to convince the judge to set bail at $200,000; but once Charlie was in New York, Dewey hit an all-time record by setting his bail at $350,000. He wanted to make sure Charlie wasn't going anywhere!

Agnes was not only a strong, devoted mother, but also an intelligent woman. As well-informed as she was, she could not resolve the dilemma with Ralph. In her heart, she had never reconciled herself to Ralph's choice of life; but outwardly, she avoided causing him further problems. To Agnes, Ralph was still the same wonderful, generous, and attentive son—and a loving father to his Joey. Once Agnes had lectured Ralph, telling him he was a grown man and, therefore, knew his risks. If ever he was found guilty, he would have to take his just punishment.

Recalling his mother's words, Ralph resolved to become involved again in something legitimate—if for no other reason than to keep the cops off his back. Five days later, he was discharged from the robbery indictment; and several months later, he followed through with his resolution. At the start of 1932, he became an investor in a trucking company—the Bayard Carton Company, located in downtown New York. The company had four trucks, which collected ashes and rubbish around the city on an independent basis. They also obtained a license from the city to collect garbage. Ralph was put on the company's payroll, and was instrumental in developing the company's growth.

In the spring of the same year, Ralph decided, in concert with his brother, Armand, to open a nightclub in Coney Island for the summer months only. They called it Reilly's Tavern, a misleading name for two Italians. Reilly's served the best drinks and boasted a floor show with eighteen strippers and a star attraction. It became the jumping-off place for the summer where many of Ralph's friends became habitués. With two new enterprises, Ralph reorganized his life, hoping to avoid further clashes with the police.

One rather hot and muggy night, Ralph, somewhat restless, cruised down to Reilly's. He parked his car, greeted the doorman, who doubled as a bouncer (to discourage carousers, to break up a fracas), and entered the club. He spotted his brother, Armand, with Ralph "Bottles" Capone and Capone's cousin, Willie Fischetti, at a front row table waiting for him. At that moment, the lights dimmed, so he silently slipped into a chair beside them to watch the show. The curtains slowly parted, and eighteen chorus girls appeared—arms linked, kicking their shapely legs to the lively music. They squealed in unison, turned, thrust out their buttocks, shuffled around, formed a long chorus line, and, finally, separated down the middle to usher in the leading lady. Ralph could feel an adrenalin rush as he beheld a very beautiful girl—slender figure, with reddish blonde hair, green eyes, and a seductive smile. *What a beauty,* thought Ralph. *Strictly show business material—a winner.* The music switched to her song, and her sequined dress glistened as she moved her body gracefully, softly, in rhythm with the music—with expertise and class. *No bones in that lady,* mused Ralph.

The audience applauded wildly for Mickey Dexter as the curtains were drawn. She came out and graciously bowed to the crowd, then disappeared. Unbeknownst to Ralph, Mickey had also spotted him, her absentee boss. She was intrigued and eager to meet him. She deliberately passed his table on her way to the bar, but Ralph, from the corner of his eye, saw her coming. He casually stood up, slipped a twenty dollar bill into her hand, and whispered, "Meet me at the Limehouse in Chinatown on Marx Street around four thirty." She nodded and discreetly left.

After several drinks, the three men rose to leave without Armand, who remained to close shop. It was about three in the morning. The streets were practically deserted. They had no trouble making it to the Limehouse in New York's Chinatown in about seven minutes (from

Coney Island, that was record speed). Bottles, Willy, and Ralph went in and treated themselves to Chinese spareribs, discussing business until Mickey arrived.

Ralph discovered that Mickey was not only beautiful, but a very serious young lady. She was working to support her son, a few years older than Ralph's Joey, and thus, they had discovered a common bond—raising their sons without partners. Ralph couldn't resist Mickey's charm and began dating her steadily. After a few months, the infatuation wore off, ending the affair as quickly as it began.

The month of October is generally thought of as a prelude to those that follow. Sometimes there are warnings of climatic changes ahead, but sometimes it is difficult to predict, surprising even the best weather experts. Some believe October is the most beautiful month of autumn, proud of its golden orange, rust-and-red-colored leaves sprawled in layers on the ground. The hot summer sun has finally retreated to higher levels, cooling the atmosphere. As the year draws to a close, the evenings become rather chilly, and Café Society's beautiful women drape their furs over their elegant evening clothes. Nightlife comes alive again, and despite the Depression, there were enough people who could still afford the luxury of dining out, escaping the harsh realities. But for most, there was no escape.

The police, however, didn't leave Ralph alone. One early morning, returning home from a night with the boys, he made a right turn and found a police car pulling up alongside.

"Pull up to the curb," a stern voice called out.

"Crap," Ralph mumbled. "Here we go again."

Ralph tried to protest, but the policeman had specific orders to take him in. He was booked at the Raymond Street Jail in Brooklyn and charged with burglary. Again in a dreary cell, indulging in self-pity, he looked up to see his brother, Armand, and his lawyer solemnly standing before him. Their faces were so grim, they startled him, and Ralph jumped up.

"What is it? You guys look like you just came from a funeral!" he exclaimed, scarcely expecting the news he was about to hear.

"That's exactly why we're here, Ralph," replied his brother, Armand, sadly. "We have some really bad news for you."

"For Chrissake, what is it?" shouted Ralph, hardly able to contain himself.

"Tony . . . Tony . . . ," babbled Sammy, his lawyer.

"Tony . . . was killed . . . ," interrupted Armand quietly. "Was killed in a freak automobile accident."

"OH . . . NO . . ." Ralph moaned. "Not Tony . . . Chrissake, not Tony!"

"He was driving . . . died instantly," Armand added, watching his brother's face contort with pain.

"No . . . no . . . Tony . . . Tony . . . ," wailed Ralph.

Tony had been driving his 1931 Ford convertible coupe, which he had purchased about six months earlier. It was one of the first cars to be fitted with an automatic shift. Ralph covered his face, bowed his head, trying to conceal the tears that were about to fall. He was completely crushed. Tony had been a very important part of his life. They had been practically inseparable—like Siamese twins. Ralph lost awareness of the present as he thought of Tony, how he would miss his best pal—the way they watched over each other, their joyful camaraderie, the fistfights they had as teenagers, the women they had fought over. He remembered Tony's funny mimicry of a gangster. He'd put a comb through his hair, slip an El Producto cigar out of Ralph's pocket, light up, then shuffle along at Ralph's side with a menacing look on his face. "Oh, Tony," cried Ralph out loud.

Armand and Sammy left Ralph in his grief, silently rocking back and forth on his cot.

Ralph's state of mind worsened the next day when he found himself in a lineup with some of the more notorious men around town: Bugsy Goldstein, Happy Maiori, Frank "the Dasher" Abbandando, and Abe "Kid Twist" Reles. With the first of those three, Ralph was on very friendly terms, but he detested Reles. The others were also surprised to see him in the lineup. Bugsy's real name was Martin. Ralph didn't know how he acquired the name Bugsy. Perhaps it was because he was short and had a pug nose. Bugsy was a heavy gambler, falling knee-deep in debt at times. He also palled around with Phil (Pittsburgh Phil) Strauss, whose reputation was very questionable, to say the least. Happy, whose front was a florist shop, was a good-looking Sicilian, about five foot six, with a smooth face, black hair and eyes, and a warm personality—a happy guy from Brownsville who belonged to the Brooklyn combination. The Dasher was also a friend but rumored to be part of Murder, Inc.

Ralph never had much to say to Abe Reles, just hello and good-bye. He had a nose for people, and Reles was not on his hit parade. Reles was a braggart, always acted like a tough guy out front. He was too neurotic, twisted, a known sex molester—something that turned Ralph off completely. There were many reasons to call Reles "kid twist." Furthermore, he was untrustworthy, and Ralph wasn't surprised when he later heard Reles had become a canary (a stool pigeon).

To say Ralph hated the lineup was an understatement; it destroyed him psychologically every time he climbed to the platform—to stand as if in a theater with hot, bright lights blazing. In the darkness of the audience, there was always someone to yell, "That's him!" Ralph heard his name called. It seemed like a nightmare.

"This is Ralph Liguori. Three arrests prior to this. Occupation: butcher."

A smart-aleck voice from the dark laughed. "Aah, he's the one that likes to chop 'em up!"

Ralph stiffened, and hatred swelled up in him. He felt naked, shorn of his self-respect, pride, dignity. The mere fact that he was in a lineup (especially with these men) led people to believe he *must* be guilty of something.

"Are you sure it's not him?" the wiseacre cop pressed.

"Well, yeah . . . it looks like him." Then the person rescinded. "No . . . no . . . the guy was a little taller."

"Look again . . . Look real hard," the detective urged.

"No . . . No . . . it's not him."

Fortunately, no one pointed out Ralph. The case against him was dismissed, and ten days later, he was released. Ralph was always in a dark mood after one of his arrests. It left him lifeless—together with the news of Tony, which had crushed his heart and soul; he could not snap out of his deep depression.

There would never be anyone like Tony!

CHAPTER NINETEEN

The plainclothesman seated next to Ralph nudged him gently in the ribs with his elbow.

"Hey, Ralph . . . wake up . . . We're almost there," he said.

Ralph had lulled himself to sleep with the *chug-chug*ging, *swoosh-swoosh*ing sounds of the train even though he was sure he had heard an occasional whistle tooting. Drained of emotion, he dozed on the train taking him to Dannemora.

He opened his eyes, rubbing his sore neck, which had awkwardly supported his head against the back cushion. Bleary-eyed, he looked out the window.

"I see the police cars are still with us," Ralph croaked groggily.

The overcautious authorities, having heard that someone might try to spring the prisoners, had instructed the train engineer to keep pace with the police cars patrolling alongside.

"Yeah, well . . . it's almost over. We'll be there in about ten minutes," replied the accommodating detective.

Dannemora is a small town in the Adirondack Mountains—the upper northeast part of New York State, near the Canadian border. A few miles east is Plattsburgh and Lake Champlain, which borders Vermont. The population then was about three thousand people. The penitentiary was commonly known as Dannemora, although its real name is Clinton Prison. The inmates, however, call it Siberia because of its remote location and the long hard, cold winters.

The train had left Sing Sing just north of New York City and took the long route due north.

Ralph heard the screeching of the wheels coming to a halt and watched from the window as the train stopped practically in front of Dannemora. The men were tired after the long ride; they stared at the enormous gray walls, its menacing turrets in the middle of nowhere, and the huge ominous gates. Depression grew deeper than ever. *This, then, is our new home,* thought Ralph.

One side of the tremendous gate was opened to admit them. Ralph glanced around at the walls, one of which jetted out going nowhere. The architectural pattern was more or less a triangle—the far end being interrupted. Here and there, following no particular criteria, stood several red buildings; and far beyond toward a hill, Ralph could see barns and silos from nearby farmhouses. He also noticed a castle-like structure. *Probably headquarters,* he thought. In fact, it was the warden's office. A guard at the gate used a phone and announced the arrival of the new inmates. They were immediately led to the receiving station.

The men went through the usual prison procedures, then stripped off their clothes for their prison uniforms. Reducing a convict to a number was part of the dehumanization process. Ralph became number 24805; Charlie, number 24804; and Davey Betillo, number 24803. The three were taken to the old cell block until the prison authorities decided what to do with them. After two or three weeks, Ralph was assigned to work in the weave factory, Charlie was sent to the laundry, and Davey was placed in the dye shop. (On the average, between sixty and seventy men worked in one shop; some accommodated as many as two hundred.) Ultimately, they were transferred to cell blocks in different wings of the prison. Charlie was taken to a new cell block and was comfortably settled. Ralph went to the A Block, cell number 113; his cell, as well as Davey's, was reasonably adequate. All the cells contained sinks with running water, a toilet, cot, and a locker. The authorities did not want them close together; however, they saw each other three times a day in the mess hall and in the yard for recreation. The three friends never had an argument in all the years they were together in Dannemora.

The reality of their new lives behind bars had hit them hard. They were convicts and had to accustom themselves to prison regimentation. They woke up, ate their meals, worked, played, and slept at the sound of the bell, marching everywhere in neat files. It was an ordinary prison routine. Ralph was up at 7:00 a.m. to wash and dress in time for breakfast at 7:30 a.m., then off to work. Lunch was served at 12:00 noon, and he had half an hour in his cell before returning to work at 1:00 p.m. Work period ceased at 3:00 p.m., and everyone marched back to his cell; out again a half hour later, they marched to the yard for recreation. At 4:30 p.m., he was back in his cell in time to freshen up for dinner at 5:00 p.m. Finally, he returned to his cell at 5:30 p.m. for the night. Ralph had roughly two and a half hours to read, write, whatever, until the bell rang at 8:00 p.m. There was to be complete silence thereafter. And the nights were long! The regime could affect any man if his nerves weren't solid. If a prisoner didn't work during the day, he could go stir-crazy with nothing to do; many went to the mental ward. There were approximately three thousand inmates, and over a thousand were in the hospital—mostly because of their idleness. It was a grave problem with the administration. Ralph was grateful to have his job.

The weekends were different. On Saturday, Ralph worked half a day. He returned to his cell at 12:00 noon to wash and dress for lunch. After lunch, the men were free to do whatever they wished: see a movie, relax in the yard, read in the library, or remain in their cells. Dinner was at five as usual. Naturally, on Sunday, no one worked. Everyone had the right to attend the religious service of his choice: Catholic mass, Hebrew or Protestant services. Otherwise, one could go out to the yard bright and early and stay out all day, except for the lunch break. When a runner called out the religion, the prisoner shouted his assent and waited for the officer to come by to obtain name, number, and cell block. The inmate would then step out of his cell to march together with the others and the escorting officer. They marched "with God at their side." The mass, like the other services, was held in the prison auditorium, which had seen better days. The priest used a makeshift altar, which was moved to one side when not in use. Ralph could not feel that he was in the house of God.

All prisoners had an opportunity to obtain medical attention. A doctor was always available. A different runner would walk by the cells, shouting, "Doctor call!" And the inmates came forward to present their data. A doctor's slip was written up, and if the prisoner worked, a shop excuse slip as well. An officer in charge inspected all the slips before signing them for approval. Everything in prison was checked and double-checked.

While the prisoners were in the mess hall, guards checked suspicious cells for irregularities. Everyone's laundry was also inspected. A runner went by rolling a huge container in which the inmates threw their dirty laundry, which was later scrutinized. Further, when an inmate cleaned and swept out his cell, he had to throw his rubbish into a huge box, which a hall guard pushed around. That too was carefully examined. They were always looking for hidden messages.

Who was a runner? He was an inmate selected by various officers throughout the prison to do their bidding—run their errands, help them in small chores, and run messages. Every shop had a runner—usually someone who was serving a short prison term. The runners had a special pass, which was signed by the screw (officer) everywhere he went. Some became stoolies. One had to be careful!

Ralph never turned in his dirty laundry. He threw it down the chute directly to Charlie, who personally took charge of Ralph's clothes. Not even in prison did Charlie and Ralph lose their clothes fetish. They had to be spotlessly clean. Ralph's shirts and trousers were all very well pressed by Charlie. Sometimes, Ralph would tease Charlie about the way he had pressed his shorts. It was all in good fun, but then, Charlie was a good sport. He was reasonably happy in the laundry because it wasn't long before he had things running smoothly—the way he wanted—with everyone. Charlie was in the laundry until the day he was transferred. He never worked in the library as some people have erroneously thought. Charlie, however, did visit the library as Ralph did—to do research and to read his favorite books.

The laundry was Charlie's haven. He established his own kitchen facilities, unobtrusively to be sure, in a corner of the laundry where he cooked his spaghetti and sauce. He had become bored with the mess hall chow like the rest, especially Ralph. Charlie was a terrific cook! Outside friends kept him supplied with spaghetti, canned tomatoes, and other foodstuff. He had more privileges than most, primarily because he had a very nice keeper whose name was McCurry—a man who respected Charlie and treated him very well. Ralph's keeper's name was Smith; later it was a Mr. Brown. Both men, however, were very strict. Ralph was also well respected because he stuck to his credo of minding his own business. He felt it was the best way to endure a prison term. Ralph was not looking for trouble. All he wanted was to get the hell out!

Prison life was not easy, but Ralph and Charlie had not lost hope of beating the rap; their appeals were ever present in their minds. As for the outside world, Ralph had to give up all of his independent enterprises. That was the price he paid for not belonging to a combination—a family. Once out of prison, he would have to start from scratch. He did worry about his son, Joey, and his family; and of course, he thought of his lovely Dotty. Charlie, on the other hand, had many interests in New York and was still boss of his organization. That had not changed. There were many reasons for him to remain determined to be released. He was needed on the outside.

For superficial conversations, sports, and fun, Charlie and Ralph joined their friends out in the yard. It was called the Big Yard because it was as huge as an Olympic stadium. Charlie held court at the far end, up on a hill. It was perfect because he could see what was happening at all times. Davey Betillo was always with them, as well as a close circle of friends from New York. They had a closely knit clique of about twenty-five inmates, but they would include anyone who appeared friendly and peaceful. All of this meant, however, that when Charlie and Ralph wanted to talk privately, they had to go elsewhere. Charlie chose the hospital where they had more of an opportunity to be alone.

One day, early in August, Charlie asked Ralph to meet him in the hospital the next day. He wanted to talk to him. As arranged, Ralph went out on sick call the following morning and met Charlie. The hospital was not a pretty scene. Men were there who were literally going buggy;

some walked around like zombies; some talked to themselves. All were stir-crazy. Some inmates had gone berserk after spending time in the icebox (solitary confinement). There were also those who just wanted a change of pace from the monotonous daily routine. Ralph and Charlie were huddled together, waiting for the doctor.

"Ralph, I want to tell you what's happening . . . ," Charlie whispered. "I have a new lawyer, James M. Noonan of Albany . . . used to handle a few things for Dutch Schultz. I'm having him petition a writ of habeas corpus for me . . . at the Clinton County Courthouse. We're basing it on the unconstitutionality of the Joinder Law—like our lawyers always said during the trial. I'm taking a stab at it . . . ," Charlie added firmly.

Ralph silently nodded his approval. He knew that if it didn't work, Charlie would continue with the direct appeal of the verdicts.

"And . . . if I'm lucky, Ralph," Charlie continued softly, "it will set the precedent for you . . . and the rest of the boys."

"Charlie," Ralph answered, "you know I'm with you all the way. All I can say is . . . I hope you make it out . . . But, you know, that Dewey bastard won't take it sitting down."

"Yeah . . . I know . . . but I have to try. We'll see what happens. Our freedom fight is just beginning!" Charlie vowed, resolute.

The doctor breezed in, and suddenly, Ralph and Charlie went into their act of backaches and stomach pains for him.

On August 12, Clinton County judge James M. Croake granted Charlie's writ of habeas corpus, setting the hearing for August 24. There was a lot of hubbub in the warden's castle when Sheriff Rudolph LaChappelle served the order to Warden Thomas Murphy for Charlie's appearance in court. It was exciting news. Charlie would go to Plattsburgh for the hearing. He learned what was happening immediately because he had his stoolies (runners). Charlie was always up on everything. Everyone wished him good luck that last day in the yard. Warden Murphy was a pleasant person, but he had his orders.

Dramatic, tenacious Dewey claimed that he had a tip from the underworld that there might be trouble—that Charlie might be sprung—and pressured everyone for heavy guard protection. Under those circumstances, Warden Murphy was obliged to send four automobiles with prison guards to escort the van in which Charlie, in his prison grays, was handcuffed to a guard. That, however, was nothing compared to what Charlie found in Plattsburgh. Detectives, policemen, and state troopers were on duty in the courtroom corridors. Everyone was searched for weapons. Dewey had *again* created the atmosphere he wanted, but he did not appear on the scene. He sent his chief assistant, Jacob Rosenblum, who was assisted by Attorney General Bennett's staff.

Attorney Noonan, in Charlie's petition, claimed that the amendments to the vice laws did not become effective until April 9, 1936; whereas the criminal acts charged to Charlie happened between April 13, 1934, and January 31, 1936. Therefore, he declared it was *ex post facto* and, hence, unconstitutional. He insisted that each count should have been tried separately. (Chapter 328 of the 1936 laws, section 279 of the Code of Criminal Procedure, permits a prosecutor to consolidate indictments to avoid delays in trials—the so-called Joinder Law.)

Dewey's man, Rosenblum, argued that the habeas corpus proceedings were not proper until the appellate courts had decided on the convictions. He stated that merging the counts constituted procedure and did not affect the prisoner's rights.

Judge Croake gave each side ten days to file their briefs. His decision would follow within twenty days, after he had received and studied them. (A judge has the option to order separate trials.)

Dewey was not taking any chances. He was prepared in case Charlie was freed. He had six warrants ready for his rearrest—two of which dealt with income tax evasion.

Charlie returned to Dannemora the next day. Everyone greeted him in the yard as though it was the return of a hero. He was in good spirits and joked about his reception in Plattsburgh.

"I swear I even saw state troopers on the roof of the courthouse," he chuckled.

Then, turning to Ralph, he mentioned one funny remark made by the judge when Rosenblum was mouthing away that Charlie's petition was "vague and indefinite." Rosenblum had added, "If we had tried him on one single count—"

Judge Croake interrupted and quipped, "Then he wouldn't be here today."

But Charlie's mood dampened on September 15. Judge Croake had reached his decision. The *New York Times* headlined: LUCIANA LOSES PLEA FOR RELEASE ON WRIT . . . JUDGE FINDS NO VIOLATION OF CONSTITUTIONAL RIGHTS . . . SUGGESTS "ORDERLY APPEAL." Attorney Noonan stated he would appeal the decision to the Appellate Division in Albany. In fact, he presented the appeal the first week of November, and on the seventeenth of that month, during a night session, he attacked Judge Croake's decision. Rosenblum repeated his arguments that the writ of habeas corpus was groundless. It was obviously too hot a potato for Judge Croake to handle, and the appeal was lost.

Solemnly, Charlie lowered his head, as some of the inmates in the yard went to pay their respects. For the moment, he was defeated and returned to the prison grind.

Ralph and Charlie had become very good friends of the chaplain, Father Booth. He inspired them, and they went to church every Sunday. Father Booth was a man's man, and all the inmates loved him. He had been at Dannemora for many years and was very definitely "pro-con." As he delivered his sermon, his eyes scanned the auditorium, as though he was taking a personal inventory of those present.

After Sunday mass, Charlie cooked in the yard with Ralph assisting; they always invited some friends to take meals to their table. Rarely did they eat in the mess hall on Sunday. Charlie could have easily become a great chef because he possessed that one necessary ingredient—a passion to cook. If, for some reason, he did not cook, he usually instructed Ralph to do the honors. Ralph was not a cook on the same level as Charlie, but as a connoisseur of food, he knew what went with what. One day it rained, and everyone rushed inside, trying to cover their plates, piled high with spaghetti and meatballs. It was a very funny scene.

Joe Zox (Fulton Fish Market) had sent a barrel of fish, and they hid it in the Big Yard about three feet in the ground. Every Sunday they took out a big codfish and made soup. They ate cod for about a month and a half. Many of the convicts asked, "Hey, you guys . . . How d'ya get the fish?" Charlie and Ralph just smiled. They were used to eating well, and *no one* could take that away from them.

It is difficult to explain how some things are done behind prison walls. Regarding clothes, Ralph and Charlie, as well as Davey, wore tailor-made trousers in prison. Ralph had four pairs in his locker. Working in the weave factory, Ralph was able to extricate a piece of pants goods, which he stealthily handed to Betillo who worked in the dye shop. Betillo processed it (shrunk it) and passed it to a friend in the tailor shop. Of course, no one was supposed to notice what was happening. (They could take the goods, but they couldn't be caught in the act.) The last person involved in the process took the trousers out to the yard. Then a few friends would circle closely around until for whomever they were meant put on the trousers. It was their prison modus operandi, and there was never a hitch. The same pattern, more or less, held true for shoes. Someone in the leather shop whipped up handmade shoes for them. It was obvious the three friends took very good care of themselves in their new home.

All the inmates received small change from the administration—enough to buy cigarettes. For those who didn't have any income at all, it was a helping hand. Once a week, farmers came to Dannemora to sell food. A large bag of apples cost a quarter. One could order anything available such as coffee, sugar, and eggs. With coffee, it was the same story. One could buy it, brew it, but couldn't be caught—a difficult feat since coffee has such an aromatic fragrance. Ralph was caught once but charmed himself out of punishment.

Ralph read a great deal in prison—three papers a day (the *New York Journal*, The *Daily Mirror*, and the *Daily News*), books, magazines, anything he could obtain from the library or from some other source. He shared them, particularly the newspapers, with the other inmates. His newspaper traveled from one cell block to another. That was also a neat trick. Ralph tossed it down to his friend a couple of cells away. Then that inmate threw it to another, and he to another, and so on and on. If an inmate happened to be in an upper tier, he hung down a string of some kind holding a magazine, or anything else available. The newspaper was then slipped into the loop, ready to be pulled up. Then it was passed around that tier. Hundreds of prisoners ended up reading the same newspaper; it went on for days and days. Reading helped many of the men who didn't work. They were locked in their cells all day with nothing to do, except for recreation at three thirty in the afternoon. The reading material kept everyone's minds occupied. Ralph spent most of his spare time in the library reading law books; so did Charlie.

About four or five months after his arrival to Dannemora (and with his wounds still fresh from his conviction), Ralph received one of his biggest surprises. A guard came into the weave shop and called out, "Number 24805, Ralph Liguori." Ralph left his bench and was told he was wanted in the warden's office for a special visitor. As he washed and changed into a clean white shirt, Ralph kept wondering who the hell the visitor could be since it was not visiting day, nor was he expecting anyone. The guard escorted him to the warden's office and remained outside the door. As Ralph entered, a distinguished, white-haired gentleman turned from a window to face him.

"Hello, Ralph . . . Do you remember me? I'm Judge McCook."

"Why, Judge," Ralph answered ironically, "how could I *ever* forget you?"

Ignoring the sarcasm, McCook gazed sympathetically at Ralph. "How are they treating you, Ralph?"

"How should they treat me?" Ralph retorted, still shocked by the strange visit. "I'm doing all right under the circumstances."

"You look fine. Fine," the judge replied quietly.

"Judge . . . can I ask you one question? Just one," Ralph remarked rudely. The judge nodded, and Ralph added blatantly, "Do you sleep nights for what you did . . . to Charlie and me?"

Judge McCook's face turned pink, as he stood back sheepishly at the unexpected outcry. He began to respond nervously, "Now . . . Ralph . . . Let's—"

But Ralph heatedly interrupted, "You knew I was telling the truth . . . that I didn't dream up all those things I said on the witness stand!"

"Ralph, don't worry. Everything's going to be all right . . . ," McCook managed to say, somewhat embarrassed.

"What's the use . . . All right . . . all right," Ralph grumbled. Only God, he thought, knew how he felt at that moment.

Judge McCook, showing his discomfort, began mumbling, "If anybody should come up here to see you, Ralph . . . don't talk to anyone . . . especially newspapermen . . . don't talk to anybody." It was a kind of plea.

Ralph stared at him irreverently. So that's why the bastard had come to see him! He definitely was afraid of something!

"Everything's going to come out all right," McCook repeated, patting Ralph lightly on the shoulder. As he walked toward the door, he added paternally, "Behave yourself, Ralph."

"Don't worry, I do," Ralph replied bitingly. Then, more politely, he managed to say, "Thanks for the visit."

And Judge McCook disappeared.

Immediately thereafter, Ralph went out to the yard; and as he approached the hill, he could see Charlie grinning.

"Judge McCook call on you?" he laughed sardonically as Ralph sat down next to him.

"Yeah . . . he called on you too, huh?" Ralph answered disgustedly.

"Yeah . . . he gave me the creeps . . . Has a guilty conscience, I guess. Can't figure it out," Charlie said, shaking his head, wondering why McCook really exposed himself.

They compared notes on the conversations they had with the judge, and both came to the conclusion that McCook was aware they did not have anything to do with the case—that they had been railroaded. Nobody could know it better than him. The two friends decided to take McCook's visit good-naturedly. What else could they do? They were behind prison bars! But Ralph kept repeating to himself, *He knows. The bastard knows I'm innocent!* That night, his mind strayed back to the trial—and to his poor Dotty with all her sufferings.

Christmas was not too far away. It gave Ralph something in which to look forward—to plan and especially to keep his mind occupied. Charlie and Ralph had sent word to their brothers to have friends send packages to Dannemora, which they could share with the rest of the prisoners for Christmas. They had discussed this with the other men out in the yard and urged those who had some influence on the outside to have their friends contact various manufacturers of shirts, socks, shoelaces, scarves, whatever; to send their packages in care of Father Booth. Ralph specifically gave his brother the names and numbers of three or four inmates to whom he could directly send packages—in order to have more to share. The packages began arriving, day after day, and Joe Zox did not forget the fish! Father Booth and his staff had quite a time reorganizing everything—foodstuff and all. Individual bags were made up for each prisoner, regardless of his religion. On Christmas morning, *everyone* received a gift package with maybe a shirt, a couple packs of cigarettes, fruit, cigars, a can of beans or coffee, and various other goodies. The holiday hustle-bustle had picked up everyone's spirits. After Christmas mass, all the inmates went out to the yard, including Father Booth, for a big party. Charlie and Ralph had a huge group at their table eating together.

Ralph was restraining his laughter when one of the fellows, to whom he had directed his brother to send a package, went to him, rather embarrassed.

"Oh, Ralph . . . I got a package . . . I forgot to tell you . . . Maybe it was your package?" the convict said nervously.

"Did you eat it?" Ralph chuckled.

"Yeah . . . ," the man replied, shamefaced.

"Well, did you like it?" Ralph prodded. The man nodded. "Well, great . . . forget about it!" Ralph grinned.

Charlie, who was listening, laughed his uproarious laugh. It was so contagious that Ralph finally burst into laughter, and every man, at that moment, tried to forget he was behind prison walls.

Dannemora Prison had been known as one of the worst prisons in the country (equaled only to Alcatraz), but Ralph and Charlie were doing their best to make it one of the best!

CHAPTER TWENTY

Dewey's crusade against the restaurant racket was in full force, and with Judge McCook again at his side, Dewey was sure to win. He claimed the two-million-dollar-a-year racket was initiated by Dutch Schultz, and that it had two unions in its pockets, plus a "protection" association. Dewey had publicly become very popular with all his gangster convictions. So much so that in February 1937, Mayor La Guardia formally proposed that he run for the office of district attorney. Meanwhile, Dewey still had unfinished business with the prostitution case.

Charlie and Ralph huddled together to compare notes. Dotty had returned from Europe, and Ralph's brother, Armand, was finally able to talk to her. She was ready to recant her story; she was completely miserable about what she had done to Ralph. Dotty was prepared to tell how she was promised her European trip and immunity, in exchange for her collaboration with Dewey and company. Cokey Flo was also disillusioned because her boyfriend, (Jimmy) Frederico, had not received a lighter sentence—despite her cooperation. She was ready to retract her statements about Charlie. Mildred Balitzer, for her own personal reasons, had also changed her mind. This was terrific news! They were the women with the most damaging testimonies in the prostitution case. On March 11, Charlie's attorney, Moses Polakoff, filed affidavits with the recantations to the Supreme Court as the basis for a new trial. In the affidavits, the girls claimed they were induced to falsify their information against Charlie. Moreover, Mildred Balitzer revealed she possessed a letter from Dewey's aide, Sol Gelb, promising her immunity. Cokey Flo and Mildred both stated they had been paid 2,500 dollars each by a magazine for their stories—through Mr. Dewey's intervention. Dewey, prompt as usual with his rebuttal, matter-of-factly asserted that the women's statements had been reconfirmed under oath after trial and signed.

Charlie informed Ralph that the girls were being hidden from the famous prosecutor so that Dewey couldn't further pressure or frighten them. Armand also knew where they were. Furious, because he didn't know where the women were hiding, Dewey turned the cards on the table and countered that the women were recanting because they were afraid of being murdered. The man was not to be defeated. The hearing on the motion for a new trial before Judge McCook was set for March 16. Both sides were told to prepare their briefs for consideration. Ralph and Charlie's spirits were definitely up, but they were still on pins and needles.

During the first week of April, Dewey received a copy of Polakoff's brief, which had to be filed with the Appellate Division in time for the oral argument set for May 7. In Polakoff's brief, Dewey and McCook were not spared! They were both attacked for unfairness—and emphasized again the unconstitutionality of the Joinder Law.

Around the last week in April, Judge McCook began investigating Dewey's charges that two well-known criminal lawyers (meaning Polakoff and Carlino) had prepared perjured evidence for a new trial; he was specifically referring to the three women. The two lawyers did not take the accusation sitting down. McCook found himself being directly charged by Polakoff with bias and prejudice. That was nothing new to Ralph or to Charlie! Lorenzo Carlino, Ralph's lawyer, had also filed an affidavit. In it Carlino stated that one of the jurors claimed the jury had been under pressure—that three of them had been threatened and had become frightened. The affidavit further stated that, although the juror was reluctant to sign, he would be willing to testify to that fact.

In the morning hearing, called to examine the validity of the affidavits, Judge McCook began by affirming that Dewey had presented evidence proving that the petitions were a fraud to the court.

"With his daring statements, Dewey wants to hide the truth," was Polakoff's immediate and vigorous rebuttal, and he warned against what he called "star chamber proceedings."

Carlino also attacked the court. When he was asked to take the stand, Carlino refused, claiming he was being treated as a common criminal. Polakoff, however, even though he considered the proceedings highly irregular, agreed. Dewey asked Polakoff where the girls were being held, and the savvy attorney finally revealed they were in Hartford, Connecticut. Thinking he could trip Polakoff, Dewey then slyly asked whether or not he was giving money to the women. Polakoff stoically answered, "I have been paying their expenses." But Polakoff emphatically added that the girls were afraid of being rearrested by Dewey and of being treated unjustly. They wanted protection.

At that point, Ralph could picture Dewey's ironic smile. Things became even more sticky. Claiming that Carlino's affidavit was nothing but perjurious material, Dewey further inflamed the usually calm

Polakoff, who turned a fiery gaze at McCook; he stated firmly that the defense would welcome a full and impartial investigation.

"In fact," Polakoff blasted, even hotter under the collar, "I am going to demand it, not from Your Honor, but from the governor of this state, or the grand jury. This is going to be a dogfight, Your Honor!"

Judge McCook pooh-poohed Polakoff's remarks as nonsense and, before adjourning, announced that the new motions would be heard on Friday morning.

That Friday, April 23, all hell broke loose at the hearing. Judge McCook had a hard time keeping things under control. The defense and prosecutor were at each other's throats, and McCook was also being drawn into the arguments. Dewey kept arguing that the women were recanting out of fear, together with their need for drugs and money. He knew however that the women were under the cure for drugs. He reiterated that the three women had signed their previous statements to him under oath. Dewey's repetitious remarks sounded like a broken record. Then he produced an affidavit from a third party, a woman missionary, who stated that Dotty had told her she would recant rather than suffer. Dewey fought very hard not to have the court hear the women directly. He *had* to! If the women were heard, he would have lost more than just a case.

Carlino became a roaring lion in court, attacking both Dewey and Judge McCook. He made a motion stating that Judge McCook should step down and let another justice hear the case—and even asked *him* to take the stand. McCook, of course, denied all motions and requests.

Referring to his affidavit, Carlino shouted, "He (Dewey) will stop at nothing! He poses as God in the courtroom. He's welcome to try to get me, or frame me . . . But he's not going to make a goat out of me!"

In his summation, Dewey stood his ground and smugly remarked, "I take back nothing. Everything I have said is proved by documentary evidence."

In the end, Polakoff, was pleading for the women to be heard, emphasizing that Charlie was sent to prison practically on the basis of the three women's testimonies. "If they testified falsely at the trial, as they now say they did, Lucania is entitled to a new trial!"

Judge McCook deferred his decision in order to study the briefs and ordered everyone to file them.

Naturally, Ralph and Charlie read all these things for themselves in the newspapers—as well as the surprising news that the Labor Department wanted to deport Charlie at the end of his term. Dewey had not forgotten that Charlie was not born in New York—that he had lied about it on the stand—and began putting the machinery in the works.

Dewey was always studying ways to destroy Charlie. Now Charlie had something else to worry about. Ralph, for his part, was not aware of what Dewey had in store for him. Their nerves had been shattered over the turn of events concerning the girls.

The prison routine, in the meantime, continued its normal course. It wasn't too depressing during the day, but the nights haunted Ralph. He often read himself to sleep. Ralph had made many friends among the inmates, and Father Booth was also comforting—great company. He sat out in the yard many times with them and talked about his favorite subject—boxing, especially the big fights, for instance, between Billy Conn and Joe Louis. He was an advocate for the prisoners, helped everyone for whom he could obtain a fair break in prison. Sometimes he interfered with administrative rules to make his point, and, of course, this was frowned upon. As a result, he had fallen out with the administration.

The last event, which triggered the warden's special disfavor toward Father Booth, involved an inmate named Rocky who, for some reason, seemed to be on his screw's (prison guard) hate list. It was a Sunday, after the call for church. The screw moved close to Rocky's cell bars and sneered under his breath, "Hey, cock sucker . . . ya gonna kiss the padre's skirt today?"

Good sense told Rocky to ignore the instant heat of his reaction. He managed to keep calm but slammed his cell shut and snapped. "Lock me up!" He wanted to be put under key block in order to seek the PK (pen keeper). When time came for recreation, however, another screw let Rocky out with the rest of the company. Rocky had by then decided to forget about the incident. Once in the yard, the screw hollered, "Break!" And everyone broke their lines.

Father Booth, spotting Rocky, beckoned him over. Rocky sauntered slowly toward the priest, expecting an inquisition.

"Rocky . . . why didn't you come to church this morning?"

The chaplain noticed everyone who attended church, and if someone was not present at mass, Father Booth knew it.

Rocky looked a little sheepish. "Father . . . let's forget it," he scowled.

But Father Booth intuitively knew something had happened. "Rocky . . . I'm your chaplain . . . Tell me! Did an inmate bother you? Did you get back news from home?"

Rocky kept nodding his head no.

"Then, the screw must have bothered you!"

"Father . . . ," Rocky practically pleaded. "Let's just drop it."

Confident that the screw had bothered Rocky, Father Booth waited for him to appear in the yard. Soon, the marching sounds of another company caught the chaplain's ear, and he caught sight of Rocky's screw. As the men dispersed, Father Booth called after him, "Bill, I want to talk to you!" The screw, however, shunned him and walked off, as if to say, *The hell with you.* That was the wrong move because it only infuriated the chaplain. He ran after the screw and swung him around, warning him, "Don't let this collar fool you . . . boy." And threw a well-trained right to the screw's chin, knocking him down.

The fallen man looked up at the tough priest with hatred in his eyes. As he wiped blood from the corner of his mouth.

Observing the action, all the inmates began screaming and clapping their hands. The chaplain prepared himself for the screw to jump him, but several guards came running while others immediately aimed machine guns at the men. It looked like a riot in the making. Two guards led the screw away, and Father Booth was summoned to the warden's office. The screw was transferred to another prison, and Father Booth was diplomatically released from his prison parish. He had been an excellent chaplain, but he had been at Dannemora too long—and had become consumed with the prisoners' problems. All the inmates missed him.

It was disheartening, but shortly thereafter, Ralph and Charlie were hit with more terrible news. On May 7, Justice Philip J. McCook refused to grant them a new trial. He claimed that the affidavits submitted were "poisonously false," insisted that the women's recantation was "induced by fear, financial pressure, and craving for drugs." He also asserted that Dewey's evidence was so good that "the hypothesis of a victimized, 'framed' Luciano is utterly destroyed." McCook and Dewey had again sung a perfect duet. As a team, they were hard to beat!

Ralph thought of the visit McCook had made to the prison. What a bastard! So that was the way "everything was going to be all right." Yet, somehow, the judge had seemed disturbed. *Were the political pressures so great? God, what a farce!* Ralph mulled in his mind. *Who said all politicians were upright citizens?*

Then to further blacken their moods, on June 2, the New York Court of Appeals in Albany upheld the constitutionality of the Joinder Law. That decision was handed down in connection with Dewey's fight against the restaurant racket defendants. The defendants had appealed the law, exactly as Charlie and Ralph had. The magistrates also added that there was no "ex post facto" argument to analyze. Ralph and Charlie realized it was a devastating blow because the decisions would also be applied to their case.

More than a month later, on July 17, the Appellate Division unanimously upheld McCook's ruling and the convictions. One of the judges, Justice Irving Untermyer, however, issued a statement in which he stated that the sentence given to Charlie was excessive and thought that the women should be heard at an open hearing.

"I concur," he wrote, "in the affirmance of the judgments as to all the defendants, *except* that, in my opinion, the *sentences are excessive* and, under the authority vested in us by section 543 of the Code of Criminal Procedure, *should be reduced*. I am further of the opinion that the new evidence, consisting of the *recantation* of *three* of the four *principal witnesses* against the defendant Luciano and of the statement tending to show that the *testimony* of the *fourth principal witness* was *false* in a material particular, was of such importance as to require the trial justice, in the exercise of the discretion, to *compel* the *production* of those *witnesses* for *examination* under oath in open court.

"I accordingly vote to modify the order denying the motion for a new trial in this respect as to the defendant Luciano."

Concurring with Justice Untermyer for a new trial was another judge, Justice Cohn. Their statements offered a gleam of hope, and the prospect of appealing the case to the New York Supreme Court kept Charlie and Ralph alive and kicking.

Praying didn't come easy to Ralph, but he did pray. Father Booth was instrumental in bringing him closer to God. His Sunday sermons made sense to him. Booth wasn't a pansy with a high-pitched voice, preaching the Gospel. Ralph felt his absence. Booth had sacrificed himself for everyone in Dannemora—had been sort of an anchor. Now the prison was buzzing with the news that a new priest had arrived to take his place. His name was Father Ambrose Hyland, and he had a rough time replacing Father Booth in the hearts of most. There was open hostility among Father Booth's die-hard followers, whose loyalty was hard to change. Still, as Ralph watched the new priest that first Sunday (sky blue eyes searching the faces of his new parishioners), it was apparent he was also a determined man.

Father Hyland stood tall, at six feet two, with a lean body and broad shoulders. A good-looking guy. His face was rather refined with a thin high-bridged nose and sensitive mouth. There he was on stage, in front of the long kneeling bench, which had been made into a makeshift altar. Somehow, Ralph could tell he wasn't happy with the auditorium as a place of worship. It did look pitiful. The administration ran movies there and other demonstrations they deemed proper. The seats were clamped to the floor—a reminder of where the prisoners were. All the clergymen took turns using the auditorium. Father Booth had dreamed of a Catholic chapel, but no one had given him the chance to fulfill that dream. Perhaps, this new priest could do something. Ralph stared at Father Hyland and thought, *This guy is no pushover. He might do just that.*

Shortly after Father Hyland's arrival, an inmate was murdered in prison. Murders were rare, but when it happened, a cloud of silence hovered over the prisoners. It epitomized all the frustrations of life behind bars. Many of the inmates felt like killing someone, at one time or another. They were in prison presumably to be rehabilitated. Somehow, the system had failed, and the realization was depressing. Ralph learned this time that the victim had been in the prison music band and had merely fought over an instrument with another inmate. It was Father Hyland's first introduction to his new position. He was especially depressed because he didn't have a decent place in which to hold a funeral. It was probably at that moment, forced with the dilemma, that he vowed to build a church. He was often overheard saying that the prison auditorium was not good enough for God!

One Sunday, he made his announcement. Father Hyland told his convict parishioners that Father Booth would have wanted him to continue in his place—to fulfill his dream of a church within prison walls at Dannemora. He stated he was determined to carry out those plans; he would talk to Warden Murphy, Governor Lehman, and to the bishop to obtain their support. He asked for everyone's prayers to help him succeed—to pray directly to Saint Dismas for his help.

"Who is Saint Dismas?" Father Hyland asked his prison congregation. "Saint Dismas was the good thief on the cross who died alongside Jesus Christ. As death approached, Christ said to him, 'This day thou shalt be with me in paradise.'

"And our church will be called Saint Dismas," he concluded with a smile. Father Hyland had proven that he had guts, just like Father Booth, and the men warmed to his personality and inner strength.

Church of Saint Dismas, the Good Thief. It was a great name and caught on easily. An immediate hit.

CHAPTER TWENTY-ONE

Sometimes dreams seem so real that one believes the dream is! Conversely, reality or things are so incredible that one thinks he is dreaming. Reality with a dreamlike quality presented itself to Ralph one night as he lay on his cot, as usual, leafing through the newspapers. He had just finished reading an article about Dewey's campaign for district attorney when suddenly, he was jolted upright at discovering his name in bold print! There, in the newspaper, heading a feature column, he read: RALPH LIGUORI, LUCKY LUCIANO'S RIGHT HAND MAN, IS INDICTED IN FEDERAL COURT ON A CONSPIRACY CHARGE. Ralph was being indicted, along with seventy-four other people, all involved in an international narcotics ring.

He panicked. "What the hell. Is everybody going crazy!"

With hands trembling, he continued to read the article. A Major Garland Williams, district supervisor of the New York Narcotics Bureau, had been investigating the ring for some time—had already arrested ten people. Another fifty-five persons were rounded up by agents in Louisiana and Texas, the latter supposedly the headquarters of the narcotics ring. The assistant United States attorney prosecuting the case was Joseph P. Martin. Other indictments and arrests were expected.

Ralph's heart began to pound fast, its rhythm accelerating, and he placed his hand on his chest, as if to stop it from leaping through his rib cage. He began to perspire, and the saliva building in his mouth tasted like burning gall.

"Shit," he choked. "I'm dreaming all this. For Chrissake, I'm in Dannemora!"

At that moment, a screw walked by and stopped at his cell. He had heard Ralph muttering and growling. "Hey, Ralph," he called. "You okay?"

"Yeah . . . just a bad dream . . . I'm okay." Ralph reassured him, feigning embarrassment. The screw walked away, and Ralph punched his pillow in frustration. He shut his eyes tightly against the vision of the words he'd read, hoping that sleep would come—hoping he would wake up from a bad dream.

But in the morning, when he picked up the paper, which had fallen next to his cot, there it was—his name, the indictment. Not a dream!

He tried to tell himself it was a mistake, kept repeating it over and over in his head. It didn't work; he was quivering with anxiety. He couldn't mention it to Charlie.

On November 2, 1937, the citizens of New York elected Thomas E. Dewey as their new district attorney. He was to assume his new title officially on January 1. Meanwhile, he was still the special prosecutor, performing his gang-busting activities nonstop. For some time he had been after Louis Buchalter (Lepke) and Jacob Shapiro (Gurrah), leaders of the garment industry, particularly after they had also gobbled up the flour-trucking and baking industries. Dewey and his staff were closing in. Following the issuance of indictments against them, Lepke and Gurrah had vanished—were nowhere to be found. Their fleeing associates, however, were picked up, one by one (if they were not already murdered by their own kind). FBI's J. Edgar Hoover, not to take second place in the limelight to Dewey, had also issued warrants for the two men. Hoover had declared Lepke the most dangerous criminal in America.

While the police hunted Lepke and Gurrah, Dewey turned his attention to Tammany Hall. In his campaign speech of October 24, 1937, he had specifically attacked Albert "Al" Marinelli, New York County clerk and Tammany Hall leader of the Second Assembly District West. Dewey had stated that Al was "a political ally of thieves, pickpockets, thugs, dope peddlers, and big-shot racketeers." He had pointed out that Al had gone to the 1932 Democratic National Convention in Chicago in the company of Charles Luciano, and that they had been together at the Drake Hotel. Dewey also specified that at the January 1935 Al Marinelli Beefsteak Dinner, many underground individuals had turned up to cheer the honoree. Dewey persisted in referring to Marinelli as a shadowy figure with a mysterious background. Nor did he spare other Democrats. He was out to destroy Al Marinelli by association and, at the same time, disgrace the Democratic Party.

When reached by reports, Al flatly replied, "No comment." But Dewey had aroused the ire of many important political leaders. After Dewey's victory at the polls, Governor Lehman found a letter on his desk from a citizen's committee, demanding Marinelli's removal from office (based on Dewey's speech). There followed a rapid exchange of letters. The governor forwarded the charges to Marinelli and, on November 24, received a nineteen-page rebuttal from Al—asserting that he was being crucified for having helped the underdog and concluding his self-defense by swearing he had never taken a dishonest dollar in his life!

On November 25, Governor Lehman requested that Dewey submit specific charges against Marinelli. A week later, Dewey complied, reiterating his October 24 charges, and submitted his affidavit, his documentation, and a cover letter, stating, "In the event you desire to treat these statements of facts as formal charges, there will be no delay."

Dewey's accusations were heavy. He named "notorious underground criminals"—such as Charlie, Adonis, Genovese, and Betillo—as Marinelli's friends. He also stated that in his office of county clerk, Marinelli surrounded himself with men of questionable backgrounds (possessing prison convictions and arrests). In addition, Dewey asserted that Marinelli had lied about the whereabouts of a known fugitive from justice—a man the Feds were hunting regarding election fraud charges. It was later discovered that the fugitive was Marinelli's personal chauffeur. Indeed, it was a sorry situation for him. But the truth was that Marinelli did know the people named. He had grown up with them in the same neighborhoods. Many did have records. It was also true that many mothers and fathers had always turned to Al Marinelli, begging him to help their sons find legitimate jobs, thereby embracing a normal life. *Whatever happened to courts' theory of rehabilitation—the idea that if given the opportunity, criminals could go straight?* thought Ralph as he followed the developments in the press.

The same day, Governor Lehman received Dewey's letter—again he sent a copy to Marinelli, ordering him to submit in writing his verified answer to the charges by noon the following Monday, December 6. A copy of that letter was also dispatched to Dewey so that everyone was informed of the matter. The governor then patiently awaited the results.

Marinelli's friends urged him to resign, especially since his term was to expire on December 31. He was not planning to run again, nor was he seeking any other public office. Therefore, to avoid public hearings and further abuse, his Tammany Hall cronies agreed on his resignation to spare the party additional humiliation. The Italian-American community was also embarrassed. Everyone wanted to end the notoriety. Marinelli resigned, thereby becoming another victim of political expediency.

Al Marinelli had been a close personal friend of both Charlie and Ralph. Huddled together in the prison yard, it was natural for them to discuss Al's predicament and all the hullabaloo in the news. It was also natural for the conversation to touch on Lepke, whose indictment—in screaming headlines—linked Ralph to the same narcotics ring. Lepke was charged with being one of the principal plotters of the drug traffic and was said to have helped finance the ring. The indictment charged Lepke with conspiracy to violate the Federal Narcotics laws and with bribery of public officials. Police were combing the country for other fugitives. Their search went as far as Marseilles and Shanghai. Agents said Lepke was hiding in the Midwest, but other experts thought he was in Palestine. It was called the most gigantic narcotics ring ever smashed in the United States. One hundred customs and narcotics agents had made simultaneous raids in Manhattan, Brooklyn, and the Bronx. A total of eighty-eight people were indicted, with only forty-five apprehended.

Ralph, still secretly concerned about himself, learned more about the ring in the paper. It had begun in the Bronx where a chemist, involved in the ring, operated a refining plant. The plant exploded in February 1935, and the chemist was arrested. That set off more than two years of investigation. The ring smuggled narcotics from China, sending some of their members (inconspicuous men and women, sometimes married couples, posing as tourists), to Shanghai. To guarantee success at customs, the ring corrupted two customs officials, who were ultimately arraigned. The disguised couriers traveled in first-class cabins (sometimes in tourist class) to confuse custom agents. They always traveled with four or five trunks; the narcotics would be hidden in one of them. At customs, the tourists pointed to the legitimate trunks and were consequently allowed through. The ring was huge, with people stationed on both sides of the ocean. In just six such trips, they made a million dollars. Lepke was said to be involved in at least two shipments for one-fifth of the financial interest. Almost two hundred pounds of pure heroin was to sell at one hundred dollars an ounce. A great deal of money was spent financing the ring, but the net return exceeded all expectations.

Ralph decided it was time to discuss his problem with Charlie.

"Charlie . . . ," he began twittering, "you may or may not know this, but I've also been indicted for this narcotics ring rap . . ."

Wide-eyed and with a disturbed expression, Charlie took his time replying. "Yeah . . . Ralph . . . you know I did see your name in the paper, but since you're here with me, I shrugged it off as a mistake. I just didn't believe it . . ."

"I wish it were . . . Charlie," a despondent Ralph shook his head. "It's like an April Fool's Day joke . . . but it's not. It's been a couple of months now, and still I haven't heard anything on it. I keep praying it's a lot of hogwash."

"What the hell's behind this . . . Who's behind this?" muttered Charlie in disgust. "More of Dewey's stuff?"

"What's to be gained by it all?" Ralph asked. "For Chrissake . . . I'm already in Dannemora!"

"Maybe they want to tie us *all* in on a narcotics rap," Charlie replied.

"So what's the point? To keep us in here forever?" Ralph sighed.

They hashed the situation over and over between them but came out with nothing that really made sense.

In January 1938, their attention was directed to their appeal in the New York Supreme Court. Charlie had hired new blood, prestigious Martin J. Conboy (former U.S. attorney of New York), who was being paid top dollar. It was a joint effort again with Ralph's lawyer, Lorenzo Carlino; David Siegel for Dave Betillo, Frederico, and Wahrman; and Caesar Barra for Pennochio. The appeal for a new trial attracted many people. The courtroom was packed on both days, January 18 and 19, 1938; folding chairs were supplied to accommodate standers. Missing were the squads of police who had been present for the prostitution case. Hell, everyone was behind bars! Ralph surmised.

Conboy spoke for two hours the first day, and his remarks were memorable for their clarity. He specifically argued that many errors were committed by Judge McCook in the conduct of the trial—that there was, in effect, little proof in any of the testimonies. In other words, there had been insufficient evidence—all of which constituted prejudice against Luciano. The court would be justified in reversing the convictions, he emphasized, and asked for a dismissal of the indictment of sixty-two counts. Conboy repeated the charge that the Joinder Law was ex post facto and unconstitutional.

Although he admitted to the court that there existed a "public revulsion" against Luciano, he added, "For that very reason, he must be given the most evenhanded kind of justice!"

The ever ready Dewey had prepared a two-hundred-page brief but spoke for only an hour. "This case can never be retried," he began dramatically. "The witnesses comprised as fine a collection of pimps, thieves, prostitutes, and criminals ever gathered together under one roof. They could never be found again. The case is here for the first and last time."

There he was, thought Ralph, posing as God in the courtroom again, dictating law. Dewey didn't get much further in his summation because it was near closing time, and the court adjourned. The next day, however, Dewey was even more adamant. He argued strongly against a new trial and cried out in defense of Judge McCook—"that McCook had meted out *evenhanded justice, leaned over backward*, and had used *scrupulous fairness*."

Ralph became nauseated upon reading those words. McCook had not even allowed Dotty, Cokey Flo, and Mildred Balitzer to reverse their testimonies. *At least hear them, by God!* he screamed inside himself.

Dewey insisted that the crimes were committed, and the only new point raised, as *he* saw it, was the contention that the prosecuting staff had suborned perjury. He had heavy words for Charlie. To say "Luciano had the underworld on call" was an understatement, Dewey said, and his credibility was "a little less than worthless."

Martin J. Conboy was a brilliant lawyer, with a profound knowledge of the law—as well as of all the tricks of the trade. After Dewey, smug as ever, sat down, Conboy rose and gave a brief rebuttal. Standing tall with an air of confidence, Conboy argued that witnesses had been held incommunicado, and that the defense had not been allowed to interview them. A snappy exchange ensued between the two lawyers, but Conboy had made his point. He definitely outclassed Dewey, but politics were involved, and the case was a cut-and-dried issue.

The gray of winter had set in, and Ralph prayed as never before for the spring to break through to bring some good news. To the contrary, on April 12, 1938, the court of appeals in Albany, New York, upheld the convictions by a five to one decision. Chief Judge Frederick E. Crane recited a ten-page opinion, highlights of which were: "Luciano planned with his lieutenants to place prostitution on a commercial basis, and to extract whatever financial profit was possible. The actual management he may have entrusted to others, but he cannot escape his criminal responsibility as the leader and principal.

"The similarity between the crimes was so striking that the inference that they were connected together, or parts of a common scheme, is well-nigh inescapable. There was no need to allege a conspiracy since the crimes were properly joined together because of their similarity.

"As the principal and leader of the whole enterprise, Luciano did not take an active part in the daily operation of the business, but that he was the directing hand and moving force behind it all. The evidence adduced in the trial leaves no doubt."

The judge topped all his remarks by saying that he didn't think the sentences were that severe. Ralph thought they could not have had worse luck than to have someone like Judge Crane preside.

One judge, however, dissented. Judge Harlan W. Rippey contradicted him. He stated that there were "*material* and *prejudicial* errors in the conduct of the trial, which could not be *overlooked*," and that "the defendants were tried for a crime with which they were not charged in the indictment."

The verdict, as far as Charlie and Ralph were concerned, was colored by prejudice, which was so deeply rooted that it was impossible to be objective (impartial). The defendants lost again; there was no doubt that the case would go to the United States Supreme Court for review.

No sooner did Ralph pick himself up after the gloom of the legal battles than he was shot down again—as Charlie whispered the startling news to him.

"Ralph, be calm now . . . but I got a tip that a warrant has arrived for you at the warden's office."

"What? You mean for that narcotics thing?" Ralph's heart leaped.

"Yeah . . . You have to appear in federal court. Now . . . look . . . don't get over excited. We'll fight this one too. Find out first what it's all about."

"Christ . . . Charlie . . . another frame!" Ralph gasped, almost choking on his words.

"Ralph . . . be calm . . . ," Charlie interrupted sympathetically. "Don't turn around . . . The warden's stoolie is coming up to get you," he added in a whisper.

It was a Sunday Ralph would never forget. The screw told him the warden wanted to see him, and without a word, Ralph stood up. He found it difficult to say good-bye, but Charlie rescued him.

"So long . . . Ralph . . . Remember what I told you. Watch what you're doing . . . ," he managed to say. He thought of Ralph as his younger brother.

Ralph nodded and hurried away with the screw.

The warden was waiting in his office with his assistants. An old electric chair stood against one of the walls, and one of the men, pointing to the chair, said, "Hey, Ralph . . . take a seat." Ralph did not appreciate the man's warped sense of humor—while everyone else hee-hawed at the tasteless joke. The smirk on the warden's face disappeared as he informed Ralph of the warrant and what it contained. A guard was assigned to escort Ralph to New York and was ordered to remain as his shadow. The warden then told Ralph to return to his cell to change into a suit; he was to leave immediately.

The guard was Sergeant Frank Duckett. He and two of his brothers were the toughest guards in Dannemora, but they were the best, if one knew them personally. Ralph was handcuffed to Duckett as they boarded the train and took their seats. Ralph sat by the window. The train whistle wailed; the wheels made several short *chug-chug*ging movements; then the train picked up speed, leaving Dannemora in the distance.

Duckett turned toward Ralph, "Ralph, I don't know what this is all about, but soon's we get farther down, I'm going to take the handcuffs off you. I don't think you'd hurt me. Would you, Ralph?"

"No, Duckett. I'd never hurt you . . . because I'd be hurting a lot of other people, if I ever did. Don't worry . . ."

Satisfied, Duckett took the handcuffs off and went into the bathroom. Ralph could have attempted an escape, had he tried, but he didn't. First, he was not guilty of the newest charge against him; and second, he had given his word. Instead, his thoughts raced along with the rhythmic percussion of the train, as it rushed down to New York City.

Duckett returned and opened the briefcase to read the warrant. "A conspiracy case of narcotics?" he half-whistled. "Hey . . . Ralph . . . that's a strong accusation."

"Duckett, I swear to you I don't know what it's all about," Ralph retorted defiantly. Without another word, he turned despondently to the window and became mesmerized by the *swoosh-swoosh* of the train.

Finally, Grand Central Station. Handcuffs neatly in place, Ralph and Duckett stepped out of the train, and as Ralph looked up the ramp, he saw them. About twenty detectives were waiting. "Duckett, we've got visitors up there," Ralph said sardonically.

"Man . . . ," Duckett remarked. "You spot them guys better than I do."

As the two walked up the ramp, the detectives began shouting.

"Ralph, welcome back to the Big Apple."

"Hey, how ya doin', kid?"

"How's Siberia?"

"How's Charlie?"

Ralph made some general responses as he and Duckett were led to a waiting police car. Destination: Tombs Prison. The next morning, Ralph was arraigned in federal court. He immediately recognized Justice Joseph P. Martin from his picture in the *New York Daily Mirror*. After a casual salutation, Martin said flatly, "Ralph . . . do you want to plead guilty? If you plead guilty . . . I'll recommend you for parole."

"Plead guilty to what?" Ralph answered hotly.

Duckett interjected, "Would you please read the indictment to me."

The indictment stated that Ralph was part of a conspiracy in narcotics, and that he had been at the scene of the crime with someone on Broadway in late 1936. Duke promptly answered, "Why, this is outrageous! This man's been in prison for over a year in Dannemora. If he were in Sing Sing, they'd probably say he went out nights selling narcotics!" Then, turning to Ralph, he exclaimed forcefully, "Don't you dare plead guilty to anything like this, Ralph!"

Ralph looked at Duckett gratefully and replied firmly, "No, I won't, Duke."

Duckett stared at Martin and exclaimed, "You heard the man!"

Martin gestured with his hands as if to say, *It's his funeral*.

Ralph went before the court and pleaded not guilty.

When his faithful guard departed, Ralph was taken to the Federal detention house on West Street. There, Ralph met Gurrah, Lepke's partner, who was in for income tax evasion. Ralph hadn't seen Gurrah for several years; the man wanted to know about Charlie and life in Dannemora. They reminisced all through the night. Gurrah was not handsome, rather a short crass-looking, thick-necked man with a protruding brow hooding his evasive eyes. Despite the fact that he was a braggart, Gurrah amused Ralph with his manner of speech. He spoke coarsely in terribly broken English, and his facial expressions were comical—especially when he imitated someone. He liked to mock people, and when they got around to talking about their common enemy (Dewey), Gurrah did not spare him, making a mockery out of him. But all that was just one side of the tough Gurrah; he was second only to Lepke in Murder, Inc., and consequently, no man would ever want to alienate him. He was extremely violent with his enemies—even when he wasn't paid to kill them.

Dewey was their constant topic of discussion as he was always in the news. Dewey had just made a lengthy speech in New York before the newspaper publishers, commending them on their fight against crime by exposing and informing the public of municipal corruption. He charged ahead with his attacks on Tammany Hall. If one listened to him long enough, one came away believing that all Democrats were crooks. It was obvious he was preparing the groundwork for the governorship.

Gurrah had Dewey's voice down packed. With Gurrah's imitations and tomfoolery, and Duckett's cheerful visits, Ralph whiled away his time in the desolate dormitory. Duke, a die-hard baseball fan, went to see the Dodgers every day, then reported the happenings to Ralph. It helped to momentarily forget.

But the big heat was on Lepke. There were multiple reasons why the authorities wanted him. In person, Lepke was easier to digest than Gurrah; he was mild mannered, but he obviously possessed a cold streak. On the short side and slim, Lepke looked like a respectable businessman and, oddly enough, was a family man. With his soft-looking eyes and dimpled left cheek, it was hard to imagine him as the brains behind Murder, Inc. He treated the corporation like everything else—as a business.

As usual, certain defendants of the narcotics ring pleaded guilty to save their necks before the trial began. On May 3, two women and fourteen men informed Justice Joseph Martin and the court of their decision. Captured was the alleged leader and organizer of the gigantic ring, Gennaro Caputo, who was also wanted by the French Guillotine for the murder of a woman named Marie Gierere. (He was eventually returned to France.) Another man, the so-called financier, Jose San Pedro, was given a separate trial; and when it began, about twenty-five defendants remained in the case. The fireworks began almost immediately. Gennaro Caputo's lawyer, Colonel Lewis Landes, an ex-army man, argued with Federal Judge Murray Hulbert over statements made on the stand by a Federal agent. He was asked to take his seat, but Landes remained standing and reiterated his objections, asking for a mistrial. The judge fined him fifty dollars for contempt of court. Another defense attorney asked for a mistrial because he didn't agree with Colonel Landes's statements—and raised his own issues.

At that point, Judge Hulbert declared a mistrial, stating, "It certainly will not be the purpose of this court to force a continuation of a trial where it seems a reasonable deduction that something has transpired, which may affect the jury's consideration of the evidence. I feel myself that here may be some prejudice, as far as some of these defendants are concerned. And, in the interest of fair play, I direct that a mistrial be declared."

Ralph thought of Judge McCook and about all the times the defense counselors had demanded a mistrial on much more serious motions, which McCook always punctually denied. It further convinced Ralph of the weighty impact politics had had in his case. Finally, the new trial began with a new jury. Ralph was still in the dark regarding his involvement. Who had fingered him? He didn't have to wait long. A young lady, modestly dressed with a sloppy hat slanted over her head, took the stand.

"Do you know Ralph Liguori?" the prosecutor asked.

"Yes, I do," she replied emphatically. "That's him over there (she pointed to Ralph). My husband used to work for him."

A guard next to Ralph half-whispered, "Ralph . . . what the hell did you do to her?"

Ralph stared intently at the woman, trying to place her. Then he remembered. Why, she was Louie "the Bum's" wife! "What did I do?" Ralph replied sarcastically. "Nothing . . . I just gave her husband a job. He came to me with broken shoes, and I put him back on his feet."

Louie "the Bum" had never amounted to much. He had returned to New York after the boys chased him out of Chicago. Apparently, he had become involved with the narcotics ring and was caught. Trying for a lighter sentence, he mentioned Ralph's name, placing him at the scene of the crime. Ralph, however, was in Dannemora and couldn't possibly have been in two places at one time. Louie "the Bum" had probably thought that the prosecutor would be more than interested since Ralph was also connected with Charlie in the vice case, thereby hopefully netting even bigger fish. As absurd as it all was, Ralph was convicted of the charge based on the woman's testimony. He was given a two-year sentence to run concurrently with the state charge. It was all so preposterous to Ralph. Of course, how could he not appeal.

Sergeant Duckett remained a true friend to the bitter end, and Ralph was grateful for his support. Duke attended the court sessions every day, and when it was over, he said in an exasperated tone of voice, "You know, Ralph . . . I can see now why all of the prisons are full!"

"You wouldn't believe it . . . if you didn't see it," Ralph responded.

Duke shook his head in disbelief.

When Ralph returned to Dannemora, Charlie was there waiting for him up on the hill, as if he had never left. All the men gathered around Ralph, wanting to hear the incredible story. No one could believe it. Another strike against justice!

Alone at last, Ralph gave Charlie all the gossip—about Lepke, Gurrah, and how Louie "the Bum" had done him wrong. It took a few days before Ralph brought him up-to-date on all the news. He also told Charlie that during his stay at the Federal detention house, an FBI man stopped to see him. The man told him that President Roosevelt was planning a special United States Senate investigation of the Luciano trial. The inquiry was going to lay it wide open—to expose whoever was responsible for the frame-up. Since the case had obviously become a political question, everyone wanted it to materialize.

"Ralph . . . you're going to appeal this conviction . . . aren't you?" Charlie pressed.

"Damn right! Hell . . . one frame is enough!" answered Ralph decisively.

In fact, his appeal went through all the courts. *Two years* later, the charge against Ralph was reversed by the United States Supreme Court.

The charge was dismissed.

CHAPTER TWENTY-TWO

Father Hyland's plans for the prison church had progressed only so far as the forefront of his mind. Surprisingly, the warden was not against the idea but would not entertain a separate chapel for Catholics. Rather, he favored one place of worship for all. Father Hyland, instead, promoted not only a Catholic church, but separate chapels for Rabbi Schoenkopf and the protestant minister, Mr. Bay. He looked the warden squarely in the eyes and stated he and the other clergymen would have it no other way. Finally, the warden acquiesced, but on condition that Father Hyland receive permission from the governor—since it meant the establishment of a denominational chapel on government property. The land belonged to the government. Would the bishop approve? They talked about tools, equipment, cement, and man power. Who would build the church?

"Why, my men!" answered Father Hyland convincingly. "We have about seven hundred idle men in prison. And that old wall that leads nowhere in the yard . . . we'll tear it down and use the old bricks as a beginning."

Up in Albany, New York, Father Hyland had problems with state politicians. His was a big order. As the legislature saw it, besides not having any money, land, or labor for the project, there was no precedent for it. They didn't know how to handle it. Father Hyland then went to Governor Lehman, who fortunately lent a sympathetic ear. The governor was ready to cooperate, *if* Father Hyland could persuade the general public and civic groups to be in favor of the plan.

Next was the bishop. Miraculously, he was very receptive, so much so that he gave Father Hyland a check, thus becoming the prison church's first contributor. Encouraged by the bishop's reception and generosity, Father Hyland visited other prominent monsignors in New York, all of whom complimented him on his project. He was left with one more stop and braced himself for the cardinal. But will miracles ever cease? He received a whopping five-thousand-dollar check! True, for what he needed, he had collected only a drop in the bucket, but the signs were positive. He returned to Dannemora with renewed faith. At his next Sunday sermon, he advised the inmates of his accomplishments and asked everyone to keep praying—because someone up there was listening!

Prayers were fine, Ralph and Charlie agreed, but they believed in action. Charlie promptly asked to see Father Hyland to determine what he could do to help. The kindly chaplain told him that the real problem was money. He admitted he felt like a beggar but added soulfully, "St. Francis of Assisi became a beggar for the church." Following the meeting, Charlie and Ralph again asked their brothers to contact all their friends on the outside to send money to the chaplain for the worthy cause. Ralph personally wrote to a few friends, and Charlie advised his closest associates. Certainly, they did not do it all, but Charlie and Ralph were ultimately responsible for a large part of the contributions. Naturally, all the other prisoners did their part. It had become the prisoners' personal project. Everyone wanted to see the church built.

The proudest inmates were those who actually began building the church. Many of them turned out to be bricklayers, carpenters, plumbers, electricians, and artists. The working squad was called the WPA (a takeoff on Roosevelt's social project), and it stood for Working Prison Association. If one of the workers was asked, "Where do you work?" The proud answer was, "WPA." The inmates involved in the construction of the church had very good jobs; they were always on the outside and reveled in a few special privileges. Temporarily, they were the envy of the prison.

Charlie and Ralph still hoped Lady Luck would not let them down on their appeals. Moses Polakoff had made a motion for a reargument to the court of appeals in Albany, based on the inability to question Peggy Weil (a prostitute witness). They argued it was a prejudicial error, and that it was a violation of one's right to due process of law guaranteed by the Constitution. On June 3, 1938, the motion was denied. Polakoff told Charlie that he had expected that to happen, but it was necessary as part of the preparation for the U.S. Supreme Court appeal.

There was another person whom Lady Luck had let down—Tammany Hall leader Jimmy Hines. Dewey had ordered him arrested more than a week earlier (May 25)—charged with intimidating, influencing, and bribing government officials, judges, and law enforcement agents in order for the underworld to operate freely. The indictment went so far as to name Dutch Schultz as having Hines on his payroll. Apparently, Dewey had all the proof he needed. Once again, he made the headlines. It was another blow to Tammany Hall and to the New Deal leaders. Dewey could already taste the governorship! Hines's bail was fixed at twenty thousand dollars, and on July 11, he pleaded not guilty. While all this was going on, Dewey and his staff also went to work on the

Taxi Chauffeurs' Union. An old friend of Ralph's, State Motor Vehicle commissioner Charles A. Harnett, who had once helped save his driver's license, was next to get the ax.

On July 11, the attorneys for Charlie and Ralph finally filed with the highest court of the land (the U.S. Supreme Court), asking for a review of their trial. The review stipulated: first, that the defendants had received a "mere pretense of a trial"; second, that it had been "inconsistent with the rudimentary demands of justice." Further, the lawyers mentioned the Joinder Law, as always, and complained that some of the women witnesses didn't tell the truth because they had been made "substantial promises of immunity."

Dewey filed his opposition brief with the U.S. Supreme Court on August 16, 1938. Naturally, he defended his Joinder Law, picking up on some of Judge Crane's remarks. Regarding the other points raised by the defense, Dewey sneered, "They didn't have a leg to stand on." He called them "baseless" and asked that the convictions be upheld.

Constantly sidestepping the issue and, at times, actually denying his interest in the candidacy for governorship of New York, Dewey finally admitted his intentions and, indeed, accepted the nomination on September 29—seventeen days after Jimmy Hines's mistrial. Governor Lehman had announced his decision to retire, which cleared the way for Dewey. But it is believed that with some coaxing from President Roosevelt, Herbert Lehman gave up his dream of the U.S. Senate (and possible retirement) to run again. It was a happy postmaster General James Farley who triumphantly announced at the Democratic Convention that Lehman would head the Democratic ticket once more. Obviously, this took Dewey down a peg or two. He would have extremely stiff competition from a very popular incumbent. Nevertheless, Dewey opened his campaign on October 10, 1938, and tackled it with a resolute mind and devotion—game to the last. He had help from the U.S. Supreme Court in boosting his popularity (when that august body upheld the convictions in the prostitution case and the Joinder Law) by refusing to review the case.

What strange political machinations lurk behind a façade of justice and righteousness, fumed Ralph. No one could tell him it wasn't political maneuvering that had brought about such a heartbreaking end. The opportunities had all been tried; the doors were definitely closed.

There would be no more appeals.

Adjusting the headset of his small radio, Ralph tuned in Dewey's broadcasts. As he had every Monday in his cell, he followed Dewey's gubernatorial campaign, trying to quell the hatred in his heart for the man who had framed him. When he heard that Dewey had lost the race to Governor Lehman, who, as the people willed, would remain in office for another four years, Ralph was among the first to send his cheers of joy echoing through the cell block.

Jimmy Hines was found guilty on February 25, 1939, on thirteen counts (including conspiracy, felony, aiding and abetting and protecting policy racketeers, magistrate manipulating, and jury fixing) to serve four to eight years. His lawyer, however, won a motion based on reasonable doubt, and Hines was out on thirty-five-thousand-dollar bail—free to await his appeal. No such privilege for Ralph and Charlie.

Dewey wielded a heavy ax and made sure to swing it in wide arcs. It was Fritz Kuhn's turn. Kuhn was the leader of the German-American Bund Movement—a National Socialist, a Hitlerite who used the swastika as his emblem, flags and armbands. He indulged in anti-Semitic propaganda, hiding behind the USA's laws of free speech and press. Dewey pursued him with impassioned zeal, ever conscious of the publicity, the limelight, the favor to be curried from the traditionally Democratic Jewish vote. Diplomatic relations between America and Germany were strained. No one wanted a man like Kuhn in the States.

Ralph was one of them. Although he had committed many misdeeds in his day, Ralph *never* went against the United States! If Kuhn didn't like what he found in the States, why didn't he get the hell out!

Dewey first investigated Fritz Kuhn on sales tax evasion, finally obtaining an indictment for grand larceny and forgery. Kuhn was jailed, and his bail was set at fifty thousand dollars. But Kuhn had friends. The bail money was posted the first of October, and he was out again. Kuhn's trial began on November 9, and on November 29, he was found guilty on five counts. Destination: Dannemora State Prison. Germany had just invaded Poland, and the Allies and Axis stood postured at each other in the dawn of World War II. Kuhn was not a popular man. The warden was worried about his safety in prison because of the Jewish population among Dannemora prisoners. For a time, Kuhn was not allowed out into the yard with the other inmates.

The warden called Charlie in for a chat, asking whether he thought Kuhn could be let out for recreation without running into serious problems. Charlie gave the warden his word that Kuhn would not be bothered. Out in the yard, Kuhn was brought up to Charlie's court, for safety's sake. No one molested him there. Kuhn was treated as any other con. He managed to make a few friends, but Ralph didn't like him—only on rare occasions would he speak to him.

Kuhn was assigned to the dye shop, and one day, he boasted to Betillo, "I can make this prison go up in the air in five minutes!" Gathering all the chemicals from the dye shop, he probably could!

Davey stared at the German, half-scared. "'Hey, man . . . You're crazy . . . You can't do that!"

Kuhn just sneered. He was soon released and sent back to Germany. That was where he belonged, as far as Ralph was concerned.

The story was different with Lepke. He was still at large, and Dewey had squads of police combing New York for him. Nationwide, the FBI and the Federal Narcotics Bureau were on the hunt as well. Dewey convinced authorities to offer a $25,000 reward. He spoke on radio and appeared in newsreels, pleading for information leading to Lepke's arrest. The media kept him in the limelight. While Dewey was screaming, "Find Lepke!" the pressure was being put on the hunted criminal by the underworld itself. The "Big Heat" was dampening everyone's activities. People were being arrested as never before! The situation could not go on! Lepke understood he had to surrender. Finally, he contacted newscaster Walter Winchell, who made a deal for leniency with District Attorney Bill O'Dwyer in order to help turn in Lepke. Lepke negotiated with Winchell to cop a plea with the FBI to receive from six months to a maximum of two years in the pen. Late in the evening of August 24, 1939, with additional weight gained and a thick dark mustache, so that no one would recognize him, Lepke climbed into Winchell's car for the trip to FBI Chief J. Edgar Hoover.

But Lepke was double-crossed. He was turned over to the Federal Narcotics Bureau. The change wasn't Walter Winchell's fault. He was a good skate. Winchell had stated many, many times in his famous radio broadcast that Dewey had the wrong information on Charlie. In his Sunday column, he wrote, "To the boys up above, our best regards" (meaning Charlie and Ralph). Now they had Lepke.

Early in 1940, the Murder, Inc. probe was going full steam ahead. Abe "Kid Twist" Reles was picked up, along with some minor hoods. Reles was a screwball; he'd punch someone, even in a restaurant, if he was so much looked at cross-eyed. But once the cops began applying the pressure, the toughness softened. Reles began to sing, saying things that weren't altogether true. He snitched on Happy Maiori, Bugsy Goldstein, the Dasher—Ralph's dancing buddies. He also sang about Siegel, Lepke, and Anastasia. It was Reles's persistent recitative that both Happy Maiori and Bugsy Goldstein went to the electric chair. Ralph called Reles a rat fink—the worst stool pigeon ever. News reports stated that while in custody at the Half Moon Hotel in Coney Island, Reles fell to his death from a window. Actually, he was thrown from the window. Reles had also begun to squeal on corruption within the police department, and when anyone started to rat on the cops, the result is a foregone conclusion.

It happened on November 12, 1941. Abe Reles was told to tie his sheets end to end, then to dangle them out the window in preparation of making a break. Somehow, Reles never got to hold on to the sheets, and it was a long way down. When the incident was over, both Charlie and Ralph said, "Good riddance!" Siegel beat his rap, as well as Albert Anastasia, but Lepke was executed.

Charlie had despised Reles. But Lepke had been Charlie's partner in the Amalgamated Clothing Union. They had had extensive holdings together in the garment district. Charlie always maintained that Lepke died like a man in the electric chair.

Many considered Dewey an egocentric individual. His opinion of himself was so high that after his defeat by Lehman for the governorship, barely a year later, in 1940, he aimed for the Republican nomination for president of the United States. Dewey hated the Democrats—even wrote a book called *The Case Against the New Deal*. He was convinced that the worst Republican was better than the best Democrat. The Republicans, however, preferred their more liberal member, Wendell Willkie (1940), who had won the hearts of his party with his folksy approach—as opposed to Dewey's cold, prosecuting ways. Although Dewey lost the nomination, to solidify party support for the future, he went on the road, campaigning for Willkie and denouncing Franklin Delano Roosevelt. But some Republicans found Dewey too exuberant in his talks. His own top party people were disturbed, even angry—said he was campaigning for himself, not Willkie, keeping his eye on the next presidential campaign in 1944. The election results were fairly predictable. World War II was under way, and the American people felt more secure with Roosevelt. Willkie was soundly defeated.

Ralph was eligible for parole in 1940, what with good behavior and other legal credits in his favor. When the guard came to get him in the weaving shop, a few inmates slapped him on the back, wishing him good luck, but Ralph was not very optimistic. He was sure Dewey wouldn't let him out—that he would do everything possible to keep him in Dannemora. He knew Dewey had his appointed men on the parole board to do his bidding.

When Ralph walked into the room, the parole officers sat waiting, their hands folded, their faces grim. He barely had time to sit down when one man sardonically quipped, "Why, Ralph Liguori, didn't your political friends help you make parole?" Ralph didn't bother answering. His parole was obviously being denied, so he stood up and walked out.

Ralph could have easily been paroled, based on his clean record in prison, but he was a "persona non grata" to Dewey. The guard escorted him back to the weaving shop, where his glum expression was enough for everyone. No one said a word; denial of his parole was understood. Work went on as usual.

At recreation break, Ralph found Charlie waiting. His group had gone on break earlier. By the expression on Charlie's face, Ralph knew Charlie had already received the news.

"Yeah . . . I know all about it," he mumbled sadly. "The stoolie in the laundry came and told me you got three more years for your minimum."

"Well, I expected that anyway . . . ," Ralph replied unhappily. "I knew I wasn't going to make the parole board . . . They're going to keep me in as much as they can."

"Come on, Ralph," Charlie coaxed brightly to change the subject, "let's go play some handball!"

That was just what Ralph needed. He had to slug something, hit something, to dispel his disappointment and force his hatred for Dewey out of his system. The vigorous game proved therapeutic.

When Ralph's brother, Armand, rushed to Dannemora the next day to find out what happened, Ralph was already in a better, calmer mood.

"I got three years for sitting on a chair," Ralph informed him.

"What!" exclaimed Armand, astonished.

"Yeah . . . ," Ralph replied sarcastically. "I went in, sat on a chair, and got three more years."

WPA workers were tearing down an old wall, as well as some old beams, to make way for the new church, and the clangor and pounding reverberated through the prison—evidence of progress.

Father Hyland donned prison overalls and helped sort out the brick, stones, slabs, and beams that could be salvaged for use. He worked alongside his men whenever he could, even taking up the shovel and helping to dig. Slowly at first, carloads of cement began arriving, followed by bulldozers, trench cutters, and steam shovels converging on the scene. If an inmate didn't actually work manually to build the church, he participated in other ways. Joe Zox sent more barrels of fish to the prison; he had continued to send large amounts of fish *gratis* to Dannemora. Once when the truck arrived, the workers hoisted one barrel and brought it out to the yard; then about ten men formed a human ring to bury the barrel under the earth. This served as Charlie's and Ralph's personal supply for their fish cookouts. The work moved steadily along, and the spirit had captured everyone. Of even greater importance, it gave everyone a purpose and kept many inmates sane.

At one point, the workers stopped work on the scaffolding because they found a bird's nest, which contained a few eggs, and heard the mother bird crying. They immediately called the chaplain; they didn't want to break up a home. What to do? Father Hyland's eyes searched the heavens for patience and fortitude.

The church received extensive publicity with newspapers covering the event. But the commentary wasn't all good. The New York League for Separation of Church and State was in opposition. Some antagonists called it the church of the "Hoodlum Saint." Father Hyland was subpoenaed to defend his project in court on April 14, 1940, but he won! The difficulties were finally overcome.

The church was an enormous piece of Gothic architecture, measuring 156 by fifty-two feet, with a wide gate to the entrance grounds. The tower, built of solid masonry, rose to a height of 125 feet. Authorities worried that someone could leap from the tower onto the wall and escape. More time was spent to look into the control of that probability, but it was agreed it would be an impossible feat. The interior would accommodate about twelve hundred persons, and in the space surrounding the church, Father Hyland planned to have gardens where one could sit and meditate. A beautiful altar was donated by a wealthy woman. It was a unique work of art—supposedly the original altar that the explorer Magellan had brought from Spain to some island, where it is said a small miracle occurred. Kneeling before it, the entire island population had become Christianized. Above the altar was a huge oil painting of Saint Dismas painted by a gifted prisoner. A fellow inmate by the name of Domenic had proudly posed for it. Tile floors glistened, and there were fourteen windows in which stained glass, representing the stations of the cross, were eventually to be inserted. For the moment, temporary plain glass let the sun's bright rays pierce through. There was a baptistery and a couple of small side chapels—one which was to house a beautiful statue of Saint Dismas—to be sculpted by another gifted prisoner.

There was still a great deal of unfinished work (like the wall that led nowhere, which had yet to come crumbling down), but the church stood ready, in all its glory, to celebrate its dedication. After weeks of preparation, its first pontifical mass was said on August 28, 1941. It was indeed quite an achievement. Everyone was excited that Sunday! One inmate, with musical talent, had written original music for the prison choir, and the celestial sounds filled the hearts of everyone present. Two thousand men participated at the mass; hundreds more were on their feet, along the side aisles, and in the back of the church. The overflow stood outside the great doorway in what would be future garden spaces. The administration had invited many important New York dignitaries and civic group leaders to share and participate in the dedication with its convict parishioners. With hands clasped, everyone stood silently as the bishop spoke; openly moved, he read the telegram from Pope Pius XII, thanking all the inmates who had participated in building the church. Many men, some hardened criminals, had tears in their eyes. It was the first time in the history of the U.S. penitentiary system that a church had been built within its walls. Dannemora had made history, and its inmates were very, very proud.

The following Sunday, Father Hyland announced that whoever had not made his first Holy Communion and Confirmation—and wished to do so—should contact him. Ralph returned to his cell, his mind wandering back to when he was a child of some eight years old. He remembered having seen an orderly procession of people walk up to the altar to receive Holy Communion. He didn't know much about the sacrament then, but he decided to join them. When the priest slipped the holy Eucharist into his mouth, Ralph began to eat it but ran outside to spit it out. He went home and related the incident to his mother, which resulted in his receiving a swift slap in the face. Ralph stood back and stared in surprise at his mother. He couldn't imagine what he had done wrong. Agnes had tried to explain, but Ralph's feelings were hurt. Defiantly, he began to play hooky from Sunday school. He later learned the meaning of it all, but he never did make his Holy Communion or, consequently, his Confirmation.

Ralph couldn't expunge that childhood experience from his mind. *Why not?* he wondered. *Why not do it now!* Ralph decided to talk it over with Charlie.

"You know . . . Charlie . . . I never took my first Holy Communion . . . or Confirmation," he remarked with an effort at nonchalance, sitting up on the hill, looking vaguely out into the distance.

"You're kidding!" exclaimed Charlie. "Every Italian kid on the block made his first Holy Communion and was confirmed . . . What happened to you?" he asked incredulously.

"Nothing much. Had a bad experience . . . never got around to it . . . I guess. Now . . . I'm thinking . . . since Father Hyland brought it up . . . ," Ralph's voice trailed off.

Charlie laughed that laugh of his. "Go on . . . ," he urged. "Go ahead and make it, Ralph . . . *I'll be your godfather!*"

They chuckled over the episode, and Ralph sent word to the runner to write him down for classes. He was excused from work to attend a few catechism lessons in preparation for the big day and truly immersed himself into the teachings. Ralph was very emotional on the designated Sunday in the Church of the Good Thief. Charlie straightened Ralph's tie, slapped him gently on the cheek, and smiled encouragingly, then stood behind him in line with his hand on his shoulder, as is customary for godfathers. Ralph felt his heart skip a few beats as he went up to receive the holy Eucharist. This time, he didn't spit it out. He felt closer to God than ever before, and he and Charlie had forged another bond between them.

According to tradition, a godfather is always supposed to look after his godchild.

CHAPTER TWENTY-THREE

The thump-pause-thump of the ball vigorously slapped against the wall reverberated in a steady rhythm throughout the yard, and the grunts and gasps of the players running and springing to wallop the ball made for interesting accompaniment. Handball offered the perfect therapy for the release of tensions and anger, and Ralph was a champion—the best server in his crowd. Usually, he played doubles with Charlie, Davey, and another friend. Sometimes he slugged it out in singles because Charlie and Davey loved playing cards, which Ralph disliked. Ralph couldn't even sit still long enough to finish a game. He was more the athletic type—loved the outdoors, running around, moving his body. That's why he loved handball. Sunday mornings he went out to the court at eight o'clock and played until noon, took a break for lunch, then went back until five in the afternoon. His frustrations seeped through his pores along with the sweat. Then, after a cold shower, he felt like a new man.

Recreation time was very important to the inmates, not only physically, but psychologically. They had an opportunity to socialize, to discuss their life's burdens, their plans, as well as to tell jokes or to indulge in ordinary horseplay. It all helped to loosen the tension and provide calm for the nerves and balm for the being.

Despite his situation and surroundings, Ralph never lost his friendly and generous attitude toward his fellow man, and he never faltered in his belief that the best policy was to mind one's own business. He had decided long ago that each man had a right to his own choices in life. In Dannemora, men came and went, each with a variety of stories on his back.

One fellow, Teddy Adonolfi, whom Ralph knew from the West Side of New York for about five years, was already in Dannemora when he arrived. Teddy had been involved in the Rosenthal kidnapping case, for which he was sentenced to sixty years in prison. Rosenthal was a New York State millionaire, and Teddy, along with three or four other men, was asking half a million dollars in ransom money. One of them squealed on the rest, and they all went to jail. The informer—who, of course, received a lesser sentence—was sent to Dannemora along with Teddy. The cohabitation was rather sticky, and the stoolie, a Jewish guy, obviously afraid of his comeuppance from Teddy, constantly sought transfer to another prison. When all else failed, he went to the warden with a far-fetched story that Teddy was planning to kidnap the warden's daughter. The warden did not fall for the fabricated tale but realized there was serious animosity between the two men. Something could break at any moment. He finally transferred the stoolie to Great Meadow Prison in Comstock, New York. Everyone sighed with relief.

Teddy was assigned to the hospital as a nurse's aide; it was a good job, and he was very happy there. As a man locked up for sixty years, he didn't want to do anything to jeopardize his job. Ralph always thought that underneath it all, Teddy was a good fellow. During outside breaks, he hung around Charlie's court. Ralph saw him often through the weave shop windows and made it a point to call him. "Hey, Teddy, how ya doin'?" And Teddy waved and grinned. In prison, it's little things that keep a human being going. Teddy died in Dannemora long after Ralph left.

During the notorious Lindbergh kidnapping case, Ralph and many others—including two men from New York, Irving Bitts and Savis Pacali—did their best to help find the child. They worked day and night trying to obtain information relating to the case, but they did not succeed. Their efforts, however, were appreciated by the warden.

But Ralph's temper was not always on even keel. In the weave shop one day, an inmate named Smithy, spurred on by an inferiority complex, lashed out in jealousy at Ralph—bad-mouthing him, calling Charlie a pimp, which was the ultimate provocation. At first Ralph ignored him, but when Smithy attacked again, calling Ralph a pimp to his face, that did it. Ralph had fashioned a knife, similar to a dagger, and kept it hidden underground in the yard. Charlie, always protective, was concerned about it, but Ralph insisted it was simply there as a precaution. Seeing his young friend white-lipped with anger, Charlie sensed trouble immediately, but Ralph denied there was any. Still outraged, however, Ralph seized his first opportunity to retrieve the knife and brought it furtively to his cell, intending to put it through Smithy's side. The next time Smithy walked toward him, apparently to badger him again, Ralph was just about to attack when reason intervened and brought him to his senses. If he pulled that knife, he'd never get out of prison. Why do it? Smithy was a poor slob, not worth the risk. *The hell with it,* he told himself. The observant Charlie heaved a sigh of relief when he saw Ralph restore the knife to its hiding place.

There were many tragic stories behind the inmates at Dannemora, and Ralph heard his fill of them. George Scalise was president of the Elevator Union in New York and part of their clique in the prison yard. Ralph remembered the man as an undertaker in Brooklyn. Scalise had been charged with embezzlement of funds and was sentenced to five to ten years in Dannemora. He was heartbroken to land in prison after having held such an important job, but he too had to make the best of it. Ralph and Charlie tried to make him feel important by treating him to handmade shoes and tailor-made pants. Scalise was out of Dannemora before Ralph.

But the person to whom Ralph became most strongly attached was an eighteen-year-old boy whom he nicknamed Zootsuit, because the boy wore his pants in the late thirties style—wide pleats tapering down to narrow cuffs at the ankle. Zootsuit had received a sentence of thirty years for manslaughter. He was sent to Dannemora because only two months earlier, he had turned eighteen. Had the fatal event happened before, he would have been considered a minor and sent to a criminal reformatory. His crime too had been the result of a bad temper. Zootsuit had graduated from high school and had gone back to school to visit a friend. Sitting on the staircase, waiting, Zootsuit had lit a cigarette. A teacher walking by had caught him smoking (not allowed on school premises) and, unaware that Zootsuit was no longer a student, slapped his face. A frenzied resentment surged up inside Zootsuit. *What right did he have to slap me?* He raged and staggered to his feet, his hand soothing his burned cheek. Cold hatred rising, it took no time for him to acquire a pistol. Still fuming, Zootsuit went back and shot the teacher, who fell instantly to death. When his rage quieted, and coming to his senses, the young man was deeply regretful, but it was too late.

Ralph, hearing the story, thought Zootsuit was a damned fool to kill his teacher over so trivial an incident. But, remembering the venom of his own rage, he understood how resentment could easily lead to violence. Revenge and the defense of one's honor had been around for a long time. In former days, gentlemen resorted to strict rules of dueling to death (using swords or pistols) to protect their sacred honor.

Zootsuit was placed in the cell next to Ralph, who treated him like a son. Ralph devised a knock signal to call him and won him over with coffee and sandwiches. They tied a rope to the prison bars nearest their two cells—a rope long enough to hold a checkerboard, which, with clever ingenuity, they tied into place. Then, with their arms and hands extending through the bars, they played dominoes or checkers—sometimes all night long.

The night before Ralph left Dannemora, Zootsuit kept him up all night playing dominoes. No one slept a wink. Zootsuit had grown very fond of Ralph and hated to see him go. With tears in his eyes, he accepted all the goods Ralph bequeathed to him—four pairs of shoes, bedding, warm blankets, a radio, a coffeepot, hot plates, books, everything Ralph had owned in prison. Ralph was misty-eyed also. He always remembered Zootsuit and what a waste of a human life the misguided youth represented.

After almost five years, Ralph was taken out of the weave shop and made a hall man. Davey Betillo, a year later, left the dye shop, and he too became a hall man in the East Hall, which was later torn down. Charlie remained in the laundry. Ralph didn't find his new job very stimulating but did his best to help the other inmates as much as he could.

Ultimately, Ralph's talents were wanted elsewhere, and he was transferred to the dye shop—a job he had till the end. He was eventually promoted to head engineer with six men under his supervision.

In prison, a man learned to pick his friends carefully. Some men accepted their prison terms philosophically while others never could. There were always those hard, cold-blooded characters who didn't give a damn about anything; it was the sensitive guys who suffered the most, especially if they didn't have visitors—no apparent ties, no one who cared about them. All the inmates looked forward to having visitors. Visitors proved they were still loved, were still part of the human race.

Visiting hours were in the afternoon. Ralph's family would alternate. Sometimes Agnes and Anna visited, but more often Armand, who came up on the train together with Charlie's brother Bart. If something out of order was discussed between prisoner and visitor, a policeman tapped the prisoner on the shoulder and escorted him back to his cell. Judge McCook was an exception and, later, a few others, about whom Ralph was kept in the dark—until much later.

Mail was also important, and it was better not to expect it. A man could go crazy waiting—especially if nothing arrived.

Dotty finally wrote. It took some courage on her part after all that had transpired, but she did. She expressed her sorry, acknowledging guilt, depressed because they hadn't given her a chance to recant. She asked to be forgiven, redeclaring her love for Ralph. Ralph, of course, had forgiven Dotty from the beginning. He knew what she had been up against—all the pressures and anxieties, which Dewey had put her through. It was another reason to hate Dewey.

Dotty also wrote Ralph about their dog; she said they were inseparable, and that the dog was a constant reminder of their love. She was forced to sign her letters using Ralph's wife's name because of the censors who read and stamped all the letters with a code in the warden's office.

But about two years after his arrival in Dannemora, Armand, on one of his usual visits, had some startling news.

"Ralph . . . I don't know how you're going to take this . . . ," Armand began solemnly, and a warning bell ran in Ralph's head. "Dotty . . . asked me . . . to ask you . . . if it's all right if she got married?"

"Married?" Ralph replied, stunned as images of the girl he loved raced swiftly through his mind.

Noticing the disappointment on Ralph's face, Armand tried to mitigate the blow. "Yeah . . . Ralph . . . now take it easy . . . She said she met a nice boy who wants to marry her. Guess she would like to return to her hometown and settle down, have a family."

Armand kept studying Ralph's reaction. Ralph sat quietly—in a trance. He loved Dotty very deeply, but he was also aware of the very difficult experiences she'd been through. He could offer her nothing locked up the way he was, not knowing what his future would be. Ralph's thoughts focused haphazardly on so many memories, bringing to life the long-buried pulsating sensations he had shared with Dotty. He recalled how she had captivated him on their first date, the time he had her cured, the day he presented her with the beautiful Pomeranian dog. Suddenly, it was too much; Ralph cupped his hands over his eyes. Perfect love was perfect freedom. Someone had said that, and the thought had remained with him. He realized a sign of his love would be to release her. Yes, that much he had to do for her—free her, even if it tore him apart.

"Okay . . . ," he finally answered, resolute.

"Okay . . . what?" Armand asked, looking puzzled.

"Tell her it's okay to get married," Ralph managed, then paused; he was choking on his words. "And tell her . . . tell her to be happy for me too."

Armand nodded sympathetically. He took one last look at Ralph's glistening eyes. He wanted to hug his younger brother, comfort him, but he knew he couldn't. Reluctantly, he rose, made a helpless gesture, then hurried away.

Ralph returned to his cell and immediately took from beneath his cot the shoebox, which contained all of Dotty's letters. He selected one letter at random, and then another, and then yet another—read and reread every one until his eyes were too blurred with tears to go on. He hid his face against his cushion; then he finally succumbed to the agonizing heartache and fell asleep, dreaming of the Dotty he had just liberated from his life.

But Dotty remained forever in his heart.

CHAPTER TWENTY-FOUR

"Tony . . . how many times have I told you . . . you've got to be more careful with the women you pick up . . . ," Ralph admonished.

Tony had picked up a slight venereal disease during one of his amorous adventures, and Ralph was driving him to see their mutual friend, Dr. Gardner, on West End Avenue.

"Yeah . . . Ralph . . . you're right . . . you're right . . ." Tony nodded repeatedly, but when he saw how serious Ralph was, he laughed and made a fraternal apology. "Hey . . . Ralphy . . . it's okay . . . I'm going to be all right. Dr. Gardner told me . . . Relax . . ." Tony was a mischievous, handsome son of a gun.

They took the elevator to Dr. Gardner's office, and as Tony opened the door, Ralph caught sight of a pair of the most beautiful legs he had ever seen, neatly crossed. He lifted his gaze and focused on the face—lovely white skin, delicate features, large blue eyes, and a mass of beautiful blonde hair. Her expression was that of a Madonna—sweet, innocent. *What a gorgeous creature,* he thought, taking an empty chair opposite her in the waiting room. The shy young woman felt the electric charge in the air. Her eyes met Ralph's, and without a smile, she acknowledged his presence. There was something strange, something different about the girl besides her unique beauty. Ralph felt drawn to her, in an unusual way, with a tremendous compulsion to know who she was. Just then, Dr. Gardner's nurse called the blonde beauty, and she vanished, breaking the spell.

Once Tony and Ralph were admitted into the doctor's office, Ralph asked, "Listen, Doc . . . who was that girl?"

"What girl?" teased Dr. Gardner.

"You know . . . *that* girl!" Ralph emphasized, pointing to the door.

"Oh . . . you mean Dotty Fletcher. Beautiful . . . eh . . . Ralph?"

"Christ . . . the most beautiful creature I ever saw!"

"Want to meet her, huh?" And before Ralph answered, "She'll be here again next week. If you stop by with Tony . . . I'll introduce you."

The week flew by, and Ralph again brought Tony to Dr. Gardner's for his checkup—anxiously waiting for his introduction to Dotty. Dr. Gardner handled the niceties very well, and it was agreed that Ralph would take Dotty home. He drove her directly to the modest rooming house on Eighty-fourth and West End Avenue where she lived and very aptly elicited her agreement for a date the next evening. Then, as a perfect gentleman, he took his leave.

The following night, Ralph spent longer than usual preparing for his date. He wore his dark blue silk suit, favorite tie, sprayed on his best cologne, and donned a wide-brimmed fedora to match his suit. He wanted to look especially good for Dotty. When she opened the door, Ralph caught his breath. She was surely a heavenly creature, something divine, nothing coarse or vulgar about her—a goddess. She wore a green crepe dress, softly draped to one side, with several strands of long white pearls reaching from her slender neck to rest gently on the rise of her young breasts. Her almost shoulder-length hair slightly brushed the silver foxtails casually wrapped around her slim shoulders. She smiled timidly, and Ralph soon learned that Dotty was a very shy, sensitive girl—someone to cherish and protect. He discovered that behind her reserved manner, she was a very defenseless child, insecure against the grim realities of life. His chest swelled. He took her arm and led her to his car.

They went to an Italian restaurant downtown, and after some fine cuisine and a glass of the best rose wine, Dotty loosened up. She told Ralph she had been born in Albany, New York, and had left home when she was seventeen. Her one ambition was to break into show business, and she had begun her career as a burlesque dancer in Manhattan. With her height of five feet six, perfect proportions, and million-dollar legs, she had worked her way up to Minsky's on Forty-second Street. At eighteen, Dotty was already working in the famous Follies chorus line, under the pseudonym Dotty Fletcher. Her real name was Nancy Presser, but to Ralph, she always remained Dotty. Dotty continued at the Follies until it closed in 1930, and at twenty-two, she was still doing bit parts here and there.

After dinner, the twosome left for a famous Broadway show in the elegant Theater District. When Ralph witnessed how thrilled Dotty was, he was riding high. During the first act, Dotty rose to go to the powder room; and when she returned, Ralph noticed her eyes glistening. An uncomfortable suspicion crossed his mind, but he shrugged it off. He took her straight home that night and, feeling strangely confused, went home.

But he couldn't shake her vision from his mind. It was more than love at first sight; an almost mystic spell had come over him. He knew he had to have her. Gathering all his self-confidence, he arranged to see her. Leaning against the door with his hat in his hands, Ralph spoke as calmly as possible, offering to move her into a lovely room at the Brent Hotel, owned by a friend of his, on Eightieth and Broadway. He expected a certain amount of resistance, but without a word of argument, Dotty quietly packed her belongings and followed Ralph to his car. She too had been smitten. Ralph was hard to resist.

That evening, they repeated the routine of their first date; Ralph knew she was crazy about Broadway shows. He was ready to do anything to make her happy. Again, during the first act, she excused herself and returned with her eyes glowing. Ralph's suspicions were now definitely aroused, especially when she practically fell asleep during the second act. Still, he said nothing. She was such a good-natured girl that he hated to upset her; besides, he was sure she would burst into tears. After the show, he almost spoke to her about it but decided to hold off. He had other plans for the evening. He had waited long enough.

"Do you have time for a drink, tonight . . . Ralph?" Dotty purred when they reached her hotel. She was anxious to continue the evening with the handsome, blue-eyed, baby-faced young man-about-town. Dotty had been with many men since leaving the Follies but always with reluctance to support herself. But her feeling for Ralph was different. She *wanted* to be seduced.

Ralph waited for her in bed, the covers drawn up to his chest. Dotty was taking a hell of a long time in the bathroom getting ready, he thought. He had never understood why women went through all the bother of dressing up for bed. But he too was vulnerable to the esthetic side of lovemaking—and loved undressing his women.

Dotty finally appeared in a pale blue negligee with a low round neckline, which exposed the upper globes of her bosom; and from her tiny waist, folds of silk fell softly about her slender hips. Her complexion was smooth and delicate, like fine porcelain, and her large blue eyes, picking up the color of her gown, were like crystals. Ralph felt his whole being aroused; he promised himself to savor every moment of the night's enchanting rhapsody. Dotty shyly approached the bed, and Ralph reached out for her with arms outstretched. He held her gently in his arms as though she were a fragile china doll, afraid she would break into tiny pieces. He was experiencing a new emotion. His heart was full of love for her—a love that was a thing apart from the passion she aroused in him.

Carefully, Dotty cradled her new lover in her arms; and as Ralph quivered with the glide of her fingertips, she treated him to sweet, fragrant kisses. He rolled over and lifted strands of her beautiful blonde hair in his hands, looked into the blue depths of her eyes, then smothered her with all the kisses he had been saving for her. Dotty took his body and pressed it tightly to her, causing the sensation of oneness, until Ralph's manhood spoke to him. Tenderly, he expertly stroked her wreath of love until, sensing her arousal, he entered her warmth, stirred to the quick by the melodic harmony he experienced. As Dotty threw back her head, uttering a low groan of pleasure, they responded to each other in a litany of endearing phrases.

Ralph couldn't see Dotty the next night, but a day later, he took her to the movies. Again, she visited the ladies' room; and again, Ralph caught her dozing. He was determined to discover whether his suspicions about her using drugs were correct. He could think of nothing else. He knew she was a loner, had no real friends, so it was up to him.

That evening in the hotel room, while she was in the bathroom getting ready, Ralph began to search the place upside down; he even stood on a chair to peek into the chandelier but found nothing. He loosened his tie and stared around the room for a clue. Then he glanced at the closet, which was half-open. He noticed her coat. The coat! He grabbed it and searched the pockets, then the lining, and there it was. He found what he was looking for—a phial of heroin. Even with his suspicions, Ralph was both surprised and sickened. Just then, Dotty appeared at the door, stopping dead in her tracks. Frightened, she gazed at Ralph, who sat on the edge of the bed with the heroin in one hand and her coat in the other.

She tried to be brave. Very quietly, she said, "I've been taking it for over a year and a half . . . I got hooked on it while I was still at the Follies . . ." She started to cry.

Ralph was shaking with anger. "Listen . . . Dotty. I could kill you! You've broken my heart! Why . . . why?" he wailed.

"When I was working . . . I used to get tired easy . . . and one of the girls persuaded me to try the stuff . . . said it would give me extra going power . . . And before I knew it, I was hooked. Oh . . . Ralph, I'm sorry. I don't want to . . . It's stronger than I am. What can I do?" She was breathlessly sobbing now.

Ralph's voice was reaching high peaks. He was a wounded animal, angry, ferocious. His goddess had lost her divinity. He wanted to crush her, smash her, but instead, he lamented.

"Listen . . . Dotty . . . I don't want to hurt you, but I can't leave you this way, in this condition . . ." With a strained voice, he exclaimed, "Dotty . . . I don't want you to take this stuff!" Then more gently, "Look . . . I want to have you cured . . . Okay . . . Do you want to take the cure or not?"

"Oh, yes . . . Ralph . . . yes . . . I'll take the cure. I want to be cured . . . honest!" She threw herself into his arms and continued sobbing.

Ralph kissed her tenderly on the cheek while he crushed the phial of heroin in his hand. Ralph never claimed to be a saint, but there was something about narcotics that left him completely cold. He was 100 percent against it.

Ralph paid a visit to his very good friend Dr. Gardner, who knew of Dotty's problem.

"Doc . . . you've got to help me . . . got to do me a favor. Do you know where I can send Dotty to be cured?"

"Sure . . . Ralph . . . there are some good sanitariums. I'll get in touch with you in a couple of days. Don't worry . . . I'll do my best."

"Okay . . . Doc . . . I'll be waiting."

About three or four days later, Ralph took Dotty to a private sanitarium in Hartford, Connecticut, for the cure. Dr. Gardner had made all the arrangements.*

The sanitarium was host to Dotty for a month. When she was released, she was the picture of health—even more beautiful. Her cheeks were rosier, and her blue eyes were as clear as the skies in early spring. She ran into Ralph's arms, and he swung her around with joy. Deliriously happy, they drove back to New York and drank champagne to celebrate Dotty's recovery. They were a happy twosome—always together. No other woman mattered to him.

Ralph kept her in style; she became a lady of leisure. Dotty's one downfall, however, was her devastating addiction to drugs, which Ralph constantly tried to cure. Only a month later, Ralph noticed the familiar sign in Dotty's eyes. Frustrated, he grew cross with everyone. He never allowed anyone to enter her room, and when he confronted her, Dotty told him he was imagining things. But Ralph was not easily fooled.

One night, he overrode all his obligations and parked in a borrowed car, a few feet up from the hotel entrance, to avoid being noticed. About 9:00 p.m., he saw Dotty leave the hotel and walk to the corner of Broadway. She handed some money to a young man who, in turn, gave her a tiny package. It was enough. Ralph had seen it all. He allowed

---

* There have been things written about Ralph that are outright lies—terrible lies, which have him introducing narcotics to Dotty and that, after meeting him, it was only downhill for her. An outraged Ralph remonstrated that the sensational writers should have, at the very least, researched their facts before slandering a person.

Dotty to return to the hotel undisturbed; then he sprang from his car and grabbed the fellow.

"What did you give that girl?" Ralph hissed, pulling the man's collar tight around his throat.

"Nothing!" the man choked.

"Don't tell me nothing . . . you bastard," Ralph's hands were tightening around his neck.

"A guy's got to make a living," the peddler managed to say.

"Listen . . . you creep . . . that's my girl . . . and I'm warning you . . . Don't let this happen again! Do you know me?"

"No!" The blood was now rushing to the peddler's face.

"Well, I'm going to tell you something . . . ," Ralph threatened. "I'm not the type to get anyone arrested . . . but I'm going to warn you . . . Don't you ever let me catch you again . . . because I'm not going to talk to you this way next time. I'm going to talk to you . . . a different way. Got me?"

The man's head bobbed up and down, and Ralph released him. He had obtained the man's word.

Ralph walked to the hotel in a sweat. He opened the door to Dotty's room and leaned against the door, removing his handkerchief to dry his damp forehead. Dotty saw the grim expression on his face and panicked.

"All right, Dotty," he began. "I saw the whole thing come off. What do you want to do now?"

At first Dotty was speechless; then she began to cry helplessly. "I'm sorry . . . I'm sorry . . . Ralph . . . Please forgive me. I do want to get well!" Her sobs became heavier. "I don't know . . . Guess I'm still weak . . . Please believe me. I want to get well for both of us. I love you so . . . Help me!" Dotty pulled at her hair in desperation.

Ralph went to her and tenderly took her in his arms. What could he do? He was desperately in love. "I believe you, Dotty. Okay . . . okay . . . let it go the way it is," he whispered, trying to comfort her. "I'll get you cured again . . . before you really get hooked bad . . ."

They both agreed to give the sanitarium another try. It was arranged she would return there in a week. Meanwhile, Ralph stayed close to her, saw her every day. He felt he had to watch Dotty for her own good. But Dotty couldn't wait out the week, and her supply of heroin didn't last. It wasn't long before Ralph caught the dope peddler hastily leaving the hotel, his neck gyrating like a snake as he searched frantically around. Ralph appeared out of nowhere and snatched him up and knocked him forcefully against the wall.

"You goddamn bastard, I thought I told you to stay away from her!" Ralph grabbed him again and, with his steel fists, hit him so hard that the pitiful drug pusher fell through a pane of glass.

Two plainclothesmen came rushing out of a police car. "What happened, Ralph?" they called out.

"Nothing . . . ," he replied, unruffled. "I just had a slight argument with this guy . . . that's all."

"You sure? Want this bum inside?"

"Naw . . . it's nothing. Let him go." Ralph looked at the bum coldly and added, "*This* time!"

"Okay . . . Ralph . . . if you say so." The policemen walked away but waited casually in front of their car.

Ralph grabbed the peddler again hard. His face was already swollen, and his broken nose was bleeding badly. "Okay . . . buster . . . I'll give you just two days to get out of town. Don't let me ever see you again . . . ever!"

Torn and tattered, the man fled like hell, and Ralph never ever saw him again.

Shattered, Ralph slowly went up to see Dotty. He was tired, emotionally drained. Even the key in his hand felt heavy, and he wearily pushed the door open. Dotty was poised with one leg on the bed, skirt hiked up, thigh exposed, syringe in hand as she gave herself a shot of dope. Ralph cringed. The sound of the door alerted her, and she turned his way, her eyes already dreamy. Ralph felt hurt, sick—a pain he could not identify. He had come to know the hell of drug addiction, how the addict would do anything when he did not have the needed narcotics, how he would sell his friends down the river, or even kill if he had to in order to obtain his dosage. Ralph later was often accused of selling narcotics, but he never did. He couldn't. He had too much heart.

Dotty, her lips pursed petulantly, moved close to Ralph like a child begging forgiveness. Exhausted, he took her into his arms and whispered, "Okay . . . Dotty . . . in a few days you'll be back in the sanitarium. We'll get you well . . . if it's the last thing I do!" He stroked her shoulder and smoothed back her hair in a loving gesture to comfort her. She smiled a gorgeous smile, but Ralph barely saw it. He was picturing the entrance to the sanitarium.

All his commitments for a few days were canceled. Ralph drove up to Hartford to fetch Dotty the day she was released from the sanitarium, after another month's cure. He had decided on a special surprise for her. Realizing Dotty needed company in his absence, he had bought a beautiful pedigree dog (a miniature Pomeranian), which he felt sure she would love. Anxious as a sixteen-year-old, he knocked on her door and stuck his head in. Dotty was tossing a few articles into her overnight bag.

"Hi . . . ," Ralph said cheerfully.

"Hi . . . you're early," she replied sweetly, and her eyes darted immediately to the fluffy little bundle in Ralph's arms. "Oooooh . . . ," she squealed, "isn't she precious! Is it for me . . . Ralph?"

Ralph nodded and smiled, happiness filling his entire being. Dotty gently took the dog and caressed it tenderly, cooing to it as though it were an infant.

"How do you feel?" Ralph asked more seriously, scrutinizing her face. It was fresh again—like that of the well-scrubbed all-American girl. Her blonde hair was brushed freely away from her face, and the white of her soft blue eyes were clear—pure. She wore just a trace of lipstick, and a sweet fragrance clung to her.

"Wonderful *now*, and so hungry!" she gasped with delight.

"You look terrific," he exclaimed. "Thought I'd take you to Albany to see your folks. Would you like that?"

"Oh . . . Ralph," she hummed, embracing him, almost forgetting the tiny creature caught between them. They looked at each other and laughed.

"Okay . . . then . . . let's go," Ralph sang.

They arrived in Albany in the early evening. Dotty's family lived in a quiet Polish neighborhood where most of the homes were of wood frame—in a variety of quaint shapes and styles. Their home was a small two-story frame with a front porch, which went around part of the way on one side, and squarely in the center was a two-seater swing. As they pulled up, they saw Dotty's mother seated in a rocker, busy with her sewing basket. When they stepped out of the car, the elderly woman rose slowly, gently putting down her sewing, and, with a look of radiant surprise, watched the young couple come toward her.

"Dotty . . . ," she murmured, stretching out her arms.

Dotty rushed into her mother's embrace. Ralph noticed the woman wore her grayish blonde hair in a low bun, which rested lightly on the nape of her neck. Age had marked her delicate features, and Ralph could see that hard work and hard times had drawn a film of weary sadness over her eyes. But suddenly, there was excitement in the air as Dotty's mother shouted for her husband and young son to come running.

"Dotty's here! Dotty's home!" It echoed from one end to the other of the small house.

The modest home seemed to come alive with a festive spirit. Although Ralph was initially ignored, he was soon properly introduced. Dotty's mother was a little apprehensive at first, and understandably so, thought Ralph. But as the hours passed, she became more congenial. Mrs. Presser was a fine woman, extremely defensive and overly protective of her daughter—and ecstatic that she had her little girl back for a few days. Dotty's father, on the other hand, was a friendly fellow and, like most Polish men Ralph knew, loved his beer. He worked in a nearby plant, and Ralph was willing to wager he made a meager living. Ralph took him out the next day to buy a few cases of beer, and that night, the men drank more than their share—in honor of the homecoming. Dotty's brother was still attending school and, from what Ralph could gather, was an honor student. The boy was happy to see his sister; they went off alone together sometimes, talking, sometimes teasing, but mostly just happy.

Dotty absorbed all the family love like a sponge and returned it in kind. Ralph would always remember how serenely Dotty behaved then. They left in only a few days, but Ralph wanted to prolong the special glow of their happy interlude. He wanted to give Dotty something extra to separate the past from the present—to cancel all the negatives they had both known and to start again, fresh and unscarred. He decided to take her to Saratoga Springs to continue their furlough from the darkness of life in the city and to provide the happiest, most memorable time of their young lives.

CHAPTER TWENTY-FIVE

Saratoga Springs, better known as Saratoga to most race fans, is a beautiful town in the southeastern foothills of the Adirondacks. Originally an Indian camping ground, its mineral springs, spectacular landscape, and mild climate made it one of the most fashionable spas in the country and, perhaps as a consequence, became the horse racing center of those years. In fact, in the late eighteen hundreds, a Saratoga association for the improvement of horse breeding was established and sponsored annual horse races. In later years, race fans could visit the National Museum of Racing, full of sweet memories depicting the importance of Saratoga in its heyday. Saratoga conjured up the thrilling excitement when the bell clanged, and the horses took off to the screams and shrills of the spectators, yelling for their favorite to pull up front.

Charlie "Lucky" silently owned a part of the tracks, and yet, he was often there to bet just like any racing fan. It was in his blood; he loved to gamble on the ponies. Ralph almost always saw Charlie in a choice box, whenever he went up to Saratoga to unwind.

With Dotty snuggled close to him, Ralph headed the car toward the Kentucky Club, a plush restaurant and bar owned by Ralph's uncle Tommy Dyke and his brother, Johnny. The décor was luxurious with fine wood paneling, nice thick red carpeting, and murals on the walls depicting some of the finest racehorses. It was close to the tracks and frequented by the top Albany politicians, celebrities, and sportsmen, as well as by the boys. Ralph stopped in every time he made an appearance in Saratoga to pay respects to Uncle Tommy, who never lost his interest in him or in the family welfare. There was no question about Ralph's fondness for him. As he and Dotty happily walked in, Ralph saw Tom Dyke sporting one of his own famous cigars, entertaining a group of cronies. He looked toward Ralph, and his face lit up. With a broad smile, Dyke left his table to meet the young couple.

"Ralph, you son of a gun, good to see you, kid." Then, turning to Dotty, he added approvingly, "I see you haven't lost your touch!" Dotty smiled shyly. She was as fresh as a morning rose, young, sweet, full of life. "Gotta hand it to you . . . ," he chuckled. "This one has to be the most beautiful yet!"

Ralph grinned from ear to ear and proudly introduced Dotty. Then Tom led the happy twosome to the table of onlookers, some of whom Ralph had recognized. As they all looked admiringly at Dotty, Tom turned to one of the younger men seated in the group.

"Charlie . . . this is my nephew, Ralph, a very respectable boy . . . and real smart. I want you to take special care of him . . . now that you've met him." He smiled.

Ralph looked at Charlie, who winked at him; of course, they knew each other but said nothing. Then Charlie, for Tom's benefit, extended his hand and strongly clasped Ralph's. "Ralph . . . ," he grinned. "This is what I call a real formal introduction."

Everyone laughed, and Ralph and Dotty joined the crowd for a round of drinks to toast for Dotty—the center of attraction.

That afternoon, Dotty and Ralph met Charlie with a girlfriend in one of the local hangouts for sandwiches and coffee. Charlie "Lucky" was indeed lucky with the girls, but he made it his business to remain footloose and fancy free. He always said he couldn't afford to be tied down, and he was right. The girls all knew it but loved him just the same. The men soon kissed their girls good-bye, leaving them on their own, while Charlie went to the races, and Ralph strolled over to a crap game. The next day, Charlie left for New York, but Dotty and Ralph enjoyed a few more days of their tryst.

Perhaps Charlie did not know that Ralph was indirectly related to Tom Dyke, but after that specific introduction, which Charlie took seriously, he became an even closer and generous friend to Ralph—very often playing the big brother role. Ralph never needed anything because he was his own boss, but if he ever did, Charlie would have complied without hesitation. Contrary to what many people have thought, Ralph always considered Charlie "Lucky" Luciano a perfect gentleman. Naturally, he could be provoked; but as Ralph reasoned, what kind of a man doesn't react in some way or another to a raw deal?

Charlie enjoyed nightclubs just as much as Ralph. Many nights they ended up together at Tilly's kitchen on 134th Street and Seventh Avenue. Tilly's was famous for its delicious Southern fried chicken. While savoring the tasty ingredients, one couldn't help noticing how the black male dancer had curled himself up like a snake, gyrating about. He had the ability to twist his hips into an incredible position, elongating his whole body to resemble a corkscrew. Tilly's was open until five in the morning, and at that hour, one could meet different types of people from all walks of life—and for all reasons.

On Sunday night, Ralph and Charlie hung out at Small's Paradise in Harlem. It was usually one of the last jumping-off places. Ralph could not resist taking Dotty there to see Gladys Bentley, a black singer-dancer who danced on her toes and picked up twenty-dollar bills with the muscles between her legs. Dotty wouldn't believe it (pooh-poohed the idea), so Ralph prearranged it with Gladys to dance her way to their table that evening. Ralph placed a twenty-dollar bill next to his glasses, and sure enough, there came Gladys.

During the week, and sometimes on Saturday, Ralph stopped at the Village Barn in Greenwich Village around the cocktail hour. Two of the most famous habitués were Pat O'Brien and Spencer Tracy, along with many other aspiring young actors. Ralph saw Pat alone often, but other times, Pat huddled together with Tracy, deep in conversation (no doubt about show business). Ralph admired Pat—a terrific guy and a fantastic storyteller. Pat's white skin would gradually turn pink, then a deeper crimson, depending on his stories, mood, and booze.

Pat loved to tease Ralph about the girls and would call out to him, "Hey . . . Ralphy . . . how ya doin'? The girls treating you right?"

Ralph blushed and grinned. "All right . . . Pat, all right."

Occasionally, they drank and chatted together at the bar. One night, Ralph, rather embarrassed, made a request. "Listen . . . Pat . . . you're already a famous guy. How 'bout giving me your autograph?"

"You're kidding . . ." He laughed.

"No, man . . . just think what it'll do for my reputation." Ralph beamed.

Pat, incredulous, was nevertheless willing to please. When he asked for something on which to write, Ralph fumbled around and came up with his driver's license, requesting the movie star to write on the back of it.

"Ralphy, you're a character," O'Brien exclaimed and signed his name.

Ralph spent the rest of the time listening to Pat's stories. What an entertainer!

That autograph came in handy for Ralph not long afterward as he drove back from a visit to Dotty in Hartford. His windows rolled down, he was enjoying the sweet summer breezes, his head full of thoughts of Dotty, when he heard a shrill whistle blow. He braked at once, realizing he had gone through a red light. A burly Irish cop came up to the window.

"Okay . . . bud . . . passing red lights your hobby," the cop sarcastically remarked.

"No, Officer . . . It must have changed on me. I'm really sorry," Ralph replied meekly.

"Oh, yeah, that story I've heard hundreds of times. Your license . . ." He snapped.

"Officer . . . believe me. I wouldn't lie to an Irishman. I was born on St. Patrick's Day!"

"You were, now," the cop said, disconcerted, examining Ralph's license. "Ahhh, so you were! What's this on the back of your license?" He referred to the autograph.

"I told you, I'm, a friend of the Irish. That happens to be Pat O'Brien's autograph. He's a very good friend of mine!"

"Ya mean the actor?"

"Ahuh . . ." Ralph nodded with pride.

"Oh, well now . . . why didn't you say so? You can tell Pat for me, that from one donkey to another, I just can't give ya a ticket. Be off now . . ." And waved Ralph on.

Ralph chuckled as he drove off. *Oh, the luck of the Irish,* he cried out, *but Italians have fun too!*

The Depression had brought with it great pain and insecurity, and people wanted to forget, to laugh, to be entertained. Many liked to dance their troubles away. It was the era of the "Ten Cents a Dance" ballrooms.

Sometimes Ralph met Charlie at the Rosemount on Fulton Street and Flatbush Avenue. At that time, the Rosemount was considered the elite of the dance halls—very high-class. One could easily catch Glenn Miller there leading his fresh young band. Ralph appreciated all forms of music; his favorites were jazz, half-time rag, and low music (the blues). He especially loved to go to the Alhambra Palace in Brooklyn to hear the Memphis Five group—the best Dixieland jazz band around town. They were sensational and always jammed the club. Ralph never forgot the trumpet player, Philly Napoli, and his high C's. On numerous nights, he and Charlie wound up in Harlem at the Cotton Club to listen to Louis Armstrong and Cab Calloway, who often joined the debonair twosome at their table for a few drinks. Ralph particularly liked Armstrong, who had a happy personality—made everyone feel good and was always ready to play someone's favorite tune.

The Cotton Club had also introduced a galaxy of talented people. Even Rudy Vallée, with his famous megaphone, made his appearance there as well as Ella Logan, the torch singer, who was also very popular on the radio and, later, became an actress. Charlie and Ralph met Ella at the Cotton Club, and immediately, it was a happy threesome. Ella's weakness, however, was for Charlie. She fell for his charm, and he helped make her famous by opening many nightclub doors for her. But Ella deserved success. In addition to her talent, she was a great gal and a close, loyal friend to the bitter end.

One of the late, late spots for the boys was Kings Terrace off Broadway, around Fifty-fifth Street, between Seventh and Eighth Avenues. It was an elegant nightclub, and Charlie and Ralph loved to get all decked out and walk in like royalty, showing off their beautiful women. There were times, however, when they went alone and had a few laughs and drinks with the showgirls. Occasionally, Ralph took Dotty to Ben Modern's Riviera Club, where Danny Kaye appeared before Hollywood grabbed him. Hollywood had absorbed much of the great talent that had sprung up in and around New York, finally gaining an opportunity for real exposure. Many became the giant pillars of show business while others emerged as great movie idols. Like everyone else, Ralph had his favorite singers, such as Bing Crosby, Kate Smith, Al Jolson, Deanna Durbin (whose lovely voice matched her radiant smile), and, later on, there was no one like Frank Sinatra.

In addition to his growing activities, Ralph was still giving a hand to his uncle Al, collecting from gin mill owners to whom Al had supplied alcohol and whiskey. Ralph had taken Dotty with him on a collection stop one cold, wintry night and had planned to step out with her later when suddenly, at Fifty-ninth Street and Ninth Avenue, near Roosevelt Hospital, Ralph felt a severe pain in his lower right side. *My god,* thought Ralph, *it's my appendix.* Dotty panicked, but with nerves of steel, Ralph pushed on the gas pedal and sped directly to the emergency entrance of the hospital.

"I'm afraid it looks like a ruptured appendix," a worried young intern said upon completing a cursory examination. "Can't leave. Very dangerous. Who's your doctor?"

Ralph's pain had sharpened significantly.

"Dr. Workman," he managed to reply.

"Get to him immediately, or we'll have to operate on you here," the young doctor cautioned.

Ralph phoned his physician in Long Island. It had snowed very heavily; the ground was solidly packed with snow, and the roads were hazardous. Dr. Workman advised Ralph to leave his car and to take a cab to the Hudson View Hospital on 152nd Street between West End and Riverside Drive. He would meet him there.

After half an hour, the resident on duty ordered Ralph wheeled into the operating room; and just as the anesthesia mask was being placed, he felt someone pinch his cheek. It was Dr. Workman in his surgical gown. Ralph relaxed and dozed off.

Fortunately, the operation was a success, although Ralph had had a close call. When Ralph came out of anesthesia, his blurred vision lightened on beautiful Dotty, who looked more relieved, as well as

Agnes, Anna, and his brothers. Dr. Workman confirmed that Ralph had had a narrow escape and had to remain in the hospital fifteen days to recuperate. Ralph hated to be confined anywhere and balked, but he was obliged to follow orders.

When he was finally discharged, he decided to do something special for the entire staff in appreciation for the royal treatment he had been given. He rented a nightclub for a night off Second Avenue from an acquaintance (Joe Dagressa)—the Rainbow Inn on East Second Street. All the hospital staff was invited, but when word spread downtown that Ralph was holding a shindig, many of his friends crashed the party. One of them had bumped into Jimmy Durante at a club, and Durante showed up with a few friends about two in the morning. The party was fantastic. Durante sang and played the piano for the crowd. Suddenly, three plainclothesmen entered and approached Jimmy, huddled over the piano in his usual style.

"You're under arrest!" they snarled.

"Under arrest? What's the charge?" Jimmy frantically screamed.

"Stolen car."

Jimmy turned to Ralph and cried, "Hey, Ralphy . . . tell these guys I'm Jimmy Durante . . . I have three cars in my garage!"

The detectives sneered. "We don't care who you are. We have orders to lock you up."

Jimmy kept pleading, "Ralphy . . . would you . . . talk to these guys!"

Ralph lifted his hands in a gesture of helplessness, grinning. "Hey, Jimmy . . . what the hell . . . I didn't know you went around stealing cars."

The crowd stood dumbfounded, watching incredulously. The detectives, however, completely detached, dragged Jimmy away—straight to the police station.

About a half hour later, Ralph and his friend Bill Ercolini left for the police station. There was Jimmy playing a minipiano, singing, "Inka Dinka Doo . . ." As soon as he saw Ralph, he stopped and burst into laughter.

"You son of a gun . . . I knew it had to be one of your wild tricks!"

Everyone, including the cops, had a good laugh over it. Then Ralph took Jimmy to Ferrara's Café for a special cup of coffee to mark *finito*, the end to a special day.

CHAPTER TWENTY-SIX

A politician (a politico) is shrewd, crafty, cunning, and, at times, not so lily-white in his dealings as one would think; some are outright ruthless. He needs contacts, people. And money—nice liquid cash to launch the campaign machinery to keep it running. How else can he win an election, secure that seat of power in which to wheel and deal? Ralph never understood people's surprise at learning that a politician was connected with an underworld figure. Not everyone is a millionaire's son, and even the rich boys need help. Money will not do it in every case. For some, it calls for favors. A businessman may support a candidate in exchange for some influence later on—for example, on a bill he wanted passed. The phrase *everyone has his price* applies to many. But there are men who cannot be bought to betray certain principles. Ralph was one such man. No price could persuade him to betray a friend. But Ralph paid an enormous price for this, and it tormented him all his life.

Charlie, through the ingenious leadership of Costello, placed many men in political office with money and votes, and they were not always grateful. As soon as they were seated behind their executive desks, they did an about-face and double-crossed the boys. Fiorello La Guardia, a man whom Charlie had once liked, had grown up in the same neighborhood as Charlie—the same that produced Augie Pisano, Joe Adonis, and Al Capone. La Guardia became congressman on the strength of Italian votes, and whether he knew it or not, Charlie had given his okay. But "Little Flower" La Guardia, once in office, was always on some crusade to wipe out the rackets. He stirred up such a fuss that he finally aroused the interest of Governor Roosevelt, and in 1931, the Seabury Commission was born to wipe out the gangsters and corruption in New York. Judge Seabury was another one of those seemingly righteous men, but he was going after Tammany Hall, also for personal revenge. Tammany Hall's support was essential for any Democratic candidate to win, and this support was once denied him. Seabury continued with his investigation, hitting hard—such as in his attacks on Mayor Jimmy Walker. But early in 1932, Governor Franklin Delano Roosevelt began pushing to become president; and he was shrewd, crafty, and cunning enough to know he had to water down the Seabury investigation. The

Democratic Convention in Chicago was coming up, and he needed Tammany Hall's support to win the presidential nomination.

Tammany Hall was originally called the Society of Tammany and was founded in New York City several years after the Revolutionary War by an Irishman, William Mooney. Initially, it was a patriotic fraternity club, but it soon turned to politics. Tammany Hall became a powerful political machine for the Democrats and wielded such authority as to influence politics, not only in New York, but throughout the country. The first leaders were Irish who, with their innate effervescent personalities, were naturals as politicians. They were great speakers as opposed to the early Italian immigrants, who had to first struggle to master the language, but they caught up in their own way.

At that particular time, Tammany Hall had two rival leaders: James J. Hines and Albert C. Marinelli. Ralph didn't know Hines personally, but Al was a very good friend whom he had met through his uncle Al. In fact, Al was his uncle's *compare*. Al was a neighborhood kid who grew up with his fists in the streets but persevered until he became district leader for the Democrats downtown. Later, with Charlie's assistance, he became state county clerk for New York. He was an attractive man with regular features—a ruddy complexion, black hair, and large luminous dark eyes. Taller than most Italians, he moved his lean, muscular body with an air of confidence. His positive, powerful appearance was combined with an easygoing personality and a smooth, modulated voice. Al was a born politician and drew people to him. A great deal of double-dealing transpired in Tammany Hall, but there were also many decent men there. Al helped Ralph several times, not for money, but simply for old-fashioned friendship. His friends were numerous, in and out of Tammany Hall: Al Smith, F. D. Roosevelt, and the latter's advisor, "Big Jim" Farley, to mention a few. Like Jimmy Hines, Al Marinelli had many allies in the underworld, and Charlie was a close friend.

There was quite a bit of unrest concerning the two 1932 presidential candidates, Al Smith and Franklin D. Roosevelt. Tammany Hall was split between them. Voters were contemplating a change. Most people were tired of Republican rule, which they blamed for the Depression—the unemployment that had driven the average man to despair. Charlie and his combination held meetings to work out their own strategies. They had no intention of losing Tammany Hall's protection. Charlie planned to go along with Al Marinelli, who was supporting Smith, and Costello joined Jimmy Hines in his campaign for Roosevelt. Politicians in their own right, they aimed to ensure that their operations would continue without too much interference from the law. And Tammany Hall needed them—that is, their money and the votes they controlled. The boys had the boroughs in their pockets.

During the Depression, money was tight. After the stock market crash, things went downhill for everyone, and the only men with ready cash were the boys. They had kept away from the stock market for obvious reasons. Not being able to stash all their money in banks like ordinary citizens, they missed out on the interest and legal investments. They had to find different ways to capitalize on the massive amount of money they had accumulated and hoarded away; they had to invest it, make it grow. They too had to expand their holdings. Later, they became real experts in laundering their money.

It was during this period that shylocking or loan sharking mushroomed into a giant business. It was already practiced by the old dons who preyed on the poor and ignorant immigrants; some were good guys, and some were bad guys. The bad dons squeezed and bled the immigrants until the poor suckers were bound hand and foot to them. With Charlie's outfit, things were different. It was a business, like everything else, and the practice spread throughout the underworld in all the major cities of the country—from the small hood all the way up to the lords and masters. Everyone needed money—rich men, poor men, beggars, thieves. The banks were reluctant (those that remained viable) to lend money even to the most respected businessman, and farmers with unharvested crops were up the creek. The average citizen didn't have a chance, let alone the worker without a job. In those days, one saw angry factory workers out of work, huddled together over a bonfire on many a cold, dark night during the Depression, grumbling about their fate. Some were bitter enough to become soldiers in the underworld; others became their allies out of necessity. People had to make a buck. They had to eat. Everyone turned to the men who had the cash. Interest, however, was higher than in a bank, and the terms and conditions were somewhat different. If someone in business could not pay his loan, he usually found himself with a new partner. That was how the boys wrapped up the garment district of New York.

What happens today? If a person is unable to meet his payments on a car, house, or boat, the loan company or bank has it repossessed, confiscated. Naturally, shylocks had their own rules, and some had no scruples whatsoever. A shark is a cheater, whether it be card shark, pool shark, or loan shark.

At times, the results of nonpayment were very painful, if not disastrous. Obviously, the boys could not use the law to assist them in their collections. Most of the combinations had their own "enforcers," whose job it was to collect the smaller loans. Some of them were very tough, mean guys who manhandled those hoods who welched; for example, on gambling debts, sometimes word went around that someone had been eliminated. There were also small-time, independent hoods who, aiming their sights higher, were merciless amongst themselves. Some guys were staked at exorbitant rates for bars or restaurants, and when they didn't pay up, musclemen threw their weight around. Police were known to find someone in the gutter—dead—with his *mouth full of paper*. They were the welchers. They had cried when they needed help, signed IOUs, but when the time arrived to meet their obligations, they didn't. One had to remember the rules.

With the ordinary citizen, the situation was different. They became indebted in other ways if they didn't pay. Less brutal methods were applied, but allegiance had to be pledged, and the debt was always paid off in some way. When election time came, they remembered those who had helped them and voted as they were told. In the Italian ghettos (as in the Irish, Polish, et cetera), the district party leader was also a very influential man. He was busy running around, doing "favors" for his constituents, getting to know everyone on a first-name basis. Generally, he too had pledged allegiance to someone for his job, so the poor and illiterate were led and strung along.

In the upper echelons, Charlie and Frank "owned" many politicians, who owed them favors for just being in office. It was like the protection racket in reverse. Small wonder that during that period, with all the usury going on, the underworld controlled many people—consequently, a high percentage of the votes. It also permitted their tentacles to stretch out and grasp part and full ownership of many legal enterprises haunted by bankruptcy and complete ruin. They had become a very powerful group.

In June 1932, the Democratic Convention was held in Chicago. The Drake Hotel was jammed, but all the important people had long before reserved their suites. Frank was in one wing with Jimmy Hines and the Roosevelt supporters while Charlie was in another with Al Smith, Marinelli, and company. As the convention rolled along, it was apparent that good ole Al "the Happy Warrior" Smith had fallen far behind. Charlie and Frank saw the handwriting on the wall and held a powwow to make their decision to dump Smith. But that wasn't easy on Charlie. He sincerely liked Smith and trusted him; he and Marinelli had started the machinery in Smith's favor. When Charlie broke the news to Smith (that they had to sacrifice themselves to back Roosevelt to become the next president of the United States), his heart was broken. Hines, instead, was ecstatic when he was told that the boys were abandoning their support of Smith to pool their efforts for Roosevelt. Erroneously, much of the credit for success was given to Hines, but it was not his. The real credit for leadership belonged to a tenacious James A. Farley, the real manager of Roosevelt's presidential campaign, who organized a terrific platform and ran a tight show. "Big Jim" Farley had been chairman of the New York Democratic Committee since 1930. Two years later, he became national chairman, and he held that seat until 1940.

After Roosevelt was nominated as the Democratic presidential candidate in Chicago, the boys recruited their soldiers to help campaign for him. Ralph did his part by distributing pamphlets and shouting the virtues of FDR—of how he was going to put the country back on its feet, save the American family, and fulfill the American dream.

Sometimes it wasn't easy to get around because the enemy wanted their competition out of the way, out of reach of the people, and Ralph's personal contribution was interrupted in the weeks before election.

He was driving back with his attorney, Sam Rosenblatt, from visiting Dotty in Hartford, Connecticut—where she had returned for another cure. They had stopped for something to eat in the wee hours of the morning, and an exhausted Sammy had gone to his hotel for some shut-eye while Ralph drove his car to the garage. He tooted his horn, and the attendant stuck his head out and asked Ralph to wait until he finished a wash job. As Ralph patiently waited behind the wheel, he saw a car coming straight at him. He thought the men in the car were drunk, and his first impulse was to duck. But the car screeched to a halt, and Ralph found himself surrounded by plainclothesmen.

One detective laughed. "Hey, Ralph, what did ya think? It was your last moment?"

"No . . . I thought you were all drunk!" Ralph retorted sarcastically.

"We have a warrant for your arrest, Ralph. We have to take you in on account of the elections," another stated more seriously. "We also got one for your friend, Charlie 'Lucky'."

Charlie, however, was in Hot Springs, Arkansas, visiting friends.

Ralph had no choice but to follow them. Fortunately, they were friendly cops; and instead of taking him directly to the station house, they drove around town—even took Ralph to a restaurant on Broadway. The detectives told Ralph they couldn't avoid taking him in. They also confided that they were getting orders from different station houses to take people in because of the elections. Ralph pleaded he was tired, but the detectives continued driving until seven o'clock in the morning, when finally they stopped in an all-night coffee shop. At that point, the detectives allowed Ralph to make a phone call to Sammy at the hotel. After much persistence with the hotel operator, he heard Sammy's groggy voice.

"Sammy, come to the Fifty-fourth Street station house court . . . They're booking me . . . I think it's for vagrancy," Ralph cried.

"What? Okay . . . Ralph . . . I'm putting my shirt on right now. Be there as fast as I can . . . don't worry."

At the station house, a detective was in the process of registering the charge, and Ralph was about to sign a bail bond when the door burst open, and in rushed Sammy. "Ralph, don't sign anything!"

The detective looked up scornfully. "Who are you?"

"I'm his attorney!" Sammy blasted.

There was a bitter exchange of words between Sammy and the detectives, but despite all the objections, Sammy was unable to stop them from booking Ralph for vagrancy.

It was an especially bad period. The Vagrancy Law was being enforced because of the Lindbergh case. (Congress had passed the Lindbergh Law in 1932 after the kidnapping and killing of Lindbergh's son, making it a federal crime if a kidnapped victim was taken out of the state. Later, it was changed to include all kidnapping cases.) This allowed the police to arrest carte blanche beggars, criminals, and even innocent men without jobs who were out on the street. Bootleggers had really big problems. Everyone had to get off the streets or risk being locked up. A vagrant (a vagabond) with no means of support was considered a menace to society; and an arrest for vagrancy brought a jail sentence, as well as a fine. Ralph was booked on that pretext.

Every arrest is mortifying, but Ralph had become accustomed to the harassment. He clearly understood the reasons. In court, to demonstrate he was not a vagrant, Ralph proved he was living with his family and, as his visible means of support, stated that he was the owner of the Bayot Company (the trucking company in which Ralph had invested), demonstrating the payroll books as evidence. As a result, he was duly discharged.

They wanted Ralph off the streets until after the elections because he was out canvassing votes for Tammany Hall, enticing the Italians to vote Democratic. He was not alone. On another front, various speakers and lawyers spoke at Italian functions. All the Democrats were pushing for Roosevelt's success. Ralph personally distributed turkeys to the poor and needy for Thanksgiving and Christmas, soliciting votes for the Democrats as well as promising favors and jobs, as he was instructed to do. One hand washes the other, he would say.

Franklin Delano Roosevelt was elected the thirty-second president of the United States. He was reelected three times. The boys were somewhat apprehensive because with Al Smith, they would have been sure of what was going to happen. With Roosevelt, it was different.

Even though he had used them, he was his own man. And he proved to be more unpredictable than they had expected. Roosevelt began with an explosion on his inauguration day by closing all the banks. It was something Ralph never forgot.

Frankie Marlowe called Ralph on behalf of a mutual friend, Dr. Marino, urgently requesting him to drive to a bank in Hartford, Connecticut. A Greek friend of theirs was opening up a restaurant and required $30,000 for the transaction. It was an errand of great trust, and the fact that Ralph had a fast car (an Auburn Cord sports car) was a plus. Ralph consented and picked up the Greek in the wee hours of the morning in order to reach Hartford before the bank opened. As he raced down the roads, he couldn't help wondering about the urgency of the trip. Once in Hartford, he drove down main street toward the bank when a traffic cop spotted his beautiful shiny car and waved him to the side. He was accused of being a New York gangster and was ordered to follow a police car to the station house.

The captain looked at the Auburn Cord and whistled in admiration.

"What are you boys doing in town at this hour?" he asked.

"My friend here has business with the bank," Ralph answered.

"Oh, he does, does he? What kind of business?" The captain demanded as his eyebrows shot up.

"Hey, what kind of town is this?" Ralph remarked, trying to avoid giving a straight answer. "Do you treat everybody who drives into town like this?"

"No, just suspicious characters who drive fancy cars. But I'm willing to be reasonable, if you can tell me who can vouch for you."

Soon the captain was calling Dr. Marino in New York, who explained that Ralph and the Greek were there on legitimate business, which seemed to satisfy the friendly officer.

"Okay, Ralph, you're in the clear. But before you go, I'd like to try out this fancy sports car."

Ralph could only consent. "Sure, why not . . . ," he replied. "In the meantime, we'll go somewhere for a cup of coffee." Then added kiddingly, "We won't get arrested for that, will we, Captain?"

The captain laughed and took off. But Ralph had to wait over an hour before he returned with the car. When he and the Greek finally reached the bank, it was closed. A large sign announced the closures of all banks by the new president. It was the day Roosevelt took his oath, March 4, 1933.

That night, Ralph met with Frankie Marlowe and Dr. Marino and reported the jinxed trip. Ralph had had his suspicions. There had been a leak that the president would close the banks, but Ralph never raised the question.

Frankie Marlowe could have been one of the big boys, but he wanted to go it alone. He treasured his independence, was kind of stubborn about it, and sometimes flew off the handle if anyone tried to give him orders. Ralph understood because he could have been with Charlie twenty-four hours a day, if he so desired. Frank was physically large, six feet tall and husky with typical Italian looks—black wavy hair and intense dark eyes. He had a quick temper, which eventually brought about his demise.

Joe Adonis, Frankie, and Good-looking Georgie were the best pickpocket trio in town; but once Joe became a boss, the other two dabbled in anything on which they could get their hands. They devised a routine where they impersonated policemen in order to shake down their victims. Frankie usually posed as a detective in a trench coat with a hat perched on one side of his head, the brim practically covering his left eye and, with his height, was quite convincing in the part.

Frankie told Ralph the story of how they were shaking down a Jewish kid who wanted to become a racketeer, and whose father was supposedly a Mr. Big in the garment district. The kid wanted to become rich fast on his own. He wanted to buy $100 worth of counterfeit money and was willing to pay $25 for every hundred. Frankie and Georgie had taken the deal. The exchange was to take place in the men's room of a downtown hotel. The boys prepared a nice bundle filled with newspaper cut the size of greenbacks, and Georgie carried it to the meeting. As the would-be racketeer turned over the money he promised to Georgie, the door burst open, and in walked Frankie, the detective.

"Hey, what's going on here?" he exclaimed with authority and grabbed the bundle of money from the boy.

At the same time, Georgie yelled, "Run, kid, run!" And the deceived young man hightailed it out of there.

According to Frankie, they had clipped him twice—the second time, Frankie was a cop on the beat.

Ralph wouldn't believe the story. "NOBODY," he said, "could be that dumb."

Frankie, half-laughing, assured him it was true, inviting Ralph to hide in the men's room where a third meet had been set up. When the act was over, Ralph emerged, astonished. He was very impressed with Frankie's impersonation. He could have fooled even him. But that poor kid, Ralph couldn't help feeling sorry for him.

Not long after, Georgie (extraordinarily good-looking with blond hair and blue eyes), tired of the risks, wanted to settle down. He had plenty of women after him from whom to choose. Finally, he opened up a restaurant on Forty-third and Eighth Avenue and went straight.

After losing Georgie to the restaurant business, Frankie began hanging around with Frank Iola, who was in good graces with Little Augie Pisano, one of the bosses. Iola was even taller than Frankie and weighed more—built something like a football player. They were quite an awesome pair. Not too many people wanted to tangle with them.

Whenever Frankie had too much to drink, he would trust only Ralph to drive him home. Frankie was in bad shape one night and brooding as Ralph drove him to his home on Fourth Avenue and Union Street. Frank spoke to Ralph in big brother tones.

"Listen . . . Ralph . . . you're getting too big. Watch yourself. Yeah . . . I know everyone likes you . . . but do me a favor. Just don't trust everybody . . . Okay?" Then with a faraway look in his eyes, he left, and Ralph went home burdened with thought.

Shortly thereafter, Frankie had a falling-out with Iola. Together they had clipped someone, and Frankie had held out on his new partner. It was a double cross. A cardinal rule had been broken. Ralph was later told that Frankie was found dead in the gutter. He felt remorse; Frankie had been a friend for many years.

Not too long after Frankie's death, Frank Iola stepped into his car, turned on the ignition, and was blown to eternity.

CHAPTER TWENTY-SEVEN

Nobody, nothing lasts forever. The year 1933 was the inception of the New Deal. After Roosevelt closed the banks (a move that made the underworld's money vaults even more attractive), he continued to keep everyone alert and anxious, like a happy child at play. One didn't know what FDR was up to—one innovation after another. Memorable during those grim years were the NRA (National Recovery Act) and the more successful WPA (Works Progress Administration). While Roosevelt was taking steps to regenerate America, he took another definite action to clean up Tammany Hall. He was not two-faced because he never promised anything to anyone. He was like a multifaceted diamond. One never knew which face he would show at any given time. The Seabury Commission, which had been passive for some time, suddenly found new impetus and resumed its investigations. After putting the squeeze on Mayor James J. Walker, he was forced to resign, leaving an opening for Republican Fiorello "Little Flower" La Guardia. La Guardia had long tired of his seat in Congress and was anxious to get his teeth into the real action as mayor of New York City. The office became his in January 1934, and he too had plans.

Roosevelt appointed James A. Farley, his campaign manager, to be postmaster general of the United States (a post he held until 1940), and Martin J. Conboy was sworn in as the new U.S. attorney of New York on December 27. As the end of the year rolled along, FDR finally persuaded Congress to pass Amendment Number 21 to end the Prohibition Era (or the "Noble Experiment," as some people had called it). Control of liquor traffic went back to the States. It was just a few weeks before Christmas—one of Roosevelt's gifts to the nation.

The boys, of course, were not idly standing by. They were aware of the Prohibition problem, knew it couldn't last forever. The smart ones had already moved into other operations, had become silent partners in the new legitimate liquor industry, diversifying their interests—legitimate and otherwise. Gambling casinos were being mapped out throughout the country. Some of the older men, who had made a great deal of money bootlegging, just retired.

During that period, there was another ambitious man. In the Republican clubhouse, Tom Dewey was programming his future, making a brilliant career for himself going after gangsters, which, of course, held him in the limelight. He had started with "Legs" Diamond (John T. Nolan); later, Waxey Gordon; and, just as he was about to close in on Dutch Schultz, Martin Conboy's appointment arrived. In January 1934, Dewey discreetly, cautiously, went into private practice to take advantage of the transition to calculate his next moves. He had already gained sufficient publicity to obtain other big clamorous cases against political figures. He did not fade away!

Dotty and Ralph were still a couple, very much in love. Ralph had moved her into the Emerson Hotel on Seventy-fifth and Amsterdam Avenue and, as usual, kept her in style, making sure she had all the money she needed, or so he thought. To fill the void she felt when Ralph went out of town, Dotty became inseparable from her dog. Unlike Ralph's other women, Dotty accepted his way of life, his late hours, which made her even more precious to him.

Immediately after Ralph's birthday on March 17, 1934, Agnes left word with Dotty that she needed to see Ralph urgently. Ralph was perplexed and rushed over to his mother's home. He found her fidgeting, an almost frightened look on her face.

"Ralph . . . I forgot to tell you something very important," she began faltering. "It's been on my mind for a long time now . . ."

"Well, what is it?" Ralph asked patiently.

"You must go to get your citizenship papers!"

"What . . . for what?" Ralph exclaimed.

Agnes struggled for the words to explain, "Well . . . you . . . know . . . Ralph . . . We never said anything. I guess we didn't think it was important." She finally blurted out, "Ralph . . . you were born in Rome, Italy."

"Mom . . . you're kidding me!" Ralph was shocked. "I thought you said I was born in Brooklyn?" For his driver's license, he had given Brooklyn as his place of birth to the police department.

"No . . . Ralph . . . Rome," Agnes replied with finality. "I'm sorry . . . I should have told you long ago," she lamented. "But it's time you straighten this out. Go now and get your papers."

Needless to say, Ralph was extremely upset over the news. He had always thought he was a native-born American. The disclosure was hard for him to digest, but he immediately contacted his friend John Foley, who personally took him to city hall to obtain his first papers. He was advised it would take at least two years before he could receive his American citizenship.

The episode was traumatic for Ralph. He wondered what triggered his mother to confess the truth now. Unbeknownst to him, this would be instrumental in changing the course of his life.

On the positive side, Ralph's affairs were going very well for him. Besides his activities in New York, he had extended his investments to Miami, which brought him an additional $800-$900 a month. Ralph, however, remained a soft touch for anyone with a sob story, which many times caused him trouble.

One evening, as he stood on the corner of Sixtieth and Broadway waiting for one of his controllers, a down-and-out-looking fellow approached him and asked if he were Ralph. At first Ralph thought the man was a runner and nodded in the affirmative as he scrutinized him. *He sure needs a cleanup,* thought Ralph.

"I'm Louie, Willie 'the Bum's' brother," the seedy character stated. "Can you help me out . . . I had a little trouble in Brooklyn . . . Got to stay away from there."

Ralph, knowing the man's brother, didn't ask questions and replied matter-of-factly, "Want to stick around here?"

"Yeah, I'm dead broke," the man lamented.

Ralph, saturated with work, thought, *Why not help the guy?* He had some poker games, which needed coverage on the West Side, which brought in from twenty to seventy-five dollars, depending on the payoff.

"All right," Ralph agreed. "You can hang around here. I have some poker games for you . . . but first, we have to spruce you up a bit."

Ralph took Louie to a high-fashion shop on Seventieth and Broadway and bought him a couple of outfits, as well as some shoes. He spent more than two hundred dollars. Then Ralph purchased a secondhand Cadillac for twelve hundred dollars for Louie to drive. "This will, at least, give you a good front," Ralph said at the car lot. If the man was to represent Ralph, well, he had to look halfway decent. Once Louie had a much more respectable appearance, Ralph took him around to the poker games and introduced him as his man.

"Okay, you take over now, and watch yourself. Don't get into any trouble, and I'll help you all I can," Ralph stated paternally.

He would be earning about $300 a week, and Ralph thought he would be grateful. Louie, however, was not an appreciative felon; instead, he kept causing problems for Ralph, embarrassing him, even soliciting more money. Ralph understood it was time to get rid of the bum. It was on the night he was going to a banquet at the Waldorf Astoria with Charlie that he met with the bum in front of his hotel to sever relations.

"Listen . . . you've got thirty seconds," he told the ungrateful wretch. "Don't let me see you around here again, because I don't like people who like money better than their friends. Take a walk . . . take a long walk!"

Humiliated, the brazen bum went downtown to see Charlie, but Charlie was cushioned by two (and sometimes three) persons. It was not easy to see the boss. When he mentioned it was about Ralph, however, he had uttered the magic word and was allowed through to him.

Charlie stared at the despicable man standing in front of him bad-mouthing Ralph and felt nothing but repugnance. He finally interrupted the bum's spiel and, with utter contempt, ordered him out.

"Look, if Ralph chased you . . . he must have had a good reason. Now, there's the door. Take a walk!"

But Louie's vindictive nature was such that he even went to the bosses in Chicago to condemn Ralph. The hot line between New York and Chicago produced the same results, and the contemptible bum was also chased out of Chicago. He naively had thought he could stab Ralph in the back, but he didn't know how close Ralph and Charlie were.

Sometime in June 1934, Ralph spent a few days in Saratoga with Johnny Orzo. Ambling along the sidewalks after leaving a poker game (in which Ralph came out a big winner), Johnny stopped to say hello to a friend. He casually introduced him; after which, Ralph stood aside to allow the two men to speak privately. In a few moments, Johnny approached Ralph, asking if he had a few hundred dollars on him.

His wallet bulging with his big winnings, Ralph said, "Yeah, sure . . . How much do you need?" He handed three hundred dollars to Johnny, who then added two bills of his own, giving the man a total of five hundred dollars.

As they walked away, Johnny assured Ralph, "Don't worry . . . Ralph, he's good for it."

Ralph said nothing. It was understood Johnny would collect.

About a month later, in New York, Dotty and Ralph had just returned from Sunday dinner when the hotel concierge gave him a message to meet Johnny. Dotty clung to Ralph, hoping to keep him with her as it was still early. But Ralph gingerly kissed her good night and strolled over to Johnny's hotel, the Embassy on Seventieth and Broadway. As Ralph had imagined, Johnny wanted to step out to Small's Paradise, and Ralph called for his car at the Emerson Garage. Once in the car, Ralph drove toward 110th Street and Central Park West to the club. He stopped for a red light when suddenly, Johnny practically jumped out of the car.

"Ralph, wait a minute . . . I gotta talk to that woman!"

Ralph swerved to the curb and waited about ten minutes for Johnny.

As Johnny slipped back into the car, he grinned. "You know who that woman was?"

"I give up, who?" Ralph replied flatly.

"Remember that guy in Saratoga we gave the money to? Well, that's his girlfriend."

"What the hell did you stop *her* for?" Ralph snapped. "You had no business stopping her!"

"Aw, what're ya worrying about . . . Ralph," Johnny moaned. "It's his girlfriend."

"That's just it. You should not have stopped her . . ."

"Relax . . . Ralph. She wants me to call her next Monday night."

Ralph didn't know what Johnny was up to, but he didn't like it. His humor changed. There were certain rules about interpersonal relationships with women, and Johnny's behavior was out of line. Something told Ralph to keep an eye on Johnny for his own sake. The following night, he walked over to the Embassy Hotel to try to dissuade Johnny from calling the woman.

"Ralph, I've got to call her," Johnny insisted.

"Will you forget about her," Ralph snapped. "Johnny, do me a favor: don't call her!"

"Why? Why the hell you always got wrong things on your mind?" Johnny sulked.

"I don't have wrong things on my mind. You've no business calling her. The guy got the money . . . You've no business telling her about it."

"Well, you don't have to come," Johnny pouted.

"Oh, no . . . Where you go . . . I go!"

There was no stopping Johnny. He called and made an appointment to meet the woman at eight o'clock in front of Walgreens Drug Store at Eighty-third Street and Broadway. They arrived by cab, and after Johnny stepped out to meet his date, Ralph had his cabby circle around—until he saw the two walking arm in arm. Ralph stopped the cab, paid the driver, and walked toward Johnny and the woman. When Ralph came within a few feet of the couple, they were suddenly surrounded by what looked like twenty plainclothesmen and detectives. They seemed to have come out of nowhere and pounced upon him and Johnny. Before Ralph could protest, he felt a sharp kick in the shins, another in the groin, and he fell to the ground—only to be kicked again and again. He courageously rose, but he was struck on the head by another policeman. Ralph's small stature allowed him to close in with his steel fists and was able to crack one cop's jaw, but there were too many for him.

Johnny was also fighting for his life. He was a big man and had already jostled and whacked a few of the cops, but he too was outnumbered.

There was such a ruckus that people opened their windows and leaned out to see what was happening. When they saw the police punching Ralph and Johnny about like puppets, they began to shout at them; some even uttered obscene remarks.

"Hey, what the hell you doin' to those fellas!"

"Hey, you rat finks . . . you sons of bitches . . . Leave them alone!"

With so many witnesses, the cops dragged and prodded their bleeding victims into their cars and drove them to Eleventh Avenue, a deserted dead end. One of the Winberry Brothers was among the police—the same cop who was involved in Charlie's famous ride. He was a tough Irish bastard, as unorthodox as the rest. With renewed vigor, the police continued their brutality. They repeatedly whacked Ralph about the head until he felt it had cracked wide open. Blood ran from his scalp to his ears and face, half-blinding his eyes, but Ralph stubbornly forced his body up and, committing a shrill cry, tried to ram two cops just lunging for him. From behind, however, another copy clubbed him on the head. As Ralph slumped onto the pavement, he heard an inspector McDermott shout to Johnny, who was also badly beaten up, his face smashed, "Run, you guinea bastard . . . Run!" Johnny began running, and one cop shot him down. Johnny fell, bleeding, his hand searching for his wound.

Just as McDermott ranted, "Hit the other guinea in the head!" the garage doors across the street opened halfway. The men inside thought a gang war was in progress. With more eye witnesses, the lawmen couldn't shoot Ralph, who was out cold by then, and couldn't finish Johnny off. Instead, the police hauled the two battered, wounded men in separate cars to Roosevelt Hospital on the ruse that they had captured them in a gang fight.

When Ralph arrived in the hospital, Johnny was already there, flat on his back on a table, with a bullet in him. Two cops dragged Ralph directly to Johnny while another snarled, "Johnny confessed."

Ralph was slumped over; his head was bleeding, his face smashed, and his eyes blurry; but he managed enough strength to snap, "He confessed to your sister . . . you rat!"

At that point, the doctors chased the cops out of the hospital. "Get the hell out of here," cried one doctor who had sensed the truth.

Johnny and Ralph were both patched up. Ralph had stitches all around his head, but they could not surgically extract the bullet from Johnny. He carried it in his body for the rest of his life. Ralph was the first to be taken to The Tombs Prison and, incredibly, booked on extortion. A week later, he was out on $50,000 bail; after which, he went to stay with his mother at Sheepshead Bay and Fifteenth Street to recuperate.

While recuperating, he received a call from Al Marinelli, who sympathetically inquired about how he felt. Then he asked, "Listen, Ralph . . . do you have your car there? Can you drive?"

"Yeah, sure," Ralph answered reassuringly.

"Okay, then come down to Ferrara's Café."

As they drank their coffee, Al asked quietly, "First, Ralph . . . I want to know . . . Did you have arms on you?"

"Arms? What the hell did I need arms for, Al? For what? They didn't find arms on us."

"Okay, Ralph," Al replied, satisfied. "I wanted to hear it from you. Now . . . tell me the whole story."

Ralph related the sad tale and also defended Johnny. He told Al that Johnny wasn't shaking down the girl for his money, if that's what he thought. Johnny was just being idiotic about the girl, which wasn't anything new. Al confided he had performed his own investigation. He had gone down to the garage to speak with the men there to obtain their testimonies—evidence of how they were beaten. It was Al who told Ralph the garage people at first thought it was a gang war and were shocked when they realized they were police. Al shook his head in disgust.

Finally, he said, "Okay, Ralph . . . here's what you do now. Go to the Sixty-eighth Street station house and ask for Inspector McDermott. When he comes out . . . just tell him I want to see him here!"

Ralph nodded, put on his hat, and went to the station house. As he walked in, one wise cop cracked, "You want to see . . . Inspector McDermott?"

"Yeah," Ralph exclaimed bitterly. "That's just who I want to see!"

Another detective approached Ralph immediately and frisked him while Ralph turned to see Inspector McDermott one flight up at the railing.

"You want to see me?" he called down with contempt.

"Yeah . . . just you I want to see!" Ralph replied sarcastically.

McDermott walked down the stairs arrogantly. "Well . . . what do you want?" he rasped.

Ralph took one step closer to him, his blue eyes blazing with hatred, and felt the impulse burning inside him to smash the man. "Al Marinelli wants to see you!"

"Al Marinelli? Why didn't you tell me you knew Al Marinelli?" McDermott was taken aback.

"I don't know anybody," Ralph retorted.

"Where is he?" he asked quietly, his demeanor no longer tough.

"At Ferrara's Café."

Ralph slipped into McDermott's car and went to Ferrara's on Grand Street. The scene was something Ralph continued to relish for a long time. McDermott walked ahead, his strut a little less imperious. He took off his cap in front of Al, who motioned him to sit down.

"You Irish bastard," Al snarled. "It's a good thing Ralph's not a rat like you, because I'd make you do twenty years in prison for what you did to these fellows. And I've plenty of witnesses to do it. Who the hell did you think you were pulling off something like this?"

McDermott was caught good and proper and was squirming like a child. "Well . . . Al," he began apologetically, "we had the wrong information. We got a story . . . but we learned later that it was a different Ralph . . . not him . . ." McDermott blabbered a cock-and-bull story about a guy—a loan shark, who had loaned this woman money and was hustling her for it, increasing the amount to two, three hundred every week. "But we got the wrong information," he repeated sorrowfully.

With the explanation out of the way, McDermott knew what he had to do. He rose from his chair and extended his hand to Ralph. "Okay . . . Ralph . . . let's shake hands and forget about everything," he said almost meekly.

Al Marinelli met Ralph's searching eyes. Imperceptibly, he nodded his okay. Reluctantly, Ralph shook hands for Al's sake—because he knew McDermott was now in Al's pocket for the rest of his career.

Ralph discovered later that the woman involved was very calculating with her favors. She apparently was also on very intimate terms with the inspector, who wanted to demonstrate what a powerful man he was.

He hadn't counted, however, on being licked by a much more important man.

CHAPTER TWENTY-EIGHT

Whenever Ralph was home, he personally checked on Dotty to see if anyone was supplying her with drugs. When it was possible, he sat watch in his car, other times in other cars, to avoid being discovered, waiting near her hotel for some action. Ralph also had his own stool pigeons working to let him know if any suspicious characters were hanging around Dotty. His heart dictated his resolve to try everything. Dotty always pleaded, "I promise . . . Believe me, Ralph. This is the last time. I swear I'll never do it again!" Ralph deeply loved her and forced himself to believe her, but there was always a next time.

It was Indian summer 1935, a September evening with the last rays of sunlight streaking the skies in luscious pigments of orange, apricot, and copper, creating a warm glow on the horizon. Ralph glanced over at Dotty beside him in the car, noting wisps of her blonde hair gently flowing in the light breeze, and he felt his heart melt. She looked lovely, despite still another bout with drugs and another sanitarium cure. Ralph wondered how long the latest remission would last. He cringed, remembering the last time he saw her—in bed, fighting for her sanity, struggling against her need for heroin. Ralph had again prepared to send her to the clinic, but to please him, she had tried on her own to detoxify herself, but it ended in disaster. He could still hear her screams.

"They're coming for me . . . Ralph . . . They want to take me . . . No . . . No . . . Go away! Ralph . . . tell them to go away!" she had babbled, twisting her body in desperation. She was hallucinating, seeing weird creatures threatening to seize her. The pupils of her eyes were widely dilating, making them look black and dead in her pale face, and she pulled her hair violently, screaming all the while.

She had been in horrible pain. Ralph, totally helpless, tried to draw her back to reality. "Dotty . . . Dotty . . . be calm . . . It's going to be all right! Dotty, please . . . ," he wailed.

Something snapped, and Dotty, still writhing in pain, clutched Ralph's arms, her eyes wildly darting, gasping feverishly. "If you get me what I need, they'll go away . . . Please . . . Ralph. Oh! They're coming back!"

Again, she screamed in a shrill, terrifying voice, her fingers scraping at the flesh of her own arms, tearing at herself hysterically, until Ralph, with tears in his eyes, grabbed her flailing hands and held them tight. It was just too much. He couldn't handle it; he called the doctor to give her a sedative but realized he couldn't leave her to her own devices. From her bureau, he pulled out a couple of silk scarves and tied Dotty's hands to the bedposts as she went into a cold sweat, twisting and turning. Dr. Gardner, who was accustomed to Ralph's frenzied calls, came running with a hypodermic needle. Once she was sufficiently sedated, Ralph carried Dotty to his car and sped through the night to the clinic in Hartford.

Now they were going home—again. Seated next to her, driving back to the city, Ralph shook his head as if coming out of a bad dream. It was now dusk; the sky had lost its earlier lustrous splendor. He looked at Dotty, who turned toward him and smiled. She was happy to be out of her nightmare.

Ralph carried Dotty's luggage up to her hotel room where she lazily removed her trench coat and hung it in her wardrobe. Suddenly, without warning, Ralph swung her around, clutching her shoulders, and his handsome features were stark with controlled fury. "Dotty . . . this is it now," he seethed. "The next time I catch you, I'm turning you over to the Narcotics Squad!"

Dotty's eyes opened wide, and she gasped, trying to gauge the sincerity of his words. Then she smiled sweetly and hugged him, whispering, "I promise . . . I promise, Ralph . . ."

At the mention of her promise, which she had so often broken, Ralph put out his fingers to her lips and murmured, "Shissssh . . ." Then he gently lifted her and placed her on the bed. "Let's not talk about it now." He smiled. "I have other things on my mind." Dotty giggled, interpreting his certain smile. She snuggled up to her man as Ralph drew her tightly to him.

Some months later, on a return trip from Saratoga, Ralph went directly to see Dotty. To his surprise, upon opening the door, he found a strange-looking girl in her apartment. Ralph sensed immediately she was a junkie. He caught that certain look around her eyes. The girl's face was haggard; she had a sallow complexion, and her clothes looked as though she had slept in them. Ralph imagined she was younger than she looked. He saw red sparks showering through his brain. Dotty had just been cured, for Chrissake! In front of the dissipated-looking young lady, with ice in his voice, he inquired, "Dotty, didn't I tell you I didn't want anyone up here?"

"Oh . . . Ralph . . . she's just an old friend. She came up to say hello," Dotty purred.

"Yeah, I'm sure," Ralph retorted, giving the girl a venomous glance. She lowered her eyes, sullen, mute.

"We're going downstairs for some coffee, Ralph. Want to come along?" Dotty asked gently.

Ralph mumbled no, and the girls left. As soon as they closed the door, Ralph began to search the apartment, turning it upside down, but he couldn't find anything. He decided to let things ride for the moment.

About a month later, Ralph left town again on business, staying away only a few days; and on the morning he returned, he went straight to the Emerson to see Dotty. The concierge told him that Dotty was not in; she hadn't been in all night. Ralph said nothing but went up to the room. Sure enough, the bed was still made. Dotty's dog was snuggled against the pillows, looking forlorn, but perked up when she saw Ralph; he fondled her a bit in his arms before taking her out for a walk. When he returned, the telephone operator told him Dotty had called and had asked him to take care of the dog. Dotty's whereabouts remained a mystery. All she told the operator was that she would be back in a few days.

Ralph was naturally worried. Dotty had never done anything like that. He shook his head in bewilderment, spent the night in the hotel room, hoping that Dotty would call again, but she didn't. In the morning, on his return from walking the dog, he found a couple of detectives waiting for him.

"Ralph . . . you're wanted in Dewey's office," one told him.

"Dewey?" Ralph exclaimed, startled. "What for?"

"Don't know. All we know is you're wanted for questioning."

"All right," he replied. "Let me take the dog up."

They arrived at Dewey's headquarters in the Woolworth Building, and Ralph was led into the office of one of his assistant district attorneys, Harry S. Cole. He was very cordial, opening with the usual banalities, asking Ralph to sit down, then deftly easing into the crux of the matter. "Now . . . Ralph . . . I don't want you to get the wrong idea about what I'm going to tell you."

"What do you mean?" Ralph asked.

"Did you read the papers this morning?" He pointed to a newspaper on his desk.

"No," quipped Ralph, "I didn't have time."

"Well . . . we have your girlfriend, Nancy Presser—Dotty—here," Cole added solemnly.

"What for?" Ralph retorted, livid.

"Don't get upset, now . . . She was caught by the police with an ounce of heroin in her possession. Dotty was in an apartment, which was listed two weeks ago as a disorderly house. That's the reason the police went there in the first place. Then we learned this girl had just moved in."

Ralph's face fell. "Who was the girl?" he asked.

"Florence Brown . . . sometimes called Cokey Flo," Cole answered.

"It must be the one I caught up in Dotty's apartment about a month ago," Ralph mumbled. He was angry with himself; he had slipped up. All the precautions he had taken had been in vain again.

"You know . . . Ralph," Cole continued sympathetically, "Dotty can get ten years for that."

"Ten years!" Ralph shouted. "Who the hell did she kill to get ten years?"

Cole allowed that phrase to pass. "She spoke very highly of you . . . Ralph. Dotty told us how good you've been to her. Said you had her cured from drugs several times."

"Yes, I did . . . four times!" Ralph shot back.

"You did a good deed to society, Ralph . . . ," Cole responded kindly, "but we also know that you've been a bootlegger, been in numbers . . . and well . . . you know."

"Yeah, that's right, but I closed my office . . . closed shop . . . closed everything," Ralph answered. (Which he did do when the investigations about Dutch Schultz began, and Dewey had assumed the role of commander in chief in the Woolworth Building.)

"Ralph, we know that you come from a good family. Don't worry." Cole rose from his desk, walked around it, and sat on the edge in front of Ralph with a friendly air. "Ralph . . . ," he said earnestly, "you're the only one who can help your girl."

"I'll get her a lawyer, right away," Ralph proposed.

"No, you won't have to. Want to see her?" he asked.

Ralph pondered on his first statement but replied emphatically to the other, "Sure, I do."

Cole went to the door and spoke to the guard. Dotty must have been in a room nearby because she was brought in rather quickly. Ralph rose from his chair to greet her, and as soon as Dotty saw him, she threw herself into his arms. "Please forgive me . . . Ralph . . . please forgive me," she cried.

"Didn't I tell you not to associate with that girl?" Ralph said sternly. Dotty continued to sob. She was in such a state that Ralph couldn't scold her further. "Okay, honey . . . don't worry. I'll do all I can. I won't let you down."

Cole motioned to the attendant, and they took Dotty away. Ralph looked at Cole, who seemed to be quite satisfied with his first act, and before he could make a comment, he said peremptorily, "That's it for today, Ralph. You'll be hearing from us."

Ralph was stunned because he wasn't on top of the situation. He returned to his hotel, puzzled about the whole predicament. After the interview with Cole, he hung around home. He had a funny feeling in his gut. He needed to feel his family's love around him—especially his son's. Ralph continued to brood about Dotty and wondered how the hell he could free her, but his hands were tied. He had to wait for Cole. He had said a lawyer wasn't necessary. Ralph could still see his smug face; Cole's words kept ringing in his ears.

Reading the newspaper in his mother's living room, he learned Charlie had been arrested in Hot Springs, Arkansas. Dewey wanted him in New York. Ralph's first thought was that it had something to do with Dutch Schultz's murder, but he soon learned differently.

Finally, Cole called Ralph back to his office. "Ralph, we're going to hold you as a material witness," he bluntly remarked, catching Ralph completely off guard.

"What for?" Ralph screamed.

"You want to help your girl, don't you?" he asked.

"Naturally," Ralph retorted. "I've been waiting all this time. What the hell must I do?"

Cole had been standing, but now he leaned against the desk, his routine when he wanted to act palsy-walsy. "You'll have to do what we tell you."

"Okay . . . ," Ralph replied, exasperated. "What do you want me to do?"

Cole smiled priggishly. "We'll tell you about it on Monday." Again, Ralph was dismissed; but this time, he was taken to The Tombs Prison and jailed.

The next morning, Ralph's brother, Armand, rushed to The Tombs to find out what was going on. Ralph said he was in the dark and explained Dotty's dilemma. Armand told him to be calm, and that he would try to learn something on the outside.

Bright and early Monday morning, Ralph was taken back to Cole's office and was greeted very fraternally. "Ralph . . . you have to cooperate with us."

"All right . . . how?"

"Do you know Charles Luciano?"

"Well . . . I've seen him around occasionally," Ralph answered cautiously.

"Listen, Ralph, I'll lay it on the line. Dewey's a very important man. He's going to become district attorney, then governor of New York, and someday, he'll run for president of the United States. He can help you a lot. Give you freelance with your numbers—all over. Nobody'll bother you. But first, we have to convict Luciano!"

Ralph kept his composure because he wanted to know how far Cole would go. "What? Why pick on me?" he asked carefully.

"Because you come from a good family," Cole answered flatly. "You've been arrested, but you've never been convicted of a crime."

After the cold turkey conversation, Ralph was told to sleep on it, and he was returned to The Tombs.

Lying on his cot, Ralph thought for hours about what was happening; what was he getting into? He, naturally, was also worried about Dotty. His instinct told him they were going to involve her also. *Poor kid,* thought Ralph. She was too fragile for all this. Armand returned to inquire about the developments.

"They want me to frame Charlie on something," Ralph whispered.

"What?" Armand looked shocked. "Don't do it, Ralph. Don't do anything. I'll be back." He hastily left, leaving Ralph in a state of confusion.

A few days later, Ralph was again taken back to the inner sanctum. Cole was busy behind his desk, arranging some papers; the guard was still behind Ralph.

"Ralph, do you want to see your girl this morning?" he stated matter-of-factly.

"Of course," replied Ralph in the affirmative, and Cole nodded to the guard to escort Ralph to another room where Dotty was waiting. When Ralph walked in, he noticed another girl sitting there but ignored her. Dotty rushed into his arms again, wailing, "Ralph, they want me to frame Luciano. What can I do? Please help me!" The tears were rolling down her cheeks, and Ralph could see by her haunted, red-rimmed eyes that she was in deep, deep trouble.

"How the hell can you do that, Dotty? You only met him once—that time in Saratoga. Don't do it. You can't do it!" Ralph stated emphatically.

"Ralph, they told me I'd do a lot of years in prison. Oh, I'll die . . . I'll just die." She was trembling with fear. Of course, Dewey later twisted around the reasons for her fear.

"Look, Dotty." Ralph stroked her hair gently. "Don't worry, they're just trying to scare you. You can't lie. You can't do anything like that. You'll only get into further trouble. Think of your family!" Dotty began to sob again, and Ralph felt impotent.

They didn't care what happened to her, Ralph fumed inwardly. It was inhuman what they were doing. She was just their pawn. They were destroying her, preying on her fragility. He could see that they were going to use all the ammunition they could. Dewey was later often accused of being more interested in convictions than justice to gain political power. Ralph could attest to that. At that moment, when he saw Dotty's despair, he wanted to smash the whole goddamn bunch of them. But he had to be in control of himself.

Cole came into the room with an air of confidence, knowing he had pushed them both up against the wall. Ralph wanted to spit in Cole's eye. As they led him out, Dotty covered her face, and he heard her sobbing. Once the guard left him alone in Cole's office, Cole leaned forward, hands folded on his desk. "Ralph, only you can help your girl. After this is over, we'll send you both on a nice trip to Europe to forget." He smiled slyly.

Ralph did not answer, overcome with gloom. "Think about it," Cole concluded. Ralph was led back to The Tombs.

Agnes had some unexpected visitors of her own. Unable to get straight answers from Armand, who wanted to spare her, she went to the source. Entering the visitors' room, Ralph saw how strained her face was—like someone who has had many sleepless nights. "Ralph, some plainclothesmen came to the house," Agnes whispered. "They told me if you didn't do what the district attorney wanted, they would give you twenty-five years in prison. Ralph, what do they want you to do? Is it the numbers? Did they catch you in something? Son, you know, you'll have to take your punishment . . ." Her voice trailed off.

"No, Mom, it's not the numbers. I've had everything closed for some time now. But I learned they want me to tell lies about Charlie . . . frame Charlie as the head of all the whorehouses. And, Mom . . . that's not true. Anything . . . but that! It's a political maneuver, and . . ." Ralph paused, trying to control himself. "These bastards also got Dotty mixed up in it."

"Dotty?" There was sudden shock in Agnes's eyes. She put her hand to her forehead, absently smoothing her hair a bit. Then sadly, she said, "Ralph, you've done a lot of things . . . not all good . . . but, Ralph, if you do anything like that . . . I don't want to know you as my son!"

"No, Mom . . . don't worry. I'll never do anything like that," Ralph reassured her.

"There just has to be a way to get you out of this. It's completely crazy," cried troubled Agnes.

Ralph looked at his mother as she rose to leave—the dearest person in the world to him—and thought about how much he loved her. Her moral support meant everything. Agnes left Ralph with his head in his hands. He had always understood her feelings. This was not what she and his father had planned for him.

Monday morning, the guard came for Ralph. This time, he was surprised to see Anna sitting solemnly with Dotty in Cole's office. *This guy is trying everything in the book to convince me,* thought Ralph. Cole attempted a smile and began with his usual phrases of persuasion. He explained that Dotty's role, which, in collusion with Ralph, would make Charlie a goner.

"It's all a pack of lies," Ralph cried.

"Don't be a damn fool, Ralph." Cole snapped. "We don't want *you*! We want *Lucky*!"

Cole looked toward Anna, who sat there dumbfounded, not wanting to believe her ears. Cole wanted her to cooperate, to influence Ralph to agree to the setup. Ralph looked at Dotty. She was running real scared; he could see she was wavering. But the interview ended in a deadlock. Ralph didn't say yes, but he didn't say no. He wanted to learn more!

The agonizing interviews had gone on for over two weeks. Ralph was called in almost every other day and given bits and pieces each time. It was their cat-and-mouse game; they were trying to break him psychologically. Armand, in the meantime, was running around on the outside, doing some investigating of his own. Friends told him Dewey was politically obsessed; that his driving ambition was to become president; that he wanted to ensure himself of the Republican nomination; and that he was out to break the Democratic Party. The politicians gave Armand a message for Ralph. "Tell Ralph to do anything those bastards want—for the moment. Then we'll tell him what to do."

Armand looked compassionately at his brother and added gently, "Try not to worry, Ralph. Everybody knows what that man has on his mind. Stand pat. Let them think you'll cooperate."

And Ralph did just that.

On the next visit, Ralph learned just how far they would go. Cole was tough. "Ralph, you'll have to cooperate with us, otherwise, we can give you up to twenty-five years in prison."

"What?" Ralph yelled. "You're crazy. I'm not doing twenty-five years in prison for nobody!"

Ralph sensed Cole was bluffing, just wanted to scare him, and Ralph was ready to play along.

"Okay, Ralph . . . what do you say?" Cole urged.

"Well . . . what if I answer the lawyers wrong?" Ralph finally asked.

"Don't worry. We'll tell you how to answer before you take the witness stand," Cole assured him. "That'll come later. You will be well protected."

"You know if I do something like this . . . I'd have to get out of town—fast." Ralph paused, then asked suspiciously, "What will I get for all this?"

Cole reminded him of the European trip, but Ralph just stared at him to make him understand that wasn't what he had in mind.

Cole rose from his chair, rather uneasy, and walked to the window. As he gazed out, he casually said, "We're willing to give you twenty thousand dollars." He turned slightly to catch Ralph's reaction.

Ralph couldn't believe his ears. "Well, now we're talking a different tune," he said, smiling, playing the game.

"Okay," said Cole, returning to his desk; he brushed the interview aside. "We'll talk about it tomorrow."

At the next meeting, a cohort of Cole's, Charles P. Grimes, another Dewey assistant plotting against Charlie, was present.

"Ralph . . . we want you to meet this woman today, a madam named Joan Martin," Cole stated, beginning the session. "She was arrested after the police raided her house of prostitution. She's cooperating with us in this case. Now . . . we're going to rehearse what you're supposed to do."

Ralph nodded apathetically. An attendant ushered in a middle-aged woman, and there was no doubt in Ralph's mind—by looking at her—that Joan Martin was one tough lady. She sat to Ralph's left, nervously adjusting her horn-rimmed glasses, and Grimes was to his right while Cole, at his desk, a bunch of papers in his hands, presided over the meeting.

"Now, Ralph . . . this is your role: you're to say that Luciano sent you to Joan Martin's house in Brooklyn to shake her down every week for $300. Then you were supposed to take the money directly to Luciano at the Grotta Azzurra Restaurant, where he usually eats!"

It was obvious the Martin woman was to be a key witness for Dewey. *What sons of bitches,* Ralph thought.

"Well . . . what if they catch me in a lie?" Ralph interrupted, still pretending to be unconvinced.

Cole tried not to lose his patience. "Look . . . Ralph . . . we have the strategy all figured out. We'll go over all the details with a fine-tooth comb."

He probably means I'll be rehearsed to death, mused Ralph. But he persisted, "And you think they'll believe me?"

"Yes, we do," Cole answered, exasperated. "I told you . . . your record shows that you've never been convicted, and you're neither a pimp, nor a prostitute. They'll believe you all right." He insisted on his ideas and schemes, and soon that day's session was over.

While Ralph was going through all this madness, Charlie was having his own problems fighting extradition in Arkansas. Day by day, the events unraveled a clearer picture of Dewey's intentions.

April 1-2: In Hot Springs to relax and gamble, Charlie was arrested upon Dewey's say-so but was soon freed on a $5,000 bond. Dewey was angered and issued some dramatic, if not harsh, statements, then immediately sent a detective with a warrant. He turned to State Attorney General Carl E. Bailey for assistance. After a few hours of freedom, Charlie was rearrested and held without bail. Charlie retaliated and declared he would fight extradition and hired two lawyers.

All of Charlie's contacts tried to help—Owney Madden was one of them. When, however, they offered $50,000 to Attorney General Bailey, they played a wrong hand, causing a ripple of negative reactions. Then a battle began to transfer Charlie from the Hot Springs jail to Little Rock. Finally, armed with machine guns, state troopers moved Charlie to the Little Rock jail.

In New York, Dewey indicted Charlie and eleven so-called underlings on twenty-five counts. The most important was Dave Betillo, whom Dewey claimed was Charlie's chief lieutenant. Betillo was held on $75,000 bail for compulsory prostitution. Dewey also revealed he had 110 witnesses scattered throughout various jails. These witnesses were costing the city of New York $400 a day.

Among the many women Dewey had picked up for questioning was Gay Orlova, a beautiful ex-Earl Carroll chorus girl. After being grilled for five hours, she finally admitted to being Charlie's sweetheart. Not being able to pin anything on her, Dewey had to release her but issued strict instructions that she be watched very closely at her apartment on West Sixty-Fourth Street.

April 3: Charlie, through his lawyers, called attention to the date of the New York warrant—October 25, 1934—and categorically denied the charges against him as "the most vicious kind of politics."

He added vigorously, "I wish to say most emphatically that the accusations are false. I am not guilty, and New York officers know it. I may not be the most moral and upright person, but I never stooped so low as to aid in the prostitution traffic, as I am accused. If those who are taking action against me were on the level, they would not have waited this long, for they have been well aware of all my movements since 1934."

Chancellor Garrett of Arkansas still refused to consider bond, and Charlie waited in his cell for the hearing on the warrant.

April 6: Dewey prepared to invoke the Lindbergh Law to get Charlie back. More detectives took off for Little Rock with a formal request for extradition. The specific charge was extortion based on the booker Al Weiner (obviously collaborating), who claimed Charlie extorted money with the threat of violence, placing the date at June 24, 1935. Charlie was ready to prove he was not in New York at that time, but Dewey was sending one detective to say that he was. The extradition was argued in Little Rock in the presence of Governor J. Marion Futrell and Dewey's aides.

April 7: Governor Futrell granted New York governor Lehman's request for extradition. Charlie's lawyers immediately issued a writ of habeas corpus in Little Rock's federal court.

April 8: District Judge Martineau dismissed the writ. "I see no reason at all why he should not be returned, except that he doesn't want to go." He did however grant the lawyers a ten-day period to fight Charlie's case.

While the police heavily surrounded the Pulaski County Jail, where Charlie was being held without bail, his lawyers prepared to appeal the court's dismissal of the habeas corpus proceedings to the federal circuit court of appeals in Kansas City.

April 9: Dewey was not too happy about the extradition delay but used the time to enhance his case—as the extraordinary grand jury continued probing into the compulsory prostitution racket.

April 11: There was a tiny spark of hope when Judge Kimbrough Stone of the circuit court of appeals in Kansas City announced that he would receive the petition for probable cause of appeal the following Monday.

In New York, Dewey was preparing a new indictment for Charlie and the others under the new anticrime or Joinder Law. In his personal fight to secure passage of the law in Albany, he was quoted as saying, "Today crime is syndicated and organized. A new type of criminal exists who leaves to his hirelings and front men the actual offenses, and rarely commits an overt act himself. The only way in which the major criminal can be punished is by connecting to him those various layers of subordinates, and the related but separate crimes on his behalf."

He went on to say that the current law was a straitjacket and didn't allow prosecution of offenses together (except in conspiracy) even though related. Separate trials were needed for each offense, in separate courts with separate juries.

The new bill now permitted the joinder of a series of related offenses in a single true bill. It was no wonder it became known as the Dewey Law. It was his primary tool in indicting everyone.

April 13-16: After receiving the petition, Judge Stone denied Charlie's lawyers the writ of habeas corpus.

April 17: The ten-day period was up for Charlie. His lawyers maneuvered to extend his stay, but it was too late. Dewey caught them in a technicality, and Charlie was his for the trip back to New York. It was a terrible defeat for Charlie.

Once in New York, Charlie was taken to the Raymond Street Jail in Brooklyn. The self-satisfied Dewey brought Charlie immediately to court, and Judge McCook set bail at an unheard-of $350,000. They wanted to make sure he wouldn't be going anywhere.

Ralph learned they had Charlie and felt badly for him, especially because he knew how they were working behind the scenes. He was called back to Cole's office for a couple more rehearsals with the Martin woman. The routine was always the same; she was an unhappy madam who was shaken down every week, and Ralph received the money to take to Charlie. Cole had pictures of the defendants, which were supposed to help Ralph and Joan Martin identify them. *What a phony setup, a lot of crap,* thought Ralph. He was always difficult, always asked all kinds of questions—what if this, what if that? And Cole would grit his teeth.

Cole was adamant when he was again alone with Ralph. "Ralph, you have to go to the grand jury to swear in what you're supposed to say."

Ralph was startled. He didn't expect the sudden conclusion and tried to gain some time. "How can I take your word for all this? Like I said, if I testify against Luciano, I'll have to get out of town!" Ralph argued.

"Don't worry. You'll get your money," Cole snarled.

"How can I take your word for it?" Ralph persisted.

"Look, if you don't believe me . . ." He paused. "Do you want to talk to Dewey?"

"Yes . . . I would," Ralph replied firmly.

Without a word, Ralph was taken to Mr. Dewey's office on the same floor. Cole walked in first and, in a very scholarly manner, said, "Mr. Dewey, this is Ralph Liguori, about whom we've been talking. He doesn't believe we will give him the money, if he testifies against Luciano."

Ralph stared at the famous Mr. Dewey, who focused in on him. Dewey's lips formed some kind of smirk—his mustache, as usual, neatly trimmed. Then, mockingly and yet always authoritative, Dewey asked, "What makes you think we won't give you the money?"

"What guarantee do I have?" Ralph replied, undaunted.

"What do you want, then?" Dewey's smile disappeared.

"Well, put the money in a bank account in my name," Ralph offered with satisfaction—maintaining a perfect pretense of cooperation—but with strings attached.

Dewey lost control. His face became crimson, and as his mustache went up, he shouted, "Get out! You're too goddamn smart!"

"Fuck you, you mustache bastard," Ralph snapped back.

Cole grabbed the belligerent Ralph's arm and, fuming, dragged him out by the arm. He had lost face with his boss. His star witness, whom he had been grooming for days, had tripped him.

As they returned to his office, Cole twisted Ralph's arm and sneered, "We're going to crucify you for this! We were going to use you and Martin to get to Luciano . . . Now we're going to use her to frame *you*. Buddy, you're a goner. You're going up the river!"

At that moment, Grimes came up and knowingly snarled, "Why you, guinea bastard . . ." And moved toward Ralph to hit him. Luckily, Cole motioned to the guard, and Ralph was roughly taken back to his cell.

Damn shysters, thought Ralph. *If I could only put my fists into all of them—the self-righteous bigots!*

April 23: Late that same afternoon, Ralph was indicted and held on $25,000 bail. His name was written in pen and ink at the bottom of the blanket indictment, becoming unlucky *number 13*. The same charges as Charlie: compulsory prostitution.

The next day, all the defendants stood before Judge McCook to be arraigned under Dewey's new blanket indictment, containing ninety counts. Total bail was around one million dollars and a maximum total of 1,950 years.

Dewey had organized what would become a spectacular trial—a trial to go down in history. And it did!

CHAPTER TWENTY-NINE

The selection of the blue-ribbon jury, which began on May 11, was a tedious task because both the prosecution and the defense wanted to make sure that no one was prejudiced about the case. In Dewey's camp, they didn't want anyone who would not believe their type of witnesses and, in particular, the prostitutes Dewey had waiting in the wings. The defense tried to eliminate those who would hang their defendants from the start, particularly Luciano, whom Dewey, with the help of the press, had already classified him as public enemy number one.

It took a couple of days to select the jurors from a long list of about two hundred talesmen, which included many prominent persons. Many declined for one reason or another, others were eliminated, and after intense interrogations, both sides finally agreed to the jury they hoped would be impartial. They were all middle-aged married men: Edwin Aderer, gold dental manufacturer; Theodore A. Isert, editor; Edward Blake, salesman; Paul Mahler, consulting engineer; Hewitt Morgan, customer's man; Robert R. Gagnon, purchasing agent; Charles H. Jones, banker; Robert I. Center, book publisher; Lincoln H. Weld, public accountant; Stephen G. Smith, art importer; John McGowan, electrical supervisor; and Martin Moses, teacher. Two alternates were designated: Henry R. Sturges, investment counselor, and Clarence Talbot Squier, accountant.

Dewey, as was his style, opened the trial in a sensational way. His assistants carried in a stand with a huge chart, five feet tall, which illustrated Dewey's preconceived idea of the vice syndicate. It showed Luciano at the top as the vice lord and, underneath, his so-called henchmen in their relative roles. Ralph was listed as the stickup man. The defense objected strenuously to this tactic, claiming that it was premature to make such claims; that it was done to impress and influence the jury. Dewey rebutted calmly that it was only to help the jurors remember the names. The objection was overruled by Judge McCook—the first of many denials yet to come. Then Dewey began with his opening address—a long discourse on the vice racket. Dramatically speaking in front of the jurors, Dewey had become a champion for the prostitutes of New York. He wanted the perpetrators of such a low, debasing crime punished and the city cleaned up. He mainly spoke about Luciano's organizational skills, quoting him on just hearsay, and stressed he would prove that Luciano stated he would turn over the racket to Dave Betillo. He talked about the rules of the syndicate, the booker fees, the bonding, and the kickbacks from madams. When Dewey mentioned the supposedly gentlemanly in-house standards, he turned to the defendants and smiled mockingly, as he promised. "I shall, however, reveal to these various defendants just how each arranged to double-cross the others, and show them where and how the chiseling was done." He closed his speech ready for the fight.

The defense counselors jumped from their seats, crying in vain for a mistrial. Many had wanted separate trials for their defendants, as did Carlino for Ralph. Judge McCook, however, refused everyone. It was now absolutely certain that the trial that Dewey so carefully planned would continue undisturbed.

George Morton Levy for Luciano opened his address by saying, "My client is no angel, but he made his money in gambling—not prostitution."

Levy made an eloquent summary of Luciano's past history, stating that as a youth, he had worked legitimately; he touched on the social environment, which led Luciano to become involved with bad company; he admitted to Luciano's brush with narcotics when he was eighteen, but that after his brief punishment, Luciano had learned his lesson. Levy claimed that in Luciano's later life, it was only gambling that brought in his revenue. He stated that Luciano knew only Betillo before the trial, and it was this friendship that led Dewey and his staff to believe that Charlie Luciano had to be the natural kingpin of the vice racket. "Not so," claimed Levy, and he was ready to prove it.

Lorenzo C. Carlino rose to address the court and the jury. "My client knows nothing of all these things," he exclaimed and proceeded to tell them that Ralph Liguori would take the stand to deny any connection with the racket. Then Carlino added dramatically that an agent of the district attorney threatened Ralph with twenty-five years in jail if he refused to testify against Luciano. The jurors now had an idea of what to expect from Ralph's defense. As Carlino spoke, Ralph watched the jury closely and sensed only a few really paid any attention to the defense attorney's remarks.

The other defense attorneys—Murray, Siegel, and Barra—one by one got up to disclaim their defendant's guilt, but it was as if no one was listening.

The prelude was over. The girls waited nervously for their cue, waiting for their moment on center stage. They were handpicked prostitutes or "Broadway Geishas," as the papers called them. Dewey called them exhibit A. They would have pathetic stories to tell, and all were willing to talk to save themselves. One was quoted as saying, "If I tell what I know, it means complete immunity. It means I go out; I don't go to the workhouse for a year, maybe three!" Actually, Dewey made no secret of the fact that he had promised them immunity. He had openly stated he would not prosecute any of the women who would expose the inner workings of the vice racket. What he didn't say was that many of their stories were prefabricated; that they were coached and briefed by his aides to suit his case.

The jurors sat fixed, eyes wide, ready for the show; the defense counselors were alert for the battle—watchful, ready to act. Then the parade started; it began with the less significant prostitutes but who were, nevertheless, still damaging to the defense. Called to the stand was Rose Cohen alias Renee Gallo. The door opened, and in walked a brunette around twenty-five, average height, in a blue crepe dress and matching hat loosely slanted to one side. Around her neck hung a scarlet scarf to match her small ruby lips. Her features were refined but hardly her obvious profession. With Dewey's shrewd guiding hand, she began to tell her life story, arriving at the point where she had settled in a house of prostitution run by a Molly Leonard. It was there that she had met Pete Harris (alias Balitzer), the booker who had pleaded guilty and who was to be one of Dewey's key witnesses. Rose told how her weekly earnings were divided: half went to the madam (in this case, Molly), 10 percent to Harris as the booker's fee, five dollars for the doctor, and eighteen dollars for board. She was left usually with a very little percentage. On her first arrest, she met Jimmy Fredericks (alias Frederico), Jesse Jacobs, Meyer Berkman, and Max Karp, the lawyer who defended her in court. Under Karp's coaching, she told a good story and was dismissed.

Some of the defendants had been named and directly connected with the racket. Samuel Siegel, counselor for Frederico, rose to cross-examine the witness and immediately branded Rose Cohen as the scarlet woman. He assailed her with questions, which exposed her dormant emotions. She replied haughtily—at times she was insolent. She boldly stood her ground, her black eyes glaring. Nearing two hours on the stand, however, she showed signs of exhaustion. Siegel kept banging away.

Q: "Do you expect to walk out of here a free woman?"
A: "Positively! I was told this was my last chance to talk, or go away for three years."
Q: "No doubt that thought has kept ringing in your ears!"
A: "Oh, yes!"

Siegel had made his point. She was buying her way out. After James D. C. Murray closed the cross-examination, in which Cohen testified she had refused to identify Luciano, she was excused. With her square shoulders held high, she swung herself off the stand. Judging from the jurors' faces, she was not hard to look at.

Next came Murial Ryan, a statuesque, lovely twenty-four-year-old with reddish brown hair. She wore an outfit that almost matched the color of her hair, and she too wore a wide-brimmed hat that slouched to one side. As she positioned herself on the stand, she crossed her slender legs purposely in the direction of the jury. When she opened her mouth to speak, there was a slight rustle in the courtroom. Her babyish lisp did not match the rest of her. In her high-pitched voice, Murial told the court about her beginnings. Getting down to brass tacks, she revealed how she had first worked for the booker Nick Montana but then had switched to Pete Harris, with whom she had thought she could make more money. She was told, however, that she would have to pay—because a "new combination" was taking over.

Again, Siegel took up the cross-examination. Murial replied with such naiveté that she caused many in the courtroom to grin.

Q: "Are you being paid expenses?"
A: "Oh, yes. One dollar and fifty cents a day as witness fee."
Q: "Where have you been staying?"
A: "Oh, at the House of Detention. Twice I was escorted out, with three of my friends, by a police matron and a policeman. We went to Radio City Music Hall twice, and to the Paramount Theatre once, and we saw *Mr. Deeds Goes to Town*, *Thirteen Hours by Air*, and *Under Two Flags*. After *Mr. Deeds*, we stopped in Chin Lee's, but nobody danced, and we all chipped in to pay the bill.

Murial, however, caused the most snickers when she was questioned about her lover. She was confused about his name; she was so dumb that even Charlie grinned at some of her remarks. It was a kind of burlesque, especially when she left the stand, swishing and swaying out of the courtroom.

Then, to enlighten the court, two madams were called. First came Dorothy Arnold alias Dixie Arnold alias Dorothy Sherman—a twenty-five-year-old blonde from Virginia. Under direct examination, she was interrogated by Barent Ten Eyck, a bright young prosecutor who skillfully led her through her story. Dorothy worked with Manhattan's number one booker, Nick Montana, but after he was arrested, she had turned to Pete Harris. He explained that his girls had to pay ten dollars a week as a bonding fee. Through Harris, she had met Jimmy Fredericks. She caused the jurors to lean forward when she mentioned the "green punch card" system. It was the first time anyone had spoken about them. They were cards with numbers on them, and as the girls earned their money, they punched the cards accordingly. At the end of the week, the amounts were tallied, and the deductions began.

Ralph listened with interest. He was gradually envisioning a picture of the racket in which he was being accused of participating. When the next madam arrived, he really perked up. Her name was Betty Winters, a plump Russian woman about thirty-two who had been a madam for seven years. Betty claimed that although she ran a disorderly house, she herself was never a prostitute. Again, Montana and Harris were mentioned, but she also included Fredericks, Dave Miller, and Jack Eller as cohorts. Then Ralph heard himself named as she pointed at him. He almost jumped up, but Carlino simply looked at him, and he froze. Betty claimed she had seen Ralph a few times, and on one occasion in particular; she had seen him at the Rainbow Inn, where a banquet was held in his honor. Ralph wanted to yell, *You bitch! You must have crashed my party!* The woman was testifying about the time he had thrown the reception for the hospital people. Ralph had never seen the woman in his life. This was a first attempt to associate Ralph with the other defendants, but it didn't stick. Carlino rose and blasted her on cross-examination. She defended the fact that she was never a prostitute, but she squirmed when Carlino popped up with a record showing she had been convicted as a prostitute in 1928, "exposing her body for the purpose of prostitution," and had been sentenced to ten days in the workhouse. Carlino had established perjury and returned to his seat satisfied.

The comedy had only just begun. More girls came and went. They all had pitiful stories to tell, and no matter how hard they tried to act the part of a lady, they couldn't sustain it. Ralph felt sorry for some of them, but others were hard as rocks. One had to hand it to Dewey. He was building up his case gradually, creating a mood and a solid foundation. Dewey had started with the women who had fallen into the lowest depths of society to gain pity from the jury—to scorn the defendants who had, through their vice syndicate, exploited them.

Up to that moment, every one of the defendants had been fingered and linked to the combination by the women, except Pennochio and Charlie. Ralph was mentioned, more or less, by the Winters woman; but he was anticipating the big bang by the whorehouse madam, Joan Martin, the woman with whom Cole (Dewey's assistant) had expected Ralph to collaborate in framing Charlie. At recess, Carlino told Ralph to stay calm, not to make any sudden outburst because that would only confirm to the jury that Ralph was a violent man. The papers had described him as mild-looking, and Ralph was to maintain that image. Ralph sat uncomfortably, waiting for Martin's entrance and the lies she would undoubtedly tell.

Joan Martin walked slowly to the stand, nervously plucking at her lightweight coat. As she settled herself on the hard wooden seat, the court saw a plain, haggard-looking woman of average height. Unlike the other girls, Joan Martin wore a dowdy hat perched slightly forward, and her horn-rimmed glasses were the schoolmarm type. She complained of a sore throat and was given a glass of milk. Her voice was hoarse; sometimes she wheezed. Barent Ten Eyck, Dewey's able assistant, took over direct examination, which seemed to be very carefully studied. She gave some background history and her age as forty-one before beginning her spiel. She claimed she opened up her disorderly house in February 1931 and worked with a booker, Charlie Spinach. When she refused to join the combination, Spinach returned with Wahrman and three other men to convince her to rethink the offer. They tore her place apart in order to frighten her into accepting orders. At this point, she sniffed into her handkerchief and pulled her collar snugly around her neck, looking toward the jury for sympathy.

Ten Eyck egged her on, and she stated that her next visitor was Jimmy Fredericks (pointing dramatically to him on the bench) and said he was even tougher. "He asked me for $250 security for the girl and $150 for myself, in addition to the weekly payment," she lamented. She finally understood that she had to agree to the payments, said she would pay the security fees on installments, which, unfortunately, she had neglected. Fredericks returned again, and this time, he meant business. According to Joan Martin, after a bitter exchange of words, Fredericks had pulled a lead pipe out of his coat and hit her on the head, knocking her out cold. She was taken to a doctor who "gave me four stitches here" (pointing to her right forehead) and "six stitches here" (indicating the back of her head). Martin continued to moan that she had to move, but even in her new place, she soon had new visitors. Two men, whom she had refused to allow in one day, returned with still another man.

Q: "Do you see any of them in the courtroom?"

She looked searchingly toward the bench and hesitated. Before she could answer, the prosecution helped her by asking Ralph to remove his glasses, which he did. Joan Martin pointed directly at Ralph.

A: "Yes, that man with the glasses."

Carlino jumped up and objected vigorously because, as he told the court, Dewey had asked Ralph to take off his glasses, thereby identifying him *in advance*! Ralph was the only defendant wearing glasses. Of course, Carlino knew it was all an act since the Martin woman had already met Ralph in Harry Cole's office. Judge McCook, as usual, did not sustain the objection.

The prosecution continued.

Q: "What's his name?"
A: "I know his first name. It's Ralph."

Martin continued to involve Ralph by saying he was a customer of one of her prostitutes, named Lillian. Ralph had supposedly come in with two other men, using the excuse that he wanted to see Lillian.

Q: "Where did they go?"
A: "They walked into the parlor, and before I knew it, one of the other two fellows pulled out a gun and said, 'All right now . . . it's a stickup.' They went through my things and my pocketbooks. They took my watch and thirty-six dollars. Then they went through coffee cans and cereal cans."
Q: "Did they find any more money?"
A: "Yes, some change in the girl's purse."
Q: "Did you bond after that?"
A: "Yes, about a week later."

Ralph couldn't help chuckling, despite everything. Now he knew how Dewey, Cole, and company wanted to get him! The stickup man! It was a well-rehearsed comedy act. She knew her part very well, but it still wasn't finished. Martin claimed that she had had still another bout with Fredericks; that he had punched her in the jaw, had even pulled out his gun to shoot her dog. The story went on with what seemed like a convincing display of facts.

After luncheon recess, Samuel Siegel, defense counsel for Frederico, was ready for her.

Q: "Ms. Martin, you say you were hit on the head by one of the defendants, Jimmy Fredericks."
A: "Yes."

Q: "Where?"
A: "Brownsville."
Q: "Well, were you bleeding?"
A: "Oh, yes, an awful lot."
Q: "Did you go to the hospital in Brooklyn?"
A: "No."
Q: "Well, where did you go?"
A: "To the Bronx."
Q: "To the Bronx? Do you mean to sit here and tell the court and jury that you were badly bleeding, and you went to the Bronx to a hospital or a doctor? Were there no clinics in Brownsville?"
A: (No answer.)
Q: "Well, will you please mention the street, what hospital, what doctor?"
A: "I don't remember."
Q: "Did you get stitches?"
A: "Oh, yes."
Q: "Well, will you please show the jurors where you were hit on the head?"

Martin nodded dutifully, took off her hat, and dramatically jumped down from the stand. "See, see!" she exclaimed, parting her black hair with her fingers to show where the stitches were. The jurors stepped down to get a closer look; some waved their hands, as if to say they couldn't see a thing; others took notes. She was so comical that the defendants had to laugh. Finally, her act was over; and despite the defense counsels' efforts to prove her a perjurer, Dewey seemed pleased.

Then a strange thing happened. The defense lawyers suddenly made a motion for a recess to speak with Judge McCook. It was granted, and the defendants were ushered into the bullpen. One of the defense counselors had spotted somebody pointing out the defendants to the girls before they took the stand. Carlino quietly told Ralph and the others to get ready to change their suits with one another. In the meantime, in the judge's chambers, the defense lawyers kept objecting animatedly, stating that the defendants were being pointed out, one by one, through the courtroom doors—to the left and right of the judge's bench—by someone on Dewey's staff. The defense demanded that the defendants be allowed to change their suits. Judge McCook looked surprised and, even though Dewey denied the accusations, granted the request. In private, the defense lawyers went into another huddle; then Carlino came into the bullpen and dictated, "Nobody changes suits. *Stay the way you are*!" The defendants exchanged glances of bewilderment.

As court reconvened, Dewey immediately asked to address the jury. "Gentlemen of the jury," he began dramatically, "I cannot tell you what is going on behind doors in this case. I'm not permitted to tell you . . ." He paused, then spoke rapidly, "But if any of the witnesses point out the wrong defendant . . . it's because all the defendants just changed their suits!"

There was complete pandemonium; the entire courtroom was in an uproar as all the defense lawyers jumped up steaming, demanding a mistrial. But Judge McCook didn't have the guts to do it. He paternally reprimanded Dewey, telling him not to do anything similar again, or he would have to grant a mistrial. Nevertheless, no matter how often the defense had asked for a mistrial, it was always denied. Dewey and McCook were a tough duo to beat.

As Judge McCook banged his gavel for silence in the courtroom, the defense lawyers sat down in complete disgust.

CHAPTER THIRTY

The squealers were not all women. The three bookers—Al Weiner, Dave Marcus (alias Miller), and Pete Balitzer (alias Harris)—had turned state's evidence before the trial opened. Ralph didn't know them and didn't want to because he had no respect for stool pigeons. To him, they were as low as their racket. Now they would have their chance to "sing" in front of the jurors. Toward the end of the first week of the trial, Al Weiner was called.

Weiner was half-crippled, and as he shuffled in, one couldn't help noticing the thick ugly shoe he wore. The jurors stared and saw a frightened, odd-looking character, about twenty-seven, already bald, roly-poly in build, with rimless glasses hanging on his nose. He mentioned Fredericks, Wahrman, and Jacobs in his testimony but, more importantly, did a beautiful job of tying in Betillo at a September 1933 meeting.

At this meeting, Betillo supposedly read the riot act to the bookers with statements like: "There are a lot of houses holding out. From now on, there's going to be a $250 fine on every house that tries to hold out on us!" and "You bookers have got to remember, we're doing you all a favor by letting you work for us." Betillo also had some very derogatory things to say about some of the men: "Dave Marcus is a dirty rat. We're going to run him out of town." "Pete Harris was a louse." and "Jack Eller is due to get his belly kicked in." Weiner was obviously laying some of the groundwork for his other squealing partners in crime.

The defense was alarmed at Weiner's testimony and hoped to trap him under cross-examination in his lies to break down the effect of his story. Weiner was terrified when they took over. He admitted to not knowing what income tax was, and that he had never paid any state or federal taxes. They tripped him up now and then, but the most poignant and damaging question was, "How do you hope to profit by testifying against your former supervisors?"

Objections from the defense resounded in the courtroom when he answered, "Mr. Dewey told me he would see that I got leniency, and that I'd get a short term in jail where I wouldn't be murdered."

More screams of objections to have the last remark stricken, but Dewey interrupted and pompously admitted, "That's exactly what I told him."

In order to cope with all the witnesses and not drag the trial out for all eternity, Judge McCook had decreed all-day sessions for Saturday as well. This enabled Dewey to end the week in glory by keeping his promise to have Charlie linked to the group. On Saturday, he called Dave Marcus to the stand. Unlike Weiner, Marcus was middle-aged, tall, spindle-legged, with jumbo ears. After arriving to New York from Pittsburgh in 1929, Marcus, then thirty-seven, had opened up a disorderly house. Things took a bad turn for him in August of 1933 when, with a fixed frown on his face, he related in detail the misadventures with the mob. Threatened with a knife against his throat, he was told to leave town in twenty-four hours. He had, however, refused and wouldn't play ball with his molesters. Consequently, one night, as he was getting into his car, six bullets fired from a passing car, practically killing him. To clear the air, he had finally taken a leave of absence from New York. He had returned sometime later and, in December 1934, had resumed his activities—this time under the syndicate rules. Soon Marcus became one of the biggest bookers in Brooklyn.

It was Dewey's expert prodding that finally made Marcus mention Charlie. First, however, Dewey threw Pennochio into the ring. Marcus testified that Fredericks had introduced him to Tommy "Bull" Pennochio in the early summer of 1935 and had been told that he was the treasurer of the organization.

Then, in June of 1935, Fredericks met Marcus again and was told there was a shift in the houses, and that they were going to give him Weiner's. Afraid of such a move, Marcus complained that Weiner could, understandably, go squealing to the coppers. Fredericks had replied impatiently, "What are you hollering for? You don't have to worry! We'll take care of you!" Marcus retorted, "Who do you mean by 'we'?" And Fredericks answered, "Well, Little Abie, Davey, and then . . ." Reluctantly, he added, "Charlie."

There were dramatic reactions in the courtroom. Defense lawyers shouted cries of objections, and the jurors sat up in attention, murmuring to one another. Dewey continued unabashedly, "Did you know what he meant?" Marcus frowned and replied solemnly, "No." The uproar ceased as they heard him utter that last word, but Dewey smiled at the jury and the court. He was satisfied. Marcus had lived up to his expectations. Everyone had thus been caught in the dragnet. In fact, Marcus had mentioned nine out of the ten defendants. Ralph was the one person he didn't know. That, naturally, didn't surprise Ralph. At the mention of

Charlie's name, Ralph glanced over at him. Charlie had his head bent, gazing disgustedly at Marcus from under veiled eyelids. Marcus avoided him altogether.

That weekend, as on all weekends to follow, the jurors were locked up in the Grosvenor Hotel, surrounded by security guards. All precautions were taken to avoid jury tampering.

When court reconvened Monday morning, a buxom thirty-seven-year-old madam by the name of Molly Leonard, a veteran in the business, took the stand. This was the first time she was arrested, and her story was similar to that of the other girls, with the exception that she mentioned Charlie. In a conversation with Pete Harris, she had been asked to join the combination and had not liked the idea.

Q: "What did he say?"
A: "He said, 'There are good people behind the combination.' I asked, 'Who?' He answered, 'Lucky.'"

Levy jumped up and shouted, "Objection, Your Honor, that's only hearsay!" It was overruled by Judge McCook.

Cross-examination by David Siegel elicited her real name as Molly Glick; then he hammered away at degrading her and her profession. He revealed that she had been a drug addict for seven years and had taken a cure once. Notwithstanding all of that history, she still enjoyed puffing her opium pipe. Levy, however, angry at his objection being overruled, went after her with vehemence. He was trying to prove she never saw Lucky in her life. "Stand up, Mr. Lucania," he stated firmly. Then he turned to the witness.

Q: "Did you ever see this man before?"
A: "No."
Q: "Have you ever spoken to him?"
A: "No."
Q: "When you were arrested in February and taken to the district attorney's office, were you asked about a man named Lucky?"
A: "No."
Q: "You had never heard his name mentioned before, had you?"
A: "No, until the time Pete Harris mentioned him."
Q: "Did anyone ever tell you that if you wanted to get immunity, you would have to mention the name of Lucky here?"
A: "No."

Molly Leonard was a tough broad and knew the ropes.

The procession of girls continued. Dewey produced them intermittently among his key witnesses, as a sort of intermission or comic relief. Some were more entertaining than others. Bonnie Connolly, Shirley Taylor, Marilyn Sommers, and Jean Mathews—all pretty prostitutes in their early twenties—were called. Connolly, a bleached blonde who had shared Pete Harris's apartment with two other girls, whispered her answers as if she were in her boudoir. Taylor cried out indignantly against the bookies, claiming they didn't have bookers in Pennsylvania. Her tiny figure erect in the witness box, Sommers smiled invitingly at the jurors and admitted she was a cruising prostitute, but her mother didn't know. Mathews, a small Spanish type, sighed she worked long hours from eleven in the morning until ten at night. Then Eleanor Jackson, an attractive twenty-eight-year-old ex-model, lamented in eloquent English that she became a prostitute out of necessity—because she was out of work.

The third bookie to squeal, Peter Balitzer, the man most mentioned by the girls, took his turn on the stand. The defense knew in advance that he would be most damaging to their clients and was prepared for the worst. Dewey beamed at what he knew would be his shining hour. Ralph realized Balitzer would also link Charlie, somehow, but was caught completely off guard when Balitzer involved *him*!

Hawk-nosed Balitzer, at age of thirty-three, had become the number one booker in New York. As he spoke, his mouth twisted nervously like the rubber band he held between his fingers, and his shifty eyes avoided the jurors throughout his testimony. Mainly, he complained about the weekly protection fee he had to pay the syndicate. When he and his brother were threatened, he settled with them. He was particularly angry with Wahrman who shook him down for $900 and, without hesitating, eagerly pointed to him on the bench. The prosecution asked Wahrman to stand up for all to see. It was Wahrman who had introduced Balitzer to Betillo (presumably chief lieutenant of the racket), and it was Betillo who, in discussion about bailing out the girls, revealed the kingpin to him.

Balitzer: "Listen, who's behind this? You get six or seven pinches a day. It costs $500."
Betillo: "Don't worry about it. Charlie 'Lucky's' behind it."

The cry, "Objection!" came up loud and clear, but as usual, it was overruled by Judge McCook. The prosecution continued to ask whether Balitzer had mentioned this to any of the madams. He replied that he did a couple of times, until Fredericks emphatically told him not to use the name Charlie "Lucky."

Another round for Dewey. Charlie this time squirmed in his seat, his face red with anger, as he realized the frame-up was definitely in the works. Up to that moment, Ralph had only half-listened to the testimony, but he perked up when he heard *his* name mentioned. Balitzer testified that Ralph Liguori, the "stickup" man for the ring, had asked him to book one of his girlfriends called Gashouse Lillian. At that point, Ralph almost burst out laughing, especially at the girl's name. Many colorful names were heard during the trial such as Jennie, the Factory, Hungarian Helen, Nigger Ruth, Violet of the Bronx, Cutrate Gus, to name a few. Balitzer crudely went on to say that he didn't like Gashouse Lil because she was too loud and fresh in experience. What followed by the prosecution was a key question, which was obviously to cue Balitzer on what he was supposed to say next.

Q: "Do you know Nancy Presser?"
A: "Yes, Ralph called me and said he had a nice blonde for me to book. He introduced me to Nancy Presser, and told me to put her to work. I said, 'Okay, if she's reliable.'"
Q: "Did you speak to Ralph about Nancy after that?"
A: "Yes, I said she wasn't reliable. She couldn't get up in the morning to get to work on time. She was a nice girl, but I couldn't put her in good joints."
Q: "Did Liguori tell you what relationship he bore to Nancy?"
A: "Yes, he told me he liked her . . . he loved her."

It was obvious that the prosecution wanted to paint Ralph as a pimp. It was no longer a laughing matter. Ralph turned to his lawyer and mumbled—seething,—that Balitzer was a goddamn liar! Because he didn't know any Gashouse Lil, and he had certainly *never* put Dotty in any whorehouse! Carlino tried to soothe his nerves because he too knew what was going on. What do you expect from a guy like Balitzer, whose own wife was a whorehouse madam and who had even tried to book minors? Ralph fumed inwardly. What the hell were a few extra lies to him, especially to save his skin! Some of the jurors looked at Ralph with disgust. Dewey was doing a fabulous job of defaming him.

As Ralph listened to the bookers testify, it was clear to him they were all very much involved in the racket, as well as those on the bench—with the exception of Charlie. Dewey obviously had a case; Ralph was not disputing that. What Ralph could not stomach was how they were weaving tales, putting Charlie at the top and involving him. A guy is hung for what he does, not for what he doesn't do.

Ralph thought that it probably was true that Charlie knew about the racket; there was little he didn't know about the action in New York. That didn't mean, however, that he was involved. For instance, Charlie knew of Ralph's numbers racket. But Ralph was independent and didn't have to give Charlie a cent out of his profits. Many independents operated in New York. There were certain things Charlie didn't touch, and prostitution was definitely one of them. Besides, if he wanted a woman, he went to Polly Adler's. Charlie mixed with a higher class of people. The whole prostitution thing was beneath him.

The heavy drama continued when the next witness, Danny Brooks, took the stand. Ralph had seen him around in the bootlegging days but didn't know Brooks was a convict serving time in Dannemora Prison. Brooks had been given time out to squeal on his former associates, partly for revenge because he blamed them for his arrest on compulsory prostitution charges and, of course, for the possibility of shortening his seven—to fifteen-year sentence. Dewey had left no stones unturned. Brooks's real name was Daniel Caputo. He was about forty-two, a short unkempt character with black hair and mustache. He maintained a cocky, know-it-all attitude. He had Levy jumping up and down constantly because Levy objected to the use of the name *Lucky* as hearsay.

Brooks used the name loosely throughout his testimony, stating that in his chats with Fredericks, he had learned that Charlie "Lucky" was behind the combination. *Objection.* That Charlie "Lucky's" mob had sent him out of town. *Objection.* That with Betillo, the big boss had been referred to as Lucky. On that point, Levy asked for a *mistrial*, but it was all denied by Judge McCook. Encouraged, Brooks went on, this time with Wahrman—Lucky again. *Objection.* Then he quoted Fredericks as saying, "I lost a decision. Lucky has just made a decision . . ." *Objection.* On still another point, he used the same story as Marcus and Balitzer; wanting to be reassured concerning who was really behind the combination, he was told it was Lucky. Again, Levy moved for a *mistrial*, that the name was repeatedly brought in as hearsay, and once more, the motion was denied by Judge McCook. No surprise!

Charlie leaned over to Polakoff, his face grim, and whispered, "He and the other bums are shooting off their mouths about something they don't know. When I really give orders, I use an entirely different name, and only through my own men." He was of course referring to his authoritative name of *General*.

The entire courtroom was in an uproar as all the shouting reached a crescendo when Brooks narrated that he and Fredericks had gone to

Betillo's house one evening on business. He was to wait in the car but instead went up to Betillo's penthouse and had found him in his pajamas with a couple of broken ribs.

Caesar Barra objected, but Betillo couldn't contain himself, jumped up, and shouted, "You're lying! You couldn't get up into my house!" Barra stood up, a reprimand in his eyes, and Betillo sat down unsteadily, mumbling, "He's a damn liar!"

To reassure the jurors, Barra turned to them, insisting it was outraged innocence that caused Betillo to shout (understandably so) even though he didn't approve of the outburst. Naturally, the prosecution was happy about the turn of events. Brooks had named everyone except Ralph and Jack Eller. A welcomed recess was called.

For a change of pace, Dewey called Peter "The Greek" Tach, a male madam, and the show was on. Pete, a little man of forty, dressed in pale green, swished to the witness box. He was not at all intimidated and testified with nonchalance; he kept everyone chuckling with his mannerisms and speech. Pete briefly told the court that he had been arrested a couple of times here and there for vagrancy and another time for maintaining a disorderly house. He also admitted to being kept by a few women.

He spoke with such a flair that he had everyone in stitches. Ralph was practically rolling in the aisle, and it was the first time he saw Charlie actually laugh. The prosecution asked Pete if he knew a Nick Montana. In his response, Pete said yes, that Montana had frightened many boys but not him—that went for Jimmy Fredericks of the pink shirts and red ties. He proceeded to bad-mouth Fredericks with such emphasis that the stocky, swarthy Jimmy couldn't help breaking up, his body rocking with laughter.

Urged to go on by the prosecution, Pete answered, "Well, another time I was slow in giving the bond money, and Jimmy, in exasperation, comes to me and says, 'Am I in trouble with you again? Why don't you pay up?' 'Why should I?' I answered, and he said, 'What are you here, the boss?'"

In cross-examination, Samuel Siegel, intent in breaking down the witness's credibility, tried very hard not to join in the merriment.

Q: "You're what is known as a male madam?"
A: "Yes."
Q: "Did you get immunity?"
A: "I didn't ask for it."
Q: "You haven't been indicted?"
A: "I don't know. I didn't ask the grand jury."

Q: "Then you haven't been incarcerated?"
A: "No, but I'm getting $3.00 a day as a witness for the court."
Q: "Are you being held in the House of Detention?"
A: "No."
Q: "Where then?"
A: "Well, you know that place is a bore." (More laughter.)
Q: "You were also a procurer, weren't you?"
A: "Call me anything you like." (He threw up his hand indifferently.)
Q: "Well, you lived off women, didn't you?"
A: "Yes . . ." He smiled with satisfaction. "So I did!"

Pete "the Greek" had managed, momentarily, to ease the tension.

CHAPTER THIRTY-ONE

All-night sessions were not uncommon among the defense lawyers. Judge McCook adjourned each day's proceedings at seven o'clock, and after they paused for dinner (where they mostly rehashed the trial), they sometimes worked through the night and into the morning—until court reconvened at nine thirty. On the outside, the defense staff worked diligently to muster up any and all evidence necessary to bolster their case. Dewey and his staff were doing the same.

The next day's opener was a lightweight witness, a prostitute named Helen Kelley. Unlike the others, she brought in a new twist of "white slavery," claiming she was kept a prisoner in Hungarian Helen's brothel. The defense was able to reveal that Kelley had been arrested and was on the lam. When asked why she had gone to Dewey, she cried out, "To get back some of my self-respect that I lost when I became a prostitute!" And, naturally, to beat her rap for jumping bail.

After the Helen Kelley sob story came a real heavyweight. Joe Bendix was a convict serving a fifteen-year to life term in Sing Sing, as a fourth offender under the Baumes Law. He was a small-time chief, who was willing to do anything to get his sentence reduced. Up until then, Dewey had only presented witnesses who mentioned Charlie's name (hearsay), to which his lawyers objected so many times. This time, he was presenting a witness who would link Charlie directly to the rackets. Dewey very carefully steered Bendix through his story, revealing first that he had known Charlie for nine years. It was through Frederico, however, that a meeting had been arranged with Charlie in order to get a collector's job with the syndicate.

Q: "And you met Luciano? Was that in June 1935?"
A: "Yes. Frederico told me to be at the restaurant, Villanova, on Forty-sixth Street. I went there, and Frederico and Luciano were at a table. I sat down with them."
Q: "What did Luciano say?"
A: "He said, 'Jimmy talked to me about you. I understand you want to be a collector. I thought you were too high-hat for that kind of job. You know there's only $40 a week in it.'"

Q: "Did you tell Luciano why you wanted the job at such pay?"
A: "Yes, I told him my record on hotel thefts was so long now that the next time it would be a Baumes Law rap for life, and I thought it would be better to work for him and stay out of jail."
Q: "What did Luciano say?"
A: "He said he would take the matter up with Little Davey."

According to his story, Bendix had met again with Luciano, who had told him to get in touch with a man named Binge, who would put him to work. Bendix, however, had difficulty in finding Binge, became discouraged, and went back to stealing.

Levy could hardly sit still after Bendix's preposterous tale. He rose slowly and sauntered up to Bendix, whose thin frame seemed to cringe, as if expecting a blow on the head. He sat waiting, eyes wary, fingering his thin mustache. Levy, instead, very gently and with a serious expression, asked him if he had ever been examined for insanity. Highly insulted, Bendix replied that he was perfectly sane. Yet Levy was out to prove Bendix was a half-wit. Challenging his acquaintance with Charlie, he asked Bendix to state where in 1929 he had met Luciano. The place turned out to be the Club Richman, a well-known and expensive nightclub. Bendix said he had been introduced to Luciano by a Captain Dutton of the U.S. Army, whom he had met once in a hotel lobby. Incredulously, Levy egged him on, "Go on with your good story." Throughout the line of questioning, Levy rather poked fun at him. His tone changed when he produced Bendix's long prison records and began jabbing him with loaded questions, setting him up for the knockout.

Q: "Were you in Sing Sing Prison?"
A: "Yes."
Q: "How many times?"
A: "Three."
Q: "Were you ever in isolation?"

Bendix would not answer, and Dewey jumped up to object. Levy turned to Judge McCook and asked that the witness answer. The judge looked down at Bendix and directed him to answer, but still, Bendix's lips were sealed. Impatiently, Levy waved in his hand the documents he had obtained from Sing Sing and showed them to the judge. "This is the kind of witness Dewey has," he said in an indignant voice. "This man is a degenerate. He was placed in isolation because he was caught more than once having immoral acts with a Negro in prison!" Levy recomposed himself and moved on to Bendix's current sentence.

Q: "While waiting in your cell thinking about the fifteen years you were serving for burglary, you wrote to Dewey, offering to pin guilt on Luciano, did you not?"
A: (Squirming in his seat.) "Yes."
Q: "But you wrote another letter to District Attorney Dodge's office, offering to pin guilt on somebody or other for another crime—the $500,000 Bank of Manhattan bond theft. Did you not?"
A: (Losing his composure.) "Yes, I did. I wanted to help myself."
Q: "Help yourself out of a fifteen-year jam by testifying against anybody, anywhere, about anything?"

The question hit home. Bendix, upset, responded, sputtering like an imbecile, that he was being double-crossed by Assistant District Attorney Morris Panger, who had promised to make sure he received a light sentence. He was double-crossed, and Bendix knew the reasons why. Levy pressed on, in obvious disgust for the man.

Q: "Oh, you know why?"
A: (Really going to pieces and shouting.) "Yes, and I'll tell you why. Panger got wise I was running over to Dewey's office. And Dewey and Dodge, they don't like each other."
Q: "So, District Attorney Dodge hates Special Prosecutor Dewey, and that is why you were double-crossed?"
A: "Absolutely! That's why. Assistant Panger admitted it to me. Panger told me, 'I understand you've been yelling to Dewey. Well, help yourself, I don't blame you, but I don't think you'll get very far.'"
Q: "What did Panger mean by those words?"
A: "I don't know, but he had a nasty sneer on his face."

Dewey made no effort to interfere in helping his pathetic witness during the interrogation but rather threw up his hands in disgust and stared into space. Judge McCook turned sideways, his eyes glued to his desk, while most of the jurors sat with their mouths wide open. Charlie chuckled, shaking his head, and the others, including Ralph, smiled with some relief. Levy, however, didn't let up and picked up what Dewey had neglected to do during direct examination. Tauntingly, he asked Bendix to identify Charlie. "Get up, Charlie. Let this gentleman get a good look at you." Charlie rose from his seat accommodatingly.

Bendix appeared to shrivel further in his seat while Levy said, "Is this the man you asked for a job collecting vice tribute at $40 a week?"

No one seemed impressed when he meekly muttered, "Sure, he is."

He really hit rock bottom when Levy brought out the fact that Bendix had tried to use his lawyer to help him commit perjury on the stand in one of his previous arrest cases.

Q: "Didn't you ask your lawyer to help you falsely testify that the hotelman made improper advances, and that he bribed you with the valuables you actually stole?"
A: (Sulking.) "It was something like that."

Levy paused, turned to the jury to make sure everyone had understood that here was a phony squealer, and ended his cross-examination. Defense counselors were quite satisfied for the moment, but they weren't through with Bendix. They had a few more surprises waiting in the wings.

Dewey, however, was a man of great resources. He was seldom discouraged and went on undauntedly, convinced that he had an airtight case against Charlie and the other defendants. And why not? He and his assistants had worked very hard to interlace even the most minute details into a complete tapestry. Smiling, sure of himself, he called his next witness, Florence "Cokey Flo" Brown. Ralph leaned over to whisper to Carlino that she was the one who had caused Dotty's problems. Carlino nodded knowingly. Ralph, however, wasn't the only one who had stirred. Jimmy Frederico squirmed in his seat, and his lawyer, Samuel Siegel, signaled for him to stay calm. Cokey Flo had been Frederico's girlfriend. Charlie stared expressionless because he had never seen the woman before, couldn't imagine what damage she was about to do to him. The smug looks on the faces of the prosecution staff alarmed the defense, and tension filled the courtroom.

The jurors' first impression was one of pity as they saw the frail, shabbily dressed, undernourished-looking girl wobble to the stand. She appeared to be an impoverished refugee rather than the tramp she was. It didn't seem to matter that she was a whorehouse madam, a drug addict, and, worse, a junkie. She somehow aroused sympathy among the jurors, who soon learned her history—hardly one to brag about. Born in Pittsburgh, she had emigrated to Cleveland and, at the age of fifteen, was operating a speakeasy with another girl. From there she went to Chicago, where she was kept by three men. She returned to Cleveland when, at a certain point, her then current lover had taken her to New York. Two months later, Cokey Flo had become a whorehouse madam. It was through her booker that she had met Jimmy Frederico. In a low, dull voice, she revealed that she and Frederico had been sweethearts and had lived together.

The prosecutor asked her if she knew Charles Lucania, better known as Charlie "Lucky," and she replied that everyone knew him in the business. But as usual, it was Dewey's expertise that led her to the point. Cokey Flo said she had first been introduced to Charlie "Lucky" in a Chinese restaurant on upper Broadway in the spring of 1934, along with Tommy "Bull" and Davey Betillo. Did they speak about the prostitution racket? "Yes," she replied. "When they left—in the car—while she drove." It was just incredulous to think that Charlie would be in the car with those people, thought Ralph. "Frederico was complaining to Charlie that some of the bookies had been holding out on the bond money."

Charlie, she reported, suggested the bookies should be called on the carpet to get in line. "Have them all come down, and we'll straighten them out," he was quoted as saying. Asked if there were any other meetings, she nodded and spoke about one meeting in a garage to which she had driven Frederico and Benny Spiller; then there was another meeting around Easter 1935.

Ralph stole a glance at Charlie and could see his jaw tighten. He must have been thinking, *What crap!*

Then Dewey cleverly threw her a leading statement, "Tell us about the Chinatown reunion." She responded and began her discourse, her voice passive, hardly audible. The same people were present. At that time, Charlie was apparently discouraged with the racket. "I'm disgusted," she heard him say. There wasn't much money in it, and he wanted to get rid of it. The houses were becoming difficult to manage; the madams didn't want to pay the bond. Jimmy had complained about a madam who was holding out, and Charlie had said, "Why don't you get the madams together, Jimmy? I told you to!"

Jimmy had answered, "I thought I could go around and talk to them."

Charlie responded, "You can't take care of them."

Cokey Flo had managed to portray Charlie as a ruthless character as well as establish him directly as the kingpin of the outfit. Occasionally, she sneaked a tender look at her ex-lover, Frederico, who stared back, devoid of expression. Charlie, instead, glared icily and jotted down notes as she spoke. Davey Betillo, Tommy "Bull," and the others sneered.

Another leading question by Dewey. "Last October, do you remember another meeting in the restaurant?" She said, "Yes," relating that it was the same old thing.

Charlie was disgusted; there wasn't much money. Davey had said, "Give it a chance. Things are a little bad now, but it might get better."

Charlie had replied, "No, there are a lot of investigations, and we may get into trouble. I think we better fold up for a while."

Dewey persisted for her to go on, "Well, there've been a lot of pinches, and that took money out of the combination." Charlie said, "But when we get them all in line, it'll be okay." Then Davey added, "Besides, I don't think it will be so tough. The Dewey investigation won't get to us. They'll just pick up a couple of bondsmen and let it go at that."

The conversation had continued to the point when Charlie supposedly said what has become a famous phrase, "We could syndicate the places on a large scale—the same as the A & P stores. We could even put the madams on a salary or commission basis. It would take a little time, because they'd object at first, but we could do it."

Everyone was aghast in the courtroom; merchandising women in that way was just too much. Judging from the jurors' faces, all upright, law-abiding citizens, it was downright scandalous. There was no doubt of it—the script had been well written. Then Dewey brought his interrogation to an end.

Q: "Did he say anything about the use of his name?"

A: "Oh, yes. Charlie said, 'I don't like the idea of people using my name. I hear they're trying to see some guys and, through them, trying to see me through Davey, so they wouldn't have to bond. I'm tired of having my name mentioned. It has to be stopped!' He didn't like it at all."

With that closing exchange, Dewey tried to cover his tracks on the hearsay point. Cokey Flo, pale and weary, asked for a recess, and Judge McCook's gavel went down, granting it.

During recess, the defense counselors huddled to plan their counterattack. Cokey Flo had named practically all the defendants (except Ralph), and Dewey, at long last, had confirmed a direct connection to Charlie. Naturally, the defense was going to assail her on her drug habits. She was an opium, morphine, and heroin addict—the reason she had been dubbed Cokey Flo. Her looks were completely ruined. At twenty-nine, she looked more like fifty. Obviously, Dewey had touched only lightly on the subject, but Cokey Flo told the court that she had not lost her memory because of narcotics. It never hampered her work, in which she had to remember thousands of girls' names. Her habit was so bad, however, that she had been rushed through a cure a week earlier in order to be in shape for the trial. David Siegel, for the defense, was the first to cross-examine her. Cokey Flo, tired from the morning session, leaned on the arm of the chair, trying to prop herself up.

Q: "Feel a little drowsy?"
A: "No." (Straightening up.) "I was just trying to think so I could answer correctly."
Q: "How many times a day were you in the habit of using the needle?"
A: "Three times every day—when I woke up, after dinner in the evening, and when I went to bed."
Q: "How much morphine in each shot?"
A: "About one-fourth or a gram—in the leg."

Siegel couldn't control himself and demanded that the witness be examined for drugs. The prosecution objected. A small battle of words ensued, only to be interrupted by Judge McCook, who agreed to a medical examination by physicians—one for each side. Satisfied, Siegel continued.

Q: "You could identify Luciano in a minute, couldn't you?"
A: "Yes."
Q: "Well, do you see him here?"
A: (She stood up.) "Yes, he's the third man back at the table. The man in the black tie."
Q: "Point to him."

She promptly pointed her finger at Charlie, who half-rose and asked, "Me?"

Her faint voice answered, "Yes."

To further provoke her, Siegel walked over and put his hand on Charlie's shoulder and asked, "This man?"

Cokey Flo was not to be swayed and stood her ground. "Yes," she repeated. "That man with the yellow pencil in his hand."

After the afternoon recess, the doctors came up with their results, which they handed to Judge McCook in a sealed envelope. The report showed that Cokey Flo had not had drugs in the last forty-eight hours. Ralph was furious. What did that mean? That in the House of Detention where she was supposed to be under surveillance at all times by a police matron, she had access to drugs—and before? He hated Cokey Flo for what she had done to Dotty.

In a brief interrogation by Pennochio's lawyer, it was brought out that Cokey Flo had switched from morphine to heroin because, as she said, it was cheaper. He also revealed that she had done time for being a junkie and for soliciting.

Levy was the toughest on her. He had her mumbling and picking nervously at her face as she answered. After more than three hours of questioning, she was tired, and her resistance began breaking down—especially when he harped about her relationship with Jimmy Frederico.

Q: "You are madly in love with Frederico, are you not?"
A: "I wouldn't say that."
Q: "But you still have a soft spot in your heart for him?"
A: "I suppose so."

Whereupon, Levy read the first love letter he had in his possession. It was written toward the end of April, after Frederico's arrest. The letter contained more feeling than she had admitted, and Levy read some of the passages.

"You will always mean everything to me. Everything that is good and fine and sweet in this world will be embodied in your image for me . . . because I know and you know, in our hearts, that you are guilty of nothing wrong. Even those who are prosecuting you must know by now that you are innocent." It was signed with love and kisses.

Then he read another letter dated as late as May 15 (the first week of the trial), a letter that revealed her true feeling toward the famous prosecutor and her concern for Frederico.

"I wish Uncle D would die of cancer, the louse. There's no justice at all. I think it is terrible to make a person do time before they are even convicted . . . . They let lousy murderers go free . . . . But a person that hasn't even been convicted yet has to stay in jail until some louse gets good and ready to bring them to trial . . . . I'm going down to see Siegel . . . . Want to know what defense he's worked out. I want him to get his head working, and not think he's going to get his money for nothing."

The letters certainly proved whose side she was on, so why the sudden change of heart? Why did she go to the prosecutor? She calmly answered that even though she had a soft spot in her heart for Jimmy, she wanted to go straight—to begin a new life. Levy, however, charged it was because she believed by pointing her finger at Charlie that Dewey would go easy on Frederico. Her story, he said, was invented (and well-rehearsed) to save her lover.

Cokey Flo grew paler and paler by the minute. The brandy she had been given during recess periods to boost her up was no longer helping. Worn-out, she could hardly answer when Levy charged heavily.

Q: "Is it not true that you took this stand for three purposes: One, to get yourself publicized as a heroine. Two, to get yourself out of jail. And three, to have the opportunity to tell these jurors just how innocent Jimmy Frederico is?"
A: (Weakly.) "No . . . but Jimmy is innocent."

Charlie had been shaken by Cokey Flo's testimony but hoped that the cross-examination had broken down some of her credibility. There was a small chance, and he was gambling on it.

On Saturday, Dewey brought in the Waldorf Astoria personnel to identify Charlie as living in the hotel on Park Avenue under the pseudonym of Charles Ross. Henry Woelfle, the manager, confirmed that Charlie had lived in a $250 suite from April 7 to October 29, 1935. When Charlie's pictures were printed all over the newspapers in connection with Dutch Schultz's murder, the hotel management asked him to leave, and Charlie did. Asked if he had seen any of the defendants visit Charlie, Woelfle said he thought he had seen Wahrman. Upon identification, however, he pointed instead to defense lawyer Moses Polakoff, and the defendants chuckled at the mix-up.

They didn't laugh for long because the next witness, a chambermaid by the name of Marjorie Brown, more than made up for Woelfle. A pretty young girl, she stood up and tiptoed over to the defendants. She first pointed to Charlie, then Wahrman, Frederico, and Dave Betillo by tapping them on the shoulder; finally, she motioned to Berkman, who was beyond her reach. They were, she said, all visitors of Charlie. Ralph thought the girl did a damn good job of memorizing the photos the prosecution provided—better than anyone else.

A waiter, Joseph "Gus" Weiman, was at best ineffectual. All he did was recall that Charlie entertained ladies in his room with tea and pastry and was a middle to average tipper.

Judge McCook adjourned at one o'clock, and everyone took a breather for the weekend.

CHAPTER THIRTY-TWO

Dewey continued his barrage of witnesses—all ready to do his bidding—to condemn Charlie "Lucky." To open the third week of the trial, he called a Thelma Jordan to the stand. She was a plump brunette prostitute and, while confessing to her twenty-six years, refused to give her real name. She didn't want to hurt her distinguished family in Kansas. Ralph stared at her because there was something familiar about her, but he couldn't place her. The questions and answers began. She had first worked with Harris, then Eller, then had met Spiller (and had become Spiller's girl). The rest was hearsay, and Levy strongly objected as she mentioned names. His motions were always denied. When she said Spiller had told her that Charlie was at the head of the racket, Levy again shouted hearsay and asked for a mistrial. Denied.

The defense team and the defendants by now were accustomed to the routine. What caught Ralph completely unaware came at the end of her testimony. Harry Cole asked her whether she remembered a conversation between Nancy Presser and Ralph Liguori in Dewey's office. A bombshell hit Ralph! Thelma was the girl he had noticed sitting in the same room with Dotty when Cole had allowed him to see her at headquarters. What came next was such a pack of lies that Ralph actually felt ill.

"Yes," she said. "Ralph told Nancy if she knew what was good for her, she wouldn't testify against him or any member of the combination, because if she did, she would be taken care of. He said if she talked, he would see to it she got her pictures in her hometown paper, so her folks would know what she was doing!"

According to Jordan's testimony, Ralph had insinuated that Dotty could be murdered if she talked, like in the Titterton case (a sensational case publicized about that time in which a woman had been murdered in her bathtub).

Carlino immediately glanced at Ralph, worried about a violent reaction, but Ralph just shook his head in disbelief. He couldn't believe his ears. Harry Cole was doing much more than he had promised.

At the time of Jordan's arrest, she was reluctant to talk but apparently had changed her mind. When David Siegel cross-examined her, asking her why she had first lied to Dewey's staff, it only worsened the situation, causing an unexpected reaction. Up to then, she had been somewhat calm; but now, on the stand, she shouted out that she was afraid because she knew what happened to girls who talked. Siegel dropped the subject, but it was all very damaging to Ralph.

The reputed telephone contact man of the combination was called next. His name was Anthony Curcio, better known to the mob as Binge—the man Bendix had mentioned in his testimony. Curcio was twenty-eight, had started out as a bootlegger, then had become a booker before going to work for Fredericks. He was a two-bit squealer, out to save his own skin, because at the time of his arrest, they found a tiny book in his apartment with the names and phone numbers of the bookers and collectors. Since Binge was a key witness for the prosecution, Dewey himself did the honor, questioning him on his role. Binge claimed he knew what was happening at all times. He knew the names of everyone—the big shots, the bookies, the bondsmen, and the names of all the girls and madams who worked through the combination. Everyone had his number. Binge was the go-between. They called him with problems, and in the case of a raid, Binge contacted the right people to give precise instructions. He named most of the defendants but did not mention Charlie or Ralph, which was in their favor. Dewey had said in one of his opening statements that he would demonstrate how the boys double-crossed one another, and he was doing a hell of a good job—his way. Curcio's testimony was without doubt detrimental to the defense.

The next morning, Ralph nervously awaited Dotty's appearance. He knew it would be a tough ordeal for both of them, and after having heard how well rehearsed all the witnesses had been, he couldn't begin to imagine how they had rehearsed Dotty. Dewey, however, had still another anticlimax for Ralph. He first called a material witness, a he-madam named James Russo—an ex-taxi driver, around thirty-eight, with a surly disposition. Russo expounded how the syndicate boys constantly harassed him. Then Ralph couldn't believe what he heard; Russo brought him and Dotty into his sordid testimony, stating that Dotty had applied to him for work. When he had refused to take her into his house, Ralph arrived to threaten him. Ralph was reported as saying, "What the hell's the matter with you . . . You don't want to put that girl to work?"

Russo said, "I suppose I got to take a girl I don't want?"

Ralph had supposedly replied, "You better put her to work . . . if you know what's good for you."

Not wanting any trouble, Russo said he put Dotty to work.

Ralph had to restrain himself from lunging forward to smash the lying bastard. What no one realized was how deeply Ralph really loved Dotty. The mere thought of sharing her with other men made him mad with jealousy, and the lies pouring forth from the witness stand completely nauseated him. Carlino gave Ralph an encouraging look and promptly cross-examined Russo.

Q: "Was immunity promised to you yesterday?"
A: "Yes, I wouldn't testify unless they promised me immunity."
Q: "When were you taken to Mr. Dewey's office?"
A: "After this case started, they took me down there. I didn't want to go. Mr. Harry Cole talked to me, then got mad at me and sent me back to jail, because I wouldn't talk."
Q: "When did you go before the grand jury?"
A: "Yesterday, I told Dewey's office, 'If you people defend me, I'll go before the grand jury and tell all I know.'"

Ralph was sure Cole had threatened Russo like he had with him—the difference being that Russo was really involved and afraid of Dewey's wrath. Carlino continued to badger him about Dotty.

Q: "Did Nancy work for you in July 1935?"
A: "Yes."
Q: "How much did Nancy earn for herself at your house?"
A: "About $70 or $80 a week."
Q: "That means she entertained about one hundred men a week?"
A: "Yes, about that."

Ralph covered his face with his hands. They were not only setting him up as a pimp, but were degrading Dotty as a cheap whore. Carlino did his best to break Russo's testimony (to humiliate and disgrace him), but the damage was done. Dotty was yet to appear, but she and Ralph had emerged as two very low characters to the jury.

The moment had arrived. The court called Nancy Presser to the stand. Ralph thought he'd have a heart attack as he saw her walk in faltering; his eyes began to smart. She wore a beige suite that showed off her figure, but her beautiful hair was severely pinned under a matching hat. Ralph's heart broke for her. Despite her makeup, Dotty looked very, very pale and ten years older. Her eyes searched for Ralph on the bench, and as their eyes locked, she tried to convey her predicament, asking for his forgiveness. Ralph strained hard to hold back his tears. Charlie looked over at Ralph to give him courage. He knew the way Ralph felt, but at that moment, Ralph felt trapped; his hands were tied. He could no longer help her. Under direct examination, the court learned that her real name was Genevieve Fletcher (Dotty to some and Nancy Presser to most) and a native of Albany, New York. She had left home at an early age to try her luck on Broadway and began first as an artist's model.

Ralph realized that Dewey would not spare him anything and was expecting the worst—but *not* what he was about to hear. Dewey took a stance a few feet away from the witness box and, in an authoritative voice, asked Dotty, "Do you know Charlie 'Lucky'?"

Dewey slyly looked toward the jury as she meekly answered, "Yes, I do." She went on to say that she had been Ralph's sweetheart first, but after Ralph had introduced her to Charlie in the winter of 1934 at Kings Tavern, Charlie had unexpectedly called her. When she had told him that she was Ralph's girl, Charlie supposedly had said, "Never mind about that. I'm the boss. I'm a bigger man than Ralph. You could go places with me." It was another one of Dewey's tricks to break Ralph to go against Charlie, right there in the courtroom, but Ralph didn't fall for anything as stupid as that. Charlie gave Ralph a swift look of disbelief, which he dismissed. Dotty continued testifying that she had met with Charlie several times—first at the Barbizon Plaza Hotel and, after that, at the Waldorf Astoria. He was, Dotty said, a perfect gentleman and a very generous man.

She then made absurd statements such as being present at a meeting that Charlie had called at Kings Tavern, to which Wahrman, Betillo, Fredericks, and Pennochio had been invited. She said she overheard the conversation they were having. Wahrman had complained about "Dago" Jean, a whorehouse madam, holding out; and Charlie, she reported, had commanded, "Go ahead and wreck the joint!"

Another time, she revealed that Charlie boasted to her that he would raise the two-dollar joints to three and the four-dollar houses to five. He would put the madams on salaries, taking their joints away from them. It should have been easy to realize Dotty had to be lying. Charlie would never talk business in front of women. It was something no one did.

Dotty was extremely nervous as she spoke; her voice quivered, and at that point, she could not even look Ralph's way. And still the worst was yet to come. Dewey kept prodding her to speak up, as she continued her story. After her brief interlude with Charlie, she supposedly had returned her affections toward Ralph. Subsequently, she testified, Ralph had told her she would have to go to work (meaning as a prostitute). When she refused, she quoted Ralph as having said if she didn't obey, he would cut her up so that her own mother wouldn't recognize her. Also, she implicated Ralph directly as the stickup man for the syndicate, stating that when she had been working in a house on Ralph's orders, she had found her madam holding out on the bond money and advised Ralph.

As a result, Ralph raided the place because, according to Dotty, he had said, "I have orders from downtown to do it." Further, Ralph had taken the madam's money and wristwatch, the latter of which he gave to Dotty. What could Ralph do but listen to this litany of lies.

Dewey was very clever indeed; he was doing his best to break Ralph's resistance. Ralph gritted his teeth and clutched his hands tightly.

Dotty went on to corroborate the Jordan woman's testimony about Ralph threatening her. She quoted him as having said, "You know what they did to Nancy Titterton. She was found murdered in her bathtub. That's what'll happen to you if you lay a finger on any of us." Again, Ralph shook his head in obvious despair. He knew Dotty had been forced to say all those horrible things, but the jurors kept looking at him as if he were dirt!

Dotty was shaking like a leaf. Ralph didn't know how she managed to contain herself on the witness box. She looked as if she would collapse at any minute. Judge McCook had called for a night session, and luckily for her, it was already close to 10:00 p.m. Dewey finally ended his interrogation, and for the moment, it appeared he had the upper hand.

The defendants slowly walked into the bullpen, each with his depressing thoughts. Charlie quickly whispered to Ralph, "Hey, Ralph, you don't believe any of that stuff, do you?"

Ralph was still uptight and testily replied, "What the hell . . . Do I have to argue with *you too*? Don't I *know* what it's all about?"

"Okay, pal," Charlie said sympathetically. "Take it easy."

In the morning, the defense lawyers were ready to attack, but Dotty was late. Dewey informed the court that the witness Nancy Presser (Dotty) had to be moved "late last night from her Jackson Heights apartment where she was being sheltered." Of course, by his statement, he inferred that the defense was trying to get to her. As a matter of fact, Dewey's office had arrested several persons for attempting to intimidate witnesses that same night. They had all been arraigned before Judge McCook and held on bail. One of the more clamorous arrests was that of Attorney Samuel Kornbluth. He was charged with trying to have a girl witness change her testimony in favor of Charlie. Through her other female friends, it was learned that Kornbluth had tried to get through to Cokey Flo to tell the truth. There was a big hubbub that night, and Moses Polakoff immediately issued a statement.

"Counsel for Luciano emphatically deny any improper methods in the investigation of this case. Naturally, an intensive investigation is being conducted, motivated solely by a desire to get the entire truth concerning the charges on credibility of the witnesses against Luciano.

The defense seeks only the opportunity to conduct a proper and unhandicapped investigation."

Armand was also trying to locate Dotty, to try to reason with her, but he couldn't find her. His efforts would have been futile anyway. The girl, at this point, was simply too terrified.

That morning in the courtroom, Dewey made another of his dramatic statements regarding the arrests.

"I'm too busy with the conduct of the court case to discuss outside matters. All I can say is that all the arrests are in connection with this case."

Dotty finally arrived, and before she had time to catch her breath, David Siegel opened the cross-examination without a trace of compassion.

Q: "You're a drug addict, aren't you?"
A: "I used to be, but I'm not now."
Q: "And you were a drug addict for about eighteen months?"
A: "About that."
Q: "How many grains of dope would you take a day?"
A: "I don't know. I took three or four doses."
Q: "What kind of drugs did you use?"
A: "Morphine and heroin."
Q: "How did you take the dope?"
A: "By a hypodermic in my knees and other parts of the body."
Q: "Have you been to a doctor between yesterday and right now?"
A: "I have not."

Up to that moment, Dotty had been holding her own, but Siegel was out to destroy her character and began to insinuate that she was a pervert. Dotty sat stiffly erect with defiance. They were going to throw everything at her. Siegel, however, was a lamb compared to Levy. Following the afternoon recess, Levy took over with a batter of questions, which left her stammering and fumbling. In his hands, she was a fish out of water. He began by also attacking her morals. Conceding that Dotty's conduct in her hometown had been above reproach, he revealed how Dotty had broken moral rules soon after her arrival in New York by living with a married man—a florist who paid her rent for six months. She admitted to only one or two other affairs with men whom she had met through friends. Afterwards, she said she had become a call girl. Ralph winced at that, wondered why Dewey and company had completely blocked out her respectable career as a chorus girl. Dotty had also neglected to do the same. Had it been programmed that way? Why?

Then she fell into one contradiction after another. A certain Betty Cook had introduced her to Charlie about nine years earlier, and then a few years later, they had met again at Kings Chop House. Charlie had winked at her, and she had given him her number. He had called her and had invited her up to his suite at the Barbizon Plaza. It was late at night; she couldn't remember the floor, only that it was high up. Levy, hard as nails, plunged into her trysts with Charlie.

Q: "What did you do when you got there?"
A: "Well, we had a few drinks."
Q: "Can you recall anything you said?"
A: "I told Charlie 'Lucky' that I needed money and had to go into a house of prostitution to get it, and he said not to. He said if I needed any money, to call on him."
Q: "Did you have an affair with Luciano that night?"
A: "No . . . oh, no."
Q: "How long were you in the room?"
A: "Maybe an hour or so."
Q: "Did you sit on the bed?"
A: "No."
Q: "Well, was there any loving and kissing?"
A: "There was not."
Q: "What did he do?" (Incredulously.)
A: "He gave me fifty dollars."
Q: "But he treated you like a perfect lady?"
A: "Yes."
Q: "Weren't you surprised to get fifty dollars for nothing but an hour's chat?"
A: "No. I was used to that. Anybody who took me out paid for it."

To knock Dotty down a peg or two, Levy reminded her and the court that under direct examination, she admitted to having worked in James Russo's $2 bordello. Without pausing, he continued grilling and produced Dotty's admission to another visit to the Barbizon where, again, Charlie had been a perfect gentleman.

Q: "Well, when was it that you visited him in the Waldorf?"
A: "In 1935."
Q: "Do you recall what apartment you went to?"
A: "I think it was 39D."
Q: "When you went there, did you announce yourself before you went up?"

A: "No, I just went right up to the room."

She added that she entered the Waldorf through the Park Avenue entrance and thought she took the regular elevators (anyway, the first one she saw). Again, she repeated she did not announce herself and went directly to the thirty-ninth floor.

Charlie leaned over to whisper to Polakoff. He was smiling because Levy had trapped Dotty. In fact, Levy pointed out to the court that no one could go up to the apartment without being first announced, and the regular elevators did not go to the thirty-ninth floor. Only special elevators to the left of the Park Avenue door went up to the tower apartments. Dotty meekly said something about getting lost in big hotels, but the defense had won its point. Sensing her errors, Dotty grew more and more agitated. Confusion had set in as Levy coldly, without compassion, continued.

Q: "Did you go into his room?"
A: "Yes."

Asked to describe the suite, she continued to flounder—no phonographs, no fireplace, maybe a piano and, yes, a radio on the table, which she played, but couldn't remember whether the French mirror was in the bathroom or bedroom.

Q: "Did you go into the bedroom?"
A: "Yes."
Q: "Was there one bed in there or twin beds?"
A: "I'm not sure. Either twin beds or a double . . . either one."
Q: "How many telephones were there in the bedroom?"

Dotty lowered her head and covered her eyes with her hands. It was devastating. She was being torn apart. Ralph's instinct told him to spring out of his seat to go to her, but naturally, he couldn't. How could she know all those things if she had never been up there? Dotty finally whispered, "Two."

Q: "All right. Now describe the bedroom as a woman would."

Dotty remained silent, her face still buried in her hands. Then, after a minute or so, she lifted her face with tears rolling down, her eyes pleading, and, in a trembling voice, begged Judge McCook for a recess. After hours of constant badgering by Levy, Dotty had finally broken down. Judge McCook granted a ten-minute recess, and a matron came in to help Dotty. She had practically collapsed on the stand. Dewey stood up and vanished with his wilted witness, and everyone in the courtroom was buzzing about the latest developments. The jurors were exchanging remarks while the defense counselors smiled because Levy had torn Dotty's story to shreds. Ten minutes went by swiftly, but Dotty did not appear. Judge McCook waited, the jury waited, everyone waited, fixed in their seats, watching the door for Dotty to reappear. Instead, Dewey returned and addressed the court.

"Your Honor, the witness says she feels sick. She feels faint and dizzy."

Levy, patiently waiting for his prey, slyly informed the court that he would try to be gentle with her, and Judge McCook snapped, "Bring her back!"

Dewey disappeared. There was complete silence as the suspense heightened. Dewey reappeared. Embarrassed at the turn of events, he apologized profusely, "Your Honor, the policewoman informs me that the witness is really very ill and unable to go on."

Levy rose, satisfied, knowing that he had won. With a grin, he said, "If Mr. Dewey feels that the witness is too ill to go on, I am perfectly willing to let her testimony stand without additional cross-examination."

"That settles it," Judge McCook exclaimed and adjourned the court. It was about 7:00 p.m. Dewey huffed and puffed, gathered his papers, and marched out of the courtroom with his boys following. Ralph, naturally, was distraught for Dotty; he was tired but happy that she couldn't go through with the farce.

Charlie grinned and congratulated his lawyers.

CHAPTER THIRTY-THREE

The prosecution staff had worked diligently, zealously, in their case against prostitution for the state of New York. They had had some setbacks (some not-so-good witnesses), but Dewey, with his never-ending optimism, transmitted his positive attitude to his staff. They were convinced that they would win in the long run. After almost three weeks in the courtroom, they were drawing their case to an end.

As an interval after Dotty's fiasco, Dewey offered the court a series of insignificant prostitutes like Betty Anderson, blonde and slender, and Kathrine O'Connor, a lovely redhead, who singled out the bookers and the bondsmen. Madams were not overlooked. Jenny Benjamin, a thirty-eight-year-old mother of three children, and Jenny "the Factory" Fisher, a fifty-year-old professional weighing in at 220 pounds, both spoke of their particular involvement. Benjamin said she did business with Fredericks but couldn't identify him on the bench. Fisher offered a history lesson on the prostitution trade—before and after Charlie "Lucky."

To further illuminate the jurors, the prosecution displayed the ticket or card that the syndicate issued to the madams for their prostitutes. State witnesses, prostitute Rose Cohen, and madam Dorothy Arnold had touched on this aspect, but now Dewey explained in great detail exactly how the card system worked. It was something like a time clock slip, except that the numbers represented dollars and not hours. Each card went up to $100, and when it was completely punched, the prostitute was given another.

In brief, as the customers paid for services rendered, the madam punched the amount on the prostitute's card and, at the end of the week, did the bookkeeping. That was also when the deductions began. Half of the girl's earnings went to the madam, and out of the other half, fees varied from house to house—such as for maid service (sometimes $2) and room and board (running from $25 to $50). Some girls had their own apartments, and this put another dent into their salary. Flat fees paid by the prostitutes were $10 bonding, $5 doctor visits, and 10 percent for the booker. It was obvious that for most, a measly pittance was left. It may have been lucrative to the syndicate (although Charlie had been quoted as having said there was not much money in it), but for the prostitute, apart from a few exceptions, it was almost slave labor.

Dewey promised to produce another interesting chart, but first he called a witness who, unbeknownst to him, plunged him into hot water. Frank Brown, assistant manager of the Barbizon Plaza Hotel, wasn't particularly happy about testifying, and his facial expression and curt, brusque answers conveyed that feeling to everyone. But there he was, a material witness for the state, being asked to identify the defendants as guests he had seen in Charlie's suite. When Brown stated that he didn't recognize any of them, Dewey became red with anger and demanded that the witness tell the court that he had identified pictures of the defendants when questioned in his office. Levy exclaimed instantly, "I object, Your Honor. The prosecutor is attempting to discredit and impeach his own witness!"

Judge McCook, instead, asked Brown to step down to take a closer look. "Well, there's not one of them I could swear to having been there," Brown answered, looking back at the judge from the floor. Dewey exploded again and asked Judge McCook to allow him to cross-examine the witness, whom he considered hostile. Levy objected again, but he was, as usual, overruled. Dewey scowled and began firing questions crudely.

Q: "Now, Mr. Witness, didn't you talk to me yesterday and to Mr. Grimes in my office?"
A: "That's right."
Q: "You didn't say last night that you had any doubts that you knew these men?"
A: "I didn't say I was positive."
Q: "You didn't tell me you weren't sure, did you?"
A: "I didn't say I was sure."
Q: "What happened to your memory overnight?"

Once more, Levy jumped up to object; and surprisingly, Judge McCook sustained the objection.

Q: "When you told me yesterday you thought you recognized these men, was that your best recollection?"
A: "Yes."
Q: "And is it still your best recollection that you recognized the men as those you saw in Luciano's room when you had drinks with him?"
A: "That's right."

Again, the witness was asked to step down to point out the defendants whom he recalled seeing. "Put your hand on them," the judge encouraged.

Levy objected strenuously, "This is the third attempt to force the witness to identify the defendants. It is an attempt to coerce and intimidate the witness!" Overruled.

Brown, however, remained intractable. "There's none there I can walk up to and put my hand on as having seen in the room." Judge McCook persisted. "Couldn't he point anyone out?" Again, the response was, "Well, as I say, there is none I can point to as having seen. I've seen thousands of men. I can't identify all of them."

Once back in the box, Dewey contemptuously threw a bunch of pictures at the witness and asked,

Q: "These are the twenty pictures I showed you yesterday?"
A: "Yes, sir."

Again and again, Dewey tried in vain to have the witness admit he could identify some of the defendants. Brown kept insisting he couldn't, that he only said he thought, and that, after all, they could have been men he had seen in the lobby. Dewey was furious that he couldn't get to first base with his *own* witness and gave up for the moment.

Levy took over the cross-examination and began by asking him about recognizing photographs in Dewey's office. Brown told him that they were very insistent about it.

Q: "Were you threatened at that office?"
A: "Well, the first day there were three or four in the room. They were talking about putting myself and others in jail, similar to what they did to the people at the Waldorf."
Q: "There was a threat to put you in jail?"
A: "Yes."
Q: "Did they say Dewey was all powerful and could put you in jail?"
A: "They didn't say it directly, but they hinted it."

Dewey was just fuming and interrupted by shouting from his table, "Didn't you tell me yesterday that there were men in the courtroom whom you had seen in Luciano's room?"

Brown replied passively, "No, they gave me pictures and said I MUST have seen them."

For Ralph, the situation was ridiculous; he understood very well, having gone through similar treatment. Levy turned to Judge McCook and exclaimed, "It has all been gone over and over. Mr. Dewey is still impeaching his own witness."

Angrily, Dewey retorted, "I'm showing exactly what kind of a witness he is!"

Levy interjected, "Your Honor, I ask that the record show the enthusiastic and vicious manner in which the statement was made, and I ask for a mistrial." Denied.

The prosecution continued with more personnel from the Barbizon. A former bellboy, William McGrath, identified Betillo, Pennochio, and Attorney Cantor. The defense revealed that McGrath hadn't been a very reliable employee and had been dismissed.

Another witness, an elevator operator, Lawrence Oberdier, also proved ineffective. He got confused between defendants and admitted that he was brought into the courtroom one day to take a peek at them. Dewey could have done better without that trio. The Frank Brown testimony was especially a painful experience for him and another setback for the prosecution. For the defense, it helped prove that some witnesses were indeed being unscrupulously pressured into testifying for the state.

On Friday morning, May 29, the state called Mrs. Hedwig Scholz, a chambermaid in the Waldorf Astoria Hotel, to the stand. She was used as an opener to give everyone time to wake up and get their senses functioning properly for Dewey's grand finale. Mrs. Scholz smiled at Charlie, identifying him as Charles Ross. She kept smiling as she revealed he was a late riser and made his bed around two every day. Damaging to the defense was her identification of Betillo, Jacobs, and Berkman. Under cross-examination, Levy tried to prove it was only because, like so many others, she had been shown pictures beforehand. More to the defense's favor was the fact that Mrs. Scholz contradicted Dotty's description of Charlie's apartment, further proving that Dotty had never gone up to his suite as she had claimed.

With grim countenances, two members of Dewey's staff carried in a large chart, four by eight feet, and placed it for all to see. It was a similar tactic Dewey used in opening his case, and it never failed to attract everyone's attention. Naturally, the defense objected, and David Siegel commented that it would be a good point to use in a possible appeal. Obviously, it pertained to the vice racket, but this one was dedicated solely to the prostitutes. Under various columns, the court learned how many prostitutes were arrested in 1935, how many were not guilty, discharged, on probation, held for special sessions, and where bail was forfeited. Based on records from the women's court, the statistics, as Dewey said, "offered to show that the guarantee made by the combination—that no girl would go to jail—was kept. It also implied that here was corruption in the magistracy."

Mildred Balitzer, wife of booker Pete Balitzer, was saved for last. She was intended to close Dewey's case with fanfare—to clinch Charlie's connection as the boss of the vice racket. An ex-madam and drug addict, she was nevertheless a polished, poised witness and rather attractive with her flashy auburn hair and a completely coordinated black-and-white outfit. She wore a fitted black-and-white flowered dress, black coat, stunning black hat with a neat white bow, black purse, and white gloves. Her silver fox hung casually around her shoulders. Not bad-looking at all. She spoke in a studied, intelligent manner, low-key, with a slight Southern accent. Looks, however, can be deceiving, and her tale was just as squalid as some of the others. Born in West Virginia, her maiden name was Henry; she had studied nursing at seventeen but had dropped everything to marry early. Before taking up with Balitzer, she had been married twice and had a child. She had become Balitzer's mistress in 1931, left him for another man while opening up a disorderly house in 1932, but returned to Balitzer in March 1933, tying the knot with him in November.

After Dewey got through with the preambles, he charged ahead into her knowledge of the syndicate. She told her story with an air of confidence. She had known Betillo and Pennochio when she had been a madam in 1932 and had learned then that a vice combination was in the works. It was Betillo who had introduced her to Charlie (as "my boss") in a Chinatown restaurant. When Pete, her husband, was having his problems paying his dues to the boys in 1935, she had gone to complain to Betillo that Pete wasn't making that much money. Betillo, however, had remained impassive to her requests to let Pete off the hook. Sometime later, she went back to Betillo and told him she wanted Pete to quit. When Betillo, still insensitive, had told her it was impossible, she had angrily replied, "I'm going to see Lucky myself about it." Betillo, according to her, had replied, "It won't do you any good. Whatever I say is okay with Lucky." Mildred was not easily dissuaded, and when she (supposedly) met Charlie in a Miami bar, she took up the case. Charlie had stalled her by saying he would look into it back in New York, but when they met again in a restaurant on West Forty-sixth Street, she had gained no ground with her pleas. Charlie had given his ultimatum: "He can't get out unless he pays the money. You know the racket!"

During the short recess, Charlie was fit to be tied, furious at the obvious frame-up. Reporters tried to obtain a comment, and he was quoted as saying, "I never saw that woman before in my life. I never heard of her before this case started, and I never knew her husband. If I did, I'd admit it, but the truth is I never saw her, and she never saw me. She's dreaming!"

In a more relaxed interview to the reporters a day earlier, Charlie had expressed a more positive attitude. "I'm going to insist on being given a chance to take the stand. They put all kinds of people on the stand to testify against me. I don't know any of them, except the hotel employees of the Waldorf and the Barbizon Plaza. All this other stuff is manufactured . . . Take all these bookers who went on the stand . . . these guys *are* in the business. They know everybody in the racket, but they didn't know me. They admitted it."

When they asked him why his name would be mentioned so freely, he replied briefly, "I don't know what their motive was in using my name . . . *if* they did use it. I don't know any of them. I know Betillo, but I don't know a thing about his business." Of course, Charlie knew more than he was saying, but he knew when to stop talking.

In cross-examination, Caesar Barra, for the defense, dug further into Mildred's past, which she didn't appreciate—especially when he mentioned her daughter. She lost some of her composure when she was asked about the birth date of her daughter, but the court saved her and ruled that she didn't have to tell. Her drug habit, it was revealed, had begun in 1932 when she had started to smoke opium, and she too had taken a cure for narcotics since her arrest. The defense had prior knowledge that some of the women witnesses had been entertained at nightclubs while awaiting trial, and Barra was more than anxious to question her on it.

> Q: "After your arrest and while you were living in an assigned apartment under custody, didn't you go to a cabaret?"

She answered yes, adding however that it was after a long session in Dewey's office. They had finished around two in the morning and had stopped off at a midtown club.

> Q: "Where?"
> A: "Leon and Eddie's."
> Q: "Who was with you?"
> A: "A policeman and Sol Gelb (of Dewey's staff)."
> Q: "Did you dance?"
> A: "No."
> Q: "But you did drink, didn't you?"
> A: "I had several brandies."

Q: "Who paid the bill?"
A: "Sol Gelb."

Mildred also admitted to having had permission to dine with Pete several times at Childs Restaurant near Dewey's office. *Very cozy,* thought Ralph.

Levy took his turn and, as always, was relentless in cutting down his adversaries. He began with her arrest for compulsory prostitution, and wasn't it true that she was testifying because she was promised immunity? Her answers were hardly audible, and the clerk had to read them back. No, she had answered, nor was she threatened with jail. She had signed a waiver of immunity. The foremost thing in her mind was to help her husband.

"Precisely," retorted Levy. "Didn't your husband, in effect, tell you to testify against Charlie 'Lucky,' or he'd go up for twenty years?"

Again, she calmly said no. Dewey sat back in his chair, looking very pleased at his witness. Ralph gazed at her intently. *What an air of self-confidence,* he thought. *The bitch would have made a damn good actress.*

Levy turned his attention to Mildred's old flame, Gus Franco, with whom she had lived before marrying Pete. She claimed she had met him on the street in the company of a policeman, and Franco had threatened her with death. "He told me to keep out of this, or I'd be killed," she said. Levy sidetracked her remarks by trying to establish, instead, the existing friendship between Mildred, Franco, and his mother; didn't they, in fact, get her a lawyer? She only partially admitted to it. She claimed she didn't see Gus's mother frequently since her arrest, and no, she did not discuss with her lawyer the matter of involving an innocent man in a serious crime.

Q: "Did you tell Gus you were going to testify against Lucky, so you could get out of town with your child?"
A: "No."
Q: "How many times did you see Lucky between October 1933 and January 1934?"
A: "Five or six times."
Q: "You were angry with Lucky when he refused your request, were you not?"
A: "I certainly was!"
Q: "And bitter too?"
A: "Naturally, I was bitter."

Q: "And you are still angry and bitter, aren't you?"
A: "I am."

It was soon all over, and Mildred Balitzer was allowed to leave the stand. The defense had tried very hard to break her, but she remained a positive witness for the prosecution. Dewey, smug as ever, smiled as he turned to Judge McCook and the jury and serenely announced that the state had completed its case. It was a little after 6:30 p.m.

Before the day was over, the reporters had still more startling news to write about. Jack Ellenstein, alias Jack Eller, one of the ten defendants, would plead guilty on Monday, June 1, to charges against him. Another score for Dewey—even if it came as a surprise. That would mean no bookers would be left on trial since Marcus, Weiner, and Balitzer had all turned state's witness. In fact, Ellenstein had desired to give in before the trial, but the defense purposely postponed it, so Dewey couldn't have him to testify against the others. Ellenstein, at forty-two, was a small fat man with protruding pale blue eyes and a few gray hairs on his bald head. He would have faced life imprisonment if found guilty and was naturally hoping for clemency from the court.

Maurice P. Cantor, Ellenstein's lawyer, informed Dewey and Judge McCook of his client's decision. Due to the new developments, McCook informed the jury they would be summoned an hour later on Monday.

An exhausted jury rose to leave, wondering what type of performance would be in store for them.

CHAPTER THIRTY-FOUR

"I'm a sporting kind of gambler, namely horses, and golf is my game. That's why it annoys me to be charged with running this prostitute racket. Look, I like money as well as anybody, but that is a lousy racket, and I wouldn't take a cent from it. What do they think I am anyway?"

During the weekend recess, Charlie had indulged in a couple of interviews. At thirty-eight, he looked younger, despite everything. Smartly dressed in a gray serge suit, white shirt, and silk tie, he appeared to be conducting a business meeting rather than an interview as the kingpin of the vice racket. Poised, affable, he said he was anxious to take the stand and prove his innocence.

"I think I will beat this rap. I'm not putting any money on it, of course, because I'm not foolish, and I realize I am handicapped by being tried with nine other guys. But if I had to bet one way or the other, I would bet the jury will believe me."

When asked what he thought about all the evidence presented against him, in a soft but emphatic voice, he replied, "Just that it is not true, and I hope I will be able to prove it. The witnesses who got up and said they knew me were lying, all except the hotel people. I know them, and I do not deny it."

Was he resentful against the prostitutes who testified against him? "No, poor things, they were just bulldozed into it."

Of course, Dewey and his staff laughed off Charlie's declarations. They were busy getting ready for the defense's counterattack, expected to take much less time than the prosecution but not necessarily less effective.

As soon as Judge McCook's gavel went down, opening up the fourth trial week, all the defense counselors had something to say; most demanded a mistrial. Caesar Barra, speaking for all the defendants, moved for the dismissal of the superseding indictment naming all the defendants in the vice charge, claiming that their constitutional rights had been violated. It was another attempt to fight the new Joinder Law where more than one crime was charged in the joint indictment, bunching all the defendants together. Carlino had tried vigorously twice on those grounds for Ralph, but his motions were denied. Nothing had changed. McCook upheld the law and dismissed everyone's motions. He ordered the defense to be ready after a short recess.

Ralph wore his dark brown silk suit and his hair neatly trimmed for his debut. Ralph was short, but he always looked good in his clothes. He wanted to look as respectable as possible for the blue-ribbon jury and was looking forward for the chance to speak out in his defense—to shout his innocence from the highest hill. The fact that he was innocent made Ralph strong, unafraid to testify. As far as he was concerned, Dewey and his tribe were no better than him. After all, they had tried to bribe him! For the sake of appearances, he wanted to look as calm as possible. Ralph had promised Carlino that he would keep his cool and not make any unnecessary outbursts. But, hell, Ralph thought, a lot depended on how Dewey treated him. Carlino and Ralph had many sessions together where the competent Carlino told him what things he could say and what he shouldn't in order to protect himself. Ralph rehearsed over and over in his mind about how he would tell his story. He was to be the first witness—and very important for the defense—because he held the dynamite in his hands. His opening testimony was going to set the scene—that he was being railroaded, and Charlie framed. Ralph knew the odds were against him, but he was fighting mad.

"Will Ralph Liguori please take the stand," a clerk called out.

Ralph felt a tug inside, his innards hurt, and his mouth was dry, but he stood up and, head erect, walked carefully to the stand. He was sworn in by the clerk, and then, once he was comfortably settled, Carlino rose slowly and walked toward him. He asked Ralph to give the court a little of his background. Ralph gave his name, age, address at 1801 Eighty-first Street, Brooklyn, and trade as a butcher. He told the court he had begun working at fifteen to help his widowed mother and had worked his way up to manager in the butcher trade. As Ralph spoke, his eyes shifted slowly around the courtroom. It was unusually packed, all wondering what the defense would pull out of the hat. The jurors, who had a couple of days rest, were fresh looking, and Ralph said to himself, *Pay real hard attention, you guys, to what I'm going to say!* Then Carlino's voice boomed.

Q: "Do you know Nancy Presser?"
A: "I do."
Q: "She was your girl?"
A: "Yes."
Q: "How many times did you have her cured for narcotics?"
A: "Four times."

Q: "Did you support her?"
A: "I did."

Asked to elaborate, Ralph told the court that he had met Dotty in 1933, and that they had gone together almost immediately—around three and a half years—and had lived together; the last place was the Emerson Hotel for nine months. And yes, he paid all the bills. They called Ralph Mr. Presser at the hotel.

Q: "Did you ever place her in a house of prostitution?"

Ralph vehemently denied that he had placed Dotty in a whorehouse. He also denied that he ordered Pete Harris, James Russo, or any madam to book Dotty. All lies. In fact, he added truthfully, he had no knowledge of her being a prostitute and still found it hard to believe. Actually, Ralph was heartbroken about the whole thing. He couldn't believe that Dotty had succumbed to prostitution, and if she did, that it had to be occasionally (behind his back) to obtain money for drugs. Ralph would never have supplied her with any. But, no, he couldn't believe it.

Q: "Did you ever beat her up?"

Ralph's face fell at that question, but Carlino soothingly reminded him of the testimonies by Dotty and the Jordan girl. Naturally, Ralph denied that he did because in all his life, he *never* hit a woman. He had loved them and left them, but never did he beat them. It was not in his character.

Q: "Ever receive any money from her?"
A: "I should say not."
Q: "Did you ever visit Nancy's home?"
A: "Yes."
Q: "Who was there?"
A: "Her father . . . mother . . . brother."
Q: "Did Nancy ever come to your Brooklyn home?"
A: "Every Sunday and all holidays . . . Christmas . . . Thanksgiving . . . and all the rest."

Carlino was great in the courtroom. He had a certain savoir-faire in his demeanor. Dewey had nothing over him as a presence of force and ability to move about. At a given moment, his piercing eyes would look sharply at a predetermined target as it suited him—the jury, the judge, the press, and the spectators in general. He had everyone listening.

Q: "Now tell us, do you know Charlie Luciano?"
A: "I've seen him around town."
Q: "Do you know any of the other defendants?"
A: "I've seen Jimmy Frederico around, but I don't know him."
Q: "Do you know any of the other people listed on Mr. Dewey's chart as connected with the case?"
A: "I have seen Danny Brooks in Dewey's office. But I don't know him."

The reason Ralph declared he didn't know Charlie personally was because it was Charlie's dictum. He didn't want either one of them to acknowledge their friendship. Charlie said it would only further jeopardize their chances, and the defense lawyers had to agree.

Q: "Were you ever a holdup man for Charlie 'Lucky' or any other defendant?"
A: "I was not."

Ralph categorically denied everything. They were all lies, and he was there to tell them that a lot of crap had been manufactured about a lot of people."

Q: "How is it then that you are a defendant in this trial?"

Ralph sat bolt upright in his chair and answered loud and clear.

A: "Because I wouldn't cooperate with the prosecution!"

That remark had the jurors sitting at the edge of their seats while Carlino continued nonchalantly.

Q: "Tell the court about it."

Slowly, Ralph began to unravel his tale—about his having been brought to Dewey's office for questioning because they had arrested his girl, Dotty. How Assistant Special Prosecutor Harry Cole had told him at first that he was the only one who could save his girl, and that he had asked Cole what did he have to do.

Q: "What did Harry Cole want you to do?"
A: "He began boasting that Tom Dewey was a big shot. That he was going to be the next governor of New York . . . that he could protect me . . . that he knew I had nothing to do with the combination . . . and that he didn't want me as a defendant. All they wanted me to do was to help them get Luciano. When I hesitated, he said, 'Don't be a damn fool. We don't want you. We want only one man, Charlie Lucky.' I said I didn't know Charlie Lucky, and he said that didn't make any difference. I said, 'But suppose I go into the courtroom and can't pick him out? What will they do to me?' He said, 'Don't worry. We'll show you so many pictures of him, you'll dream about them all night.'"
Q: "What else did Cole say?"
A: "Well, he showed me pictures of Lucky, Betillo, Frederico, and Pennochio, and said they wanted all four. He said, 'Now remember, Lucky's the boss, Dave's the strong-arm man, Tommy's the treasurer, and Jimmy's the man who told you to collect $400 from a madam. You brought the money down to Mulberry Street where Betillo and Charlie were waiting. Charlie 'Lucky' put the money in his pocket and gave you $10 for your trouble.' I said that never happened, but he didn't like my answer. He repeated, 'We know you had nothing to do with this. We want to get the rest, and if you will cooperate with us, it will help Nancy.' He wanted me to say that I was hired by the combination as a stickup man."
Q: "Go on."
A: "He said he would get a madam to back up my story. He said, 'Don't worry. We got bums, prostitutes, and madams up here who will do anything to save themselves. We've arrested a hundred of them, and none of them is going to jail.' They had me coming and going for days from my cell to the offices to kind of persuade me at first, but then they began to threaten me."
Q: "Now, what about Nancy?"
A: "When I told him it was all baloney, he said he didn't care if it was true or not. It was the only way to save Nancy, whom they caught dead to right in a room with a man. Well, I didn't believe him, because they had told me at first it was for heroin. I knew they were throwing a lot of crap my way. I asked him why he never told me Nancy was caught like that, and he said that Nancy begged him not to tell me. They wanted me and Nancy to get together on a story against Luciano."
Q: "What did Cole say about Nancy?"

A: "He said, 'We picked Nancy because she's just the type Charlie Lucky would go for. The jury will believe that.' He wanted me to say I introduced Nancy to Lucky in 1927, and that Lucky slept with her a week."

Q: "Did you talk to Nancy?"

A: "Yes, Nancy begged me to do what Cole wanted, 'cause they had threatened her with three years in prison, and when I refused, she got angry. They even had my brother and sister trying to convince me. I also saw Assistant Special Prosecutor Jacob Rosenblum in the office there, and he said, to get wise to myself and to 'give Cole what he wants.'"

Q: "Did Cole promise you anything?"

A: "Yes, he promised if I would cooperate and tell the story he wanted me to, he would pay me and my girl's way to Europe for six months and also give me protection. Said Dewey's got plenty of state dough back of him. He also offered to put Nancy and me in an apartment together pending trial."

Q: "What did he say he would do if you didn't cooperate, as he called it?"

A: "He said he would see that I got twenty-five years in jail. He said Dewey had all the authority in the world."

Q: "What happened in your last interview?"

A: "They gave me my last chance. They even had me see Dewey personally, who reassured me, 'That's right. If you testify before the grand jury, you go scot-free.' He said I was the peddler, and he was the buyer. I told him I had nothing to sell. For $20,000 they wanted me to frame Luciano." (Ralph's voice went up an octave as he turned in defiance toward the jury box. He wanted them to understand he was telling the truth.) "I told them, 'It's a pack of lies. It's perjury, and I won't perjure myself for nobody!' When I refused everything, Dewey had me indicted."

Then Ralph mentioned how he had met Grimes in the hall, who angrily called him a "guinea" and wanted to hit him. The courtroom was really animated now. Ralph had exploded a bombshell. Dewey was visibly embarrassed, but he recovered fast. His staff had nothing but hatred in their eyes for Ralph. He had unmasked them, but would the jury believe him?

The reporters in the press box were fidgeting, anxious to run out with their scoops. Some managed to run out because at that point, one of the jurors got sick, and a doctor had to be called. McCook declared that juror number 11, John McGowan, could not continue and pulled out alternate

Clarence Talbot Squier's name to replace him. Squier was sworn in, and soon the cross-examination began.

Ralph sat waiting for the famous prosecutor to go after him. He had to be calm because he knew Dewey was going to provoke him into anger. When Dewey sauntered forward with the usual smirk on his face, Ralph felt the hatred in his soul swell. Dewey had what looked like a white index card in his hand. He came very close to Ralph and asked evenly, "How old are you?"

"Thirty years old."

Dewey walked back to his table, turned, and came to him again. All the time Ralph's mind was on that piece of paper. Again, "How old are you?"

"Thirty."

As Dewey turned his back again, he snickered, walked toward the jury, and stopped midway. All the while, Ralph concentrated on the paper, wondering what the hell it could be. Dewey turned toward him and asked slyly, "Ralph, how old are you?"

"I'm *still* thirty." Then the light hit Ralph. It was his driver's license. Dewey was balking at his age.

Now for the last time, Dewey charged up to Ralph, his fist under Ralph's nose, waving the paper in his face, shouting angrily, "Is this your handwriting?"

Ralph was somewhat flippant when he answered, "Why, Mr. Dewey, the brilliant prosecutor. Yes, that is my handwriting, and that's my driver's license."

"Then you lied!" Dewey shouted.

Still on the sarcastic side, Ralph said, "No, I didn't. I was always taught from kindergarten on up that you don't lie, unless you go before the judge of a court, or a notary public. Well, when I got my driver's license, I didn't sign my name before either one. Therefore, I did not lie."

"Ah, so . . . ," Dewey responded caustically. "Well, why did you do it?"

"Now, I'll tell you why I did it," Ralph replied in monotone. "My father had passed away when I was ten, and at fifteen, I had begun working to help my mother. One of my brothers had been called into the army. I had gotten a job in a butcher shop where I rode a bicycle to deliver orders. To make more money to help the family, I needed a driver's license, so I had said I was eighteen years old."

A few people in the courtroom clapped, and that only infuriated Dewey all the more. He attacked Ralph by challenging his claim of having been an honest Brooklyn butcher boy.

It was obvious there was no love between them, and Ralph snarled back, "Mr. Dewey knows me better than myself. Go on, call up the people I worked for . . . It'll only cost you a nickel. Don't be a cheapskate!"

Dewey didn't answer, only walked away from Ralph with sheer disgust on his face. He picked up other papers on his table and returned, rustling them in his hands. Methodically, he went into Ralph's arrest record even though he had never been convicted. Then he produced a check for $200 from Dotty's father, which Ralph endorsed, like he was some kind of thief—also because Ralph had said he had never received money from Dotty. But Ralph readily admitted it as one-time only loan. Dewey really had nothing on Ralph, and he kept pulling at straws. Still, he tried to degrade Ralph with side remarks like didn't Ralph share Dotty's room except when she had customers? But Ralph flatly stated he was her only customer. Tired himself of the line of questioning, Dewey was ready for a different approach. Always jostling around, he now came back with renewed vigor to continue his cat-and-mouse game.

Q: "Do you know Charles Luciano?"
A: "I've seen him around—nightclubs like Kings Terrace, at the tracks at Saratoga."
Q: "Did you ever do any business with him?"
A: "No . . . I didn't."
Q: "Who are my assistants who asked you to commit perjury?"
A: "Harry Cole, Mr. Ariola, Charles Grimes."
Q: "Didn't Mr. Hogan ask you to perjure yourself?"
A: "No . . . Mr. Hogan frightened me every time he saw me, threatening me with twenty-five years in jail."

Dewey's facial expressions did not conceal his contempt for Ralph, and the feeling was mutual. It ended up being a shouting match.

Q: "Did I ask you to frame Luciano?"
A: (Ralph pointed his finger angrily at Dewey.) "Yes . . . you did! When Cole took me to your office. He told you that I didn't believe you would give me the money, and when I asked you to put it in a bank in my name, you chased me out, and I cursed you!"

Dewey was quick on the draw; he insinuated that Charlie was paying Ralph to testify in his behalf as he roared, "Who paid for your lawyer in this case . . . Charlie?"

"No!" Ralph shouted back. "My mother and sister paid for my lawyer. Charlie paid nothing!"

Dewey waved his hands in disgust, as if to say, *This guy is a nut*, and looked at Judge McCook. "That's all, Your Honor."

During recess, Carlino had his arms around Ralph as Charlie came up and commented, "Ralph, that's the way it went?"

"Yeah . . . Charlie, that is the way it went."

Charlie called Dewey a few obscene names and walked away with Polakoff, who had patted Ralph on the back. All the defense lawyers were complimenting Ralph on the good show, and naturally, he was happy. He had had his day in court, and he would never forget it. Neither would Dewey.

The New York papers went berserk. Even the radio newscasts were blaring away. Walter Winchell did his share. The papers came out all blazing with front-page headlines: LIGUORI'S EVIDENCE GIVES NEW HOPE TO LUCKY; LIGUORI BATTLES DEWEY—CHARGES BRIBE OFFER; ACCUSED HOLDUP MAN OF VICE RING CHARGES FRAME-UP; WITNESS SAYS DEWEY PLOTTED LUCKY FRAME; SUSPECT ACCUSES DEWEY ASSISTANT; LIGUORI, ALLEGED LUCIANO STRONG ARM MAN, "TOO TRUTHFUL," HE TOLD COURT; and many others. One paper wrote that after seventeen days since the trial had started, the defense had really scored.

During the night session, Anna took the stand. She was of course a little nervous but, like her mother, a fighter and was ready to tell it as it was. Carlino, however, to spare her, was very brief.

Q: "Do you know Mr. Cole?"
A: "Yes, soon after April 4, I was in his office. Ralph and Nancy were there."
Q: "What did Mr. Cole want with you?"
A: "He said he wanted Ralph to say certain things, that they had a puzzle, and if Ralph would say what he wanted him to, they could get the last link. And that was Charlie 'Lucky'."
Q: "Did Nancy say anything?"
A: "Yes . . . She said she would say anything to get out of that darned place."
Q: "Anything else?"
A: "Well . . . Cole pleaded with me to have Ralph testify against Luciano. He threatened to crucify Ralph on the stand, if he didn't do as he was told. He told me Mr. Dewey was a powerful and influential man, and that if Ralph was wise, he might go absolutely free."

The cross-examination was even more brief. She was asked whether she was sure of her recollections, to which she replied, "Absolutely!" Then added, "Are you implying that I may have lied?"

"No . . . let's say biased?"

Anna stood her ground and very strongly remarked, "Some truths are hard to take. And, I believe you are taking very lightly the fact that I swore in."

Anna was quickly dismissed but walked out with great dignity.

There were many other small pluses for the defense, such as the testimony of Sol Parken, clerk of the city prison, who verified the number of times Ralph left The Tombs Prison to go to Dewey's offices. There was also John L. Ryan, the manager of the Emerson Hotel, who confirmed that Ralph paid the bills and was known as Mr. Presser. For the defense, in general, five Pittsburgh policemen, which included a county detective named Thomas Calig, testified that Dave Miller had lied under oath about his arrest, and his wife's on prostitution charges. They all told of a raid in 1927 in Miller's Pittsburgh house of prostitution. Dewey had admitted that Miller had lied and asked that it be put on the record, but the defense demanded that he be arrested for perjury. Judge McCook said he'd think about it.

To complete Ralph's defense, early the next morning, Agnes took the stand. Ralph was concerned about her but knew his mother would be prepared. Her testimony was scheduled to be short and simple. As soon as she was sworn in, however, the defense counselors gathered together for a consultation while Dewey complained that the sketchy introduction of witnesses was making it impossible for them to work. To placate him, Levy informed the court that as soon as the Liguori defense was through, he would start with Luciano's.

Attention was finally given to Agnes, who sat patiently—the picture of respectability. With sad eyes and a drawn face, she quietly stated that she had received a telephone call from Dewey's office imploring her to influence her son to testify against Luciano, as they wanted him to. Carlino walked halfway between the judge and jury, looked at one and then the other, and rested his case. The prosecution had no questions.

Carlino had done his best. Everyone knew that Judge McCook was in Dewey's camp, so all anyone could do was to hope and pray that some of the jurors had listened and believed.

CHAPTER THIRTY-FIVE

Everyone was looking forward to Charlie's appearance on the stand, but the defense used their own suspense tactics. While all those present waited with bated breath and straining ears, the defense programmed a series of witnesses first to build up Charlie's true reputation as a gambler of sorts, not the low character of which he had been accused, with the title of Vice King of Manhattan. Their case ran on two tracks: one to disprove the testimonies against Charlie, and the other to demonstrate that his bad habits were to be found elsewhere—specifically, that he made his money gambling.

The first witness called didn't last long on the stand. He was Captain George Paul Dutton of Albany, a department supervisor of the New York State Police. Captain Dutton denied that he had introduced Luciano to Joe Bendix (a fourth-time offender and a witness for the prosecution). In fact, he said he had never seen Luciano before entering the courtroom that morning. Dewey, in an effort to discredit Dutton, said he was not an army captain, which Bendix claimed. They squabbled about that for a while, but Dutton stood his ground.

Max Kalik, a bookmaker, took the stand next. He said he had known Lucky for about eight years and had seen him almost daily at the racetracks. A colorful character, Kalik revealed that Charlie did not risk much; instead, he was a hedger when it came to "laying a horse." Asked what that meant, he replied, "Well, say I have a large bet that I couldn't handle. I'd say, 'Charlie, do you want to hedge a little?' And he'd say yes. He'd take $500 of that bet. In order words, he'd book $500."

Charlie seemed to get a kick out of the explanation and smiled, but Levy wanted more specifics, wanted to make it clearer, and asked, "Suppose at two to one Lucky bet $300, then the price would go down to even money. He'd lay $300 the other way so that he'd lose nothing?"

"That's correct," answered Kalik with a grin.

In cross-examination, Dewey tried to disqualify Kalik as a lawbreaker, to which he replied sweetly, "I've been a bookmaker for thirty years, and I've had such nice people trading with me that I didn't think it was criminal."

"Like 'Legs' Diamond . . . Lepke . . . Gurrah?" Dewey snapped.

Kalik denied the accusation, and that was the end of him.

Then Henry Golstone, another bookmaker, testified to very much the same. Charlie had placed bets with him, about $200 to $300, and had been seen frequently in Saratoga at crap games.

A more intimate friend, Thomas Francis, a handicapper and owner of a racing stable, stated that he personally went with Charlie every afternoon to the racetrack. A frequent visitor at the Waldorf, Francis swore that he had not seen any of the other defendants in Charlie's suite. He was loaded down with several books—apparently to use as reference, if need be. Dewey, however, didn't lend him or his books any importance.

After a succession of professional gamblers, bookmakers, and "horsey" gentlemen swore to Luciano's gambling habits, very respectable "Bobby" Crawford, the Broadway music publisher, took the stand. He spoke of the first time he had seen Lucky in 1932, dressed like a society man, mingling with the blue bloods of the sporting world, at private gambling sessions in Saratoga. One could look down the tables and find people like Mr. and Mrs. Bing Crosby, Sam Rosoff (the subway tycoon), and other famous Broadwayites like George White (Scandals) and Mazda Lane. In fact, Crawford stated, Lucky had also been, on occasion, in the Saratoga mansion rented for the season by the Crosbys and himself. He talked about the craps games at Smith's, a famous gambling house in Saratoga, which Charlie ran wide open during racing season. Here, too, millionaires and top-notch gamblers brushed elbows to place their bets. Other times, Crawford continued, they had gone to Charlie's place around the corner from the United States Hotel. Once, he and Rosoff had to borrow money from Charlie to continue playing. Crawford had told the truth as he knew it, and as he left the stand, he had every reason to give Charlie a broad smile of encouragement.

Levy was confident that these testimonies confirmed where and how Charlie made his money, and that he definitely associated with a higher class of people than with the lowest dregs of humanity—as in prostitution. Also scheduled to testify to Charlie's character were George White (the famous impresario), Mazda Lane, and Charlie's girl, Gay Orlova, who, by only her entrance into the courtroom, could sway the hearts of many.

After the lunch break, all eyes and ears perked up when Morris H. Panger, an assistant district attorney, arrived to testify. He was a key witness for the defense. His credentials were top-notch. An aide to District Attorney William C. Dodge, he had been with the New York County since 1920. His testimony helped Ralph's story as well as the defense's contention that Charlie was being "legally" framed. Panger shot holes through Joe Bendix's tale that Charlie okayed a collector's job for him in the vice syndicate. He came well prepared with documentation relating to Bendix's arrests and criminal life. Levy had him directly tell how it was that he knew Bendix and of his involvement in the Luciano case.

Panger stated that while Bendix was in jail on a burglary charge (his fourth offense), he had written many letters to the district attorney's office offering valuable information in exchange for leniency. Levy read some of them to the court. Bendix had tried to bargain for a misdemeanor plea rather than to the burglary rap to avoid the Baumes Law life term. He finally had come up with a wild story that he knew something about the Bank of Manhattan bond robbery. Panger, however, had refused to negotiate any deals with him. "I made him no promises," said Panger. Later, Bendix had admitted it was a hoax.

After failing with Panger, Bendix became angry and had decided to sell his wares to Dewey's office. "After he had talked with Mr. Dewey's aides," added Panger, "I did not change my recommendations that he be released after two and a half to four years." The court had heard all this before, but what the prosecution wasn't ready for was what the defense still had in the bag. In one of the envelopes addressed to Panger, Bendix had enclosed, by mistake, a letter he had written to his wife. Then to complicate matters, Bendix had followed it with another note to Panger asking him to destroy the letter. Dewey obviously suspected something and objected strenuously. This time, oddly enough, he was overruled. Levy asked Panger to read Bendix's letter to his wife.

> "My beloved wife, I do so hope to be able to see you tomorrow . . . It may mean that even after sentence, I may be held over and transferred to Fifty-second Street until May 4, the date set for Lucky's trial. Pray, my precious darling . . . that again our prayers will be answered.
>
> "It will mean so much what impression you and Joan will make on Mr. Ariola (special prosecutor's office) . . . Try to think up some real clever story, which would prove of interest to Mr. Ariola—anything to show your willingness to help him. The chances are he may not need it, but it will help, nevertheless. In some unknown reason, my implicit faith lies with him, and his promises are worth far more than coming from the other DA's office.
>
> "Sweetheart, want to get this off in time . . .
>
> "Your devoted husband, Joe."

Everyone in the courtroom turned to look at Dewey, who was objecting. Overruled again. Levy continued questioning Panger.

Q: "Did Mr. Dewey know of this letter?"
A: "Under orders from District Attorney Dodge, I sent photostatic copies of Bendix's letter to Dewey on May 22."

Again, all eyes went to Dewey. He was in deep trouble. The letter had cinched the fact that Bendix was a big liar, that he had manufactured his tale to save his neck. The defense felt it was all very damaging to Dewey's case, which he had worked into shape with great artistry. It was another terrific boost for the defense. Charlie was all smiles and content as could be. He was really stimulated by the positive turn of events. Charlie was more convinced than ever before to take the stand. Just another couple of witnesses and he would have his chance.

Lorenzo Bressio was a curly haired young man with an olive complexion and extremely broad shoulders. He gave his trade as a wholesale beer distributor and stated he lived in Queens. This did not stop him from staying over with Charlie in his suite at the Barbizon Plaza from time to time. Levy got to the point.

Q: "Did Mr. Luciano ever have any women visit him there?"
A: "Only one."
Q: "Well, who was the one?"
A: "I saw Ms. Gay Orlova, who was known as Charlie's girlfriend."
Q: "Now, will you please tell the court, did you see any of the defendants visit Mr. Luciano?"
A: "No, I stayed there a lot. The only one that came was Little Dave Betillo, and he came to see me, not Charlie."

On cross-examination, Bressio was not exactly cooperative with Dewey. When he was asked sarcastically if, in effect, he was not Charlie "Lucky's" bodyguard, Bressio very matter-of-factly replied, "No, just a close buddy, sort of a companion." From then on, Dewey couldn't extract any straight answers. Bressio couldn't remember dates or names, and the more Dewey pressed, the more "I don't knows" and "can't remembers" he received.

Since Levy had more than once suggested that Gay Orlova would take the stand, the court was still being held in suspense. Levy had said it would be nice if she testified to confirm the things that she had already publicly admitted to the newspapers. But Ralph knew differently. Charlie wouldn't let her. That morning, before court opened, in a brief interview with the press, Charlie had said his peace. "I hope Ms. Orlova won't be mixed up in this dirty mess." And that, of course, meant no.

Gus Franco was a swanky, unmarried young man of twenty-nine from Manhattan. He was the nephew of a local district political leader and the son of a Sicilian coffeehouse owner. Franco was called to put a dent in Mildred Balitzer's testimony. After denying he knew Luciano personally, Levy asked him about his relationship with Mildred. Franco was a smooth talker and readily admitted to having lived in a penthouse with her. He claimed, however, that he had never known she had been running a house in the same building. When he had found out, he had told her to quit the racket.

Then Franco plunged into his conversation with Balitzer regarding Charlie. "Just before the trial, when Mildred was locked up, she went to an outside phone and called me. She was sobbing and yelling and she said, 'Gee, it's good to hear an honest voice once more, Gus . . . They got me in a spot. I can't help my husband . . . unless I put the finger on Lucky in court. They're pounding me, Gus . . . They're killing me. I gotta do what they say!'"

Q: "Did you ask her whether she really knew Charlie 'Lucky' or not?"
A: "Yes, I said, 'But, Mildred, if you don't know the man, that's the wrong thing to do.' She said she didn't know Lucky from beans, but she had to back up Pete."

Dewey didn't waste time informing the court in cross-examination that Franco had one Federal Narcotics conviction on his record. Then he mysteriously suggested that wasn't it true he was coming to the aid of Luciano on orders from the counselors of L'Unione Siciliana?

"Objection, Your Honor!" Sustained.

This was one man Dewey seemed eager to get his hands on. Off guard, he threw another stinger.

Q: "Did you ever kill a man in Brooklyn, say in 1931, in a holdup?"
A: (Vigorously.) "That's a lie."
Q: "Aren't you really a dope runner, a Dutch Schultz policy racketeer, murderer, kept lover of Mildred Harris, and a thief whose only true virtue is that you were caught only once?"

Franco didn't bother to answer and looked at Levy, who was already on his feet objecting, charging that there was no record Franco ever committed any such crimes, and that Dewey was stabbing in the dark. Surprisingly, Levy's objection was again sustained.

The court adjourned for lunch, and Charlie, as usual, was hounded by reporters for comment. He obliged by making a statement similar to most others. "This is distinctly a wrong rap. I do not pretend to be an angel, but I am far from being public enemy number one or even public enemy number 1,000. I am just a guy around the tracks and occasionally around the dice tables."

Charles Lucania (alias Charles Luciano, alias Charlie "Lucky," alias Charles Ross) took the stand at 2:10 p.m. Nattily dressed in a fine gray suit with thin blue threads, hair neatly combed and shoes highly polished, he walked to the stand; all eyes remained fixed on his every move. He spoke in his usual low-modulated voice. Charlie was not a shouter, vulgar, or gruff. When, on occasion, he became angry or was provoked, his voice was never shrill but rather restrained, in a strong, firm tone. He tried always to be in control. His only loud display was his laughter, which was usually a spontaneous outburst, contagious to those around him. But now, he was heading for a non-laughing matter, and his self-control would be bitterly tested by Dewey.

With one hand on the Bible and the other raised, Charlie swore to tell the truth, nothing but the truth. He gave his parentage and personal data. (His mother had died and his father was still living at seventy-seven; the family address was 265 East Tenth Street.) It had been agreed beforehand that the direct examination would be brief. There were denials on just about everything that had occurred during the prosecution's bombardment of witnesses who had named him as the vice lord. Levy guided him rather paternally as Charlie answered leading questions matter-of-factly, with a certain amount of confidence.

Q: "Did you go to school on the east side?"
A: "Yes . . . five years."
Q: "What grade were you in when you left?"
A: "The sixth."
Q: "Where did you go to work?"
A: "The shipyards."
Q: "How long did you work there?"
A: "Three . . . four years."
Q: "How much salary?"
A: "Five to seven dollars a day."
Q: "You said you worked three to four years. Did you then get into some trouble over the sale of narcotics?"
A: "I did."

Q: "What happened?"
A: "I served six months in the reformatory."

Charlie spoke candidly, almost nostalgically, his gaze at times absent like most people when speaking of their childhood—even the worst kind. He mentioned that after he came out of the reformatory, he went to work for his father. Soon afterward, he started his gambling career with floating dice games and later graduated into running his own gambling houses, expanding to horseracing, handicapping, betting, and booking.

Q: "Tell us what you have done since."
A: "I have been a gambler for ten years."
Q: "Have you run craps games in Saratoga?"
A: "Yes . . . in several clubs."
Q: "Do you remember being at the Barbizon Plaza?"
A: "Yes."
Q: "How many of these defendants did you know before this trial started?"
A: "Only one. Dave Betillo. I've known him eight or ten years."
Q: "Did you have any business with him?"
A: "No. The closest I came to it was when he asked me to operate a gambling enterprise on a boat, but I turned it down. I learned later that the boat was seized." (He smiled at his near escape.)
Q: "There has been testimony that Frederico, Berkman, Jacobs were in your room?"
A: "They were not."
Q: "Now . . . all these witnesses you have seen here . . . do you know any of them?"
A: "I never saw any of them."
Q: "Did you ever in your life place a girl in a house of prostitution?"
A: "I never did."
Q: "Did you ever take the earnings of a prostitute?"
A: "I always gave . . . never took." (Grinned at that one.)
Q: "Ever engage in bonding houses of prostitution?"
A: "I never had to make my money that way."
Q: "Now, about Nancy Presser, did she visit you in your hotel?"
A: "I told you. I never saw any of those witnesses."

Charlie knew who Dotty was, all right, knew she was Ralph's girl, but he had to say that because he wasn't admitting that he knew Ralph either. He had to be coherent in that; it was an agreement between him and Ralph. Levy kept going, giving him a gentle workout, preparing him for the big match.

Q: "Cokey Flo . . . Did you meet her in any restaurant in New York?"
A: "Never saw her until she came in here."
Q: "Did you have a conversation with others in her presence that you would monopolize the houses in New York and raise the prices—to create a chain store system of the vice?"
A: "No . . . sir!" (Most emphatically.)

Charlie categorically denied ever meeting or knowing Mildred Balitzer—neither in New York nor in Miami. And he continued to deny.

Q: "You heard the testimony of Joe Bendix that Captain Dutton introduced you to him in the Club Richman with a woman called Cashmere?"
A: "I did."
Q: "Was it so?"
A: "It was not. I never met any of these people."
Q: "You heard him say you offered him a job. Did you?"
A: "I never met him in my entire life."
Q: "Did you ever take a dollar from a prostitute directly or indirectly in your entire life?"
A: "I never did!"

Then Levy went into Charlie's extradition fight in Hot Springs. He asked Charlie when had he first heard that Dewey was looking for him. Charlie replied he was in a gambling house when he had heard about it. He had returned to his hotel, where he found a detective hanging around, but nothing happened. The next day at the golf course, a young boy had come running to tell him that a detective and sheriff were waiting for him at the hotel. Again, Charlie had returned and, this time, had submitted to arrest. The rest of the story is known. When asked why he fought so hard against extradition, Charlie answered his lawyer had informed him that Dewey would have had him on trial within forty-eight hours for putting a girl in a house of prostitution, which was not true. He had to gain time to see things clearly.

Q: "You were arrested in Florida in 1930."
A: "Yes . . . for maintaining a gambling house. I was fined one thousand dollars."

Q: "Did you ever issue any order to have any madams beaten up?"
A: "No." (With emphasis.)

With that last no, Levy concluded. Almost half an hour had gone by. Levy looked directly into Dewey's eyes and said briskly, "Your witness," then secretly crossed his fingers because as an astute lawyer himself, he knew what traps were waiting for Charlie.

Dewey nodded slyly. He gave everyone a moment to adjust his thoughts because he intended to reduce Charlie to putty in his hands. Dewey was less agitated than he had been with Ralph. This time, his attitude and approach were entirely different. He paused slightly at the stand, looked around him, then quietly began his interrogations. Dewey, skillful in his maneuvers, made Charlie repeat when and where he was born, and Charlie again made the same error. He said he was born in New York and not in Sicily. Charlie knew better, but he also was aware Dewey knew the truth; that sooner or later, he would use it against him. Charlie was perhaps ill-advised or just obstinate in not mentioning it; for the moment, he surmised, did not need an additional handicap. Dewey smiled at the answer and then made Charlie suffer through his narcotics experience.

Q: "How old were you when you were convicted of selling narcotics?"
A: "Oh . . . 'bout eighteen."
Q: "Wasn't there a trunk of dope seized?"
A: "Yes."
Q: "Oh . . . then you were a stool pigeon?"
A: "I told what I knew."

Ralph had to chuckle at that one, and all the defendants grinned, except Charlie. He was dead serious.

Q: "Oh . . . just a decent citizen who told what he know . . . for a consideration perhaps?"
A: "I didn't get anything for it."
Q: "Well . . . you served six months for narcotics selling. What next?"
A: "I worked for a hat company."
Q: "And next?"
A: "I began the crap games."
Q: "That would make you about twenty or twenty-one. You didn't go into the army?"

A: "No . . . I was too small."
Q: "How tall are you?"
A: "I meant too young. They didn't call my class."

Dewey appeared to enjoy tripping Charlie on his English; there seemed to be a personal satisfaction in this.

Q: "You told the whole truth about your arrest in Miami?"
A: "Yes."
Q: "What about the gun you were carrying?"
A: "I didn't mention it because my lawyer hadn't asked me. Besides, possession of a revolver is not illegal in Florida."
Q: "Well, you were quoted by a newspaper as saying, 'I thought to make a little hunting trip to the Everglades while I was down there.'"
A: "They say a lot of things in the newspapers that are not true."
Q: "On July 27, weren't you found in an automobile with Joe Scalise, and in that car, wasn't there found two revolvers, a shotgun, and 45 rounds of ammunition?"

Charlie sat back in his chair, as if trying to recollect the incident, while Dewey impatiently waited for his answer. "Oh, yes," Charlie finally said. "We had been on a hunting expedition in the country."

Q: "And what were you hunting?"
A: "Peasants."
Q: "You mean pheasants?" (Dewey sarcastically interposed this, enjoying the correction once more.)
A: "That's right."
Q: (Shouting dramatically with his arms waving.) "What . . . you mean to tell me you were shooting pheasants in July—out of season in July?"
A: "That's right."
Q: "Were you shooting pheasants with a pistol?"
A: "No . . . we had a shotgun."

Charlie squirmed in his seat, knew he was in trouble, but he had to play the scene out. And Dewey was going all the way. He asked whether Charlie and Scalise passed the shotgun to each other every time they wanted to shoot. Charlie replied no, that he used the shotgun; Scalise had left his in the country.

Sometimes it seemed as if the questions were coming faster than the answers, and Charlie felt sweat on his brow. Dewey was laying clever traps for him. He accused Charlie of being a habitual liar, revealing that he had lied about his pistol permit. Dewey also wanted to know what Charlie had told the police his legitimate business was, during all the years he claimed to be a gambler. After a weak "I don't recall," Charlie managed to remember that he did have a restaurant at one time downtown. But Dewey kept badgering him for more answers. He even mentioned the famous ride and charged that Charlie had lied to the grand jury about that too. Charlie tried to inject the fact that he was telling the truth, but Dewey's voice overpowered his; hardly anyone heard him, let alone believe him at that point. He was definitely feeling the heat, uncomfortable as hell; he was too tired even to sit straight. He tried crossing his legs and slouched a bit. Dewey was exhausting him. *What next?* thought Charlie.

Q: "You're a friend of Ciro Terranova, aren't you?"
A: "I don't know him at all." (His lips twisted slightly.)
Q: "Then why did you call his house with his private telephone number, Pelham 3061?"

Charlie straightened up at the startling evidence. He should have known that his phone calls were checked. Trying his best to save himself, Charlie, of course, denied it. Dewey, however, kept cornering him.

Q: "Are you questioning the records kept by the hotels?"
A: "No, but lots of people used to come to my room. I let 'em all use the phone. I don't know who made that call."
Q: "So you don't know Terranova?"
A: "I've heard of him. Know some of his friends."
Q: "Do you know Bugsy Siegel?"
A: "Yes."
Q: "And Jacob Gurrah Shapiro?"
A: "Yes."
Q: "Louis Buchalter?"
A: "Yes."

His answers hardly audible, Charlie did manage to say that he only knew the men slightly, and of their businesses, only what he read in the newspapers. Dewey was, in effect, accusing Charlie of being public enemy number one—not necessarily the vice king. It was a tactic that worked on the jury because it was reasonable to assume that by admitting he knew these gangsters, he had also classified himself.

At that point, the whole courtroom seemed to be drained from the emotion that this duel caused. After all, Dewey had planned for this moment a long time as it meant a whole new bright future for him. He had to nail Charles Luciano. It seemed as if everyone was relieved when Judge McCook called for a short recess. It was four in the afternoon.

During the break, Charlie unwound a little over a cup of coffee with his counselors, who tried their best to bolster his morale. Some people will ask, why did they let him take the stand? Because Charlie had his own rule of thumb regarding justice. He was innocent of this crime. Prostitution was literally repulsive to him, and he felt he should be freed from that stain and the charges against him. In his obsession to be freed, he underestimated Dewey and his ambition. Just as Charlie had his men and contacts in his world, Dewey was more than influential in his. On the other hand, because of the tremendous buildup by the prosecution, and of his nefarious reputation, not to take the stand—as far as he was concerned—would have been seen as admitting guilt. It was the lesser of two evils. Dewey, in the meantime, was conferring with his staff for a smash finale.

In the courtroom, Dewey stood at the table, rippling through his dossier, and pulled out a few papers. The courtroom was buzzing. Judge McCook's gavel went down; silence returned. No one knew what to expect next while Dewey—papers in his hand—walked back to the stand to continue the third degree.

Q: "Understand you've been paying your taxes?"
A: "Yes, I paid up a year and a half ago. I filed my returns for the last six years."

Dewey asked if Charlie's sudden burst of conscience, after cheating the government all these years, was because he knew the governor had started a massive investigation on the rackets. Charlie denied that was the reason and claimed he just decided it was time he did pay his taxes. Dewey kept jabbing at him, wanting to know why he had stopped at the six years. Wasn't it because he knew the statute of limitations expired in *six* years? Charlie stubbornly replied that he thought he had paid enough. Energetically, Dewey shook the papers in his hands and began shouting, "$15,000 for 1929, $16,500 for 1930, $20,000 from 1931 to 1934, and $22,500 for 1935! Did you just pick out the figures out of the sky?"

Charlie was just as agitated and retorted, "I paid the government more than I made at that time." Then more quietly, "I thought it was the proper amount to pay the government."

When Dewey made Charlie reveal that he did not pay state taxes, Dewey had the last word. "And that's because the federal government prosecutes big gangsters and the state does not!"

Charlie started to sputter his answer, but Dewey just turned back smiling. He had concluded his cross-examination.

Completely exhausted, Charlie stepped down from the stand, walked back to the bench, looked at his defense counselors, and said for all to hear, "Well . . . I did my best."

CHAPTER THIRTY-SIX

Everything that followed Charlie's testimony seemed to be unimportant, superfluous, even if the defense still had something to say—as though a huge balloon had slowly been deflated. One hears the sizzling sound but really waits for all the air to escape, finish, end. Therefore, it took a crazy personality like Joseph Barth to jolt the jury and court back to attention.

Barth was the janitor of the apartment in the East Seventies where the Martin woman (alias Joan Garry) had maintained her bordello. Brought to the stand as a minor witness by David Siegel, on behalf of Wahrman who was primarily accused of wrecking her place, Barth became the center of a bitter battle between prosecution and defense.

Under direct examination, Barth had stated that he had been offered hush money from the madam in exchange for closing his eyes and ears to the male traffic in her apartment, but Barth refused it. Further, he stated that he had no knowledge of her furniture having been smashed by the defendants as the Martin woman testified.

Until then, all went reasonably well; but the next day, he was recalled by Dewey, and the fireworks began. Dewey claimed the witness had visited his office desiring to change his testimony. Siegel protested that the witness's testimony had been tampered with by the state, and that the testimony should be considered concluded.

"I request that the witness not be recalled. That's the least Your Honor can do, and it's your duty to do it," wailed Siegel. The defendants exchanged disgusted looks while the defense lawyers frowned amongst themselves. Judge McCook denied the request. The defense team was extraordinary and, under normal circumstances, would have won easily.

Barth nervously took the stand again as Dewey smugly proceeded. With his eyes fixed intensely on the fidgety janitor, Dewey had him tell the court a different tale. Barth admitted that he had lied on the stand the day before, that the meeting with Mrs. Martin in Dewey's office had refreshed his memory. Still objecting, Siegel interposed that the witness had not even changed his clothes since he last testified, but Barth repeated, shamefully, that he had been in error the previous day. Then Dewey revealed other damaging facts. Barth had been in the Greystone

Park Insane Asylum for three months in 1931. With that bit of news, he turned to Siegel and, in his most contemptuous way, said, "He's *your* witness."

Siegel defiantly replied that he was not and asked instead that Judge McCook charge Barth with perjury. The judge declined the request. Siegel was a very angry lion as he approached Barth on the stand. In his interrogation, the court learned that Dewey's aides had used unorthodox methods in having a grand jury subpoena issued to Barth at practically eleven o'clock at night, to appear immediately in Dewey's office. There they had worked him over until four in the morning until he finally had agreed to the story that corroborated with that of Joan Martin—one of Dewey's precious key witnesses.

Continuing to blast Barth, Siegel pursued his line of questioning.

Q: "Yesterday, you said the woman offered you hush money?"
A: "Yes."
Q: "And you said you refused it?"
A: "Yes."
Q: "So, you lied yesterday when you said you never took ten dollars a week?"
A: "Yes, I lied. I didn't want to implicate myself."
Q: "Did anyone on the defense ask you to lie? Did Moe Wahrman, Abie's brother, who talked to you, ask you to lie? Did I ask you to lie? Did my assistant ask you to lie?"
A: "No . . . you told me to tell the truth."
Q: "Did we pay you?"
A: "No . . . you didn't."
Q: "All right now. You are sure we asked you to tell the truth and promised you nothing. Now, what did Mr. Dewey or his aides threaten would happen to you, if you didn't change your story?"
A: "They didn't threaten me."
Q: "Tell me just what was said to you at Mr. Dewey's office."
A: "They said my testimony didn't match up with Mrs. Garry's, and they wanted me to talk to her and try to remember what happened three years ago, try to make it match."

Certainly, Dewey had a way of having his witnesses say what suited him.

In an attempt to prove "Cokey Flo" Brown had lied when she stated she had known and met with Luciano in connection with the vice racket, Levy called Samuel J. Siegel, attorney for James Frederico, to the stand. Cokey Flo had admitted on the stand going into Siegel's office several times but maintained he had never questioned her regarding Luciano in the case.

Siegel instead testified that yes, she had come to his office to try to help her boyfriend, Frederico, and on the third visit, he asked her, "Where does Luciano fit into the picture?" And she had replied she didn't know. "Then I asked her if she knew him," continued Siegel, "and she had said . . . no . . . she had never seen him."

From the prosecution table, a stiff voice said, "No questions, Your Honor."

The last witness for the defense was patrolman George Heidt of the New York police force—a most reluctant one but, nevertheless, a witness for the defense. The defense's objectives in having him testify were threefold: the most important, if possible, to establish that Mildred Balitzer did not know Luciano; secondly, to dispute the fact that Gus Franco had accosted Mildred on the street, threatening her with death if she testified against Lucian; and lastly, to prove to the court and jury to what extent Dewey's aides went to keep their women witnesses happy—while waiting for the trial to begin. Under lock and key in the apartment Dewey had for them, Heidt guarded not only Mildred, but Thelma Jordan, Peggy Weil, and Jenny "the Factory" Fisher.

A never-tiring Levy began the direct examination. Embarrassed to the point of begging off, Heidt was forced to tell about his nightclubbing with the girls.

Q: "Did you take the girls to restaurants during the evening?"
A: "Yes. Sometimes we got back as late as two thirty in the morning, if we went to the movies."

Levy asked if he had taken Mildred to Leon and Eddie's as she had testified, and Heidt confirmed that he had. That was also the day she had stated that Franco threatened her.

Q: "What time did you get there?"
A: "At two thirty in the morning."
Q: "Who was with you?"
A: "Mildred and Sol Gelb, the assistant prosecutor."
Q: "How long did you stay there?"
A: "About three-quarters of an hour."
Q: "Did anyone approach her while you were with her from that time until you went to Leon and Eddie's?"
A: "No. We went directly to the building in a cab."

Q: "From noon until 2:30 a.m., had any strangers spoken to Mildred Balitzer in your presence?"
A: "No."

It was also ascertained that the several brandies Mildred had claimed she had at Leon and Eddie's turned out to be enough to get her somewhat drunk. The gang had left Leon and Eddie's around three fifteen for the Dizzy Club across the street; from there they had gone to the Club Richman and stayed until closing, with Mildred by then pretty well intoxicated. Contrary to what Mildred had said, Heidt admitted to other evenings out, and that Mildred definitely liked her booze. Levy also inquired about the night before the trial.

Q: "And was Mildred Harris again plied with drinks by you the night before she took the stand in the courtroom?"
A: "I wouldn't say, 'plied'."
Q: "Well, how many drinks, and drinks of what?"
A: "Twelve to fourteen drinks of brandy."

When asked if Mildred had been permitted to drink all she wanted, Heidt answered, "Not quite as much as she wanted." Levy nodded, indicating he understood, and then, to determine still another factor in her personalized treatment, asked:

Q: "Was she sober when she went into the Woolworth Building? Dewey's office?"
A: "Yes."
Q: "How did she come out of the building?"
A: "I don't know, Counselor. You place me in a funny position. You're asking me things that I'm not supposed to tell. This means my job."

Suddenly, everyone heard Dewey shouting sarcastically from his table, "Speak up! Speak up, Officer. It's your business to tell the truth!" Slightly relieved, Heidt responded.

A: "Well, she came out slightly intoxicated."
Q: "How many times?"
A: "Once or twice."
Q: "And at what time?"
A: "About two or three in the morning."

Now that Levy had unequivocally established that Mildred Balitzer was a lush and given drinks freely by permission of Dewey's staff, he pushed even harder.

> Q: "Did you ever hear Mildred Harris and Peggy Weil discuss Luciano?"
> A: "I'll say. That was the topic of conversation all the time. I had to walk away from them sometimes. They talked so much!"
> Q: "Well . . . what did you hear Mildred say?"
> A: "She asked Peggy if that bum eye of his was glass. How tall he was. Things like that."

"Your witness," emphasized Levy in a rather forced, polite tone.

Dewey, however, didn't seem to want to waste time with him but did extract from Heidt that he was reprimanded regarding Mildred's drinking. Heidt admitted, "Sol Gelb bawled me out a couple of times for feeding Milly too much booze."

Anxious to counteract Heidt's statement that no one approached Mildred on the street, Dewey dropped Heidt quickly to put his police partner, James F. Cooney, on the witness stand. According to Cooney, Mildred had been, indeed, accosted in his presence by what he called a menacing individual. Dewey turned around for all to see his wide smile. As usual, he thought he had won that round also and returned to his table pleased.

Moses Polakoff then rose from the defense counselors' table to address the court and jury and, on behalf of his colleagues, announced, "Your Honor, the defense rests."

No sooner were the words pronounced, everyone began talking at once, and Judge McCook had to bang his gavel several times before silence returned. Once in control, the judge announced that the summations would begin after a ten-minute recess.

Caesar Barra was a cannonball in shape and, as is the case with many his size, was limber and quick on his feet. In fact, he had jumped up practically a hundred times during the trial, only to be overruled constantly by Judge McCook. He was the first to address the court and jury in the summations, on behalf of Dave Betillo and Tommy "Bull" Pennochio, and caused some commotion with his daring statements. Barra looked sternly at the jury and told them that Dewey was using the trial to get Luciano for his own publicity to become governor of New York. He must have hit home because Dewey jumped up and protested wildly to Judge McCook that the charge was "absurd" and "preposterous." Strangely, the judge ordered Dewey to sit down. Barra, undisturbed by the interruption, continued to address the jurors, "You are not here as a nominating committee. You are not here to name Mr. Dewey or anyone else governor of this great state. Neither is it up to you to justify the spending of a large sum of money for this investigation."

Excitedly, he came to his point. "What is perjury to people like Dewey's pimps? What is perjury when it is sold to the prosecutor for the people of New York? Mr. Dewey told them they were peddlers, and he was the buyer, and I tell you they sold him a gold brick!" Barra looked directly at Judge McCook to make sure he was listening, as he added most earnestly, "I always understood it to be according to the best ethics of the American Bar that when a lawyer learns that his witness had conducted willful perjury, it is the duty of that advocate to call it to the attention of the court, and I have known of the disbarment of a lawyer, because he retained that information."

Finally, Barra concluded that he was resting his case on that important fact because the persons testifying against his clients had their "lips seared with perjury." Glancing at Dewey, he said, "I never would believe Mr. Dewey to be so dumb as to swallow hook, line, and sinker the propositions that these procurers made to him."

The defendants almost cheered him. He had expressed the sentiments of many of the defense lawyers, and as he returned to his seat, Barra was greeted with wide smiles of approval from everyone.

Next to speak was David Paley, attorney for Benny Spiller. He was brief, but he made the jurors laugh as he argued that Dewey's witnesses were all liars. Carried away with passion, he shouted, "But, while I don't believe a single one of them, if you believe them, then my client can't be guilty. Not one of the twenty-eight of Dewey's women witnesses said Benny ever put them in houses of prostitution, or took their earnings. Benny was a shylock. That and nothing more!"

Lorenzo Carlino was something else. They called him the loud speaker for the group. Strange, but his attacks against Dewey had a personal flavor. Not just professional rivalry—something different. Perhaps it was because he sincerely felt outright indignation about the injustices Dewey was performing. Whatever, his speech was very effective. He struck hard right from the beginning, charging that Dewey had kept his precious witnesses supplied with booze and drugs while they waited for trial. Carlino also charged him with suborning perjury. "If you can buy a Dewey prostitute, body and soul, for fifty cents," he shouted, "how much do you think it would cost to buy a few words from her on the witness stand?"

He hit hard at Dewey's vanity. "Mr. Dewey had the opportunity to do the state of New York the greatest service ever given a man to do.

And it has slipped through his fingers. Why? Because he had to gratify that vanity of his—he had to get one man. And to do it, he set free all those people who, he says, make up the prostitution machinery of New York. From the deals he has made, they are all going to be set free." Then, indignantly, he turned toward Dewey, pointing his finger. "You have legalized prostitution," he shouted, "by giving immunity to these prostitutes and bookers. You've given them carte blanche to go out and begin all over again, and you can't do a thing about it, because your hands are tied."

Carlino walked closer to Dewey, and shaking his fist under his nose, he exclaimed dramatically, "Here is a man of supreme ego and enormous vanity. You have seen him sitting here, smirking at the press table. You have seen him moving, oh so slowly and gracefully, as he performed before you like some fine snake, some beautiful cobra." Turning to the jury but keeping one eye on Dewey, he bellowed, "Much of this trial centers around the personality of the distinguished special prosecutor. He is the greatest actor I've ever seen in my day with a striking smoothness, perfect balance and poise.

"Mr. Dewey is the lawyer for all the people of the state of New York, but he has been guilty of suppressing evidence in this case. He refused to have the grand jury minutes brought into court. He concealed the Joe Bendix letters for two weeks, he declined to bring back Dave Miller into the courtroom to change his testimony after he caught him in perjury. Gentlemen," he continued gravely, "there is a terrible danger in trusting great power to the judgment of an immature boy, and after all, he is nothing more." And again wagged his finger at Dewey.

Then Carlino vigorously attacked Dewey and his assistants for their failure to take the stand to deny Ralph's charge that he was framed and threatened, if he wouldn't testify for them. "No assistant prosecutor dared to take the stand to deny the charges of a frame-up!" he shouted.

He reprimanded Dewey for keeping Ralph incommunicado for three days after his arrest while they tried to "proposition" Ralph to turn state's evidence. "The reason my client is being persecuted, as well as prosecuted, is because he refused to become part and parcel of a frame-up against these other defendants or some of them." Carlino told the court that obviously, when Ralph refused, "there was nothing for them to do but make him one of the defendants.

"If Ralph Liguori had been a part to their nefarious schemes, what a perfect picture Mr. Dewey would have had. He wouldn't have needed to put on the stand Cokey Flo, Mildred Balitzer, and Joe Bendix—Joe Bendix who was the biggest mistake Mr. Dewey ever had in a courtroom."

Lightly discussing Dotty's testimony, he accused her of trying "with her woman's wiles" to induce Ralph to lie for the prosecution. "When he refused," Carlino continued, "she turned against him, for hell hath no fury like a woman scorned." Then he startled everyone in the courtroom when he made the statement that he would however go easy on Dotty (by far the most damaging testimony against Ralph) and leave her to the other lawyers. "Do you know why? I'll tell you why!" he screamed at the jury. "It is because only this morning, that damned fool client of mine said, 'Go easy on Dotty. Don't knock her, Counselor. I still love the girl.' Believe me, gentlemen, I could have shot the damned fool through the head!" The jurors chuckled, and Ralph smiled sheepishly. Carlino walked up close to the railing of the jury box and intensely looked at them while he pleaded, "Gentlemen of the jury, do not send an innocent man to jail!"

He had spoken over two hours and had had the courtroom completely entranced by his speech. A great orator. When it was over, everyone caught his breath. Ralph felt very lucky to have Carlino. He was an exceptional person and did a superior job in defending him. Carlino took Ralph's innocence—what happened to him—like a personal affront. He was indeed an extraordinary human being.

James D. C. Murray, counselor for Jesse Jacobs and Meyer Berkman, had a different approach. Murray captivated the jurors with a little story to demonstrate that his clients, as bondsmen, had a legal right to accept bond payments from women. Murray compared the action to that of a department store salesman who took a down payment for a bed from a prostitute, and who agreed that the balance could be paid on the installment plan from her earnings while using the bed. He considered the bed a legal consideration, and the salesman had every right to take the money. "When Jesse Jacobs put up his money to bail out these women, he gave a legal consideration," he reasoned, "and is no more guilty of compulsory prostitution than would be the department store I have cited." Ralph and the defendants laughed, but he could see the jurors looked confused, to say the least. Judge McCook frowned.

One by one, the defense attorneys took turns defending their clients. Next was Samuel Siegel who, before delivering his main argument, attacked Dewey fiercely. "In my thirty-four years at the bar, I've never heard of a prosecutor supplying a witness with liquor as Mr. Dewey did!" He dismissed Dewey's claims that the vice ring was a colossal twelve-million-dollar-a-year business by citing figures given by witnesses. "I'll tell you why this has been painted to you as a gigantic racket!" he yelled. "It is done to justify Mr. Dewey's job."

Siegel stressed that it was not against the law for his client, James Frederico, to take money from madams to bond prostitutes in the event of arrest. "There existed no form of insurance for women of this sort against the risk of the profession—police raid and incarceration. Reputable bail bond houses refused the risk of bailing these unfortunates. My client, Jimmy Frederico, supplied that want. He bailed out prostitutes, yes. What of it?" he argued, waving his hands.

It was definitely another slant just as David P. Siegel, lawyer for Abe Wahrman, had his. As aggressive as ever, he emphasized the culpability of the three original squealers—Miller, Weiner, and Harris—who had turned state's evidence. "There you have the combination Mr. Dewey speaks about!" he shouted angrily. "They were the vice czars of New York, and they tried to make you believe these defendants were the real combination just so they could save their own skins." He touched on Cokey Flo's testimony (the letter) and her addiction to drugs and finally urged the jurors for fair play and a "verdict uncolored by any prejudice or sentiment."

Charlie had more than one lawyer, and at the moment, they had their heads together, whispering last-minute touches to the upcoming summation. Moses Polakoff, who was considered the brains, was joined by George Morton Levy, an eminent New York lawyer and brilliant mouthpiece. Charlie also had an elderly advisor with vast experience. Levy rose slowly and walked solemnly toward the jury box. Then dramatically, as befitting his speech, he charged that the prosecutor had created nothing but an atmosphere, "upon which Dewey hopes to convict these men, and he can't do it by evidence."

His twist was superb. He called Dewey a stage manager—a producer/writer who changed the script as he went along. It was burlesque (an extravaganza) with a cast of madams, pimps, and prostitutes. The star, he said, was Mildred Harris Balitzer who played more than one role. "I call her Sara Bernhardt Balitzer. We see her continually begging Simon Legree Luciano to free the bonds of her distinguished husband, Peter, so that he may not be stultified by a trade in women, which, by his own testimony, was paying two hundred dollars a week for the privilege of carrying on." Levy continued animatedly, "Down in Miami, begging Luciano to release her husband, Mildred played Little Eva!"

Levy reviewed Dewey's opening remarks—one of which was Dewey's claim that he would give evidence that Luciano had said he would turn over the business to Little Davey. "But," Levy jeered, "we never heard it here. And I'll tell you why. There was no actor who learned his lines on that part of the play, so it had to be eliminated from the script."

He went on to show significant differences between what Dewey said he would prove and what he actually did. "You didn't deliver what you promised, Mr. Dewey, and you made reckless promises."

Referring to the restaurant meeting, Levy pointed out, "Mr. Dewey told you in his opening that Charlie Luciano lived in regal splendor in his Waldorf Tower—so great a figure that even those nearest to him did not dare breathe his name. Yet, he showed you that Luciano went around telling his business on street corners, in dives, in restaurants, in front of dope fiends, and women he had only seen casually. Oh, no, gentlemen. You see, the play was altered. Parts were changed by the astute stage manager."

He mockingly brought out how Dewey had risen disgustedly, with great indignation when patrolman Heidt had revealed that Mildred Balitzer had been wined and dined. He also picked up on the Joe Bendix fiasco. "Tom Dewey is a brilliant man," Levy said sarcastically. "He knew that Joe Bendix is a liar, and he should have known it before he put Bendix on the stand. A twelve-year schoolboy could have detected it.

"I don't accuse Tom Dewey of deliberately suborning any witness. That would be unthinkable," Levy declared. "But he didn't have to do that. He was dealing with a class of people only too eager to find out what he wanted them to say."

Levy changed the argument, admitted frankly that Luciano had lied to obtain a pistol permit and a chauffeur's license, but that it had nothing to do with his guilt or innocence in this case.

"Gentlemen, there is prostitution in New York, and the evidence here is overwhelming that women were, indeed, booked into houses and bonded," Levy said earnestly. "Whether the bonding was legal or illegal, we are not concerned. Luciano is charged with being the brains of the outfit, but he had nothing to do with prostitution, booking, or bonding. That is where we stand.

"I predict that 80 percent of Mr. Dewey's summation will be atmosphere. I want you to consider Luciano as a human being, not an animal. Give this poor man the benefit of the doubt. He wanted to elevate himself and, of late, had been associating with the better element at the racetracks—and not with prostitutes and procurers.

"Luciano did not have to take the stand, and expose himself to every art and barb of the learned prosecutor," Levy exclaimed. "He knew that every act of his life would be disclosed, yet he took the witness stand. The case for the prosecution is unreliable and unstable, and you, men on the jury, cannot possibly find a verdict for the state on the evidence.

"Gentlemen of the jury, give Charles Luciano a square deal!"

Charlie was as pleased as he could be with his defense. Levy had given an excellent oration and deserved an ovation. The defendants almost clapped. It was already late (around a quarter to nine), and most everyone looked tired. They had heard enough for one day, and Ralph wondered if the jurors would remember everything when it was time to cast their votes. Judge McCook shut his desk lamp and adjourned the day's session until ten thirty the next day when Dewey, he announced, would begin his summation.

In the morning, Dewey arrived with his crew, nice and fresh, as if they had been polished up—especially Dewey who appeared immaculate and cocky. As Ralph sat listening, everything became like a mirage. There was Dewey with his hands in his vest pockets, marching back and forth in front of the jury box, sometimes gripping the railing, preaching dramatically; and Charlie looking bored at him, at times coldly with the kiss-of-death look. Then Judge McCook's face appeared, first speaking like a stern father, then in a palsy-walsy manner with the jurors. Superimposed were the defense lawyers moving up and down like jumping jacks, waving their hands and shouting their objections. Ralph couldn't concentrate. He had a terrible headache. The weeks of stress had caught up with him. Everything had become distorted, blurred. He looked at the witness box and saw Dotty's figure like an apparition, pale and fainting, as the matron appeared to help her. Then the scene dissolved to Charlie squirming in the box with Dewey prancing about. Ralph even saw himself shouting and pointing his finger at Dewey, and again, there was Dewey in front of the jury. That faded to Judge McCook wiping his brow and again to the defense counselors.

The noise in his head had become excruciating, so much so that Ralph placed his hands to his temples. He didn't know whether to laugh or cry at the scenes—both real and imaginary!

CHAPTER THIRTY-SEVEN

Ralph was tossing and turning in his bed; he could not sleep. In the darkness of his cell, he fumbled for his radio and switched it on for company. It was his direct contact with the outside world, and it was turned on constantly when he was confined to his cell.

"Give us the tools, and we'll do the job!" It was Winston Churchill on the radio speaking to America, who was still trying to stay out of World War II. But Hitler and Mussolini were making it more and more difficult. Nevertheless, America had become involved. President Roosevelt had asked the nation to become "the great arsenal of democracy" by keeping the Allies supplied with war materials. But he was soon stabbed in the back by Japan. The United States was not enjoying a particularly good relationship with the Japanese. It had extended credit to China, Japan's deadly enemy, and later placed an embargo on gasoline, iron, and steel to Japan. The Japanese were not happy about that, and when Tojo became premier of Japan, things took a turn for the worse. He was a military extremist, and while he was secretly planning to declare war on the United States, he sent his ambassador Namura and a special representative to talk peace with President Roosevelt's secretary of state, Cordell Hull. They were in the office talking peace while the Japanese fleet was quietly, secretly, moving toward Hawaii.

On December 7, 1941, launching the biggest surprise attack in history, the Japanese fleet, led by Vice Admiral Nagumo, started bombing Pearl Harbor in Hawaii. Bombs from the almost four hundred planes whirling overhead were dropped down on the U.S. Pacific Fleet. The American naval base, caught off guard, didn't know what hit them; they were completely unprepared. When the raid was over, the casualty list was heavy. Battleships such as the *Arizona*, *Oklahoma*, and *Utah* were destroyed. A total of eighteen U.S. ships were hit and almost 170 planes destroyed. Some four thousand people, including civilians, were either killed or wounded. President Roosevelt called it "a date which will live in infamy."

The United States was now forced into the war. The next day, December 8, 1941, the president signed the Declaration of War against

Japan; and a few days later, on December 11, the United States declared war on Germany and Italy. It was a shock to everyone.

Ralph listened to the news with tears in his eyes. There wasn't an inmate with a smile on his face. They would have been happy to fight in the war without a minute's notice. Instead, they worked twenty-four hours a day in the prison shops, making pants and shoes for the armed forces. Actually, all the U.S. prisons had their men working night and day to help the war effort.

Occasionally, there were blackouts. No one could light a cigarette after dark. Occasionally, they had air raid drills; and at the sound of the siren, the inmates rushed out of their cells. The authorities wanted to see how long it would take the prisoners to get out—in the event something should happen. Thank God, nothing ever did.

A short time after Pearl Harbor, Ralph received a letter from his sister telling him that his son, Joey, wanted to join the navy, but he wasn't of age. Then the next thing he heard, Joey had joined the army. Ralph felt badly, but he realized it had to do with a sense of duty. Sometime later, Joey sent Ralph a letter from England, telling him he was going to Germany. The inmates constantly spoke about the war during recreation. It was depressing, and they prayed that it would end—because in the beginning, things were not going well for America and its allies.

Then the French superliner the *Normandie*, which had been requisitioned by the U.S. to be turned into an aircraft carrier (and to be renamed USS *Lafayette*), was burned. There it lay, capsized in the Hudson River pier at West Forty-eighth Street, Manhattan. This was really too much. The Germans attempted to take credit for it and spread their propaganda, aiming at the American morale. The truth was that it was an accident caused by flames spreading rapidly from burning burlap bales containing kapok-filled life preservers, which had apparently caught fire by a burning torch used by the workers. Frank S. Hogan, Manhattan district attorney, after a thorough investigation, stated that there was no evidence of sabotage. The FBI, however, quietly continued their own investigation. Later they too concurred.

Having been the victim of falsehoods, Ralph was always upset when he heard some of the absurd accounts—as in the case of the *Normandie* being burnt down by Albert Anastasia, and that Charlie had given his word to do it. Simply not true! Many crimes could be traced to the men of the waterfront, but they would never help the enemy to do anything against America! Just fantastic stories. What is true is that some of the boys did help the Navy Intelligence at the waterfront—in fact, all along the coast. It was natural that they should do their patriotic duty. Charlie knew about it, but there was no planned operation as some people continue to insist. It may seem odd, but the gangsters all loved America and would do anything to help their country. The rackets were a thing apart.

Business was being run as usual, with the boys making out with ration stamps—but traitors to America, *never*; there was talk about Joe Zox being one of the key persons to help the Navy Intelligence during the war. Why not? He was head of the Fulton Fish Market and a bigwig in the unions. The boys had the ports in their pockets, and they were all friends of Charlie's. It was natural for them to do their part.

What was Dewey doing during the war? His term as district attorney had ended, but he didn't go after it again. He wanted to be free to prepare for the New York gubernatorial race, and he did. In August 1942, at the Republican Convention in Saratoga, Dewey was officially nominated their candidate for governor.

He made one of his classic promises, "Let me say right now that I shall devote the next four years exclusively to the service of the state of New York."

On the whole, his campaign was dull, apathetic. He did spark his speeches with talks of non-isolationism; he even talked favorably about social benefits (at least some). People, however, were primarily preoccupied with the war. Therefore, partially because the Democratic Party was not united behind their candidate John J. Bennett, and because Charlie had his secretive plans to get out of prison (something Ralph was not aware of at the moment), Dewey won! It was a great triumph for the Republican Party because it was the first time in twenty years that a Republican had succeeded in capturing the governorship of New York. The seat in Albany had been a Democratic powerhouse for a long time. Dewey may have become the governor, but he was not very popular, no matter how hard he worked at his trade. He was too cold, aloof. People just didn't take to him.

Charlie didn't waste time in prison. He hired a well-respected attorney of the New York Bar Association, George H. Wolf (also Frank Costello's lawyer), to represent him in another appeal. In the early days of February 1943, Wolf filed an appeal in the New York Supreme Court to reduce Charlie's sentence, based primarily on his good behavior and that of his family, stressing the point that Charlie had repented and showed signs of redeeming himself. It seemed to be destiny (or politically programmed) that Judge McCook should hear the appeal. McCook's eyebrows went up as Wolf also introduced his potent argument, without going into detail—the fact that consideration should be given because Charlie had helped the navy in the war effort. Even if Judge McCook had received confirmation of this, it apparently didn't sway him because on February 10, 1943, the appeal was denied. In his decision, however, McCook left a ray of hope when he stated that if Charlie continued to collaborate with the authorities, maintaining his record of good behavior in prison, it was possible that, in the future, clemency could be found justified by the executive—meaning Governor Dewey. Charlie knew the groundwork had been laid, and Ralph was still unaware of any intrigue.

In November 1942, the Allies had invaded North Africa, and subsequent war strategies had to be prepared. President Roosevelt and Prime Minister Winston Churchill met in Casablanca, Morocco, to do just that. The conference opened on January 14, 1943, and lasted ten days. In the end, one of their decisions was to invade Sicily as a stepping stone to the invasion of the mainland. Preliminary plans were laid out. General Dwight D. Eisenhower, supreme commander of the Allied Forces, was head of the military project Husky, the code name given to the Sicilian plan. The attacks were to be made in the southern ports of Licata and Gela by General George Patton, leading the U.S. Seventh Army, and on the eastern coast at Syracuse and Noto by General Montgomery, commanding Britain's Eighth Army. After months of preparation, the Allies invaded Sicily on July 10. Fighting took over a month, especially because the German garrison in Messina was tough to beat, but it fell on August 17, and finally, the Allies conquered Sicily.

In prison, many of the Sicilian and Italian Americans, including Ralph, kept abreast of the news, ears glued to their radios. Many of them had relatives in Sicily and Southern Italy and had kept ties with their homeland. Charlie, on the other hand, was completely out of touch with Sicily. To him, it was a forgotten land. He and Ralph felt they were Americans. It was no secret that most Sicilians were pro-American and wanted no part of Mussolini's war. They were ready-made collaborators for the Allies.

During recreation one day, the conversation turned to Vito Genovese, and Charlie wondered how he was making out in Italy during the war. Vito had gone to Italy shortly after the prostitution trial. He was implicated in the murder of a man named Ferdinand Boccia and decided to hightail it out of the States for a while. Vito also saw what Dewey had done to Charlie and wanted to stay away from his hatchet. With a pile of money fit for a king, he made his headquarters in Naples, not too far from the little town where he was born. While Charlie and Ralph were sweating it out in Dannemora, Vito was wheeling and dealing in Naples, playing ball with the Fascists to enhance his pockets. With them behind him, he had plenty of freedom to move about. He was a natural during the war to become the number one black market agent in the area. It was easy for a pro like him. Vito had been operating in Italy for seven years before the Allies invaded Sicily. Naturally, he went against the Fascists and, after the invasion, became a liaison officer (interpreter) for the Americans. He was well respected in the Allied Military Government. His luck ran out, however, when a young CID (the army's Criminal Intelligence Division) sergeant, Orange C. Dickey, discovered his black market activities. Vito was arrested in Foggia toward the end of 1944, and after keeping him on ice in Italy, Dickey finally received word to send him back to New York on the old Boccia murder rap. Ralph was still in Dannemora when this happened. Vito left on a ship leaving from Bari the early part of 1945. But he was acquitted. They had no witnesses to testify against him, and with Charlie in prison, he spread his wings to take on more and more of the command.

Many life-changing situations happened toward the latter part of 1944. Ralph received another letter from his son in which he told him that while combing the forests in Germany with two MPs, they caught some German soldiers. Joey disarmed one and wrote, "I could have killed that fellow like a dog, but, Dad, I refused to do it, because I felt he was a soldier like me, so I gave him a shot in the chin, and out he went. I wanted to show that Americans can also use their fists."

Ralph proudly read the letter to the men out in the yard, after which they howled with approval.

About this time, Ralph had finished preparing a new brief. He had worked on it for quite some time and wanted to get it to Armand—since he didn't know what was going to happen to him. The brief contained the points of law for an appeal and an outline of the mistakes made in Ralph's case. This was very important to Ralph, and he was anxious to know whether he could trust the situation. Ralph had a talk with Charlie. "I want to send my brief out with the priest's runner, Charlie . . . Do you think it's all right?" he asked.

Charlie looked at Ralph curiously but, without commenting, said, "Yeah . . . sure . . . give it to him. He'll see that it gets out."

When the runner came around, Ralph told him what he wanted to do and gave him the brief. The runner nodded and left. Although Ralph was uneasy about it all, he didn't suspect anything. A couple of days later, Ralph met the runner and, with some apprehension, asked him quietly, "Did you send the brief out? Did you give it to the priest?"

The runner acted as though he were in a hurry on some assignment and hastily replied that he had. Little did Ralph know that Charlie had intercepted the passage. The brief never got to Ralph's home.

Not too long after the incident, Ralph went to the mess hall for breakfast, and he didn't see Charlie. He began wondering if, perhaps, he was sick and had gone to the prison hospital. Later in the dye shop, a guard came up to Ralph and confidentially whispered, "Ralph . . . they took Charlie out early this morning."

"What?" Ralph exclaimed in an undertone. "Where did they take him?"

"He's been transferred to Comstat, Great Meadow."

Disguising his complete surprise, Ralph casually mumbled, "Oh, yeah? Well . . . at least he's closer to home." In fact, Comstat, which was a more lenient prison, was close to Albany—and to the governor's mansion. Ralph went on with his work, but his mind began working—thinking, thinking. Charlie had to have known he was being transferred. Why didn't he tell Ralph? They had always discussed things between them. Something was wrong! For two days, Ralph couldn't stop thinking. He had a foreboding feeling and somehow was sure that Dewey was involved. The second day, Armand came running. Ralph was called out to the visiting room and saw Armand's contorted face.

"Armand . . . what's wrong? You look like someone who's been through the wringer," Ralph asked, suspecting it had to do with Charlie.

"Ralph, what happened?" Armand gasped, trying to keep composed.

"What happened? Nothing," Ralph replied, waiting for Armand to tell him something.

"What do you mean nothing? It's all over the New York papers that you and Davey wanted to cut Charlie's face!" Armand ran nervous fingers through his hair.

"What!" Ralph practically shouted. "Who the hell ever said that? Look, there's the officer behind my shoulder. Ask him!" Ralph turned halfway around and spoke to the officer, "Officer, tell my brother. Did I try to harm Charlie?"

The officer was equally surprised. "Why, no, sir. They're the best of friends."

Ralph leaned forward and whispered to Armand, "Look . . . I don't know what's happening, but all I know is that Charlie has been transferred to Comstat. This had to be some kind of excuse to get him away. Don't worry. I haven't done anything wrong. I want to get out of here real bad! Did you get my brief?"

"What brief?" Armand asked, startled.

"You didn't get my brief through the priest?"

"Ralph . . . I haven't seen anything," Armand replied, perplexed.

Deciding not to burden his brother further, Ralph dismissed the subject and made light of it. Armand was relieved that Ralph hadn't spoiled his prison record and left.

Ralph went into depression. He hated enigmas. He didn't feel like talking to anyone; he stopped going out to the yard; instead, he remained in his cell and listened to the radio. He didn't know what he expected to hear, but he listened attentively until he thought the walls were closing in on him. His mind was very confused. He was both angered and hurt by Charlie's actions. Finally, he fell asleep.†

Dewey's promise to concentrate on the governorship was short-lived. In June 1944, he was nominated Republican candidate over Wendell Willkie for the presidency. There was no love or fanfare about it. Dewey had convinced them (cajoled them) into believing, with all his facts and figures and Gallop polls, that he was the only man to oust FDR. He tried very hard to persuade the American people; his speeches, however, didn't make sense to them because America was much more concerned with the war. Roosevelt, who had both the Pacific and European war theaters to worry about, didn't pay much attention to Dewey and, in the beginning, didn't do any campaigning. Ralph listened every evening to the newscasts—every hour until eleven o'clock. Whenever Dewey went on the air, the inmates in the cells around Ralph would yell, "Hey, Ralph . . . get on . . . get on!" They knew Ralph didn't want to miss him. Ralph personally felt Dewey had diarrhea of the mouth—attacking, attacking, attacking. Then President Roosevelt gave one of his famous speeches on the radio.

"People of America, my friends. A lot of things have been said in this campaign. They spoke about my wife, they spoke about my sons, they even spoke about my daughters-in-law, but when they speak about my little dog, Fala, I must defend him, because he can't speak for himself!"

The inmates all cheered. Almost knocked the prison down. The next day, Ralph was called into the warden's office because the guards heard Ralph's name being called out by the prisoners. The warden wanted to know what all the rumpus was about. Ralph gave a polite explanation, but he never forgot the incident.

Politically, America was not about to change horses in midstream, especially during such a crucial period, and Roosevelt won his unprecedented fourth term as president of the United States. Dewey returned to the governor's mansion and licked his wounds for a while.

---

† Contrary to other reports that Charlie Luciano was transferred to Great Meadow, Comstat Prison, on May 12, 1942, Ralph had always insisted, "It was a deal to change the rest of my life. Someone wrote that Charlie was transferred to Comstat Prison in 1942. That was another lie. He was with me in Dannemora, until the latter part of 1944."

During Ralph's last year in prison, he resembled a robot, a tired man at thirty-nine. The last mysterious events had taken their toll on him. His one thought was that of being released and beginning a new life. Finally, he came up for parole. Ralph's sentence had been seven and a half to fifteen years and with good conduct; they had given him four months a year off the maximum, which brought him up to ten years. It was also two-thirds of his sentence, and they couldn't hold him any longer. In the warden's quarters, Ralph stared at the parole board members propped erect in their seats, so sure of themselves, judges in his fate. The parole board (political appointees) had received their instructions, and Ralph was due for still another big surprise. The head of the board spoke patronizingly and informed Ralph that he would be granted parole, but the condition was that he be deported! Ralph thought his head would explode when he heard the words. Most of his life he had thought he had been born in America, and when his mother finally told him about the citizenship papers, it was too late. He was already involved in the prostitution case. They had him over a barrel—on technicalities. Ralph wanted to scream, *Isn't it enough that I was framed and have done practically ten years? Now they want me out of the country!*

The officer passively continued to advise Ralph that if he fought deportation proceedings, they would bring him back for violation of parole, and he would have to do five more years. *Hell,* Ralph thought, *then they probably would still want to deport me.* Someone shoved a piece of paper in front of Ralph to sign, acknowledging that he agreed to their terms. It was an extremely difficult moment for Ralph. He did not want to do five more years and still have the same problem hanging over his head. With a heavy heart, he signed, knowing he would definitely fight the deportation issue.

His family immediately obtained the services of a lawyer. About a week later, Ralph was taken to New York and turned over to the emigration authorities on Ellis Island. He arrived around midnight from Dannemora and proceeded directly to court for his hearing. Ralph's lawyer asked the court's indulgence since he was expecting his assistant to arrive with pertinent documentation. The judge was a benevolent person and granted a few minutes. After a short time, however, the judge said the hearing had to begin, and Ralph was called to the bench.

The first words out of the judge's mouth were, "Son . . . do you want to go to Italy?"

Ralph looked pleadingly at the judge. "No, Your Honor . . . I'd rather you send me to prison."

"Well, you're not going back to prison. You're going home where you belong!" the judge replied firmly.

One of the federal authorities, an FBI man, stood up and began to defame Ralph, stating that he was an undesirable, a racketeer, a non-American. He kept reading off a sheet, and it sounded as if Ralph was public enemy number one.

Ralph's lawyer jumped to his defense and mentioned that Ralph arrived in America when he was less than a year old; that his family was exemplary; that his prison record was excellent; that he had always claimed his innocence to the crime for which he was convicted; and that Ralph had a son in the U.S. Army fighting for America.

The judge turned to Ralph with sympathy, "Son, do you have a boy serving this country?"

"Yes, Your Honor."

"Where's your son now?"

"Your Honor, I don't know whether he's living or dead. The last time I heard from him, he wrote that he went into the invasion of Germany."

The judge banged his gavel, shouting, "This is a darn shame! I happen to know something about this man's previous case, and I'm not going to be the second goat!"

Then someone from the parole board rose from his seat to corroborate what the FBI man had stated, but the judge was impatient with him. Instead, he turned to Ralph and asked, "Have you anyone here from your family?"

"Yes, Your Honor . . . My sister is here."

The judge called out, "Ms. Liguori, would you please take the witness stand?" Anna stood straight with dignity, walked over, and took the stand. "Do you mind, Ms. Liguori," the judge continued, "if I ask you a few questions?"

"Not at all, Your Honor," Anna answered politely.

"Do you know the whereabouts of your nephew?"

"I'll have to say the same thing as my brother. We haven't heard anything for some time now. We're all worried about him."

"That's all, Ms. Liguori. Your brother will be home tomorrow!"

The judge was definitely on Ralph's side. He looked at everyone present and exclaimed again, "This is a darn shame. This man is a good man—American as anyone else sitting in this courtroom. I will not sign this warrant!" There were protests, but he banged his gavel.

Case dismissed.

Ralph was ecstatic. He thanked the judge over and over again, thanked his lawyer, and hugged Anna. A guard took him away to another part of Ellis Island—to a different room where he no longer would be deported to Italy.

The bliss Ralph felt didn't last long. In the wee hours of the morning, three Federal men arrived and handcuffed him, taking him into custody. Ralph protested. He wanted to know where they were taking him, but it was no use. They didn't answer, just dragged him away.

The judge had ruled in Ralph's favor, and he was to have gone home that day to his family. Instead, he was being shanghaied out of the country. Rage began to swell within him. If they didn't agree with the judge's ruling, then, according to the United States Constitution, Ralph was entitled to an appeal before they could arbitrarily deport him, as they were doing.

A bell rang in Ralph's head. It must be Dewey! He and his men were powerful. Ralph was sure they had programmed his exile. Dewey had to move Ralph *out* of the country because he knew once free, Ralph would have the opportunity to blackball him from there to kingdom come.

The Feds put Ralph on board the ocean liner the *Gripsholm*, which was sailing that very day for Italy. They didn't want to lose a precious second.

Ralph trembled with fury for what they were doing to him. He felt helpless, hopeless. Nothing, of course, was of any use; he was convinced. The special prosecutor was still giving commands, could not rest easily if Ralph remained a threat to his ambitions. Yet another campaign beckoned, and Dewey was determined to rid himself of his primary stumbling block—Ralph Liguori.

BOOK II

THE MEETING PLACE OF THE ENGLISH-SPEAKING WORLD
BROADWAY CLUB
EX COLIBRI
The most Modern & Smartest Night Club in Town.
BEST DRINKS - FLOOR SHOW
HOT & SWEET MUSIC
DANCING NIGHTLY FROM 9 PM
Via Boncompagni, 87 - Tel. 42433

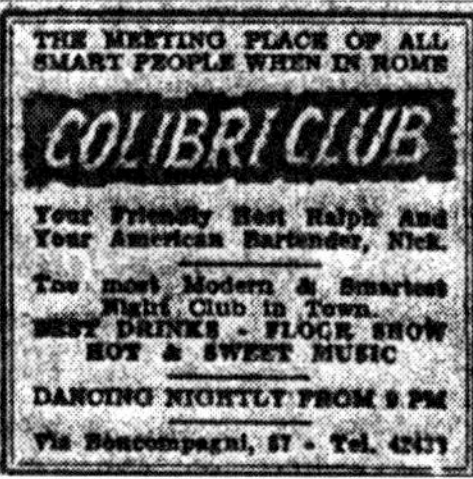

CLUBS MANAGED
BY RALPH LIGUORI
IN ROME, ITALY
WHILE IN EXILE

4 AUG 1948 CASINA
DELLE ROSE

4 AUG 1948
COLUMBIA CLUB

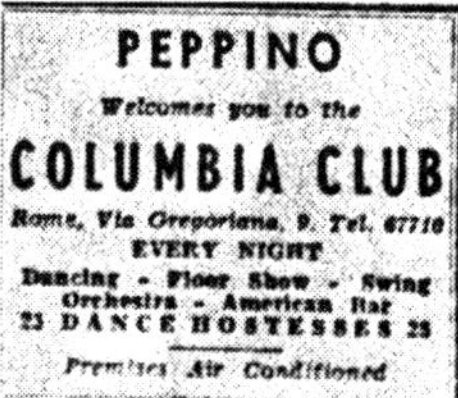

FORMERLY THE
"LA STIVA CLUB
OWNED BY RALPH

The American Legion Club
(Downstairs in Teatro Odescalchi)
Club Open from 4 P.M.
American Snack Bar
Hamburgers - Hot Dogs - Iced Beer
MUSIC EVERY NIGHT
DANCING SATURDAYS
Visiting Americans are Welcome

WHEN
IN
ROME

ENGLISH SPEAKING DRIVER
FOR
GOOD SIGHTSEEING TOUR
CALL OR WRITE

RALPH LIGUORI

190, VIA GIOLITTI
ROME

TEL. 7314086

CHAPTER THIRTY-EIGHT

On August 25, 1945, the ocean liner *Gripsholm* sailed from the American Export Lines's pier in Jersey City for distant shores. Aboard the vessel, Ralph as well as one hundred other deportees were handcuffed to prevent anyone from jumping ship out of desperation. They stood grimly at the railing, watching the Statue of Liberty fade into the distance. About five miles out, the handcuffs were finally taken off; the deportees walked around, scrutinizing the ship and their fellow passengers. The *Gripsholm* was a Swedish Red Cross ship, which acted also as a diplomatic exchange carrier during the war, and it was on one of its routine crossings. The first stop was Naples (Ralph's destination), then Greece, and, ultimately, Israel and Egypt. There was a mishmash of people on board (diplomats, missionaries, refugees returning home, military families); and of the almost fifteen hundred passengers, about half were deportees of one sort or another. Ralph's tearful family had rushed down to the pier to say good-bye, just in time before the ship sailed at six o'clock in the evening.

Carlino did not have an opportunity to appeal, or to write up a habeas corpus, or to perform any other legal action to stop the madness. Ralph was simply shanghaied out of the United States. He had two thousand dollars and the suit on his back—not very much to begin a new life in a foreign country alien to him in every way. Ralph didn't even know the language. He was given a decent cabin to himself and was grateful for the privacy. Once alone in his new quarters, Ralph threw himself on his bed, and his eyes became blurry. The tears slowly rolled down his cheeks as he silently cried himself to sleep.

The *Gripsholm* was also host to a large group of Greek nationals, deported as undesirables, who were on their way to Athens. The captain was afraid to let them out of their cabins for fear they would clash with the Italians. He called Ralph into his office for a consultation. Would it be all right for him to release the Greeks? He asked. Or did Ralph think there would be friction between the two groups? Ralph told the captain to allow the men full freedom on board because everyone had his own problems. No one was looking for additional troubles. They were all fellow sufferers under the skin, looking for peace. The captain relaxed his manner, thanked Ralph for his thoughts, and the next day, the Greeks began to mingle freely.

One afternoon, Ralph came upon a group of men shooting craps. A young Swede who worked on board decided he wanted to cut the game. A very rough, tough deportee, however, who was throwing the dice, sneered menacingly, "Get lost, Sonny, or you'll find yourself overboard!" Ingenuously, the Swede insisted. Ralph quickly grabbed the youth and pulled him aside.

"Listen, kid," Ralph pointed out firmly, "that guy just came out of prison, and you're no match for him. You'd better take a walk and mind your own business." The young sailor understood Ralph's message and never came back.

It was a voyage Ralph would remember all his life. The food wasn't bad; some days it was better than others, and it sure beat what they had been served at Dannemora. They did have some interesting company. Ralph looked out the portholes and stared wide-eyed at the sharks following the ship, as they did every day—scavengers, ready to devour the refuse, which was thrown out daily. Sometimes Ralph sat out on the deck with a fellow deportee, but mostly, he sat alone, meditating, trying to cope with his confused state of mind. He thought about where the hell he was going. After ten years in prison, he was being rewarded with a one-way trip to Italy! He didn't know where to find it on the map, and yet, he was being exiled there—to a country where he didn't know a soul, didn't know who he was going to meet or what he was going to do. Would he find work? How would he manage? Those questions continued to whirl around in his head. He had been advised that it would be difficult to find candy, sugar, and other goodies in Italy, so he purchased a suitcase on board and stocked up on whatever he could buy, including health and sanitary articles. Ralph really didn't know what he would be facing.

It took the *Gripsholm* almost two weeks just to cross the Atlantic because the ship was slowly navigating through the waters due to the mines still known to be active in the ocean. On the tenth of September, the ship arrived in Naples, coming through the most torrential storm Ralph had ever seen. It was rather frightening—all the bolts of lightning, the deafening clap and roar of thunder, the high waves breaking against the sides of the ship, and the rain. It seemed like an ocean upside down, the waters gushing around in torrents. A thorough deluge. The captain made a remark about Noah and the ark, and although Ralph was not the most religious man, he thought, *What does God have in mind this time?* The weather made it impossible for the *Gripsholm* to pull into the Bay of

Naples, and it had to ride at anchor some distance from shore. No one left the ship until the next day, when rowboats and small motorboats were provided to take the passengers ashore. As they approached the port, Ralph could see that it had been devastated by bombing; and as usual, a large crowd was waiting to greet those arriving. With a hammering heart, Ralph prepared himself for the unknown.

The port of Naples was one of the liveliest ports in Europe. Ralph knew the New York docks well, but Naples was something else. People hawked whatever little they had to sell after the bleak postwar days. Black market runners huddled here and there, making contacts, and military men wandered around with little Neapolitan boys chasing after them. It was a colorful and chaotic sight; the only serious expressions were on the faces of the Italian carabinieri (Italian State Police force) waiting for Ralph. There was also a group of American military police (MPs), and much to Ralph's surprise, out of the crowd, he heard voices calling out to him.

"Hey, Ralphy, I got a telegram saying you were coming."

"Hey, *paesano*, welcome to sunny Italy."

Ralph had barely made his way up to the wharf when a tall imposing carabinieri officer, flanked by two of his men, saluted and introduced himself. He informed Ralph that an uncle was waiting for him in a nearby hotel, and that they were to take him there. Next to him, a young man in civilian clothes extended his hand and embraced Ralph in the Italian fashion. In grammar school English, he told Ralph that he was his cousin Mario, his mother's sister's son. Ralph was shocked. He knew he had relatives in Rome, but he had never met them, didn't know them or anything about them. His logical thought was that his mother had immediately cabled them about his arrival. Ralph almost wept on the spot from the emotion surging within him; he no longer felt completely alone, abandoned. When he and Mario arrived at the small hotel near the port, Ralph found his uncle Emilio, his mother's brother, waiting to embrace him. Ralph would have recognized him anywhere; he looked so much like Agnes. Before leaving, the carabiniere advised Ralph that he had to report the next morning to the police commissioner at Naples headquarters for registration formalities. Ralph's uncle thanked the young officer, and once alone, the three relatives cried, laughed, embraced, and clasped one another's arms while Emilio and Mario babbled rapidly in Italian. Although Ralph knew a few words, he could not speak Italian; but with hand gestures and his cousin's limited English, they somehow communicated. Ralph could not have had a better welcoming committee. His uncle had reserved a room for him, so Ralph freshened up a bit before the happy trio took off for lunch at

Zia Teresa's Restaurant on the waterfront. Ralph devoured the delicious spread set before him, and just for a fleeting moment, his loving father crossed his mind. They sat there for over two hours, relaxing, taking time to become acquainted, until Ralph became restless. He thought he'd like to do some sightseeing. Emilio understood and returned to the hotel, leaving Mario and Ralph alone to explore Naples.

The harbor was destroyed, but the old fort, which had protected Naples in Roman times, was still standing. The men wandered over to take a closer look. The weather was still gray and cloudy, but they could see the shadow of Mount Vesuvius in the background. Ralph learned that the Bay of Naples was called Santa Lucia. Chuckling, he told his cousin he didn't know any saints, but sinners! Mario laughed. Then the two men hit all the nightclubs in town, met a couple of nice girls, and wound up at the hotel at six o'clock in the morning. Ten years in prison was a long time.

After breakfast, Ralph reported to police headquarters; and instead of receiving what he had expected would be a cold reception, he found a very sympathetic, accommodating commissioner who said he had heard something about Ralph's story. The commissioner smiled and extended his hand, assuring Ralph he would have no problems in Italy. Ralph considered himself very lucky; things were not as black as he had imagined. Emilio and Mario were waiting for him for the drive to Rome. In the early postwar years, one had to have a special permit to drive a car, that is, if one was lucky enough or rich enough to own one. Ralph's two uncles, well-known jewelers in Rome, had managed both.

The drive to Rome was a mixture of sights, especially along the coastline. It had been beautiful under normal circumstances, but Ralph now saw bombed structures, deserted hovels, carcasses of military vehicles here and there, rotting leather boots, and dirty helmets. As they traveled inland, the beautiful countryside offered splendid panoramas of green rolling hills—but always blighted here and there with ruins. When they arrived at Monte Cassino (about seventy-five miles south of Rome), the war came alive for Ralph. He had had his ears glued to the radio during that period in Dannemora, and there wasn't one phase of the war with which he wasn't familiar. He thought of his son, Joey, and his heart was heavy, for he still had not received word from him. Monte Cassino was one of Germany's last strongholds in Italy and successfully resisted the Allies for some time. An ultimatum was said to have been given before the Allies heavily bombarded it, sending hundreds of tons of explosives down, almost completely demolishing the monastery.

The destruction of the monastery by the Allies had remained controversial. The Germans before and after the bombing claimed they were not stationed in the monastery, having conceded to the Vatican's pleas that it be considered a neutral area. The Allies, however, disputed their claims that they were not in the monastery. Early in the war, President Roosevelt and the other Allied leaders—prompted by appeals from Pope Pius XII—had given instructions that historical monuments, including religious edifices, should be protected wherever possible if it did not seriously hamper Allied Military operations. General Eisenhower had issued his own orders relative to these pleadings and confirmed that historical monuments of a nation would be respected as long as the war permitted. "If, however," he insisted, "we have to choose between destroying famous buildings or sacrificing men's lives, then men's lives count infinitely more, and the buildings must go." This obviously was the case at Monte Cassino even though General Mark Wayne Clark later revealed that he thought it was a tragic mistake.

Ralph turned to Mario and asked where were the "Germani." He wanted to know where the Germans had made their headquarters. Mario couldn't understand Ralph, who kept repeating "Germani." Finally, Ralph blurted out, "Hitler . . . Hitler's *soldati* (soldiers)."

Mario laughed and said, "Oh, you mean the *Tedeschi*." And waved toward some buildings that had been razed to the ground. He patiently explained to Ralph that Germans in Italian are called *Tedeschi* and not *Germani*, as most Americans of Italian descent called them. They laughed over that one. Then Ralph's uncle, who obviously was well versed in Italian culture and history, began to enlighten him about Monte Cassino's ancient past. He told him that the Benedictine order was founded by St. Benedict about AD 529 when the saint fled persecution and found seclusion there. Even at that time it was a ruined city, but soon, St. Benedict built a monastery on the highest point of the town. It later became a cathedral and, sometime thereafter, became a national monument. It was supposed to have had a library filled with precious manuscripts and paintings, and their fate after the war was unknown. Ralph just listened because he knew nothing of those things. He just sighed and took his last look.

Rome in 1945 was not the hustling, bustling city it became more than a decade later. The Germans had surrendered to the Allies in May, ending the European phase of World War II; but most of Europe, including Italy, was devastated—not to mention the lives of most people. The Allies were generally true to their word during the war, had abstained from bombing the Eternal City, although some of the surrounding towns had been bombed. One exception, which Ralph saw later, was the bombing of the San Lorenzo district in Rome. The basilica there was practically demolished; even the Catholic Verano Cemetery next to the basilica was damaged as well as some of the buildings in the area, which were blown to smithereens. When the Allies arrived in Rome, the Italians had declared it an "open city," thereby avoiding any further destruction to its archeological and historical patrimony. This, of course, kept the Vatican intact.

Now just four months after the war, Ralph was driving into Rome—a Rome that still showed the signs of war. The Marshall Plan, which was to help rebuild war-torn Western Europe, was still a dream of Dean Acheson, but it was soon finalized. It was put into action in 1948 under George C. Marshall's guidance. As he had in Naples, Ralph saw black market stands along the streets of Rome, shoe shine boys bent over swinging their buffing rags, shining shoes and boots to a high polish as American GIs smiled down at them. American flags waved in the breeze here and there; beautiful girls hung on the arms of young Allied soldiers; and American jeeps were jogging down the streets. In the midst of it all, Ralph also saw hungry-looking people—men in jackets, which had seen better days—women with babushkas on their heads heading for church—and an occasional priest sauntering along in his long skirt with a group of Italian children at his heels. Most people were out of work, food was scarce, and survival was the game everyone played.

They drove straight to Mario's home on Via Dandolo in Trastevere, the southwestern part of Rome. It was a very large apartment in a huge building, and even though the times were bad, Ralph could see that his mother's sister, Mina, had been one of the privileged before the war. She along with other cousins gathered there to welcome Ralph to Rome. He also met his other jeweler uncle, Pio, who had temporarily left his business to join the family reunion. Everyone sat down to a wonderful lunch, which Aunt Mina had prepared and which, of course, started with pasta. It was almost like being home, and Ralph became misty-eyed thinking of his mother and how happy she would be if she could see him surrounded by her loved ones. A room was made ready for Ralph, and he soon retired for the evening (exhausted) to his new four walls.

The next morning, Ralph rose early, ready to stretch his legs around town. After walking up and down the main streets, he ended up at one of his uncle's jewelry stores in Piazza della Rotonda, across the street from the famous Pantheon—one of ancient Rome's architectural masterpieces. To his surprise, he found some GIs in the store and began talking to them. It was great to speak his own language; the soldiers' American slang was music to his ears. He learned where all the good nightclubs were from them and, that night, didn't waste any time in taking a personal look at one of them—the Colibri Club on Via Boncompagni, close to Piazza Fiume. Ralph found the place packed with military men. It was a beautiful club with an obviously good clientele; he later learned it was strictly for officers in the Allied Armed Forces. Ralph began to unwind, to break the shell built by his confinement in Dannemora. He was laughing again. The American soldiers made him forget, for a while, that he was exiled to a strange country.

During the weeks that followed, Ralph began making the rounds of the other clubs: Columbia Club on Via Gregoriana, off Piazza di Spagna; Nirvanetta on Via Maroniti near Largo Tritone; Casino delle Rose in the beautiful Villa Borghese Gardens; and Grotte Del Piccione off the Corso on Via della Vite. Clubs that soon would become an intricate part of Ralph's life in Rome.

With his winning personality, it wasn't long before Ralph made many friends among the officers and sometimes met them at one of the clubs. Naturally, he didn't fraternize only with the boys; he found himself some very beautiful girls. At thirty-nine, he had to make up for lost time. Dannemora had taken the best ten years of his life. Living with Aunt Mina soon cramped his style, so he spoke to his uncle Emilio about finding a place of his own. Emilio learned that above his store in the Hotel Abruzzi, there was a vacancy, and he was only too delighted about the arrangement; he was convinced with Ralph's presence (reputation), he would have ready-made protection from thieves. Apparently, word was out that Ralph Liguori, intimate friend of Charlie Luciano, was in Rome. About a month later, he kissed his aunt good-bye and moved to his new quarters. Like all mothers, she was apprehensive but gave her blessing; she understood that at his age, he would want some privacy, especially with all he had gone through.

The window in Ralph's new room was right above the jewelry store in the piazza, as Emilio had told him. Ralph opened it for some air and leaned out to gaze at the Pantheon in all its splendor. Of course, his uncle had filled him in on its history. Ralph mused over some of the facts. The Pantheon was a national shrine, first built about 27 to 25 BC by the Roman emperor Hadrian and was reconstructed and redesigned by the Roman statesman Agrippa between AD 120 to 125. A unique building. An open dome on top (twenty-seven feet in diameter) provided the only light. Although it boasted a majestic entrance, its unsurpassed beauty was inside, with its Corinthian columns and pilasters all around. The floors and walls were decorated with beautiful colored marble designs. It was used as a church by the Christians. Kings were buried there as well as the famous painter Raphael. Ralph promised himself to visit the Pantheon in the morning. As he stared at the fascinating structure, his thoughts wandered back to the States. He thought about Charlie and if and when he would ever see him again. He had a few things he wanted to straighten out with Charlie!

Ralph focused back on the Pantheon. Little did he know it would become the backdrop (the meeting place) for him and the man responsible for his exile in Rome.

CHAPTER THIRTY-NINE

Ralph's Rome sojourn was just beginning, and soon he found that he had become a drawing card for the clubs. His love for nightlife had not diminished in Dannemora. To him, it was still stimulating—an intoxicating atmosphere, especially now when he needed to release some of his bottled-up emotions, needed to feel alive, to feel like a man again. No matter how good one had it in prison (mainly through connections), it is nevertheless always a prison. One night at the Columbia Club, which had become home for the Allied Forces, Ralph was introduced to the Allied commissioner, Colonel Ross. Ralph liked him immediately, and all night long, the colonel kept pouring Ralph drinks to celebrate his liberation. It was a long time since Ralph had any whiskey; consequently, he became sick as a kid on his first binge. Ralph's circle of friends among the officers and GIs kept growing. His popularity became such that they went looking for him during the day at his uncle's jewelry store, which looked like another Allied headquarters. It was great for Ralph, but he still was without a job.

Colonel Ross assumed a protective role toward Ralph, becoming more or less his mentor. While nursing their drinks one evening at the Colabri Club, he carved the path for Ralph's future.

"Ralph, the GIs love you. You're a natural to manage these clubs around town. They click with you . . . People like you almost instantly."

Ralph stared at his drink, afraid to look up, wondering what the colonel had on his mind.

"Besides," he continued, "we'd like to have someone on our side in these clubs . . . to kind of see that our guys get a fair shake. I know you're looking for something to do, Ralph . . . so I've already talked to the owner of the Nirvanetta. He's ready to take you on."

Ralph was pleasantly surprised. Here was an important colonel in the U.S. Army—the Allied commissioner in Rome—giving him his trust. Ralph was not just an ex-con to him. His eyes full of appreciation, Ralph replied gratefully, "That's really big of you, Colonel. I don't have the words to thank you."

"Ralph . . . don't thank me. As I said, you're a natural for the job." The colonel clinked Ralph's glass with his in a salute. Just then, a few officers walked in and stopped by the table to say hello. The private talk had ended. After his good-byes, Ralph went straight to the Nirvanetta to conclude the deal—and what a deal! He could manage the club as he wished, as host to the Allied Forces. His hours would be flexible (something Ralph had insisted upon due to his phobia about confinement), and he would receive 10 percent of all the gross. Certainly not bad for a beginning!

Christmas was just around the corner, and Ralph's aunt Mina announced that he had to share Christmas Eve and Christmas Day with them—a strict family tradition in Italy. Ralph regretfully advised her he had business at the club on Christmas Eve, but he definitely would be with the family on Christmas Day. He wanted to give a great Christmas party, an old-fashioned celebration, for the boys away from home who, like his son somewhere in Germany, as well as himself, were displaced persons. With great enthusiasm, he began planning to make it a memorable night. He bought a huge pine tree to decorate. It was difficult to find all the trimmings because at that time, Christmas trees were not the custom in Italy. Italians, instead, decorated their homes, churches, and offices with the *presepio*, the Christmas nativity scene. Some of these, especially in churches (where small chapels were turned into a *presepio*), were works of art. Even those in private homes were elaborate with the little town of Bethlehem as the stage setting with townspeople, animals, and the traditional manger scene—Baby Jesus, Mary, Joseph, the three wise men—all carefully arranged in their places. With the help of some of his officer friends, Ralph was able to find everything he needed in the Army PX. To complete the atmosphere, Ralph had one GI dressed as Santa Claus, and the band managed to play American Christmas carols. It was a fantastic night with food and drinks on the house. The GIs later gathered around the tree and sang carols, hanging on to some of their Italian girlfriends who were entranced by the magic of an American Christmas Eve.

The war was finally over. The bad times, hopefully, were fading away; clouds were lifting and people began to think about normalizing their lives. Some of the soldiers were scheduled to return to their families, their jobs, and many would hopefully marry and have children. Ralph looked at them and again thought of Joey. It had been ten years since he had seen him. He wondered what he looked like after all this time and hoped that wherever he was, he was well taken care of on that special night. Interrupting his thoughts were the voices of several of the boys, calling out in unison for Ralph to join them under the tree. When he shook his head no, a young captain pulled Ralph by the arm toward the tree, and Ralph too began singing. He couldn't remember the last time he sang, and everyone laughed at his flat notes.

That carefree, happy ambience continued on Christmas Day with the family. Aunt Mina's house had been beautifully decorated, *presepio* and all, and gaiety filled the rooms. There was a concerted effort on everyone's part to overdo the festivities—perhaps as a subconscious force striving to compensate for all the terrible war years. Food was abundant. They all bowed their heads in silence as Ralph's uncle said grace; then everyone dug into the antipasto. Ralph couldn't keep track of the number of courses, and naturally, the wine flowed. Ralph felt a certain contentment. Christmas Eve was a big success and now this! He closed his eyes for a second and glimpsed a flash of the old days—a time when he was young and his father was still alive.

Nirvanetta was an attractive club. It had an indoor garden and a nightly floor show, which periodically changed. The regular dancers (twenty-five beautiful hostesses) mingled with the boys between acts, and Ralph saw many a romance bloom. It was crowded every night, and it was not uncommon to see many of the officers dropping by to see the action. Nirvanetta was successfully launched, and Ralph became known as the master host and manager. He also became considered a sort of mascot for the Allies; they went to him with their problems, and somehow, maybe miraculously, he solved them. As time passed, Ralph began to change their scrip (military money) for them. It had started as a favor to one of the boys; then others came. They went looking for him at the jewelry store; by now, everyone knew he lived upstairs. Ralph never took advantage of anyone; it would have been like cheating his own son. The colonels and the majors learned of his benevolent ways toward their men, and in no time, they were recommending him to the newcomers in town, sometimes giving him special jobs to do for them. Ralph was in his glory. He couldn't have been happier; he was a respected man again.

On his own time, Ralph made the rounds of restaurants in town, and there weren't many that he missed. Ralph loved to eat, had long possessed a sort of sensuous attachment to food, but that wasn't anything new. In New York, Charlie and he had been great bon vivants when it came to fine table delicacies. In prison, deprived of their fine habits, they still managed to eat better than the others—with the aid of their friends on the outside. Italians are great chefs by nature, and Ralph pampered himself with the best. He became a steady customer at some of the finer restaurants such as Passetto's and Fagiano's, to name two. Since fish was his favorite dish, Mario introduced him to a colorful restaurant at the seaside in Ostia Lido Beach, a few kilometers from Rome, called *Il Pescatore* (the Fisherman). Not since the days of Fulton's Fish Market had Ralph eaten such choice fish. He became an assiduous client, praising the chef to high heaven. During one of Ralph's numerous visits, the owner complained that the Americans (he was actually referring to *all* the Allied Forces) were not allowed to eat in his restaurant and asked if Ralph could help. Always careful about making promises he couldn't keep, Ralph said only that he would look into it. The next weekend, he invited the provost marshall (head of the MPs in Rome) out to dinner.

"Captain Vallendorf, I'm going to take you to a special restaurant for dinner."

"Where to, Ralph?"

"Out on the beach," Ralph replied.

"Out on the beach?" The officer laughed into the phone. "Okay, Ralph . . . you're not my type, but I'm, game."

The provost marshall was soon licking his fingers; he patted his stomach in delight and pulled out a cigarette to complete the ritual. Ralph knew it was now time to begin his talk.

"Captain, isn't it a shame that the Americans can't come out here to enjoy this seafood?"

"You're kidding?" Then Vollendorf's eyes leveled with Ralph's. "Oh, I get you . . . It's off-limits . . . right?"

"Right! It's a pity, because the food is great . . . and reasonable. It's a family run place . . . and besides, they're good people. Friends of my cousin."

"Okay, Ralph . . . you tell the owner that from tomorrow, this place will be ON limits," the provost marshall responded emphatically. The Il Pescatore was on its way to becoming a favorite haunt for many of the boys, as well as some officers who, perhaps, initially dropped in to check out the restaurant. After that, Ralph became known as a connoisseur of eating places. "Go ask Ralph!" was a common phrase among the boys.

There were many things happening at once to Ralph, and at that particular time, he fell in love. But really in love! Ever since Dotty had married, Ralph had felt a void, and suddenly, that all changed. Shortly after moving in to the Abruzi Hotel, he was standing outside the jewelry shop, sharing a smoke with a young GI, when he saw a spectacular-looking girl walk by, looking at the store. Tall and slender she was, with an easy-swinging gait that made her gorgeous mass of long black hair bounce gently behind her exquisite neck. Her red-and-white flowered dress hugged her bosom, which Ralph was sure had been molded by the gods, and the loosely fitted skirt clung and swayed just so as she swung by. The color of the dress accentuated her big brown eyes, rosy cheeks, and sensuous lips.

"Hubba-hubba," murmured the GI as his eyes followed her down the street.

She was the most sexually attractive woman Ralph had seen in ten long years, but he didn't say anything; he couldn't. He was struck. Something went *POW* inside him. He was hit by what the Italians call *Il colpo di fulmine* (a dramatic phrase meaning love at first sight). Ralph had to know who she was; he had to meet her. He began asking around the neighborhood—the barman, the grocer. His Italian was still not great, but the people all smiled, shaking their heads, as if they understood his dilemma. No one knew her, but he wouldn't give up. He asked Mario to help him. They finally traced the lovely girl down to an aunt who lived, as luck would have it, just up the street from Ralph's hotel. All he needed now was a proper introduction, and that was not easy—especially in those postwar days; a family girl was not allowed out after a certain hour. With all the military men floating around, a girl's reputation was at stake. At long last, through friends, Mario was able to find a contact, a distant relative of the aunt, and a proper meeting was arranged at the aunt's house.

The much-desired girl was not the shy type, but she behaved with decorum despite Ralph's obvious ardor. Ralph, on the other hand, was beside himself; so great was his passion, but he somehow managed to act the part of a worldly gentleman. During the rather stiff and proper conversation Ralph was discreetly having with the aunt, he discovered his new beloved had a sense of humor. She smiled at both of them sympathetically, as though she were not involved. He had the impression the lovely girl was intrigued by it all, and ultimately, she consented that some kind of courtship could begin. This was necessary, they all agreed, for the two to become better acquainted. Ralph learned her name was Elena, and that she came from Northern Italy, which, Ralph thought, probably accounted for that certain something different from the Roman girls he had met. Elena had only recently arrived in Rome to stay with her aunt and to hopefully find work. She was twenty-three years old—sixteen years younger than Ralph. There was no doubt in anyone's mind, especially Ralph's, that Elena would soon be his in marriage. There was no other way!

Ralph was consumed by thoughts of Elena, and he became possessive. He didn't want anyone else to see her. If he could have performed witchcraft, he would have made her invisible to everyone except to him. Her beauty had him mesmerized, and his jealousy was becoming absurd. At least once a day, he had to see her, even if for only five minutes, to feast his eyes upon her and to reassure himself. It was fortunate that he had the club to manage.

Apart from the turbulence in his heart, Ralph was doing well. At least he thought so, until that brisk November morning when he met her for their usual walk. Elena was as beautiful as ever but rather tense and somewhat aloof. Her lovely eyes revealed she was definitely agitated about something. Ralph decided to bide his time, to try to determine what had caused the change in her. They chatted uncomfortably as they walked toward the piazza with embarrassing pauses between them. They stopped for ice cream and continued walking in silence until Ralph couldn't take it any longer. He stopped dead in his tracks and demanded to know what was wrong. Elena's face became contorted, and her eyes opened wide with horror as she blurted out, "You're a gangster! Someone told me you're a gangster!"

Ralph's first reaction was one of rage, but he was smart enough to know that losing his temper wouldn't help. He was nevertheless speechless. They resumed their tormented walk toward the Pantheon and found a place to sit. Ralph took her hands gently and gazed at her with longing.

"Look . . . honey . . . I don't know who told you such nonsense . . . but I'm not a gangster," he said, selecting his words so that she could understand. Turning away in shame, he continued, "But I have been in prison." Painfully and succinctly, Ralph told her his sad tale. Elena remained mute, did not interrupt, her head bowed. Ralph stared at his clenched fists, then searched her eyes, fearing the worst. "Did you understand me?" he asked sadly. "My Italian is not so good." He tilted her chin so that he could see her misty eyes.

"Yes," Elena murmured, "but it doesn't matter. It's too late. I love you."

Ralph embraced her tenderly, and the matter was closed. Later, he discovered the evildoer who had tried to destroy his love and beat the hell out of him. It had been a long time since Ralph had used his fists.

The first part of the New Year was packed with a busy schedule. Ralph took stock of everything that had happened to him since his arrival in Rome and decided he couldn't complain. He had his girl, his job, money in his pocket, family and friends. He had temporarily pushed all his anxieties and insecurities to the back of his mind. But if only he could see Joey, he constantly thought. He was dying to see his son, and it was no secret to the Allied officers, for he talked incessantly about him—especially when he was with a group of young GIs or if he saw a young soldier who reminded him of Joey. The officers knew Ralph had not seen his son in ten years, and they tried to console him whenever he went into one of his monologues.

One evening at the Columbia Club, Ralph sat talking with a few officers, enjoying one last drink before calling it a night. He had been going on and on again about not having had a chance to be a father because he had spent ten years in prison. (Ralph had never allowed anyone to bring Joey to visit him in prison. He couldn't bear the thought of his son seeing him behind bars.) He did know that Joey had married at eighteen, "almost like his old man," Ralph had remarked. "The point is," Ralph continued to lament, "Joey lacked the strong guidance of a father . . . and believe me . . . I would have been strict. I know too much about life, also made too many mistakes, sometimes trusted the wrong people. I'll always be grateful to my mother and sister for bringing him up to be a good boy." Ralph was truly commiserating his fate when Colonel Ross, who had been listening attentively, stood up.

"Ralph, stop thinking about it, or you'll go crazy. Besides, I have a funny feeling you'll be seeing him soon. After all, Germany is not so far away." He winked, put on his cap, and left.

With Ralph's late-night schedule, he slept late in the morning, rising around ten o'clock. After showering, he walked to the corner bar to have his breakfast, Italian style: espresso coffee and a brioche. Then he went into the jewelry store to gab with his uncle before taking off to do any number of odds and ends for the military.

January in Rome can be unpredictable. It can give you a taste of sudden coldness, sharp and unpleasant, or it can kindle you with bright sun, offering the illusion that spring was just around the corner. It was one of those fantastically sunny mornings when a handsome young GI entered the jewelry store and stood just inside the door, shy and hesitating.

Ralph turned to see who had entered the shop and saw a uniformed boy.

"Need to change your scrip, kid?" he said matter-of-factly.

The young lad's eyes widened. "Dad . . . Dad . . . don't you recognize me?" He took off his cap and rushed forward. "It's me, Joey, your son!"

Dumbfounded, Ralph's heart skipped a beat; he stood staring, not believing his eyes. *This clean-cut, good-looking blond kid is my Joey?* he said to himself. Instinctively, he grabbed Joey's arms and searchingly looked into his face. "Joey . . . Joey . . . is it really you?" Ralph's eyes began to tear.

"Yeah, Dad . . . it's me," Joey laughed. They clutched each other in a tight embrace, both sobbing with joy.

Ralph's uncle rushed forward from around the counter to kiss and embrace Joey, chattering words of affection in Italian, which Joey obviously didn't understand. "Joey, this is your great uncle, your grandmother's brother," Ralph cried. Joey responded with still another big hug. He was a handsome lad, and Ralph was very proud that he had fought bravely for his country. To him, Joey was a hero. "Damn it, Joey," he continued, "you're a sight for sore eyes. I've been waiting for this moment a long, long time." Ralph's mind raced back to when Joey was a tot, to when he had fought to have him back, to the last time Joey had tears in his eyes when Ralph had told him he was going away for a while. Joey had been ten years old then, and yet here he was, a young man of twenty—and married.

"Look, Dad," Joey exclaimed, pulling out a couple of pictures from his wallet. "This is Jean . . . Jinnie, my wife. Beautiful, heh? And this is Baby Linda, your granddaughter," he added proudly.

"You mean I'm a GRANDFATHER?" Ralph practically screamed. "At my age?" Joey laughed.

As Ralph grinned in appreciation at the photos, his thoughts dissolved to his last months in Dannemora—to the time he received Joey's last letter (through the American Red Cross). Joey was being shipped to destination unknown, told his dad about his newborn child and how happy he was to learn that Ralph was finally going home.

Unfortunately, Ralph did not go home; he was instead exiled to Italy. Ralph never heard from Joey after that.

Noticing the faraway look in Ralph's face, Joey cried out, "Hey, Dad, anything wrong?"

Ralph looked up, his eyes smarting. "No, son, I'm just one very happy guy! Come on, let's go."

The party was on. Ralph couldn't wait to introduce Joey also to Elena, to the rest of the family, to his friends. He wanted to show him off to everyone! In a tender father-and-son chat, Ralph told Joey he had met a nice girl whom he intended to marry, and Joey must meet her. "You can call her Grandma," Ralph teased as they walked up the street to Elena's house. It was a meeting Ralph never forgot. When Elena opened the door, and Joey saw such a beautiful girl, he almost fainted. Elena looked both surprised and embarrassed when she learned the young soldier standing before her was Ralph's son. They were practically the same age.

"Daddy . . . where'd you get this lovely girl?" Joey said admiringly.

"Well, son . . . it took me a little time, but I finally found her." Ralph kissed Elena lightly on the cheek.

Elena threw a jacket over her shoulders, and the three merrily walked toward the piazza for their favorite ice cream. Ralph showed Joey the Pantheon, and as they entered, Ralph began speaking like a guide about all the things he had only recently learned himself. That night, he took Joey to the Nirvanetta Club and introduced him to everyone—proud as a peacock. (Elena was not allowed out at night, which suited Ralph because he did not want her in the clubs.) Joey had a great time dancing with the girls. Father and son were like two long-lost souls, savoring the taste of their long-lost love. As they made the rounds of the clubs, Joey met his father's friends and was equally proud to see Ralph so well liked and respected. Then his furlough, like all good things, had come to an end. Just the thought of losing Joey again made Ralph sick in the pit of his stomach. *There's only one man who can help me,* he thought and remembered that Colonel Ross had made it a point of wanting to meet Joey.

"Ralph, when he comes, bring him up to the office," he had said.

Colonel Ross's secretary greeted Ralph and Joey cordially, then picked up the phone to announce them. The door burst open, and an exuberant Colonel Ross came out, extending his hand. "So this is Joey. Well, boy . . . we've been waiting a long time to see you." He looked at Ralph and winked. Meanwhile, Joey had jumped up to salute him. "You know, your father has been pining away for you," the colonel added, amused. "We're happy to see one of his dreams come true. He deserves it."

Smiling at both of them, Ralph interrupted, "Colonel, can I talk to you for a minute . . . in private?"

"Sure, Ralph . . . come in." The colonel turned to Joey and smiled. "Good to see you, Joey. Have a good holiday." Again, they saluted.

Behind closed doors, Colonel Ross's eyes narrowed a bit. "What is it, Ralph? Something wrong? You should be happy these days."

"That's the problem . . . I am very happy," Ralph replied meekly. "Colonel Ross, you're the only person I can turn to. Joey's furlough is practically up. Can you . . . as a special favor to me . . . can you get an extension for him? He's got to go back in two days. Frankly, I can't bear it." Ralph was wearing his heart on his sleeve, and the colonel knew it.

"Well, Ralph . . . how much time do you want?" he asked matter-of-factly.

Ralph hesitated, not wanting to go overboard. "Oh . . . at least another three . . . four days?"

"I'm sorry, Ralph, I can't do it. I'd like to help you out." And he paused to watch Ralph's reaction. The color in Ralph's face drained. "But let me see . . ." The colonel was toying with him. "I'll tell you what I can do . . . How about a month?" Colonel Ross smiled broadly with satisfaction.

Ralph couldn't believe his ears. "Well, what are we waiting for?" He cried as the colonel picked up the phone to call the Seventh Infantry Allied Command in Frankfurt. In a brief conversation with Germany, he obtained an extension for Joey. The colonel was just as pleased as Ralph and cheerfully waved him out of the room.

Ralph, full of happiness, decided to play the same trick on his son.

As he walked out of the office, he put on a long face, and Joey jumped up in alarm. “Well, Dad?”

“I’m sorry, Joey . . . They won’t give me five . . . not even four days.”

“How much, Daddy? Not even two?” Joey moaned.

Ralph looked solemnly down at the floor, not wanting to betray himself. “No.”

“Gees . . . I heard you knew all the big shots in Rome, and you can’t get this favor for me?”

“No, Joey . . . The colonel said he’d give me only”—Ralph paused, took a deep breath—“a month!” he yelled, laughing at Joey.

“Yahoo!” Joey shouted, tossing his hat in the air. “Well, Daddy, let’s get a move on.” And the two lovebirds sailed out.

In the days that followed, Ralph considered himself the happiest man in the world. Everything was on the up and up. Joey, of course, eventually had to go back to Germany. After four and a half months, he returned to his wife and child, his grandmother, aunt and relatives, and to the United States of America.

Ralph was never to see Joey again.

CHAPTER FORTY

The Nirvanetta was a success, enjoying capacity crowds every night. Ralph's reputation was spreading to other clubs, which began clamoring for his services. (They were aware of his popularity with the Allied Forces.) Ralph finally consented to take a break from the Nirvanetta for a few months to assist in managing the Colibri Club and, simultaneously, the Casino delle Rose. The Casino delle Rose was larger than most of the downtown clubs, with a high outdoor dance floor set in the beautiful Villa Borghese Gardens. It had become a rendezvous place for many personalities. Ralph never forgot the evening Sophia Loren, at the start of her career, walked in with her then boyfriend (later husband) producer Carlo Ponti. Ralph did not know him. All he saw was a lovely young girl no more than sixteen, and he flatly refused to let her come into the club. The headwaiter approached Ralph and discreetly explained who they were, but Ralph, obsessed with obeying the laws in Italy, exclaimed, "I don't care *who* he is. *That* girl is too young to come in here!" Mr. Ponti and his entourage had a quiet conference with the owner, who calmly gave Ralph the okay, claiming full responsibility. Ralph finally had to give in. He remained at the Casino delle Rose until 1948.

The Colibri Club was probably his favorite. It was an elegant place and, at the same time, rather cozy—with a good clientele, composed mostly of Allied officers. It also became a meeting place for a drink—to relax, to unwind. Ralph had become acquainted with some of the top military brass in Rome. Colonel Ross, his mentor, was a regular; General Keel stopped in occasionally; and colonels Clark, Peeler, Taylor, as well as the provost marshall were good customers. Ralph enjoyed talking to them, and they began to know the *real* Ralph, which strengthened their trust in him. He remained on duty from ten in the evening to around four in the morning.

One chilly February morning, Ralph read in the newspaper that Charlie Luciano was being deported to Italy! The article stated that he had been transferred back to Sing Sing, after Dewey's pardon in January—a pardon given with the *excuse* that Charlie had helped the Allies during the war in Sicily. There was one condition however: Charlie was to be deported to Italy. If he violated this order (escaped, jumped ship, or whatever), he would be taken back to prison for another forty-one years. Immigration agents had taken Luciano to Ellis Island for the usual deportation proceedings before escorting him aboard the ocean freighter *Laura Keene*.

"Ah, Charlie, at least you knew what was in store for you!" Ralph remarked, growing more and more resentful as he continued to read. "You weren't shanghaied in the middle of the night!" There was a bitter taste in Ralph's mouth. He was forced to curb his inner fury regarding the injustice of his ten years in prison for something he didn't do, then denied parole due to obvious political pressures, and, ultimately, shanghaied out of the country on Dewey's orders. Who else but Dewey? Ralph was convinced of it. It was a tough pill to swallow for any man, and Ralph was obsessed by the illegality of it all. He repeatedly reviewed the trial in his mind, asking himself the same questions. Why didn't his brief get out of prison for his appeal? How did Charlie cleverly maneuver his pardon with his lawyers, using pretentious reasons, to be transferred to Great Meadow, in Comstock (oddly, in close proximity to the governor's mansion in Albany)? And why was it necessary to whisk Ralph away? Ralph couldn't wait to see Charlie face-to-face, to look him straight in the eyes to obtain some straight answers.

While Ralph was musing about Charlie, the last group of officers broke up their party. One major approached him at his corner table. "Hey, Ralph, you look tired . . . done in. Why don't you call it a night . . . I mean a day?" He laughed.

"Yeah . . . guess you're right," Ralph answered. "I am a little tired tonight." He dared not reveal what was really on his mind!

Joey was gone, but Ralph had his hands full with many boys, military and otherwise, always in need of one thing or another. One day at the Hotel Abruzzi, the hotel owner called Ralph, advising him there was a woman in the lobby who wanted to speak to him. When Ralph came down, he found a woman in her forties, although she looked much older. *No doubt scars of the war,* thought Ralph. She was shabbily but cleanly dressed in black, with heavy black stockings a little wrinkled at the ankle and shoes that needed care. He learned she was a widow with a young son of thirteen. She begged Ralph to put her boy to work in one of the clubs and kept brushing wisps of hair over her ears—wisps falling from a bun, which she had tried to pin neatly at the nape of her neck. Ralph took one look at the obviously poverty-stricken woman and was filled with charity. But he couldn't have her small boy in his clubs.

"Look, ma'am, I can't put your son to work in my clubs," Ralph explained kindly. "There are dancers, adult shows . . . a lot of drinking! He's too young. I just can't have him." He spoke in sympathetic tones but clearly was not about to have a young boy in that atmosphere. As he might have expected, the desperate woman began to weep, sobbing that she had no money, didn't know how she could manage. They were destitute. Ralph tried to give her some money, but she refused. She wanted her son to work! Well, Ralph had never turned anyone away, especially a woman in tears. Finally, against his better judgment, he complied with her request.

"*Va bene*, okay, signora." Ralph sighed. "*Facciamo la prova*, let's give it a try. Bring him to the Colibri Club tomorrow."

Ralph put him to work as a busboy helping the waiters, providing champagne bottles for them and whatever else they needed. He was sent home at eleven before the real action began. One night, while the lad was walking with four bottles of champagne on a tray, he turned his face toward the stage. When he saw one of the dancers doing a semistriptease, his mouth opened wide, and his eyes bulged. The hapless boy stumbled backwards and fell, while broken glass flew everywhere. The music, however, continued, and the girls went on dancing, uninterrupted. Ralph quickly rushed to the boy's side, helping him up off the floor, while one of the waiters hurriedly cleaned up the mess. In the back room, Ralph ordered the boy to go home. The youngster rebelled and lambasted him with a slew of Italian swear words, some of which even Ralph did not understand. There was no doubt the boy was a street urchin who had picked up a lot of wicked talk.

The next day, the boy's mother showed up to apologize, but Ralph flatly refused her. "No, signora, keep your son at home. I'll give you the money just the same." The grateful woman kissed Ralph's hands, and the boy kept his distance from the clubs.

About five months later, she was back in the hotel, crying to the owner that she had to see Mr. Ralph, that her son was dying in the hospital and needed penicillin. She obviously understood that Ralph was prey to sad stories.

The owner tried to calm her. "Don't be afraid. Ralph is a good man. If he can help you, he will." He called Ralph with a certain urgency in his voice, and when Ralph saw the woman, his first thought was, *Now what?* But as she sobbed her dreadful story, he was filled with compassion.

"Okay, okay, signora, be calm. I'll do the best I can!"

Ralph went directly to the Allied Commission office to see Colonel Ross. He was warmly greeted, as usual. "Colonel . . . I've got a problem to talk to you about," he said, almost breathlessly.

"Sure, Ralph . . . What is it?" The colonel smiled reassuringly, his brows going up slightly.

Ralph explained his latest dilemma, and as the colonel uttered a few comforting, positive words, he picked up the phone to call Frankfurt. Two hours later, Ralph went to the Allied Commission to retrieve the penicillin and took it directly to the hospital; the doctors were very grateful. When the boy saw Ralph later, he began to cry, sorry that he had cursed him in the club, apologizing and asking forgiveness. Ralph patted him on the cheek and told him to save his strength to get well. The fortunate boy lived to become a fine lad. He never forgot Ralph. And Ralph never forgot his good friend and mentor, Colonel Ross.

Ralph was running back and forth between the Colibri and the Casino delle Rose and occasionally stopped by the Nirvanetta to keep in touch. He sandwiched in all his chores for the military. He was also constantly looking for lodgings for incoming soldiers in order that they wouldn't wind up in sleazy flophouses. Ralph loved his now vocation because it involved contacts with people. He truly had become something of a mascot for the U.S. military in Rome.

He never, however, neglected his girl. Elena was still not completely his, and the role of the patient lover was new for him. Her scent permeated the air he breathed; the thought of her, the fragrance of her remained with him, seeped through his pores. He was burning the candles at both ends (slept very little), but Ralph had never felt so terrific. He and Elena never missed their *passeggiata* (walk) together. At times they went bicycling or took long hikes. The months rolled by, and suddenly, it was summer. The June sun was magnificent, inviting. Ralph took his beloved swimming at the Lido Beach in Ostia in the afternoons. Elena was great in everything she did. Between clowning around in the water, the two lovers lolled around the beach, trying to break down their language barrier. Ralph taught Elena English, and she kept repeating the Italian words to improve Ralph's pronunciation, which was pretty bad. Ralph was a new man, happy, even though there was still something very ambiguous, something undefined in his life; and at odd moments, he groped for the missing link, like a detective intent on solving his case.

Something was happening every night. The Colibri had gained publicity and had become the talk of the town. Anyone who was anybody at all went there. Even though the rest of Italy still displayed the scars of war (towns devastated, people homeless, desperate, paying the price for the ugly sins of man), Rome, the capitol, the Eternal City, was the first to bask in the sunshine to prosper (thanks to the Allied Forces). It had the good fortune to bounce back on its feet, even with the confusion of the Italian government (still in an unorganized state) and the local chaos. These things, however, were all foreign to Ralph. He was working day and night and leading a full life.

One particular night, the Colibri was jumping with servicemen three deep at the bar, and Ralph was enjoying a few laughs with a group of air force officers. Suddenly, around three in the morning, Ralph saw *the* man before him smiling from ear to ear.

"NO! It can't be . . . CHARLIE!"

Ralph leaped toward him. Charlie stretched out his arms and grabbed Ralph in a tight embrace. They kissed each other on the cheeks like two lost brothers. It was all they could do to not start weeping like two small babies.

"Ralphy . . . you son of a gun . . . Christ! It's great to see you!" Charlie cried, trying to control his emotion.

"When did you get here?" Ralph gasped, studying his friend. *He looks good,* thought Ralph, and he could see that Charlie had on a tailor-made suit. His face was fuller and not as pale as it had been in Dannemora.

"I've been in Italy since February. First I landed in Genoa, then I went to Sicily . . . ‡ Man . . . what I haven't been through." Charlie sighed.

"Christ . . . Charlie, why didn't you let me know?"

"Ralphy . . . I didn't want to make waves for you. Anyway . . . I wanted it to be a complete surprise!"

"Well, man, it sure is a surprise!" Ralph responded, embracing Charlie again.

Some of the officers were impressed by meeting Charlie. In his way, Charles Luciano had become, with his reputation, somewhat of a celebrity with all the notoriety surrounding his name. Bottles of champagne began popping as the two friends reminisced about the past for more than an hour, both overcome with emotion. Charlie and Ralph were, in effect, very close pals—although Ralph was not a business associate; the bonds between them were deeper, stronger. That was why Ralph's hurt was so intense, but at that moment, he was just happy—truly happy to see Charlie. He finally closed the doors to the public for some privacy.

"Charlie . . ." Ralph began quietly after the euphoria had died down. "What's this I read in the papers about you helping the war effort in the invasion of Sicily?" His gaze was fixed on Charlie's face, waiting for an explanation.

---

‡ Regulations for deportation state that prisoners must return to their place of birth. That's the reason Charlie went to Lercara Friddi in Sicily, and Ralph was sent to Rome.

"Ralph, you know . . . that's all a lot of bullshit. Dewey was paid off! A deal was made." And Charlie downed his drink.

"Yeah, Charlie, BUT—" Ralph wanted to pursue the issue.

"Ralphy . . ." Charlie interrupted gently, "let's forget about it tonight. Too complicated to talk about it now. Let's drink and be merry, for tomorrow's another day."

Ralph had always surmised that the Sicily affair was a trumped-up excuse, but he too didn't want to spoil their first night. Charlie was Charlie. He let the matter pass for the time being.

Charlie moved into a separate hotel (Hotel Milano) in the Piazza di Montecitorio, not far from the Italian Senate building and practically around the corner from Ralph. Ralph introduced Charlie to his uncles, cousins, and friends, and he could see Charlie was impressed with the way Ralph had set up shop in Rome. They met at the jewelry store in front of the Pantheon, and over a late breakfast, they gossiped like two old ladies at tea. Uncle Al and Tommy Dyke had sent Ralph their best regards. Charlie also filled him in on their friends, those who had died and those who were in and out of prison. He revealed that Bugsy Siegel had gone to Las Vegas to open up the Flamingo and was using up a great deal of the boys' money for the project. Ralph remembered Bugsy when he had a barbershop on West Forty-Seventh Street, but he had gone a long way since then. Bugsy Siegel was no pushover.

"Well, the thing is dragging out, and some of the guys are not satisfied," Charlie confided, speaking slowly, quietly. "Lansky reported that he's working with millions of dollars. I left Frank in charge. He's the guy with the brains and guts to keep things under control. I can rely on his judgment. He's sensible and fair. Some of the boys, however, are getting itchy. Then, there's Vito, who keeps pushing his weight around. Ever since he came back from Italy, he's been putting the screws into people. I think the Naples sun got to him. I've got to get back . . . somehow. Somehow," he repeated. Charlie looked up into space as though he were mentally reviewing his decisions. He was practically talking to himself.

These matters, however, didn't concern Ralph. Actually, Charlie never went into great detail about his personal business deals. He told Ralph only what he wanted to and oft times after the fact, treating him like a younger brother. At that moment, Ralph had many other things on his mind.

"Charlie . . . ," he tried to interrupt Charlie's ramblings.

"Being in prison didn't help things," Charlie continued, ignoring the interruption.

"Precisely, Charlie," Ralph replied, his lips tightened. Hell, he understood Charlie had his problems, but he too wanted some answers. "About Dewey," he asked rather rudely.

"Oh, Ralph . . ." Charlie looked at his friend sympathetically. "Let it go. You had fifteen, I had fifty years. We're out now. Let it go!" he said, dismissing the subject again. He definitely had many pressing things on his mind. There was one thing prison had taught Ralph, and that was patience. He knew that sooner or later, he would know the whole truth. Ralph told Charlie about Elena, and he seemed pleased to hear the news. It wasn't long, however, before Charlie also found himself a girl—a beautiful, ravishing, olive-skinned Roman girl who soon moved in to the Hotel Milano with him. Charlie didn't waste much time.

The September skies gave signs of the ending summer, and Ralph still hadn't received the answers from Charlie that he wanted. After breakfast one morning, Charlie and Ralph strolled toward the Pantheon. There were many Italians and soldiers hanging around the magnificent building, so they entered for privacy. As they stood in the center of the Pantheon, the sun's rays blazed through the open dome above their heads, illuminating the ancient, colored marble floors. Staring at the beautiful designs, Charlie spoke in low tones.

"Ralph, I'm going to be leaving for Cuba any day now."

"Cuba!" Ralph exclaimed.

"Yeah . . . I didn't say anything before, 'cause I wanted to make sure all the arrangements were ready."

Ralph immediately guessed that this must have been one of the angles Charlie thought about before being deported.

"To tell you the goddamn truth, Ralph," Charlie continued, "I planned this move before I left. Now it's time."

"Hell, Charlie . . . that's great!" Ralph tried not to raise his voice in the exciting news. "You'll be only a stone's throw away from home. It sure beats being across the ocean, far from the action—your family . . . and friends," he added solemnly.

"Well, you know . . . Batista is a very good friend . . . He's given me his full support in Havana. It can't be too soon, 'cause I got word that my presence is badly needed," Charlie looked away as he quietly, evenly added, "for a lot of pending matters." It was evident at that particular moment he wasn't going to elaborate.

Ralph remained silent. His mind was suddenly confused. Charlie knew Ralph was happy for him but also sensed his somewhat disturbed state. In fact, Ralph had acquired mixed emotions over Charlie. It had begun in prison after Charlie had been transferred and had haunted him ever since.

"Ralph, don't worry," Charlie said fraternally. "I won't forget you. I'll go first . . . then I'll let you know what's happening, and you can come after."

"Okay, Charlie . . . okay." Ralph nodded in consent.

They agreed to celebrate before Charlie's departure with the girls, with a sumptuous dinner at Fagiano's right around the corner from Charlie's hotel. Everyone was in a merry mood. They had quite a few laughs, except Charlie's girl, who would not accept the fact that her lover was leaving. Kept pretending it was all a big joke. Charlie was especially charming that night, full of high expectations. The gay foursome remained for some time, savoring their last reunion. They walked Elena home; then, standing in front of Charlie's hotel, saying good-bye, Charlie's girl cried out desperately, "Charleee . . . if you leave me, I cut your face!"

Charlie took one look at Ralph and laughed hysterically, which, of course, was contagious; and Ralph, instantly reading his mind, also burst into laughter. With all the tough guys Charlie knew in America, he had to come to Italy to be told by an Italian girl that *she'd* cut his face! The two pals continued laughing, but the unhappy woman didn't understand their sense of humor and fled into the hotel in tears.

Then Charlie became serious. "Ralphy . . . this is it. I'll see how things are over there, then if everything's okay, I'll write to you to come.

"But . . . remember . . . you wait till I write you. Okay?"

"Okay, Charlie. Happy landings." Ralph smiled warmly.

"Behave yourself, Ralphy." And they embraced in a final farewell.

A despondent Ralph walked back to his hotel in the impenetrable darkness of a moonless Roman night.

CHAPTER FORTY-ONE

Joey's departure, then Charlie's brief stay threw Ralph into a psychological crisis. One of the most successful ways to rid oneself of depression was to keep busy, Ralph knew, and he became a workaholic, working around the clock. The owner of the Columbia Club on Via Gregoriana (the first club he had visited upon his arrival in Rome) asked him to help promote it—to act as part-time host. It was no secret in Rome that the military boys went where Ralph was. His clubs had become the popular places. Ralph could never say no, and although he had his hands full, he arranged his schedule in order to divide his time among all the clubs. Some received more of his services than others, depending on his financial arrangements. For a special opener at the Columbia Club, Ralph had invited a few of his top brass friends for champagne on the house, and it was on that night that the provost marshall suggested he branch out on his own.

Rubbing his glass in his hands, he said, "As long as you can generate all this business for these clubs, Ralph . . . why don't you consider opening a place of your own? You know . . . we'd like to have a place where the boys can eat late at night, like when they come in from Germany. What do you say?" the provost marshall concluded with a smile.

Ralph looked at him appreciatively because he knew this was another confirmation of the trust bestowed upon him. "Well, I've been so damn busy that I've never really given it a thought . . . but . . . I guess I could look into it," Ralph replied, mulling over the idea. "I'd definitely need some help in running it, because I can't give up these other clubs, not for some time." Ralph paused for a moment; then more positively, he answered, "Sure . . . why not, Captain? I'll start looking for a place right away!" He raised his glass in agreement with the provost marshall.

Ralph talked it over with Elena, who agreed to help him in purchasing the food for the club (a chore she later faithfully did every morning at five o'clock). The idea mushroomed into reality, and Ralph enthusiastically began looking for a place. He found an interesting structure located right off one of the main streets, Via Del Corso on Via S.S. Apostolli, 20. It was a movie theater entrance; to one side was the cinema, and toward the back, about ten steps down, was the restaurant. The place was very rundown, but Ralph could see the possibilities. It was perfect—away from the street, which would help muffle the sounds of music and merriment in the early hours. The restaurant had about twenty portholes around the walls, and Ralph played with the idea of a ship's stowage. He finally decided on Stiva, which, translated, refers to the lower part of a ship. To Stiva he added the name of the theater: Odescalchi (named after an aristocratic Italian family). And it was baptized La Stiva Odescalchi. It became a chic super club, restaurant and bar.

Ralph was very proud of it. Upon entering, one saw the bar slightly elevated, and to the left were several booths. Separated by lush drapes was the dining area, which had a more elaborate booth effect. In the center was a dance floor backed on one side by a five-piece band. The kitchen was up a few steps to the right of the entrance. Ralph hired an exceptional cook (the most important element) who would leave (at the jewelry store) a list of all the things he needed: meat, vegetables, fruit, whatever. And Elena did the shopping regularly. Everyone in the club—the hatcheck girl, the bartender, waiters, and busboy—were all dressed in Italian Navy uniforms. The hours were from five o'clock in the afternoon until four in the morning. Ralph was at the restaurant every two or three days, depending on his schedule, but he had placed the management in the hands of a young man who was already doing errands and handling money for him. He had been highly recommended by family friends, and Ralph trusted him completely as the accountant for La Stiva.

While Ralph was hustling around Rome, Charlie was having his problems in Cuba. A few months later, in December, Ralph read in the newspapers that a reporter had spotted Charlie in Havana, and that the heat was on. He also received newspaper clippings from home about it; even columnist Drew Pearson wrote against Charlie, specifically that he was too close to the United States. Ralph felt sick for Charlie. He felt Charlie was being persecuted all over again.

Why the hell didn't they leave him alone? He fumed. Let him have his first Christmas outside of the pen in peace! It appeared as though the reporters were writing about Charlie every day; newspapers were having a field day with it. Most said he was too close for comfort, that it was easy for him to set up contacts in America, and some blatantly referred to narcotics traffic. Ralph was extremely upset about that. *The guy hardly lands there, and already they're trying to pin the narcotics racket on him,* Ralph seethed to himself. His spirits dampened for Charlie, for himself, because he feared his dream of the possibility of returning to the States one day (somehow linked with Charlie) was being annihilated. Was Charlie going to be plagued by the newest, most infamous charge?

The Bureau of Narcotics soon began charging that Charlie was organizing drug traffic and leaned on the State Department to put pressure on the Cuban government to expel Charlie. Fulgencio Batista, however, ex-president and dictator of Cuba and personal friend to Charlie, was an extremely powerful man. Although Ramon Grau San Martin was then president, he was a figurehead—Batista's man. Batista was still number one. No one made an important move without his okay, and Batista kept protecting Charlie. The State Department threatened to stop sending health legal drugs, much to the outrage of the Cubans, but Batista held fast and told Charlie, "It's a two-way street. They need our sugar." To clinch matters, he invited Charlie to stay with him. When rumors to this fact hit the capitol, the State Department rebelled furiously and declared, as a final warning, that if Luciano was not expelled, they would break diplomatic relations and recall their ambassador.

"Well, Ralph . . . at this stage of the game, I knew better," Charlie solemnly explained on his return to Rome.

Ralph had taken him to see La Stiva (which pleased Charlie); they sat, drowning their sorrows over some drinks, alone in a corner booth with only the bartender cleaning up. "I told Batista that I didn't want to cause hardships between the two countries. That it was no use fighting city hall. That Cuba was a tiny country compared to America, and needed to be at peace with one another."[§]

"How did he take it?" Ralph asked earnestly.

"How did Batista take it? Hell, how do you think *I* was feeling? The last thing I wanted to do was leave Cuba," Charlie moaned. "Well, Batista was mad as hell at what he called 'interference in internal affairs,' but he finally agreed to my sound judgment. He promised to protect my interests in Havana, and I was grateful for that."

"So then what happened?"

"Shit . . . before I know it, they put me on this lousy freighter, and I was pretty sore about that. But I won one battle. They wanted to deport me to Sicily . . . I mean make me stay there, but I said . . . no way! I still had to go to Lercara Friddi to present my documents to the carabinieri. You know . . . those are the rules. Then I hightailed it out of that hick town to Palermo, where I had to register other papers . . . I talked my way out of there to Naples, where I finally rested my weary bones. Man . . .

§ Neither of them had heard of Castro yet.

was I tired . . . I'd been through the mill, so I relaxed and took in sunny Napoli," he concluded with sort of a secret smile on his face, pleased about something.

Ralph stared at him for a moment and saw that he was on the thin side; his cheeks a little hollow, and he had lost a lot of weight; but despite everything, Charlie still looked young for his fifty years. Charlie continued to relate part of his Cuban experience; he saw some of his old friends who flew to Havana to be with him and miraculously, with everything going on, managed to have a nice Christmas with some of his closer pals. He also brought Ralph up-to-date about Bugsy Siegel's fiasco at the Flamingo in Las Vegas, at a semi-opening for the Christmas period, and how they had put him on a short probation to straighten things out. He again cursed Vito as a troublemaker (called him a rat bastard) and generally grumbled about his fate.

"Well . . . here I am, Ralph." He threw up his hands slightly in disgust.

Ralph didn't probe. He never concerned himself with all the gritty details of Charlie's world. After all, he was not a part of his so-called combination. Charlie always treated him as a younger brother, protecting him from certain things.

Shaking his head sadly, Ralph responded, "Charlie, I'm real sorry things turned out this way. I know how much you counted on getting back in shape there. Christ, what a rotten deal!" Ralph forgot his own troubles at that moment—the many personal questions surrounding his future. As he stared at his dear friend, he noticed a strange look of resignation on Charlie's face.

Charlie shrugged and said, "What the hell, Ralph, it was a wild dream, but . . ." He sighed. "You have to make the best of what life gives." Charlie acted as though he had another ace up his sleeve, but Ralph wasn't sure what.

Ralph finally drove him back to the San Giorgio Hotel where he had temporarily checked in. It was a first-class hotel near the railroad station (Stazione Termine), right in the heart of Rome.

During Charlie's absence, Ralph had acquired a car (he had been using a friend's jeep), but not in the normal way. He had had his first mishap with the clubs, and it was an American colonel who did him wrong. The colonel's bill had run up to a grand. A thousand dollars in those days was a lot of money, so Ralph advised him to settle it before the debt became even larger. The colonel agreed and gave Ralph a check. Ralph tried to cash it, but it bounced. The colonel didn't have sufficient funds. At first Ralph was furious because he had gone out of his way for the man, and he didn't appreciate being taken. Ralph was truly proud to be working with the military and was disappointed in the one rotten egg. It was his first catastrophe in Rome, and he was anxious to resolve the problem. He discovered that the colonel lived in Livorno, several miles up the coast from Rome, and drove there to see what he could do. Nothing! Ralph learned everything was in his wife's name. Ralph then spotted a beat-up motorcycle and a late '40s model Chevrolet, which looked as if part of it had been burned. Without hesitating, he confiscated both and took them back to Rome. Ralph had no trouble selling the motorcycle, but he kept the Chevy for himself. He was always a sucker for cars, and he had it overhauled completely, then painted it a beautiful green—a lush sea green. Everyone knew *that* was Ralph's car. It was always sparkling clean.

Sitting in the car, hearing the story, Charlie laughed, remembering how they used to take care of welchers in the early days of New York, when they were both young and starting out. Some fifteen years later, the colonel wrote Ralph a letter wanting to settle his old debt, no doubt a matter of conscience.

Needless to say, Charlie was way ahead of Ralph financially; he had his things going for him in the States, had money coming in from his gambling interests. Ralph, instead, was starting out fresh. But it didn't matter to Ralph because he wanted it to be the *right way* this time.

As Charlie closed the car door, he leaned in at the window and said, "Let's have lunch tomorrow. I'll meet you in front of the Pantheon at noon."

"Okay," Ralph replied.

"And . . . oh . . . bring Elena with you." Charlie winked.

"Yeah, sure," Ralph responded, and as he pulled away, he shook his head. Charlie was acting as if he had a surprise in store for him.

The taxi pulled up slowly in front of the Pantheon. Ralph saw Charlie lean over to pay the driver, then carefully step out from the driver's side. He waved to Ralph and Elena and smiled as he walked around the taxi to open the door for his companion. Ralph watched Elena, who was staring at the blonde head she saw through the back window. Then, gracefully, a lovely slender woman stepped out, hanging on to Charlie's hand as he gently ushered her out. "So, this is the surprise," Ralph said to himself as they walked up to him.

"Igea, this is my friend, Ralph," Charlie said politely.

In a ladylike manner, Igea Lissoni stretched out her hand and, in a soft voice, said, "*Molto lieta*, pleased to meet you. Charlie has told me all about you . . . and that you are also his godson." Her light, gentle eyes met Ralph's, expressing sincerity in her words.

"Pleased to meet you," Ralph replied smiling, and he noticed that Charlie was beaming from ear to ear. "Yes, it's true. He's my godfather," he added but was not about to tell her how it happened.

"And this is Elena, his fiancée," Charlie continued the introduction.

Igea turned her attention to Elena and exchanged niceties while they both gave each other the once-over. Igea wore a dark blue suit, which, to Elena's dressmaker eyes, was a little too tight, but it didn't detract from her refined look, in general. Her speech denoted a certain class about her as she measured her words, speaking quietly, calmly. Ralph also noticed that her almost frail five-foot-four frame went well with Charlie's build, and her alabaster skin contrasted becomingly with his Mediterranean looks. Charlie was at his best. He exuded charm, and the way he looked, touched, and spoke to Igea, Ralph knew that it was for real. Charlie knew how to handle women! In the past, Ralph had seen him charm his way into the hearts of many, but this was something different—not the usual sexual attraction like the Roman woman he had latched on to during his first arrival. Even his feelings for Gay Orlova, with whom Charlie had had a long relationship, was not the same burning love one has for the woman taken in marriage. No doubt about it, Charlie was hooked. The group had more than the semblance of a romantic foursome as they strolled over to Fagiano's Restaurant. While everyone slowly savored the spread of seafood delicacies, Ralph and Elena heard Charlie's brief love story. It was brief because Charlie never went into detail about his women. It was the same with Ralph. Their women were part of them and yet a thing apart—never to be involved in the business world.

With the two women present, however, the conversation, this time, was a little more open. They learned that as soon as Charlie had arrived in Naples, he had gone to a nightclub with friends to unwind after his hectic experience in Cuba and had met Igea. She was a leading chorus girl in a nightclub act that was on tour in Naples, and Charlie had instantly understood she was not the wiggling burlesque type, that her movements expressed classical training. In fact, Igea had her training at the ballet school of the La Scala Opera Company in Millan, where she was born. She had also danced in the opera company's corps de ballet but had left when she realized that there was more money and recognition in the nightclub circuit than at the opera house. Also in those days, to become a prima ballerina in Italy meant continued years of sacrifice without any guarantee of success. To Charlie's good fortune, he was at the right place, at the right time.

Contrary to other stories, it was love at first sight for both of them, so much so that she left the show without hesitation, packed her bags, and accompanied Charlie to Rome. Her family soon learned of Igea's romantic decision, and whether they approved or not, they accepted the situation, knowing that Igea was not a promiscuous girl. If she had fallen madly in love, then it had to be the real thing. As far as they were concerned, Igea and Charlie were married, and Igea's sister became a frequent visitor in Rome. According to Elena, Igea was truly in love, partially fascinated by this man, Charlie Luciano, who offered her a life of luxury—the status of a signora, lady of leisure, all combined with his passion for her. She didn't care about the twenty-two years age difference. (Igea had confided to Elena that she was born in 1920.) Also, she didn't care whether he married her or not, as long as they were together. Whether they had a private ceremony or not, Igea later wore a plain wedding band for all to see.

After a long leisurely lunch, the party finally broke up, and Charlie and Igea returned to their suite at the San Giorgio Hotel while Ralph walked Elena home. On the way to his hotel, Ralph made one big decision. Perhaps it was Charlie's love tryst acting as a stimulus, but Ralph promised himself he would marry soon.

Then BANG, startling news arrived. On June 20, 1947, Bugsy Siegel was riddled to death in his posh home in Beverly Hills by unknown assassins. Ralph felt some remorse, remembering him as a kid in New York, but Charlie didn't bat an eyelash. Ralph knew better not to ask questions. Anyway, what the hell did he care? It was none of his business. Bugsy, obviously, had to pay his dues. The ripples of the killing reached even across the ocean. Charlie was immediately summoned by the Italian police, but it was only a formality. They couldn't charge him with anything. It was just to appease Interpol. To make matters worse, who showed up in Rome but Virginia Hill, Bugsy's girlfriend. And the Italian police became agitated again. Charlie had stopped into the Colibri Club to see Ralph, and as they stood drinking at the bar, Virginia Hill walked in with some friends. Ralph happened to notice her as the group was being escorted to a table, and instantaneously, Charlie, glass in hand, followed his gaze. She was barely seated when she began to look around, her dark eyes darting here and there, checking the action. Suddenly, Virginia spotted Charlie, and her face turned the color of death, the mask of fear. She quickly mumbled something to her friends, and they scrambled out. It was the fastest exit Ralph had seen in a long time. She caused such a fuss rushing out that Ralph could not help commenting.

"Did you see that?"

"Yeah," Charlie replied with a smirk.

"I swear she looked familiar!" Ralph continued.

"That was Virginia Hill," Charlie coughed up a chuckle.

"Well . . . what the hell was that all about?" Ralph asked.

"Guess she's got a guilty conscience. She's either going or coming from Switzerland," he sneered, alluding to the money she probably had stashed away there. Perhaps Charlie was right, thought Ralph, because they learned from a friendly source that she had also gone to Paris. Suddenly, it hit Ralph; he remembered her. He used to see Virginia around New York with some of the boys. "She's still a good-looking broad," Ralph commented, "but not my type!"

"It's a good thing for you," laughed Charlie.

Virginia Hill ran straight to the Italian *questura* (police headquarters) to demand protection. She told them she was afraid of Luciano because he was the one who ordered the Bugsy Siegel killing. The Italian police commissioner frowned over the whole episode but could not disregard her accusations. He ordered protection for her. Ralph was automatically involved, for he was erroneously known as Charlie's *luogotenente* (lieutenant) and *braccio destra* (right-hand man) by the Italian newspapers and policemen. Charlie and Ralph were followed night and day. They couldn't walk the streets without having a tail behind them. Even the FBI was in town to surveil them. It was a very discouraging period. Finally, when the police forces couldn't pin anything on them, they tired of the affair; and when the Hill woman left for the States to act as the bereaved beloved of Bugsy, things eased up a bit for Charlie and Ralph.

Because of the Kefauver hearings, where the gun moll was subpoenaed to appear, Hill wound up behind the eight ball for blabbing about her money. The Federal agents charged her with income tax evasion. Virginia Hill's unhappy existence and/or her conscience caught up with her. She managed, after several attempts, to take enough pills to call it the end. Virginia Hill died of an overdose in 1966.

CHAPTER FORTY-TWO

Ralph and Elena chose an ancient basilica, Santa Croce (Holy Cross) in Gerusalemme, for their wedding; and as the name implied, it contained relics of the Holy Cross of Christ. The basilica is a beautiful Baroque structure whose origin dates back to the empress Saint Helena in the fourth century. She had brought back soil from Jerusalem—precisely from Calvary—to cover the grounds of the basilica she had planned. Since then, it has been enlarged, restored, and, after centuries, still stands erect in all its architectural splendor. A solid construction. And that's what Ralph desired for his marriage. Something for keeps, and he didn't want anyone or anything to spoil it. There were no invitations. In fact, Charlie knew he was going to take the step, but he didn't participate. It was top secret, with only two witnesses present. Ralph didn't want his wedding day to be made public, afraid of the publicity with probable headlines screaming: CHARLIE LUCIANO'S LIEUTENANT, RALPH LIGUORI, TAKES ITALIAN BRIDE. No photographers and no reporters.

Elena was beautiful, radiant as all brides. The church was practically empty; soft lights hit the beautiful frescoes, which forgotten artists had immortalized, and as they knelt in silence with only the ghosts of the past watching, a young priest joined them in the holy sacrament of marriage. It was beautiful, simple, and true—unstained by petty gossip. The basilica, San Croce, not only contained the religious relics (signs of the Passion of Christ), but also a beam of the cross of the Good Thief. Ralph's mind flashed back to Dannemora and Father Hyland—to the time the inmates built the church of Saint Dismas, the Good Thief. He thought it was sort of symbolic, and although not a devout man, Ralph became very fond of that church.

There was no time for a honeymoon, but that night, Ralph took his beloved to his hotel room, which had been especially prepared with flowers, fruit, and champagne. Ralph closed the door quietly and leaned his back against it, staring at Elena in all her white splendor as she slowly approached the bed. She stood there immobile, then turned toward Ralph and smiled sweetly. His heart took a giant leap, but he was lost, his mind confused. With all the women he had had in his life, here he had one without experience (a virgin); and it was new to him, fascinating, stimulating, and, at the same time, scary. He wanted a beautiful first night—a truly sensational one to consummate his passion and his marriage. He was sure their mutual love would overcome all barriers.

"Ralph, help me," Elena called bewitchingly.

Ralph walked over and switched on the bed lamps, then turned off the ceiling light to create a more subdued atmosphere, casting flirting shadows into the four corners of the room.

"Help me," she repeated demurely, sitting on the edge of the bed, trying to unzip her dress.

Ralph timidly went to her and gently helped her to undress. In so doing, his senses returned, and he began kissing her bare shoulders. He turned her slightly toward him and pressed his lips to her ear, her neck, slowly leading to her sensuous parted lips. As he engulfed her tender mouth, he touched the softness of her full breast, and his passion soared.

Elena gently pulled away, took his hands lovingly, raised him from the bed, and when they were both on their feet, she mischievously pushed him into the bathroom.

Ralph wasn't sure whether it was shyness on her part to finish undressing on her own or whether she was simply afraid.

When he reentered the room, the lights were out; it was completely dark, except for some streaks of light fighting their way through the blinds. Ralph slipped into bed and found Elena lying on her back, her eyes glistening. As he tenderly pulled her to him, he was pleasantly surprised to find her body was bare of all the feminine frivolities, and the contact of her flesh enflamed his own. He felt her silken body quiver at his touch and reassuringly took her into his arms. Elena, in response to her husband's passion, brazenly extended her legs to grasp Ralph's, bringing their bodies into a oneness. He loved her eagerness, which aroused his excitement, making him swing gracefully on top of her. She clung to him, enraptured, and he gently prepared her for the moment he would transport her to the height of ecstasy. As he parted her limbs and carefully took her, she gasped—half in pain, half in blissfulness. At that moment, he felt an undefined satisfaction surging throughout his being. She drew him closer with her arms, pressed him tighter to her breasts, not wanting to release her man. Ralph made no attempt to escape his enslavement.

It was September. Enter Autumn. The sweet climate promised a beautiful Indian summer, prolonging a happy period. And Ralph wanted his life to continue its good course. It was important to him. Optimistically, he kept plugging away, but 1947 had given him a jolt when the Hill woman blew into town. At the time, he sensed she was a bad omen. He was having problems with his club, La Stiva Odescalchi (it wasn't making money), and began to suspect that he was being taken by his accountant. Ralph was shelling out, but the profits didn't add up. He was becoming a little uneasy. But because he trusted the boy, he played a waiting game.

Charlie took Igea quite often to La Stiva; he loved to eat there because the chef was close to being a cordon bleu chef. He improvised dishes for Charlie whenever he had time. It was not unusual for Ralph to meet them for lunch. One day, he joined them for a drink and sat facing the bar. As they made small talk, Ralph kept staring at the bottles of whisky lined up on the shelf behind the bartender. Charlie noticed they had lost Ralph and said, "Hey, Ralph, stop thinking about work and relax for a change." Ralph nodded absently and kept staring at the Seagram's bottle; the color looked rather pale. *It could be the way the light is hitting it,* he thought. There was one way to find out. He called the bartender to bring him a glass of Seagram's. He didn't want to expose his suspicions, but the whisky was so watered down that he wanted to throw the glass against the wall. He was furious. Here he was breaking his back to prove himself, to do good, to demonstrate that people could trust him; and in his *own* club, he was being cheated, along with the customers.

Ralph clenched the glass when he saw his account manager coming down the stairs from the kitchen. He was a good-looking boy, clean-cut, and Ralph noticed that lately, he had started dressing very well. He saw Ralph immediately and smiled as he came toward him. "Ralph, I didn't know you were here. I was about to call you. That damn refrigerator is broken again."

"Again?" Ralph snapped, irritated. "Well, get it fixed!" It was odd; only three days before, he had told Ralph the refrigerator had broken down, and Ralph had given him money to repair it.

"Okay, Ralph, I'll get on it right away." As he walked away, he nodded to Charlie, who nodded back, silently observing everything, but not a word was spoken.

Ralph did not let it pass this time. It took a few more days of suspicion, and things began coming to a head. Ralph was being solicited for bills he thought he had paid, and when he checked the restaurant books, he found they were registered as paid. In further investigations, he noted that other paid bills were padded. On top of all this, Ralph could not swallow the fact that his whisky was diluted.

He picked up the phone to call the embezzler and sharply dictated.

"Bring the club keys down to my uncle's store. I don't want to see you anymore—not in the club, nowhere! Do you get me?" Ralph banged down the receiver with anger, not wanting to hear another word. To Ralph, the boy had done it raw. The accountant must have been dumbfounded, being caught off guard like that, because a week later, he tried to see Ralph at the Columbia Club. The doorman brought him the news, and Ralph snapped back, "Tell him to go away. I don't want to see him, ever!"

"But, Ralph . . . ," the doorman interrupted, "he told me he's been sick."

"Tell him to drop dead!" Ralph was hurt; he had had so much faith in the boy when he took the club and remembered his words. "Look, there's no boss here. Behave yourself and I'll take good care of you. But remember, walk straight." The entire affair was very depressing. Ralph closed the club. It was the only way.

Ralph, however, didn't have much time to be depressed. He was too busy; besides, he was still in the honeymoon stage. Elena was also disappointed in the boy, but she never interfered in Ralph's business. It turned his stomach when he thought about it. He and Charlie were discussing it alone at lunch, and apart from trying to console Ralph, Charlie was giving him the usual brotherly advice, "Ralph, you'll never learn. You can't give your complete trust to anyone. Man is what he is . . . corruptible!"

That, I suppose, includes you too, Ralph bitterly thought. He looked up from his plate and rather heatedly said, "Yeah, like ending up doing time for something I didn't do . . . and being shanghaied out of the States!"

Charlie was taken aback but again tried to avoid the subject, but for the first time, Ralph saw real remorse on his face. "Ralph . . . like I said," and he repeated the same phrases, "you had fifteen years . . . I had fifty . . . What's the difference? We're out now. Let's try and forget the whole thing."

"How the hell am I going to forget the ten years I did? And not only that . . . the worst thing . . . to go to a country I never knew." Having to close the club had definitely put Ralph in a bad mood.

With infinite patience, Charlie solemnly responded, "Let's forget it . . . you know . . . Let's try to make the best of it." He tried to calm Ralph, but suddenly, he looked older, unusually distressed.

Soon after this heated but unfinished conversation, three gentlemen whom Ralph knew slightly from the clubs came down to the Nirvanetta: the commander of the American Legion in Rome, Carmen Casolini; the chief of the American Export Lines, "Reggie" Perkins, an impressive guy standing six feet; and another gentleman from the American Express. One of them asked Ralph, "Can you do us a favor, Ralph?"

"Sure, why not? If I can . . ."

"We're looking for a club—a nice place. You know all the places around here . . ."

"You're the one guy we feel can give us some good information," said another.

"We want to open a club, an American Legion club," joined in the third.

Ralph did not suspect, at the moment, that they had been tipped off regarding the closure of his club. "Look, I have a place I just closed a few weeks ago," he replied in a businesslike manner. "You look at it. If you like it, you can have it."

The men appeared very pleased and very anxious to see the place, so Ralph made an appointment for the next day. As Ralph led them into the club, he felt nausea again thinking about his bad luck, but he was able to shrug it off. The three men were enthusiastic in their appraisal when they saw the interior, its layout. "Oh, boy . . . Ralph, this is just what we've been looking for!"

Instantly, Ralph's thoughts went to Joey—of how patriotic he was—and decided he would be doing a good deed by giving the club to the American Legion. "What the hell," he exclaimed, "I'll give you a good deal on it." And Ralph sold the club for a song—$5,000; he practically gave it away because he also had around $2,000 in whisky alone in there. But he was so disgusted over what had happened that he no longer gave a damn. That behavior was part of Ralph's makeup.

Anxious to close the deal, Casolini said, "Ralph, do you mind if we pay you next week?"

"No, don't worry about it," Ralph replied benevolently. "Here are the keys." And Ralph turned over the keys without receiving a cent.

A week passed, and the three looked for Ralph at the Nirvanetta. "Here, Ralph . . . Here's five hundred dollars. It's all we can give you . . . now," Casolino said.

"We'll give you more later on," Perkins assured Ralph.

"Sure, okay. I don't need the money now," Ralph said, with complete trust. "You can give it to me in the next weeks. But . . . look," Ralph added, "the club's license is not in my name. It's under someone else's, but you can still run the place. You must renew the license about two months from now. So remember, check it out and renew it. It's not complicated. You just go and pay whatever it is, and they'll renew it." Ralph spoke very emphatically about that point.

One of the men arrogantly quipped, "Oh, we don't care anything about the license. We have Ambassador Dunn behind us."

Upon hearing those words, Ralph kept quiet. If they had such good contacts, who was he to talk? Besides, it was possible since they all represented very important companies. They advised Ralph that they were starting to remodel a little—making repairs, installing special effects they wanted. Ralph encouraged them as they left and occasionally dropped by to say hello and watched the progress. Everyone seemed happy, and Ralph proceeded not to pressure them for the money. For their part, the men kept reassuring Ralph that they would pay but first had to take care of the remodeling expenses.

The days and weeks passed; then two months later, Ralph found a slip in his mailbox, summoning him to the district police commissioner's office—something concerning his affairs, the slip said. Ralph couldn't imagine what it was about, but by now, he was used to checking in with the police. Most of them had become very good friends. He was watched constantly, and he made sure that he didn't make any mistakes. When he entered the police station, he was surprised to see the American Legion commander Casolini and the American Express man there. They both pretended not to see him, but Ralph didn't dwell on it; some men could be that way. Then he saw Perkins walk in, and a warning bell rang in his head as he noticed their hostility toward him. When the police commissioner called them in, Ralph refrained from shaking hands with them due to their cold attitude. *What the hell is going on?* he thought. Fortunately, it was the same police commissioner who had given him prior permission to run La Stiva Odescalchi. He was a friend and had given Ralph his personal okay.

"*Ciao*, hi, Ralph, are these the people you sold the club to?" he asked.

"Yeah . . . ," Ralph replied, "why?"

"*Bell' affare hai fatto!* What a deal you made!" he replied sarcastically.

"Why?" Ralph repeated.

"Nice people," the commissioner frowned. "They tell me you sold them a club without a license."

"*Dottore* (a title of high regard), I'm glad I'm talking to you and not someone else. Why did you give me permission to open the club?" Ralph asked.

"Because there was a license, and everything was in order."

"Well, I told them all about the license, that they had to renew it." Ralph glared at his accusers. "They told me they had Ambassador Dunn behind them, so what do they want from me?"

The police commissioner turned toward the three grim men and snapped, "So . . . what do you want from Ralph?" He dismissed them, giving orders to close the club. The three so-called distinguished gentlemen were surprised at the outcome of the session and lost some of their composure. Apparently, they thought of Ralph only as an ex-con, and that they could easily take him for a ride. They were surprised to find out differently.

Personally, Ralph was shocked at their behavior and left the station in a ruffled state. Bitter thoughts raced through his mind. Prison had branded him, and some people would never let him forget it. He was victimized—an easy prey for four-flushers who pretend to be law-abiding citizens. He was making it his business to play it straight; he was not looking for trouble because his dream was to return to the United States. His Italian police blotter had to be clean! The three men thought they were smart by stringing him along regarding the money, not that he cared about it, but when they tried to make him look like a liar and a thief, Ralph was fuming. He went home trembling.

Ralph's upright friends apparently did have good contacts because they soon obtained permission to open up again—without a license, just for legionnaires, they said. But non-legionnaires were allowed to enter; no one bothered them. They did not however want to pay Ralph because they insisted he sold them the club without a license. To make matters worse, Ralph learned through his sources that the trio had taken the money from a man named Angeletti, a war veteran with no arms and legs, to pay for the club. Instead, they used the money to remodel it to their liking and for whatever else. They continued to refuse Ralph payment, and he was now seeing red. *Those bastards are taking me for a swindler!* he screamed to himself. They were not going to get away with it. He hired a well-recommended lawyer to represent him. The case, however, kept being postponed, and the lawyer gave no details. Ralph was getting weary of it all, suspecting foul play. A friend of his in the Ministry of the Interior contacted the judge involved to discover what was wrong. The wise and benevolent judge advised him. "If Ralph is a friend of yours, tell him to change his lawyer!" Ralph's suspicions were correct, and he wasted no time in dismissing his lawyer and obtaining a new one. Things then started to roll.

Ralph hired a big criminal lawyer, Federico Turano, who was tops. When Turano heard the story, he was appalled at the behavior of the gentlemen who hid behind the prestigious name of the American Legion. "If they don't pay you," he cried, "I'll blow the American Legion off the map of Italy!" He immediately subpoenaed all of them. That move caused Colonel Broad, head of the CID (Criminal Investigation Division) with whom Ralph enjoyed mutual respect, to summon Ralph.

After cordial salutations, Ralph sat down. He knew damn well why the colonel wanted to speak to him. Consequently, he said briskly, "Colonel, give it to me straight!"

"Ralph, please withdraw your attorney. I'll give you the money," the colonel pleaded.

"Listen, Colonel, I don't want any money from you. You know me. I don't give a damn about the money," Ralph blurted since it was an emotional topic with him. "It's the principle! What I'm mad about is that they made me look like a thief, and even took the money off that poor guy, Angeletti."

"I know, Ralph . . . I know . . . but please . . . Look . . . I'll give you one thousand dollars tomorrow." Colonel Broad was doing his best to end an embarrassing situation.

"No!" Ralph was adamant. I don't want the money from you. I want the money from them . . . because they got the money . . . off Angeletti."

"Ralph . . . just do me a favor. Come up tomorrow . . . will you?"

"Yeah, okay . . . but I'm not changing my mind." And they shook hands.

As Ralph promised, he went up the next day; and to his surprise, he found Charlie and Colonel Charles Poletti, the military governor of Rome, an old friend from New York. Poletti was lieutenant governor of New York City in 1942 after Governor Herbert H. Lehman left for military service—and before Dewey became governor in 1943. Poletti was in the invasion of Sicily and landed in Gela with the troops on July 10, 1943. Having had achieved recognition for his active role in the war, he had become, first, military governor of Palermo, then Naples, and, finally, Rome. His office was in the beautiful Palazzo Delle Assicurazioni Generali (the largest Italian insurance company at the time) in front of the historic Palazzo Venezia. They were all good friends, and they tried to release some of the tension by joking around a bit, but it didn't work. Ralph understood that underneath it all, they were on his side but had to do their job. He was ready for them.

Poletti began trying to convince Ralph to drop the case; that they would provide the money. He was a terrific person, and Ralph sincerely liked him, but this was one favor he couldn't do for him.

"Look . . . ," argued Ralph, "you all know that the place was worth three times what I asked of them. Those sons of bitches were trying to pull a fast one on me."

"But . . . Ralph," Colonel Broad tried to interrupt.

"No, Colonel . . . Before you say anything, it's like I said yesterday. I don't want the money from you guys. They're trying to make me look like a swindler . . . when all the time they're the rat bastards!" Ralph was stubborn, but what the hell; he knew he was right, and there was no budging him.

Then Charlie tried, "Ralph . . . I warned you not to trust anyone. Now listen . . ."

Ralph was exasperated, and before Charlie could start the "forget about it" routine, Ralph butted in and brusquely said, "No . . . Charlie . . . you're my godfather. I have known you a long time. We're good friends . . . We'll still be good friends, but just this one time, I must say NO to you. Those rat bastards went to the police commissioner and made me look like a thief . . . when *they're* the real thieves. I say NO and it's NO!"

There was complete silence. Then Charlie turned to the others. "Ralph is right . . . What can I do?" he said contritely. "Ralph is 100 percent right."

He shook his head in resignation. Ralph stood up and walked out on everybody.

Two days later, Ralph received another surprise. His lawyer, Turano, called him to go down and pick up his money. They wanted the case settled out of court to avoid scandal. For all Ralph knew, Charlie could have given him the money. He had a hunch that perhaps he did. But the case against the American Legion was dropped. Ralph was sorry about the whole mess. He didn't have anything against the American Legion but against the three upright gentlemen.

Imagine taking money from a guy with no arms and legs, and then not meeting their obligations, Ralph sizzled.

CHAPTER FORTY-THREE

History has shown that after the war, the winners meet to divide the spoils, and World War II was no different. Even though the terrible war had not ended yet, the Yalta Conference in February 1945 among the Big Three more or less did just that—almost immediately, the United States and Great Britain were double-crossed by Stalin. For Europe, they agreed upon Germany and Austria being occupied until their fate could be further discussed; Poland was to form a new government, but Stalin never allowed free elections (and the Polish people became political prisoners); Italy lost some territory (some of which Mussolini had conquered) but, for the most part, came out fairly well, considering it was a leading Axis partner. Italians were allowed to get on with forming their new government almost immediately. For everyone involved in the war, final decisions came later; boundaries and territories were exchanged, modified, and taken over; and Russia had already begun its expansionist dreams of Communism, causing Europe to become divided into east and west blocks. Talk about gangsters!

The reconstruction of Italy was not easy, not only because of the obvious destruction brought about by the war, but because it had long experienced internal problems of its own. Political parties, which had gone underground during Fascism, had resurfaced, and they all wanted a piece of Italy. Each one had his own particular dream for the future. The monarchy that existed during the days of Mussolini, if only as a figurehead, became temporarily important again. It was certainly not popular, for it had played buddy-buddy with Fascism, but did change—that is, it did an about-face—in 1943, after the Allies landed in Sicily. At a Grand Council meeting, the monarchy arrested Mussolini and placed a military man (an ex-Fascist) named Badoglio in charge, who immediately declared war on Germany—after an armistice was signed with the Allies. The Resistance received another boost when the Italian political parties formed the Committee of National Liberation on September 9, 1943. A few days later, Mussolini was rescued by the Germans and lost no time in forming his own party, claiming an Italian Social Republic, still as an ally of Germany.

The Allies soon put an end to it all. After Rome was liberated (June 5, 1944), the monarchy knew its time was running out and agreed to the Italian parties forming a new government for the interim period—that is, until the country could go to the polls. As soon as the war was won in Italy, the Allies handed back the country to the people but remained with a military government (AMGOT) to make sure it received a democratic chance of survival. The coalition government, formed in 1944, was headed by a man named Ivanoe Bonomi, and it comprised seven parties—the three strongest being the Christian Democrats (Alcide De Gasperi), the Socialists (Pietro Nenni), and the Communists (Palmiro Togliatti).

Italy then became engrossed in the Fascist Purge. It relentlessly set out to remove Fascists from private, public, and political offices. In sum, to weed them out and punish them. One of the chief promoters was U.S. Colonel Charles Poletti (then military governor of Rome), who fought an exhaustive battle eliminating and expelling the Fascists. He appointed a committee to locate and process the dismissals and personally issued a detailed outline of where to look for them. He pressed hard for a law of sanctions against the Fascists, and indeed, the government soon passed a law more severe than even Poletti could have imagined. In his zealous effort to help rebuild Italy, Poletti authorized a radio program explaining the makings of a democracy to the Italian population—and even had a program to teach hygiene and sanitation, which was certainly needed. Most Italians, however, were going hungry. "Never mind the sermons. Give us something to eat and a place to work!" was their cry. But those things also came. Later, in 1948, the American European Recovery Program (or the Marshall Plan, as it was more popularly called) began to send funds to rebuild Italy's economy. Everyone was proud of Poletti; he had a dynamic personality, and some Italians never forgot him.

Then the bickering between the parties began. Some wanted it hot, some wanted it cold, and some wanted it in between. Therefore, a new coalition government was formed in 1945, headed by a compromise candidate (between De Gasperi and Nenni) named Feruccio Parri of the Action Party. This too collapsed with the threat of Communism in the background, and the political ideological difference pulled them farther and farther apart. De Gasperi took over and, supported by the Allies, began to get down to business. His government had a vote of confidence in the local government elections in April 1946, and a month later, weary of all the strong political pressures, King Victor Emmanuel III finally abdicated in favor of his son, Prince Umberto II. In June, a national constitutional referendum was held; and the Italians, also tired of it all, voted for a republic to replace the monarchy, which forced the king into exile. A constituent assembly was elected to prepare a new constitution.

The Allies, satisfied with the course of events and with De Gasperi and his moderate democratic government, finally signed a peace treaty in February 1947, in Paris, calling for a withdrawal of troops within ninety days. It would have been too simple if all went smoothly. The conflicts continued, and De Gasperi resigned in May 1947 because of his bitter quarrels with Nenni and Togliatti. Nenni would not break away from Togliatti, who was very pro-Soviet. His Socialist Party did not only split, but it was excluded along with the Communist Party from De Gasperi's new coalition government. The new constitution went into effect in January 1948, and finally, in the national elections of April 1948, De Gasperi's Christian Democrats won an overwhelming majority. De Gasperi was now in the driver's seat and proved to be one of Italy's greatest statesmen. He held office until 1954.

This was briefly the Italy to which Ralph was exiled. He found a country struggling to be reborn, and that was just what he was trying to do.

Sicily's fate was different. Things hadn't changed much since Garibaldi had unified it to Italy in 1860. Internal conflicts—exploitation—had never ceased. Wars had continued, with Italy's endless problems regarding territory. First the World War I; then Mussolini's regime, which paid more attention to the colonization of Africa than to Sicily; and the terrible Second World War postwar chaos and starvation ran rampant throughout the island. World War II further impoverished the Sicilians. Disease, such as malaria, was widespread; and when the Allies arrived with soap and drugs, they were blessed and cheered as heroes. The island was turned back to the Sicilians in February 1944, but unlike Italy, the political situation was not organized; there was no real partisan movement, and so the old structure still more or less had its hold on the people.

The Mafia was very securely ensconced and powerful. Some land reform was put into effect by the acting government. Peasants went back to work on the large estates, but this time, they were assigned land on the *mezzadria* system (crop sharing). As usual, the conflicting internal interests obstructed justice again, and the land reform was difficult to carry out. While their lot seemed to improve a little, nothing really changed for the Sicilians. Repelled by the continuous treatment of neglect, of always being considered the poor colony (that wretched relative to whom charity should be given), they began to rebel. It was in this climate right after the war that the Separatists Party, which had its small beginning in 1941, grew stronger, gaining impetus. It was strongly supported by the Mafia and, strangely enough, by the rich landowners who did not relish the thought of their land being given to the peasantry. Backed by the Mafia, a break with the central government in Rome would leave them to their own devices. The leading Mafia exponent at the time was Don Calogero Vizzini of Villalba, an almost illiterate man but whose cunning, conspiratorial, and paternal ways combined with his tough methods had won him the title of a Sicilian Mafioso "Capo."

Vizzini was the one who supposedly helped the Allies in the invasion of Sicily together with Luciano. Vizzini, perhaps; Luciano, no. Charlie didn't even know the man. Fairy-tale stories probably spread by newspapermen, which have Luciano landing in Sicily with the troops in 1943. As the fable goes, four days after the invasion, an American plane, which displayed a strange yellow gold cockade with the black letter *L* on it, flew over Villalba (practically in the heart of Sicily). According to this legend, the *L* stood for Luciano. As the plane flew over, it supposedly dropped a package for Don Vizzini, and lo and behold, in it was a silk handkerchief with the same emblem and letter on it. A few days later, two armored tanks, with that emblem again, is said to have arrived to pick up Vizzini and, incredibly, Lucky Luciano. He was supposed to be in one of the tanks that whisked Vizzini away, disappearing for a week. The story ends with General George Patton's march into Palermo on July 22, a march that met with no resistance—all due to Vizzini's contribution on orders from Luciano. If one is to believe the emblem and black letter *L* story, it would be more realistic to have the *L* stand for *Liberty* since that was the slogan of the Separatists Party of which Vizzini was a chief promoter. Nothing could be more false, as far as Charlie's participation was concerned. It's strange that no one has been able to conjure up a story of how Luciano could have left prison to perform such patriotic feats.

Charlie was not influential in Sicily, had no connections with the local Mafia. It is possible that other Mafia chieftains in the United States had ties because of relatives in their homeland. Charlie did not. When Charlie was deported there, the thought of how he lived as a child made him quiver. He couldn't stand small town life and wasted no time in escaping the island altogether upon his arrival. The entire Sicily affair only added to Charlie's mystique—just another fantastic fable!¶

¶ Insisting that Luciano was with him in Dannemora in 1943, Ralph comments, "Charlie and I were very good friends. We were together every day in prison. Talked about the war. If he really did go to Sicily, he had to leave the prison around nine o'clock at night, and come back to prison for breakfast around seven thirty in the morning. See how ridiculous the story is?"

During those days of ferment, there was one man who was making spectacular headlines in Sicily and Italy: the *bandito* (the bandit) Salvatore "Turiddu" Giuliano. His name has become legendary, and his story lives on with an adventuresome, somewhat pathetic, romantic aura around it, albeit controversial. To the destitute in Sicily, he was a hero—a Robin Hood—who stole from the rich and gave to the poor; to the Mafia, the politicians, he was a tool to use for their own sometimes devious means; and to the police, he was simply a criminal, a murderer who killed in cold blood. And to himself? From personal accounts of people who knew him well (family, friends, and journalists who were allowed to interview him in his hideout in the barren, rugged, jaggedly shaped, and impossible to reach hills near Montelepre where he was born, a stone's throw away from Palermo), and from his own writings, he thought of himself first as an idealist who wanted to break the chains that bound the Sicilian people. Also a paladin. It was no wonder the Sicilians tried to protect him.

Some facts are nebulous, depending on the source. He was a good boy, religious, studious, serious, and handsome; and it was the latter attribute, together with his charm and flair, that enhanced his reputation. His father was one of the early immigrants to America at the turn of the nineteenth century and, after years of labor in the promised land, returned to Montelepre. With his savings, he bought a house and a small farm, which became productive; and the family, with the standards of the day, was regarded as well-to-do. Giuliano, born on November 16, 1922, was considered *un buon partito* (a good catch). He was talented in everything he did—even strummed the guitar. In school he excelled, was above average, and even though at the time only elementary schools existed, his teachers saw to it that he continued his studies with private tutors.

Then the war broke out. Giuliano's brother was called to arms, and Giuliano took his place working in the family fields. After some time, he also joined the armed forces, but only long enough to handle a machine gun and learn about ammunitions in general since the Allies had invaded Sicily. He, along with many others, abandoned the fight, tired of a war in which they didn't believe and because of their natural inclination against Fascism. Like all wars, World War II brought destruction and left famine and disease in its wake. Youth were disoriented, and Giuliano was no exception.

Wheat was at a premium during the war (was rationed), and the peasants had to consign their grain to the government pool, where it was then distributed according to need. This situation remained even after the invasion. People were exasperated, and when hunger ran rampant, it was difficult to preach patience, especially to the young. In the autumn of '43, Giuliano was able to buy some wheat and was trying to smuggle it home when he was accosted by two carabinieri (state police), who inquired about the contents of the two sacks saddled on each side of his horse. Giuliano knew that he was caught and tried to plead his way out, imploring them to let him go, that it was to feed his family in dire need of food. It didn't work. Refusing to be taken into custody, he took off, running toward the hills trying to escape. While he was making his way through the uneven rocks, the carabinieri opened fire, wounding him. Giuliano returned fire, killing one of the carabinieri. Then with swift catlike movements, he escaped, for he knew the rugged, jagged way, and soon, with the help of the scrubby underbrush, disappeared from sight.

Another version is that he had been trying his hand at black marketing the wheat, and it was his third attempt. He had been prepared against pirates along the way with a pistol in his hip pocket. Instead, he was approached by two carabinieri, who were deaf to his pleas, and Giuliano was forced to surrender the wheat. As they conducted him back to town, Giuliano, after a struggle, freed himself and pulled out his gun. Faster on the draw, he fatally shot one carabinieri. He ran into the woods, but a carabinieri's bullet caught him in the hip, wounding him slightly. With astounding courage, he leaped through the rocky terrain to his safety.

Whichever version, it was a tragic consequence of a war, which drastically, irreversibly changed Giuliano's destiny. He became an outlaw in the remote hills near his home, protected by his small band of men with his cousin, Gaspare Pisciotta, as first lieutenant—and by the omerta (code of silence) of the people. He thought of himself as a defender of the oppressed. He was both judge and executioner and committed himself to this mission with an almost fanatical dedication. They stole arms and munitions from abandoned army warehouses, held up trains, and obtained ransom money by threatening to kidnap rich *latifondisti* (large landowners)—the barons, princes, in short, the aristocracy—with letters of extortion. Giuliano was however also a one-man show, venturing out as a highwayman alone in broad daylight. All that he succeeded in obtaining, he shared ostentatiously with the poor, doing everything with style; and his charismatic quality drew people to him. Sometimes he needed a fence for his stolen goods. Enter the Mafia. His contacts with the "honored society" grew due to their similar political views.

Giuliano's zealous youth and his confused, distorted idealism convinced him in 1945 to wholeheartedly embrace the Separatists Party ideology: Liberty for Sicily. In Giuliano's case, his infantile idealism moved him, whereas for the Mafia, it was shrewd calculation to be on the winning side. Early in 1947, Giuliano shifted his allegiance to the Christian Democrats, warning the Sicilians against leaning to the left. He began to combat Communism with the same forceful conviction as he held for a liberated Sicily.

Still a Separatist at heart, Giuliano openly loved America, land of liberty with freedom for all, and wrote a very moving letter to President Harry S. Truman, pleading to annex Sicily to the United States as the forty-ninth state. In his letter, he warned against the Russian menace, "who long to appear in the Mediterranean Sea . . . We can no longer put up with the spread of the Red tumult. The leader, Stalin, who spends millions to conquer the hearts of our people, with a political system based on falsehood, has met the people's favor . . . We will not allow these base people to take away our freedom, which, for us Sicilians, is the most precious element in life."

He asked President Truman for moral support. What was the outcome of that letter? Whatever, it was another dream of Giuliano's that did not come true.

Again a tool in the hands of the high lords of political intrigue, Giuliano embarked in the role of savior against Communism. He agreed to their orders once more and bloodied his reputation forever in the much publicized massacre on May 1, 1947, in a village called Portella della Ginestra (a few kilometers from Montelepre). This was part of Giuliano's kingdom, and although he cited the evils of Communism, he was unable to convince the people not to attend the Communist rally there. The inevitable happened. Machine gun fire reached the crowd, killing eleven and wounding thirty-three (other reports vary). It didn't matter who had fired the guns; Giuliano was blamed. There are those, however, who say that the real trigger was pulled by those who ordered the massacre—if a massacre was intended in the first place.

However unwelcome on the surface, the support of the Mafia-feudalists-Giuliano combination helped double the Christian Democrats in 1948, and it remained (with De Gasperi in Rome) the majority party for years to come. Giuliano had served his purpose. He had been promised pardon by the Separatists who never made it to power, but it was the Christian Democrats (although not openly) who declared that Giuliano and his group would be granted amnesty. They later changed their tune to asylum in another country. But the rewards did not arrive. Some of his Mafia friends began to brazenly betray him, holding out on ransom money. Giuliano's alliance with the Mafia was one of mutual assistance, never one of subordination, so he thought. This trickery only outraged him since he was taking all the risks. Unpredictable as always, Giuliano laid a trap for them and, in the battle, killed a Mafia boss of Partinico (not far from Montelepre) and four of his men. Of course, this audacious act brought repercussions from several fronts. The Mafia surely would not just sit back, and the government in Italy had had enough. In August 1948, the Ministry of the Interior ordered the formation of a special police force led by Carabiniere Colonel Ugo Luca to repress banditry—specifically to get Giuliano.

The Mafia-feudalists by now were secretly plotting to help in his demise, and Giuliano, under pressure from his own men for their freedom, felt his world closing in on him.

Ever since his arrival in Rome, Ralph had heard of Giuliano, who was the topic of conversation almost everywhere—bars, stores, piazzas, wherever people gathered. There were daily bulletins on the radio of Giuliano's latest escapades, and during those postwar years, he had many secret sympathizers.

Charlie was one.

It was September; the sun had decided to retire late and blazed fiercely. It was hot and muggy, and Ralph couldn't wait for the relief that would come from the soft evening breezes. Charlie had asked Ralph to join him for dinner at Fagiano's before going to the club, but it took sheer willpower to dress up in the heat. Ralph felt so sluggish; he moved in slow motions. Finally, he reached Fagiano's and found Charlie already looking over the menu at his favorite table.

Charlie looked up casually and said, "How 'bout *prosciutto* and *melone*?"

"Sure, sounds good. It's been too godddamn hot today." Ralph sighed, loosening his tie.

"And *mazzancolle alla griglia* with mixed salad," Charlie continued.

"Have them throw in some shrimp too!" Ralph loved fish.

Charlie rattled off the dinner to the waiter, put down the menu, and, rather relaxed, looked at Ralph. "Well, how goes it, Ralph? You look all done in," Charlie inquired in his brotherly fashion.

"Naw, it's just the heat," replied Ralph.

"And the clubs?"

"Good. I'm glad I gave up the Nirvanetta and Casino delle Rose. I was spreading myself too thin. Now, I can concentrate on the Columbia and the Colibri. It's better this way." Ralph didn't mention the fiasco with La Stiva. Neither did Charlie.

The waiter brought the first course, and Charlie wasted no time in digging in. "Glad to hear it, Ralph. Mmmm, this melon is really good. Sweet."

It was one of their typical dinners together where they exchanged small talk and brought each other up-to-date. However, that night, Ralph was anxious to bring up the man he had been reading about in the newspapers. Charlie appeared to be in a good mood, so Ralph thought he'd try.

"Have you been reading about Dewey's presidential campaign?"

Ralph expected to be cut off, but instead, Charlie placed his knife and fork neatly across his plate and reached for his wine glass, still in a pleasant vein.

"Yeah, he's sure plugging away," he smirked. "Have to give him credit. The political writers have made him their unanimous choice."

"What do you really think, Charlie?"

Ralph hoped Charlie would open up. His suspicions told him that Charlie had been helping Dewey for a long time now. Ralph had been following Dewey's career very closely—as far back as 1938 when he made his first try for governor of New York while still the DA and lost to Lehman; when Willkie beat him in the presidential bid; and when, in 1942, he tried again for the governorship. Dewey, up to then, hadn't done so well on his own, and everyone knew it cost a great deal of money to campaign, not to mention the votes necessary to win. That time he made it. It was the behind-the-scene intrigue that Ralph wanted to hear from Charlie's lips. He wanted to know all the things that had been haunting him all those years—ever since Charlie was transferred to Great Meadow with the trumped-up excuse that he and Betillo had tried to cut Charlie's face in Dannemora. They wanted Charlie away from Ralph at all costs. Why? Ralph had filled in the pieces of the puzzle for himself; what else but another double cross? But he wanted to hear it from Charlie.

After a short pause, unaware of Ralph's thoughts, Charlie replied, "Well . . . Wallace is out of the picture.[**] Didn't have a chance! Read where they threw eggs at him in Pittsburgh." Charlie laughed in his unmistakable way.

"Yeah . . . well . . . Dewey had tomatoes thrown at him more than once," Ralph retorted, not displeased.

Charlie ignored the pleasure on Ralph's face and continued lightly, "Truman is the only one that keeps the public in stitches. The papers said that when his microphone had disturbing sounds . . . he quipped, 'It sounds like the Russians on the wire, trying to mess up the Voice of America's broadcast.' He's a regular guy. Gutsy style. More folksy than Dewey. But you never know. It's too soon to tell. You know . . . Dewey

---

** Henry A. Wallace, independent candidate of the Progressive Party.

has come a long way. Has matured. Has a good record . . ." His words trailed off.

"Sure . . . ," Ralph rebutted. "He's got that crime buster reputation!"

Charlie still paid no attention to Ralph's sarcasm, and as the waiter set down their second course of fish on the table, he looked at his food as though he were studying the quantity, quality, and preparation by the chef. "Yeah, but now he's counting on our boys," he said absently.

Ah, so, thought Ralph as he dug into his shrimp, but he was too excited to really enjoy it. He repeated the words to himself, "Counting on our boys." His thoughts again returned to 1942, when Dewey became governor with a little help from "his" friends. His last attempt for the presidency against Roosevelt in 1944 had been unsuccessful, but after FDR died and Truman became president, Dewey went at it again, bruised and scarred but still out front, fighting for his place in the sun, to become what he had always dreamed of when he was a boy: the president of the United States of America.

"Look, Charlie . . ." Ralph focused into the present. "I want to know! Where do we come in?"

"Ralph, look, it's very important this time," he finally started to say something, but the waiter interrupted him.

"*Mi scusi*, Signor Luciano," he said, handing Charlie a note.

Charlie placed the note nonchalantly next to his plate and then carefully, discreetly, opened it. Ralph could see a look of surprise on his face. He casually glanced up and looked across the room, then looked at Ralph and said, "Don't turn around now, Ralph . . . but do you know who's behind you?" And before Ralph could answer, he added, "Giuliano!"

"You're kidding," Ralph said, truly surprised. Without being conspicuous, Ralph tried to glance sideways, but all he could see was a glimpse of an Italian army officer.

"Yeah, it's that lieutenant." Charlie sensed Ralph's observation. "He wants to talk to me. I'll be right back. Just act normal and DON'T TURN AROUND!" Charlie rose nonchalantly, and sauntered over to the lieutenant's table, and shook hands with the man like old friends. Giuliano asked him to sit down, and they talked no more than ten minutes. Ralph was picking at his salad when Charlie returned, just as casually, sat down, and said, "Ralph, you got any money on you?"

"Not too much, Charlie, just a couple hundred."

"No, that's not enough. Listen, you stay right here until I come back. Order more fish, dessert, wine . . . but stay here. DON'T GO OVER THERE. It's dangerous! I'll be back as soon as I can. Remember . . .

don't move!" Charlie slowly stood up and walked out of the restaurant unruffled.

Ralph called the waiter over and ordered another dish of grilled fish and more wine. In so doing, he was able to see Giuliano better, sitting about five tables behind him against the wall. Ralph had heard that Giuliano was great at disguising himself; he was known to walk right under the noses of the carabinieri in Sicily in various disguises without ever being recognized. Giuliano was now perfect in his uniform as the Italian army lieutenant, which he completed with a little vandyke beard, mustache, long sideburns, and dark sunglasses. Ralph sipped his wine and thought, *That son of a gun. All of Italy is looking for him, and here he is in the center of town, leisurely having dinner.* Everyone knew that Colonel Ugo Luca had more than one thousand men in Sicily combing the hills for him. One had to admit it. Giuliano had plenty of guts. He was only twenty-six years old. They both stayed at their tables, casually eating, as if nothing was happening. Charlie finally returned, about forty minutes later, which seemed an eternity, and sat down.

"Anything happen?" he asked.

"No. Nothing. He hasn't moved from his table," Ralph replied. "Now what?"

"As soon as we finish our wine, we'll get up and take a cab. I've already told him to follow us in another cab, but not to be obvious when we walk out." Charlie motioned to the waiter to bring the bill.

"Okay . . . whenever you're ready," Ralph said.

Charlie placed some money on the table, and they left. They hailed a cab, and Charlie told the driver to wait a few minutes until a friend came out. Soon Giuliano appeared and climbed into another cab. Charlie then gave word to take off, and Giuliano followed them slowly. They took the old Appian Way, which was deserted at that hour, and just past the San Sebastian Catacombs, they stopped at a little restaurant-bar. The cabs pulled over to the side and turned off their lights to wait. The place was just a dive but was a good hiding place. Charlie had no intention of mentioning Giuliano's name inside, so just before they went in, he finally introduced Ralph to Giuliano. He seemed like a nice young man to Ralph—very mannerly, not pompous or arrogant as he had sometimes been described. His facial muscles revealed he was under great stress—the tension was high. The three men took a table in a dimly lit corner and ordered drinks. As Giuliano briefly spoke, Ralph had the impression that he was confused, that he didn't really know what his next move would be. He told them how he hated Communism and how disgusted he was with conditions in Sicily—about the way politicians began to snub him, and that there were very few people whom he trusted anymore. His primary interest was to have his family members released from custody. He had sent a message to Interior Minister Mario Scelba, promising to leave Italy in exchange for their release, and asked for amnesty and a passport. His plan was to try to leave for the United States—the only country he respected.

That's where Charlie came in. As soon as the waiter brought the drinks and was again out of hearing range, Charlie discreetly handed Giuliano an envelope with two thousand dollars, a great amount of money then, which, apparently, was to help Giuliano reach the States. Giuliano's dark eyes smarted with gratitude, and he quietly thanked Charlie. Ralph downed his drink and gave Charlie the eye. He did the same; Charlie also wanted to move out of there, fast. Ralph could just imagine if the newspapers latched on to the story—if someone had discovered the lonely trio sipping drinks in a dark corner. What a field day they'd have with it. Giuliano also sensed the urgency to leave, and simultaneously, everyone stood up. Ralph paid the check as the other two walked out ahead of him. Everyone kissed and embraced one another Italian style; they said their good-byes and wished Giuliano *buona fortuna* (good luck). Then Giuliano climbed into his cab and took off in the dark of the night.

In the backseat of the cab, Charlie looked relieved that it was all over, and Ralph couldn't help commenting, "Did you have an appointment or something with that guy?"

Charlie looked stoically, straight ahead. "No, it was accidental." Then he turned to look at Ralph, his eyes narrowing a bit, and half-thinking, he added, "A lot of people know I almost always eat at Fagiano's! He must have gotten word."

"Yeah . . . could be. Charlie . . . could be," Ralph murmured absently and dropped the subject. Ralph stared out the window, into the darkness of the night, and Charlie leaned back and gazed into nothing. The two friends remained silent, each with his own thoughts on the episode, as the cab sped along the lonely Appian Way.

CHAPTER FORTY-FOUR

The horses charge forward at the start; the gray Arabian leaps ahead, but the others are all steadily working their way up; after the first curve, the chestnut beauty races ahead; now they are neck to neck, but the others are still coming. Through the binoculars, one can see the jockeys in their colorful windbreakers—purple, flaming red, turquoise, gold-and-black striped—manipulating the reins with expertise, their leg muscles hugging the horse, moving the spurs just so, whispering words of love, all coaxing their horse to "go, baby, go!" Not until the last bend in the track, when each horse makes his last great stretch toward victory, does the crowd become really animated. They begin to scream; people jump up and down; those against the rail shake their fists, everyone urging "his" horse to come in; and then the final wild roar as the chestnut beauty springs forward victoriously through the finish line. Suddenly, everything subsides, and the murmuring crowd slowly moves away, out of the booths to bet on their next horse. Charlie and Ralph are among them.

They had won, thanks to Charlie. In the States, he always personally knew the horses and the jockeys; and in Rome, it was the same. His love for the racetracks had never waned; he was addicted to the ponies, so it wasn't unusual to see them at the Capannelle racetracks (off Via Appia) in Rome, mingling with other devotees of the races. Sometimes they went to Villa Glory (behind the Stadio Flaminio) to see the trotters. Later, when Charlie moved to Naples, Ralph occasionally drove down to join him at the Agnano racetrack, and it was also the same there.

Once Charlie had a big bet on a horse at Agnano. The horses were off and running, and Charlie handed Ralph his glasses. "Here," he said, "see if you can see something." Ralph took the binoculars and focused on his horse, which was stretching his legs in a fine gallop reaching the lead horse, when suddenly, the horse in front kicked up a stone with his hind leg and hit Charlie's jockey right in the nose. It was bleeding terribly. Ralph told Charlie, who quickly took the glasses to see for himself. Unfortunately, Charlie's horse came in second; but like a pro, he took it in stride. He slowly ripped his slip in two. Win some, lose some. The jockey, instead, was very upset; he went looking for Charlie near the stables and began to cry about it. Charlie soothed his aching heart. "Forget about it. Never mind," he said. "As long as you're all right, the hell with the money." Ralph and Charlie left the racetrack and went to eat. It was just another day.

On this particular afternoon at Capannelle, Charlie and Ralph walked out of the main pavilion with the crowd to collect their winnings. It was a beautiful racetrack, well kept, and included a small park with a few palm trees. Baroque staircases led up to the four pavilions—one was for the owners, a sort of clubhouse—where beautiful azaleas in shades of pink, soft reds, and violet drooped from huge ornate ceramic vases on the banister posts. The bleachers faced the tracks on one side and were separated from the rest of the ground by a neatly trimmed green hedge. To the right of the tack, in the distance, one could see the beautiful Castelli Romani—the small hills outside of Rome. It was an oasis, and if the weather was good, some people spent all day at the races.

The voices of the crowd seemed to mesh like the undulating hum of a beehive, and the faces were a spectacular study of types, of various individuals, most of them clutching wrinkled race sheets, studying the horses as though they were experts at the game. Some were huddled together softly, exchanging tips on the favorite, while shrewd bookies bent over, taking bets and giving the odds-on. There were the usual derelicts and degenerates, as well as family types, with binoculars hanging around their necks, enjoying a day of fun.

From habit, Ralph's eyes roamed everywhere. He seldom missed a trick as he surveyed the surroundings.

"Charlie . . . ," he mumbled. "Don't turn around. The law's behind us."

"The hell with them. What do we care?" Charlie shrugged as he folded his winnings into his pocket. "Come on, let's go congratulate our jockey." They went toward the stables, not caring whether they were followed or not.

Ralph suspected it, but it still was a surprise when he found a slip the next morning in his hotel, requesting his presence at police headquarters.

"Ralph, where do you get the money to bet on the horses?" the captain asked.

"What? Did I ever come up here and ask anybody for money?" Ralph replied angrily.

"Nooo," his voice went up like a question mark.

"Well . . . what do you want to know? Where I get the money?"

The captain glared in affirmation.

"I don't steal it, if that's what you want to know, and I don't ask anybody. Where do I get it? Why, I wouldn't even tell my own brother, if he was here. Why should I tell you?" Ralph was disgusted; he didn't even bother to say that he worked for the money because the captain damn well knew he did. "Is that all?" Ralph concluded.

"That's all." And he was dismissed.

"What the hell did they want this time?" Charlie asked, his back to the bar, sipping his coffee at their favorite coffee shop near the Pantheon.

"The general routine. Where did I get the money to bet on the horses, as if I went out and stole it," Ralph replied bitingly.

"Well . . . I got a slip too. I have to report tomorrow morning," Charlie said quietly.

"Okay . . . So we bet a little heavy on the horses . . . So do a lot of other people," Ralph continued, still irritated. "There's nothing wrong in that. We didn't steal the money!"

Charlie looked at Ralph sideways. "There's always some cop wanting to make a career, always looking to make that one big arrest. Guys like us are ready target for them."

"Well, I don't care about anybody else! We didn't do anything wrong, and that's what counts! They can all go to hell!" Ralph snapped, convinced he was right. Ralph did have opportunities to make easy money, but he didn't want any part of it. Sometimes at their breakfast meetings, Charlie clued Ralph when someone from the States blew into town. He knew better than anyone what was cooking and warned Ralph, always in his brotherly fashion.

"If that guy contacts you, stay away from him!" Ralph listened because they were guys involved in narcotics, and Charlie didn't want him to mingle with any of those people. Charlie also avoided the men offering narcotics deals, contrary to what he was accused.

The next day, Charlie went to the police, and it was the same. That evening, Charlie called. "Ralph, let's go for a ride tonight, get some fresh air along the sea, get away from it all."

"Okay, Charlie. Shall I pick you up?"

"No, no. I'll come by the hotel around eight o'clock."

Ralph hung up without giving the invitation a second thought. They were both in a sour mood, angered at the police harassment, and it was one way to forget. At eight sharp, there was Charlie, behind the wheel of a beautiful 1948 Oldsmobile, beeping the horn. Ralph couldn't believe his eyes. He walked around the car admiringly and noticed it had New Jersey license plates.

"Come on, Ralph, get in," Charlie called. Ralph looked perplexed as he climbed in, and Charlie laughed. "Great, isn't it?"

"It's a beauty. Where'd you get it?"

"That crazy Willie Moretti sent it to me. What a peach, wanted to do something for me."

Ralph smiled and shook his head approvingly, remembering Willie who was always a generous guy. Some people knew him as Willie Moore. Ralph always thought it was funny how guys took Irish names as an alias. He was happy for Charlie. Being exiled was harder on him—to be free and yet not to be free. Then Ralph glanced down, and between them on the front seat was a box. Charlie continued laughing almost to himself and said, "Open it!" At that point, it could have contained anything. Ralph opened it slowly, as though he expected a jack—in-the-box to pop out, but all he could say was, "Christ, these are beautiful!" And they were. Ties and ties—expensive silk ties. Willie always wore loud ties, but these obviously had been specially picked for them.

Willie's note said, "These are for you and Ralph, with love."

"Well, I'll be damned," Ralph chuckled and shook his head in appreciation.

"He also said to say hello, and that your uncle Al also sends his regards." Charlie continued to beam behind the wheel of his Oldsmobile. It was a new toy, and Ralph understood. They ended up at the Il Pescatore Restaurant and treated themselves to various dishes of fish. They talked all evening, raked up the past, and then, finally, Charlie dropped Ralph off at the Colibri Club.

It was a night for reminiscing. Ralph was mingling with the customers; making the rounds of the tables, when he saw someone with a familiar face walk in.

"Ralph . . . you son of a gun," the man exclaimed, and before Ralph could blink, the man grasped his arms and embraced him.

"Ben . . . Ben Grauer! I don't believe it. Man, it's been a long time." Ralph was sincerely moved to see the great American sports commentator again. Brought him back many years.

"Yes . . . a long, long time, Ralph. You look great!" he replied, and then the fun was on. Out came the champagne, and Ben sat at the piano to play their favorite tunes. It was a memorable night. The next day, a write-up in the paper said, "He had done it for a good friend he hadn't seen in twelve years."

About that time, Robert Conway of the *New York Daily News* wrote a very tongue-in-cheek article, using derogatory remarks about Ralph such as "ex-convict lieutenant, pint-sized partner," stating that Charlie and Ralph were operating nightclubs in Rome "New York style" (meaning girlie shows). The article also said Ralph was fronting the clubs for Charlie; that he was Ralph's silent partner, and that Ralph and Charlie were trying to ace out the owner of another club who was balking at their offers. Ralph was obviously furious about the article. It was pure bunk for the sake of sensationalism. Charlie never had anything to do with the clubs except to come in for dinner, lunch, or drinks. On the other hand, Ralph loved the clubs. They were like a pastime for him—a gathering place for friends, old and new, like Orson Welles who always stopped in for a drink to say hello. Ralph thought he was a genius. Many people didn't like Orson because he was too brilliant; they were intimidated by his incredible brain.

Once Ralph and Elena bumped into Welles and a girlfriend at the Kursaal Beach Club at the Ostia Lido. While they were sitting around chewing the fat, Ralph mentioned to Welles that his car had broken down.

"Don't worry about it, Ralph," Welles said kindly. "I'll tow you in."

They enjoyed the rest of the day in peace, and when it was time to leave, true to his word, Welles towed Ralph into Rome. A regular guy. He was dating an Italian girl—a high-class one. Ralph never knew he was going out regularly. Welles was having his problems with Rita Hayworth at that time; she was suing him for a divorce. "It's difficult to live with a genius," was her excuse. Meanwhile, she was being courted by the world's renowned playboy of the times, Prince Aly Khan, whom she eventually married in 1949 after a lot of notoriety. But Ralph believed she was right—to him, Orson Welles was a genius.

Celebrities weren't the only ones to fraternize Ralph's clubs. There was the regular Roman crowd—friends who, directly and indirectly, involved him in a variety of episodes. But not as much as his new bartender, Diamond Dick.

Diamond Dick had also been deported. He was supposed to be exiled to Salerno, the town of his birth near Naples, but was able to convince the authorities that he would be a good boy in Rome. He had scraped up some funds (enough for a beginning), and with a GI pension from the U.S. government, he was set. He even obtained an allowance under the GI Bill of Rights to learn Italian. Ralph was surprised to see him walk into the Colibri Club one night. It had been more than thirteen years since Ralph had seen him, and he gave Dick a hearty welcome, as he did routinely with everyone. Dick hadn't changed much, just a little gray at the temples, which, against his black hair, gave him a look of maturity; but knowing him, Ralph knew it was only an illusion. Even though he was forty-two, his slight five-feet-five frame still made him look youthful. As he spoke to Ralph, his dark eyes darted all over the place. Ralph could tell he was sizing up the club, wondering where he could fit in.

"Hey, Ralph," he began in a confidential manner, "how 'bout getting me the bartender job here? You know I'm the best in the business," he added smugly.

Nothing like coming right to the point, thought Ralph. Unfortunately, he was never one to say NO, and he replied, "Sure, why not? I'll talk to the owner." Diamond Dick was hired, and Ralph's headaches began.

Initially, he was efficient; he *was* the best bartender around, but he was just as unreliable as ever. His old habits crept in; he began to play hooky and involved himself in many escapades. Ralph was being constantly called to police headquarters to vouch for him. Dick soon lost his job at the Colibri Club, and both Charlie and Elena were happy. Elena didn't like him, considered him a playboy. When they thought they were rid of him, with Ralph's okay, he began work at the Columbia Club. Elena was furious. She literally hated him because he was such a mooch, always sponging meals and even expecting Elena to do his laundry. To her, he was simply overbearing. She couldn't stand his arrogant ways, but mostly, she considered him a bad influence on Ralph, didn't want Ralph to vouch for him anymore because it put him in a bad light.

Charlie felt the same. He definitely did not like the fact that Dick was tending bar at Ralph's club. "Too close for comfort," he commented. Then he continued, "you're not hanging around with that guy, are you? Stay away. He's bad news!" He even asked Elena on the QT; he was that concerned. Charlie and Ralph occasionally argued over it, especially when Diamond Dick was involved in some escapade, which implicated Ralph. Charlie, playing his godfather role to the hilt, kept telling Ralph to get rid of Dick. But Ralph was a fool and stood by the man. Perhaps because he was rebellious, for underneath it all, Ralph was still resentful. He felt things between him and Charlie were not yet resolved.

It all finally came to a head however. Diamond Dick began pushing the friendship too far. He still came to the house for his free meals, but Ralph began to notice something amiss with his eyes and his mannerisms. It didn't take long to figure it out, especially one night when Dick arrived at Ralph's apartment with his shoulder out of joint. He looked in bad shape—and intoxicated—that he fell flat on his face. Ralph and Elena picked him up and positioned him on the couch. Then Ralph told Dick he knew he was on drugs (just for a moment, with a painful twinge, he thought of Dotty) and ordered him out, shouting angrily, "I don't want you near me or my wife anymore. Stay away from me and this house, if you know what's good for you!" Finally, Ralph had some peace from Elena and Charlie. Years later, when he ran into Dick accidentally, the latter tried to apologize. Ralph listened stoically, then replied, "Look . . . there's nothing to talk about. You like that stuff better than a friend. It's your life. Stick to that stuff, but forget about Ralph!"[††]

The unresolved problem between Charlie and Ralph regarding Dewey kept gnawing at Ralph. Since the night he and Charlie had met with Giuliano, and Charlie had almost revealed what Ralph wanted to know, Ralph had been unable to approach the subject again in the right mood, time, or place. All year, Ralph had been reading everything he could find about the 1948 presidential campaign. Wallace, still in the race, was calling Truman names; they were all calling each other names, creating a really colorful race. Wallace, however, lagged far behind and, as Charlie predicted, was out of the picture. Truman and Dewey were running neck and neck; either one could take that final leap to victory. The Gallup Polls gave Dewey a wide edge over Truman, and the Democrats were seriously divided when Strom Thurmond and the Conservatives in the South bolted the party, forming the Dixiecrats, which, as a third party, weakened the Democrats. Truman would get a larger popular vote, most experts agreed, but not enough to win the Electoral College.

In November 1948, Americans went to the polls. Would it be Truman or Dewey? Charlie had all his machinery in the States working to elect Dewey. Ralph had understood that. He wasn't a complete fool; he didn't need Charlie to tell him that the outcome of the election would create a major turning point in their lives. Ralph, however, believed that Charlie would tell him all sooner or later. Needless to say, Ralph hated Dewey with a passion. Just the thought that Tom Dewey could become president of the United States made him ill.

[††] About 1971, in Naples, drug abuse brought Diamond Dick to his death.

CHAPTER FORTY-FIVE

There is a great deal of pain in the world, physical and mental, various kinds. Some people cannot cope. They look for an escape—a relief from the pain, the torment they feel. Like the bully who picks on the skinny kid, there are always those who profit from the weaknesses of others—and not just in the rackets. One sees it in everyday life in all circles of society—in politics, wars, and in big business. And narcotics is big business! Ralph had expressed his views on the subject many, many times, stating that there wasn't enough money in the world to involve him in that filthy, inhuman racket—something he considered the lowest dregs of vice. But when a man has a prison record and has certain friends, like Ralph, it is difficult to be believed. Ralph felt that society saw him as being tainted (forget about the talk that ex-cons are treated with the same equal rights) and kept looking for him to make a false move. He believed that even if he tried to lead a normal life, some people felt they had a license to keep calling him names, to continue to ruin his existence. There was always someone (some ambitious person) who wanted a promotion, fame, who was waiting in the bushes for his chance. This reality, at times, was difficult for Ralph to digest.

"Ralph . . . can I talk to you?"

Ralph was walking up Piazza Barberini toward the club when an Italian he knew, only by sight, came up to him. He stopped. "Sure, what is it?"

The man looked furtively around and then half-whispered, "There's an American here, and he wants to buy some stuff—$20,000 worth."

"What stuff?" Ralph asked, as if Ralph didn't know to what he was referring.

"Narcotics," the Italian whispered uneasily.

"What!" Ralph yelled. "Did I ever sell you any narcotics?"

"No."

"Well . . . get the hell out of here . . . or I'll kick you in the pants. Don't you ever stop me again!"

Ralph was fuming. When was he going to have some peace? The next day, another Italian approached him. The same thing occurred. Ralph sent the second man on his way with greater vehemence. "Get the hell away from me, if you know what's good for you. Don't let me see your face again!"

At that point, Ralph figured something was going haywire. Something was wrong. Ralph had noticed a few FBI men around and put two and two together. *They're out to frame me and Charlie on a narcotics rap,* he thought immediately. But, unable to come up with any answers, he did what he thought best. He went to his friend, Police Commissioner Giampaoli, to report what was happening.

"Dottore, I'm telling you . . . there's a frame in the works," Ralph complained energetically.

"Ralph, don't worry. We know you're not selling narcotics."

"But there are some people around offering people money . . . trying to frame me and Charlie."

"Look, I know you're minding your own business. You're clean. Don't you worry about anybody. Nobody's going to bother you."

Ralph thanked him and left but was far from assured. *Famous last words,* he thought. A few days went by, and Ralph lived them like a man waiting for the ax to fall. Sure enough, one morning, he picked up the newspaper, and there it was—a story about a ship from Naples; its destination, New York. As it approached the New York harbor, a garbage tanker moved in rather closely, and a bag that was meant to be thrown aboard the tanker fell instead into the bottom of the ocean. The police later hauled it out and found about $200,000 worth of heroin. And who was to blame? The article said that the hand of Luciano was obviously behind such a daring act. He and his lieutenants had purchased all the police in Italy and were sending narcotics to the States. There it was! Everything Ralph was afraid of was beginning.

Early that evening, Ralph met Charlie at the Excelsior Bar. It was a rendezvous place for them; the service and ambience suited them, and they avoided the more obvious: being spotted together in Ralph's clubs.

"Charlie, did you see the papers?"

"No. Haven't touched them yet. Why?"

"Well, there's a scandal about narcotics in New York. They found a garbage bag with $200,000 worth of heroin in the ocean . . . was supposed to be thrown aboard this ship. Who do you think got the blame for it?"

"Let me guess." He paused, arched his eyebrows, and said, "We did."

"Naturally," Ralph replied.

"Hell . . . let them write what they want. They blame us for everything. The only thing they haven't accused us of is robbing a baby." Charlie was just as disgusted as Ralph. What could anyone do? Ralph sighed. The chips were against them.

Precisely on October 3, 1948, the *Rome Daily American* carried another story entitled, $200,000 HEROIN SEIZED IN US; LUCIANO BLAMED. An Italian liner—this time it was the Vulcania from Genoa—was inspected by U.S. Customs upon its arrival in New York. Officials found a $200,000 cache of heroin hidden in a cabin occupied by six stewards. The inspector, a Mr. Harry Durning, expressed his belief that Luciano was involved in smuggling drugs into the U.S. and was the brains behind an organized gang operating in Italy. Ralph became agitated all over again. What gave that man the right to spout off without proof? Just because Charlie was living in Italy! The gray clouds were growing darker, and Ralph felt the FBI men closing in.

Vera, one of the club's showgirls, came up to Ralph and asked to speak to him. "Mr. Ralph, can I speak to you?"

"Sure, what is it?" he replied.

"About six o'clock tonight," the girl began nervously, "I was having my supper at the Tavernetta restaurant . . . on Via Sistina . . . when two men at another table asked me to join them. I refused, but they were persistent. First, one comes over to my table and sits down. Then the other comes, and they insisted on ordering drinks. So . . . I finally let it go, and had a few drinks with them. Then I got scared."

"What happened?" Ralph asked, not really knowing what to expect.

"Well, one guy says, 'Young lady, do you know where I can get some heroin?' I told them I didn't know what that was, but if they were sick, I could take them to a doctor. They started to laugh at me. I got mad and told them off. Then the other guy tells me they wanted to buy narcotics, but I still didn't know what they were talking about. 'Are you making a damn fool out of me?' I asked. 'I don't know what a narcotic is!'"

"Yeah, go on. What else did they say?" Ralph urged because now he was seeing things a little more clearly. His suspicions were right. He smelled a rat.

Vera was wringing her hands but went on. "Then one says, 'Do you know Charlie Lucky?' and I told them I had seen him around. Then he goes on and asks me if I knew Ralph Liguori. I told them, of course, that I worked for you. When one of them asked where . . . I told them at the Columbia Club."

They damned well knew she worked for him. Ralph interrupted her and said, "Listen, Vera, did they mention what hotel they were staying at?"

"Yeah, they told me the Ambassador Hotel on Via Veneto, and even gave me their room number."

How convenient, thought Ralph. "Okay, girl, don't worry about it. Don't say anything to anybody, and if you see them again . . . walk the other way." He dismissed her and went to the phone to call Diamond Dick. He was the only one he could use for what he had in mind. They met, but not before Ralph learned that the name of his enemy was George White, a crackerjack narcotics agent.

"Dick, you've got to do me a favor. Just do as I tell you and NOTHING else!" Diamond Dick nodded, seeing the serious look on Ralph's face. Ralph then proceeded to give him a few instructions. "There are some FBI guys around . . . trying to frame me and Charlie. Last night they stopped Vera, asking her for narcotics. Now, I know the trail is on me and Charlie. So here's what you do. You go to the Ambassador Hotel and call 'em up. Here's the phone number. Tell them, 'I heard you want to buy some stuff.' Don't worry. Stuff can mean anything. He'll probably tell you he'll be right down to talk to you. When he comes down, you just repeat what I told you. That you heard they wanted to buy some stuff. NOTHING ELSE. Understand?"

"Yeah, Ralph. I git ya."

"Okay . . . then bring me back the news."

For once, Dick did as he was told. He met the men, briefly talked, and made an appointment for dinner. At dinner, they were cagey with one another. The two men suspicious of the encounter coyly played along—sizing up the character before them. Dick, however, was no amateur and did the same. Nothing came out of the meeting. They agreed to meet again for lunch the next day. This time, they opened up a little, and one said, "You know I'd like to invest some money here—at least $20,000. I have plenty of money on me, but I don't trust these dagos. These Italian guys will cut me. I want somebody I can trust. And I'm looking to get a good deal."

Dick was still playing a cagey game and said, "Well, I don't know what you want to buy?"

"Come on, don't play fox with us," one of them replied.

"Hey . . . look . . . you guys . . . I can't be wasting my time with you. See you around." Dick stood up to leave, but not before one called out.

"Let's meet tomorrow, same time, same place."

"Yeah, sure." And Dick left them to phone Ralph of the developments.

Ralph had them on his mind all that night at the Columbia Club. He couldn't help being irritable. It was not easy to sit by and watch people's conspiracies. After ten years in prison for something he didn't do, Ralph had understandably become a little paranoid. He found suspicious entanglements everywhere. His insides were rumbling like a volcano, and he feared the consequences of the explosion. He was talking to the bartender on duty when he happened to turn at the sound of people coming down the stairs. Instinctively he knew. They were the two FBI men!

He motioned to the bartender to fill his drink, and as he poured, he whispered, "Tell Ms. Vera to go into the ladies' dressing room, and not to come out until I get there. Then, when the phone rings, call me, whether it's for me or not." Ralph needed an excuse to get up so the men would not suspect he knew who they were. Sure enough, about ten minutes later, the phone rang. After he hung up, Ralph went straight to the dressing room, which was just a few feet way. He found Vera fidgeting and calmly took her by the arm. "Come here, Vera, look through these drapes. Do you remember what you told me yesterday about those two guys you saw in the Tavernetta? Look through here and tell me if that's them over there."

"Oh, Mr. Ralph . . . how did you know it was them?"

"Never mind, Vera. I have a little more experience than you. Just casually go out and sit down."

After a few minutes, Ralph nonchalantly returned to his bar and resumed his drink. The men sat as though they were unconcerned, sipping their drinks—long enough to get a good look at Ralph and his club.

The next day, Dick had another meeting with the agents; and when they asked him if he had any news for them, the sparks began to fly. "Look," Dick began, "let's cut out the cat-and-mouse game. I still don't know what you guys want to buy."

"What do you do here?" One snapped.

"I'm a GI in Rome, studying Italian under the GI Bill of Rights," Dick retorted.

"Well, what we want to buy is narcotics," the other finally blurted out.

"Narcotics? I don't know anybody who sells narcotics!" Dick gasped.

"Don't you know Ralph Liguori and Lucky Luciano?" they growled.

"Sure I do, but if I'd go to them with a thing like this, they'd kick me in the pants."

"Well, all we want is protection."

But Dick did not budge.

When they saw that they were getting nowhere, the men pulled out their badges and told Dick they were FBI men. Their tone softened as they asked for his help, collaboration, but Dick still maintained that he knew nothing, that he could be of no assistance.

After their usual progress report, Ralph left Dick up to his own devices and went to the Broadway Club. He stood at the bar, facing the door. It was a habit with him in order to check on the action, but that night, he was obsessed with what was happening—what he would do about it. Three years had gone by since his arrival in Rome, and he had a clean record. It was important to him because his dream was to apply for reentry to the United States. After five years, completing his fifteen-year maximum with good behavior on the outside, he would be eligible to do so. Therefore, he was especially nervous, on edge, because he thought someone was trying to force a monkey wrench into his plans.

When he noticed George White walk in with a big cigar propped haughtily in his mouth, Ralph smoldered with murder in his eyes. What stung him even further was that behind White was Hank Manfredi, a good friend of his and Charlie's. Hank was head of the FBI in Italy. His office was in Trieste, but from time to time, he came to Rome. Ralph knew him from when he had been a CID man for the American Armed Forces. Hank was also surprised to see Ralph and immediately gave him the eye—winked as if to say, *Is this guy coming after you?* Ralph didn't budge, didn't say anything. He pretended he didn't know White, and the two men took their table near the dance floor. Ralph's eyes were fixed on George White—so smug, so sure of himself.

White was about fifty, with a stocky build, and Ralph could tell he was a fast operator. He had learned that White was one of Washington's Narcotics Chief Anslinger's best men. As he watched White smiling and talking to Hank, making believe he did not notice Ralph, something snapped, and Ralph beckoned the waiter. "Listen," Ralph said, "see that man with the cigar in his mouth? Tell him somebody wants to talk to him at the bar. He'll know!" Ralph added firmly.

Sure enough, White casually strolled over.

"Sir, did you want to speak to me? I'm afraid I don't know you."

Ralph grabbed him by the lapels and snarled, "Why . . . you rat bastard . . . so you don't know *me*!"

"Just a minute, Ralph, don't get excited," White pleaded.

"I thought you didn't know who I was. You lying bastard," Ralph interrupted, squeezing the lapels a little more.

"Don't lose your temper, Ralph. The Italian police know I'm here."

"I don't give a goddamn about you and all the FBI put together!" Ralph released him and put both his hands in his pockets.

When White saw Ralph's new stance, he became edgy. "Do you have a pistol permit? Do you have a gun on you?"

Ralph almost laughed because that was the last thing he would be carrying in his pocket, but he played along. "None of your goddamn business. You have no jurisdiction over me." White tried to interrupt, but Ralph continued sharply, "Look, never mind about what pistol I have. If I wanted to hit you, I wouldn't do it with a small Beretta. I'd shoot you with a .45, so you wouldn't get up anymore. I'm going to give you two hours to get the hell out of Rome, if you know what's good for you. Otherwise, I'll send you home in a macaroni box!"

Manfredi had shot up to join them. "Ralph, what's the matter? What's the trouble?"

"Why, this son of a bitch is going around town trying to bribe people to frame me and Charlie on narcotics with a $20,000 stake!" Ralph raged.

"Take it easy," Hank said, trying to calm him. "He told me he was on someone's tail, Ralph . . . ready to make an arrest, and called me in on this . . . told me to come to Rome. But I'll tell you now in front of him. If I knew he was gunning for you and Charlie, I would not have come down. I would have told him that he was wasting his time. I'll swear for you and Charlie. Come on . . . Ralph . . . let's forget it. Let's have a drink."

White seconded the invitation, but Ralph simply glared at him and said, "No, I don't drink with a rat bastard like you. I'll drink with a bum out on the street before I would drink with a person like you." Then he turned to Manfredi, "Hank . . . sorry . . . I'll drink with you anytime, but not with him. That's it. Some other time."

White headed for the door, but Hank took Ralph's arm gently. "Meet me tomorrow at the Excelsior, and we'll have a drink together, okay?"

Ralph nodded and turned to his drink at the bar. His nerves were shot. He needed cooling off.

As agreed, the next day, Ralph met Hank at the Excelsior Bar, and Hank tried to reassure his faith in Ralph over a couple of drinks. They had known each other since Ralph's early arrival in Rome, and Hank knew how fairly he had treated the armed forces boys. He tried to console Ralph.

"You know how it is, Ralph . . . They're always writing about Charlie and you. Don't worry. Once in a while some loners come around and try things on their own, for what they believe to be the 'big one'. Like I said, Ralph . . . if I knew it was you and Charlie, I wouldn't have wasted my time coming down here." They shook hands, and Hank left to go back to Trieste. Ralph stuck around because he was expecting Charlie; he couldn't wait to tell him what happened.

It was October, and the night air had become chilly. Charlie walked in wearing a handsome tailor-made light wool coat and a beautiful Borsalino in the same brown hues. He could have made the best-dressed list if he were from the right side of the tracks, Ralph thought cynically. They sat at a table near the bar, and when Ralph brought Charlie up-to-date, he shrugged off the affair, telling Ralph that since they were clean, they had nothing to worry about. But Ralph couldn't be convinced so easily. Once before he had been clean, yet he had done time anyway.

They tossed around a few other arguments, and then Charlie left to meet Igea. Ralph joined Orson Welles at the bar. Orson was always interesting, and his conversations had a soothing effect on Ralph, making him forget his blues for a while. Welles was a triple threat. While he was talking to Ralph, drinking, he was eating a sandwich and writing a script at the same time. He told Ralph about a new film *(Prince of Foxes)* that he had just signed to do with 20th Century Fox. He was to play Cesare Borgia, and Tyrone Power had the leading role of Count Orsini. Welles was also working on many other things in Italy. After some time, he also left—almost simultaneously with George White's entrance. White headed for the bar, eased himself onto the stool, turned toward Ralph, and, with his lily-white finger, motioned to him to come over.

"Who you calling, your sister?" Ralph said loud and clear, his anger returning.

White noticed that Ralph's color had changed and went to him. "Ralph, I'm sorry. Maybe, I was a little rude. Excuse me."

Ralph was completely untouched by his remarks. "You better get out of here before it's too late," he whispered.

"Well, will you do me a favor?" White asked.

"What is it?"

"Please don't tell anyone that I'm here in Rome."

"Look, I don't give a goddamn about you and the others like you. I don't care who's here. Just leave Charlie and me alone. We've had enough of the likes of you. We're sick and tired of you all!"

Ralph never did see White again, but he had a feeling his troubles were just beginning.

CHAPTER FORTY-SIX

On January 20, 1949, Harry S. Truman took the oath as the thirty-third president of the United States of America and, the next day, returned to his desk in the Oval Room in the West Wing of the White House to resume his duties.

A few months later, on May 5, Thomas E. Dewey, accompanied by his wife and secretary, Paul E. Lockman, sailed for Europe on the Cunard Line's *Queen Mary*. After the stress and strain of the presidential campaign and the disappointment of his defeat, he was quoted as saying to a reporter at a press conference, "I was just as surprised as you are, and I gather that it's shared by everybody in this room." Dewey decided to take a holiday, a six-week tour of Europe.

Ralph was sitting alone at the Excelsior Bar, reading the daily newspaper, searching for news of Dewey, when his heart skipped a beat. The article read, "DEWEY IN VENICE; NEXT STOP: ROME." It was Sunday, June 5. His blood drummed in his ears—with orchestra cymbals crashing against his eardrums. He had subconsciously waited for the moment—even dreamed of it for a long time—and now consciously faced the possibility of seeing Dewey. What would he do when Dewey came to Rome? What would he say if he saw him? He wondered whether Charlie knew. Oh, of course! Charlie ALSO read the papers. Ralph stood up trembling, paid for the coffee, and walked out onto the Via Veneto. The fresh air helped clear his head. He thought he'd walk to the Columbia Club, where he could pull himself together, and he wasn't there five minutes when the phone rang. It was a friend, Major Brennen from the American embassy, asking to see him in the morning.

The major was sitting behind his desk, mulling through some papers, when Ralph entered. They shook hands cordially and exchanged banalities. Then the major went right to the point. Dewey was coming to Rome, and he was concerned. Ralph said nothing, waiting to hear more.

"Listen, Ralph . . . I know you got a bad deal in the States. You didn't deserve it. We understood that here . . . also because of how you've treated all the military around Rome. If I were you, I would say hello to him. After all, Dewey is still governor of New York, and he can help you go back to the States." The major was looking at Ralph very sympathetically, hoping to convince him. It made Ralph feel good, knowing the major believed in him.

"I don't know, Major. I'm kind of afraid of my emotions after all these years. When I read about it yesterday, I was practically a basket case!"

"Ralph, you have a couple of days to get yourself under control. On Wednesday, June 8, Dewey will take a sightseeing tour of Rome. I'll tell you his tour route, and your best bet to see him is at the Pantheon. Plan to be there around ten in the morning. When you see him, go right up and talk to him." The major's eyes were intense as he waited for an affirmative answer.

Ralph played with his hat on his lap, embarrassed by the major's interest in him. He thanked the embassy man for his concern and drew a deep breath. "I don't know how I'll handle it," he continued, "but . . . okay . . . Major, I'll go and talk to him."

Back in his hotel room, Ralph sat on the edge of the bed, thinking. Revenge could be so sweet. He was happy that Dewey didn't become president. The office of the president was almost sacred, and Ralph felt Dewey did not belong in such a high place—not after what he had done. The fact that Dewey was taking his defeat badly made Ralph feel good. Sometimes there was some justice.

Ralph put in a call to Charlie at the Quirinale Hotel and tried to be casual.

"Guess who's coming to Rome?"

"I give up. Who?" Charlie asked expectantly.

"Dewey's coming to Rome," Ralph steamed. "That rat bastard."

Some moments passed before Charlie spoke. "Listen, Ralph . . . what's on your mind? Leave him alone!"

Ralph was hurt by the tone of Charlie's voice.

Charlie repeated his words slowly, firmly.

Ralph mumbled an agreement and hung up. He was finally convinced of a conspiracy between Charlie and Dewey. The short conversation told him everything. Ralph decided to keep away from Charlie, at least until he cooled off, because he couldn't promise himself what he would do.

Somehow, he got through the days, but his nights were sleepless. The newspaper, always in his pocket, reported Dewey's moves around Rome. The tour was described as nonpolitical. While in Europe, Dewey planned no comment on political or international matters. *But how can he resist the spotlight?* wondered Ralph. In London, Dewey had met with Winston Churchill, Foreign Secretary Bevin, and even addressed members of the House of Commons. In Rome, he was being wined and dined by all the bigwigs—having dinner with Prime Minister De Gasperi, lunch with Foreign Minister Sforza, talks at the Quirinale, a tête-à-tête with American Ambassador Dunn, and a brief audience with the pope. It was Ralph's turn.

That eventful morning would remain etched in Ralph's mind forever. He had spent the night in the hotel because of its proximity to the Pantheon, and he was mindful of Elena's anxieties. He took longer than usual to shower and dress. He wanted to be impeccably dressed—to look his best. He savored every move, every gesture, all the while thinking of what he would do. At the corner coffee shop, he had his espresso, sipping and thinking, almost ceremoniously. He picked up a newspaper, then waited for his cousin Mario to open the jewelry store. Too nervous to read the paper, he leaned against the wall, eyes fixed on the Pantheon, remembering the first night he had admired it from his hotel window. Soon it would be the backdrop for his encounter with Dewey. Ralph had harbored his hatred for thirteen long years—from the moment he had refused Dewey's bribe against Charlie. Afterwards, in prison, sacrificed by Dewey's ambition, Ralph had planned—dreamed—of a vendetta. The thought of Charlie made him grit his teeth in bitter remembrance. "Leave him alone," Charlie had said, which infuriated Ralph. That phrase was part of an enigma, which had begun in Dannemora. He understood that Dewey had Charlie transferred to another prison, back then, to ultimately help prepare for Charlie's release. In the process, Ralph was to be sacrificed again.

"Hey . . . Ralph . . . you look like you're sleeping with your eyes open."

Ralph hadn't seen his cousin saunter up to the store. "Yeah, almost," he chuckled and followed Mario into the shop.

They had breakfast delivered and conversed over coffee when suddenly, Ralph's ears picked up the faint wail of sirens. *This is it,* he thought. The police sirens grew louder, and Ralph rushed out in time to see the motorcycle escort of Dewey's car coming into the square. They passed right by Ralph, turned, and stopped in front of the Pantheon. Immediately, the square was full of police. The motorcycle escort remained in position while other police cars pulled into the square. In the center, a crowd of plainclothesmen and detectives surveyed the action. The sirens had attracted early morning shoppers who stopped to stare, and people leaned out of their windows.

Dewey's car remained parked for some time, and Ralph swallowed hard before crossing the square toward the car when three policemen stopped him, saying, "Sorry, you can't pass." Just then, Dr. Fontana, police commissioner of the political squad, came up, signaling permission for Ralph to be allowed through. "Let him pass," he ordered. "He knows the man!"

Ralph proceeded slowly with the three policemen close behind, his heart pounding as he sensed a hundred eyes watching him. But he was focused on only one man. The police moved Ralph to the opposite side of the car from where Dewey was sitting, and at that moment, Elena came rushing toward him, shouting his name. She knew the anger in his heart and feared he would do something rash like pull out a revolver to shoot Dewey. Just as Ralph reached out to open the car door, the frantic Elena tugged at his arm, but he ignored her plea. Slowly, he drew open the door and leaned in. "Hello, Tom . . . ," he managed. "Welcome to Rome."

Dewey's face went stone white in shock and fear; then he gasped, "Hello, Ralph."

Mrs. Dewey, her hand on her husband's, maintained her composure, leaning forward to say, "Hello, Mr. Liguori. How are you?" Dewey's secretary, Mr. Lockman, mumbled some inaudible greeting, but Ralph had eyes only for Tom Dewey.

Feverish with emotion, Ralph uttered the question that had burned inside him for years.

"Tom . . . I want to ask you one thing. Do you sleep nights for what you've done to Charlie and me?"

No answer.

"You knew we had nothing to do with that case!"

After a long tense silence, Dewey found his voice.

"Let's forget it, Ralph."

It was a sad voice, perhaps even remorseful, as though he wished Ralph would disappear, that it was just a bad dream. But Ralph's voice pressed on. "Forget it? I was innocent. How can I forget ten years in prison for something I had nothing to do with?"

"Let's just try and forget it," Dewey repeated, embarrassed, his tone pleading.

Ralph had heard the same plea from Charlie over and over again. Elena's hand, trying to pull him away, had a calming effect on him. "It's not so easy," Ralph said softly, more in control of himself, and backed away slightly to let the Dewey party out.

Lockman emerged awkwardly, followed by Mrs. Dewey. Dewey was the last to step out, and Ralph noticed he was as dapper as ever. In 1948, Dewey had been voted one of the ten best dressed men in America. He seemed to have difficulty looking at Ralph, his color still pale; then finally, he turned to Ralph and asked, "Are you coming with me, Ralph? Do you want to come in with us?"

"Sure . . . I'll come with you," Ralph surprised himself by his reply, and they all walked together into the Pantheon. They were the center of attraction, surrounded by security personnel. Once inside, Ralph saw that ropes had been placed in a circle directly under the open dome, which was done whenever it rained. (The architects of old had provided for a drainage system in the center, perforating some of the center floor mosaics in a harmonious pattern.) In all the confusion, Ralph decided to hang back against the huge doors, telling Dewey to go ahead.

"Okay, Ralph," Dewey replied, noticeably trembling, and began walking with his escort toward the center of the Pantheon, the organ music playing in his honor. He looked back over his shoulder to keep an eye on Ralph and, in doing so, did not see the ropes in front of him and suddenly stumbled over them. There was a murmur from the crowd, and someone quickly took Dewey's arm to help him regain his balance.

Ralph was some yards back when it happened, and a policeman said, "Hey, Ralph . . . He's sure scared of you!"

"If you did what he did, you'd be scared too," Ralph replied. "Remember . . . in America they called us gangsters, but I can tell you one thing. When a man walks the way he did, his conscience can't be clean."

"He's got a lot of nerve coming to Italy," another detective said.

Ralph made no comment. Dewey was still a famous politician, governor of New York. If Ralph were to do anything out of line, some policeman would love to lock him up and get a promotion. Ralph decided to keep quiet.

The welcoming ceremony soon over, the whole entourage began to leave the Pantheon. Dewey approached Ralph at the door, and the two walked out together toward the car.

"Look, Tom . . . ," Ralph began. "I want to apply to return to the United States. Are you going to blackball that too?"

Dewey took a deep breath, avoiding Ralph's eyes. "No . . . Ralph, go ahead. Do it." He agreed, then, more relaxed, asked, "Where's Charlie?" Dewey dared a swift glance at Ralph, unwilling to reveal his feelings. They were standing together at the car, his wife and secretary already in the backseat, but Dewey waited for Ralph's answer.

"He's in the hotel," Ralph replied, concealing his displeasure.

"Tell him to come and see me. I'm at the Hassler Hotel," Dewey said with another sneak look at Ralph. Then urged, "Will you tell him?"

"Sure, I'll tell him. I'll call him right up." Ralph reassured him, wondering if his smirk was showing. He wouldn't *think* of preventing Dewey from seeing Charlie, his partner in crime. Ralph enjoyed the prospect. It confirmed all his suspicions.

"Thanks, Ralph. Good-bye and . . . behave yourself," Dewey breathed, and Ralph never saw a man so relieved. Dewey's ordeal had ended.

"Yeah . . . so long, Tom. My regards to the States," he replied, sarcastically. And as he watched the car drive off, Ralph sneered quietly, "Fuck off, you mustache bastard!"

From the jewelry store, Ralph phoned Charlie, and they met for lunch at Passetto's near the Piazza Navona—Charlie eager for the news. "You should have seen the way he looked, Charlie . . . when I opened the door and he saw me!"

"Well, he probably thought it was his last moment. It's a wonder he didn't have a heart attack." Charlie laughed.

"But that's not all! When he went into the Pantheon, he fell over the ropes, trying to watch what I was going to do," Ralph added animatedly.

"You can't blame the guy for being worried," Charlie snickered. "You're the last man he ever wanted to see."

Ralph let that one pass, mentioned a few other events, then stopped abruptly. "He wants to see you, Charlie. He asked me to tell you to call him at the Hassler." Ralph stared hard at Charlie for his reaction. Nothing. Suddenly, he exploded. "Jesus Christ . . . Charlie . . . it's all so clear to me now! Why didn't you tell me about this before? You must have known I always had my suspicions. Charlie . . . I always respected you as my friend . . . as the General . . . For Chrissake, you're my godfather! You should have come clean with me! You did me a raw one . . . Charlie!" Ralph seethed, trembling with hurt.

Charlie turned red with guilt, knowing the time had come for confession. Wearily, with the contorted features of a drowning man, he tried to plead his case. "What the hell, Ralph, after all the appeals failed, I had to do something. Everyone knew we had nothing to do with the case. They gave me a maximum of fifty years and could have kept me for thirty. You had a maximum of fifteen. I didn't feel like dying in jail, so I made a deal!"

"A deal?" Ralph repeated, despair building.

"Yeah . . . a deal."

Charlie was now bent on telling all. "I had the boys pay him off: I gave Meyer Lansky a hundred grand to give to Dewey. But that wasn't enough for him. Part of the deal was my promise to get him elected governor of New York, which we delivered in 1943, and the other condition was that we would support him, when the time came, for the presidency."

Ralph was on fire. "Couldn't you have told me?" he cried. "Did you take me for a jerk? Did you forget I went up the river for you? All I had to do was accept Dewey's bribe, and I would have been a free man! But YOU, Charlie . . . you know the rules of betrayal . . . and yet . . . Charlie . . . Charlie!"

Ralph cried, shaking his head despondently.

"Can't you see, Ralph, I had no choice. I weighed everything in the balance, and I had no choice," Charlie insisted, relieved that it was finally all coming out.

"But you should have told me! Maybe things would have been different for me too!" wailed Ralph.

"I couldn't. That was also part of the deal. Dewey wanted you out of the way, Davey and everyone else in Dannemora who could have gotten wind of it, but especially you . . . Ralph. You knew too much. After all, they tried to buy you. He couldn't afford to have you running around loose, blabbing, while he's trying to campaign."

"So . . . *that's* why my brief never got out of prison?"

Charlie lowered his eyes, ashamed.

"And then that phony story in the newspaper that Davey and I tried to cut your face was a ready-made excuse to separate us." Ralph contemplated his clenched hands with disgust. He had finally put the pieces of the puzzle together.

"Ralph . . . I heard about that farce, and I want you to know I had nothing to do with it. All I was told was that we would be separated."

"Yeah . . . sure . . . ," Ralph replied sarcastically. "Ralph, the patsy, the number one fall guy! That rat bastard made me the scapegoat twice!" Rage surged through Ralph's body. He wanted to break the dishes and glassware on the table, but Charlie exclaimed, "Come on . . . let's get out of here." He signaled the waiter, and the two weary men left to walk around the Piazza Navona. Charlie broke the heavy silence.

"Everything was carefully planned. The navy was facing problems on the waterfront with German U-boats. They had sunk a lot of ships, and Nazi saboteurs were all along the Atlantic coast. After the *Normandie* burned, some of the boys on the waterfront were approached to help, but the catch was no one would do anything on a large scale if I didn't get into the act. It was no big deal. You know as well as I do, they can say they want about us, but traitors we're not. All the guys wanted to do their bit for the war. So we built up the whole thing to make it look like a big war effort on my part, because that was supposed to be our cover-up story—the excuse for Dewey to release me. It was because of all these things that Dewey transferred me to Great Meadow away from everybody. The rest of the stuff about me and Sicily . . . I already told you . . . It's a lot of crap! We didn't do anything to deny the rumors at the time, because it helped magnify my war effort. Christ . . . Ralph . . . can you understand I wanted out!"

"And the plans included my being shanghaied out of the States—out of Dewey's hair?" Ralph interrupted. "Christ, Charlie . . . what a double cross! Can you imagine how I've been tormented all these years?"

"Ralph . . . I'm sorry . . . but you've got to believe me. There was no other way. If Dewey had become president, we'd both be back in the States today. That was to be the real payoff. He didn't make it, and we're still here. At least, we're not behind bars."

Charlie's remorse calmed Ralph. He was glad—not that he felt any better about any of it, but at least the air had been cleared. "Well, Charlie . . . I knew it had to be a fix, but you just should have told me. That's all."

Ralph was resigned to his destiny, but he felt he could never feel the same way about Charlie.

They parted. Ralph walked to his hotel, and Charlie grabbed a cab. Ralph walked up to his room in a fog, feeling the need for a nap to soothe his nerves. As he undressed, he thought of Charlie and Dewey, tried to imagine Charlie's phone call to Dewey, knowing that Charlie would make it short and sweet. Sleep wouldn't come. He was still turning and tossing when the phone rang.

"Ralph?"

"Yeah, Charlie."

"I'm seeing Dewey at nine thirty tomorrow night at the Hassler. Want to come along?"

"Naw, Charlie. You go by yourself, 'cause I'm known more than you around here. It's best we're not seen together going up. We're liable to get stopped."

"Yeah . . . you're probably right. Okay . . . just wanted you to know."

"Thanks, Charlie . . . Give him my regards." And Ralph smiled because he was sure that was one thing Dewey didn't want to hear.

"Yeah, okay . . . Ralph. Call me late tomorrow, and I'll let you know." Ralph could tell he was anxious to cut the conversation short.

"Yeah . . . okay . . . *Ciao*."

Somehow, the fact that Charlie had called soothed Ralph. He knew that Charlie didn't want to break the ties that bound them, and that, just maybe, the General had begun to fear his "lieutenant." With a sense of morbid satisfaction, Ralph rolled over and slept like a lamb.

Ralph stood outside the Columbia Club, restless, unable to work. In half an hour, they would meet. It was the only thing ringing in Ralph's head. Hands in his pockets, he walked up and down the streets and found himself heading toward the Piazza della Repubblica (near

Charlie's hotel, at the time the Quirinale)—not stopping to look at one of his favorite fountains, at the tantalizing maidens of the four seasons, which seemed to reach out for him. Unconsciously, he turned onto Via Nazionale, reached Via Torino, and slipped around the corner into the dark shadows of the night. He stood staring at the entrance of the Quirinale Hotel across the street, and as he expected, at nine fifteen sharp, Charlie walked out, dressed to kill with a huge bouquet of long-stemmed pink roses. *For Mrs. Dewey, no doubt,* Ralph sneered to himself. The cab was waiting for Charlie, and as he drove off, Ralph automatically continued his walk down Via Nazionale, turned right at the tunnel, and, at the end, found himself on Via del Tritone at the foot of Francesco Crispi. He was subconsciously walking to the Hassler Hotel, expecting God knows what. Casually, he looked up and saw the neon sign for the Florida Club and, in a semitrance, walked toward it. Luckily, the doorman, an ex-carabiniere and friend, called him. His voice broke the spell, lifting the heavy, dull pressure in his head.

"How d'ya feel? Heard you saw Dewey?" the doorman remarked.

Word sure got around fast, thought Ralph. As the two exchanged a word on the subject, a familiar young plainclothesman walked up and leaned toward Ralph confidentially, whispering, "Ralph . . . in a couple of days, I want to tell you something."

"Well, tell me. Tell me now," Ralph replied.

"No. I can't tell you . . . no . . . no . . . I can't."

"Why? Why can't you tell me? What is it . . . a secret?" Ralph teased.

"Yeah, a big secret."

"Oh, yeah," Ralph chuckled. "Are you trying to tell me that . . . Dewey's here?"

The young man looked startled.

"How d'ya know?" he gasped.

The doorman started laughing and said, "This man could put you and many more like you in his hip pocket."

Ralph laughed, then turned to the young policeman. "What the hell were you trying to say—and not say—by not telling me that Dewey's here? What's your position in all this?"

"Well . . . I'll tell you now that you know," he answered, embarrassed at his blunder. "I was stationed here to tell you that you couldn't pass."

"Couldn't pass here?"

"Yeah . . . We had orders to stop you, if we saw you going down Via Sistina toward the Hassler!"

"Suppose I had wanted to?"

"Then . . . we had orders to take you to the police commissioner."

"Ah, so?" Ralph sang. "Well . . . don't worry. He doesn't interest me anymore." Again, Ralph's suspicions were correct about being stopped. The police commissioner, however, had always told Ralph not to be seen too much with Charlie around Rome, especially since he was running the clubs.

"Come on," Ralph said, "I'll let you escort me back to the Columbia Club." He winked at the doorman, and they took off. The Columbia Club was on Via Gregoriana—a stone's throw from the Hassler.

For the remainder of the evening, Ralph drank and mixed with his guests until he could no longer keep up the pretenses. The suspense was too much. He slipped away into his little office to polish off some work. It was already quite late, but he preferred to wait a little longer before he called Charlie. He didn't want to seem too anxious. Finally, he dialed the number.

"Hey . . . Charlie . . . It's a good thing I didn't go with you," Ralph said sprightly. "They had cops stationed all around the Hassler. We would have been stopped."

"Well . . . it's just as well," Charlie replied softly.

"How'd it go?" Ralph asked.

"Oh . . . okay . . ."

"What'd he have to say?"

"The same old things. If he had been elected president . . . blah . . . blah . . . you and I would be back in the States by now. It went wrong for him, and it went wrong for us too."

"Yeah . . . but we got the dirty end of it," Ralph responded firmly.

"Yeah . . . we did, Ralph. Let's hope for the best." His voice sounded like that of a tired old man. "Good night, Ralph."

"Good night, Charlie." Ralph hung up, closed the lights, the club, and went home to Elena.

The next day, Dewey left Rome to return to New York to finish his term as governor—and to plan his next moves.

"Ralph . . . I want to ask you something as a friend."

Ralph was sitting in the police commissioner's office. His presence had been requested. Instinctively, he knew it was about Dewey.

"Sure, *Dottore* . . . What is it?"

"Why did we have orders to watch only you? We had strict orders to control you closely while Dewey was here, and not Luciano? I can't figure it out."

"*Caro, Dottore*, a lot of people would like to know that. It's a personal story about three guys and a political payoff—a long story, but someday, it will all come out."

As the police commissioner shook his head in bewilderment, Ralph put on his Borsalino, tipped the brim in a salute, and walked out.

Yeah, thought Ralph as he briskly turned the corner toward Via Nazionale. *It's a story about a general, a would-be president, and a little guy named Baby Face Ralph.*

CHAPTER FORTY-SEVEN

Early in January, Charlie gave a heated interview to a reporter after U.S. Customs officials said they had "positive" information that Charlie was involved in all the illegal transfers of narcotics from Italy and (they stated) from the "other Mediterranean countries." Charlie was furious and denied everything. "It looks like an old-style frame-up," he told the reporter. It was further charged that Charlie was linked to $1,000,000 worth of narcotics and perfume seized aboard a French liner. "That's a big lie," Charlie said. "Everywhere I go, it's the same thing—smuggling, smuggling, smuggling. Now they even got me in the perfume business. I'm fed up!" Ralph too had problems. After the George White episode, he thought he'd have some peace, but he also constantly denied his involvement. He was glad Charlie had told reporters the attacks were an insult to the Italian authorities. "Do you think I'd be walking 'round here with no police bothering me, if I were tied up in this kind of thing? If they really want to frame me proper, they ought to arrest somebody and get 'em to say I'm running the business." No one knew then, but his suggestion was soon to materialize.

Charlie and Ralph spent the winter months in relative peace until the end of March. Ralph was at the bar in the Columbia Club, examining some invoices, when the doorman came downstairs, all smiles. "Ralph . . . a young lady wants to see you . . . a foreigner," he announced.

"Tell her to come downstairs," Ralph said matter-of-factly. It could have been just anybody. When he heard the footsteps, he casually looked up and instinctively guessed who she was. By her looks, the description in the newspapers, it had to be Giuliano's girlfriend, Maria Cilyakus. He had recently read about her arrest in Palermo. They had made a big thing about it. The police had apprehended her on her way to Giuliano's hideaway. Furious, she had broken all the windows in the police station because they had wanted her to divulge Giuliano's whereabouts. "I'm a newspaperwoman, not a stool pigeon," she answered stubbornly. They had locked her up, claiming she had highly insulted the police. Giuliano wrote a public letter to her, which he sent to the newspapers and the Palermo court, asking that it be forwarded to Maria in jail. He condemned the harsh police action, talking about freedom of the press. He took the advantage in pleading for his cause. Maria's lack of collaboration resulted in her sentence to four months detention with a suspended sentence, and she was expelled from Italy. They gave her a furlough to Rome to catch her plane home to Sweden.

Ralph stood up to greet her. "Hello . . . you asked for me?"

"I have to make sure you're Ralph," she said. "Have you an identification card?"

Ralph smiled and said, "Just ask anyone around here. Everybody knows me, but if you insist"—at that time, Ralph had a pistol permit, and he pulled it out to show it to her—"here!"

The young woman laughed. "Oh, I knew it was you, because Giuliano had described you perfectly to me. He told me to give you a lot of kisses." And she leaned over and kissed Ralph on both cheeks.

Ralph flushed and gestured for her to sit down, then motioned to the bartender for a couple of drinks. Maria was a beautiful girl, reddish blonde hair with intelligent eyes. She was all keyed up over her experience with Giuliano, with the police, and began to tell Ralph about it. She told him how she had tried to interview Giuliano, but that it was very difficult. She had faced a wall of silence surrounding his name in Sicily. Finally, through another contact, she was escorted to Giuliano in the hills. Her eyes sparked as she mentioned his name, and she confessed she had fallen in love with him almost immediately. Her interview went on for days, and she learned more about Giuliano than most journalists. Their tryst, however, couldn't last forever. It was a dangerous game for both. After a few days, Giuliano begged her to leave for her own good, adding that he had plans to go to the States. Her eyes glistened with tears as she recalled her separation from him. "You know, he had this dream of annexing Sicily to the United States," she added.

Ralph turned away, embarrassed for her, and spied two men walking down the stairs. *Here we go again,* thought Ralph. "Don't look now," Ralph interrupted, "but those guys who just came down are FBI agents."

"Oh, to hell with them," Maria said scornfully. "But are you sure?"

"I'd know those guys anywhere," Ralph snarled. He tried to size them up. One had the look of a well-educated man—distinguished-looking. The other was an obvious sidekick. "Now what the hell do they want?" Ralph said to himself.

"Are those men giving you trouble, Ralph?" Maria asked softly.

"Not yet, Maria, not yet," Ralph replied.

"Never mind," she said, trying to cheer Ralph. She lifted her glass. "Here's to Giuliano. Hope he makes it out of here!" Then she rose to leave. Her last words, as she gently held Ralph's hands, were, "Giuliano wanted me to tell you and Charlie . . . thanks . . . for what you did for him. He'll never forget you!" The next day, Maria Cilyakus left for Sweden, and Ralph lost track of the two Feds.

It was a splendid Sunday morning. Summer had just started, sending its message of love; the sun seemed to make one forget everything that was ugly. Elena and Ralph were leisurely having breakfast while he consulted his U.S. connection (the daily newspaper) about things back home. Dewey had been gone a little more than two weeks, but in the back of Ralph's mind, he had not forgotten Dewey's "okay" about applying for readmission to the States. Like a kid, he was homesick for the sidewalks of New York, his family, and friends, but he knew he had to do more time in Italy. He had to be patient. To pass the time, Ralph read everything he could in English. Thus, it wasn't surprising that he found a tiny, insignificant article on the back page of the *Rome Daily American*, June 26, 1949. He felt someone had unexpectedly punched him. He put down his coffee cup slowly and carefully read, U.S. MAN CARRYING DRUGS JAILED HERE. The article stated that at the Rome Ciampino Airport, the Italian Customs police had picked up a man named Vincent Trupia with sixteen pounds of cocaine in two of his suitcases and another two in a waterproof pouch strapped to his body. Trupia was about to board a plane for New York. "Here we go again," Ralph groaned. Should he tell Charlie right away? *No. Why ruin his day? Why ruin my day,* he told himself and decided to forget the article for the moment. Instead, he took Elena to the beach to enjoy a day of sunshine.

Two days later, he read Washington Narcotics Chief Harry S. Anslinger's comments about the case. He wasn't familiar with Trupia's name. The arrest, he said, was part of a campaign to stamp out international drug traffic, and he had ordered the Italian police to watch Lucky Luciano. He further commented that he had sent one of his experienced agents, District Supervisor Garland Williams, to Rome earlier in the year to delve into the narcotics smuggling racket. Ralph remembered the name. He was the same agent involved in the narcotics rap they had tried to pin on him when he was in Dannemora. He wondered if Williams was the man he suspected of being an FBI agent in the club during Maria's visit. That man fit Williams's description. *But what the hell do I care? I'm clean,* thought Ralph.

About a week went by, and Ralph met Charlie at the Excelsior. He noticed that Charlie's spirits weren't in the least dampened over Trupia, a small-time operator. Finally, they were alone, and Ralph spoke softly, "Charlie, I know you've been reading the papers, so what do you think?"

"Aw, Ralph, don't be a killjoy. Do you always have to worry about everything? Do you know the guy? No. Do I know the guy? Hell, no. Have we been keeping our noses clean? Damn right! You know the cops are watching us all the time, so don't think about it. I'm sick and tired of having to tell everyone that I'm not that desperate to be in the dope business."

"How do you think I feel?" Ralph pressed. "Remember that rap they tried to pin on me in Dannemora? And remember what I went through with Dotty trying to cure her? I will never forget what that stuff did to her . . . And that rat bastard, Dewey, said at the trial that I had started her on the habit. Christ. As far as I'm concerned, it's the crappiest racket. I don't care how much money some guys make."

"Yeah . . . yeah . . . Ralph . . . I remember. Let's not talk about it. I never wanted to handle the stuff back home . . . (Charlie had always fought his associates on this subject.) Frank (Costello) and a couple of others agreed with me . . . yet my name is always plastered around as the kingpin. Well, I'm fed up. I don't give a damn about anybody anymore. Let's forget about it, okay?"

"Yeah, okay . . . Maybe I'm exaggerating, but I can't help having the creeps about this one." Ralph looked up from his drink and saw about six detectives hanging around the lobby. He sighed. "Charlie, you're probably going to say that I'm imagining things again . . . but don't turn around. The whole squad is here!"

"Oh, Christ . . . the hell with them. What do we care?" He shrugged disgustedly.

Ralph looked toward them again and saw one detective whom he knew very well. He gave Ralph the eye, calling him over. Casually, Ralph rose and nonchalantly walked by them when the detective greeted him, amicably taking him aside. "Ralph, it's nothing important, but tomorrow we have orders to pick up you and Charlie. So be ready!"

Ralph was mesmerized, and all he could say was, "Yeah, thanks." He went on to the men's room and returned to Charlie, who still had his back to the action. Charlie shoved his drink aside in complete disgust as he listened to Ralph. "Christ, here we go again," he lamented. "I'm going, Ralph. I want to stay with Igea, kind of prepare her."

Ralph sat there and watched him walk past the detectives, head high and indifferent. He ordered another drink and pulled out his newspaper, trying to drown out his worries. But he couldn't concentrate. He thought about Elena and all the anxiety she had been through lately—and now this. One thing was definite: he would sleep at the hotel. He couldn't bear for her to see him arrested. It was just too demeaning.

Ralph was propped up in his bed, reading, ready for them. The clock read five in the morning, and he knew they would be at his door any minute. Sure enough, he heard the heavy, banging knock.

"*Avanti*, come in," Ralph called.

"*Mani in alto,* hands up," a policeman cried as the door burst open. About ten detectives—all armed—walked in and took different positions. One had a gun, which looked like a small machine gun. It was a MAB (Moschetto Automatico Beretta). Ralph chuckled and said in English, "Put that water pistol away." But the lawman didn't understand. One detective went up close to Ralph and half-whispered, "Ralph, if you have anything, let me know. I'll hide it for you." Ralph looked up at him as if to say, *Do you think I was born yesterday?* And, in a voice for everyone to hear, replied, "No, you look real good 'cause Ralph has nothing to hide."

The police captain ordered Ralph to rise, and as he put on his robe, another cop searched his bureau drawers and found a little German pistol. It had been given to Ralph as a present (a souvenir of the war) by an American officer friend. The police commissioner of the district had given Ralph a permit and authorization to keep it in his room, but it wasn't loaded. The policeman almost leaped with joy. "Aha, *Dottore*, we have him!" And ecstatically held up the pistol. Then he looked at Ralph triumphantly. "Ah, Ralph . . . we finally got you."

Ralph started to laugh. "You got me? Hey, kid . . . you'll have to get up earlier in the morning to get me." Ralph walked over to the bureau, opened another drawer, and pulled out the permit. "Here . . ." He chuckled and gave the permit to the captain.

As the captain read the document, another cop opened the wardrobe and, seeing all of Ralph's suits, called out, "Wow . . . Look how many suits he's got!" Then to Ralph, "Hey, Ralph . . . is it true you wear $100 ties?" Ralph could see they were taken aback by his extensive wardrobe. The rookies were having fun caressing the suits, but he was in no mood for their kid stuff and snapped, "Never mind the ties and suits!" Finally dressed, he turned to the captain. "I'm ready. Let's get this over with." The captain waved everyone out, and Ralph was escorted to police headquarters.

In another part of town, in his elegant Pairoli apartment on Via Lima, Charlie was restless, waiting for the police intrusion. He had prepared Igea and had given her some money to tide her over, in case they kept him more than a couple of days for questioning. Igea, however, couldn't reconcile herself; she was still nervous but bravely held back her tears. The suspense continued all morning. They had decided to have a cup of *cappuccino* (milk and coffee) together while they waited. The doorbell rang, and Igea's cup began to rattle in her trembling fingers. Charlie put down the paper and went to Igea. Gently, reassuringly, he put his hands on her shoulders, then opened the door for his unwanted guests. *Maresciallo* Miniti of the Squadra Mobile stood calmly at the entrance, surrounded by his men, in position for any unpleasant skirmish. He stepped inside and told Charlie he was wanted for questioning at the questura (police headquarters). To his surprise, Charlie cordially told him he was expecting the visit. He asked him kindly to wait a few minutes until he said good-bye to Igea, who was still frozen in her chair. Whispering words of encouragement, he lightly kissed her as the maresciallo motioned him out. Surrounded by police, they walked out side by side to the waiting Fiat 1100 police car, which whisked them away.

While Ralph was being given the preliminary honors at the questura, Dott. Migliorini, assistant to the commissioner, came in to interrogate him personally.

"*Ciao*, Ralph, so we finally got you. Do you know how long I've been following you?"

"No. How long?"

"Six months."

"Why, *Dottore*, I haven't the words to thank you. In America, I had to pay someone to watch my back, but here in Italy, I get it for free. Thank you very much for watching me." Ralph was sarcastic. Migliorini ignored his remarks and plunged right into his questioning.

"Do you know where the Torino Hotel is?" he asked stubbornly.

"If I was ever there, I would have been registered with a girl." Ralph smiled, continuing his sardonic attitude.

"Leave women out of this!" the man practically yelled. Then more calmly, "Do you know a man by the name of Trupia?"

"No . . . I don't know any Trupia. Listen," Ralph added impatiently, "what do you want? Hell, write whatever you want. I'm sick and tired of this treatment!"

Ralph wanted to walk away, the situation was so intolerable, and he turned abruptly, only to see Charlie go by with the squad. Charlie looked at Ralph, paused a second, and remarked in Sicilian.

"Cca' si?" (You here?)

"Cca' sugnu." (Here I am.)

Immediately, Charlie was hustled into another office, and he waited there while Migliorini continued to write. *God knows what he's writing*, thought Ralph. After a few minutes of shuffling his feet, Ralph saw Hank Manfredi walk by, who quickly called to him and came up close.

"Hank, what the hell is going on here?"

"Don't worry, Ralph. I'll swear by you and Charlie."

"Why the hell don't you tell these people to leave us alone!"

"Ralph, don't blame these people. The pressure is on from Washington. They're blaming the Italians for allowing shipments of narcotics to go to New York. And they're convinced it's you and Charlie. They had to pick you up to keep things quiet. Take it easy. It'll be all right." He did his best to restore Ralph's confidence and then disappeared into another room.

Ralph heard a great deal of commotion down the hall, and later, he learned that some other men were also picked up. Three were Sicilians: Francesco Catalano (a resident of Rome), Andrea Mafione, and Antonio Lomanto—all legitimate businessmen whose only crime was that they knew Luciano. Charlie and Ralph (especially Charlie) were constantly contacted for far-fetched business ventures. Everyone believed Charlie was loaded. Ralph definitely wasn't, but his lifestyle gave that impression. These men were also dragged into the mess. While all the questioning was going on, the police thoroughly searched Charlie's apartment and Ralph's hotel room but found nothing that could implicate them.

Sometime later, there was more commotion. Everyone was taken to the Regina Coeli Prison. They were put into the same cell, their nerves shot, comforting each other. Charlie, in his usual big brother act, said, "Relax . . . Ralph . . . They can't pin anything on us. We're clean!"

"What the hell do they want, blood?" Ralph snapped.

"It's like Hank said. The heat is on Italy to lock us up. It'll be over soon. Don't worry."

Ralph nodded skeptically. Another bad dream! He lay back on the cot and tried to release some of the tension. A short time later, a guard showed up at the cell. Charlie was wanted in the warden's office. "Now what?" Ralph asked.

Charlie shrugged and left. When he came back, he smirked. "Guess what happened?"

"What?"

"They showed me a telegram from Washington, which said that we are not to be in the same cell together—not even for a day. We've got to be far apart."

"Maybe they think we can burn down the prison together." Ralph chuckled.

"Yeah," Charlie smiled and picked up his belongings. "Remember, take it easy. They've got nothing on us. We'll be out soon. Just formalities until things cool down." The two pals were separated in different sections of the prison.

Charlie's parting words calmed Ralph, but he began thinking of contacting a lawyer, just in case. He was not aware that Elena, shocked as she was, would do exactly that as soon as she heard the dreadful news. The lawyer contacted someone in the police department and, afterwards, advised Elena to stay calm, that he had reassurance from the police it would all blow over soon—no lawyers were necessary. According to the police, Ralph and Charlie were not arrested, only being held for questioning.

The papers went wild on both sides of the ocean. The *New York Times* building headlined: LUCKY LUCIANO AND RALPH LIGUORI ARRESTED FOR NARCOTICS. Agent Garland Williams was quoted as saying, "The United States is working in close coordination. The importance of the case makes it inadvisable to give out any information." The Italian papers gave daily results of the investigation, some more sympathetic than others, but they were handicapped by the Italian police, who were very reticent about information. Oreste Barranco, chief of the Squadra Mobile, repeated the same phrases, such as, "Nothing important had emerged. Investigations are continuing actively. Nothing new." And he repeated that to the end. Instead, chief of the Italian Interpol Giuseppe Dosi was more emphatic. He chastised the American Press for the inaccuracies—distortion of the facts concerning the questioning of Luciano and possible connection with the international drug ring. "All I can say is that interrogations are going on. But I would caution reserve, since we haven't anything on Luciano yet," he pronounced. Around the fifth day, when questioned again by reporters, Dosi replied, "Luciano and the others are in good spirits. There is nothing else to say. We are still working on our case."

Elena and Igea met often during the detention to console each another and to exchange notes. They would change meeting places because they were afraid of being followed and disturbed by reporters, police, or whomever. Once it was a certain café on Piazza Barberini; another time, a theater near Quattro Fontane; then a restaurant; once in church, Santa Maria degli Angeli; and so it went. Igea was caught several times by reporters—once in her apartment, where she gave brief statements about Charlie's innocence. Elena was different, shy and very much a family person; she managed to avoid all publicity. The women brought food, cigarettes, and clean clothes every day to their men, content to see they were reasonably comfortable. The prison director was quoted as saying, "Luciano is a model prisoner. He chain-smokes, reads a few newspapers, and spends most of his time reading books from the library. He had made no trouble for anyone and is always calm and cheerful. He has not seen Liguori, except for periods during questioning when they are brought in together."

Igea kept pining about Charlie's incarceration. Finally, after waiting five days, she languidly coaxed the chiefs of the Squadra Mobile—using her soft blue eyes to her advantage—and convinced them to allow her to talk to Charlie. He was driven to the questura where they met and chatted briefly. As usual, Charlie reassured her that he would be home soon. Naturally, the newspapers picked up on the visit, but the police would not comment.

Trupia would not sing. After repeated interrogations, he would not reveal the names of his accomplices in the United States. When asked if he knew Luciano, he answered, “Who doesn’t know of him? But I’ve never had anything to do with him or Liguori.” Of course, that didn’t satisfy the Feds, and the Italian police continued to hold them for further questioning. Then came the confrontation with Trupia—first with Charlie, then with Ralph, and, lastly, with the others. Charlie was cool about the meeting, and Ralph was reasonably calm. Again, the Feds banged their heads against the wall. It was simple. They did not know each other.

The vaudeville act continued until the police acted on a tip that the white stuff was being shipped out in confetti. Naturally, Charlie’s candy factory in Palermo was searched and personnel interrogated. The candy story was laughable. Many tales were fabricated about it—imaginations running wild. The results were again negative. There just weren’t any elements (facts) to prove such a fantasy. In later years, Charlie had to finally close the factory; the harassment from the narcotics agents was so great.

Finally, after all the trails and tips had been exhausted, on the eve of July 15, Charlie and Ralph were released, along with the others. Police had absolutely nothing on them. Many people were waiting outside the gates with reporters and photographers, as usual, swarming around. Ralph couldn’t count the police on hand but did see one policeman fall off his motorcycle in the excitement. Fortunately, they were swiftly driven away to their respective homes. Ralph had little trouble when he arrived at his hotel, but Charlie, well, Charlie was Charlie. He found an army of reporters waiting at his apartment in Via Lima. When he stepped out of the car, it was like a blitz; they all pounded upon him, hurling questions. Charlie’s nerves were still on edge, and he snapped, “Can’t I have any peace yet?” He spotted one well-known reporter, who had instantly taken a picture of him. Charlie never did like him; he grabbed the camera and smashed it. “You better not be here when I come down,” he snarled. Then he pushed and shoved everyone aside as he tried to get to his apartment. The party broke up for the moment.

Later, after Charlie had seen Igea and had relaxed, he allowed reporters to come in for a short press conference. He was smiling and serene again, philosophized about the entire affair, commenting about

Agent Garland Williams's morbid persecution of him—behind which was his archenemy, Harry S. Anslinger.

While they were in jail, Charlie's close business associate Meyer Lansky, who had remarried, had decided to take his new wife on a European tour as a delayed honeymoon—and had every intention of seeing his old friend once they arrived in Italy. The ocean liner *Italia* docked in Naples on July 12, and the Lanskys were among the two hundred or so passengers to disembark. They checked in to the Excelsior Hotel, and Lansky was immediately aware of the plainclothesmen in the lobby. He ordered some drinks to his room and, on his way to the elevator, picked up a few newspapers while the young porter followed with the luggage. Lansky took off his jacket, loosened his tie, and slipped into an oversized armchair. The busboy soon came with drinks, and as he slowly savored his drink, he browsed through the papers. There was marked surprise on his face when he read Charlie was in jail on a trumped-up narcotics charge. He shook his head in dismay. What next? Naturally, he could not meet Charlie, especially since the Feds were also on his back. Lansky was deeply disappointed, but there would be another opportunity to see his friend. Throughout their stay in Italy, Lansky continued to follow the case and was greatly relieved to read about Charlie's release. Still, there was too much heat on Charlie. Too risky to see him. It had to be another time. He would send word.

Although the Trupia affair was over, the problems did not cease for Charlie and Ralph. They were cleared of all complicity in the drug traffic, yet the relentless Federal agents weren't satisfied. Ralph believed they were angry because they were innocent—that they were unable to keep them behind bars. They had to find a way to punish them. So much pressure was put on the Italian authorities by Washington that the Italians had to do something to placate them in the face of good relations. Legal retaliation was the answer, even if unjust. It was rumored all along, even after Charlie was released, that he would be declared *persona non grata* and banished from Rome. When a reporter asked Charlie about it, he sighed. "I don't know the rules here. I'm in a fog. Sometimes I think I'm going nuts. In the States I know what I can and can't do, but here, it's different. They got laws I don't know nothing about." In the end, he accepted his fate. Charlie had five days to leave Rome and to return to his birthplace, Lercara Friddi, with a curfew to boot. Even the other men were expelled from Rome and had to return to their hometowns in Sicily.

Ralph, on the other hand, was born in Rome. The only thing they could do was give him a curfew. Ralph knew it was being prepared because he received a tip from friends in the police department. They also told him to find something to do—obtain some kind of normal job. It was obvious that with all the unwelcome publicity and, more importantly, with the curfew, Ralph had lost his position with the clubs. His livelihood was badly affected, and he had no choice but to look elsewhere to make a living. *What do guys in Washington care?* he fumed. *They just send their hotshots around. Do they ever stop to think about the lives they've ruined with their overzealous activities?* The only thing Ralph could think of at the time was renting apartments, something he had done for the armed forces. He still had a lot of contacts. But he was going to fight that godddamn curfew. They had no right to pin that on him. It was not justifiable. He had done nothing wrong.

It wasn't easy hiring a lawyer because very few wanted anything to do with the police department. Some Fascist laws were still on the books (a leftover from Mussolini's reign), and the *ammonizione* (curfew law) was one of them. Fortunately, Ralph was able to hire his old counselor from the American Legion episode, Federico Turano, to represent him. Turano was one of the best criminal lawyers in Rome. "Ralph, are they still molesting you?" he said over the phone.

"*Dottore*," he replied, "if I'm innocent, how can they give me a curfew? I haven't taken a crooked dollar since I've been in this country!"

Turano agreed to take the case because for him, it was a pure case of police harassment. "*Va bene*, Ralph," he said. "Stai calmo. Ci penso io." (Okay, be calm, I'll take care of it.) He immediately appealed the curfew, and Ralph gained some time.

A friend in the police department sent Ralph to one of his colleagues whose wife operated an Italian rental agency in Castelfidaro (a few miles out of Rome). With his personality and know-how, he immediately convinced the woman, and Ralph was hired. He handled all the American and international clientele, and word soon went around that Ralph was in action again. He ran ads in the newspaper, put up bulletins at all the embassies and other international offices, including the U.S. military, where he had friends. He wasn't making very good money, but it was an honest living. He kept thinking that after he won the curfew appeal, and the scandal blew over, he would be able to return to the clubs.

Charlie and Igea arrived in Lercara Friddi on July 21 and stepped out of their car like a royal couple. Friends and relatives were on hand, and a large crowd of the local people had gathered to greet them. The hot noon sun did not deter their enthusiasm, and suddenly, the crowd swooped upon them. "Let them breathe!" shouted relatives forming a wedge in front of the crowd. It was too hot for that sort of thing. Finally, a procession lined up as they followed their two celebrities to a cousin's house where Charlie, smiling, waved good-bye to his people.

The next day, Charlie presented his documents to the authorities at the municipal court, but it was not a hostile meeting. They would have loved to have had him remain among them, but that was the last thing Charlie had in mind. He was lucky because he and his counselors had found a quirk in article 37 of the law, which had him expelled. It did not specify—not in writing—that Charlie was obligated to permanently stay in Lercara Friddi, his birthplace. Consequently, after a few days of festivities, he and Igea left for Palermo—always under authorization. In October, they were already comfortably settled in Naples. His curfew, however, continued without interruption. That was when rumors revealed that he had secretly married Igea, but it wasn't true. Just sensational newspaper copy. Charlie had gone soft but not crazy.

At the time of their release, the Italian police announced that three individuals had been uncovered: two in America who had ordered the drugs and one in Italy who had provided them. They added that investigations were continuing on both sides of the ocean. In fact, by the end of July, Ralph read in the newspapers that three persons were arrested in Malden, Massachusetts, as Trupia's accomplices: Angelo Ciccola and Domenic and Angelo Isabella. Ralph was very happy because that kind of news would certainly exonerate them completely and would help in his appeal. But Anslinger and Williams were not content with the arrests. It was, according to them, just a beginning, and investigations were still under way. They kept insisting that Luciano was behind the narcotics operation in Europe. Anslinger was obsessed with Charlie (reminiscent of Dewey). Consequently, all his underlings continued to persecute him. It meant that indirectly, being a close friend of Charlie's, Ralph was also on their hate list.

Elena thought it was an act of providence that Charlie left Rome, not that she didn't like him. Quite the contrary. She thought of him as a gentleman and a person with whom she could speak whenever she had doubts. Unbeknownst to Ralph, she had asked Charlie why Ralph was not as wealthy as he. With gentle eyes, and without alarming her with details, Charlie informed her that long, long ago, Ralph had refused to be a business associate. Elena understood; she sincerely liked Charlie and had a good rapport with Igea. In her naïve way, she thought Ralph would not be involved in unsavory affairs with the distance between the two friends.

CHAPTER FORTY-EIGHT

Charlie was taking his godfather role seriously. He kept in touch with Ralph by phone, wanting to know if he was staying out of trouble. Theirs was an unexplainable relationship—a strange human bond. In November, Charlie obtained permission—a ten-day police pass—from the Rome questura to come into the capitol to clear up some private affairs. He and Igea arrived discreetly by train from Naples on November 15 and quietly slipped into their luxurious apartment, which they were to use for the last time. That afternoon he, Igea, Ralph, and Elena lunched at the La Biblioteca Restaurant. Ralph enjoyed Charlie's story of his eviction from their Pairoli apartment.

It had all started months before when the contessa Clotilde Rossi di Montelera had begun legal action to evict the tenants in her Via Lima apartment. She stated it was being occupied abusively—that she never directly made a contract with them. (In effect, Charlie had a contract, but with a third party.) The contessa needed the apartment for herself. The truth, however, was that when the Trupia scandal broke out, she was shocked to learn her tenant was none other than the notorious Lucky Luciano. She immediately sent her daughter, Marchesa Sandra Rossi di Montelera, to Rome and to their lawyer to solicit the eviction. Charlie, for his part, was too involved to pay any attention to anyone. Now, definitely settled in Naples, he thought it was time to iron everything out and to take care of his furniture. He also had to make some decisions about the land he had purchased in Santa Marinella, a lovely sea resort area near Rome. Even though the clouds loomed heavy over their heads, the foursome managed to enjoy themselves, forgetting their problems during Charlie's ten-day visit.

The year 1949 was drawing to a close. On Christmas Day, Pope Pius XII opened the huge right center doors of St. Peter's Basilica in the Vatican, announcing the beginning of the 1950 Holy Year—something that occurs every twenty-five years. Ralph took this as an auspicious sign. He was still optimistic about his appeal and threw himself into his work with the same enthusiasm he always had. Perhaps like a greenhorn snatching at straws, he always tried to be of good cheer, even if he had reason to be heartbroken. It wasn't long before the police began again to break down his spirits. First, the carabinieri showed up at the office inquiring about his activities in the agency. Then the finance police visited, followed by the regular police—people coming and going, all asking more or less the same thing. "Have you someone working here by the name of Ralph Liguori? What does he do exactly? Well . . . do you know *who* he is?"

The owner, who had become a very good friend, answered the last question rather animatedly.

"Yes, I certainly do know who he is. That's why he works for me . . . That is why he's welcome in my home. I have two daughters. He wouldn't come into my home if I didn't know who he was!" With all the harassment, the prospects of winning his appeal appeared dimmer and dimmer.

One morning, Ralph found an Italian in his office, waiting for him. He thought it odd since he did not locate apartments for Italians. As soon as Ralph entered, the man jumped up with a piece of paper in his hand.

"You must sign this," he said anxiously.

Ralph paid almost no attention to him and went to his desk. The man followed with the paper, laid it on Ralph's desk folded, and repeated, "You must sign this . . . here!"

The paper was folded in such a way that Ralph could not read the contents, and although he couldn't read Italian, it angered him.

"Look, I don't sign anything. What do you think . . . I came on a banana boat from the States? I will not sign it."

"Then, I've got to take you in," the man replied, somewhat frightened of Ralph.

Just then, the owner walked in. "What is it, Ralph?" she asked.

"The usual crap. He doesn't want me to read it, but I guess it's a summons of some kind. He wants me to sign it. Look, I don't want to cause you any unwanted publicity. You have a family, and this is your livelihood. What the hell. I don't give a damn anymore. I'll sign it." As soon as he lifted his pen from the paper, the eager man grabbed his copy, left one for Ralph, and ran out. It was a subpoena to appear in front of the police commission. Ralph picked up the phone and called his lawyer.

The hearing was set for the middle of February. That day, his cousin, Mario, who was to appear before the commission as a character witness, went with him. Ralph also needed him for moral support. Mario couldn't believe all the police harassment. As they walked toward the room, they saw three policemen on each side of the door, guns on their shoulders. Ralph said to Mario, "That's a special thing they're doing for me."

"Naw . . . ," replied Mario incredulously.

To prove his point, Ralph asked one of the guards, "Is there something special here today?"

The guard looked at Ralph unknowingly and responded, "Yes . . . they're supposed to give a curfew to a big gangster from America."

"Yeah . . . ," Ralph said. "What's his name?"

He couldn't pronounce Ralph's first name and sputtered, "Raf Liguori."

Ralph turned to Mario. "Well . . . did you hear that?"

"Unbelievable . . . ," Mario said, shaking his head.

They strolled away from the door and waited until Ralph was called. As Ralph approached the guards again, he could see the stupefied looks on their faces.

Upon entering, Ralph saw what seemed like thirty-five to forty men sitting around a huge table. Seeing all their glum faces, he thought it looked like a declaration of war. The men were all the big authorities: from the Ministry of the Interior, the Guardia della Finanza, the head of the Italian Intelligence (something similar to the FBI), heads of the police department, the top brass of the carabinieri, the mayors of Rome and adjacent communities. *Christ,* thought Ralph, *all this for me? To pin a lousy curfew on me? The pressure from Washington must be dynamite!* It was a grim-looking group, the faces almost sinister. Ralph spotted his lawyer, Turano, sitting among them and was relieved to see he had a friend in the enemy's camp. Turano nodded to Ralph, who stood off to one side flanked by two guards. The silence was broken when one man stood up, lifted some papers from a thick dossier in front of him, addressed the commission, and began to read Ralph's life history: Ralph Liguori was a little baby when he went to the United States . . . et cetera . . . That he was arrested many times but never convicted because of friends and political influence (went through the entire record) . . . That Thomas E. Dewey finally came along to convict both Luciano and Liguori . . . et cetera . . . et cetera.

Turano couldn't wait for the finish; he jumped up and said, "I want to know why Ralph Liguori is here?" No one answered. Some men shifted their feet; others glanced embarrassingly at one another. Turano waited a few minutes and then, in his powerful voice, half-mockingly said, "Is it possible, among all these men here, not one has the courage to get up and answer my question?"

One man rose bravely and said rather contemptuously, "For suspicion!"

"We're all suspicious around here," Turano roared. "We're all suspicious in this room." And he pointed his finger around the table.

At that point, Ralph walked out of the room rather shaken and was glad to see Mario waiting outside the door; he was talking to Anna, the owner of the real estate office, who was also summoned. Before Ralph could begin relating his experience, Anna was called. She took a deep breath, patted Ralph's hands, and walked proudly into the den of lions. Meanwhile, the two cousins paced up and down the corridor, waiting for her, which wasn't long. *Somebody made mincemeat out of somebody,* Ralph thought.

Anna quietly joined them. "They asked me what you did in the office. I told them that you took care of the American clients . . . that you rented apartments . . . and that we went half and half on whatever you made. Then they asked me how long did I know you. I answered that I knew you for about a year or something like that. I told them about the parade of policemen and carabinieri that came to the office asking about you. I said that I had met you through my husband. At that point, one of them asked me, 'Who is your husband?' And I looked at him coldly and answered, 'He's a policeman!' Well, they practically chased me out of the room. They didn't want to hear me anymore. Those sons of bitches!"

Ralph looked at Mario in disgust. Mario still couldn't believe what was happening. *He's learning how it must feel to be cornered by a bunch of rats,* thought Ralph. Before Ralph's agency friend left, she wanted to reassure him. "Ralph, curfew or no curfew . . . you're always welcome to work with me." Ralph thanked her, but he knew he would not go back for her sake.

A thunderous voice called Mario, and he too disappeared behind the thick doors. His turn was also short and sweet, and he soon came out with an expression of shock.

Behind the huge doors, however, Turano continued to dramatically defend Ralph. He had more style than all of them put together and knew the laws like the back of his hand. "You state he is socially dangerous," he ranted, "BUT you don't have any specific facts to authenticate the charge! You state he is suspect of criminal actions without giving—not even in brief form—specific facts. And you go on in this way. If he was dangerous to society, then he was at the time of his arrival in Italy. Why wait four years to condemn him?" he exclaimed.

He also reviewed Ralph's unfortunate history but with a different slant—to demonstrate that the charges against Ralph were based on a prejudiced past. "Now they want to deliberately hit him because of the drug scandal for which he was—mind you—discharged and recognized to be absolutely without fault of any kind. Completely innocent!

"We have proven with documentation and testimonies that the defendant has been a law-abiding citizen, working honestly for a living."

He went on eloquently to mention the testimonies of the agency woman and that of Mario, who attested to the fact that Ralph belonged to a reputable, well-to-do family, and that his work allowed him to live comfortably. In sum, Ralph did not need the rackets. But the commission didn't pay any attention to the evidence—even neglected to hear some of the defense witnesses.

"The defendant was condemned without legal motive and the law erroneously applied.

"As for the vague and general statements regarding 'suspicion of prostitution' and 'instigation of drug traffic'"—he waved his hands disdainfully—"the commission has reported investigating all—said suspicions in vain. There has been no proof to substantiate the accusations. They have built their case around doubts and hazy, obscure facts. The commission knows all this and yet, went ahead and sentenced him. This sentence is unjust, illegitimate, illegal, and violates articles 164, 167, and article 169 of the Police Ordinance. Therefore, the appellant is confident that this sentence will be revoked—annulled in the name of justice."

Ralph couldn't remember how much time elapsed. All he thought about was Turano trying to defend him with people he called hypocrites. Something inside him said it was another cut-and-dried case. When the doors finally swung open, and everyone walked out, Ralph was sure he guessed right by the way some men avoided looking at him and by Turano's long face, still arguing with one man. Turano felt Ralph's presence and looked up. Ralph noticed his painful expression as he put his arms around his shoulders. And Ralph knew. Two years curfew confirmed. Indoors before dark! All this because they had said "suspicion." It was a tragic moment for Ralph.

What did it all really mean? The sentence? It meant that Ralph's chances to return to the United States were ruined. All his hopes and dreams crumbled. He had done ten years of his maximum, and if his record in exile had been clean for the remaining five years of his sentence, he could have applied for readmission to the States. The five years were almost over, and with good lawyers representing him (and especially with Dewey's personal okay), Ralph thought he couldn't possibly be refused. But they didn't want him back. They had hit below the belt with the curfew fiasco.

Ralph could just hear the special commission in Washington pronounce, "Denied." Liguori has not behaved himself. His mind went to Dewey—to whether he was ever really serious about approving his return, to whether he had a part in the pressure against him. Surely, Ralph was a thorn in his side.

Dewey must have sighed a sigh of relief, for Ralph's enemies had done their job well. One could say that Dewey had won again.

CHAPTER FORTY-NINE

For some people, 1950 will stand out in history as the beginning of many of the postwar problems around the world. Certainly, there were both physical and psychological adjustments to be made. It was also the start of another decade—a new era. Some events are remembered more than others, depending on how strong the emotional involvement. In Italy, a headline read, Holy Year Pilgrimages Smashing Records Despite War and Communist Travel Bans; and Italians were immersed in the reconstruction of their nation as a democratic state.

Americans, instead, were struggling with the Korean War, McCarthyism, and the FBI were rounding up atomic bomb spies; color TV was approved; fans were enjoying great fighters like middleweight champion Jake La Motta, dancing welterweight Sugar Ray Robinson, heavyweight champion, Ezzard Charles and exciting bouts by the new heavyweight contender and knockout king of the moment Rocky Marciano. Joe DiMaggio had become famous in the New York ballparks, and Sinatra packed them in at the Palladium theater in London. There was an attempt on President Truman's life. It was an election year for Congress, but before November rolled around, Americans had their eyes glued to their TV sets. It was the first time in the history of TV—still in its infant stage—that viewers found themselves spectators of a Senate crime investigating committee. The novelty (the sensationalism) helped the Americans forget the Korean War. It was the hottest issue across the nation and gave them a firsthand look at reputed American gangsters. Chairman of the Committee Estes Kefauver, Democratic senator from Tennessee, opened the hearing on May 10, and it gained impetus in the weeks and months ahead. It was the smash hit of the season!

Unlike Americans, Italians then had no television, not even black-and-white. Italian politicians were still arguing over what system to approve, so Ralph listened to the daily radio newscasts. Occasionally, he saw newsreels in the movies, which were very popular then; and as usual, he scanned all the newspapers for news. He knew many of the guys being investigated, and it was natural that he'd be interested in how they made out. Almost immediately after the opening, Senator Charles W. Tobey of the committee urged Congress to convict Frank

Costello and Frank Erickson on perjury, "if that is the only crime in which such characters can be nailed." Frank was not worried, and when the reporters met him at his New York estate, he said, "What do I need with a syndicate? I've got all the money I need." And he sure had plenty. When asked about narcotics, he denied the charges strenuously, said he detested "the narcotics racket and anyone connected with it."

Then came the unexpected—a sensational breakthrough in June that was to haunt not only the underworld, but any citizen who was harboring thoughts about cheating the U.S. government. President Truman signed an executive order to open income tax files of racketeers to Senate investigators and ordered all federal agencies to cooperate with them. Now everyone was worried. Ralph also read that an old friend—Frank Erickson, the king of the bookmakers, and as sharp as they come—pleaded guilty to charges of conspiracy and bookmaking at a special sessions court. He was sentenced to two years in prison and fined $30,000. Erickson was no fool. He had the best lawyers money could buy. They had advised him to throw himself at the mercy of the court; otherwise, he could have received sixty years.

It was a good thing for Charlie that he was in Italy, or he would have had a hard—humiliating—time as Frank Costello. The most they could do in Italy was haul him in for questioning, which they did as soon as the Senate crime probers announced that Luciano's activities in Europe would be investigated; that a top-notch agent would be sent abroad. Time and time again, Charlie was brought in for questioning, only to repeat and repeat he was not dealing in narcotics. All of this was also prompted by Anslinger's testimony that Charlie was involved. One of the things that still linked Charlie was the committee's knowledge that he was receiving money from his friends in the States, but Charlie had never made a secret of that.

The Senate committee hearings continued all year long with a parade of witnesses, and when Virginia Hill testified, Ralph almost vomited. The committee found her a diversion. Ralph considered her a troublesome dame, a misfit. None of the guys had any respect for her. Later in October, Ralph read where his old boyhood friend, Willie (Charles) Fischcetti, and his brother, Rocco, were sunning themselves in Mexico away from the vigilant eyes of George White, who had been sent to Chicago to serve them with subpoenas to testify. Strange how White was always in the picture. The papers said that the Chicago boys had a secret meeting at Ralph Capone's estate in Wisconsin and were told to scatter. Ralph believed it. Months later, however, they finally caught the boys. Charlie and Ralph both felt sorry when they heard Willie Fischetti had died of a heart attack shortly after, in April 1951, while the hearings were still going on.

New York was saved for last, and all America was anxiously waiting to see and hear the "big boys." It was like a lineup of all-time stars—and all from Ralph's old neighborhoods. Meyer Lansky refused to say anything much about anything—even refused to discuss whether he had seen Charlie in Italy (said they talked on the phone). Joe Adonis hid mostly behind the Fifth Amendment: "I refuse to answer on the grounds it might incriminate me." When Willie Moretti testified, the fun began. Willie had started as an independent like Ralph, but as the years went by, his outfit grew to a large number and eventually went in with Costello, his cousin. Willie also stood behind the Fifth on some questions, but when they did obtain some answers, his remarks seemed to make everyone laugh. The committee, however, didn't think it was a laughing matter, and he and Adonis were both up for contempt of Congress. The committee also heard the Anastasia brothers, Albert and Anthony, but the man they couldn't wait to get their hands on was Frank Costello, the star attraction.

Everyone knew Frank was the man in charge in Charlie's absence (that's why some called him the prime minister). They tried to pick him apart—on everything. They kept hammering away on his various activities, trying to determine how much he was worth. They questioned his bootlegging days, his bookmaking involvement with Erickson, slot machines, and his political connections. The 1943 wiretap scandal about Judge Aurelio was discussed. They worked him over the coals until Frank's voice cracked; his vocal chords were strained. He had always had trouble with his throat and had undergone surgery for a tumor, which had left him with a raucous voice. He now used it as an excuse to take a break. The committee had another choice personality on their list, ex-mayor of New York William O'Dwyer, and Frank wanted him to have his day in court first to avoid stepping on his toes. Up to then, American TV audiences were enthralled by the voice and hands of the controversial gangster; Frank had refused to be televised, seen in front of the camera. As a result, the cameramen had cleverly focused on the gesturing of his hands, which, as any Italian knows, is a dead giveaway. Everyone was in for another surprise climax. Claiming he could no longer go on, Frank suddenly stood up and walked out of the courtroom with his lawyer following; the frustrated senators and counselors watched angrily.

William O'Dwyer was at that time ambassador to Mexico; he had been swiftly and mysteriously appointed by President Truman as a means of getting him out of the country—to avoid the airing of his complicity in the NY Fire Department scandal. O'Dwyer's career had soared, and Ralph shook his head in amazement, remembering him in the twenties when he was a cop on the New York police beat (a patrolman). O'Dwyer was a personable guy and knew how to get along with people; everyone liked him. He had studied hard to become a lawyer, slowly working his way up—first as a judge, then as district attorney of Kings County, before becoming mayor of New York.

The committee was now questioning him about his career, about the police and fire department corruption, and crime during the time he held these offices. They badgered him about Abe Reles's unexpected plunge to death from the window of the Half Moon Hotel, charging that his version and that of an ex-police commissioner, Frank Bals, who had testified earlier, were both nonsensical. The really hot item was his friendship with Costello. "Yes, I knew him," was his answer. O'Dwyer had a rough time but, all in all, kept his cool.

Costello was rescheduled to testify, but perjury and contempt charges were already in progress. It was clearly written on the wall that the senators were going to get him, and they did. Frank went to jail in 1952 for income tax evasion and was in and out of prison for the next several years. He had beaten the other charges, including one to denaturalize him. They had hoped to deport him, said he had lied on his naturalization papers. The Kefauver Senate crime hearings were a disaster for Frank and the start of all his real troubles.

Ralph had no real opinion of Kefauver; he was a senator with a job to do, obtaining a great deal of publicity. Some said that he was making the most out of the hearings for his own personal career, programming it for a dramatic finish. Perhaps he too wanted to become president. Senator Tobey had also become a personality but irked Ralph. Tobey pretended to be shocked at some of the things he heard; one would think he had led a sheltered life. Ralph was always leery of self-righteous guys; it reminded him of what he had gone through with Judge McCook and Dewey. Senator Tobey and some of the others had much to learn about the hard facts of life. Was it possible they couldn't understand how a street kid became involved in troubles? thought Ralph. Especially an immigrant kid, with all the strikes against him. Some of them quit school, and once they were involved and had a taste of easy money, it was not easy to abandon their friends. Ralph knew that from experience, from when he was a kid on the streets of New York. No, the committee couldn't understand certain codes. They did understand at the end, what Ralph had said all along, that the racketeers couldn't have existed if the so-called honest citizen, cop, or politician were not corruptible. As Ralph listened (read), he wondered what his life would have been like had he not gone to prison, had he not been exiled. Would he too have been on the stand before these senators? He was happy to be out of it, but he also felt sorry for some of his friends.

Ralph received great satisfaction when he heard Governor Thomas E. Dewey had refused the invitation to appear at the open hearings. Kefauver and the others wanted to know about gambling in Saratoga and the real story about Charlie's parole. They were all disappointed, especially Senator Tobey, a Republican. He thought it was a strike against the Republicans. Of course, it would have been an insult to subpoena the governor. But if justice was to be achieved, why not? thought Ralph. Why was he so untouchable? Dewey was however as clever as always. His was not a flat refusal; he invited the senators, counselors, and everyone else involved in the court hearings to Albany, knowing beforehand that they would refuse, would not budge. (Who would pay for all the expenses for such a move?) Dewey removed himself from the squabbles—as he always did. Ralph considered it another reconfirmation of Dewey's personal involvement with unsavory characters and the General and wondered about the fine line that divides good from evil.

During all this furor, Ralph was living out his curfew and hating it. He had to be in before dark or else! It was a hard pill to swallow since he had done nothing to merit it. He also had to give up his room at the hotel—too expensive. He and Elena rented an apartment up the street on Via del Pantheon. With the police, he had worked out an arrangement where they would ring the front door buzzer downstairs; he'd open the window to wave, indicating he was indoors. Ralph heard that buzzer in his sleep! But he persevered and soon opened up his own rental agency. A friend lent his name for the license, and Ralph began to spread word that he was again in business.

While Ralph was scuffling to make an honest living, Charlie received his monthly income from the States, but Ralph was not bitter. It was Charlie's money—money he had invested a long time ago. Charlie, confined in Naples, also began to look for something to do. He began investing in various things in Sicily—first, with a cousin here and there, but nothing important like the candy factory, which eventually he had to close. Later, one of the more successful enterprises was his electrical appliance store, which he opened in Naples. It featured a North Italian line of electrical implements and machines. Charlie had the exclusive for Southern Italy and Sicily. As in the States, he and Ralph did not have any joint ventures. All their lives they were friends, not business partners. Ralph, however, always had his eyes open to make some extra money on his own. Although he was making a decent income, renting apartments didn't bring in the kind of money to which he was accustomed. Then a friend came around with an idea, and he listened.

It was still spring, and the days were warming, announcing an early summer. There was a lull in the office; the room was stuffy. Ralph opened the window and leaned out (something he did often) to watch the action down the streets. Hearing some commotion, he turned in time to see a motorcycle escort and an open car cruising along toward the Hassler Hotel. As it came closer, Ralph recognized the police inspector seated in the car while the other man, he thought, looked familiar, an American face he knew. By coincidence, the police inspector looked up and noticed Ralph; he waved, calling out, "Ciao, Ralph!" Then whispered something to the man beside him, obviously identifying Ralph. The inspector's passenger began waving wildly, shouting, "Hey, Ralph, how are you? Impellitteri, remember?" Ralph sure did. He smiled and waved back, thinking, *My god, he remembers me!* He had met the attorney Vincent Impellitteri back in the early thirties in New York. He was the present acting mayor of New York City—and on the ballot in the November elections. It felt good to be remembered, and suddenly, Ralph felt very nostalgic for home.

The phone rang, breaking his trance, and he went back to his desk to work. As he jotted down some information, Sam Vavali (an ex-inmate from Dannemora who had also been deported) entered with another man named Laduga. Ralph learned that the man was a big exporter in Britain interested in obtaining the Coca-Cola franchise for all of Catania and part of Sicily.

"Do you think you can come up with a good contact?" Laduga asked.

"Well, I know a few guys," Ralph replied.

"Ralph, if you get this contract for me, there's one hundred million lire in it for you," he offered.

He had said the magic words. That was an excellent commission, an attractive sum for anybody. It was roughly $17,000 then. "Hell," Ralph said, "for that kind of money, I'll take a crack at it." And they shook hands on the deal.

Ralph was sure of himself because he knew the Coca-Cola men in Rome and went to work on it immediately. The idea keenly interested them, and Ralph was given a letter of introduction to take with him to the Coca-Cola headquarters in Milan. The catch was he had to have special permission because of the curfew, so he went to the police commissioner, who gave him his okay. A few days before leaving, Ralph treated himself to a personal send-off, stopping in at the Excelsior Bar for a drink, and was very surprised to see Jim Farley! It was a stroke of good luck because Farley at the time was chairman of the Coca-Cola Corporation in

New York. Ralph had great respect for Jim Farley. He had always been an important Democratic leader of Tammany Hall and a great political strategist. Over a drink, Ralph told him about the deal he had going, told him he already had a letter from the head man in Rome. Jim looked at Ralph fraternally. He had a pleasant face. His fringe of hair had turned white, but his expressive eyes were the same—piercing eyes that read a situation at a glance. Right then, they read Ralph. He smiled and said, "Ralph, you should also go up there under my name. Tell them I said to take good care of you." Ralph thanked him and left, feeling great about seeing him. No one ever forgets good friends.

As soon as Ralph arrived in Milan, he reported to the police commissioner, who was curious about his visit. Ralph had to demonstrate the contract, and the police were astonished at the amount of money offered in the deal. Fortunately, Ralph was given the okay and allowed to leave. He went directly to the Coca-Cola headquarters, showed them his credentials (references), and, after preliminary talks with the top men, the deal was practically in the bag. He returned to Rome, satisfied with his mission. Once in his office, he called Laduga and asked for a meeting. Laduga hesitated on the phone, then mustered up some courage. "Ralph . . . look . . . the people in Sicily advised me there's lots of oranges in Sicily," he sorrowfully announced.

"Yeah, we all know that," Ralph answered rudely.

"Well, I don't think I'll do it. They advised me against it. Thanks anyway. Thanks for everything," he concluded shamefully.

"Yeah . . . sure . . . anytime." Ralph banged the phone on its receiver and lowered his head onto the desk. Suddenly, he was completely exhausted. The whole affair was dropped. About six months later, when someone else closed the deal, Laduga bit his hands.

The Holy Year not only inspired the faithful, it also stimulated tourism, trade, and the motion picture industry. And Ralph had a crack at being a movie star. One of his cousins, who worked for Dino De Laurentiis, then a young movie producer in Rome, stopped by the office to chew the fat and to offer him a bonus.

"Ralph, I'm going to ask permission for you to stay out tonight," he said.

"Yeah . . . why?" Ralph looked at him suspiciously.

"Why? I'm going to make you a cardinal. You've the perfect face!" he added smugly.

Ralph laughed. "Me, Baby Face Ralph, a cardinal. It has to be one for the books. Listen, cuz, you've got the wrong guy!"

"No . . . Ralph . . . I'm serious. You don't have to do any real acting. You just have to look pretty in your red robes." He chuckled.

Ralph looked at him, shaking his head in laughter, but before he could comment, his cousin added, "And I'll throw in another bonus. I'll get Elena a job in the wardrobe department as a seamstress." He threw up his hands in complete satisfaction. "Well?"

"Well, what can I say? Get the cameras rolling. Just don't tell the pope!" Ralph laughed.

Permission was obtained for Ralph to participate in the movie, and Elena and Ralph began to work in their respective roles. The film, an Italo-French production, was entitled *Santa Teresa*. Most of the scenes were shot outside Cinecitta (in Hotel Cavour, the Palazzo Farnese), surrounded by the beautiful frescoes of famous Italian artists, as well as around the Vatican. Ralph actually enjoyed the work. It was fun. He met many nice people.

It was late, around seven thirty at night, and fifteen make-believe cardinals sat around a big table holding a conclave—a scene in the movie. Ralph sensed that some of the actors were restless.

"Ralph," one of them whispered, "we're going on strike. The director doesn't want to pay us overtime." There was about another two hours of work.

"Oh yeah?" Ralph replied. "That's not very nice . . ." He saw that the men were very serious. "Well . . . okay . . . don't worry. I'll tell you how to do it," Ralph instructed in a low voice. "Just stay seated . . . then when they start rolling again . . . one by one, you get up and walk away. I'll sit down for last, otherwise, they'll blame me."

The men nodded in agreement, and that was exactly what happened. When they began to stand up and walk away, the director came running over to Ralph. "Ralph . . . help me out . . . please help me out," he cried. "It'll cost me a lot of money to send these guys back to Cinecitta. It'll cost me three times more. Give me a break. Tell them I'll pay."

Ralph called the boys back, and they smiled with satisfaction. They were about to roll the cameras again when there was another interruption. "Break!" the director yelled, exasperated. It was the police. They had come to check on Ralph—to see whether he was really working in the film. When they saw him in his red robes, one crackled, "Jesus, Ralph . . . if we didn't know you . . . we'd take you for a real cardinal!" Everyone laughed heartily. The players were all paid, and the picture was soon finished.

It was just another episode in Ralph's Roman exile.

CHAPTER FIFTY

Ralph was having his problems, but there was one man whose life was hanging on a string. Giuliano's days were numbered. His life was in peril from within and from without. Minister Scelba (once said to have been a secret ally and now an archenemy) promised the Senate that Giuliano would be captured soon. The police combed Palermo for him, but Giuliano seemed to be invisible. Then Ralph read an article headlined: Calling All Cars! Giuliano Reported Escaped to Boston. Was it possible that he did get away? Was it true, as the article said, that he was smuggled into the U.S. by the Mafia? Remembering their secret meeting, Ralph was tempted to call Charlie, but he thought better of it. About two weeks later, he read sadly that Giuliano was trapped and killed in the early morning of July 5 in a hideout in Castelvetrano, Sicily—machine-gunned by the police. They had caught him in a home where he had been hiding. Leaving the home to make his way to another building, the police cornered Giuliano in the courtyard. They overpowered him, and his riddled body fell to the ground. Around his waist was his belt with the famous gold lion buckle, which he had worn proudly. That was the first official version.

Ralph's phone rang. "Ralph, did you read about Giuliano?" It was Charlie.

"Yeah . . . man . . . what a shame. I thought at first that maybe he got away."

"He was supposed to. It's a lot of crap about the police. It was no doubt an inside job. A double cross?" Charlie's voice expressed sincere grief.

"Charlie . . . he had too many enemies. He knew too much," Ralph commented. Giuliano's life and political involvement had long intrigued him. "They had to get rid of him!"

"Yeah . . . you're right about that. Things were getting too hot for a lot of people," Charlie replied sorrowfully.

Little by little, it all came out in the wash. Two days later, the newscasts reported that Giuliano had planned to escape to Tunis by air. Toward the end of the month, the newspapers were full of the news relating to the carabinieri's version. Responsibility for Giuliano's death claimed by Captain Ferenze and Colonel Luca, chief of the Banditry Repression Squad, was now being doubted. The Italian parliament stated it was not satisfied with the version because they had reason to believe it was done by two civilians acting under police orders. It further claimed no one in the area had heard the presumed gun battle; there was no evidence of bullet scars—not in the walls of the courtyard, nor in or around it. Other facts seemed to prove that Giuliano was killed elsewhere and brought to the courtyard. The police version, however, was backed by Interior Minister Scelba; and the captain became a major, and the colonel, a general, as rewards for their outstanding work in nabbing Giuliano.

Still, the controversy continued; and at the end of the year, Gaspare Pisciotta, Giuliano's cousin and right-hand man, was arrested, and Pisciotta had all intentions to tell everything. He was taken to the jail in Viterbo, where he was kept for more than three months with no attempt to question him. They *didn't* want to hear him. Finally, he was brought to the court of Viterbo, where the already tedious and elaborate trial of the massacre of Portella della Ginestra was in progress. He was put in a cage (a cell-like contraption in the courtroom) with the other gang members. They still did everything possible to avoid hearing from him. In an effort to make his voice heard, Pisciotta wrote his confession, which made the rounds of the courtroom. The short confession stated that in a personal agreement with Minister Scelba, he had killed Giuliano—and reserved the details for the court of Viterbo.

He caused a pandemonium when he finally spoke. He revealed that in exchange for a written statement claiming all responsibility for the massacre, the Christian Democrats had promised Giuliano the necessary documents and means to escape overseas. Pisciotta knew about the arrangement and felt he would be left holding the bag. He had no faith in the politicians. They were known betrayers, so he took action into his own hands. In another cross-examination, he stated that the band had enjoyed protection from the police and high officials. His famous statement can still be heard. "We were a single body. Bandits, police, and Mafia—like the Father, the Son, and the Holy Ghost!"

Pisciotta was handling dynamite. He worried for his own personal safety. Pisciotta had a copy of Giuliano's memorial—the story of his life, complete with names of his friends and enemies. It was obvious that *no one* wanted this memorial to come out. Pisciotta was sentenced to life imprisonment for his participation in the massacre and transferred to the notorious prison Ucciardone in Palermo, a prison where jailed Mafia leaders were able to continue their rule without interruption. Attempts were made to force Pisciotta to retract his damaging statements, but he refused. Gaspare Pisciotta had to go, and it is said the Mafia was again enlisted. Fearing for his life, he carefully examined his food every day; but instead, his medicine was cleverly poisoned, and he died in agony. The real instigators (perpetuators) were now safe.

Later in 1961, a memorial from another gang member, Frank Mannino, was made public, confirming Giuliano was assassinated in Monreale, then transferred to Castelvetrano, but that it was not Pisciotta who killed him. Mannino's most startling declaration was that Pisciotta committed suicide in prison—had poisoned himself. Was all this the truth? Was he put up to it by someone? The controversy went on and on. Certainly, Giuliano's death brought the end of the myth of the handsome bandit for whom ballads have been written and for whom Sicily had mourned. Some people still believe that Giuliano lives, and that one day, his memorial will come to life.

That autumn, Ralph's attention turned to the elections in the United States and particularly those in New York. As far back as June 1950, Governor Thomas E. Dewey said he wouldn't run again, fulfilling his plans to retire. This paved the way for Lieutenant Governor Joe R. Hanley to announce his intentions to run for governor. Hanley began his campaign. Ralph's eyes widened when he read that the Democrats were charging Dewey with buying off his rival for the GOP gubernatorial nomination. Supposedly, Dewey was accused of persuading Hanley to the tune of $70,000 in exchange for dropping his campaign and the promise of a lifetime income. *Christ,* Ralph thought, *Dewey is at it again.* Paying off people wasn't a new trick for him. Oh, how vivid were Ralph's memories. Democratic candidate for governor Walter W. Lynch, at a Democratic leaders meeting, quoted portions of a letter written by Hanley to Republican Representative W. Kingsland Macy. The letter had been released in Albany on the eve of the state's Republican Convention in September. Dewey was foiled by his own people—Republicans in the anti-Dewey faction of the party. Ralph was ecstatic. What juicy news. He didn't take his eyes off the newspapers.

In the letter that Hanley admitted writing, he revealed that Dewey had made "certain unalterable and unquestioningly definite propositions" to him, if he would withdraw his candidacy for the governorship. He continued, "If I consent to take the nomination to the U.S. Senate, I am definitely assured of being able to clean up my financial obligations within ninety days.

"I am assured of an adequate living compensation if elected, in perfectly legal and unquestionable ways. Also, I have an ironclad, unbreakable arrangement, whereby I will be given a job with the state, which I would like and enjoy (I have been told what it is) at sufficient compensation to make my net income more than I now have."

What a bomb! Ah, politics. What a cunning, conniving, underhanded, sweet, delectable game. Ralph smacked his lips in sheer pleasure. He wouldn't have missed it for anything in the world. With morbid gratification, he read about Dewey's dilemma, but he had no doubts about him or his potent ways. Avidly, he followed the developments. Sure enough, the mudslinging began. The headlines were smashing: DEWEY HIT AGAIN ON HANLEY CASE; NEW YORK GROUP URGES DEWEY INVESTIGATION; and DEWEY STILL JUGGLING "PAYOFF" HOT POTATO AS MAJOR PARTIES THREATEN COURT ACTION. Senator Clinton A. Erson, chairman of the Democratic Senatorial Committee, accused Dewey of letting his "ruthless ambitions" push Lieutenant Governor Joe R. Hanley out of the race. The Senate Elections Subcommittee was asked to investigate the charges regarding the $70,000 deal between Dewey and Hanley. The New York left-wing third party also demanded that the gubernatorial payoff scandal be investigated.

In his defense, Dewey denied the charges and mentioned that Franklin D. Roosevelt had agreed to run as governor in 1928, after being promised that his debts would be paid by his backers. How Dewey connected that to the payoff was beyond Ralph's logic, but Dewey was an excellent mudslinger himself. The next day, a sympathetic letter written in 1948 by Democratic Senator Herbert H. Lehman to Alger Hiss was thrown into the bitter, vicious New York State political campaign. Senator Lehman was seeking reelection against Joe R. Hanley, who, under the circumstances, was running for the Senate. Lehman had no apologies for the letter because, as he said, it was "before the indictment trial and subsequent convictions" for espionage. It was a neat maneuver to blacken Lehman's name to ensure Hanley's election.

Christ, thought Ralph, *what a mess.* All the political double-crossing intrigued him.

And the blazing headlines continued: LEHMAN LETTER TO HISS ENTERS NY VOTE FIGHT; NEW SENSATIONS PROMISED IN NEW YORK POLITICAL BATTLE; SENATE MOVES TO CONDUCT WIDE PROBE OF CHARGES AGAINST DEWEY; and HANLEY IGNORES DOCTOR TO SEE TWO VOTE PROBERS. As the headlines promised, a special Senate committee began investigating the payoff scandal, and Lieutenant Governor Hanley agreed to talk to the probers in his sickbed.

In the midst of it all, Charlie's name came into the act. The Democratic candidate Walter Lynch, in another attempt to damage his opponent, demanded that Dewey tell the people what was the consideration that made him pardon Charles "Lucky" Luciano. Ralph wasn't surprised. Everyone who was anyone suspected the truth, but Dewey always escaped it—sometimes by a thread, but he escaped. Frederick Moran, Democratic chairman of the state's parole board, when asked to comment, said, "After independent investigation and unanimous favorable recommendations by the parole board, Charles 'Lucky' Luciano was released from prison." Well phrased, but there was never any doubt that there was pressure being made in both camps for his release.

Then a strange thing happened. Ralph read in the Italian paper *IL TEMPO*: Lucky Denies All. Charlie was quoted as saying, "It's a vulgar lie to say that I was discharged as a reward for the information I gave to the Allied troops prior to the landing in Sicily in 1943." That Charlie finally blurted out part of the truth floored Ralph. He was angry at first because he had kept his mouth shut for so long. Then he worried about Charlie and called him.

"Hey . . . Charlie . . . what the hell. You tell me not to say anything, and then I read in the papers what you said about Sicily. Christ, what hit you?" Ralph asked animatedly.

"Ralph, I'm fed up with everybody. I've dished out so much money in my life, and here I am, still confined. Look at the pressure that's on us now—for doing nothing!"

"Charlie . . . you sound really pissed off. Are you okay?" Ralph hadn't heard Charlie so angry—depressed—for a long time. It had to be a bad moment.

"Yeah . . . I'm okay. They caught me on an off day. It's not like me . . . but they'll never believe the truth anyway . . . but someday we'll tell our story . . . Ralph."

It was the first time Charlie spoke about telling their story, but Ralph bypassed it. "Yeah . . . okay . . . Charlie. I'll talk to you again."

"Don't worry . . . Ralph. It's this goddamn curfew. Ciao, Ralph."

Ralph hung up and shrugged his shoulders. It was a good thing Charlie had Igea. She was good for him.

As election day drew closer and closer, the fight intensified on both sides. The campaign managers were busy at work shelling out the dirt. One million copies of Hanley's letter in pamphlet form were being mailed by the Democrats, and the Republicans were studying how to best use Lehman's letter. Dewey, with his personal charisma, went on TV to placate the people on the eve of the election and, in an eighteen-hour marathon, answered hundreds and hundreds of questions—sincerity reeking all over. When Dewey was before an audience, a microphone, or a TV camera, he was transformed—an actor of infinite talents.

New York City was also a hot seat. Another political battle was raging. Acting Mayor Vincent Impellitteri, in an audacious act, charged Frank Costello with handpicking the Democratic candidate for mayor of New York, adding a few slanderous remarks. Costello was supporting Tammany Hall's boy, Justice Ferdinand Pecora, who also enjoyed President Truman's backing. Impellitteri had left the Democratic Party to run as an independent and, fortunately for him, had Jim Farley on his side. He knew he was up against the Tammany Hall machinery and, in still another bold act, ordered the police to haul in anyone on the streets who might cause trouble in the political campaign. Hundreds of detectives combed the streets for petty crooks and suspicious characters and immediately arrested a couple hundred—many of whom were not released. As a retaliation (Impellitteri should have expected it), vandalism spread against his own campaign offices. "This is the dirtiest, filthiest, rottenest campaign in the city of New York," Impellitteri was quoted as saying. *My god,* thought Ralph, *nothing has really changed since the 1930s.*

Election day arrived, and Ralph waited for the results of "the dirtiest, filthiest, rottenest campaign." Despite all the dirt, Dewey became governor of New York for a third term. Democrat Herbert H. Lehman was reelected senator, and Vincent Impellitteri won his fight to become mayor of New York. Impellitteri was born in Sicily, and his victory was big news in the Italian papers. Even Prime Minister De Gasperi sent him a congratulatory cable. Ralph was happy for him.

Ralph wasn't surprised that Dewey won. He had an almost supernatural resiliency. To Ralph, the scandal was enough to prove that he wasn't lying on the stand way back then. It was however Dewey's last political fight and his last political office.

CHAPTER FIFTY-ONE

It was a time for celebration! The terrible days and nights of the curfew were finally over. After pressure from lawyers, friends, and relatives, the police harassment also seemed to stop. Ralph rejoiced in his grand opening of the Stork Club. Charlie couldn't go, but everyone else was there—his followers, old friends and new, and curious newspapermen—to see what Ralph was up to now. Free drinks and champagne were on the house, and Ralph was smiling from ear to ear.

The new club came about accidentally. When the curfew ended, Ralph took over the Columbia Club again for a few months. While he was there, the owner of a nightclub called the Grotte Del Piccione on Via Della Vite, stopped in to see him. The owner was up against it; he was in the red and needed help. Ralph knew the place and liked it very much. It was a sprawling cavern, which lent itself to a special atmosphere. It had many possibilities. Ralph informed him if he took over, he would have to do some repairs, change the band, and hire different waiters who spoke some English. The desperate owner agreed to Ralph's new arrangements but swallowed hard when Ralph told him he wanted to also change the name. They compromised by keeping the Italian name for identification and rebaptizing it the Stork Club.

On April 10, 1952, the headline in the *Rome Daily American* read: LUCKY's PAL OPENS 6th ROME NITERY SINCE HE WAS DEPORTED. No matter what Ralph did, he was destined to be connected with Charlie. The article even inferred that Charlie was a silent partner. Ralph wasn't surprised. Newspapermen had tried that angle back in 1948 when Ralph was running the other clubs. As always, Ralph told them they were on the wrong track—that they had to look elsewhere for their sensational scoops. Ralph didn't care much about them anymore because he was used to their tongue-in-cheek articles, even though it left a bitter taste.

Ralph ran his own advertisement in the paper to attract attention: "DINING, DANCING, AMERICAN BAR. Rome's most ancient and characteristic club. We specialize in *cannelloni* and *fettuccine*, good music, and singing. Your New York Host, Ralph." Almost immediately, the place did extremely well. Ralph was always around to see that everyone was happy. And now the owner smiled ear to ear.

Ella Logan had always remained one of Ralph's favorite people, and she was a sight for sore eyes when Ralph saw her walk into the Excelsior Bar one night. She was hanging on to the arm of a man whom she introduced as John Ringling North. When Ella caught Ralph's eye, she practically ran into his arms, elated. Ralph told her about the Stork Club, and she promised to stop by, which she did two nights later with a big party. That was Ella—all heart. She and her friends, including John Ringling North, became regulars whenever they were in town. On a particularly gay evening, Ella slipped up close to Ralph and asked, "Ralph, how is Charlie?"

"Just fine," Ralph smiled.

"Can we get in touch with him?"

"Sure! Come on . . . let's phone him." And Ralph led her into the office. As Ralph dialed Charlie's number, he smiled, imagining Charlie's expression. "Charlie . . . I've got a surprise for you," he exclaimed. "Who do you think is in the club?"

"Ralph, *ciao*. I give up . . . Who?"

"Ella Logan!"

"No foolin'. Let me talk to her," Charlie replied, very pleasantly surprised.

Ella took the phone and chitchatted with Charlie. It was obvious to Ralph that they were having a good time joking around. She handed the phone back to Ralph.

"Ralph?"

"Yeah . . . Charlie."

"I'm coming up tomorrow. Can you meet me on the highway around two o'clock?"

"Yeah . . . sure," Ralph replied. Ella was beaming with joy.

As planned, Ralph met Charlie on the Rome-Naples highway at their designated place. Ralph parked his car near a gas station, then drove Charlie's Oldsmobile to Ella's villa on Via Aventino. Charlie was all decked out. Very elegant. Ralph could see he wanted to look his best for Ella. The two reminisced about her; neither one of them could forget how wonderful Ella had been to them in prison, sending books to read and small surprise packages.

"She looks great, Charlie," Ralph remarked. "Wait and see!" Charlie just smiled to himself.

Ralph pulled up to the villa, and as Charlie stepped out, he said, "Pick me up early tomorrow night, okay? And take care of the car for me."

"Okay . . . don't worry. Have fun!" Ralph winked, swung the car around, and headed for Via Veneto. He smiled as he thought, *Hey, why not?* Once on Via Veneto, he stopped the car in front of the American embassy and climbed out to talk to the guards—friends who came into the clubs regularly. When they saw the car, one guard remarked, "Ralph, you better not park that beauty in the street. They'll steal it. Pull it in here, and we'll watch it for you."

"Oh, yeah . . . okay . . . you're probably right. Thanks a lot, guys. You know it's not my car . . . I'll feel better." Ralph thanked them profusely and pulled inside the gates. *Wait till Charlie hears about this,* Ralph chuckled to himself.

Sure enough the next day, "Ralph, where did you leave the car?" Charlie asked curiously.

"Charlie . . . if I tell you . . . you're going to laugh."

"Where . . . Ralph?" His eyebrow went up a little.

"At the American embassy."

"WHERE?" Charlie gasped.

"The American embassy."

"You're crazy!" Charlie said, shaking his head.

"Honest, Charlie . . . it's true. They're all good friends. Of course, they didn't know whose car it was," Ralph responded in a conciliatory tone.

Charlie broke into that unmistakable laugh of his. "Ralph . . . you're too much!" They both had a good laugh.

On the way to Naples, the two pals kidded and had a few more laughs. At their parking spot, Ralph left Charlie in high spirits to go the rest of the way on his own. Ralph mischievously wondered what he'd say to Igea, and he mused over that a bit as he drove back to Rome. Theirs was a good friendship, despite everything.

Two nights later, Ella entered the club with a very refined woman, all decked out in the finest jewelry, diamonds and all, the finest Ralph had ever seen. He began to shake, worrying about her safety. Ella introduced her as the wife of the owner of the Lockheed Aircraft Company. As much as Ralph was fond of Ella, the women's presence in the club that night made him nervous. The women, however, were oblivious of his concern and indulged themselves with dinner and drinks all evening. About three in the morning, Ella called Ralph to her table. "Ralph, will you call a cab for me and my friend?"

"No, Ella," Ralph replied, the jewelry still dazzling him. "She's not going home in a taxi. She's going home in my car, and somebody else is going to follow her!"

Ella tried to reassure Ralph that it wasn't necessary, but Ralph was firm. "No way, Ella. If anything happened to her leaving my club, I'd be responsible. And seeing my name is Ralph Liguori, they'd say that I steered the people to her."

She looked at Ralph sympathetically and kissed him on the cheek. "Okay, Ralph . . . have it your way." And Ralph did. His driver, an ex-policeman, drove the women home with another car following them. Ralph didn't relax until the driver called, telling him that the girls were tucked in safely.

About that time, Ingrid Bergman was having problems waiting for the birth of her twins. Her controversial marriage to Roberto Rossellini caused many waves across the Atlantic. Bergman had been condemned in Hollywood—even the U.S. Congress. Now she was in a legal battle with her first husband, Peter Lindstrom, to have her daughter, Pia, visit her in Italy. To make matters worse, Rossellini was having his own problems with a couple of films. It was all in the newspapers. Everyone read about Ingrid's trials and tribulations, and Ralph was no exception. Ella and Ingrid were very good friends, and almost every day, Ralph drove Ella to the Salvator Mundi International Hospital on the Gianicolo Hill to visit the expectant actress. On these frequent trips, Ella kept Ralph up-to-date on the happenings. Ingrid was overdue, and Ella worried about this. The attending physician, the noted obstetrician-gynecologist Professor Piero Muto Nardone, a discreet man, would not answer any questions about the subject to the press. Finally, on June 19, after two and a half hours of labor, Ingrid Bergman gave birth to twins—first Isabella and then Isotta. Her joy overcame the sadness, if only temporarily, of the news she had received two days earlier. Her daughter, Pia, refused to visit her. Ella was ecstatic over the twin births. Ralph thought she acted as though she had given birth to them. Women—never understand them!

One day, Ella swept into the club and said, "Ralph, my husband's coming tomorrow. Is there anything you'd like from New York? I'm going to call him." Ella was married to a Jewish fellow from Dave's Blue Room in New York.

"Oh, yeah . . . Ella . . . listen . . . will you do me a favor? Will you tell him to bring me some pastrami?"

"Sure, Ralph," she laughed, "I'll tell him. Come over to the villa tomorrow night. We're going to have a great party!"

That night, Ralph had another visitor in the club, a priest friend—a chaplain in a San Francisco prison. "You know . . . Ralph," the chaplain said, "I'd like to visit the Regina Coeli Prison here in Rome. Is it possible?"

"Sure . . . I'll take you there."

The next day, they went to the justice department to obtain passes. Once inside the Regina Coeli Prison, the chaplain commented that the prison was in terrible shape. "Oh . . . you think so?" Ralph remarked. "And they're only showing us the good part—the front part. You should see the other side. It's the pits." The shocked chaplain didn't comment further, and for a minute, Ralph's thoughts flew back to Dannemora and Father Hyland.

They went back to the club, and Ralph called Ella to ask permission to bring the chaplain along. "Sure, bring him with you, Ralph," was Ella's immediate response. It was a small get-together with a few of Ella's friends. John Ringling North was there and a few other people Ralph recognized from the club. The chaplain was never so happy, and Ralph noticed that he too liked pastrami. There must have been about ten pounds of pastrami on the table, and it was all gone inside of an hour's time. Between the wine and the pastrami, everyone was flying high. The chaplain remembered his Roman night long after he was back in the States saving souls.

Ella enjoyed the races, so they often went to the Capannelle racetrack, sometimes with Elena and another friend, Dr. Nunzio Stallone. Dr. Stallone was from Brooklyn but had gone to Italy with the army and stayed on. He had studied medicine in Italy and later opened the Salvator Mundi Hospital together with another friend, Colonel Camp, then chief of the American Medical Center in Rome. The races provided a fun time for all; even Elena, who was a homebody, became animated, shouting for her horse to come in.

Months later, Ella called Ralph. "Ralph . . . so long . . ."

"What?" Ralph interjected.

"I'm leaving Rome. I'll see you in about a year or so . . . Ralph. I have to go back to the States." And added melancholically, "I've got a divorce pending."

Ralph was shocked at the news. "Gees, Ella . . . I'm sorry, I hate to see you go. Come back soon. Take care . . . and . . . good luck." And Ralph truly missed his great friend Ella.

1952 was seemingly a good year for Ralph. He was busy working and leading the life he enjoyed most. But Charlie had some problems. To begin with, around the first of April, his dear friend Frank Costello was convicted to eighteen months in prison. Then after Ralph opened the Stork Club, the Italian finance men hit Charlie with a $4,000 fine. The Italian Treasury Ministry fined him for illegally exchanging $50,000 into Italian currency. (There were limits at the time.) The newspapers had him quoted as saying, "If I gotta pay, I'll have to scrape up the money and pay, I guess. I want to be a law-abiding citizen. I didn't know the laws of the country."

About the same time, Giuseppe Dosi, chief of the Italian Bureau of International Criminal Police Commission, gave Charlie a clean bill of health on narcotics before the UN Narcotics Commission in New York. Dosi said there was no evidence to substantiate charges that Luciano was the mastermind directing international dope traffic. He assured the group if there was such evidence, Luciano would be behind bars. Further, he said that because of the persistent reports in the U.S. press about Luciano being the mastermind, the Italian police had put him under the strictest surveillance. "We have had our suspicions, but no proof to substantiate charges against him whatsoever. We have interrogated him many times. Of course, he denies all. He is under strict police control in Italy, and no proof had ever been found to connect him with international narcotics smuggling. We must come to the conclusion that he does not direct the traffic." Dosi added that they would continue to question him whenever a big case of narcotics smuggling developed in Italy.

When the reporters questioned Luciano on the hearing, he said, "Somebody had to tell the truth. Anyway, it makes no difference. All I try to do is live here and obey the laws." Then he went on, "But nobody's going to print anything about me that ain't bad. I don't know why I talk to all you newspaper fellas. But I do. Even when a columnist tried to write something good, he gets criticized." (He was referring to an interview he had given to Earl Wilson.)

Charlie was right. So was Dosi. Ralph became very well acquainted with Giuseppe Dosi, and they often discussed the ensuing problems. Dosi knew Charlie wasn't the kingpin, and certainly, Ralph didn't have anything to do with drugs. There were other deportees in Italy probably wheeling and dealing, unsuspected because they didn't have a popular name like Luciano. Joe Pici and Frank Collace, for example, were picked up a year before in Milan for smuggling drugs. They were later released. There were men handling the stuff and doing very well at it. But no matter how much the Italian police tried to tell Washington that Charlie was behaving himself, they wouldn't buy it. The pressure was always on.

Around the middle of July, the Italian Ministry of the Interior took away Charlie's passport. It was the same passport he obtained in Naples about a year and a half earlier, when he thought about going to Germany.

He never went because they wouldn't give him a visa. Now the ministry declined to disclose the reason for seizing the passport. "They'll never stop persecuting me," he lamented to Ralph one night on the phone. Later that year, the papers had him in Austria at some health spa. It was all so absurd, thought Ralph. With no passport, visas, where the hell was he going to go? Further, to be caught with a false one would have been the end. Of course, Anslinger was always on his back, so much so that Charlie had sarcastically invited him to put him back in jail, then prove in court that he was involved in the narcotics racket. Naturally, it never happened.

Toward the end of the year, the negative publicity seemed to have repercussions on Ralph. The Stork Club was a complete success, so Ralph couldn't understand why the owner was acting rather peculiar toward him. Ralph suspected a double cross but wasn't sure how and when, so one day, he and the owner had their talk. The owner squirmed in his seat as he went round and round, trying to tell Ralph that to maintain the high standards of the club, expenses were running sky-high. What he didn't have the courage to say was that he was afraid of antagonizing the police by having Ralph as his manager. What he did say was that he had to reduce Ralph's percentage, that he was sorry, but there was no other way. Ralph almost told him to shove it, but he didn't want to give him the satisfaction. Instead, Ralph diplomatically told the owner that he didn't want to be the cause of his *fallimento* (bankruptcy, downfall); and if things were that bad for him, he'd need the measly cut he proposed to give. Ralph wished him luck and went home quite a bitter, bitter man.

Some weeks before, Ralph had read an article that had Charlie talking about making a film on his life. It mentioned a movie producer, Tucker, who supposedly was going to come to Italy to discuss the story with Charlie. The film, the article continued, was not going to glorify gangsters but would point out that they were pawns in the hands of their social environment. Certainly, Ralph felt it was true in his case. He understood that in his youth, his life's circumstances—beginning with the death of his father—led to many of the wrong choices; and that his inclination to trust people brought about many difficulties. But that he was dealt a raw deal in life, no one could tell him differently.

The story about the film being produced was not true. Charlie would have certainly mentioned it to Ralph. Nothing materialized, but Ralph knew Charlie had begun thinking seriously about it, and now Ralph felt he too was ready.

CHAPTER FIFTY-TWO

Sightseeing was a natural offshoot from Ralph's former jobs. It wasn't anything he planned. It just happened. He was always being asked in and out of the clubs—what to see in Rome, where to buy this or that; and sometimes he took them around in his car. Now, without a job, the most natural thing seemed to hire his car out for sightseeing—with him as a guide. It was a perfect transition but, as usual, not without problems.

Ralph had no real documents, not even residence papers. That was one reason why he obtained the pistol permit—at least he had some kind of document. For eight years, Ralph drove without a driver's license. The problem was the authorities wouldn't give him a residence status. That was true for all newcomers to Rome after the war, including Italians. It was a merry-go-round. If one had a job, one could obtain residence papers, but one could not be hired without a residence status. It was difficult to figure out. Ralph was born in Rome, deported to it, and no one thought he had any right to a legal residence. It was ironic. Ralph needed a driver's license to work.

On his way to the CIT office (Italian tourist agency) to inquire about license possibilities, he met his friend Sam Ravali. During the brief conversation, Ralph told him of his problems, and Sam, with an air of confidence, promised he would obtain the license for him. "Give me everything you have . . . and I'll take care of it for you," he said. Ralph mustered up whatever identification papers he had, and a few weeks later, Sam gave him some documents. Ralph took them to an authorized auto school (an official agency in Italy that provides licenses) and, after taking various tests, was given his driver's license.

Ralph somehow wasn't exactly happy about the situation because he didn't know how Sam obtained the documents. Sam lived in Catania, Sicily, and Ralph knew he had friends such as Minister Scelba's brother, but Ralph's sixth sense told him it would be only a matter of time until the authorities found out. As he expected, one day he was summoned to police headquarters for questioning. "Ralph . . . how did you get your driver's license?" At this point, Ralph knew the best thing was the truth, and he explained exactly what had happened. When the police learned of Ralph's connections, they allowed him to leave.

"Leave?" Ralph exclaimed. "And what do I do with this?" And waved his license in the air. "Tear it up . . . or what? Or must I get phony documents again?" Disgustingly, Ralph threw the license on the commissioner's desk and left. He was however no fool; prior to his visit, he had made a copy of the license.

Like a guardian angel, Ralph's dear friend Father Carlo Blandino entered the scene. He was a Franciscan monk who lived and worked in the Istituto Madonna degli Angeli, in Lavinio, about forty-five kilometers from Rome. Blandino dedicated his time to children of convicts who were sometimes abandoned completely, trying to make up for what society, obviously, couldn't give them. In Lavinio, he took care of the younger children; but in Milan, Father Blandino had an institute for young adults—a place where they could learn a trade in order to be self-sufficient in life. He was openly known as *Fratello dei* Gangsters (the Gangsters' Brother). Father Blandino was a burly man with bright, gentle eyes, a little taller than Ralph, and some fifteen years younger. He was all heart and as honest as the day is long. He never took advantage of anyone, but he could put pressure here and there with the right people for a just cause. And he thought Ralph needed a break. He practically took Ralph by the hand to the *Comune di Roma* (city hall), and under his instructions, Ralph was allowed to be registered as a resident in Rome. He was a true friend whom Ralph never forgot.

The U.S. military learned of Ralph's hangout at the Hotel Nord Bar on Via Amendola, near the train station and a stone's throw away from Via Nazionale, one of the main streets. It was a central location, and everyone went there looking for Ralph. Ralph's reputation as a most congenial and excellent guide spread, and many American tourists also showed up, asking for Ralph. But the bureaucracy in Rome dictated that Ralph also needed a tourist license, which was necessary, together with a normal license, to perform touristic service. He had had so much trouble in obtaining his normal driver's license that he thought it would be a monumental feat and kept neglecting it. Because of this, however, he was harassed throughout 1953. His Italian colleagues were envious of his success. Ralph was called in by the police many times on anonymous tips that he was working illegally. He was constantly reprimanded, but the police commissioner, aware of Ralph's problems, closed an eye in his favor.

Since Ralph spoke English, which many Italians did not, American tourists waited as long as two hours for him. The other drivers were not only jealous of this, but also of the special treatment Ralph received from the police. Even though they repeatedly received the anonymous calls that a car without a license was operating, the police shrugged it off because they knew it was Ralph. In addition, Ralph was the only one allowed to drive up to the plane with the military officials. He considered it, however, a very small privilege after all the harassment. *Let them be jealous,* Ralph sneered to himself. *If I take care of the Americans, it's because I am an American!*

But there's always the day of reckoning. Ralph had had it one day and went straight to police headquarters to raise holy hell. He began ranting, "If I run nightclubs, they say I sell narcotics. If I take people sightseeing, they say I sell narcotics. What the hell must I do here? If you don't want me in Italy, give me a passport so I can get the hell out!" Ralph's explosion was such that he began shaking like a madman.

The police commissioner understood Ralph's frame of mind and tried to placate him. "Ralph, *calmati* (calm yourself)! I understand how you feel. We'll get this thing settled once and for all. Tell your wife to come up here."

Apparently, Ralph's anger was very convincing because with a little push from the commissioner, Ralph obtained the tourist license in Elena's name. Another blow to Ralph's dignity, but again, he shrugged it off. At least he could work in peace—at something he enjoyed.

One of the most colorful people Ralph ever met was King Farouk of Egypt—a man whose life story remains controversial. Farouk's first marriage was dissolved because of the old monarchy story—no sons. Soon it was rumored that he would marry a beautiful sixteen-year-old commoner. He was not known as a great ruler but rather one that shirked his duty, allowing corruption to seep through his government. In the meantime, he led a life of luxury and dissipation. In 1950, Farouk took a cruise to Italy, his first visit out of Egypt in eleven years. A born gambler, he was seen in all the well-known casinos in Italy and Europe. In March 1952, he was reported hurt in an assassination plot and escaped to the north of Egypt. The country was in a turmoil, and he continued to fear for his life. In July of that year, he abdicated, requesting and obtaining asylum in Italy. Later that month, he arrived in Capri aboard his luxurious yacht with his young queen, baby son, and two daughters of his previous marriage. He was accused by his people that he left with a fortune in gold. King Farouk, of course, denied it.

In Egypt, the new government began to confiscate his various palaces, and the scandal hit all the Cairo papers. It seemed that for a man who claimed he didn't drink because of his religion, his private rooms had well-supplied liquor cabinets. But that was minor. What really shocked the Egyptians—and probably the rest of the world—was his perverted interest in sex. He was a pornographic buff. They found his four palaces full of erotic paintings and statues—bronze and marble statues of nude men and women. In one palace in Alexandria, paintings on the ceiling of a high dome depicted nude women riding horses. It was no secret to anyone that King Farouk loved his women. He went to Switzerland early in 1955 and, shortly thereafter, declared that his finances were low and he needed a job. Farouk returned to Rome in April 1955.

The first time Ralph bumped into King Farouk was at the famous *Fontana di Trevi*, popularly called Three Coins in the Fountain because of the movie. There was a great deal of commotion, people running around. When Ralph saw the roly-poly figure, he instantly knew that it was King Farouk. Farouk was always escorted by two policemen and a caravan of three cars—a Mercedes, a Pontiac, and a Dodge. At one time, he also had a Cadillac. He lived in the elegant Parioli section of Rome on Via Archimede and never went out before two or three in the morning. Ralph continued to see him around the nightclubs; and one night, as he sat in the Florida club with a friend, Charles Templeton (a Canadian with the Canadian Broadcasting Company), an army major strutted over to Ralph. He was half-drunk and slobbered, "Hey, Ralph, there's King Farouk over there. I'm gonna go say hello to him." Before Ralph could respond, the major swayed toward the table, but two plainclothesmen stopped him. Ralph could see that the officer was becoming involved in an argument, so he walked over and pulled him away.

"Come on, Major . . . let's go," Ralph said quietly. "Farouk doesn't talk to anyone."

In fact, the police made sure everyone kept his distance from Farouk. If it were a lady, the rules were overlooked. King Farouk noticed Ralph and watched the whole scene with seeming indifference. Many people were not aware that the king always carried a small pistol, a Beretta caliber 6, for his protection.

A few days later, Ralph was formally introduced to Farouk, and the two men sympathized immediately. One night, Farouk invited Ralph to dinner. Ralph consented but told the king it would have to be after working hours. Therefore, around four o'clock in the morning, the two new friends went to an all-night place near the station. It was there that Ralph saw Farouk eat a four-and-a-half-pound chicken all by himself. Ralph too loved to eat, but he had his limits. Farouk confided in Ralph that even though he liked Italy and Europe in general, he missed Egypt. But terrible things were happening there, and he had to leave. Ralph understood because he had read about the scandals, like everyone else. He also knew that the new Egyptian regime wanted the Italian government to hold Farouk for back taxes, but the Italian government turned a deaf ear. Farouk was very popular in Italy, and this gave him another problem in 1962. He sued and won a case against an Italian candy factory, which used his name on their chocolate candy without permission.

There was always some action when Farouk was in the clubs; that's why he went out very late at night—to find some privacy. One night, with a couple of friends, Ralph saved his life. They were again at the Florida club, and Ralph sensed a certain tension in the air as he singled out four Egyptians sitting at different tables. He knew they were up to something by the way they were snooping around. Ralph also spotted the cops, ready to pounce at the first false move. The tension in the room kept rising. Something like, *On your mark, get set, GO.* Ralph's reflexes were excellent. As soon as he saw one Egyptian stand up, he rushed over to Farouk while the police stood in between. The other Egyptians had also risen from their seats, but it was too late. Ralph and his friends had Farouk out the back door. It all went lightning fast. Hustling him out the door, however, wasn't easy. Farouk was huge, but they finally squeezed him through, and he was escorted home. When Ralph and his friends returned to the club, two of the Egyptians came over and asked if they could join them. Ralph nodded suspiciously, but he knew they were harmless. They wanted to explain why they had it in for Farouk. They had terrible stories to tell about the king, mostly concerning women. According to them, if Farouk favored a married woman, he would have the husband killed to have his wife. Ralph listened with skepticism.

After Farouk's close call incident, he and Ralph became very friendly, and they often did the nightclub circuit together; sometimes they saw a floor show. At that time, Farouk sported a snappy mustache, goatee, and shaded glasses; and even though he was huge in size, not particularly good-looking, he had not lost his charm with women. If he saw a young lady pleasing to him, he did not hesitate in courting her. One of his best girlfriends always said that he would die either two ways: eating or making love to a girl. On March 18, 1965, King Farouk died at the age of forty-five. Some said after making love, but the records show that it was after eating a large meal in a restaurant on Via Aurelia. Heart attack. He had gone there sometime after midnight with his latest Italian girlfriend.

And Charlie? With the excuse that Ralph took tourists down to Sorrento-Capri-Naples sightseeing, he saw him quite often. He was doing all right; he seemed to be a very content man with Igea. In May, because of good behavior, they gave him permission to go to his home at Santa Marinella near Rome, the same seaside town where Bergman and Rossellini had their villa. Charlie and Igea enjoyed the change of scenery. Charlie's name, however, still cropped up in the papers every time there was a narcotics story. Around August, the Federal agents picked up Sam Accardi in New York in what they called a three nationwide distribution ring. Accardi was described as a former associate of Charlie's, and the insinuation was that Charlie was "back there somewhere in the shadows." Charlie denied all for the thousandth time.

Another man was making the news. Charles Siragusa, district bureau supervisor for Europe and the Middle East, had broken up a ring between Detroit and the Middle East; and like the rest of the Federal agents, he too saw Charlie as the narcotics kingpin. When the big heroin scandal broke out in Italy around April the following year, which involved several chemical and pharmaceutical companies, they screamed that Charlie had to be involved. Instead, the Italians sent a man named Migliardi of Schiaparelli Laboratories to prison in Turin for eleven years. Siragusa, however, kept harassing Charlie at every turn.

Meanwhile, Charlie was still trying to go legitimate. He was involved in his electrical appliance outlet in Naples and had a few people working for him. He often told Ralph, "Everyone here has his hand out, Ralph . . . worse than in the States . . . You have to watch your step." Ralph understood what he meant.

Naturally, many deportees contacted Charlie—some to pay their respects and others with specific messages. Charlie always knew what was happening in the States. Joe Adonis was the latest friend up against it. His appeal was rejected (Kefauver perjury charge), and he was sentenced to serve eight to twenty-four months in jail. In November, Joe Adonis weighed all the pros and cons and decided that, instead of doing time, he would offer to deport himself. It seemed a little whacky to Ralph because with good behavior, he probably would not have done all two years; and afterwards, he could have stayed in America. There had to be other strong reasons. Maybe it was because he knew they also had an airtight denaturalization charge against him. Adonis was another victim of not knowing his real birthplace. He thought all along that he was born in New Jersey. The government had evidence he was a native of Italy—that he had gone to the United States when he was five months. Perhaps another reason was that he didn't like the climate in the underworld anymore and, at fifty-seven, was anxious to retire. Adonis definitely had a large amount of money stashed away, and sunny Italy was a fine choice for retirement. Whatever his reasons, he came up with the crazy proposition, and the courts agreed. Adonis spent Christmas with his family before leaving for exile in January. At the same time, Costello's tax evasion case was being reviewed by the Supreme Court;

and unfortunately, his term was upheld. Costello was sentenced to five years in prison. Charlie and Ralph discussed the fates of the two men with remorse. Their friendships went back a long way. Almost twenty years, however, had passed, and Ralph felt he was now far removed from that world.

All during 1955, Ralph worked mostly for the American and Canadian Air Force—hundreds of them. He was practically their official guide in town. That was how he met Charles Templeton, who, after taking a stab at entering the Canadian parliament, had become involved in the broadcasting business. Ralph thought he was an amiable and intelligent person. Since his first visit to Italy, Templeton had been nursing an idea and requested Ralph's help.

"Ralph . . . would you do something for me?" he said one day over a drink.

"Sure . . . if I can," Ralph replied.

"I'd like to make a film on a sightseeing tour of Italy with some Canadians."

"Okay . . . why not?"

"You know the spots, Ralph . . . The Colosseum, the Vatican, the hills around Rome," Templeton suggested.

"Sure . . . don't worry. I know where to go."

As he requested, Ralph took Templeton and his men around Rome while they made a newsreel of the tour. Happy with what they had so far, that evening at dinner, Templeton asked, "Ralph . . . how about going to Naples?"

Ralph instinctively knew what he meant; Templeton was also interested in Charlie, but Ralph said nothing. Instead, he said, "Okay, we can go tomorrow morning. Be ready at seven o'clock."

As soon as they arrived in Naples, Ralph pulled over to a bar and excused himself. On the QT, he called Charlie. "Listen, Charlie . . . I'm doing a little work for some friends. Is it all right if I take a picture of your home?"

"Sure, Ralph . . . but make out I don't know anything," an accommodating Charlie answered.

"Okay, thanks. How's everything . . . Igea?"

"Fine. Just fine . . . everything's okay."

"Okay . . . *ciao*. Talk to you."

Ralph returned to his car, said nothing, and continued the tour to Capri, Sorrento, Pompei while the camera kept rolling. On their return to Naples, Ralph took a pleased Templeton directly to Charlie's luxurious apartment on Via Tasso, 474—an exclusive area called Parco Como-Ricci. There, Ralph gathered several deportees he knew around

Naples and had them say something into the mike. Templeton was able to make a very good film out of everything and was very appreciative. Ralph, for his part, was happy to help him out in that way.

After Templeton returned to Canada, Ralph received a letter from him, advising that a young lady from his office would be visiting Rome. Would Ralph take good care of her? Of course. But Templeton had a surprise for Ralph. The girl brought him a copy of the newsreel they had made in Italy. Ralph was elated. It was the kind of gesture a nice guy like Templeton would do.

Ralph had his small rewards.

CHAPTER FIFTY-THREE

Ralph's life was running a smooth course, but toward the end of 1956, he was hit on the head with still another whopper. The Colibri Club had changed names, becoming the Broadway Club, and the new manager was having his problems. He was crying to Ralph about it one night at the bar of the club, offering him a partnership. But Ralph subsequently learned from the owner that the manager was not to be trusted.

Ralph was grateful for the offer and would occasionally stop into the club after work—although he still had not made any decisions. One night, the hatcheck lady approached him.

"Ralph . . . listen," she said maternally, "there's a young lady here. She hasn't a place to sleep. Can you get her a place, some pension somewhere?"

"Well, if I can, why not? I'll do my best," Ralph replied and although he was in a hurry—he had to leave for Naples with some GIs around eleven o'clock. He phoned several pensions he knew, but nothing was available. Noticing the late hour, he made a hasty call as a last resort to Elena. He explained the situation quickly. Would she take the unfortunate girl until she found something else? Elena, who was used to Ralph's missionary ways, agreed. Ralph told the hatcheck lady, but when he saw the girl, he shuddered. She was tall, on the thin side, and her sleazy clothes, a size too small, had seen better days. She also looked as if she needed a bath. Ralph's first impulse was to get away—fast. Instead, he rattled, "Okay, you can go over to my house. My wife will take care of you. You can sleep there for a few nights." He wrote down his address, and as the women thanked him profusely, he hurried off.

When Ralph returned from Naples, he asked Elena if the girl had showed up. Did she present any documents? With a frown on her face, Elena told him that the girl had been hired by the Broadway Club. Ralph could tell Elena did not like the girl as she added, "She gave me her contract from the club. It said she was twenty-three years old." It sounded okay, and for the moment, Ralph blotted it out of his mind, turning to other things.

About three days later, Ralph was again in the club when the manager approached him. "Ralph . . . you know that girl, Laura . . . She hasn't come in for two days!"

Ralph didn't like the smell of things. "Listen, you do me a favor. When she does come in, tell her to give you the keys. I don't want to have her in my home anymore. My wife's complaining, and I need peace on the home front."

The manager agreed, but Ralph didn't trust him, and the next night went down to see for himself. He found the girl sitting at the bar, her light brown hair fluffed out more than usual and her face overly made up. "Where've you been?" Ralph asked sharply.

"To my mother's," she replied matter-of-factly.

"I thought you said you didn't have a mother," Ralph retorted.

"Did I?" she said in mock innocence.

Ralph let it go. What the hell did he care? Then, rather brusquely, he said, "Listen . . . you better find yourself another place, because I can't have you up at my house anymore. Do you have the keys with you?" She fumbled in her handbag and came up with them. As she handed him the keys, Ralph made a gesture of good riddance and walked out.

A few nights later, Ralph stopped in the club, ready to tell the manager he wasn't interested in the partnership. Before he could speak, the manager anxiously approached Ralph, breathlessly informing him that Laura was only seventeen, therefore a minor, and that the police were looking for her!

Ralph harshly reprimanded the nervous man for not being more careful, happy that she was no longer in his home. It was not his problem, and he left the man more shattered than before.

The next morning, Ralph was alone at home, waiting for his driver; Elena had gone shopping. Around nine o'clock, as he was sipping his coffee and listening to the radio newscasts, he heard a loud pounding on the door. He thought it was his driver, but when he opened the door, he yelled, "What the hell is this?"

Outside the door on the stairs were about eight detectives. The one closest to him sneered, "Dottore Dante wants to see you. He's *very* anxious to see you!"

Ralph gave him a frosty look and quipped, "Oh, yeah? Don't you guys have something better to do?" Still, Ralph never thought it had anything to do with the girl Laura. When he arrived at the Vice Squad headquarters, he saw her there, sitting with one leg on top of another, smoking a cigarette with a smirk on her face. Dante acted as though he had finally caught the big fish.

"You know her?" he said severely.

"Yeah . . . I know her," Ralph replied sarcastically. "I gave her an act of charity!" He proceeded to relate how he had given her a place to sleep for a few days.

When Dante asked, "Didn't you know she was only seventeen?" Ralph replied, "No, I didn't. She showed my wife a contract that said she was twenty-three. I only found out last night that she was seventeen."

"Who told you?" Dante retorted.

"The manager of the club," Ralph snapped. "I didn't know it. If I knew it, I would never have accepted her in my home." Then, exasperated, Ralph exclaimed, "Look . . . I'm sick and tired of all you damn people. Want to send me to prison? Do what the hell you like!" He knew that Dante was going to implicate him in something, but Ralph still didn't know what it was all about.

Sure enough, Ralph was arrested; and once in his cell, the mystery began to unravel. The Roman police and Interpol had cracked down on a gang operating among Beirut, Damascus, and Rome in what they called *tratta delle bianche* (white slavery). The leader of the gang was a wealthy Greek still at large (presumably in Beirut) who personally directed all the traffic. The group had collaborators throughout Europe who recruited young girls in Rome to become dancers (chorus girls), and once polished off and under contract, they were sent to the Mid Orient with a little spending money. On the surface, everything looked aboveboard, except that some of the girls were minors; and once abroad, their fate was dubious. Not always did they dance; and the Lebanese police began to suspect foul play when some of the Italian girls died mysteriously, committed suicide, or just plainly disappeared. The alarm was called, and detectives began investigating. Apparently, when the girls arrived at their destinations, there wasn't always work for them. As an alternative to starving to death, they were forced to accept unsavory jobs about which some girls, obviously, were not happy. Some turned to prostitution. This was the kettle of fish Ralph was dragged into—just because he generously offered shelter to the girl. Laura knew the heat was on and had disappeared. The police found her near the railroad station about three in the morning. When they asked where she had been all those days missing from home, without batting an eyelash, she gave Ralph's address. Whammo, that was it.

Because his name was Ralph Liguori (once supposedly involved in the biggest prostitution rap in the United States), he was, accordingly to police mentality, a natural to be involved in the despicable gang. Ralph's name was liberally mentioned in the newspapers. The words *undesirable* and *gangster* were used indiscriminately, and according to the papers, Ralph was operating throughout Italy. The police had also arrested practically all the Italian accomplices of the group—men Ralph did not know and had never heard or seen in his life.

Sitting in his cell, commiserating his fate and waiting for Judge Gerace to interrogate him, another prisoner was brought into his cell. When Ralph learned he was part of the gang, he exclaimed, "Listen . . . do me a favor. Call the guard and get the hell out of my cell! You're with those other fellas, and I don't want to be seen with any of you, period! Call the guard!" he yelled. Finally, the man left the cell, and Ralph's interview with the judge began.

Ralph declared his innocence, but the judge wasn't too impressed, took everything with a grain of salt. When the judge had interrogated the girl, an obvious prostitute on the side, she stated that Ralph had taken her out one night and had sexual intercourse with her. Of course, this was absolutely not true; but since she was a minor, it was another strike against Ralph. The judge did not look favorably upon him. There was no real evidence against Ralph, but he was not released. Instead, he was sentenced to stand trial with the others.

It was a sad—terrible—Christmas for Ralph in the cold cell. It was especially hard on Elena, who had every reason to be bitter. However, being a very determined woman, she took charge of Ralph's defense. Upon Ralph's advice, she hired two of Rome's best criminal lawyers, Philip Lupus and Giorgio Angelozzi Gariboldi, who were ready to go all the way with the case. After three and a half months (101 days), Ralph was released on *liberta provvisorio* (released on bail) awaiting trial. Because he needed the money, he returned to work immediately. Very late one night, he stopped at a local bar with an American friend when he saw Laura enter with a male companion. As soon as she saw Ralph, she made a turn about-face and ran out. But before anyone could say anything, she had a change of heart and returned. Contritely, she excused herself and mumbled, "You know, Ralph . . . they even wanted me to say that I'd seen narcotics in your home!"

"What!" Ralph screamed. "They wanted you to say that?"

"Yeah . . . narcotics . . . but I was afraid to say something like that."

"Aw . . . listen," Ralph said disgustedly, "go away . . . just get out of my sight." He turned his back on her, closing the issue.

Charlie's reaction to all this was a mixture of complete disapproval where Ralph was concerned and a nauseating repugnance toward the cops. "Somebody's going to get a promotion after all this is over," he sniffed.

He was in better spirits since they had lifted his latest two-year curfew. After all the noise Washington kept insisting that he was the man behind the international drug trade (and even though Inspector

Dosi had said there was no evidence to prove such activities), the Italian authorities were pressured (with the help of Palermo's police commissioner, Giorgio Florita) to put Charlie on another curfew to appease them. They had used the same old excuse: *persona non grata* (socially dangerous). Ralph thought that it was enough crap to make you want to vomit. At the end of November 1956, it was all over, and now Charlie was free again to move around. Ralph met him now and then when he took tourists down in his area. Charlie scolded Ralph for letting himself get involved in what he called a stupid frame-up. "You should have been on your toes more." He sighed paternally. "Anyway, keep your nose clean, and your lawyers will have you exonerated." He agreed with Ralph, however, that if necessary, he should appeal all the way.

Then Ralph read in the papers a claim that Charlie had signed an appeal to President Eisenhower for readmission to the States. Ralph laughed to himself; they write a lot of crap in the papers. If Charlie did appeal, he did it for laughs because with all the adverse publicity he was having, his chances were zero. It was a touchy subject with Charlie, so Ralph didn't mention it.

A couple of months later, they had lunch at one of Charlie's favorite restaurants in Naples (Giacomini's), but this time, Charlie's face was grim. His closest associate and friend, Costello, had just escaped death. He was shot (May 2, 1957) in front of his Central Park West apartment and miraculously was saved. Frank had just been released on bail from his tax evasion sentence but wouldn't talk about his would-be assassin. He was jailed in the New York Tombs Prison for contempt and spent fifteen days in the company of local hoods and derelicts.

Costello knew, as well as everyone else in the underworld, that it was Vincent Gigante, one of the Genovese's hired hands; but as usual, Frank, a nonviolent man, wanted no more bloodshed and wouldn't finger Gigante in the trial that followed. If that wasn't enough, Charlie's tone became even more melancholy, his face contorted in a faraway expression, as he talked about his old friend Johnny Torrio. Torrio had died of a heart attack at the age of seventy-five, alone and abandoned in a Brooklyn hospital—a forgotten man. It happened around the first week of May 1957, and Charlie was clearly mourning his death. They had gone a long way together, had been friends and associates, and Charlie had always considered him a wise counselor. Then his face filled with anger again when he told Ralph about his good friend Frank Scalise—that he had been murdered on June 7. All hell was breaking loose in the States, and Charlie was completely disgusted.

The more Charlie talked, the more it felt to Ralph to be the end of an era. Many of the guys from the old neighborhoods were retiring, one way or another. On a lighter note, Charlie revealed that he had seen Joe Adonis, who seemed to be more relaxed; he was still on an extended tour of Italy with his wife and two daughters and enjoying himself. Adonis was becoming used to the idea of his new home and glad to be away from the pressures from all sides in the States. And no wonder! The year 1957 was a bad one for the boys; it was another turning point in their history. Greed and quest for personal power were as usual the damning ingredients that were causing the latest surge of disobedience, insubordination, rebellion. New loyalties were being bought and exchanged, and new heads of families were being contemplated. Underneath all of this was Genovese's constant obsession to be number one, and his open rebellion stated that Charlie's word or wishes no longer counted. In fact, later that year, on October 25, 1957, Albert Anastasia, a devoted friend to Charlie and Costello, was shot to death while having a shave in the New York Sheraton barbershop. They tried to say that Lansky had had it in for Anastasia because of some interests in Cuba, but it was Genovese cleaning up on his adversaries. This happened even though Costello had let it be known that he would step down.

No doubt things would have been different if Charlie had stayed in the States. All these negative events not only angered Charlie but spiritually were removing him farther and farther away from the organization he had once created. He felt hopelessly detached, and Ralph surmised the only thing he came to care about now was getting his monthly salary, so to speak, from his remaining interests. The final clincher was when Vito Genovese pulled the asinine blooper of calling for a supposedly secret meeting of all the bosses in Apalachin, New York, on November 14, 1957. In his zeal to become Boss of all Bosses, he naively picked out the wrong place. The exposed affair, unknowingly discovered by a New York state trooper, made a laughing stock of all those who attended. A few lost face as they were seen running into the woods like petty thieves. "What a mess! How things had deteriorated," Charlie wailed.

It was now clear to everyone that Vito had been crowned top banana, and Frank was just tired of it all.

But there are still strange quirks in life, and the rivalry between the two men was still not completely ironed out. Fate threw a mean curve at Vito because he would not be free to wheel and deal as he would have liked. In the summer of 1958, he was trapped on a narcotics charge with his sidekick, Vincent Gigante, the same man who tried to kill Costello. It was a big case; the indictment named thirty-six other guys. The trial was held in the spring of 1959, and Vito was sentenced to fifteen years in prison. He was sent to the Atlanta penitentiary, to which Frank had returned after his appeals on the tax evasion case had failed. The warden was not happy about having two powerful men in his prison, aware of all the tension among the prisoners. It wasn't strange that most of them were on Frank's side. In effect, it was now Vito's life that was in danger. Frank had sized up the situation, and it was then that the famous meeting between the two bosses took place. Charlie told Ralph it was Frank who called the meeting to save Vito, and Ralph did not doubt it because Frank had the smarts and class. By calling the shots and shaking hands with Vito, Frank had given his blessings to the new Boss of all Bosses and was assured of a tranquil retirement. Frank wasn't called Prime Minister for nothing! Unfortunately for Vito, he had to rule behind bars.

Now perhaps he could imagine how Charlie felt all those years in Dannemora. There was a difference, however; Charlie, like Frank, was well liked and respected by all. Vito died in prison a tired and bitter man in 1969, and again, the scramble for the top brought about new skirmishes. And so it went. Frank, on the other hand, enjoyed a reasonably peaceful retirement and died comfortably in his bed on February 21, 1973, at the ripe old age of eighty-two.

CHAPTER FIFTY-FOUR

As far as Ralph was concerned, Charles Siragusa was, besides being the European and Mideast director of the Narcotics Bureau, a man without scruples who happened to work on the side of the law. He was a sidekick of Harry Anslinger's, still determined to apprehend Charlie. If Ralph fell into the dragnet, all the better. Siragusa was always convinced that Charlie was involved in the drug racket but could never come up with anything concrete, which frustrated him all the more. He never gave up; he was relentless in his pursuit to hang Charlie.

Siragusa also enjoyed his nightlife—always, of course, in the line of duty. *Good excuse,* thought Ralph. He hobnobbed with the jet set to keep his eyes open for drug peddlers, wined and dined at the more posh clubs around Rome, and danced with showbiz beauties. During the day, he was seen in sports jackets and loud ties; but at night, he wore a tux and a Papillon neatly tied under his chin—around a high, starched white collar. His thick tortoiseshell-rimmed glasses were always the same, as was his receding hairline. One of his gimmicks was to disguise himself as different characters to infiltrate the world of drug addicts, pushers, and, hopefully, that of the men at the top. When together, Charlie and Ralph discussed Siragusa many times. Charlie couldn't stomach him, obviously because he was always putting the pressure on the police in Naples to pull him in for this and that. Articles in the paper regarding drug traffic always had Charlie running the game, and Charlie would naturally lose his temper. There just wasn't any peace with Siragusa around. The heat was always on!

Siragusa was just another thorn in their side. To make matters worse, Charlie and Ralph were having personal problems. Charlie was depressed because Igea wasn't in the best of health, and he was constantly worrying about her. Ralph was nervous and tense because his trial was coming up. As usual, Ralph kept working as much as he could, trying to put some money away just in case. He still hung around the corner of the Nord Bar; had his personal table—the second one near to the door. He sat there between one tour and another. One day, a nondescript man at the next table kept trying to hold a conversation with Ralph, but he ignored him. The next day, the man returned. This time he mentioned to Ralph that he was a newspaperman. Ralph laughed to himself and made him believe he had swallowed the story.

"How's business, Ralph?" the man asked.

"Fine," Ralph replied casually, and he talked about sightseeing to keep the conversation light. Ralph knew who he was all the time. He wasn't fooling anybody, but Ralph never let on.

He wasn't, however, the only person who came around the corner; some of Ralph's best friends were cops, and they stopped by occasionally to see how he was doing. About five or six days after the fake newspaperman hounded Ralph, one of his cop friends came along.

"Hey . . . Ralph . . . did you see the papers?"

"No . . . I don't read Italian. What is it?" The cop went to the newsstand and bought the paper to read to Ralph. Ralph couldn't understand very much, but it was enough to hear Charles Siragusa's name. It was the usual type of article where he and his cohorts had arrested someone in Turin or Milan. Inevitably, Charlie's name—and Charlie's mob—were thrown in. In the days that followed, there were more articles, and Ralph was becoming more and more irate. Again, his friend returned one day with another newspaper, but Ralph was quick.

"Don't read it to me. I don't want to hear any more!" Something wild came over Ralph. He stood up, said good-bye to the cop, and headed toward the American embassy on Via Veneto. He stopped across the street and used the phone booth at a nearby newsstand. He didn't want anyone to hear him. He dialed the embassy and asked for *him*.

"Charles Siragusa. Who's speaking?" an official voice said.

"Ralph Liguori."

"Oh . . . hello . . . Ralph. How are you?" a more casual voice replied.

"I'm fine," Ralph answered coldly.

"What can I do for you . . . Ralph?"

"I'd like to talk to you," Ralph responded firmly.

"Well . . . come on up!" Siragusa invited.

"No . . . I don't want to come up there. You come downstairs and bring whomever you want with you!" Ralph retorted hotly.

Ralph walked a few feet away from the phone booth for a better view. He waited and watched for a few minutes. First, two men came out, walked to the left of the embassy, and waited on the corner, expecting something to happen. Ralph looked at them and smirked. Then he crossed the street and stood just inside the huge iron gates of the embassy. Walking alongside Charles Siragusa was the man who had claimed to be a newspaperman at the Nord Bar. Ralph stood erect, his feet straddled a bit with his chest out. He watched them come forward, and he could tell they were trying to size up the situation. Siragusa was quick and broke the ice by immediately extending his hand.

"Hello . . . Ralph. How are you?" he said with an almost smile.

"Fine," Ralph said curtly, glaring at the other man. "What the hell are you doing here?" Ralph grimaced. "Aren't you a newspaperman anymore? Who the hell did you think you were kidding? I can smell guys like you a mile away. Buddy, I was playing with you." And Ralph gave him a look to kill.

Siragusa broke Ralph's monologue. "What can I do for you, Ralph?" he said hurriedly.

"Listen, Charlie, I'm going to talk to you like a friend," Ralph turned to face him. The sun was warm, and now and then its rays hit Siragusa's glasses just so. The glare hurt Ralph's eyes a little, but that didn't stop him from holding his stance. "Look!" Ralph shouted angrily, "in America that guy wanted to become president of the United States . . . framed me and Luciano. What the hell do you want to be . . . J. Edgar Hoover? I'm sick and tired of all this stuff going on. Leave my godddamn name out of the newspapers . . . out of your mouth . . . because now I don't know what I'm doing anymore. I lost everything I had in the States . . . I lost everything here. Now, I'm losing my head!" Ralph wailed. "Now, I'm not going to tell you anything else. Do you understand what I'm trying to tell you?"

Siragusa nervously pushed his glasses up his nose and uttered, "Yeah . . . Ralph . . . okay . . . don't worry." He shook hands again and went away.

Nothing was said about Ralph anymore, but then Siragusa's tenure in Italy had come to an end; he was scheduled to return to the United States. Siragusa had a much-publicized career; he was frequently in the news because of his sometimes bizarre escapades. Sometimes he came out smelling like a rose, but in others, he goofed such as the time when he was in Paris. Two French dope peddlers had outsmarted him by giving him flour and sugar instead of the real McCoy. Siragusa, however, was not a coward; he risked his life at times, but Ralph thought he was a braggart. He left the Narcotics Bureau in 1963, waited ten years to return to Italy to participate in a film on Lucky Luciano's life—directed by the Italian director Franco Rossi. Siragusa played himself like some kind of hero, shadowing Charlie around Naples, which was a lot of hooey. That Charlie was his public enemy number one was known to everyone; he had a personal hatred—obsession—for him. Charlie was his nemesis.

To make sure they didn't mention him in the film, Ralph went to the opening with Elena and a lawyer friend, Fausto Cavalaro. If they had said just one word against Ralph, Cavalaro would have had the movie cut off right then and there. For love of money and fame, men have often been defamed, their names thrown around loosely. Caught in this web was Charlie and, of course, Ralph, who always declared they were victims of sensationalism. Luckily for the producer, Ralph was not mentioned; but in Ralph's opinion, the movie was a lot of crap. Charlie didn't even bother to see the film.

A few days after his meeting with Siragusa, Ralph went to Naples with two American colonels. He didn't have much time off (only three hours) to see Charlie. They met at the Sombrero Club and had a drink together. Ralph was anxious to tell him what had happened. Charlie was in a nervous mood because Igea wasn't feeling well that day, and that always upset him. "Did you get to see that bastard in Rome?" he asked intensely, meaning Siragusa.

"Yeah . . . I saw him. I told him to cut it out," Ralph replied forcefully.

"You should have whacked him! You would have been better off whacking him . . . to teach that bastard a lesson!" Charlie retorted heatedly. He hated Siragusa's guts and for good reason. It must have been his mood, but it was the first time Charlie didn't play the protective role with Ralph.

"Well . . . Charlie . . . I wanted to do it as a gentleman . . . you know? I spoke the best I could," Ralph replied soothingly. It was no use arguing over it. As usual, Ralph could see Charlie's mind already drifting as he simply said, "Okay . . . okay . . . Ralph . . ."

The rest of the year and into March of 1958, things were reasonably calm until one night, Charlie called Ralph at home. His voice was somewhat altered, and Ralph could tell something was wrong.

"*Ciao* . . . Charlie," Ralph said cheerfully.

"Ralph . . . *Ciao* . . . Listen . . . can you come down?" he asked quietly.

Sensing it had to be something urgent, Ralph didn't hesitate to say, "Sure, Charlie. Anything wrong?"

"Igea is going to be operated on tomorrow morning," his voice almost cracked. "It doesn't look too good."

"Gees . . . Charlie . . . I'm real sorry. What hospital?"

"She's in the Clinica Villa Bianca in Pozzuoli."

"Okay . . . Charlie. Try to take it easy. Don't worry. We'll be there." Ralph hung up the phone, a bit shaken himself. Igea had become a part of Charlie, and he was running scared of losing her. He needed somebody close to him. Charlie had many guys hanging around him, including a couple of so-called bodyguards, but Ralph was like family to him. Charlie and Ralph were tied to each other, and Ralph knew he needed him there. Elena had put down her knitting, waiting to hear the worse, and Ralph gave her the sad news. They left early the next morning.

They arrived at the clinic a little late and found that Igea had already been operated. The nurse gave them her room number, and when they entered, they found Charlie sitting at Igea's side like a drowned man. Hearing them come in, he looked up and whispered, "She's still sleeping from the anesthesia." He rose slowly, kissed her on the forehead, and they all walked out together, deciding to let Igea sleep it out. Ralph took Charlie by the arm and said, "Come on . . . Charlie, you look all done in. Let's have some lunch in the meantime." Ralph thought it would do him some good to be away for a while.

They drove down to Naples (a twenty-minute drive) to Charlie's haunt, Giacomini's. All during lunch, he was singing Igea's virtues—what a wonderful woman she was; how she had dedicated herself to him; that she was too young to suffer, et cetera. Try as Ralph and Elena did to change the subject, it was impossible. It was as though he were talking to himself. Once in a while, he glanced at his watch, anxious to return to the clinic. "I hope everything turns out all right," he finally said, eyes downcast.

Ralph broke up the solemn lunch by telling Charlie he'd drive him back to the clinic. They drove in an uncomfortable silence; no one knew what to say. As Ralph pulled up to the clinic, he said, "Charlie, I think you want to be alone with Igea, so we'll drive back to Naples. I have some business there, anyway. We'll see her on the way back. Okay?" Charlie nodded his head and thanked his dear friends for their moral support.

The next day, to clear the air a bit, Ralph took Elena to Capri; but immediately after lunch, they drove back to Pozzuoli. When they arrived at the clinic, they were told Igea had been released just an hour before. Disappointed to have missed her, they decided to drive back to Rome since it was late, and it had started to rain. The next day, Elena called Igea to ask how she felt and how everything went. Igea told her the doctors had removed one of her breasts, but she felt better. Charlie, however, later told them that the cancer had spread, and the doctors were unable to remove it all. They were heartbroken for Igea and for Charlie.

One bright spot for Charlie during this bleak period was his victory in court. The Naples police, tired of all the tension with Charlie in their midst, had (as a last resort) requested the courts to exile him to some remote region in Italy. A special magistrate's commission looked into the matter. After a full investigation and the convincing defense by Charlie's dynamic lawyer, a young Neapolitan named Giovanni Passeggio, the commission ruled on March 20, 1958, that there were no grounds to proceed against him. Charlie was naturally very happy about the verdict, but his concern for Igea had dampened any celebration, which may have taken place. He shrugged it off and hoped it would be the end of the harassment.

Ralph had his own bad streak going. His trial had come up, and it turned out to be another three ring circus. As usual, the prosecutor made a big issue out of his name. Although he didn't even know any of the men, they made it appear as though Ralph was the main defendant in the trial. To make sure he would be involved, the delinquent girl sat on the stand and repeated the lie that Ralph had had sexual intercourse with her. Ralph wanted to spit. *What a tramp. I'm not so hard up that I have to make it with her, a minor no less,* he raged inwardly. Nobody else mentioned Ralph on the witness stand. Nevertheless, he could see they were not about to exonerate him; they couldn't lose face after all the publicity they had given his involvement. To prolong the agony, the judge postponed sentencing until the sixth of June.

Outside the courtroom doors, Ralph's lawyer Lupus told reporters that the trial had been blown up by some zealous police officials who thought that by denouncing the Italo-American Ralph Liguori, they had created a sensational case. The day of the trial, Ralph's other lawyer, Angelozzi Gariboldi, had summed up the case eloquently, but it was no use. When the judge sentenced Ralph to one year and five months, Lupus picked up his papers and threw them in the air as a sign of protest. "If I don't beat this case in the court of appeals, I'll never practice law again!" he shouted. Then he turned to Ralph, "Don't worry, Ralph. You're not going to court again. We're not even going to court. If this case isn't won without us, I'll know the reason why!" Both lawyers, furious, stomped out of the courtroom indignantly. A distressed Elena sighed hopelessly. "When will it end?" Ralph was released pending his appeal.

The trial was a terrible disappointment to Ralph. He was truly depressed. To complicate matters, his eyesight was deteriorating, and that made him even more nervous. Perhaps there was truth in what Elena had hinted—that he had a knack for getting himself into trouble. But that didn't help his morale. Ralph kept very busy the following months with sightseeing, and whenever he was in Naples, he checked in with Charlie. During his visits, he could be of no assistance to his friend Charlie's morale. Igea was slowly expiring, and he was dying a little himself inside.

They received the terrible news late one night in September. Igea was dead at thirty-eight. Her suffering had finally come to an end. At the request of her family, she was taken to Milan, and Charlie was given special permission to attend the funeral services. On October 1, she was buried in the Musocco Cemetery in Milan, a long way from sunny Naples. There was practically nothing in the papers about her death or her association with Charles "Lucky" Luciano—America's famous gangster.

Could Ralph believe there was some decency left?

CHAPTER FIFTY-FIVE

Every four years the Olympic Games move around the world, promoting sportsmanship, friendship, and fair play with its white flag of peace waving in the winds. In 1960, Italy was the host country for the summer games, and Rome was a perfect setting. It was an opportunity for Italy to demonstrate to the world its postwar progress, to show its capacity for recovery, and the whole atmosphere was one of great jubilee. The Italians, known for their outgoing, warm, and generous personalities, were at their best; the mood was festive. The games lasted two weeks from August 22 to September 9, but preparations had long been under way. Villaggio Olimpico was constructed to house the athletes, and the Stadio Olimpico nearby was finally completed for the occasion. Another stadium, Palazzetto dello Sport, was built in the modern section of Rome called EUR—a district initiated by Mussolini. It was to have been completed by 1942, but obviously, due to the war, construction had been interrupted. Now plans were under way to finish as much of the area as possible. They even built a bicycle track for the racers. Most of the main athletic events were to be divided among the new Palazzetto dello Sport, the older Stadio Flaminio, and the recently completed Stadio Olimpico.

In the Castelli Romani hills near Nemi, fields were plowed and beautifully laid out with the proper apparatus for horsemen to demonstrate their skills at riding events. Lago Albano was spruced up and filled to the necessary level for rowing competitions and other water sports. Rome was beautiful and bustling twenty-four hours a day. The colors were flying with many different flags waving, and the city itself received a thorough cleaning; flowers were not spared, street signs were elaborated, and indications to the sports events were clearly visible to all.

The Olympics began in Greece long before Christ. After its decline, the Romans took it over under Nero; but he was not an athlete, not interested, and the games slowly deteriorated. The real comeback was in 1896, again in Athens, and the games—including those scheduled for the winter—have been going strong ever since. Tradition has it that the torch or flame of peace is lit on the site of the ancient games and is carried by ship to the host country. That year, the ship *Amerigo Vespucci* arrived at Bari (on the Adriatic Sea) with the torch of sacred fire. It was then carried by foot by athletes, carabinieri, and military men, all taking turns until they arrived to the Eternal City of Rome. It was a spectacular sight along the way. This ritual was perhaps surpassed only by the inauguration of the games. The ceremony was the height of pageantry—bands played, the crowd cheered, and high officials and guests all decked out, bowed their heads at the solemn reading of the pledge. The athletes stood tall in the field.

Amid that scenario, Ralph was working night and day for the many air force personnel—Canadians and American boys from all parts of the United States who had come to Rome. Most of them came for the Olympics, and they all needed hotel rooms and assistance of one kind or another. Some were accompanied by their wives and children. Others came with groups. Ralph received calls at all hours, just like the old days. "Ralph, you old son of a gun, I need a hotel for me and my family." *Couldn't Ralph find a room* was everyone' s cry. Once Ralph didn't sleep for three days and three nights because he couldn't let anybody down. Rome was jam-packed. When he couldn't find rooms in Rome, he took them to Castel Gandolfo, the pope's summer home, or anywhere else in the outlining areas where accommodations were possible. Ralph never tired. He was having the best time. Sometimes he joked with some of his military friends. "Now, don't tell your wife about all the beautiful girls you used to dance with!" Everyone had a good laugh. When someone's wife wanted to know how her husband had behaved, Ralph winked and laughed. "I'll never tell." Ralph was also busy going up and down Ciampino Airport. The new Leonardo Da Vinci Airport in Fiumicino was under construction. Therefore, Ciampino was handling all the heavy traffic. Ralph saw many interesting people like Princess Grace Kelly and Prince Rainier, ex-king Constantine of Greece, Charles De Gaulle, and even the mayor of Tokyo, plus many, many stars. It was still the *la dolce vita* (sweet life) period, and the Olympics only added to the glitter. It was a very big year for Ralph—a good year.

During those hectic weeks, Ralph didn't have much of an opportunity to see Charlie, working practically around the clock. He spent his free time with the many old friends who came looking for him. He did not, however, neglect Charlie. Since Igea's death, Ralph made it his business to go to Naples at least twice a month. Around the first part of 1959, on one of his trips to see Charlie, he met an old friend, Joe Rice, who had just come in from Cuba. He was lucky to get out alive. All three were having a drink at the Sombrero Club, and Charlie said laughingly, "Hey,

Ralph . . . can you imagine this guy? They asked him at the airport if he knew you . . . and he says NO!"

Ralph looked at Joe and exclaimed, "What the hell did you say no for?"

"Well, I figured I'd probably get you into trouble," Joe said apologetically.

"Naw . . . Joe . . . I'm known there," Ralph replied assuredly. "Maybe they would have helped you out, done you a favor or something. It probably was someone who knew me real well . . . otherwise they wouldn't have said anything."

"Well . . . what the hell," interrupted Charlie. "Next time he'll know better."

The reason Ralph felt badly was because he heard Joe had come with only a pair of overalls on his back. He could have given him a suit of clothes, helped him out a bit. Joe had to leave Cuba fast. They had caught him working in a gambling house, and when they found out who he was, they shipped him back to Italy.

"Man . . . if they knew I was American, they would've killed me," he moaned.

When Ralph asked how things were in Cuba, Joe replied, "Scary!" He told them about the revolution and Castro; that Cuba had gone Communistic because of him. Castro not only wouldn't allow gambling; he wouldn't allow anything! He wrecked the whole works, but the boys just patiently, philosophically, packed their bags and moved over to the Bahamas. What Castro really ruined was the country; he set the island and its people back many years. Charlie just sat there. He had memories of his own.

After the Olympics and all the hubbub was over, Ralph went down to say hello to Charlie. He knew Charlie had met a young girl, Adriana Risso, but it went very slowly at first. He couldn't forget Igea that easily. Like everything else, the affection grew, and he even began to take her to Santa Marinella. *What the hell,* thought Ralph. *A guy has to have some company!* When he met her, Ralph thought Adriana was a good kid (about twenty-two years old), but nobody could ever take Igea's place in Charlie's heart. That was something special! When Ralph went down, however, he and Charlie went out alone; sometimes they went to the Agnano racetracks, and sometimes they met just to eat and gab together. The conversation always centered around the happenings in the States. Nostalgia can be very strong, especially if one is exiled; sometimes it can reach abnormal heights. It's talk, talk, and talk. On this particular visit, it was the McClellan Senate Crime Committee whose investigations after the Apalachin fiasco had begun to interest them. It was like discussing the current gossip. The fires had been rekindled. The FBI and Washington were bearing down, and things were going full blast with the added leadership of Bobby Kennedy. His brother, John Fitzgerald Kennedy, had become the thirty-fifth president of the United States in 1961, and Bobby, appointed attorney general, began an all-out war against organized crime.

In 1961, Ralph was up to his ears with his appeal case. True to word, he didn't go to court; Lupus and Gariboldi handled everything, but it was another merry-go-round. In March, the case was postponed to April 24, then to July 8, and, finally, it was postponed to the middle of December—in time to spoil the Christmas holidays. *Rat bastards,* seethed Ralph.

Apart from all the tension, Ralph's eyesight was deteriorating. It had started back in 1955, and after being in a damp cell for three months at Regina Coeli for the white slavery rap, things became worse. He had complained of severe headaches to Elena; sometimes his eyes watered, but Ralph, as usual, wouldn't listen to Elena's pleas to see a doctor. Charlie, on the other hand, was having trouble with his heart; he had an attack, which weakened him, but he recovered beautifully. Charlie had to learn to take it easy—to be calm. They were two aging cronies growing old together with their aches and pains.

One day, around September, Ralph received the usual phone call from Charlie to go down—that he wanted to talk to him. Ralph met him at Giacomini's for lunch with Joe Rice. Charlie didn't say anything because he never talked serious matters with a third party around, and knowing him, Ralph didn't say anything either. After lunch, they went to the races and even won a little. They made a day of it and, around eight o'clock, ended up in the California Bar for coffee. It was getting late, and Ralph knew Charlie still wanted to talk privately to him. Sure enough, Charlie called him aside, and Joe discreetly kept his distance.

"Listen, Ralph . . . I want to tell you something I should have mentioned before. I spoke to a guy who was here from California—by the name of Martin Gosch—about making a movie. I had a few words with the guy, but I said no and chased him. A few days ago, he called me again on the phone and wants to come back and talk to me about doing my life story. When it's set and he comes, I'm going to call you at home, and you come right down to Naples. You talk to him. Tell him everything, but don't tell him about how we met Dewey in Rome. Don't tell him anything about the payoff. Don't say anything about that . . . but say anything else you want. Don't forget . . . don't mention that we met him. Remember now!"

Ralph stared at him. They had talked about telling their story many times, but he didn't understand his bit about Dewey. He shook his head slowly. "Charlie, the only thing I've understood is that I was right all along about you and Dewey." And Ralph felt some of the old bitterness creeping up.

"Ralph . . . ," Charlie said quietly, "let's not go into that again. I told you I didn't want to die in prison. Look . . . I'm in favor of telling everything. Tell him all you want except that . . . okay?"

"Okay . . . ," Ralph replied, for the moment.

A couple of weeks later, Ralph took some other people to Naples. He didn't have much time to see Charlie, but he took a chance and passed by the restaurant. As luck would have it, he missed him. It was late, and Ralph couldn't wait; he had to return to Rome with his clients. So he left word that he was there. While Ralph was driving, the lights began to bother him; then around two in the morning, his eyes started to play tricks on him. He saw rainbows around the lights. It was scary.

"Do you mind if I stop? I have a bad headache," Ralph politely asked his clients. Of course, they agreed, and Ralph pulled into a roadside bar. He turned off the ignition, leaned his head back, and closed his eyes for about fifteen minutes to rest. Soon the pounding in his head lessened. He went in to wash his face, apologized for the delay, and rode off again.

Almost as soon as he arrived, the phone rang. It was Charlie.

"Why didn't you wait for me?"

"Charlie . . . I'm sorry, but I couldn't. Had these people in the car . . . you know."

"Well . . . all right. When are you coming down again?" he persisted.

"I'll be down in a couple of days . . . okay?" Ralph replied in an appeasing tone.

"Yeah . . . okay . . . Let me know," Charlie answered, somewhat disappointed.

Ralph just shook his head; he was so tired. Could it be that Charlie was becoming possessive in his old age? After Igea's death, he seemed to want him around more. All his attempts in various legitimate businesses went sour, and his latest try with a furniture store near Capodimonte had also failed. Ralph was glad Charlie had Adriana for company because his health was not the greatest.

Elena noticed that Ralph was all done in and asked, "What's wrong? You have a strange look about you." Ralph explained what had happened, and this time she won. Ralph went to see a specialist named Leonardi for his eyes. He was told he had a touch of glaucoma, but it was not serious. He prescribed special drops to arrest the condition. Ralph, however, was never good at these things, and he neglected to use the drops regularly. Of course, he didn't improve, and he continued to suffer. Ralph's eyesight was definitely deteriorating.

Around the end of the year, on another trip to Naples, the same thing happened; his eyes were playing tricks on him. This time, Ralph went to Professor Strampelli, the famous surgeon at the San Camillo Hospital. The professor told Ralph he was in really bad shape and needed an operation in both eyes. It was a shock to Ralph, but he was prepared to do anything to obtain some relief—and hopefully some improvement in his vision. The operation was set for March (1962). Ralph now had two things to look forward: his appeal, which was postponed again to March, and the operation. Wasn't he a lucky guy!

Late one night, toward the end of January, he received another urgent call from Charlie telling him that Martin Gosch would arrive any day that week. Ralph assured him that he would definitely be down as planned.

It hit Ralph like a bomb! It was Friday, January 26, 1962. He had called it a day and was about to return home to dress. He had promised Charlie he would go down for the weekend. While Ralph stood on the corner of the Hotel Nord waiting for his driver, a friend, Inspector Fontana of the Interpol, walked up to him.

"Ralph . . . did you hear the news?"

"No . . . what news?" Ralph replied curiously.

"Charlie just dropped dead!"

"No foolin'," Ralph said stupidly, but he didn't believe it. He thought the inspector was trying some black humor on him. "Come on . . . Dr. Fontana . . . you're kidding me."

"No . . . no . . . Ralph . . . believe me. I'm not kidding. He dropped dead at Capodichino Airport in Naples."

Ralph became paralyzed; the shock was too much. Charlie dead, so sudden, no warning! His appointment with him that day was to meet Martin Gosch. Just then, the bar boy called Ralph to the phone. It was Elena confirming the news. Ralph came out stunned; his feet were wobbling, and Dr. Fontana took his arm sympathetically.

"Listen . . . Ralph. Listen to what I'm going to tell you. You know I'm a friend. I know you got a raw deal, but the heat's off you now. People from all over will be in Naples. Police, newspapermen, TV people . . . I'm telling you . . . don't go down. I know you'd like to be there for Charlie, but I know you've had enough. They're leaving you alone . . . so *don't* go down," he repeated, practically begging Ralph.

Ralph mumbled thanks to Fontana, told him he was probably right, but he still didn't know what to do. Ralph's driver came and, seeing in what state he was, steered him toward the car to help him. Ralph was home in ten minutes. Elena met him at the door and helped him to a chair. Ralph was still in a daze; he wanted desperately to go down to see Charlie, but now it was Elena who was weeping.

"Ralph . . . I know how you feel. Charlie . . . it's awful, but you can't go. Think of all those radio, TV people, the newspapermen and photographers—AND the police. Your name will be splashed in the papers again: Charlie Luciano's *Luogotenente*, Ralph Liguori, Mourns the Death of His Longtime Friend, et cetera! You *can't* go. I won't let you! It will be more bad publicity. We've had enough!" Elena pleaded.

Ralph remained silent. He was thinking of Charlie stretched out at the airport, of their appointment, and how their plans were obliterated by destiny. He was confused, but he knew Elena and Fontana were right. Like a robot, he undressed and went to bed. He lay there with his eyes wide open. Elena came in and asked if he wanted the radio on for the news. Ralph still didn't answer, but she turned it on anyway. Soon Ralph heard it for himself. Charlie was dead; he had keeled over with a massive heart attack at the Naples Capodichino Airport.

During those days of the funeral, Ralph secluded himself in his apartment. He was in for no one, and Elena was very good at seeing that his whereabouts remained unknown. To everyone who called, he was in a clinic incognito, preparing for an eye operation. She bought all the papers for Ralph to read all the news about the tragedy. He knew he would later know more from his friends, but for the moment, like everyone else, he followed the events on the radio and newspapers.

Charlie had gone to the airport a little before five o'clock to meet Martin Gosch, as planned, accompanied by a police inspector in plainclothes, Cesare Resta. What Ralph didn't know until he read it in the papers was that a nucleus of finance police had searched Charlie's apartment the night before. He was again suspected of being involved in narcotics. The only thing they did discover was the cable from Gosch announcing his arrival from Spain. All this new suspicion revolved around three drug peddlers—Frank Caruso, Vincent Mauro, and Salvatore Maneri—who had been arrested back in June 1961. They had jumped bail and had fled the country. The Narcotics Bureau in Washington had discovered that Charlie knew one or two of the men, and for them, that was an important link. Charlie had to be involved. Yet they had no real evidence. On January 23, the three men were arrested in Spain, and the coincidence of Gosch's arrival to Rome from Madrid automatically made him also suspect. The police were convinced that Charlie was going to meet one of his accomplices. To assure the police that he was clean, Charlie had invited Maresciallo Resta to accompany him to the airport to see for himself.

Charlie was impeccably dressed, as usual, but his pallor was such that one could tell he wasn't well. He had acquired a touch of diabetes, but primarily he suffered from heart trouble, was on pills for some time. Just a few weeks before, he had had another small attack. All this constant harassment definitely didn't help him. Charlie had parked his white Alfa Romeo Giulietta and, together with his escort, walked into the airport with a special pass in his pocket. Gosch's plane was to arrive at 5:20 p.m. The suspense was mounting because there were other plainclothesmen around just in case. The Finance Custom Police were also surveilling the encounter.

There are two main versions of the episode. One is that since it was early, Charlie and Resta had decided to stop at the bar. Charlie had an orange drink; Resta had coffee. Suddenly, Charlie felt ill and, gasping for air, tried to grab Resta to balance himself. He uttered a few words and fell to the floor. Gosch arrived in time to see Charlie on the floor, dead, near the counter.

The other version is one that Gosch had confirmed to reporters. He saw Charlie waiting as he came down the ramp. They smiled and acknowledged each other. As soon as Gosch approached him, Charlie introduced Resta as a friend, and they all walked toward the bar, a few feet away, for a drink. Charlie had his orange drink and felt ill. He grasped his chest and leaned on Resta to avoid falling; then gasping for air, he uttered a couple of words while collapsing to the ground. He died instantly. Whichever version one chooses to believe, one thing is certain. Charlie died near the bar in the arrivals area where he had fallen.

Everyone was shocked, especially Gosch, who remained stupefied. The airport police commissioner, Mario Forino, came running. Someone threw a cloth over Charlie. The airport medic arrived, and Charlie was taken to the airport infirmary, where they tried their best to resuscitate him, but there was nothing to do. The authorities had now taken over. After a few hours, Charlie was taken to the mortuary on Via Cesare Rossarol. Found on his person, the police listed: one gold watch, a gold neck chain, a white gold ring, a St. Rita medal, a mother-of-pearl-handle pocketknife, a pair of glasses, a key, a comb, a gold pillbox with pills, a prescription by his doctor Prof. Giacomo De Martino, personal documents (including his driver's license), the airport permit, plus about sixty-six thousand lire in cash (between $10 to $15).

The next day, around eleven in the morning, an external preliminary examination was made by Dr. D'Arona. The body was then made ready for an autopsy to determine the exact cause of death. About an hour or so later, Prof. Pietro Verga, director of pathology at the University of Naples, performed the examination while Dr. Ballusci, assistant public prosecutor, watched. The autopsy revealed lesions around the heart and nothing else, confirming that Charlie had died of a massive heart attack.

Of course, to be expected, there were malicious people who began to spread rumors that Charlie had been poisoned. However, the diagnosis by Professor Verga remains as the correct cause. No outsiders could see the corpse.

When Ralph read the different accounts, he felt nauseous. There was Charlie, dead, laid out on a cold slab without any of his loved ones or friends around. He was just a corpse to the people who were prodding—probing—here and there. Poor Charlie! Ralph hated himself because he wasn't there. But what could he do? He knew that Charlie would have understood. Ralph sent him anonymous flowers.

In the meantime, Martin Gosch was having a hard time. After the police had searched his luggage and found nothing, he had been allowed to check in to the Hotel Turistico, where he had reservations. Gosch, still in a stupor about what had happened, voluntarily made himself available to the police to clear up any doubts they may have had about his arrival. In fact, the next day, he was called to the Commando della Guardia di Finanza di Napoli headquarters. He was questioned on and off by Colonel De Luca for almost five hours. On Sunday, he was again interrogated, this time assisted by Captain Speciale of the Anti-Drug Nucleus. Gosch was in the clear.

On Saturday, Charlie's brother Bart arrived from the States. The family had made partial arrangements by phone; a casket had been ordered, and now the funeral services were finalized with Bart's presence. Saturday evening, the body was transferred to the morgue chapel for viewing; and on Sunday in the late afternoon, it was taken to the Holy Trinity Church on Via Tasso—the same street where Charlie had lived. Prayer services were performed by the parish priest Don Giulio Sammartino, but the official mass was held Monday morning at eleven o'clock. Don Francesco Scarpato, Charlie's old friend, had come down from Vesuvius to recite the High Mass with Don Sammartino. Charlie had always helped Don Scarpato (Don Cheech as he was called by his close friends). Charlie was his benefactor. Among many other things, Charlie had helped Don Cheech build a hospital and restore the San Sebastian Church at Vesuvius. Whenever Don Cheech went to Rome, Ralph was his personal chauffeur, and many times he was a guest in his home to enjoy Elena's superb lunches and dinners.

Ralph and Mother

The mass lasted fifty minutes. Not everyone who was someone to Charlie was there. Those already in Naples had paid their respects, but there were more police, photographers, and newspapermen than friends. *How sad,* thought Ralph. His brother Bart was accompanied by a nephew, Salvatore, and a cousin, Giuseppe "Pippo" Lucania. They were surrounded by close family friends and relatives. Charlie's girlfriend, Adriana Risso, mourning in black, was escorted by her parents and brother. The flashbulbs were firing away—all very irritating to the intimate circle. There was just one mishap. As one young and zealous photographer tried to get a close-up of Adriana, her brother grabbed the camera and punched the photographer in the nose. He was removed from the premises. Ironically, Diamond Dick was there, grieving as if he was a long-lost friend, more thin and pale than ever. There were also Joe "Cockeyed John" Raimondi and Joe Di Giorgio. Ralph was surprised to learn that Pat Eboli was there—and Joe Adonis, trying to be as inconspicuous as possible, standing in the back of the church—among the shadows of the holy statues. He and Charlie had had many things in common. Charlie had been the General; he had always remained the real *padrino* (godfather). No one ever really took his place. Adonis also lived his last days in Italy, changing residences often, never really finding himself. He too died of a heart attack in Ancona on November 27, 1971.

Everyone was solemn in black tie, and some men wore a black button in their lapel—an Italian custom for men mourning their loved ones. Also present were Charlie's few business associates and his lawyers, Passeggio and Bifulco. Dr. Giuseppe Dosi, retired Interpol commissioner, was also there. Ralph wasn't surprised because Dosi had liked Charlie despite his official role. Hank Manfredi flew in from Washington, perhaps in his heart to say good-bye, but most likely, officially, to see what he could discover in the international drug traffic. *They wouldn't give up, not even after his death,* thought Ralph. Henry Giordano, a deputy commissioner of the U.S. Narcotics Bureau, issued a statement that Charlie's arrest had been imminent. The Italian authorities, however, as usual, tried to appease the capitol hotshots.

Ralph had his own thoughts. It unnerved him to think that after all the *intensified* surveillance, the search of his apartment, and Charlie's request for a police official escort to the airport (to disavow any involvement), it was to no avail. He always believed it was an injustice to jail a person just because he happened to know certain individuals. Ralph certainly knew Charlie better than most. Charlie would not have told him to stay clear of men offering deals in narcotics, then turn around and involve himself. No way! He hated the stuff just as much as Ralph did—in Italy and in the States. There will be people who will always believe he was involved, but Charlie was clean in that racket. There never was any real proof. They just wouldn't let him retire in peace. The pressure finally killed him. Ralph considered them all inhuman characters.

After the funeral, the coffin was carried out of the church and placed in a magnificent black carriage drawn by eight majestic horses—a Sicilian tradition that was reserved for the rich and the mighty. This was however the only sumptuous funeral arrangement. All the rest was performed in quiet simplicity. Many solemnly followed the carriage by foot, blocking traffic here and there. Others took their cars to the English Cemetery, Santa Maria del Pianto, on the hill of Poggioreale. Don Cheech Scarpato recited the burial prayers with unashamed emotion while some chanted the responses. The cross of violets from Adriana was placed on the coffin, and other wreaths and flower pieces were arranged around it. The one that especially caught the reporters' eyes had a long ribbon, which said, "So long, pal." Some attributed it to Joe Adonis, but Ralph knew better. It was a sentiment many shared.

The postmortem items were that Charlie's body would remain at the English Cemetery until the necessary paperwork and authorization was obtained to transport the body to the United States for final burial in the family tomb in Brooklyn. Many presumed that Charlie's *notaio* (notary public), Nicola Monda, had some kind of will in his vault, but Charlie left no will or testament. To avoid any legal entanglements, he had wisely put his brother Bart's name on his various properties: the apartment on Via Tasso, the land and house in Santa Marinella, and the small place he had on the tiny island of San Martino in the bay.

Ralph had considerable time to think—isolated at home as he was. Indeed, his mind went to Dewey. He wondered how Dewey took the news. Was he relieved that now, maybe, his secret would never come out? Behind his cold veneer, did he nurse some remorse? Ralph thought about his visit to Rome when he and Charlie had their chitchat. One thing Ralph was sure of was that Dewey couldn't feel completely free from guilt. After his governorship ended in 1954, Dewey had left public office forever. He had finally retired to count his blessings and to reflect on his mistakes—political and otherwise; to ruminate about his vanished dream of becoming president of the United States. He died in 1971 with the honors of an honest statesman.

When Ralph began to circulate again, he didn't want to talk to anyone about Charlie—not even to Elena. He had enough heartaches at losing his friend. Slowly, but surely, he loosened up. Many people wanted to dig into their private relationship, but some things cannot be easily explained. To most, Ralph just said Charlie was a great guy.

One evening with Elena, he finally broke down and, close to tears, wailed, “I didn’t want it to happen so fast. I’ll miss him. Although he did me wrong, I knew how *it* was. I knew how *he* was. Charlie knew I had sacrificed myself to try to save him. He knew all about this. That was the real bond between us.”

CHAPTER FIFTY-SIX

Ralph was out like a newborn babe deep in slumberland as they wheeled him down the corridors of the San Camillo Hospital. His eye operation was not postponed; surgery was on schedule. Ralph had no illusions; he knew there were no miracles around the corner but did some private praying anyway. They had him on the table about five hours for just one eye. A few days later, there was a repeat performance for the other. Doctors Guadelupe and De Michele took turns. Both times they gave Ralph a heavy dose of anesthesia in order to keep him from stirring in bed. He slept for almost the whole day after each operation. The first time, Elena was hysterical; she thought Ralph was in a coma. She kept feeling his pulse, afraid it would stop.

After a couple of days, Ralph began to feel his senses returning—his appetite in particular, the barometer of his health. When Ralph told Elena he was hungry, she laughed and promised a homemade meal the next day. If it weren't for her . . . Even though Ralph couldn't see with the bandages, he could tell Elena was in a very good mood. She was joking with a policeman friend who had come to visit. Ralph was still kind of dopey under the sedation, but he asked why they were so damn cheery. What was the big deal? Elena came over and held his hand while their friend ruffled what Ralph thought to be a newspaper.

"Ralph," she said, "we have some wonderful news for you!"

"Yeah?" Ralph whispered. "What?"

"Let me read it to you," the friend replied. "The Italo-American, Ralph Liguori, was acquitted with *formula dubitative* [insufficient evidence] yesterday (March 7) by the Rome Court of Appeals (President Fumnu assisted by P. G. Ricciardi) for not being in the fact against him (white slavery and prostitution) . . ."

Still groggy, the only thing Ralph managed was a big smile while he mumbled, "Now isn't that nice!"

He heard Elena giggle and his friend laugh, but he fell fast asleep.

Finally, Ralph had won. It had taken 4 years from the beginning of the trial (1958)—but justice prevailed. His name was cleared! Lupus and Gariboldi had kept their word—especially Lupus, who had promised that if he didn't win the case, he would have torn up his sheepskin as an attorney. As Ralph thought about his case, he remembered what Charlie had said (about somebody being promoted from all the sensationalism), and his mind went back to the first time he had gone to court. He had bumped into the cop who had locked him up. For his role in the case, he had become an assistant police commissioner and practically snubbed Ralph.

Now in his hospital bed, he just didn't care. All he cared about was that his name had been cleared. The good news helped his spirits; as for his eyes, Ralph was realistic about his eyesight. He obtained some relief from the pain, but his eyesight didn't improve. His lenses became only thicker. Around May, Professor Strampelli advised Ralph that he had to be operated again. This time, he would personally do the honors, which he did—first in June and then again in December. The operations went a little better. Ralph returned to work, hoping for the best. A year later, he was in the hospital again for a cataract in one eye; and in 1964, he had an operation on the other. With all the operations, it was no surprise that Ralph's eyes were definitely in very bad shape. By 1966, he saw very little and had a full-time driver to assist in his work.

To brighten up his life, one day in September 1967, Ralph received a telegram from his sister Anna, advising that she and Agnes would be coming to Rome for a visit. Ralph was ecstatic over the news. He hadn't seen his mother in twenty-five years—since the last time she went to visit him in 1942 in Dannemora. It was all he could do to contain his joy. Unfortunately, glaucoma ran in the family, and Agnes had also practically lost her eyesight. She saw only shadows.

Ralph and Elena rose very early that morning (Friday, September 15), anxious not to miss the plane at ten. Ralph was all decked out for his best gal. He put on his best suit and his best tie. His hair had been trimmed just so, and he even splashed on some cologne. Ralph's driver, Aristide Harris, arrived, and they drove happily to the Leonardo Da Vinci Airport. When they pulled up, Ralph told Harris to go in first to check whether there were any newspapermen or photographers nosing around.

"Nobody's there," he said smiling, returning to the car. "All clear." Aristide parked the car, and Elena and Ralph entered the arrivals section. All the passengers seemed to have come out except Agnes and Anna. Ralph became nervous and approached the customs brigadier.

"Listen," Ralph said, agitated, "I'm expecting my mother, but I don't see her. Everybody has come out. Can I go in?"

"Sure, Ralph," he replied. "Go ahead . . . but don't do anything wrong now."

"What the hell am I going to do," Ralph scoffed, "take the plane and fly away?"

"Naw . . . I'm only kidding." The officer smiled. "We know you, Ralph . . . Go ahead."

Elena thought she had spotted them. "Could that be Anna?" she asked.

"Yeah, maybe," Ralph replied. Since he couldn't see very well, he called out, "Anna!"

Sure enough, Anna cried out, "Ralph," and she rushed toward him. They all emotionally embraced each other, tears streaming down. They had been the last to come out due to the wheelchair that was ordered for Agnes.

"Ralph . . . newspapermen are looking for you," Anna said anxiously.

"What?" Ralph cried. "They're here?" He looked around and added, "Never mind. Where's Mom?"

"There she is in the wheelchair. She's almost blind, Ralph," Anna replied, her tone full of sadness.

Ralph left Elena with Anna to help her through customs. Anna had a great amount of luggage. Ralph leaned over to kiss his mother, handing her a beautiful bouquet of flowers.

"Ralphy," Agnes murmured. "It's been so long, my son. I can't see too well, but I don't need my eyes to see you."

As Ralph gently touched her face with his hands, he saw a camera flash. A newspaperman had snapped their picture. Ralph's face changed expression as he grabbed the man by the lapel of his coat. "Listen," Ralph snapped, "this is my mother. Watch out what you write in the paper, because I'll come looking for you all over Italy. It's the first time my mother's been here, since she left Italy years ago. Remember what I'm telling you!"

"Baciamo le mani," he remarked. (A Sicilian expression meaning *no wrong would be done*.)

Ralph released him. "All right," he menaced, "BUT remember."

The next day, Ralph learned there were other journalists at the airport, because the story and picture of his mother's arrival were in more than one newspaper. The headlines, as usual, were: Boss of the New York underworld . . . *Braccio destra di* (right hand of) Lucky Luciano . . . et cetera . . . The articles, however, were somewhat more generous. Perhaps word had been passed around to give Ralph a break.

Agnes and Anna stayed in a pension across the street from Ralph's apartment, but they only slept there. In order to spend all her time with her son and daughter-in-law, Agnes didn't mind the five flights of stairs she had to climb to their apartment. AND she would eat *only* Elena's cooking.

As Ralph promised, he took Agnes to Professor Strampelli for an eye examination, but there was nothing he could do for her. He advised that the cataracts were too far gone, and because of her glaucoma, complete blindness was imminent. Agnes didn't bat an eyelash. She had known it for some time and had accepted her fate—as she had always courageously done in her life.

They had many long talks. Sometimes it was just the two of them, mother and son, reminiscing and hashing out Ralph's past—his problems in New York, the trial, Charlie, how maybe his life could have been different.

The last night they were together, they sat side by side, arm in arm, consoling each other. Agnes lifted her hand and searched for Ralph's face, gently touching his eyes, nose, cheeks, mouth—like a mother caressing her small child.

"Ralphy, you always had a clean face," Agnes murmured. "My Baby Face Ralph . . . you stuck by your friend. My little Ralphy."

And they quietly wept in each other's arms.

EPILOGUE

In the beginning, Ralph was very reluctant to reveal what he knew about certain murders. As our interviews progressed, he confirmed those details already known; and, in fact, only in certain episodes did he really open up to shed light on any murder. But it was never his intention to tell a "who done it" story, and certainly, he was not a stool pigeon. As far as he was concerned, there were more important things he wanted to reveal—primarily his relationships with Charles "Lucky" Luciano and Thomas E. Dewey.

The following are excerpts of one particularly heated discussion we had in one of our early interviews, when he angrily defended his position.

"What'd I gotta tell you that guys got killed there? NO! I don't say that!"

"Why not?"

"Because I don't say that. How'd you know he got killed there? Why did he get killed? (They'd ask.) You know a murder? There's no statute of limitation. That's why I had the arguments with Schiraldi (an Italian writer). I told him to go to hell. Who killed this guy? Who killed that one? Oh, go to hell and find out for yourself. I gotta tell 'em? I don't wanna be called in the States for murder. Try and put this in your head, Rosemary!"

"Ralph, you're not responsible for the murders of others."

"Oh yeah? How'd you know about it? How do I know? If I say John Doe killed so and so, you know, they'd come and pick me up in twenty-four hours here. How you know he killed him?

"A murder trial is never closed. It can go on fifty years after. A burglary, a robbery, extortion, no, it's a statute of limitation—three . . . four years. And, if they see a little string they can tie this on to, they tie on to that string, Rosemary. Don't let nobody tell you different. I studied law in prison. I know all about these things. A murder case is never, never, *never* closed!"

INDEX

L

M

S

T

U

V

W

Y

Z

ABOUT THE AUTHOR

Rosemary Valenti Guarnera, born in Cleveland, Ohio, began her career at the ABC affiliate WEWS-TV Channel 5; almost ten years later, she left for Rome, Italy, to pursue other challenges. Started at the Institute of American Poultry, attached to the American Embassy (which introduced American turkey to Italy), followed by co-ownership of the European Coach & Travel Co. (met Ralph Liguori). Joined FAO (Food and Agriculture Organization of the UN), World Bank, and, ultimately, Rockwell International (first shuttle to the moon). Married Italian Captain Eugenio Guarnera (deceased). Divides time between the two countries.

CPSIA information can be obtained at www.ICGtesting.com
Printed in the USA
LVOW06s2310200115

423623LV00003BA/3/P

9 781493 158324